COPYRIGHT LAW

LexisNexis Law School Publishing Advisory Board

COPYRIGHT LAW

EIGHTH EDITION
2010 CUMULATIVE SUPPLEMENT

Craig Joyce

Marshall Leaffer

Peter Jaszi

Tyler Ochoa

ISBN: 978-1-4224-8151-6

NOTE TO USERS

To ensure that you are using the latest materials available in this area, please be sure to periodically check the LexisNexis Law School website for downloadable updates and supplements at www.lexisnexis.com/lawschool.

Editorial Offices
121 Chanlon Road, New Providence, NJ 07974
201 Mission St., San Francisco, CA 94105-1831 (415) 908-3200
www.lexisnexis.com

MATTHEW BENDER

(2010–Pub.210)

ABOUT THE AUTHORS

Craig Joyce
Andrews Kurth Professor of Law and Co-Director,
Institute for Intellectual Property & Information Law
University of Houston Law Center
www.law.uh.edu/faculty/main.asp?PID=21

Marshall Leaffer
Distinguished Scholar in Intellectual Property Law and University
Fellow Indiana University School of Law
http://info.law.indiana.edu/sb/page/normal/1421.html

Peter Jaszi
Professor of Law and Director,
Glushko Samuelson Intellectual Property Law Clinic
Washington College of Law
American University
www.wcl.american.edu/faculty/jaszi

Tyler Ochoa
Professor of Law
Santa Clara University School of Law
http://law.scu.edu/faculty/profile/ochoa-tyler.cfm

PREFACE

This publication complements COPYRIGHT LAW: EIGHTH EDITION ("The Statute of Anne Edition") by providing access to a variety of materials which we hope will be of use to students and teachers alike. Together, the Eighth Edition and this Supplement provide the most comprehensive, up-to-date materials on copyright available in legal education today.

Part One of the Supplement contains the Copyright Clause of the U.S Constitution, the current version of Title 17, the Copyright Act of 1909, and miscellaneous legislative materials.

Part Two provides a rich assortment of international materials, including the Berne Convention and the Berne Convention Implementation Act of 1988, NAFTA, GATT/TRIPS, the treaty texts adopted by the World Intellectual Property Organization in December 1996, and the European Union Internet Copyright Directive — plus materials relating to copyright in the networked information environment.

Part Three collects excerpted legislative histories of interest to teachers and students of modern copyright law.

Part Four offers updated text and case law materials. We have included opinions newly released or revised by the courts, as well as additional and substitutional text notes updating developments since publication of the Eighth Edition.

Finally, Part Five contains a Cumulative Bibliography of important secondary materials on copyright (and related bodies of law). It is organized to mirror the casebook chapter-by-chapter for maximum utility.

In addition to annual bound supplements to the casebook available from the publisher, further helpful information concerning recent developments in copyright law may be obtained by consulting the following works: Marshall Leaffer, UNDERSTANDING COPYRIGHT LAW (LexisNexis, 5th Ed. 2010), Robert C. Lind, COPYRIGHT LAW: STUDENT STUDY GUIDE, and the standard treatises by David Nimmer, William Patry, Paul Goldstein, and Howard Abrams (all referenced topically in Part Five hereof).

We hope that readers will let us know what materials, or additional types of coverages, they would like to see added in the future!

Craig Joyce
Peter Jaszi
Marshall Leaffer
Tyler Ochoa
May 31, 2010

ACKNOWLEDGMENTS

At the University of Houston Law Center, special thanks to Dean Raymond T. Nimmer, Associate Dean Richard Alderman, and Andrews Kurth LLP, as well as the University of Houston Law Foundation, for their generous support of this Supplement. Thanks also to: Director Spencer Simons, Associate Director Mon Yin Lung, Reference Librarian Christopher Dykes and Document Services Librarian Helen Boyce, all of the University of Houston O'Quinn Law Library; and Associate Dean Scott Smith of the University of Houston Law Center Legal Information Technology Department.

At the Washington College of Law, American University, abundant thanks to Adeen Postar, Deputy Director of the Pence Law Library.

TABLE OF CONTENTS

PART ONE: CONSTITUTIONAL, STATUTORY, AND LEGISLATIVE MATERIALS

PART TWO: INTERNATIONAL PROTECTIONS AND THE NETWORKED INFORMATION ENVIRONMENT

PART ONE

CONSTITUTIONAL, STATUTORY, AND LEGISLATIVE MATERIALS

SYNOPSIS

COPYRIGHT (AND PATENT) CLA
CONSTITUTION OF THE UNITED S

Article I, Section 8, Clause 8

The Congress shall have Power ... To promote the Progre and useful Arts, by securing for limited Times to Authors and In exclusive Right to their respective Writings and Discoveries.

U.S. CODE: TITLE 17

COPYRIGHT ACT OF 1976

17 U.S.C. §§ 101-805
(AS AMENDED THROUGH DECEMBER 19, 2009)

TITLE 17—COPYRIGHTS

CHAPTER 1—SUBJECT MATTER AND SCOPE OF COPYRIGHT

§ 101 Definitions

Except as otherwise provided in this title, as used in this title, the following terms and their variant forms mean the following:

An "anonymous work" is a work on the copies or phonorecords of which no natural person is identified as author.

An "architectural work" is the design of a building as embodied in any tangible medium of expression, including a building, architectural plans, or drawings. The work includes the overall form as well as the arrangement and composition of spaces and elements in the design, but does not include individual standard features.

"Audiovisual works" are works that consist of a series of related images which are intrinsically intended to be shown by the use of machines or devices such as projectors, viewers, or electronic equipment, together with accompanying sounds, if any, regardless of the nature of the material objects, such as films or tapes, in which the works are embodied.

The "Berne Convention" is the Convention for the Protection of Literary and Artistic Works, signed at Berne, Switzerland, on September 9, 1886, and all acts, protocols, and revisions thereto.*

---

* Section 2 of the Berne Convention Implementation Act of 1988, Pub. L. 100-568, 102 Stat. 2853 (Oct. 31, 1988), provides the following declarations:

(1) The Convention for the Protection of Literary and Artistic Works, signed at Berne, Switzerland, on September 9, 1886, and all acts, protocols, and revisions thereto (hereafter in this Act referred to as the "Berne Convention") are not self-executing under the Constitution and laws of the United States.

The "best edition" of a work is the edition, published in the United States at any time before the date of deposit, that the Library of Congress determines to be most suitable for its purposes.

A person's "children" are that person's immediate offspring, whether legitimate or not, and any children legally adopted by that person.

A "collective work" is a work, such as a periodical issue, anthology, or encyclopedia, in which a number of contributions, constituting separate and independent works in themselves, are assembled into a collective whole.

A "compilation" is a work formed by the collection and assembling of preexisting materials or of data that are selected, coordinated, or arranged in such a way that the resulting work as a whole constitutes an original work of authorship. The term "compilation" includes collective works.

A "computer program" is a set of statements or instructions to be used directly or indirectly in a computer in order to bring about a certain result.

"Copies" are material objects, other than phonorecords, in which a work is fixed by any method now known or later developed, and from which the work can be perceived, reproduced, or otherwise communicated, either directly or with the aid of a machine or device. The term "copies" includes the material object, other than a phonorecord, in which the work is first fixed.

A "Copyright Royalty Judge" is a Copyright Royalty Judge appointed under section 802 of this title, and includes any individual serving as an interim Copyright Royalty Judge under such section.

"Copyright owner", with respect to any one of the exclusive rights comprised in a copyright, refers to the owner of that particular right.

A work is "created" when it is fixed in a copy or phonorecord for the first time; where a work is prepared over a period of time, the portion of it that has been fixed at any particular time constitutes the work as of that time, and where the work has been prepared in different versions, each version constitutes a separate work.

A "derivative work" is a work based upon one or more preexisting works, such as a translation, musical arrangement, dramatization, fictionalization, motion picture version, sound recording, art reproduction, abridgment, condensation, or any other form in which a work may be recast, transformed, or adapted. A work consisting of editorial revisions, annotations, elaborations, or other modifications which, as a whole, represent an original work of authorship, is a "derivative work".

A "device", "machine", or "process" is one now known or later developed.

---

(2) The obligations of the United States under the Berne Convention may be performed only pursuant to appropriate domestic law.

(3) The amendments made by this Act, together with the law as it exists on the date of the enactment of this Act, satisfy the obligations of the United States in adhering to the Berne Convention and no further rights or interests shall be recognized or created for that purpose.—*Eds.*

ligital transmission" is a transmission in whole or in part in a digital ..her non-analog format.

To "display" a work means to show a copy of it, either directly or by means of a film, slide, television image, or any other device or process or, in the case of a motion picture or other audiovisual work, to show individual images nonsequentially.

An "establishment" is a store, shop, or any similar place of business open to the general public for the primary purpose of selling goods or services in which the majority of the gross square feet of space that is nonresidential is used for that purpose, and in which nondramatic musical works are performed publicly.

A "food service or drinking establishment" is a restaurant, inn, bar, tavern, or any other similar place of business in which the public or patrons assemble for the primary purpose of being served food or drink, in which the majority of the gross square feet of space that is nonresidential is used for that purpose, and in which nondramatic musical works are performed publicly.

The term "financial gain" includes receipt, or expectation of receipt, of anything of value, including the receipt of other copyrighted works.

A work is "fixed" in a tangible medium of expression when its embodiment in a copy or phonorecord, by or under the authority of the author, is sufficiently permanent or stable to permit it to be perceived, reproduced, or otherwise communicated for a period of more than transitory duration. A work consisting of sounds, images, or both, that are being transmitted, is "fixed" for purposes of this title if a fixation of the work is being made simultaneously with its transmission.

The "Geneva Phonograms Convention" is the Convention for the Protection of Producers of Phonograms Against Unauthorized Duplication of Their Phonograms, concluded at Geneva, Switzerland, on October 29, 1971.

The "gross square feet of space" of an establishment means the entire interior space of that establishment, and any adjoining outdoor space used to serve patrons, whether on a seasonal basis or otherwise.

The terms "including" and "such as" are illustrative and not limitative.

An "international agreement" is—

(1) the Universal Copyright Convention;

(2) the Geneva Phonograms Convention;

(3) the Berne Convention;

(4) the WTO Agreement;

(5) the WIPO Copyright Treaty;

(6) the WIPO Performances and Phonograms Treaty; and

(7) any other copyright treaty to which the United States is a party.

A "joint work" is a work prepared by two or more authors with the intention that their contributions be merged into inseparable or interdependent parts of a unitary whole.

"Literary works" are works, other than audiovisual works, expressed in words, numbers, or other verbal or numerical symbols or indicia, regardless of the nature of the material objects, such as books, periodicals, manuscripts, phonorecords, film, tapes, disks, or cards, in which they are embodied.

"Motion pictures" are audiovisual works consisting of a series of related images which, when shown in succession, impart an impression of motion, together with accompanying sounds, if any.

The term "motion picture exhibition facility" means a movie theater, screening room, or other venue that is being used primarily for the exhibition of a copyrighted motion picture, if such exhibition is open to the public or is made to an assembled group of viewers outside of a normal circle of a family and its social acquaintances.

To "perform" a work means to recite, render, play, dance, or act it, either directly or by means of any device or process or, in the case of a motion picture or other audiovisual work, to show its images in any sequence or to make the sounds accompanying it audible.

A "performing rights society" is an association, corporation, or other entity that licenses the public performance of nondramatic musical works on behalf of copyright owners of such works, such as the American Society of Composers, Authors and Publishers (ASCAP), Broadcast Music, Inc. (BMI), and SESAC, Inc.

"Phonorecords" are material objects in which sounds, other than those accompanying a motion picture or other audiovisual work, are fixed by any method now known or later developed, and from which the sounds can be perceived, reproduced, or otherwise communicated, either directly or with the aid of a machine or device. The term "phonorecords" includes the material object in which the sounds are first fixed.

"Pictorial, graphic, and sculptural works" include two-dimensional and three-dimensional works of fine, graphic, and applied art, photographs, prints and art reproductions, maps, globes, charts, diagrams, models, and technical drawings, including architectural plans. Such works shall include works of artistic craftsmanship insofar as their form but not their mechanical or utilitarian aspects are concerned; the design of a useful article, as defined in this section, shall be considered a pictorial, graphic, or sculptural work only if, and only to the extent that, such design incorporates pictorial, graphic, or sculptural features that can be identified separately from, and are capable of existing independently of, the utilitarian aspects of the article.

For purposes of section 513, a "proprietor" is an individual, corporation, partnership, or other entity, as the case may be, that owns an establishment or a food service or drinking establishment, except that no owner or operator of a radio or television station licensed by the Federal Communications Commission, cable system or satellite carrier, cable or satellite carrier service or programmer, provider of online services or network access or the operator of facilities therefor, telecommunications company, or any other such audio or audiovisual service or programmer now known or as may be developed in the future, commercial subscription music service, or owner or operator of any other transmission service, shall under any circumstances be deemed to be a proprietor.

A "pseudonymous work" is a work on the copies or phonorecords of which the author is identified under a fictitious name.

"Publication" is the distribution of copies or phonorecords of a work to the public by sale or other transfer of ownership, or by rental, lease, or lending. The offering to distribute copies or phonorecords to a group of persons for purposes of further distribution, public performance, or public display, constitutes publication. A public performance or display of a work does not of itself constitute publication.

To perform or display a work "publicly" means—

(1) to perform or display it at a place open to the public or at any place where a substantial number of persons outside of a normal circle of a family and its social acquaintances is gathered; or

(2) to transmit or otherwise communicate a performance or display of the work to a place specified by clause (1) or to the public, by means of any device or process, whether the members of the public capable of receiving the performance or display receive it in the same place or in separate places and at the same time or at different times.

"Registration", for purposes of sections 205(c)(2), 405, 406, 410(d), 411, 412, and 506(e) [17 USCS §§ 205(c)(2), 405, 406, 410(d), 411, 412, and 506(e)], means a registration of a claim in the original or the renewed and extended term of copyright.

"Sound recordings" are works that result from the fixation of a series of musical, spoken, or other sounds, but not including the sounds accompanying a motion picture or other audiovisual work, regardless of the nature of the material objects, such as disks, tapes, or other phonorecords, in which they are embodied.

"State" includes the District of Columbia and the Commonwealth of Puerto Rico, and any territories to which this title is made applicable by an Act of Congress.

A "transfer of copyright ownership" is an assignment, mortgage, exclusive license, or any other conveyance, alienation, or hypothecation of a copyright or of any of the exclusive rights comprised in a copyright, whether or not it is limited in time or place of effect, but not including a nonexclusive license.

A "transmission program" is a body of material that, as an aggregate, has been produced for the sole purpose of transmission to the public in sequence and as a unit.

To "transmit" a performance or display is to communicate it by any device or process whereby images or sounds are received beyond the place from which they are sent.

A "treaty party" is a country or intergovernmental organization other than the United States that is a party to an international agreement.

The "United States", when used in a geographical sense, comprises the several States, the District of Columbia and the Commonwealth of Puerto Rico, and the organized territories under the jurisdiction of the United States Government.

For purposes of section 411 [17 USCS § 411], a work is a "United States work" only if—

(1) in the case of a published work, the work is first published—

(A) in the United States;

(B) simultaneously in the United States and another treaty party or parties, whose law grants a term of copyright protection that is the same as or longer than the term provided in the United States;

(C) simultaneously in the United States and a foreign nation that is not a treaty party; or

(D) in a foreign nation that is not a treaty party, and all of the authors of the work are nationals, domiciliaries, or habitual residents of, or in the case of an audiovisual work legal entities with headquarters in, the United States;

(2) in the case of an unpublished work, all the authors of the work are nationals, domiciliaries, or habitual residents of the United States, or, in the case of an unpublished audiovisual work, all the authors are legal entities with headquarters in the United States; or

(3) in the case of a pictorial, graphic, or sculptural work incorporated in a building or structure, the building or structure is located in the United States.

A "useful article" is an article having an intrinsic utilitarian function that is not merely to portray the appearance of the article or to convey information. An article that is normally a part of a useful article is considered a "useful article".

The author's "widow" or "widower" is the author's surviving spouse under the law of the author's domicile at the time of his or her death, whether or not the spouse has later remarried.

The "WIPO Copyright Treaty" is the WIPO Copyright Treaty concluded at Geneva, Switzerland, on December 20, 1996.

The "WIPO Performances and Phonograms Treaty" is the WIPO Performances and Phonograms Treaty concluded at Geneva, Switzerland, on December 20, 1996.

A "work of visual art" is—

(1) a painting, drawing, print, or sculpture, existing in a single copy, in a limited edition of 200 copies or fewer that are signed and consecutively numbered by the author, or, in the case of a sculpture, in multiple cast, carved, or fabricated sculptures of 200 or fewer that are consecutively numbered by the author and bear the signature or other identifying mark of the author; or

(2) a still photographic image produced for exhibition purposes only, existing in a single copy that is signed by the author, or in a limited edition of 200 copies or fewer that are signed and consecutively numbered by the author.

A work of visual art does not include—

(A) (i) any poster, map, globe, chart, technical drawing, diagram, model, applied art, motion picture or other audiovisual work, book, magazine, newspaper, periodical, data base, electronic information service, electronic publication, or similar publication;

(ii) any merchandising item or advertising, promotional, descriptive, covering, or packaging material or container;

(iii) any portion or part of any item described in clause (i) or (ii);

(B) any work made for hire; or

(C) any work not subject to copyright protection under this title.

A "work of the United States Government" is a work prepared by an officer or employee of the United States Government as part of that person's official duties.

A "work made for hire" is—

(1) a work prepared by an employee within the scope of his or her employment; or

(2) a work specially ordered or commissioned for use as a contribution to a collective work, as a part of a motion picture or other audiovisual work, as a translation, as a supplementary work, as a compilation, as an instructional text, as a test, as answer material for a test, or as an atlas, if the parties expressly agree in a written instrument signed by them that the work shall be considered a work made for hire. For the purpose of the foregoing sentence, a "supplementary work" is a work prepared for publication as

a secondary adjunct to a work by another author for the purpos
concluding, illustrating, explaining, revising, commenting up
in the use of the other work, such as forewords, afterwords, pi
tions, maps, charts, tables, editorial notes, musical arrangei
material for tests, bibliographies, appendixes, and indexes, an
tional text" is a literary, pictorial, or graphic work prepared fo ... ication
and with the purpose of use in systematic instructional activities.

In determining whether any work is eligible to be considered a work made for hire under paragraph (2), neither the amendment contained in section 1011(d) of the Intellectual Property and Communications Omnibus Reform Act of 1999, as enacted by section 1000(a)(9) of Public Law 106-113, nor the deletion of the words added by that amendment—

(A) shall be considered or otherwise given any legal significance, or

(B) shall be interpreted to indicate congressional approval or disapproval of, or acquiescence in, any judicial determination, by the courts or the Copyright Office. Paragraph (2) shall be interpreted as if both section 2(a)(1) of the Work Made For Hire and Copyright Corrections Act of 2000 and section 1011(d) of the Intellectual Property and Communications Omnibus Reform Act of 1999, as enacted by section 1000(a)(9) of Public Law 106-113, were never enacted, and without regard to any inaction or awareness by the Congress at any time of any judicial determinations.

The terms "WTO Agreement" and "WTO member country" have the meanings given those terms in paragraphs (9) and (10), respectively, of section 2 of the Uruguay Round Agreements Act [19 USCS § 3501].

(Oct. 19, 1976, P. L. 94-553, Title I, § 101, 90 Stat 2541; Dec. 12, 1980, P. L. 96-517, § 10(a), 94 Stat. 3028; Oct. 31, 1988, P. L. 100-568, § 4(a)(1), 102 Stat. 2854; Dec. 1, 1990, P. L. 101-650, Title VI, § 602, Title VII, § 702, 104 Stat. 5128, 5133; June 26, 1992, P. L. 102-307, Title I, § 102(b)(2), 106 Stat. 266; Oct. 28, 1992, P. L. 102-563, § 3(b), 106 Stat. 4248; Nov. 1, 1995, P. L. 104-39, § 5(a), 109 Stat. 348; Nov. 13, 1997, P. L. 105-80, § 12(a)(3), 111 Stat. 1534; Dec. 16, 1997, P. L. 105-147, § 2(a), 111 Stat. 2678; Oct. 27, 1998, P. L. 105-298, Title II, § 205, 112 Stat. 2833; Oct. 28, 1998, P. L. 105-304, Title I, § 102(a), 112 Stat. 2861; Aug. 5, 1999, P. L. 106-44, § 1(g)(1), 113 Stat. 222; Nov. 29, 1999, P. L. 106-113, Div B, § 1000(a)(9), 113 Stat. 1536; Oct. 27, 2000, P. L. 106-379, § 2(a), 114 Stat. 1444; Nov. 2, 2002, P. L. 107-273, Div C, Title III, Subtitle B, § 13210(5), 116 Stat. 1909; Nov. 30, 2004, P. L. 108-419, § 4, 118 Stat. 2361; April 27, 2005, P. L. 109-9, Title I, § 102(c), 119 Stat. 220.)

§ 102 Subject matter of copyright: In general

(a) Copyright protection subsists, in accordance with this title, in original works of authorship fixed in any tangible medium of expression, now known or later developed, from which they can be perceived, reproduced, or otherwise communicated, either directly or with the aid of a machine or device. Works of authorship include the following categories:

(1) literary works;

(2) musical works, including any accompanying words;

(3) dramatic works, including any accompanying music;

(4) pantomimes and choreographic works;

(5) pictorial, graphic, and sculptural works;

(6) motion pictures and other audiovisual works;

(7) sound recordings; and

(8) architectural works.*

(b) In no case does copyright protection for an original work of authorship extend to any idea, procedure, process, system, method of operation, concept, principle, or discovery, regardless of the form in which it is described, explained, illustrated, or embodied in such work.

(Oct. 19, 1976, P. L. 94-553, Title I, § 101, 90 Stat 2544; Dec. 1, 1990, P. L. 101-650, Title VII, § 703, 104 Stat. 5133.)

§ 103 Subject matter of copyright: Compilations and derivative works

(a) The subject matter of copyright as specified by section 102 includes compilations and derivative works, but protection for a work employing preexisting material in which copyright subsists does not extend to any part of the work in which such material has been used unlawfully.

(b) The copyright in a compilation or derivative work extends only to the material contributed by the author of such work, as distinguished from the preexisting material employed in the work, and does not imply any exclusive right in the preexisting material. The copyright in such work is independent of, and does not affect or enlarge the scope, duration, ownership, or subsistence of, any copyright protection in the preexisting material.

(Oct. 19, 1976, P. L. 94-553, Title I, § 101, 90 Stat 2545.)

---

* The Act's provisions concerning architectural works apply to—

(1) any architectural work created on or after December 1, 1990 (the date of enactment of the Architectural Works Copyright Protection Act); and

(2) any architectural work that, on December 1, 1990, was unconstructed and embodied in unpublished plans or drawings, except that protection for such architectural works, by virtue of the Architectural Works Copyright Protection Act, terminates on December 31, 2002, unless the work is constructed by that date.—*Eds.*

§ 104 Subject matter of copyright: National origin

(a) **Unpublished Works.** The works specified by sections 102 and 103, while unpublished, are subject to protection under this title without regard to the nationality or domicile of the author.

(b) **Published Works.** The works specified by sections 102 and 103, when published, are subject to protection under this title if—

(1) on the date of first publication, one or more of the authors is a national or domiciliary of the United States, or is a national, domiciliary, or sovereign authority of a treaty party, or is a stateless person, wherever that person may be domiciled; or

(2) the work is first published in the United States or in a foreign nation that, on the date of first publication, is a treaty party; or

(3) the work is a sound recording that was first fixed in a treaty party; or

(4) the work is a pictorial, graphic, or sculptural work that is incorporated in a building or other structure, or an architectural work that is embodied in a building and the building or structure is located in the United States or a treaty party; or

(5) the work is first published by the United Nations or any of its specialized agencies, or by the Organization of American States; or

(6) the work comes within the scope of a Presidential proclamation. Whenever the President finds that a particular foreign nation extends, to works by authors who are nationals or domiciliaries of the United States or to works that are first published in the United States, copyright protection on substantially the same basis as that on which the foreign nation extends protection to works of its own nationals and domiciliaries and works first published in that nation, the President may by proclamation extend protection under this title to works of which one or more of the authors is, on the date of first publication, a national, domiciliary, or sovereign authority of that nation, or which was first published in that nation. The President may revise, suspend, or revoke any such proclamation or impose any conditions or limitations on protection under a proclamation.

For purposes of paragraph (2), a work that is published in the United States or a treaty party within 30 days after publication in a foreign nation that is not a treaty party shall be considered to be first published in the United States or such treaty party, as the case may be.

(c) **Effect of Berne Convention.** No right or interest in a work eligible for protection under this title may be claimed by virtue of, or in reliance upon, the provisions of the Berne Convention, or the adherence of the United States thereto. Any rights in a work eligible for protection under this title that derive from this title, other Federal or State statutes, or the common law, shall not be expanded or reduced by virtue of, or in reliance upon, the provisions of the Berne Convention, or the adherence of the United States thereto.

(d) **Effect of Phonograms Treaties.** Notwithstanding the provisions of subsection (b), no works other than sound recordings shall be eligible for protection under this title solely by virtue of the adherence of the United States to the Geneva Phonograms Convention or the WIPO Performances and Phonograms Treaty.

(Oct. 19, 1976, P. L. 94-553, Title I, § 101, 90 Stat. 2545; Oct. 31, 1988, P. L. 100-568, § 4(a)(2), (3), 102 Stat. 2855; Oct. 28, 1998, P.L. 105-304, Title I, § 102(b), 112 Stat. 2862; May 20, 2002, entry into force of WIPO Performances and Phonograms Treaty.)

§ 104A Copyright in restored works

(a) **Automatic Protection and Term.**

(1) *Term.*

(A) Copyright subsists, in accordance with this section, in restored works, and vests automatically on the date of restoration.

(B) Any work in which copyright is restored under this section shall subsist for the remainder of the term of copyright that the work would have otherwise been granted in the United States if the work never entered the public domain in the United States.

(2) *Exception.* Any work in which the copyright was ever owned or administered by the Alien Property Custodian and in which the restored copyright would be owned by a government or instrumentality thereof, is not a restored work.

(b) **Ownership of Restored Copyright.** A restored work vests initially in the author or initial rightholder of the work as determined by the law of the source country of the work.

(c) **Filing of Notice of Intent to Enforce Restored Copyright Against Reliance Parties.** On or after the date of restoration, any person who owns a copyright in a restored work or an exclusive right therein may file with the Copyright Office a notice of intent to enforce that person's copyright or exclusive right or may serve such a notice directly on a reliance party. Acceptance of a notice by the Copyright Office is effective as to any reliance parties but shall not create a presumption of the validity of any of the facts stated therein. Service on a reliance party is effective as to that reliance party and any other reliance parties with actual knowledge of such service and of the contents of that notice.

(d) **Remedies for Infringement of Restored Copyrights.**

(1) *Enforcement of copyright in restored works in the absence of a reliance party.* As against any party who is not a reliance party, the remedies provided in chapter 5 of this title [17 USCS §§ 501 et seq.] shall be

available on or after the date of restoration of a restored copyright with respect to an act of infringement of the restored copyright that is commenced on or after the date of restoration.

(2) *Enforcement of copyright in restored works as against reliance parties.* As against a reliance party, except to the extent provided in paragraphs (3) and (4), the remedies provided in chapter 5 of this title [17 USCS §§ 501 et seq.] shall be available, with respect to an act of infringement of a restored copyright, on or after the date of restoration of the restored copyright if the requirements of either of the following subparagraphs are met:

(A) (i) The owner of the restored copyright (or such owner's agent) or the owner of an exclusive right therein (or such owner's agent) files with the Copyright Office, during the 24-month period beginning on the date of restoration, a notice of intent to enforce the restored copyright; and

(ii) (I) the act of infringement commenced after the end of the 12-month period beginning on the date of publication of the notice in the Federal Register;

(II) the act of infringement commenced before the end of the 12-month period described in subclause (I) and continued after the end of that 12-month period, in which case remedies shall be available only for infringement occurring after the end of that 12-month period; or

(III) copies or phonorecords of a work in which copyright has been restored under this section are made after publication of the notice of intent in the Federal Register.

(B) (i) The owner of the restored copyright (or such owner's agent) or the owner of an exclusive right therein (or such owner's agent) serves upon a reliance party a notice of intent to enforce a restored copyright; and

(ii) (I) the act of infringement commenced after the end of the 12-month period beginning on the date the notice of intent is received;

(II) the act of infringement commenced before the end of the 12-month period described in subclause (I) and continued after the end of that 12-month period, in which case remedies shall be available only for the infringement occurring after the end of that 12-month period; or

(III) copies or phonorecords of a work in which copyright has been restored under this section are made after receipt of the notice of intent.

In the event that notice is provided under both subparagraphs (A) and (B), the 12-month period referred to in such subparagraphs shall run from the earlier of publication or service of notice.

(3) *Existing derivative works.*

(A) In the case of a derivative work that is based upon a restored work and is created—

(i) before the date of the enactment of the Uruguay Round Agreements Act [enacted Dec. 8, 1994], if the source country of the restored work is an eligible country on such date, or

(ii) before the date on which the source country of the restored work becomes an eligible country, if that country is not an eligible country on such date of enactment, a reliance party may continue to exploit that derivative work for the duration of the restored copyright if the reliance party pays to the owner of the restored copyright reasonable compensation for conduct which would be subject to a remedy for infringement but for the provisions of this paragraph.

(B) In the absence of an agreement between the parties, the amount of such compensation shall be determined by an action in United States district court, and shall reflect any harm to the actual or potential market for or value of the restored work from the reliance party's continued exploitation of the work, as well as compensation for the relative contributions of expression of the author of the restored work and the reliance party to the derivative work.

(4) *Commencement of infringement for reliance parties.* For purposes of section 412 [17 USCS § 412], in the case of reliance parties, infringement shall be deemed to have commenced before registration when acts which would have constituted infringement had the restored work been subject to copyright were commenced before the date of restoration.

(e) **Notices of Intent to Enforce a Restored Copyright.**

(1) *Notices of intent filed with the copyright office.*

(A) (i) A notice of intent filed with the Copyright Office to enforce a restored copyright shall be signed by the owner of the restored copyright or the owner of an exclusive right therein, who files the notice under subsection (d)(2)(A)(i) (hereafter in this paragraph referred to as the "owner"), or by the owner's agent, shall identify the title of the restored work, and shall include an English translation of the title and any other alternative titles known to the owner by which the restored work may be identified, and an address and telephone number at which the owner may be contacted. If the notice is signed by an agent, the agency relationship must have been constituted in a writing signed by the owner before the filing of the notice. The Copyright Office may specifically require in regulations other information to be included in the notice, but failure to provide such other information shall not invalidate the notice or be a basis for refusal to list the restored work in the Federal Register.

(ii) If a work in which copyright is restored has no formal title, it shall be described in the notice of intent in detail sufficient to identify it.

(iii) Minor errors or omissions may be corrected by further notice at any time after the notice of intent is filed. Notices of corrections for such minor errors or omissions shall be accepted after the period established in subsection (d)(2)(A)(i). Notices shall be published in the Federal Register pursuant to subparagraph (B).

(B) (i) The Register of Copyrights shall publish in the Federal Register, commencing not later than 4 months after the date of restoration for a particular nation and every 4 months thereafter for a period of 2 years, lists identifying restored works and the ownership thereof if a notice of intent to enforce a restored copyright has been filed.

(ii) Not less than 1 list containing all notices of intent to enforce shall be maintained in the Public Information Office of the Copyright Office and shall be available for public inspection and copying during regular business hours pursuant to sections 705 and 708.

(C) The Register of Copyrights is authorized to fix reasonable fees based on the costs of receipt, processing, recording, and publication of notices of intent to enforce a restored copyright and corrections thereto.

(D) (i) Not later than 90 days before the date the Agreement on Trade-Related Aspects of Intellectual Property referred to in section 101(d)(15) of the Uruguay Round Agreements Act [19 USCS § 3511(d)(15)] enters into force with respect to the United States, the Copyright Office shall issue and publish in the Federal Register regulations governing the filing under this subsection of notices of intent to enforce a restored copyright.

(ii) Such regulations shall permit owners of restored copyrights to file simultaneously for registration of the restored copyright.

(2) *Notices of intent served on a reliance party.*

(A) Notices of intent to enforce a restored copyright may be served on a reliance party at any time after the date of restoration of the restored copyright.

(B) Notices of intent to enforce a restored copyright served on a reliance party shall be signed by the owner or the owner's agent, shall identify the restored work and the work in which the restored work is used, if any, in detail sufficient to identify them, and shall include an English translation of the title, any other alternative titles known to the owner by which the work may be identified, the use or uses to which the owner objects, and an address and telephone number at which the reliance party may contact the owner. If the notice is signed by an agent, the agency relationship must have been constituted in writing and signed by the owner before service of the notice.

(3) *Effect of material false statements.* Any material false statement knowingly made with respect to any restored copyright identified in any notice of intent shall make void all claims and assertions made with respect to such restored copyright.

(F) **Immunity from Warranty and Related Liability.**

(1) *In general.* Any person who warrants, promises, or guarantees that a work does not violate an exclusive right granted in section 106 shall not be liable for legal, equitable, arbitral, or administrative relief if the warranty, promise, or guarantee is breached by virtue of the restoration of copyright under this section, if such warranty, promise, or guarantee is made before January 1, 1995.

(2) *Performances.* No person shall be required to perform any act if such performance is made infringing by virtue of the restoration of copyright under the provisions of this section, if the obligation to perform was undertaken before January 1, 1995.

(g) **Proclamation of Copyright Restoration.** Whenever the President finds that a particular foreign nation extends, to works by authors who are nationals or domiciliaries of the United States, restored copyright protection on substantially the same basis as provided under this section, the President may by proclamation extend restored protection provided under this section to any work—

(1) of which one or more of the authors is, on the date of first publication, a national, domiciliary, or sovereign authority of that nation; or

(2) which was first published in that nation.

The President may revise, suspend, or revoke any such proclamation or impose any conditions or limitations on protection under such a proclamation.

(h) **Definitions.** For purposes of this section and section 109(a)—:

(1) The term "date of adherence or proclamation" means the earlier of the date on which a foreign nation which, as of the date the WTO Agreement enters into force with respect to the United States, is not a nation adhering to the Berne Convention or a WTO member country, becomes—

(A) a nation adhering to the Berne Convention;

(B) a WTO member country;

(C) a nation adhering to the WIPO Copyright Treaty;

(D) a nation adhering to the WIPO Performances and Phonograms Treaty; or

(E) subject to a Presidential proclamation under subsection (g).

(2) The "date of restoration" of a restored copyright is—

(A) January 1, 1996, if the source country of the restored work is a nation adhering to the Berne Convention or a WTO member country on such date, or

(B) the date of adherence or proclamation, in the case of any other source country of the restored work.

(3) The term "eligible country" means a nation, other than the United States, that—

(A) becomes a WTO member country after the date of the enactment of the Uruguay Round Agreements Act [enacted Dec. 8, 1994];

(B) on such date of enactment is, or after such date of enactment becomes, a nation adhering to the Berne Convention;

(C) adheres to the WIPO Copyright Treaty;

(D) adheres to the WIPO Performances and Phonograms Treaty; or

(E) after such date of enactment becomes subject to a proclamation under subsection (g).

(4) The term "reliance party" means any person who—

(A) with respect to a particular work, engages in acts, before the source country of that work becomes an eligible country, which would have violated section 106 if the restored work had been subject to copyright protection, and who, after the source country becomes an eligible country, continues to engage in such acts;

(B) before the source country of a particular work becomes an eligible country, makes or acquires 1 or more copies or phonorecords of that work; or

(C) as the result of the sale or other disposition of a derivative work covered under subsection (d)(3), or significant assets of a person described in subparagraph (A) or (B), is a successor, assignee, or licensee of that person.

(5) The term "restored copyright" means copyright in a restored work under this section.

(6) The term "restored work" means an original work of authorship that—

(A) is protected under subsection (a);

(B) is not in the public domain in its source country through expiration of term of protection;

(C) is in the public domain in the United States due to—

(i) noncompliance with formalities imposed at any time by United States copyright law, including failure of renewal, lack of proper notice, or failure to comply with any manufacturing requirements;

(ii) lack of subject matter protection in the case of sound recordings fixed before February 15, 1972; or

(iii) lack of national eligibility;

(D) has at least one author or rightholder who was, at the time the work was created, a national or domiciliary of an eligible country, and if published, was first published in an eligible country and not published in the United States during the 30-day period following publication in such eligible country; and

(E) if the source country for the work is an eligible country solely by virtue of its adherence to the WIPO Performances and Phonograms Treaty, is a sound recording.

(7) The term "rightholder" means the person—

(A) who, with respect to a sound recording, first fixes a sound recording with authorization, or

(B) who has acquired rights from the person described in subparagraph (A) by means of any conveyance or by operation of law.

(8) The "source country" of a restored work is—

(A) a nation other than the United States;

(B) in the case of an unpublished work—

(i) the eligible country in which the author or rightholder is a national or domiciliary, or, if a restored work has more than 1 author or rightholder, of which the majority of foreign authors or rightholders are nationals or domiciliaries; or

(ii) if the majority of authors or rightholders are not foreign, the nation other than the United States which has the most significant contacts with the work; and

(C) in the case of a published work—

(i) the eligible country in which the work is first published, or

(ii) if the restored work is published on the same day in 2 or more eligible countries, the eligible country which has the most significant contacts with the work.

(Dec. 8, 1993, P. L. 103-182, Title III, Subtitle C, § 334(a), 107 Stat. 2115; Dec. 8, 1994, P. L. 103-465, Title V, Subtitle A, § 514(a), 108 Stat. 4976; Oct. 11, 1996, P. L. 104-295, § 20(e)(2), 110 Stat. 3529; Nov. 13, 1997, P. L. 105-80, § 2, 111 Stat. 1530; Oct. 28, 1998, P. L. 105-304, Title I, § 102(c), 112 Stat. 2862; March 6, 2002, entry into force of WIPO Copyright Treaty; May 20, 2002, entry into force of WIPO Performances and Phonograms Treaty.)

§ 105 Subject matter of copyright: United States Government works

Copyright protection under this title is not available for any work of the United States Government, but the United States Government is not precluded from receiving and holding copyrights transferred to it by assignment, bequest, or otherwise.

(Oct. 19, 1976, P. L. 94-553, Title I, § 101, 90 Stat 2546.)

§ 106 Exclusive rights in copyrighted works

Subject to sections 107 through 122, the owner of copyright under this title has the exclusive rights to do and to authorize any of the following:

(1) to reproduce the copyrighted work in copies or phonorecords;

(2) to prepare derivative works based upon the copyrighted work;

(3) to distribute copies or phonorecords of the copyrighted work to the public by sale or other transfer of ownership, or by rental, lease, or lending;

(4) in the case of literary, musical, dramatic, and choreographic works, pantomimes, and motion pictures and other audiovisual works, to perform the copyrighted work publicly;

(5) in the case of literary, musical, dramatic, and choreographic works, pantomimes, and pictorial, graphic, or sculptural works, including the individual images of a motion picture or other audiovisual work, to display the copyrighted work publicly; and

(6) in the case of sound recordings, to perform the copyrighted work publicly by means of a digital audio transmission.

(Oct. 19, 1976, P. L. 94-553, Title I, § 101, 90 Stat. 2546; July 3, 1990, P. L. 101-318, § 3(d), 104 Stat. 288; Dec. 1, 1990, P. L. 101-650, Title VII, § 704(b)(2), 104 Stat. 5134; Nov. 1, 1995, P. L. 104-39, § 2, 109 Stat. 336; Aug. 5, 1999, P. L. 106-44, § 1(g)(2), 113 Stat. 222; Nov. 2, 2002, P. L. 107-273, Div C, Title III, Subtitle B, § 13210(4)(A), 116 Stat. 1909.)

§ 106A Rights of certain authors to attribution and integrity—

(a) **Rights of Attribution and Integrity.** Subject to section 107 and independent of the exclusive rights provided in section 106, the author of a work of visual art—

(1) shall have the right—

(A) to claim authorship of that work, and

(B) to prevent the use of his or her name as the author of any work of visual art which he or she did not create;

(2) shall have the right to prevent the use of his or her name as the author of the work of visual art in the event of a distortion, mutilation, or other modification of the work which would be prejudicial to his or her honor or reputation; and

(3) subject to the limitations set forth in section 113(d), shall have the right—

(A) to prevent any intentional distortion, mutilation, or other modification of that work which would be prejudicial to his or her honor or reputation, and any intentional distortion, mutilation, or modification of that work is a violation of that right, and

(B) to prevent any destruction of a work of recognized stature, and any intentional or grossly negligent destruction of that work is a violation of that right.

(b) **Scope and Exercise of Rights.** Only the author of a work of visual art has the rights conferred by subsection (a) in that work, whether or not the author is the copyright owner. The authors of a joint work of visual art are coowners of the rights conferred by subsection (a) in that work.

(c) **Exceptions.**

(1) The modification of a work of visual art which is a result of the passage of time or the inherent nature of the materials is not a distortion, mutilation, or other modification described in subsection (a)(3)(A).

(2) The modification of a work of visual art which is the result of conservation, or of the public presentation, including lighting and placement, of the work is not a destruction, distortion, mutilation, or other modification described in subsection (a)(3) unless the modification is caused by gross negligence.

(3) The rights described in paragraphs (1) and (2) of subsection (a) shall not apply to any reproduction, depiction, portrayal, or other use of a work in, upon, or in any connection with any item described in subparagraph (A) or (B) of the definition of "work of visual art" in section 101, and any such reproduction, depiction, portrayal, or other use of a work is not a destruction, distortion, mutilation, or other modification described in paragraph (3) of subsection (a).

(d) **Duration of Rights.**

(1) With respect to works of visual art created on or after the effective date set forth in section 610(a) of the Visual Artists Rights Act of 1990 [note to this section], the rights conferred by subsection (a) shall endure for a term consisting of the life of the author.

(2) With respect to works of visual art created before the effective date set forth in section 610(a) of the Visual Artists Rights Act of 1990 [note to this section], but title to which has not, as of such effective date, been transferred from the author, the rights conferred by subsection (a) shall be coextensive with, and shall expire at the same time as, the rights conferred by section 106.

(3) In the case of a joint work prepared by two or more authors, the rights conferred by subsection (a) shall endure for a term consisting of the life of the last surviving author.

(4) All terms of the rights conferred by subsection (a) run to the end of the calendar year in which they would otherwise expire.

(e) **Transfer and Waiver.**

(1) The rights conferred by subsection (a) may not be transferred, but those rights may be waived if the author expressly agrees to such waiver in a written instrument signed by the author. Such instrument shall specifically identify the work, and uses of that work, to which the waiver applies, and the waiver shall apply only to the work and uses so identified. In the case of a joint work prepared by two or more authors, a waiver of rights under this paragraph made by one such author waives such rights for all such authors.

(2) Ownership of the rights conferred by subsection (a) with respect to a work of visual art is distinct from ownership of any copy of that work, or of a copyright or any exclusive right under a copyright in that work. Transfer of ownership of any copy of a work of visual art, or of a copyright or any exclusive right under a copyright, shall not constitute a waiver of the rights conferred by subsection (a). Except as may otherwise be agreed by the author in a written instrument signed by the author, a waiver of the rights conferred by subsection (a) with respect to a work of visual art shall not constitute a transfer of ownership of any copy of that work, or of ownership of a copyright or of any exclusive right under a copyright in that work.

(Added Dec. 1, 1990, P. L. 101-650, Title VI, § 603(a), 104 Stat. 5128.)

§ 107 Limitations on exclusive rights: Fair use

Notwithstanding the provisions of sections 106 and 106A, the fair use of a copyrighted work, including such use by reproduction in copies or phonorecords or by any other means specified by that section, for purposes such as criticism, comment, news reporting, teaching (including multiple copies for classroom use), scholarship, or research, is not an infringement of copyright. In determining whether the use made of a work in any particular case is a fair use the factors to be considered shall include—

(1) the purpose and character of the use, including whether such use is of a commercial nature or is for nonprofit educational purposes;

(2) the nature of the copyrighted work;

(3) the amount and substantiality of the portion used in relation to the copyrighted work as a whole; and

(4) the effect of the use upon the potential market for or value of the copyrighted work.

The fact that a work is unpublished shall not itself bar a finding of fair use if such finding is made upon consideration of all the above factors.

(Oct. 19, 1976, P. L. 94-553, Title I, § 101, 90 Stat. 2546; Dec. 1, 1990, P. L. 101-650, Title VI, § 607, 104 Stat. 5132; Oct. 24, 1992, P. L. 102-492, 106 Stat. 3145.)

§ 108 Limitations on exclusive rights: Reproduction by libraries and archives

(a) Except as otherwise provided in this title and notwithstanding the provisions of section 106, it is not an infringement of copyright for a library or archives, or any of its employees acting within the scope of their employment, to reproduce no more than one copy or phonorecord of a work, except as provided in subsections (b) and (c), or to distribute such copy or phonorecord, under the conditions specified by this section, if—

(1) the reproduction or distribution is made without any purpose of direct or indirect commercial advantage;

(2) the collections of the library or archives are (i) open to the public, or (ii) available not only to researchers affiliated with the library or archives or with the institution of which it is a part, but also to other persons doing research in a specialized field; and

(3) the reproduction or distribution of the work includes a notice of copyright that appears on the copy or phonorecord that is reproduced under the provisions of this section, or includes a legend stating that the work may be protected by copyright if no such notice can be found on the copy or phonorecord that is reproduced under the provisions of this section.

(b) The rights of reproduction and distribution under this section apply to three copies or phonorecords of an unpublished work duplicated solely for purposes of preservation and security or for deposit for research use in another library or archives of the type described by clause (2) of subsection (a), if—

(1) the copy or phonorecord reproduced is currently in the collections of the library or archives; and

(2) any such copy or phonorecord that is reproduced in digital format is not otherwise distributed in that format and is not made available to the public in that format outside the premises of the library or archives.

(c) The right of reproduction under this section applies to three copies or phonorecords of a published work duplicated solely for the purpose of replacement of a copy or phonorecord that is damaged, deteriorating, lost, or stolen, or if the existing format in which the work is stored has become obsolete, if—

(1) the library or archives has, after a reasonable effort, determined that an unused replacement cannot be obtained at a fair price; and

(2) any such copy or phonorecord that is reproduced in digital format is not made available to the public in that format outside the premises of the library or archives in lawful possession of such copy.

For purposes of this subsection, a format shall be considered obsolete if the machine or device necessary to render perceptible a work stored in that format is no longer manufactured or is no longer reasonably available in the commercial marketplace.

(d) The rights of reproduction and distribution under this section apply to a copy, made from the collection of a library or archives where the user makes his or her request or from that of another library or archives, of no more than one article or other contribution to a copyrighted collection or periodical issue, or to a copy or phonorecord of a small part of any other copyrighted work, if—

(1) the copy or phonorecord becomes the property of the user, and the library or archives has had no notice that the copy or phonorecord would be used for any purpose other than private study, scholarship, or research; and

(2) the library or archives displays prominently, at the place where orders are accepted, and includes on its order form, a warning of copyright in accordance with requirements that the Register of Copyrights in accordance with requirements that the Register of Copyrights shall prescribe by regulation.

(e) The rights of reproduction and distribution under this section apply to the entire work, or to a substantial part of it, made from the collection of a library or archives where the user makes his or her request or from that of another library or archives, if the library or archives has first determined, on the basis of a reasonable investigation, that a copy or phonorecord of the copyrighted work cannot be obtained at a fair price, if—

(1) the copy or phonorecord becomes the property of the user, and the library or archives has had no notice that the copy or phonorecord would be used for any purpose other than private study, scholarship, or research; and

(2) the library or archives displays prominently, at the place where orders are accepted, and includes on its order form, a warning of copyright in accordance with requirements that the Register of Copyrights shall prescribe by regulation.

(f) Nothing in this section—

(1) shall be construed to impose liability for copyright infringement upon a library or archives or its employees for the unsupervised use of reproducing equipment located on its premises: Provided, That such equipment displays a notice that the making of a copy may be subject to the copyright law;

(2) excuses a person who uses such reproducing equipment or who requests a copy or phonorecord under subsection (d) from liability for copyright infringement for any such act, or for any later use of such copy or phonorecord, if it exceeds fair use as provided by section 107;

(3) shall be construed to limit the reproduction and distribution by lending of a limited number of copies and excerpts by a library or archives of an audiovisual news program, subject to clauses (1), (2), and (3) of subsection (a); or

(4) in any way affects the right of fair use as provided by section 107, or any contractual obligations assumed at any time by the library or archives when it obtained a copy or phonorecord of a work in its collections.

(g) The rights of reproduction and distribution under this section extend to the isolated and unrelated reproduction or distribution of a single copy or phonorecord of the same material on separate occasions, but do not extend to cases where the library or archives, or its employee—

(1) is aware or has substantial reason to believe that it is engaging in the related or concerted reproduction or distribution of multiple copies or phonorecords of the same material, whether made on one occasion or over a period of time, and whether intended for aggregate use by one or more individuals or for separate use by the individual members of a group; or

(2) engages in the systematic reproduction or distribution of single or multiple copies or phonorecords of material described in subsection (d): Provided, That nothing in this clause prevents a library or archives from participating in interlibrary arrangements that do not have, as their purpose or effect, that the library or archives receiving such copies or phonorecords for distribution does so in such aggregate quantities as to substitute for a subscription to or purchase of such work.

(h) (1) For purposes of this section, during the last 20 years of any term of copyright of a published work, a library or archives, including a nonprofit educational institution that functions as such, may reproduce, distribute, display, or perform in facsimile or digital form a copy or phonorecord of such work, or portions thereof, for purposes of preservation, scholarship, or research, if such library or archives has first determined, on the basis of a reasonable investigation, that none of the conditions set forth in subparagraphs (A), (B), and (C) of paragraph (2) apply.

(2) No reproduction, distribution, display, or performance is authorized under this subsection if—

(A) the work is subject to normal commercial exploitation;

(B) a copy or phonorecord of the work can be obtained at a reasonable price; or

(C) the copyright owner or its agent provides notice pursuant to regulations promulgated by the Register of Copyrights that either of the conditions set forth in subparagraphs (A) and (B) applies.

(3) The exemption provided in this subsection does not apply to any subsequent uses by users other than such library or archives.

(i) The rights of reproduction and distribution under this section do not apply to a musical work, a pictorial, graphic or sculptural work, or a motion picture or other audiovisual work other than an audiovisual work dealing with news, except that no such limitation shall apply with respect to rights granted by subsections (b), (c), and (h), or with respect to pictorial or graphic works published as illustrations, diagrams, or similar adjuncts to works of which copies are reproduced or distributed in accordance with subsections (d) and (e).

(Oct. 19, 1976, P. L. 94-553, Title I, § 101, 90 Stat 2546; June 26, 1992, P. L. 102-307, Title III, § 301, 106 Stat. 272; Nov. 13, 1997, P. L. 105-80, § 12(a)(4), 111 Stat. 1534; Oct. 27, 1998, P. L. 105-298, Title I, § 104, 112 Stat. 2829; Oct. 28, 1998, P. L. 105-304, Title IV, § 404, 112 Stat. 2889; April 27, 2005, P. L. 109-9, Title IV, § 402, 119 Stat. 227.)

First Sale Doctrine

§ 109 Limitations on exclusive rights: Effect of transfer of particular copy or phonorecord

(a) Notwithstanding the provisions of section 106(3), the owner of a particular copy or phonorecord lawfully made under this title, or any person authorized by such owner, is entitled, without the authority of the copyright owner, to sell or otherwise dispose of the possession of that copy or phonorecord. Notwithstanding the preceding sentence, copies or phonorecords of works subject to restored copyright under section 104A that are manufactured before the date of restoration of copyright or, with respect to reliance parties, before publication or service of notice under section 104A(e), may be sold or otherwise disposed of without the authorization of the owner of the restored copyright for purposes of direct or indirect commercial advantage only during the 12-month period beginning on—

(1) the date of the publication in the Federal Register of the notice of intent filed with the Copyright Office under section 104A(d)(2)(A), or

(2) the date of the receipt of actual notice served under section 104A(d)(2)(B),

whichever occurs first.

(b) (1) (A) Notwithstanding the provisions of subsection (a), unless authorized by the owners of copyright in the sound recording or the owner of copyright in a computer program (including any tape, disk, or other medium embodying such program), and in the case of a sound recording in the musical works embodied therein, neither the owner of a particular phonorecord nor any person in possession of a particular copy of a computer program (including any tape, disk, or other medium embodying such program), may, for the purposes of direct or indirect commercial advantage, dispose of, or authorize the disposal of, the possession of that phonorecord or computer program (including any tape, disk, or other medium embodying such program) by rental, lease, or lending, or by any other act or practice in the nature of rental, lease, or lending. Nothing in the preceding sentence shall apply to the rental, lease, or lending of a phonorecord for nonprofit purposes by a nonprofit library or nonprofit educational institution. The transfer of possession of a lawfully made copy of a computer program by a nonprofit educational institution to another nonprofit educational institution or to faculty, staff, and students does not constitute rental, lease, or lending for direct or indirect commercial purposes under this subsection.

(B) This subsection does not apply to—

(i) a computer program which is embodied in a machine or product and which cannot be copied during the ordinary operation or use of the machine or product; or

(ii) a computer program embodied in or used in conjunction with a limited purpose computer that is designed for playing video games and may be designed for other purposes.

(C) Nothing in this subsection affects any provision of chapter 9 of this title [17 USCS §§ 901 et seq.].

(2) (A) Nothing in this subsection shall apply to the lending of a computer program for nonprofit purposes by a nonprofit library, if each copy of a computer program which is lent by such library has affixed to the packaging containing the program a warning of copyright in accordance with requirements that the Register of Copyrights shall prescribe by regulation.

(B) Not later than three years after the date of the enactment of the Computer Software Rental Amendments Act of 1990 [enacted Dec. 1, 1990], and at such times thereafter as the Register of Copyrights considers appropriate, the Register of Copyrights, after consultation with representatives of copyright owners and librarians, shall submit to the Congress a report stating whether this paragraph has achieved its intended purpose of maintaining the integrity of the copyright system while providing nonprofit libraries the capability to fulfill their function. Such report shall advise the Congress as to any information or recommendations that the Register of Copyrights considers necessary to carry out the purposes of this subsection.

(3) Nothing in this subsection shall affect any provision of the antitrust laws. For purposes of the preceding sentence, "antitrust laws" has the meaning given that term in the first section of the Clayton Act [15 USCS § 12] and includes section 5 of the Federal Trade Commission Act [15 USCS § 45] to the extent that section relates to unfair methods of competition.

(4) Any person who distributes a phonorecord or a copy of a computer program (including any tape, disk, or other medium embodying such program) in violation of paragraph (1) is an infringer of copyright under section 501 of this title and is subject to the remedies set forth in sections 502, 503, 504, and 505 [17 USCS §§ 502, 503, 504, and 505]. Such violation shall not be a criminal offense under section 506 or cause such person to be subject to the criminal penalties set forth in section 2319 of title 18.

(c) Notwithstanding the provisions of section 106(5), the owner of a particular copy lawfully made under this title, or any person authorized by such owner, is entitled, without the authority of the copyright owner, to display that copy publicly, either directly or by the projection of no more than one image at a time, to viewers present at the place where the copy is located.

(d) The privileges prescribed by subsections (a) and (c) do not, unless authorized by the copyright owner, extend to any person who has acquired possession of the copy or phonorecord from the copyright owner, by rental, lease, loan, or otherwise, without acquiring ownership of it.

(e) [Caution: For termination of application of this subsection, see § 804(c) of Act Dec. 1, 1990, P. L. 101-650.] Notwithstanding the provisions of sections 106(4) and 106(5), in the case of an electronic audiovisual game intended for use in coin-operated equipment, the owner of a particular copy of such a game lawfully made under this title, is entitled, without the authority of the copyright owner of the game, to publicly perform or display that game in coin-operated equipment, except that this subsection shall not apply to any work of authorship embodied in the audiovisual game if the copyright owner of the electronic audiovisual game is not also the copyright owner of the work of authorship.

(Oct. 19, 1976, P. L. 94-553, Title I, § 101, 90 Stat 2548; Oct. 4, 1984, P. L. 98-450, § 2, 98 Stat. 1727; Nov. 5, 1988, P. L. 100-617, § 2, 102 Stat. 3194; Dec. 1, 1990, P. L. 101-650, Title VIII, §§ 802, 803, 104 Stat. 5134, 5135; Dec. 8, 1994, P. L. 103-465, Title V, Subtitle A, § 514(b), 108 Stat. 4981; Nov. 13, 1997, P. L. 105-80, § 12(a)(5), 111 Stat. 1534; October 13, 2008, P. L. 110-403, § 209(a)(1), 112 Stat. 4260.)

§ 110 Limitations on exclusive rights: Exemption of certain performances and displays

Notwithstanding the provisions of section 106, the following are not infringements of copyright:

(1) performance or display of a work by instructors or pupils in the course of face-to-face teaching activities of a nonprofit educational institution, in a classroom or similar place devoted to instruction, unless, in the case of a motion picture or other audiovisual work, the performance, or the display of individual images, is given by means of a copy that was not lawfully made under this title, and that the person responsible for the performance knew or had reason to believe was not lawfully made;

(2) except with respect to a work produced or marketed primarily for performance or display as part of mediated instructional activities transmitted via digital networks, or a performance or display that is given by means of a copy or phonorecord that is not lawfully made and acquired under this title, and the transmitting government body or accredited nonprofit educational institution knew or had reason to believe was not lawfully made and acquired, the performance of a nondramatic literary or musical work or reasonable and limited portions of any other work, or display of a work in an amount comparable to that which is typically displayed in the course of a live classroom session, by or in the course of a transmission, if—

(A) the performance or display is made by, at the direction of, or under the actual supervision of an instructor as an integral part of a class session offered as a regular part of the systematic mediated instructional activities of a governmental body or an accredited nonprofit educational institution;

(B) the performance or display is directly related and of material assistance to the teaching content of the transmission;

(C) the transmission is made solely for, and, to the extent technologically feasible, the reception of such transmission is limited to—

(i) students officially enrolled in the course for which the transmission is made; or

(ii) officers or employees of governmental bodies as a part of their official duties or employment; and

(D) the transmitting body or institution—

(i) institutes policies regarding copyright, provides informational materials to faculty, students, and relevant staff members that accurately describe, and promote compliance with, the laws of the United States relating to copyright, and provides notice to students that materials used in connection with the course may be subject to copyright protection; and

(ii) in the case of digital transmissions—

(I) applies technological measures that reasonably prevent—

(aa) retention of the work in accessible form by recipients of the transmission from the transmitting body or institution for longer than the class session; and

(bb) unauthorized further dissemination of the work in accessible form by such recipients to others; and

(II) does not engage in conduct that could reasonably be expected to interfere with technological measures used by copyright owners to prevent such retention or unauthorized further dissemination;

(3) performance of a nondramatic literary or musical work or of a dramatico-musical work of a religious nature, or display of a work, in the course of services at a place of worship or other religious assembly;

(4) performance of a nondramatic literary or musical work otherwise than in a transmission to the public, without any purpose of direct or indirect commercial advantage and without payment of any fee or other compensation for the performance to any of its performers, promoters, or organizers, if—

(A) there is no direct or indirect admission charge; or

(B) the proceeds, after deducting the reasonable costs of producing the performance, are used exclusively for educational, religious, or charitable purposes and not for private financial gain, except where the copyright owner has served notice of objection to the performance under the following conditions:

(i) the notice shall be in writing and signed by the copyright owner or such owner's duly authorized agent; and

(ii) the notice shall be served on the person responsible for the performance at least seven days before the date of the performance, and shall state the reasons for the objection; and

(iii) the notice shall comply, in form, content, and manner of service, with requirements that the Register of Copyrights shall prescribe by regulation;

(5) (A) except as provided in subparagraph (B), communication of a transmission embodying a performance or display of a work by

the public reception of the transmission on a single receiving apparatus of a kind commonly used in private homes, unless—

(i) a direct charge is made to see or hear the transmission; or

(ii) the transmission thus received is further transmitted to the public;

(B) communication by an establishment of a transmission or retransmission embodying a performance or display of a nondramatic musical work intended to be received by the general public, originated by a radio or television broadcast station licensed as such by the Federal Communications Commission, or, if an audiovisual transmission, by a cable system or satellite carrier, if—

(i) in the case of an establishment other than a food service or drinking establishment, either the establishment in which the communication occurs has less than 2,000 gross square feet of space (excluding space used for customer parking and for no other purpose), or the establishment in which the communication occurs has 2,000 or more gross square feet of space (excluding space used for customer parking and for no other purpose) and—

(I) if the performance is by audio means only, the performance is communicated by means of a total of not more than 6 loudspeakers, of which not more than 4 loudspeakers are located in any 1 room or adjoining outdoor space; or

(II) if the performance or display is by audiovisual means, any visual portion of the performance or display is communicated by means of a total of not more than 4 audiovisual devices, of which not more than 1 audiovisual device is located in any 1 room, and no such audiovisual device has a diagonal screen size greater than 55 inches, and any audio portion of the performance or display is communicated by means of a total of not more than 6 loudspeakers, of which not more than 4 loudspeakers are located in any 1 room or adjoining outdoor space;

(ii) in the case of a food service or drinking establishment, either the establishment in which the communication occurs has less than 3,750 gross square feet of space (excluding space used for customer parking and for no other purpose), or the establishment in which the communication occurs has 3,750 gross square feet of space or more (excluding space used for customer parking and for no other purpose) and—

(I) if the performance is by audio means only, the performance is communicated by means of a total of not more than 6 loudspeakers, of which not more than 4 loudspeakers are located in any 1 room or adjoining outdoor space; or

(II) if the performance or display is by audiovisual means, any visual portion of the performance or display is communicated by means of a total of not more than 4 audiovisual devices, of which not more than 1 audiovisual device is located in any 1 room, and no such audiovisual device has a diagonal screen size greater than 55 inches, and any audio portion of the performance or display is communicated by means of a total of not more than 6 loudspeakers, of which not more than 4 loudspeakers are located in any 1 room or adjoining outdoor space;

(iii) no direct charge is made to see or hear the transmission or retransmission;

(iv) the transmission or retransmission is not further transmitted beyond the establishment where it is received; and

(v) the transmission or retransmission is licensed by the copyright owner of the work so publicly performed or displayed;

(6) performance of a nondramatic musical work by a governmental body or a nonprofit agricultural or horticultural organization, in the course of an annual agricultural or horticultural fair or exhibition conducted by such body or organization; the exemption provided by this clause shall extend to any liability for copyright infringement that would otherwise be imposed on such body or organization, under doctrines of vicarious liability or related infringement, for a performance by a concessionnaire, business establishment, or other person at such fair or exhibition, but shall not excuse any such person from liability for the performance;

(7) performance of a nondramatic musical work by a vending establishment open to the public at large without any direct or indirect admission charge, where the sole purpose of the performance is to promote the retail sale of copies or phonorecords of the work, or of the audiovisual or other devices utilized in such performance, and the performance is not transmitted beyond the place where the establishment is located and is within the immediate area where the sale is occurring;

(8) performance of a nondramatic literary work, by or in the course of a transmission specifically designed for and primarily directed to blind or other handicapped persons who are unable to read normal printed material as a result of their handicap, or deaf or other handicapped persons who are unable to hear the aural signals accompanying a transmission of visual signals, if the performance is made without any purpose of direct or indirect commercial advantage and its transmission is made through the facilities of: (i) a governmental body; or (ii) a noncommercial educational broadcast station (as defined in section 397 of title 47); or (iii) a radio subcarrier authorization (as defined in 47 CFR

73.293–73.295 and 73.593–73.595); or (iv) a cable system (as defined in section 111(f));

(9) performance on a single occasion of a dramatic literary work published at least ten years before the date of the performance, by or in the course of a transmission specifically designed for and primarily directed to blind or other handicapped persons who are unable to read normal printed material as a result of their handicap, if the performance is made without any purpose of direct or indirect commercial advantage and its transmission is made through the facilities of a radio subcarrier authorization referred to in clause (8)(iii), Provided, That the provisions of this clause shall not be applicable to more than one performance of the same work by the same performers or under the auspices of the same organization;

(10) notwithstanding paragraph (4), the following is not an infringement of copyright: performance of a nondramatic literary or musical work in the course of a social function which is organized and promoted by a nonprofit veterans' organization or a nonprofit fraternal organization to which the general public is not invited, but not including the invitees of the organizations, if the proceeds from the performance, after deducting the reasonable costs of producing the performance, are used exclusively for charitable purposes and not for financial gain. For purposes of this section the social functions of any college or university fraternity or sorority shall not be included unless the social function is held solely to raise funds for a specific charitable purpose; and

(11) the making imperceptible, by or at the direction of a member of a private household, of limited portions of audio or video content of a motion picture, during a performance in or transmitted to that household for private home viewing, from an authorized copy of the motion picture, or the creation or provision of a computer program or other technology that enables such making imperceptible and that is designed and marketed to be used, at the direction of a member of a private household, for such making imperceptible, if no fixed copy of the altered version of the motion picture is created by such computer program or other technology.

The exemptions provided under paragraph (5) shall not be taken into account in any administrative, judicial, or other governmental proceeding to set or adjust the royalties payable to copyright owners for the public performance or display of their works. Royalties payable to copyright owners for any public performance or display of their works other than such performances or displays as are exempted under paragraph (5) shall not be diminished in any respect as a result of such exemption.

In paragraph (2), the term 'mediated instructional activities' with respect to the performance or display of a work by digital transmission under this section refers to activities that use such work as an integral part of the class experience, controlled by or under the actual supervision of the instructor and analogous to the type of performance or display that would take place in a live classroom setting. The term does not refer to activities that use, in 1 or more class sessions of a single course, such works as textbooks, course packs, or other material in any media, copies or phonorecords of which are typically purchased or acquired by the students in higher education for their independent use and retention or are typically purchased or acquired for elementary and secondary students for their possession and independent use.

For purposes of paragraph (2), accreditation—

(A) with respect to an institution providing post-secondary education, shall be as determined by a regional or national accrediting agency recognized by the Council on Higher Education Accreditation or the United States Department of Education; and

(B) with respect to an institution providing elementary or secondary education, shall be as recognized by the applicable state certification or licensing procedures.

For purposes of paragraph (2), no governmental body or accredited nonprofit educational institution shall be liable for infringement by reason of the transient or temporary storage of material carried out through the automatic technical process of a digital transmission of the performance or display of that material as authorized under paragraph (2). No such material stored on the system or network controlled or operated by the transmitting body or institution under this paragraph shall be maintained on such system or network in a manner ordinarily accessible to anyone other than anticipated recipients. No such copy shall be maintained on the system or network in a manner ordinarily accessible to such anticipated recipients for a longer period than is reasonably necessary to facilitate the transmissions for which it was made.

For purposes of paragraph (11), the term "making imperceptible" does not include the addition of audio or video content that is performed or displayed over or in place of existing content in a motion picture.

Nothing in paragraph (11) shall be construed to imply further rights under section 106 of this title, or to have any effect on defenses or limitations on rights granted under any other section of this title or under any other paragraph of this section.

(Oct. 19, 1976, P. L. 94-553, Title I, § 101, 90 Stat 2549; Oct. 15, 1982, P. L. 97-366, § 3, 96 Stat. 1759; Nov. 13, 1997, P. L. 105-80, § 12(a)(6), 111 Stat. 1534; Oct. 27, 1998, P. L. 105-298, Title II, § 202, 112 Stat. 2830; Aug. 5, 1999, P. L. 106-44, § 1(a), 113 Stat. 221; Nov. 2, 2002, P. L. 107-273, Div C, Title III, Subtitle B, § 13210(6), Subtitle C, § 13301(b), 116 Stat. 1909, 1910; April 27, 2005, P. L. 109-9, Title II, § 202(a), 119 Stat. 223.)

§ 111 Limitations on exclusive rights: Secondary transmissions

(a) **Certain Secondary Transmissions Exempted.** The secondary transmission of a performance or display of a work embodied in a primary transmission is not an infringement of copyright if—

(1) the secondary transmission is not made by a cable system, and consists entirely of the relaying, by the management of a hotel, apartment house, or similar establishment, of signals transmitted by a broadcast station licensed by the Federal Communications Commission, within the local service area of such station, to the private lodgings of guests or residents of such establishment, and no direct charge is made to see or hear the secondary transmission; or

(2) the secondary transmission is made solely for the purpose and under the conditions specified by clause (2) of section 110 [17 USCS § 110]; or

(3) the secondary transmission is made by any carrier who has no direct or indirect control over the content or selection of the primary transmission or over the particular recipients of the secondary transmission, and whose activities with respect to the secondary transmission consist solely of providing wires, cables, or other communications channels for the use of others: Provided, That the provisions of this clause extend only to the activities of said carrier with respect to secondary transmissions and do not exempt from liability the activities of others with respect to their own primary or secondary transmissions;

(4) the secondary transmission is made by a satellite carrier pursuant to a statutory license under section 119 [17 USCS § 119]; or

(5) the secondary transmission is not made by a cable system but is made by a governmental body, or other nonprofit organization, without any purpose of direct or indirect commercial advantage, and without charge to the recipients of the secondary transmission other than assessments necessary to defray the actual and reasonable costs of maintaining and operating the secondary transmission service.

(b) **Secondary Transmission of Primary Transmission to Controlled Group.** Notwithstanding the provisions of subsections (a) and (c), the secondary transmission to the public of a performance or display of a work embodied in a primary transmission is actionable as an act of infringement under section 501 [17 USCS § 501], and is fully subject to the remedies provided by sections 502 through 506 [17 USCS §§ 502–506], if the primary transmission is not made for reception by the public at large but is controlled and limited to reception by particular members of the public: Provided, however, That such secondary transmission is not actionable as an act of infringement if—

(1) the primary transmission is made by a broadcast station licensed by the Federal Communications Commission; and

(2) the carriage of the signals comprising the secondary transmission is required under the rules, regulations, or authorizations of the Federal Communications Commission; and

(3) the signal of the primary transmitter is not altered or changed in any way by the secondary transmitter.

(c) **Secondary Transmissions by Cable Systems.**

(1) Subject to the provisions of clauses (2), (3), and (4) of this subsection and section 114(d) [17 USCS § 114(d)], secondary transmissions to the public by a cable system of a performance or display of a work embodied in a primary transmission made by a broadcast station licensed by the Federal Communications Commission or by an appropriate governmental authority of Canada or Mexico shall be subject to statutory licensing upon compliance with the requirements of subsection (d) where the carriage of the signals comprising the secondary transmission is permissible under the rules, regulations, or authorizations of the Federal Communications Commission.

(2) Notwithstanding the provisions of clause (1) of this subsection, the willful or repeated secondary transmission to the public by a cable system of a primary transmission made by a broadcast station licensed by the Federal Communications Commission or by an appropriate governmental authority of Canada or Mexico and embodying a performance or display of a work is actionable as an act of infringement under section 501 [17 USCS § 501], and is fully subject to the remedies provided by sections 502 through 506 [17 USCS §§ 502–506], in the following cases:

(A) where the carriage of the signals comprising the secondary transmission is not permissible under the rules, regulations, or authorizations of the Federal Communications Commission; or

(B) where the cable system has not deposited the statement of account and royalty fee required by subsection (d).

(3) Notwithstanding the provisions of clause (1) of this subsection and subject to the provisions of subsection (e) of this section, the secondary transmission to the public by a cable system of a performance or display of a work embodied in a primary transmission made by a broadcast station licensed by the Federal Communications Commission or by an appropriate governmental authority of Canada or Mexico is actionable as an act of infringement under section 501 [17 USCS § 501], and is fully subject to the remedies provided by sections 502 through 506 [17 USCS §§ 502–506] and section 510 [17 USCS § 510], if the content of the particular program in which the performance or display is embodied, or any commercial advertising or station announcements transmitted by the primary transmitter during, or immediately before or after, the transmission of such program, is in any way willfully altered by the cable system through changes, deletions, or additions, except for the alteration, deletion, or substitution of commercial advertisements performed by those engaged in television commercial advertising market research: Provided, That the research company has obtained the prior consent of the advertiser who has purchased the original commercial advertisement, the television station broadcasting that commercial advertisement, and the cable system performing the secondary transmission: And provided further, That such commercial alteration, deletion, or substitution is not performed for the purpose of deriving income from the sale of that commercial time.

(4) Notwithstanding the provisions of clause (1) of this subsection, the secondary transmission to the public by a cable system of a performance or display of a work embodied in a primary transmission made by a broadcast station licensed by an appropriate governmental authority of Canada or Mexico is actionable as an act of infringement under section 501 [17 USCS § 501], and is fully subject to the remedies provided by sections 502 through 506 [17 USCS §§ 502–506], if (A) with respect to Canadian signals, the community of the cable system is located more than 150 miles from the United States-Canadian border and is also located south of the forty-second parallel of latitude, or (B) with respect to Mexican signals, the secondary transmission is made by a cable system which received the primary transmission by means other than direct interception of a free space radio wave emitted by such broadcast television station, unless prior to April 15, 1976, such cable system was actually carrying, or was specifically authorized to carry, the signal of such foreign station on the system pursuant to the rules, regulations, or authorizations of the Federal Communications Commission.

(d) **Statutory License for Secondary Transmissions by Cable Systems.**

(1) A cable system whose secondary transmissions have been subject to statutory licensing under subsection (c) shall, on a semiannual basis, deposit with the Register of Copyrights, in accordance with requirements that the Register shall prescribe by regulation—

(A) a statement of account, covering the six months next preceding, specifying the number of channels on which the cable system made secondary transmissions to its subscribers, the names and locations of all primary transmitters whose transmissions were further transmitted by the cable system, the total number of subscribers, the gross amounts paid to the cable system for the basic service of providing secondary transmissions of primary broadcast transmitters, and such other data as the Register of Copyrights may from time to time prescribe by regulation. In determining the total number of subscribers and the gross amounts paid to the cable system for the basic service of providing secondary transmissions of primary broadcast transmitters, the system shall not include subscribers and amounts collected from subscribers receiving secondary transmissions pursuant to section 119 [17 USCS § 119]. Such statement shall also include a special statement of account covering any nonnetwork television programming that was carried by the cable system in whole or in part beyond the local service area of the primary transmitter, under rules, regulations, or authorizations of the Federal Communications Commission permitting the substitution or addition of signals under certain circumstances, together with logs showing the times, dates, stations, and programs involved in such substituted or added carriage; and

(B) except in the case of a cable system whose royalty is specified in subclause (C) or (D), a total royalty fee for the period covered by the statement, computed on the basis of specified percentages of the gross receipts from subscribers to the cable service during said period for the basic service of providing secondary transmissions of primary broadcast transmitters, as follows:

(i) 0.675 of 1 per centum of such gross receipts for the privilege of further transmitting any nonnetwork programming of a primary transmitter in whole or in part beyond the local service area of such primary transmitter, such amount to be applied against the fee, if any, payable pursuant to paragraphs (ii) through (iv);

(ii) 0.675 of 1 per centum of such gross receipts for the first distant signal equivalent;

(iii) 0.425 of 1 per centum of such gross receipts for each of the second, third, and fourth distant signal equivalents;

(iv) 0.2 of 1 per centum of such gross receipts for the fifth distant signal equivalent and each additional distant signal equivalent thereafter; and in computing the amounts payable under paragraph (ii) through (iv), above, any fraction of a distant signal equivalent shall be computed at its fractional value and, in the case of any cable system located partly within and partly without the local service area of a primary transmitter, gross receipts shall be limited to those gross receipts derived from subscribers located without the local service area of such primary transmitter; and

(C) if the actual gross receipts paid by subscribers to a cable system for the period covered by the statement for the basic service of providing secondary transmissions of primary broadcast transmitters total $80,000 or less, gross receipts of the cable system for the purpose of this subclause shall be computed by subtracting from such actual gross receipts the amount by which $80,000 exceeds such actual gross receipts, except that in no case shall a cable system's gross receipts be reduced to less than $3,000. The royalty fee payable under this subclause shall be 0.5 of 1 per centum, regardless of the number of distant signal equivalents, if any; and

(D) if the actual gross receipts paid by subscribers to a cable system for the period covered by the statement, for the basic service of providing secondary transmissions of primary broadcast transmitters, are more than $80,000 but less than $160,000, the royalty fee payable under this subclause shall be (i) 0.5 of 1 per centum of any gross receipts up to $80,000; and (ii) 1 per centum of any gross receipts in excess of $80,000 but less than $160,000, regardless of the number of distant signal equivalents, if any.

(2) The Register of Copyrights shall receive all fees deposited under this section and, after deducting the reasonable costs incurred by the Copyright Office under this section, shall deposit the balance in the Treasury of the United States, in such manner as the Secretary of the Treasury directs. All funds held by the Secretary of the Treasury shall be invested in interest-bearing United States securities for later distribution with interest by the Librarian of Congress upon authorization by the Copyright Royalty Judges.

(3) The royalty fees thus deposited shall, in accordance with the procedures provided by clause (4), be distributed to those among the following copyright owners who claim that their works were the subject of secondary transmissions by cable systems during the relevant semiannual period:

(A) any such owner whose work was included in a secondary transmission made by a cable system of a nonnetwork television program in whole or in part beyond the local service area of the primary transmitter; and

(B) any such owner whose work was included in a secondary transmission identified in a special statement of account deposited under clause (1)(A); and

(C) any such owner whose work was included in nonnetwork programming consisting exclusively of aural signals carried by a cable system in whole or in part beyond the local service area of the primary transmitter of such programs.

(4) The royalty fees thus deposited shall be distributed in accordance with the following procedures:

(A) During the month of July in each year, every person claiming to be entitled to statutory license fees for secondary transmissions shall file a claim with the Copyright Royalty Judges, in accordance with requirements that the Copyright Royalty Judges shall prescribe by regulation. Notwithstanding any provisions of the antitrust laws, for purposes of this clause any claimants may agree among themselves as to the proportionate division of statutory licensing fees among them, may lump their claims together and file them jointly or as a single claim, or may designate a common agent to receive payment on their behalf.

(B) After the first day of August of each year, the Copyright Royalty Judges shall determine whether there exists a controversy concerning the distribution of royalty fees. If the Copyright Royalty Judges determine that no such controversy exists, the Copyright Royalty Judges shall authorize the Librarian of Congress to proceed to distribute such fees to the copyright owners entitled to receive them, or to their designated agents, subject to the deduction of reasonable administrative costs under this section. If the Copyright Royalty Judges find the existence of a controversy, the Copyright

Royalty Judges shall, pursuant to chapter 8 of this title [17 USCS §§ 801 et seq.], conduct a proceeding to determine the distribution of royalty fees.

(C) During the pendency of any proceeding under this subsection, the Copyright Royalty Judges shall have the discretion to authorize the Librarian of Congress to proceed to distribute any amounts that are not in controversy.

(e) **Nonsimultaneous Secondary Transmissions by Cable Systems.**

(1) Notwithstanding those provisions of the second paragraph of subsection (f) relating to nonsimultaneous secondary transmissions by a cable system, any such transmissions are actionable as an act of infringement under section 501 [17 USCS § 501], and are fully subject to the remedies provided by sections 502 through 506 [17 USCS §§ 502–506] and section 510 [17 USCS § 510], unless—

(A) the program on the videotape is transmitted no more than one time to the cable system's subscribers; and

(B) the copyrighted program, episode, or motion picture videotape, including the commercials contained within such program, episode, or picture, is transmitted without deletion or editing; and

(C) an owner or officer of the cable system (i) prevents the duplication of the videotape while in the possession of the system, (ii) prevents unauthorized duplication while in the possession of the facility making the videotape for the system if the system owns or controls the facility, or takes reasonable precautions to prevent such duplication if it does not own or control the facility, (iii) takes adequate precautions to prevent duplication while the tape is being transported, and (iv) subject to clause (2), erases or destroys, or causes the erasure or destruction of, the videotape; and

(D) within forty-five days after the end of each calendar quarter, an owner or officer of the cable system executes an affidavit attesting (i) to the steps and precautions taken to prevent duplication of the videotape, and (ii) subject to clause (2), to the erasure or destruction of all videotapes made or used during such quarter; and

(E) such owner or officer places or causes each such affidavit, and affidavits received pursuant to clause (2)(C), to be placed in a file, open to public inspection, at such system's main office in the community where the transmission is made or in the nearest community where such system maintains an office; and

(F) the nonsimultaneous transmission is one that the cable system would be authorized to transmit under the rules, regulations, and authorizations of the Federal Communications Commission in effect at the time of the nonsimultaneous transmission if the transmission had been made simultaneously, except that this subclause shall not apply to inadvertent or accidental transmissions.

(2) If a cable system transfers to any person a videotape of a program nonsimultaneously transmitted by it, such transfer is actionable as an act of infringement under section 501 [17 USCS § 501], and is fully subject to the remedies provided by sections 502 through 506 [17 USCS §§ 502–506], except that, pursuant to a written, nonprofit contract providing for the equitable sharing of the costs of such videotape and its transfer, a videotape nonsimultaneously transmitted by it, in accordance with clause (1), may be transferred by one cable system in Alaska to another system in Alaska, by one cable system in Hawaii permitted to make such nonsimultaneous transmissions to another such cable system in Hawaii, or by one cable system in Guam, the Northern Mariana Islands, the Federated States of Micronesia, the Republic of Palau, or the Republic of the Marshall Islands, to another cable system in any of those three territories, if—

(A) each such contract is available for public inspection in the offices of the cable systems involved, and a copy of such contract is filed, within thirty days after such contract is entered into, with the Copyright Office (which Office shall make each such contract available for public inspection); and

(B) the cable system to which the videotape is transferred complies with clause (1)(A), (B), (C)(i), (iii), and (iv), and (D) through (F); and

(C) such system provides a copy of the affidavit required to be made in accordance with clause (1)(D) to each cable system making a previous nonsimultaneous transmission of the same videotape.

(3) This subsection shall not be construed to supersede the exclusivity protection provisions of any existing agreement, or any such agreement hereafter entered into, between a cable system and a television broadcast station in the area in which the cable system is located, or a network with which such station is affiliated.

(4) As used in this subsection, the term "videotape", and each of its variant forms, means the reproduction of the images and sounds of a program or programs broadcast by a television broadcast station licensed by the Federal Communications Commission, regardless of the nature of the material objects, such as tapes or films, in which the reproduction is embodied.

(f) **Definitions.** As used in this section, the following terms and their variant forms mean the following:

A "primary transmission" is a transmission made to the public by the transmitting facility whose signals are being received and further transmitted by the secondary transmission service, regardless of where or when the performance or display was first transmitted.

A "secondary transmission" is the further transmitting of a primary transmission simultaneously with the primary transmission, or nonsimultaneously with the primary transmission if by a "cable system" not located in whole or in part within the boundary of the forty-eight contiguous States, Hawaii, or Puerto Rico: Provided, however, That a nonsimultaneous further transmission by a cable system located in Hawaii of a primary transmission shall be deemed to be a secondary transmission if the carriage of the television broadcast signal comprising such further transmission is permissible under the rules, regulations, or authorizations of the Federal Communications Commission.

A "cable system" is a facility, located in any State, Territory, Trust Territory, or Possession, that in whole or in part receives signals transmitted or programs broadcast by one or more television broadcast stations licensed by the Federal Communications Commission, and makes secondary transmissions of such signals or programs by wires, cables, microwave, or other communications channels to subscribing members of the public who pay for such service. For purposes of determining the royalty fee under subsection (d)(1), two or more cable systems in contiguous communities under common ownership or control or operating from one headend shall be considered as one system.

The "local service area of a primary transmitter", in the case of a television broadcast station, comprises the area in which such station is entitled to insist upon its signal being retransmitted by a cable system pursuant to the rules, regulations, and authorizations of the Federal Communications Commission in effect on April 15, 1976, or such station's television market as defined in section 76.55(e) of title 47, Code of Federal Regulations (as in effect on September 18, 1993), or any modifications to such television market made, on or after September 18, 1993, pursuant to section 76.55(e) or 76.59 of title 47 of the Code of Federal Regulations, or in the case of a television broadcast station licensed by an appropriate governmental authority of Canada or Mexico, the area in which it would be entitled to insist upon its signal being retransmitted if it were a television broadcast station subject to such rules, regulations, and authorizations. In the case of a low power television station, as defined by the rules and regulations of the Federal Communications Commission, the "local service area of a primary transmitter" comprises the area within 35 miles of the transmitter site, except that in the case of such a station located in a standard metropolitan statistical area which has one of the 50 largest populations of all standard metropolitan statistical areas (based on the 1980 decennial census of population taken by the Secretary of Commerce), the number of miles shall be 20 miles. The "local service area of a primary transmitter", in the case of a radio broadcast station, comprises the primary service area of such station, pursuant to the rules and regulations of the Federal Communications Commission.

A "distant signal equivalent" is the value assigned to the secondary transmission of any nonnetwork television programming carried by a cable system in whole or in part beyond the local service area of the primary transmitter of such programming. It is computed by assigning a value of one to each independent station and a value of one-quarter to each network station and noncommercial educational station for the nonnetwork programming so carried pursuant to the rules, regulations, and authorizations of the Federal Communications Commission. The foregoing values for independent, network, and noncommercial educational stations are subject, however, to the following exceptions and limitations. Where the rules and regulations of the Federal Communications Commission require a cable system to omit the further transmission of a particular program and such rules and regulations also permit the substitution of another program embodying a performance or display of a work in place of the omitted transmission, or where such rules and regulations in effect on the date of enactment of this Act [enacted Oct. 19, 1976) permit a cable system, at its election, to effect such deletion and substitution of a nonlive program or to carry additional programs not transmitted by primary transmitters within whose local service area the cable system is located, no value shall be assigned for the substituted or additional program; where the rules, regulations, or authorizations of the Federal Communications Commission in effect on the date of enactment of this Act [enacted Oct. 19, 1976] permit a cable system, at its election, to omit the further transmission of a particular program and such rules, regulations, or authorizations also permit the substitution of another program embodying a performance or display of a work in place of the omitted transmission, the value assigned for the substituted or additional program shall be, in the case of a live program, the value of one full distant signal equivalent multiplied by a fraction that has as its numerator the number of days in the year in which such substitution occurs and as its denominator the number of days in the year. In the case of a station carried pursuant to the late-night or specialty programming rules of the Federal Communications Commission, or a station carried on a part-time basis where full-time carriage is not possible because the cable system lacks the activated channel capacity to retransmit on a full-time basis all signals which it is authorized to carry, the values for independent, network, and noncommercial educational stations set forth above, as the case may be, shall be multiplied by a fraction which is equal to the ratio of the broadcast hours of such station carried by the cable system to the total broadcast hours of the station.

A "network station" is a television broadcast station that is owned or operated by, or affiliated with, one or more of the television networks in the United States providing nationwide transmissions, and that transmits a substantial part of the programming supplied by such networks for a substantial part of that station's typical broadcast day.

An "independent station" is a commercial television broadcast station other than a network station.

A "noncommercial educational station" is a television station that is a noncommercial educational broadcast station as defined in section 397 of title 47.

(Oct. 19, 1976, P. L. 94-553, Title I, § 101, 90 Stat. 2550; Aug. 27, 1986, P. L. 99-397, §§ 1, 2(a), (b), 100 Stat. 848; Nov. 16, 1988, P. L. 100-667, Title II, § 202(1), 102 Stat. 3949; July 3, 1990, P. L. 101-318, § 3(a), 104 Stat. 288; Dec. 17, 1993, P. L. 103-198, § 6(a), 107 Stat. 2311; Oct. 18, 1994, P. L. 103-369,

§ 3, 108 Stat. 3480; Nov. 1, 1995, P. L. 104-39, § 5(b), 109 Stat. 348; Nov. 29, 1999, P. L. 106-113, Div B, § 1000(a)(9), 113 Stat. 1536; Nov. 30, 2004, P. L. 108-419, § 5(a), 118 Stat. 2361; Dec. 8, 2004, P.L. 108-447, Div J, Title IX, Title I, § 107(b), 118 Stat. 3406; October 6, 2006, P.L. 109-303, § 4(a), 120 Stat. 1478; May 8, 2008, P. L. 110-229, § 807, 122 Stat. 874; October 13, 2008, P. L. 110-403, Title II, § 209(a)(2), 122 Stat. 4260.)

§ 112 Limitations on exclusive rights: Ephemeral recordings

(a) (1) Notwithstanding the provisions of section 106 [17 USCS § 106], and except in the case of a motion picture or other audiovisual work, it is not an infringement of copyright for a transmitting organization entitled to transmit to the public a performance or display of a work, under a license, including a statutory license under section 114(f) [17 USCS § 114(f)], or transfer of the copyright or under the limitations on exclusive rights in sound recordings specified by section 114(a) [17 USCS § 114(a)], or for a transmitting organization that is a broadcast radio or television station licensed as such by the Federal Communications Commission and that makes a broadcast transmission of a performance of a sound recording in a digital format on a nonsubscription basis, to make no more than one copy or phonorecord of a particular transmission program embodying the performance or display, if—

(A) the copy or phonorecord is retained and used solely by the transmitting organization that made it, and no further copies or phonorecords are reproduced from it; and

(B) the copy or phonorecord is used solely for the transmitting organization's own transmissions within its local service area, or for purposes of archival preservation or security; and

(C) unless preserved exclusively for archival purposes, the copy or phonorecord is destroyed within six months from the date the transmission program was first transmitted to the public.

(2) In a case in which a transmitting organization entitled to make a copy or phonorecord under paragraph (1) in connection with the transmission to the public of a performance or display of a work is prevented from making such copy or phonorecord by reason of the application by the copyright owner of technical measures that prevent the reproduction of the work, the copyright owner shall make available to the transmitting organization the necessary means for permitting the making of such copy or phonorecord as permitted under that paragraph, if it is technologically feasible and economically reasonable for the copyright owner to do so. If the copyright owner fails to do so in a timely manner in light of the transmitting organization's reasonable business requirements, the transmitting organization shall not be liable for a violation of section 1201(a)(1) of this title [17 USCS § 1201(a)(1)] for engaging in such

activities as are necessary to make such copies or phonorecords as permitted under paragraph (1) of this subsection.

(b) Notwithstanding the provisions of section 106 [17 USCS § 106], it is not an infringement of copyright for a governmental body or other nonprofit organization entitled to transmit a performance or display of a work, under section 110(2) [17 USCS § 110(2)] or under the limitations on exclusive rights in sound recordings specified by section 114(a) [17 USCS § 114(a)], to make no more than thirty copies or phonorecords of a particular transmission program embodying the performance or display, if—

(1) no further copies or phonorecords are reproduced from the copies or phonorecords made under this clause; and

(2) except for one copy or phonorecord that may be preserved exclusively for archival purposes, the copies or phonorecords are destroyed within seven years from the date the transmission program was first transmitted to the public.

(c) Notwithstanding the provisions of section 106, it is not an infringement of copyright for a governmental body or other nonprofit organization to make for distribution no more than one copy or phonorecord, for each transmitting organization specified in clause (2) of this subsection, of a particular transmission program embodying a performance of a nondramatic musical work of a religious nature, or of a sound recording of such a musical work, if—

(1) there is no direct or indirect charge for making or distributing any such copies or phonorecords; and

(2) none of such copies or phonorecords is used for any performance other than a single transmission to the public by a transmitting organization entitled to transmit to the public a performance of the work under a license or transfer of the copyright; and

(3) except for one copy or phonorecord that may be preserved exclusively for archival purposes, the copies or phonorecords are all destroyed within one year from the date the transmission program was first transmitted to the public.

(d) Notwithstanding the provisions of section 106 [17 USCS § 106], it is not an infringement of copyright for a governmental body or other nonprofit organization entitled to transmit a performance of a work under section 110(8) [17 USCS § 110(8)] to make no more than ten copies or phonorecords embodying the performance, or to permit the use of any such copy or phonorecord by any governmental body or nonprofit organization entitled to transmit a performance of a work under section 110(8) [17 USCS § 110(8)], if—

(1) any such copy or phonorecord is retained and used solely by the organization that made it, or by a governmental body or nonprofit organization entitled to transmit a performance of a work under section 110(8) [17 USCS § 110(8)], and no further copies or phonorecords are reproduced from it; and

(2) any such copy or phonorecord is used solely for transmissions authorized under section 110(8) [17 USCS § 110(8)], or for purposes of archival preservation or security; and

(3) the governmental body or nonprofit organization permitting any use of any such copy or phonorecord by any governmental body or nonprofit organization under this subsection does not make any charge for such use.

(e) **Statutory License.**

(1) A transmitting organization entitled to transmit to the public a performance of a sound recording under the limitation on exclusive rights specified by section 114(d)(1)(C)(iv) [17 USCS § 114(d)(1)(C)(iv)] or under a statutory license in accordance with section 114(f) [17 USCS § 114(f)] is entitled to a statutory license, under the conditions specified by this subsection, to make no more than 1 phonorecord of the sound recording (unless the terms and conditions of the statutory license allow for more), if the following conditions are satisfied:

(A) The phonorecord is retained and used solely by the transmitting organization that made it, and no further phonorecords are reproduced from it.

(B) The phonorecord is used solely for the transmitting organization's own transmissions originating in the United States under a statutory license in accordance with section 114(f) [17 USCS § 114(f)] or the limitation on exclusive rights specified by section 114(d)(1)(C)(iv) [17 USCS § 114(d)(1)(C)(iv)].

(C) Unless preserved exclusively for purposes of archival preservation, the phonorecord is destroyed within 6 months from the date the sound recording was first transmitted to the public using the phonorecord.

(D) Phonorecords of the sound recording have been distributed to the public under the authority of the copyright owner or the copyright owner authorizes the transmitting entity to transmit the sound recording, and the transmitting entity makes the phonorecord under this subsection from a phonorecord lawfully made and acquired under the authority of the copyright owner.

(2) Notwithstanding any provision of the antitrust laws, any copyright owners of sound recordings and any transmitting organizations entitled to a statutory license under this subsection may negotiate and agree upon royalty rates and license terms and conditions for making phonorecords of such sound recordings under this section and the proportionate division of fees paid among copyright owners, and may designate common agents to negotiate, agree to, pay, or receive such royalty payments.

(3) Proceedings under chapter 8 shall determine reasonable rates and terms of royalty payments for the activities specified by paragraph (1)

during the 5-year period beginning on January 1 of the second year following the year in which the proceedings are to be commenced, or such other period as the parties may agree. Such rates shall include a minimum fee for each type of service offered by transmitting organizations. Any copyright owners of sound recordings or any transmitting organizations entitled to a statutory license under this subsection may submit to the Copyright Royalty Judges licenses covering such activities with respect to such sound recordings. The parties to each proceeding shall bear their own costs.

(4) The schedule of reasonable rates and terms determined by the Copyright Royalty Judges shall, subject to paragraph (5), be binding on all copyright owners of sound recordings and transmitting organizations entitled to a statutory license under this subsection during the 5-year period specified in paragraph (3), or such other period as the parties may agree. Such rates shall include a minimum fee for each type of service offered by transmitting organizations. The Copyright Royalty Judges shall establish rates that most clearly represent the fees that would have been negotiated in the marketplace between a willing buyer and a willing seller. In determining such rates and terms, the Copyright Royalty Judges shall base their decision on economic, competitive, and programming information presented by the parties, including—

(A) whether use of the service may substitute for or may promote the sales of phonorecords or otherwise interferes with or enhances the copyright owner's traditional streams of revenue; and

(B) the relative roles of the copyright owner and the transmitting organization in the copyrighted work and the service made available to the public with respect to relative creative contribution, technological contribution, capital investment, cost, and risk.

In establishing such rates and terms, the Copyright Royalty Judges may consider the rates and terms under voluntary license agreements described in paragraphs (2) and (3). The Copyright Royalty Judges shall also establish requirements by which copyright owners may receive reasonable notice of the use of their sound recordings under this section, and under which records of such use shall be kept and made available by transmitting organizations entitled to obtain a statutory license under this subsection.

(5) License agreements voluntarily negotiated at any time between 1 or more copyright owners of sound recordings and 1 or more transmitting organizations entitled to obtain a statutory license under this subsection shall be given effect in lieu of any decision by the Librarian of Congress or determination by the Copyright Royalty Judges.

(6) (A) Any person who wishes to make a phonorecord of a sound recording under a statutory license in accordance with this subsection may do so without infringing the exclusive right of the copyright owner of the sound recording under section 106(1) [17 USCS § 106(1)]—

(i) by complying with such notice requirements as the Copyright Royalty Judges shall prescribe by regulation and by paying royalty fees in accordance with this subsection; or

(ii) if such royalty fees have not been set, by agreeing to pay such royalty fees as shall be determined in accordance with this subsection.

(B) Any royalty payments in arrears shall be made on or before the 20th day of the month next succeeding the month in which the royalty fees are set.

(7) If a transmitting organization entitled to make a phonorecord under this subsection is prevented from making such phonorecord by reason of the application by the copyright owner of technical measures that prevent the reproduction of the sound recording, the copyright owner shall make available to the transmitting organization the necessary means for permitting the making of such phonorecord as permitted under this subsection, if it is technologically feasible and economically reasonable for the copyright owner to do so. If the copyright owner fails to do so in a timely manner in light of the transmitting organization's reasonable business requirements, the transmitting organization shall not be liable for a violation of section 1201(a)(1) of this title [17 USCS § 1201(a)(1)] for engaging in such activities as are necessary to make such phonorecords as permitted under this subsection.

(8) Nothing in this subsection annuls, limits, impairs, or otherwise affects in any way the existence or value of any of the exclusive rights of the copyright owners in a sound recording, except as otherwise provided in this subsection, or in a musical work, including the exclusive rights to reproduce and distribute a sound recording or musical work, including by means of a digital phonorecord delivery, under sections 106(1), 106(3), and 115 [17 USCS §§ 106(1), 106(3), and 115], and the right to perform publicly a sound recording or musical work, including by means of a digital audio transmission, under sections 106(4) and 106(6) [17 USCS §§ 106(4) and 106(6)].

(f) (1) Notwithstanding the provisions of section 106 [17 USCS § 106], and without limiting the application of subsection (b), it is not an infringement of copyright for a governmental body or other nonprofit educational institution entitled under section 110(2) [17 USCS § 110(2)] to transmit a performance or display to make copies or phonorecords of a work that is in digital form and, solely to the extent permitted in paragraph (2), of a work that is in analog form, embodying the performance or display to be used for making transmissions authorized under section 110(2) [17 USCS § 110(2)], if—

(A) such copies or phonorecords are retained and used solely by the body or institution that made them, and no further copies or phonorecords are reproduced from them, except as authorized under section 110(2) [17 USCS § 110(2)]; and

(B) such copies or phonorecords are used solely for transmissions authorized under section 110(2) [17 USCS § 110(2)].

(2) This subsection does not authorize the conversion of print or other analog versions of works into digital formats, except that such conversion is permitted hereunder, only with respect to the amount of such works authorized to be performed or displayed under section 110(2) [17 USCS § 110(2)], if—

(A) no digital version of the work is available to the institution; or

(B) the digital version of the work that is available to the institution is subject to technological protection measures that prevent its use for section 110(2) [17 USCS § 110(2)].

(g) The transmission program embodied in a copy or phonorecord made under this section is not subject to protection as a derivative work under this title except with the express consent of the owners of copyright in the preexisting works employed in the program.

(Oct. 19, 1976, P. L. 94-553, Title I, § 101, 90 Stat. 2558; Oct. 28, 1998, P. L. 105-304, Title IV, §§ 402, 405(b), 112 Stat. 2888; Aug. 5 1999, P. L. 106-44, § 1(b), 113 Stat. 221; Nov. 2, 2002, P. L. 107-273, Div C, Title III, Subtitle C, § 13301(c)(1), 116 Stat. 1912; Nov. 30, 2004, P. L. 108-419, § 5(b), 118 Stat. 2361.)

§ 113 Scope of exclusive rights in pictorial, graphic, and sculptural works

(a) Subject to the provisions of subsections (b) and (c) of this section, the exclusive right to reproduce a copyrighted pictorial, graphic, or sculptural work in copies under section 106 includes the right to reproduce the work in or on any kind of article, whether useful or otherwise.

(b) This title does not afford, to the owner of copyright in a work that portrays a useful article as such, any greater or lesser rights with respect to the making, distribution, or display of the useful article so portrayed than those afforded to such works under the law, whether title 17 or the common law or statutes of a State, in effect on December 31, 1977, as held applicable and construed by a court in an action brought under this title.

(c) In the case of a work lawfully reproduced in useful articles that have been offered for sale or other distribution to the public, copyright does not include any right to prevent the making, distribution, or display of pictures or photographs of such articles in connection with advertisements or commentaries related to the distribution or display of such articles, or in connection with news reports.

(d) (1) In a case in which—

(A) a work of visual art has been incorporated in or made part of a building in such a way that removing the work from the building will cause the destruction, distortion, mutilation, or other modification of the work as described in section 106A(a)(3) and

(B) the author consented to the installation of the work in the building either before the effective date set forth in section 610(a) of the Visual Artists Rights Act of 1990 [17 USCS § 106A note], or in a written instrument executed on or after such effective date that is signed by the owner of the building and the author and that specifies that installation of the work may subject the work to destruction, distortion, mutilation, or other modification, by reason of its removal, then the rights conferred by paragraphs (2) and (3) of section 106A(a) shall not apply.

(2) If the owner of a building wishes to remove a work of visual art which is a part of such building and which can be removed from the building without the destruction, distortion, mutilation, or other modification of the work as described in section 106A(a)(3) the author's rights under paragraphs (2) and (3) of section 106A(a) shall apply unless—

(A) the owner has made a diligent, good faith attempt without success to notify the author of the owner's intended action affecting the work of visual art, or

(B) the owner did provide such notice in writing and the person so notified failed, within 90 days after receiving such notice, either to remove the work or to pay for its removal.

For purposes of subparagraph (A), an owner shall be presumed to have made a diligent, good faith attempt to send notice if the owner sent such notice by registered mail to the author at the most recent address of the author that was recorded with the Register of Copyrights pursuant to paragraph (3). If the work is removed at the expense of the author, title to that copy of the work shall be deemed to be in the author.

(3) The Register of Copyrights shall establish a system of records whereby any author of a work of visual art that has been incorporated in or made part of a building, may record his or her identity and address with the Copyright Office. The Register shall also establish procedures under which any such author may update the information so recorded, and procedures under which owners of buildings may record with the Copyright Office evidence of their efforts to comply with this subsection.*

(Oct. 19, 1976, P. L. 94-553, Title I, § 101, 90 Stat. 2560; Dec. 1, 1990, P. L. 101-650, Title VI, § 604, 104 Stat. 5130.)

* This subsection (d) was effective June 1, 1991. 104 Stat. 5132.—*Eds.*

§ 114 Scope of exclusive rights in sound recordings

(a) The exclusive rights of the owner of copyright in a sound recording are limited to the rights specified by clauses (1), (2), (3) and (6) of section 106 [17 USCS § 106], and do not include any right of performance under section 106(4) [17 USCS § 106(4)].

(b) The exclusive right of the owner of copyright in a sound recording under clause (1) of section 106 [17 USCS § 106] is limited to the right to duplicate the sound recording in the form of phonorecords or copies that directly or indirectly recapture the actual sounds fixed in the recording. The exclusive right of the owner of copyright in a sound recording under clause (2) of section 106 [17 USCS § 106] is limited to the right to prepare a derivative work in which the actual sounds fixed in the sound recording are rearranged, remixed, or otherwise altered in sequence or quality. The exclusive rights of the owner of copyright in a sound recording under clauses (1) and (2) of section 106 [17 USCS § 106] do not extend to the making or duplication of another sound recording that consists entirely of an independent fixation of other sounds, even though such sounds imitate or simulate those in the copyrighted sound recording. The exclusive rights of the owner of copyright in a sound recording under clauses (1), (2), and (3) of section 106 [17 USCS § 106] do not apply to sound recordings included in educational television and radio programs (as defined in section 397 of title 47) distributed or transmitted by or through public broadcasting entities (as defined by section 118(g) [17 USCS § 118(g)]): Provided, That copies or phonorecords of said programs are not commercially distributed by or through public broadcasting entities to the general public.

(c) This section does not limit or impair the exclusive right to perform publicly, by means of a phonorecord, any of the works specified by section 106(4) [17 USCS § 106(4)].

(d) **Limitations on Exclusive Right.** Notwithstanding the provisions of section 106(6) [17 USCS § 106(6)]—

(1) *Exempt transmissions and retransmissions.* The performance of a sound recording publicly by means of a digital audio transmission, other than as a part of an interactive service, is not an infringement of section 106(6) [17 USCS § 106(6)] if the performance is part of—

(A) a nonsubscription broadcast transmission;

(B) a retransmission of a nonsubscription broadcast transmission: Provided, That, in the case of a retransmission of a radio station's broadcast transmission—

(i) the radio station's broadcast transmission is not willfully or repeatedly retransmitted more than a radius of 150 miles from the site of the radio broadcast transmitter, however—

(I) the 150 mile limitation under this clause shall not apply when a nonsubscription broadcast transmission by a radio station licensed by the Federal Communications Commission is retransmitted on a nonsubscription basis by a terrestrial broadcast station, terrestrial translator, or terrestrial repeater licensed by the Federal Communications Commission; and

(II) in the case of a subscription retransmission of a nonsubscription broadcast retransmission covered by subclause (I), the 150 mile radius shall be measured from the transmitter site of such broadcast retransmitter;

(ii) the retransmission is of radio station broadcast transmissions that are—

(I) obtained by the retransmitter over the air;

(II) not electronically processed by the retransmitter to deliver separate and discrete signals; and

(III) retransmitted only within the local communities served by the retransmitter;

(iii) the radio station's broadcast transmission was being retransmitted to cable systems (as defined in section 111(f) [17 USCS § 111(f)]) by a satellite carrier on January 1, 1995, and that retransmission was being retransmitted by cable systems as a separate and discrete signal, and the satellite carrier obtains the radio station's broadcast transmission in an analog format: Provided, That the broadcast transmission being retransmitted may embody the programming of no more than one radio station; or

(iv) the radio station's broadcast transmission is made by a noncommercial educational broadcast station funded on or after January 1, 1995, under section 396(k) of the Communications Act of 1934 (47 U.S.C. 396(k)), consists solely of noncommercial educational and cultural radio programs, and the retransmission, whether or not simultaneous, is a nonsubscription terrestrial broadcast retransmission; or

(C) a transmission that comes within any of the following categories—

(i) a prior or simultaneous transmission incidental to an exempt transmission, such as a feed received by and then retransmitted by an exempt transmitter: Provided, That such incidental transmissions do not include any subscription transmission directly for reception by members of the public;

(ii) a transmission within a business establishment, confined to its premises or the immediately surrounding vicinity;

(iii) a retransmission by any retransmitter, including a multichannel video programming distributor as defined in section 602(12) of the Communications Act of 1934 (47 U.S.C. 522(12)), of a transmission by a transmitter licensed to publicly perform the sound recording as a part of that transmission, if the retransmission is simultaneous with the licensed transmission and authorized by the transmitter; or

(iv) a transmission to a business establishment for use in the ordinary course of its business: Provided, That the business recipient does not retransmit the transmission outside of its premises or the immediately surrounding vicinity, and that the transmission does not exceed the sound recording performance complement. Nothing in this clause shall limit the scope of the exemption in clause (ii).

(2) *Statutory licensing of certain transmissions.* The performance of a sound recording publicly by means of a subscription digital audio transmission not exempt under paragraph (1), an eligible nonsubscription transmission, or a transmission not exempt under paragraph (1) that is made by a preexisting satellite digital audio radio service shall be subject to statutory licensing, in accordance with subsection (f) if—

(A) (i) the transmission is not part of an interactive service;

(ii) except in the case of a transmission to a business establishment, the transmitting entity does not automatically and intentionally cause any device receiving the transmission to switch from one program channel to another; and

(iii) except as provided in section 1002(e) [17 USCS § 1002(e)], the transmission of the sound recording is accompanied, if technically feasible, by the information encoded in that sound recording, if any, by or under the authority of the copyright owner of that sound recording, that identifies the title of the sound recording, the featured recording artist who performs on the sound recording, and related information, including information concerning the underlying musical work and its writer;

(B) in the case of a subscription transmission not exempt under paragraph (1) that is made by a preexisting subscription service in the same transmission medium used by such service on July 31, 1998, or in the case of a transmission not exempt under paragraph (1) that is made by a preexisting satellite digital audio radio service—

(i) the transmission does not exceed the sound recording performance complement; and

(ii) the transmitting entity does not cause to be published by means of an advance program schedule or prior announcement the titles of the specific sound recordings or phonorecords embodying such sound recordings to be transmitted; and

(C) in the case of an eligible nonsubscription transmission or a subscription transmission not exempt under paragraph (1) that is made by a new subscription service or by a preexisting subscription service other than in the same transmission medium used by such service on July 31, 1998—

(i) the transmission does not exceed the sound recording performance complement, except that this requirement shall not apply in the case of a retransmission of a broadcast transmission if the retransmission is made by a transmitting entity that does not have the right or ability to control the programming of the broadcast station making the broadcast transmission, unless—

(I) the broadcast station makes broadcast transmissions—

(aa) in digital format that regularly exceed the sound recording performance complement; or

(bb) in analog format, a substantial portion of which, on a weekly basis, exceed the sound recording performance complement; and

(II) the sound recording copyright owner or its representative has notified the transmitting entity in writing that broadcast transmissions of the copyright owner's sound recordings exceed the sound recording performance complement as provided in this clause;

(ii) the transmitting entity does not cause to be published, or induce or facilitate the publication, by means of an advance program schedule or prior announcement, the titles of the specific sound recordings to be transmitted, the phonorecords embodying such sound recordings, or, other than for illustrative purposes, the names of the featured recording artists, except that this clause does not disqualify a transmitting entity that makes a prior announcement that a particular artist will be featured within an unspecified future time period, and in the case of a retransmission of a broadcast transmission by a transmitting entity that does not have the right or ability to control the programming of the broadcast transmission, the requirement of this clause shall not apply to a prior oral announcement by the broadcast station, or to an advance program schedule published, induced, or facilitated by the broadcast station, if the transmitting entity does not have actual knowledge and has not received written notice from the copyright owner or its representative that the broadcast station publishes or induces or facilitates the publication of such advance program schedule, or if such advance program schedule is a schedule of classical music programming published by the broadcast station in the same manner as published by that broadcast station on or before September 30, 1998;

(iii) the transmission—

(I) is not part of an archived program of less than 5 hours duration;

(II) is not part of an archived program of 5 hours or greater in duration that is made available for a period exceeding 2 weeks;

(III) is not part of a continuous program which is of less than 3 hours duration; or

(IV) is not part of an identifiable program in which performances of sound recordings are rendered in a predetermined order, other than an archived or continuous program, that is transmitted at—

(aa) more than 3 times in any 2-week period that have been publicly announced in advance, in the case of a program of less than 1 hour in duration, or

(bb) more than 4 times in any 2-week period that have been publicly announced in advance, in the case of a program of 1 hour or more in duration, except that the requirement of this subclause shall not apply in the case of a retransmission of a broadcast transmission by a transmitting entity that does not have the right or ability to control the programming of the broadcast transmission, unless the transmitting entity is given notice in writing by the copyright owner of the sound recording that the broadcast station makes broadcast transmissions that regularly violate such requirement;

(iv) the transmitting entity does not knowingly perform the sound recording, as part of a service that offers transmissions of visual images contemporaneously with transmissions of sound recordings, in a manner that is likely to cause confusion, to cause mistake, or to deceive, as to the affiliation, connection, or association of the copyright owner or featured recording artist with the transmitting entity or a particular product or service advertised by the transmitting entity, or as to the origin, sponsorship, or approval by the copyright owner or featured recording artist of the activities of the transmitting entity other than the performance of the sound recording itself;

(v) the transmitting entity cooperates to prevent, to the extent feasible without imposing substantial costs or burdens, a transmission recipient or any other person or entity from automatically scanning the transmitting entity's transmissions alone or together with transmissions by other transmitting entities in order to select a particular sound recording to be transmitted to the transmission recipient, except that the requirement of this clause shall not apply to a satellite digital audio service that is in operation, or that is licensed by the Federal Communications Commission, on or before July 31, 1998;

(vi) the transmitting entity takes no affirmative steps to cause or induce the making of a phonorecord by the transmission recipient, and if the technology used by the transmitting entity enables the transmitting entity to limit the making by the transmission recipient of phonorecords of the transmission directly in a digital format, the transmitting entity sets such technology to limit such making of phonorecords to the extent permitted by such technology;

(vii) phonorecords of the sound recording have been distributed to the public under the authority of the copyright owner or the copyright owner authorizes the transmitting entity to transmit the sound recording, and the transmitting entity makes the transmission from a phonorecord lawfully made under the authority of the copyright owner, except that the requirement of this clause shall not apply to a retransmission of a broadcast transmission by a transmitting entity that does not have the right or ability to control the programming of the broadcast transmission, unless the transmitting entity is given notice in writing by the copyright owner of the sound recording that the broadcast station makes broadcast transmissions that regularly violate such requirement;

(viii) the transmitting entity accommodates and does not interfere with the transmission of technical measures that are widely used by sound recording copyright owners to identify or protect copyrighted works, and that are technically feasible of being transmitted by the transmitting entity without imposing substantial costs on the transmitting entity or resulting in perceptible aural or visual degradation of the digital signal, except that the requirement of this clause shall not apply to a satellite digital audio service that is in operation, or that is licensed under the authority of the Federal Communications Commission, on or before July 31, 1998, to the extent that such service has designed, developed, or made commitments to procure equipment or technology that is not compatible with such technical measures before such technical measures are widely adopted by sound recording copyright owners; and

(ix) the transmitting entity identifies in textual data the sound recording during, but not before, the time it is performed, including the title of the sound recording, the title of the phonorecord embodying such sound recording, if any, and the featured recording artist, in a manner to permit it to be displayed to the transmission recipient by the device or technology intended for receiving the service provided by the transmitting entity, except that the obligation in this clause shall not take effect until 1 year after the date of the enactment of the Digital Millennium Copyright Act [enacted Oct. 28, 1998] and shall not apply in the case of a retransmission of a broadcast transmission by a transmitting entity that does not have the right or ability to control the programming of the broadcast transmission, or in the case in which devices or technology intended for receiving the service provided by the transmitting entity that have the capability to display such textual data are not common in the marketplace.

(3) *Licenses for transmissions by interactive services.*

(A) No interactive service shall be granted an exclusive license under section 106(6) for the performance of a sound recording publicly by means of digital audio transmission for a period in excess of 12 months, except that with respect to an exclusive license granted to an interactive service by a licensor that holds the copyright to 1,000 or fewer sound recordings, the period of such license shall not exceed 24 months: Provided, however, That the grantee of such exclusive license shall be ineligible to receive another exclusive license for the performance of that sound recording for a period of 13 months from the expiration of the prior exclusive license.

(B) The limitation set forth in subparagraph (A) of this paragraph shall not apply if—

(i) the licensor has granted and there remain in effect licenses under section 106(6) [17 USCS § 106(6)] for the public performance of sound recordings by means of digital audio transmission by at least 5 different interactive services: Provided, however, That each such license must be for a minimum of 10 percent of the copyrighted sound recordings owned by the licensor that have been licensed to interactive services, but in no event less than 50 sound recordings; or

(ii) the exclusive license is granted to perform publicly up to 45 seconds of a sound recording and the sole purpose of the performance is to promote the distribution or performance of that sound recording.

(C) Notwithstanding the grant of an exclusive or nonexclusive license of the right of public performance under section 106(6) [17 USCS § 106(6)], an interactive service may not publicly perform a sound recording unless a license has been granted for the public performance of any copyrighted musical work contained in the sound recording: Provided, That such license to publicly perform the copyrighted musical work may be granted either by a performing rights society representing the copyright owner or by the copyright owner.

(D) The performance of a sound recording by means of a retransmission of a digital audio transmission is not an infringement of section 106(6) [17 USCS § 106(6)] if—

(i) the retransmission is of a transmission by an interactive service licensed to publicly perform the sound recording to a particular member of the public as part of that transmission; and

(ii) the retransmission is simultaneous with the licensed transmission, authorized by the transmitter, and limited to that particular member of the public intended by the interactive service to be the recipient of the transmission.

(E) For the purposes of this paragraph—

(i) a "licensor" shall include the licensing entity and any other entity under any material degree of common ownership, management, or control that owns copyrights in sound recordings; and

(ii) a "performing rights society" is an association or corporation that licenses the public performance of nondramatic musical works on behalf of the copyright owner, such as the American Society of Composers, Authors and Publishers, Broadcast Music, Inc., and SESAC, Inc.

(4) *Rights not otherwise limited.*

(A) Except as expressly provided in this section, this section does not limit or impair the exclusive right to perform a sound recording publicly by means of a digital audio transmission under section 106(6) [17 USCS § 106(6)].

(B) Nothing in this section annuls or limits in any way—

(i) the exclusive right to publicly perform a musical work, including by means of a digital audio transmission, under section 106(4) [17 USCS § 106(4)];

(ii) the exclusive rights in a sound recording or the musical work embodied therein under sections 106(1), 106(2) and 106(3) [17 USCS §§ 106(1), 106(2), and 106(3)]; or

(iii) any other rights under any other clause of section 106 [17 USCS § 106], or remedies available under this title, as such rights or remedies exist either before or after the date of enactment of the Digital Performance Right in Sound Recordings Act of 1995 [enacted Nov. 1, 1995].

(C) Any limitations in this section on the exclusive right under section 106(6) [17 USCS § 106(6)] apply only to the exclusive right under section 106(6) and not to any other exclusive rights under section 106. Nothing in this section shall be construed to annul, limit, impair or otherwise affect in any way the ability of the owner of a copyright in a sound recording to exercise the rights under sections 106(1), 106(2) and 106(3) [17 USCS §§ 106(1), 106(2), and 106(3)], or to obtain the remedies available under this title pursuant to such rights, as such rights and remedies exist either before or after the date of enactment of the Digital Performance Right in Sound Recordings Act of 1995 [enacted Nov. 1, 1995].

(e) **Authority for Negotiations.**

(1) Notwithstanding any provision of the antitrust laws, in negotiating statutory licenses in accordance with subsection (f), any copyright owners of sound recordings and any entities performing sound recordings affected by this section may negotiate and agree upon the royalty rates and license terms and conditions for the performance of such sound recordings and the proportionate division of fees paid among copyright owners, and may designate common agents on a nonexclusive basis to negotiate, agree to, pay, or receive payments.

(2) For licenses granted under section 106(6) [17 USCS § 106], other than statutory licenses, such as for performances by interactive services or performances that exceed the sound recording performance complement—

(A) copyright owners of sound recordings affected by this section may designate common agents to act on their behalf to grant licenses and receive and remit royalty payments: Provided, That each copyright owner shall establish the royalty rates and material license terms and conditions unilaterally, that is, not in agreement, combination, or concert with other copyright owners of sound recordings; and

(B) entities performing sound recordings affected by this section may designate common agents to act on their behalf to obtain licenses and collect and pay royalty fees: Provided, That each entity performing sound recordings shall determine the royalty rates and material license terms and conditions unilaterally, that is, not in agreement, combination, or concert with other entities performing sound recordings.

(f) **Licenses for Certain Nonexempt Transmissions.**

(1) (A) Proceedings under chapter 8 shall determine reasonable rates and terms of royalty payments for subscription transmissions by preexisting subscription services and transmissions by preexisting satellite digital audio radio services specified by subsection (d)(2) during the 5-year period beginning on January 1 of the second year following the year in which the proceedings are to be commenced, except in the case of a different transitional period provided under section 6(b)(3) of the Copyright Royalty and Distribution Reform Act of 2004 [17 USCS § 801 note], or such other period as the parties may agree. Such terms and rates shall distinguish among the different types of digital audio transmission services then in operation. Any copyright owners of sound recordings, preexisting subscription services, or preexisting satellite digital audio radio services may submit to the Copyright Royalty Judges licenses covering such subscription transmissions with respect to such sound recordings. The parties to each proceeding shall bear their own costs.

(B) The schedule of reasonable rates and terms determined by the Copyright Royalty Judges shall, subject to paragraph (3), be binding on all copyright owners of sound recordings and entities performing sound recordings affected by this paragraph during the 5-year period specified in subparagraph (A), a transitional period provided under section 6(b)(3) of the Copyright Royalty and Distribution Reform Act of 2004, or such other period as the parties may agree. In establishing rates and terms for preexisting subscription services and preexisting satellite digital audio radio services, in addition to the objectives set forth in section 801(b)(1) [17 USCS § 801(b)(1)], the Copyright Royalty Judges may consider the rates and terms for comparable types of subscription digital audio transmission services and comparable circumstances under voluntary license agreements described in subparagraph (A).

(C) The procedures under subparagraphs (A) and (B) shall also be initiated pursuant to a petition filed by any copyright owners of sound recordings or any eligible nonsubscription service or new subscription service indicating that a new type of eligible nonsubscription service or new subscription service on which sound recordings are performed is or is about to become operational, for the purpose of determining reasonable terms and rates of royalty payments with respect to such new type of service for the period beginning with the inception of such new type of service and ending on the date on which the royalty rates and terms for preexisting subscription digital audio transmission services or preexisting satellite digital radio audio services, as the case may be, most recently determined under subparagraph (A) or (B) and chapter 8 expire, or such other period as the parties may agree.

(2) (A) Proceedings under chapter 8 [17 USCS §§ 801 et seq.] shall determine reasonable rates and terms of royalty payments for public performances of sound recordings by means of eligible nonsubscription transmission services and new subscription services specified by subsection (d)(2) during the 5-year period beginning on January 1 of the second year following the year in which the proceedings are to be commenced, except in the case of a different transitional period provided under section 6(b)(3) of the Copyright Royalty and Distribution Reform Act of 2004 [17 USCS § 801 note], or such other period as the parties may agree. Such rates and terms shall distinguish among the different types of eligible nonsubscription transmission services and new subscription services then in operation and shall include a minimum fee for each such type of service. Any copyright owners of sound recordings or any entities performing sound recordings affected by this paragraph may submit to the Copyright Royalty Judges licenses covering such eligible nonsubscription transmissions and new subscription services with respect to such sound recordings. The parties to each proceeding shall bear their own costs.

(B) The schedule of reasonable rates and terms determined by the Copyright Royalty Judges shall, subject to paragraph (3), be binding on all copyright owners of sound recordings and entities performing sound recordings affected by this paragraph during the 5-year period specified in subparagraph (A), a transitional period provided under section 6(b)(3) of the Copyright Royalty and Distribution Act of 2004, or such other period as the parties may agree. Such rates and terms shall distinguish among the different types of eligible nonsubscription transmission services then in operation and shall include a minimum fee for each such type of service, such differences to be based on criteria including, but not limited to, the quantity and nature of the use of sound recordings and the degree to which use of the service may substitute for or may promote the purchase of phonorecords by consumers. In establishing rates and terms for transmissions by eligible nonsubscription services and new subscription services, the Copyright Royalty Judges shall establish rates and terms that most clearly represent the rates and terms that would have been negotiated in the marketplace between a willing buyer and a willing seller. In determining such rates and terms, the Copyright Royalty Judges shall base its decision on economic, competitive and programming information presented by the parties, including—

(i) whether use of the service may substitute for or may promote the sales of phonorecords or otherwise may interfere with or may enhance the sound recording copyright owner's other streams of revenue from its sound recordings; and

(ii) the relative roles of the copyright owner and the transmitting entity in the copyrighted work and the service made available to the public with respect to relative creative contribution, technological contribution, capital investment, cost, and risk.

In establishing such rates and terms, the Copyright Royalty Judges may consider the rates and terms for comparable types of digital audio transmission services and comparable circumstances under voluntary license agreements described in subparagraph (A).

(C) The procedures under subparagraphs (A) and (B) shall also be initiated pursuant to a petition filed by any copyright owners of sound recordings or any eligible nonsubscription service or new subscription service indicating that a new type of eligible nonsubscription service or new subscription service on which sound recordings are performed is or is about to become operational, for the purpose of determining reasonable terms and rates of royalty payments with respect to such new type of service for the period beginning with the inception of such new type of service and ending on the date on which the royalty rates and terms for preexisting subscription digital audio transmission services or preexisting satellite digital radio audio services, as the case may be, most recently determined under subparagraph (A) or (B) and chapter 8 expire, or such other period as the parties may agree.

(3) License agreements voluntarily negotiated at any time between 1 or more copyright owners of sound recordings and 1 or more entities performing sound recordings shall be given effect in lieu of any decision by the Librarian of Congress or determination by the Copyright Royalty Judges.

(4) (A) The Copyright Royalty Judges shall also establish requirements by which copyright owners may receive reasonable notice of the use of their sound recordings under this section, and under which records of such use shall be kept and made available by entities performing sound recordings. The notice and recordkeeping rules in effect on the day before the effective date of the Copyright Royalty and Distribution Reform Act of 2004 shall remain in effect unless and until new regulations are promulgated by the Copyright Royalty Judges. If new regulations are promulgated under this subparagraph, the Copyright Royalty Judges shall take into account the substance and effect of the rules in effect on the day before the effective date of the Copyright Royalty and Distribution Reform Act of 2004 and shall, to the extent practicable, avoid significant disruption of the functions of any designated agent authorized to collect and distribute royalty fees.

(B) Any person who wishes to perform a sound recording publicly by means of a transmission eligible for statutory licensing under this subsection may do so without infringing the exclusive right of the copyright owner of the sound recording—

(i) by complying with such notice requirements as the Copyright Royalty Judges shall prescribe by regulation and by paying royalty fees in accordance with this subsection; or

(ii) if such royalty fees have not been set, by agreeing to pay such royalty fees as shall be determined in accordance with this subsection.

(C) Any royalty payments in arrears shall be made on or before the twentieth day of the month next succeeding the month in which the royalty fees are set.

(5) (A) Notwithstanding section 112(e) [17 USCS § 112(e)] and the other provisions of this subsection, the receiving agent may enter into agreements for the reproduction and performance of sound recordings under section 112(e) [17 USCS § 112(e)] and this section by any 1 or more commercial webcasters or noncommercial webcasters for a period of not more than 11 years beginning on January 1, 2005, that, once published in the Federal Register pursuant to subparagraph (B), shall be binding on all copyright owners of sound recordings and other persons entitled to payment under this section, in lieu of any determination by the Copyright Royalty Judges. Any such agreement for commercial webcasters may include provisions for payment of royalties on the basis of a percentage of revenue or expenses, or both, and include a minimum fee. Any such agreement may include other terms and conditions, including requirements by which copyright owners may receive notice of the use of their sound recordings and under which records of such use shall be kept and made available by commercial webcasters or noncommercial webcasters. The receiving agent shall be under no obligation to negotiate any such agreement. The receiving agent shall have no obligation to any copyright owner of sound recordings or any other person entitled to payment under this section in negotiating any such agreement, and no liability to any copyright owner of sound recordings or any other person entitled to payment under this section for having entered into such agreement.

(B) The Copyright Office shall cause to be published in the Federal Register any agreement entered into pursuant to subparagraph (A). Such publication shall include a statement containing the substance of subparagraph (C). Such agreements shall not be included in the Code of Federal Regulations. Thereafter, the terms of such agreement shall be available, as an option, to any commercial webcaster or noncommercial webcaster meeting the eligibility conditions of such agreement.

(C) Neither subparagraph (A) nor any provisions of any agreement entered into pursuant to subparagraph (A), including any rate structure, fees, terms, conditions, or notice and recordkeeping requirements set forth therein, shall be admissible as evidence or otherwise taken into account in any administrative, judicial, or other government proceeding involving the setting or adjustment of the royalties payable for the public performance or reproduction in ephemeral phonorecords or copies of sound recordings, the determination of terms or conditions related thereto, or the establishment of notice or recordkeeping requirements by the Copyright Royalty Judges under paragraph (4) or section 112(e)(4) [17 USCS § 112(e)(4)]. It is the intent of Congress that any royalty rates, rate structure, definitions, terms, conditions, or notice and recordkeeping requirements, included in such agreements shall be considered as a compromise motivated by the unique business, economic and political circumstances of webcasters, copyright owners, and performers rather than as matters that would have been negotiated in the marketplace between a willing buyer and a willing seller, or otherwise meet the objectives set forth in section 801(b) [17 USCS § 801(b)]. This subparagraph shall not apply to the extent that the receiving agent and a webcaster that is party to an agreement entered into pursuant to subparagraph (A) expressly authorize the submission of the agreement in a proceeding under this subsection.

(D) Nothing in the the Webcaster Settlement Act of 2008 or any agreement entered into pursuant to subparagraph (A) shall be taken into account by the United States Court of Appeals for the District of Columbia Circuit in its review of the determination by the Copyright Royalty Judges of May 1, 2007, of rates and terms for the digital performance of sound recordings and ephemeral recordings, pursuant to sections 112 and 114 [17 USCS §§ 112 and 114].

(E) As used in this paragraph—

(i) the term "noncommercial webcaster" means a webcaster that—

(I) is exempt from taxation under section 501 of the Internal Revenue Code of 1986 (26 U.S.C. 501);

(II) has applied in good faith to the Internal Revenue Service for exemption from taxation under section 501 of the Internal Revenue Code [26 USCS § 501] and has a commercially reasonable expectation that such exemption shall be granted; or

(III) is operated by a State or possession or any governmental entity or subordinate thereof, or by the United States or District of Columbia, for exclusively public purposes;

(ii) the term "receiving agent" shall have the meaning given that term in section 261.2 of title 37, Code of Federal

Regulations, as published in the Federal Register on July 8, 2002; and

(iii) the term "webcaster" means a person or entity that has obtained a compulsory license under section 112 or 114 [17 USCS § 112 or 114] and the implementing regulations therefor

(F) The authority to make settlements pursuant to subparagraph (A) shall expire at 11:59 p.m. Eastern time on the 30th day after the date of the Webcaster Settlement Act of 2009 [enacted June 30, 2009].

(g) **Proceeds from Licensing of Transmissions.**

(1) Except in the case of a transmission licensed under a statutory license in accordance with subsection (f) of this section—

(A) a featured recording artist who performs on a sound recording that has been licensed for a transmission shall be entitled to receive payments from the copyright owner of the sound recording in accordance with the terms of the artist's contract; and

(B) a nonfeatured recording artist who performs on a sound recording that has been licensed for a transmission shall be entitled to receive payments from the copyright owner of the sound recording in accordance with the terms of the nonfeatured recording artist's applicable contract or other applicable agreement.

(2) An agent designated to distribute receipts from the licensing of transmissions in accordance with subsection (f) shall distribute such receipts as follows:

(A) 50 percent of the receipts shall be paid to the copyright owner of the exclusive right under section 106(6) of this title [17 USCS § 106(6)] to publicly perform a sound recording by means of a digital audio transmission.

(B) 2 1/2 percent of the receipts shall be deposited in an escrow account managed by an independent administrator jointly appointed by copyright owners of sound recordings and the Amer-ican Federation of Musicians (or any successor entity) to be distributed to nonfeatured musicians (whether or not members of the American Federation of Musicians) who have performed on sound recordings.

(C) 2 1/2 percent of the receipts shall be deposited in an escrow account managed by an independent administrator jointly appointed by copyright owners of sound recordings and the American Federation of Television and Radio Artists (or any successor entity) to be distributed to nonfeatured vocalists (whether or not members of the American Federation of Television and Radio Artists) who have performed on sound recordings.

(D) 45 percent of the receipts shall be paid, on a per sound recording basis, to the recording artist or artists featured on such sound recording (or the persons conveying rights in the artists' performance in the sound recordings).

(3) A nonprofit agent designated to distribute receipts from the licensing of transmissions in accordance with subsection (f) may deduct from any of its receipts, prior to the distribution of such receipts to any person or entity entitled thereto other than copyright owners and performers who have elected to receive royalties from another designated agent and have notified such nonprofit agent in writing of such election, the reasonable costs of such agent incurred after November 1, 1995, in—

(A) the administration of the collection, distribution, and calculation of the royalties;

(B) the settlement of disputes relating to the collection and calculation of the royalties; and

(C) the licensing and enforcement of rights with respect to the making of ephemeral recordings and performances subject to licensing under section 112 [17 USCS § 112] and this section, including those incurred in participating in negotiations or arbitration proceedings under section 112 [17 USCS § 112] and this section, except that all costs incurred relating to the section 112 [17 USCS § 112] ephemeral recordings right may only be deducted from the royalties received pursuant to section 112 [17 USCS § 112].

(4) Notwithstanding paragraph (3), any designated agent designated to distribute receipts from the licensing of transmissions in accordance with subsection (f) may deduct from any of its receipts, prior to the distribution of such receipts, the reasonable costs identified in paragraph (3) of such agent incurred after November 1, 1995, with respect to such copyright owners and performers who have entered with such agent a contractual relationship that specifies that such costs may be deducted from such royalty receipts.

(h) **Licensing to Affiliates.**

(1) If the copyright owner of a sound recording licenses an affiliated entity the right to publicly perform a sound recording by means of a digital audio transmission under section 106(6) [17 USCS § 106(6)], the copyright owner shall make the licensed sound recording available under section 106(6) [17 USCS § 106(6)] on no less favorable terms and conditions to all bona fide entities that offer similar services, except that, if there are material differences in the scope of the requested license with respect to the type of service, the particular sound recordings licensed, the frequency of use, the number of subscribers served, or the duration, then the copyright owner may establish different terms and conditions for such other services.

(2) The limitation set forth in paragraph (1) of this subsection shall not apply in the case where the copyright owner of a sound recording licenses—

(A) an interactive service; or

(B) an entity to perform publicly up to 45 seconds of the sound recording and the sole purpose of the performance is to promote the distribution or performance of that sound recording.

(i) **No Effect on Royalties for Underlying Works.** License fees payable for the public performance of sound recordings under section 106(6) [17 USCS § 106(6)] shall not be taken into account in any administrative, judicial, or other governmental proceeding to set or adjust the royalties payable to copyright owners of musical works for the public performance of their works. It is the intent of Congress that royalties payable to copyright owners of musical works for the public performance of their works shall not be diminished in any respect as a result of the rights granted by section 106(6) [17 USCS § 106(6)].

(j) **Definitions.** As used in this section, the following terms have the following meanings:

(1) An "affiliated entity" is an entity engaging in digital audio transmissions covered by section 106(6) [17 USCS § 106(6)], other than an interactive service, in which the licensor has any direct or indirect partnership or any ownership interest amounting to 5 percent or more of the outstanding voting or non-voting stock.

(2) An "archived program" is a predetermined program that is available repeatedly on the demand of the transmission recipient and that is performed in the same order from the beginning, except that an archived program shall not include a recorded event or broadcast transmission that makes no more than an incidental use of sound recordings, as long as such recorded event or broadcast transmission does not contain an entire sound recording or feature a particular sound recording.

(3) A "broadcast" transmission is a transmission made by a terrestrial broadcast station licensed as such by the Federal Communications Commission.

(4) A "continuous program" is a predetermined program that is continuously performed in the same order and that is accessed at a point in the program that is beyond the control of the transmission recipient.

(5) A "digital audio transmission" is a digital transmission as defined in section 101 [17 USCS § 101], that embodies the transmission of a sound recording. This term does not include the transmission of any audiovisual work.

(6) An "eligible nonsubscription transmission" is a noninteractive nonsubscription digital audio transmission not exempt under subsection (d)(1) that is made as part of a service that provides audio programming

consisting, in whole or in part, of performances of sound recordings, including retransmissions of broadcast transmissions, if the primary purpose of the service is to provide to the public such audio or other entertainment programming, and the primary purpose of the service is not to sell, advertise, or promote particular products or services other than sound recordings, live concerts, or other music-related events.

(7) An "interactive service" is one that enables a member of the public to receive a transmission of a program specially created for the recipient, or on request, a transmission of a particular sound recording, whether or not as part of a program, which is selected by or on behalf of the recipient. The ability of individuals to request that particular sound recordings be performed for reception by the public at large, or in the case of a subscription service, by all subscribers of the service, does not make a service interactive, if the programming on each channel of the service does not substantially consist of sound recordings that are performed within 1 hour of the request or at a time designated by either the transmitting entity or the individual making such request. If an entity offers both interactive and noninteractive services (either concurrently or at different times), the noninteractive component shall not be treated as part of an interactive service.

(8) A "new subscription service" is a service that performs sound recordings by means of noninteractive subscription digital audio transmissions and that is not a preexisting subscription service or a preexisting satellite digital audio radio service.

(9) A "nonsubscription" transmission is any transmission that is not a subscription transmission.

(10) A "preexisting satellite digital audio radio service" is a subscription satellite digital audio radio service provided pursuant to a satellite digital audio radio service license issued by the Federal Communications Commission on or before July 31, 1998, and any renewal of such license to the extent of the scope of the original license, and may include a limited number of sample channels representative of the subscription service that are made available on a nonsubscription basis in order to promote the subscription service.

(11) A "preexisting subscription service" is a service that performs sound recordings by means of noninteractive audio-only subscription digital audio transmissions, which was in existence and was making such transmissions to the public for a fee on or before July 31, 1998, and may include a limited number of sample channels representative of the subscription service that are made available on a nonsubscription basis in order to promote the subscription service.

(12) A "retransmission" is a further transmission of an initial transmission, and includes any further retransmission of the same transmission. Except as provided in this section, a transmission qualifies as a "retransmission" only if it is simultaneous with the initial transmission. Nothing in this definition shall be construed to exempt a transmission that fails to satisfy a separate element required to qualify for an exemption under section 114(d)(1) [17 USCS § 114(d)(1)].

The “sound recording performance complement” is the sion during any 3-hour period, on a particular channel used by a ing entity, of no more than—

(A) 3 different selections of sound recordings from any one norecord lawfully distributed for public performance or sale in the United States, if no more than 2 such selections are transmitted consecutively; or

(B) 4 different selections of sound recordings—

(i) by the same featured recording artist; or

(ii) from any set or compilation of phonorecords lawfully distributed together as a unit for public performance or sale in the United States, if no more than three such selections are transmitted consecutively:

Provided, That the transmission of selections in excess of the numerical limits provided for in clauses (A) and (B) from multiple phonorecords shall nonetheless qualify as a sound recording performance complement if the programming of the multiple phonorecords was not willfully intended to avoid the numerical limitations prescribed in such clauses.

(14) A “subscription” transmission is a transmission that is controlled and limited to particular recipients, and for which consideration is required to be paid or otherwise given by or on behalf of the recipient to receive the transmission or a package of transmissions including the transmission.

(15) A “transmission” is either an initial transmission or a retransmission.

(Oct. 19, 1976, P.L. 94-553, Title I, § 101, 90 Stat. 2560; Nov. 1, 1995, P.L. 104-39, § 3, 109 Stat. 336; Nov. 13, 1997, P.L. 105-80, § 3, 111 Stat. 1531; Oct. 28, 1998, P.L. 105-304, Title IV, § 405(a)(1)–(4), 112 Stat. 2890; Dec. 4, 2002, P. L. 107-321, §§ 4, 5(b), (c), 116 Stat. 2781, 2784; Nov. 30, 2004, P.L. 108-419, § 5(c), 118 Stat. 2362; October 6, 2006, P.L. 109-303, § 4(b), 120 Stat. 1478; October 16, 2008, P.L. 110-435, § 2, 122 Stat. 4974; June 30, 2009, P.L. 111-36, § 2, 123 Stat. 1926.)

§ 115 Scope of exclusive rights in nondramatic musical works: Compulsory license for making and distributing phonorecords

In the case of nondramatic musical works, the exclusive rights provided by clauses (1) and (3) of section 106 [17 USCS § 106], to make and to distribute phonorecords of such works, are subject to compulsory licensing under the conditions specified by this section.

(a) **Availability and Scope of Compulsory License.**

(1) When phonorecords of a nondramatic musical work have been distributed to the public in the United States under the authority of the

copyright owner, any other person, including those who make phonorecords or digital phonorecord deliveries, may, by complying with the provisions of this section, obtain a compulsory license to make and distribute phonorecords of the work. A person may obtain a compulsory license only if his or her primary purpose in making phonorecords is to distribute them to the public for private use, including by means of a digital phonorecord delivery. A person may not obtain a compulsory license for use of the work in the making of phonorecords duplicating a sound recording fixed by another, unless: (i) such sound recording was fixed lawfully; and (ii) the making of the phonorecords was authorized by the owner of copyright in the sound recording or, if the sound recording was fixed before February 15, 1972, by any person who fixed the sound recording pursuant to an express license from the owner of the copyright in the musical work or pursuant to a valid compulsory license for use of such work in a sound recording.

(2) A compulsory license includes the privilege of making a musical arrangement of the work to the extent necessary to conform it to the style or manner of interpretation of the performance involved, but the arrangement shall not change the basic melody or fundamental character of the work, and shall not be subject to protection as a derivative work under this title, except with the express consent of the copyright owner.

(b) **Notice of Intention to Obtain Compulsory License.**

(1) Any person who wishes to obtain a compulsory license under this section shall, before or within thirty days after making, and before distributing any phonorecords of the work, serve notice of intention to do so on the copyright owner. If the registration or other public records of the Copyright Office do not identify the copyright owner and include an address at which notice can be served, it shall be sufficient to file the notice of intention in the Copyright Office. The notice shall comply, in form, content, and manner of service, with requirements that the Register of Copyrights shall prescribe by regulation.

(2) Failure to serve or file the notice required by clause (1) forecloses the possibility of a compulsory license and, in the absence of a negotiated license, renders the making and distribution of phonorecords actionable as acts of infringement under section 501 [17 USCS § 501] and fully subject to the remedies provided by sections 502 through 506 and 509 [17 USCS §§ 502–506 and 509].

(c) **Royalty Payable Under Compulsory License.**

(1) To be entitled to receive royalties under a compulsory license, the copyright owner must be identified in the registration or other public records of the Copyright Office. The owner is entitled to royalties for phonorecords made and distributed after being so identified, but is not entitled to recover for any phonorecords previously made and distributed.

(2) Except as provided by clause (1), the royalty under a compulsory license shall be payable for every phonorecord made and distributed in accordance with the license. For this purpose, and other than as provided in paragraph (3), a phonorecord is considered "distributed" if the person exercising the compulsory license has voluntarily and permanently parted with its possession. With respect to each work embodied in the phonorecord, the royalty shall be either two and three-fourths cents, or one-half of one cent per minute of playing time or fraction thereof, whichever amount is larger.

(3) (A) A compulsory license under this section includes the right of the compulsory licensee to distribute or authorize the distribution of a phonorecord of a nondramatic musical work by means of a digital transmission which constitutes a digital phonorecord delivery, regardless of whether the digital transmission is also a public performance of the sound recording under section 106(6) of this title [17 USCS § 106(6)] or of any nondramatic musical work embodied therein under section 106(4) of this title [17 USCS § 106(4)]. For every digital phonorecord delivery by or under the authority of the compulsory licensee—

(i) on or before December 31, 1997, the royalty payable by the compulsory licensee shall be the royalty prescribed under paragraph (2) and chapter 8 of this title [17 USCS §§ 801 et seq.]; and

(ii) on or after January 1, 1998, the royalty payable by the compulsory licensee shall be the royalty prescribed under subparagraphs (B) through (E) and chapter 8 of this title [17 USCS §§ 801 et seq.].

(B) Notwithstanding any provision of the antitrust laws, any copyright owners of nondramatic musical works and any persons entitled to obtain a compulsory license under subsection (a)(1) may negotiate and agree upon the terms and rates of royalty payments under this section and the proportionate division of fees paid among copyright owners, and may designate common agents on a nonexclusive basis to negotiate, agree to, pay or receive such royalty payments. Such authority to negotiate the terms and rates of royalty payments includes, but is not limited to, the authority to negotiate the year during which the royalty rates prescribed under this subparagraph and subparagraphs (C) through (E) and chapter 8 of this title [17 USCS §§ 801 et seq.] shall next be determined.

(C) Proceedings under chapter 8 shall determine reasonable rates and terms of royalty payments for the activities specified by this section during the period beginning with the effective date of such rates and terms, but not earlier than January 1 of the second year following the year in which the petition requesting the proceeding is filed, and ending on the effective date of successor rates and terms, or such other period as the parties may agree. Such terms and rates shall distinguish between (i) digital phonorecord deliveries where the reproduction or distribution of a phonorecord is incidental to the transmission which constitutes the digital phonorecord delivery, and (ii) digital phonorecord deliveries in general. Any copyright owners of nondramatic musical works and any persons entitled to obtain a compulsory license under subsection (a)(1) may submit to the Copyright Royalty Judges licenses covering such activities. The parties to each proceeding shall bear their own costs.

(D) The schedule of reasonable rates and terms determined by the Copyright Royalty Judges shall, subject to subparagraph (E), be binding on all copyright owners of nondramatic musical works and persons entitled to obtain a compulsory license under subsection (a)(1) during the period specified in subparagraph (C), such other period as may be determined pursuant to subparagraphs (B) and (C), or such other period as the parties may agree. Such terms and rates shall distinguish between (i) digital phonorecord deliveries where the reproduction or distribution of a phonorecord is incidental to the transmission which constitutes the digital phonorecord delivery, and (ii) digital phonorecord deliveries in general. In addition to the objectives set forth in section 801(b)(1) [17 USCS § 801(b)(1)], in establishing such rates and terms, the Copyright Royalty Judges may consider rates and terms under voluntary license agreements described in subparagraphs (B) and (C). The royalty rates payable for a compulsory license for a digital phonorecord delivery under this section shall be established de novo and no precedential effect shall be given to the amount of the royalty payable by a compulsory licensee for digital phonorecord deliveries on or before December 31, 1997. The Copyright Royalty Judges shall also establish requirements by which copyright owners may receive reasonable notice of the use of their works under this section, and under which records of such use shall be kept and made available by persons making digital phonorecord deliveries.

(E) (i) License agreements voluntarily negotiated at any time between one or more copyright owners of nondramatic musical works and one or more persons entitled to obtain a compulsory license under subsection (a)(1) shall be given effect in lieu of any determination by the Librarian of Congress and Copyright Royalty Judges. Subject to clause (ii), the royalty rates determined pursuant to subparagraph (C) and (D) shall be given effect as to digital phonorecord deliveries in lieu of any contrary royalty rates specified in a contract pursuant to which a recording artist who is the author of a nondramatic musical work grants a license under that person's exclusive rights in the musical work under paragraphs (1) and (3) of section 106 [17 USCS § 106] or commits another person to grant a license in that musical work under paragraphs (1) and (3) of section 106

[17 USCS § 106], to a person desiring to fix in a tangible medium of expression a sound recording embodying the musical work.

(ii) The second sentence of clause (i) shall not apply to—

(I) a contract entered into on or before June 22, 1995, and not modified thereafter for the purpose of reducing the royalty rates determined pursuant to subparagraph (C) and (D) or of increasing the number of musical works within the scope of the contract covered by the reduced rates, except if a contract entered into on or before June 22, 1995, is modified thereafter for the purpose of increasing the number of musical works within the scope of the contract, any contrary royalty rates specified in the contract shall be given effect in lieu of royalty rates determined pursuant to subparagraph (C) and (D) for the number of musical works within the scope of the contract as of June 22, 1995; and

(II) a contract entered into after the date that the sound recording is fixed in a tangible medium of expression substantially in a form intended for commercial release, if at the time the contract is entered into, the recording artist retains the right to grant licenses as to the musical work under paragraphs (1) and (3) of section 106 [17 USCS § 106].

(F) Except as provided in section 1002(e) of this title [17 USCS § 1002(e)], a digital phonorecord delivery licensed under this paragraph shall be accompanied by the information encoded in the sound recording, if any, by or under the authority of the copyright owner of that sound recording, that identifies the title of the sound recording, the featured recording artist who performs on the sound recording, and related information, including information concerning the underlying musical work and its writer.

(G) (i) A digital phonorecord delivery of a sound recording is actionable as an act of infringement under section 501 [17 USCS § 501], and is fully subject to the remedies provided by sections 502 through 506 [17 USCS §§ 502–506], unless—

(I) the digital phonorecord delivery has been authorized by the copyright owner of the sound recording; and

(II) the owner of the copyright in the sound re-cording or the entity making the digital phonorecord delivery has obtained a compulsory license under this section or has otherwise been authorized by the copyright owner of the musical work to distribute or authorize the distribution, by means of a digital phonorecord delivery, of each musical work embodied in the sound recording.

(ii) Any cause of action under this subparagraph shall be in addition to those available to the owner of the copyright in the nondramatic musical work under subsection (c)(6) and section 106(4) [17 USCS § 106(4)] and the owner of the copyright in the sound recording under section 106(6) [17 USCS § 106(6)].

(H) The liability of the copyright owner of a sound recording for infringement of the copyright in a nondramatic musical work embodied in the sound recording shall be determined in accordance with applicable law, except that the owner of a copyright in a sound recording shall not be liable for a digital phonorecord delivery by a third party if the owner of the copyright in the sound recording does not license the distribution of a phonorecord of the nondramatic musical work.

(I) Nothing in section 1008 [17 USCS § 1008] shall be construed to prevent the exercise of the rights and remedies allowed by this paragraph, paragraph (6), and chapter 5 [17 USCS §§ 501 et seq.] in the event of a digital phonorecord delivery, except that no action alleging infringement of copyright may be brought under this title against a manufacturer, importer or distributor of a digital audio recording device, a digital audio recording medium, an analog recording device, or an analog recording medium, or against a consumer, based on the actions described in such section.

(J) Nothing in this section annuls or limits (i) the exclusive right to publicly perform a sound recording or the musical work embodied therein, including by means of a digital transmission, under sections 106(4) and 106(6) [17 USCS §§ 106(4) and 106(6)], (ii) except for compulsory licensing under the conditions specified by this section, the exclusive rights to reproduce and distribute the sound recording and the musical work embodied therein under sections 106(1) and 106(3) [17 USCS §§ 106(1) and 106(3)], including by means of a digital phonorecord delivery, or (iii) any other rights under any other provision of section 106 [17 USCS § 106], or remedies available under this title, as such rights or remedies exist either before or after the date of enactment of the Digital Performance Right in Sound Recordings Act of 1995 [enacted Nov. 1, 1995].

(K) The provisions of this section concerning digital phonorecord deliveries shall not apply to any exempt transmissions or retransmissions under section 114(d)(1) [17 USCS § 114(d)91)]. The exemptions created in section 114(d)(1) [17 USCS § 114(d)(1)] do not expand or reduce the rights of copyright owners under section 106 (1) through (5) with respect to such transmissions and retransmissions.

(4) A compulsory license under this section includes the right of the maker of a phonorecord of a nondramatic musical work under

subsection (a)(1) to distribute or authorize distribution of such phonorecord by rental, lease, or lending (or by acts or practices in the nature of rental, lease, or lending). In addition to any royalty payable under clause (2) and chapter 8 of this title [17 USCS §§ 801 et seq.], a royalty shall be payable by the compulsory licensee for every act of distribution of a phonorecord by or in the nature of rental, lease, or lending, by or under the authority of the compulsory licensee. With respect to each nondramatic musical work embodied in the phonorecord, the royalty shall be a proportion of the revenue received by the compulsory licensee from every such act of distribution of the phonorecord under this clause equal to the proportion of the revenue received by the compulsory licensee from distribution of the phonorecord under clause (2) that is payable by a compulsory licensee under that clause and under chapter 8 [17 USCS §§ 801 et seq.]. The Register of Copyrights shall issue regulations to carry out the purpose of this clause.

(5) Royalty payments shall be made on or before the twentieth day of each month and shall include all royalties for the month next preceding. Each monthly payment shall be made under oath and shall comply with requirements that the Register of Copyrights shall prescribe by regulation. The Register shall also prescribe regulations under which detailed cumulative annual statements of account, certified by a certified public accountant, shall be filed for every compulsory license under this section. The regulations covering both the monthly and the annual statements of account shall prescribe the form, content, and manner of certification with respect to the number of records made and the number of records distributed.

(6) If the copyright owner does not receive the monthly payment and the monthly and annual statements of account when due, the owner may give written notice to the licensee that, unless the default is remedied within thirty days from the date of the notice, the compulsory license will be automatically terminated. Such termination renders either the making or the distribution, or both, of all phonorecords for which the royalty has not been paid, actionable as acts of infringement under section 501 [17 USCS § 501] and fully subject to the remedies provided by sections 502 through 506 [17 USCS §§ 502–506].

(d) **Definition.** As used in this section, the following term has the following meaning: A "digital phonorecord delivery" is each individual delivery of a phonorecord by digital transmission of a sound recording which results in a specifically identifiable reproduction by or for any transmission recipient of a phonorecord of that sound recording, regardless of whether the digital transmission is also a public performance of the sound recording or any nondramatic musical work embodied therein. A digital phonorecord delivery does not result from a real-time, non-interactive subscription transmission of a sound recording where no reproduction of the sound recording or the musical work embodied therein is made from the inception of the transmission through to its receipt by the transmission recipient in order to make the sound recording audible.

(Oct. 19, 1976, P. L. 94-553, Title I, § 101, 90 Stat. 2561; Oct. 4, 1984, P. L. 98-450, §3, 98 Stat. 1727; Nov. 1, 1995, P. L. 104-39, §4, 109 Stat. 344; Nov. 13, 1997, P. L. 105-80, §§ 4, 10, 12(a)(7), 111 Stat. 1531, 1534; Nov. 30, 2004, P.L. 108-419, § 5(d), 118 Stat. 2364; October 6, 2006, P.L. 109-303, § 4(c), 120 Stat. 1478; October 13, 2008, P.L. 110-403, § 209(a)(3), 122 Stat. 4260.)

§ 116 Negotiated licenses for public performances by means of coin-operated phonorecord players

(a) **Applicability of Section.** This section applies to any nondramatic musical work embodied in a phonorecord.

(b) **Negotiated Licenses.**

(1) *Authority for negotiations.* Any owners of copyright in works to which this section applies and any operators of coin-operated phonorecord players may negotiate and agree upon the terms and rates of royalty payments for the performance of such works and the proportionate division of fees paid among copyright owners, and may designate common agents to negotiate, agree to, pay, or receive such royalty payments.

(2) *Chapter 8 proceeding.* Parties not subject to such a negotiation may have the terms and rates and the division of fees described in paragraph (1) determined in a proceeding in accordance with the provisions of chapter 8.

(c) **Determinations by Copyright Royalty Judges.** License agreements between one or more copyright owners and one or more operators of coin-operated phonorecord players, which are negotiated in accordance with subsection (b), shall be given effect in lieu of any otherwise applicable determination by the Copyright Royalty Judges.

(d) **Definitions.** As used in this section, the following terms mean the following:

(1) A "coin-operated phonorecord player" is a machine or device that—

(A) is employed solely for the performance of nondramatic musical works by means of phonorecords upon being activated by the insertion of coins, currency, tokens, or other monetary units or their equivalent;

(B) is located in an establishment making no direct or indirect charge for admission;

(C) is accompanied by a list which is comprised of the titles of all the musical works available for performance on it, and is affixed to the phonorecord player or posted in the establishment in a prominent position where it can be readily examined by the public; and

(D) affords a choice of works available for performance and permits the choice to be made by the patrons of the establishment in which it is located.

(2) An "operator" is any person who, alone or jointly with others—

(A) owns a coin-operated phonorecord player;

(B) has the power to make a coin-operated phonorecord player available for placement in an establishment for purposes of public performance; or

(C) has the power to exercise primary control over the selection of the musical works made available for public performance on a coin-operated phonorecord player.

(Added Oct. 31, 1988, P. L. 100-568, § 4(a)(4), 102 Stat. 2855; Dec. 17, 1993, P.L. 103-198, § 3(b)(1), 107 Stat. 2309; Nov. 13, 1997, P. L. 105-80, § 5, 111 Stat. 1531; Nov. 30, 2004, P. L. 108-419, § 5(e), 118 Stat. 2365.)

§ 117 Limitation on exclusive rights: computer programs

(a) **Making of Additional Copy or Adaptation by Owner of Copy.** Notwithstanding the provisions of section 106 [17 USCS § 106], it is not an infringement for the owner of a copy of a computer program to make or authorize the making of another copy or adaptation of that computer program provided:

(1) that such a new copy or adaptation is created as an essential step in the utilization of the computer program in conjunction with a machine and that it is used in no other manner, or

(2) that such new copy or adaptation is for archival purposes only and that all archival copies are destroyed in the event that continued possession of the computer program should cease to be rightful.

(b) **Lease, Sale, or Other Transfer of Additional Copy or Adaptation.** Any exact copies prepared in accordance with the provisions of this section may be leased, sold, or otherwise transferred, along with the copy from which such copies were prepared, only as part of the lease, sale, or other transfer of all rights in the program. Adaptations so prepared may be transferred only with the authorization of the copyright owner.

(c) **Machine Maintenance or Repair.** Notwithstanding the provisions of section 106, it is not an infringement for the owner or lessee of a machine to make or authorize the making of a copy of a computer program if such copy is made solely by virtue of the activation of a machine that lawfully contains an authorized copy of the computer program, for purposes only of maintenance or repair of that machine, if—

(1) such new copy is used in no other manner and is destroyed immediately after the maintenance or repair is completed; and

(2) with respect to any computer program or part thereof that is not necessary for that machine to be activated, such program or part thereof is not accessed or used other than to make such new copy by virtue of the activation of the machine.

(d) **Definitions.** For purposes of this section—

(1) the "maintenance" of a machine is the servicing of the machine in order to make it work in accordance with its original specifications and any changes to those specifications authorized for that machine; and

(2) the "repair" of a machine is the restoring of the machine to the state of working in accordance with its original specifications and any changes to those specifications authorized for that machine.

(Oct. 19, 1976, P. L. 94-553, Title I, § 101, 90 Stat. 2565; Dec. 12, 1980, P.L. 96-517, § 10(b), 94 Stat. 3028; Oct. 28, 1998, P. L. 105-304, Title III, § 302, 112 Stat. 2887.)

§ 118 Scope of exclusive rights: Use of certain works in connection with noncommercial broadcasting

(a) The exclusive rights provided by section 106 shall, with respect to the works specified by subsection (b) and the activities specified by subsection (d), be subject to the conditions and limitations prescribed by this section.

(b) Notwithstanding any provision of the antitrust laws, any owners of copyright in published nondramatic musical works and published pictorial, graphic, and sculptural works and any public broadcasting entities, respectively, may negotiate and agree upon the terms and rates of royalty payments and the proportionate division of fees paid among various copyright owners, and may designate common agents to negotiate, agree to, pay, or receive payments.

(1) Any owner of copyright in a work specified in this subsection or any public broadcasting entity may submit to the Copyright Royalty Judges proposed licenses covering such activities with respect to such works.

(2) License agreements voluntarily negotiated at any time between one or more copyright owners and one or more public broadcasting entities shall be given effect in lieu of any determination by the Librarian of Congress or the Copyright Royalty Judges, if copies of such agreements are

filed with the Copyright Royalty Judges within 30 days of execution in accordance with regulations that the Copyright Royalty Judges shall issue.

(3) Voluntary negotiation proceedings initiated pursuant to a petition filed under section 804(a) for the purpose of determining a schedule of terms and rates of royalty payments by public broadcasting entities to owners of copyright in works specified by this subsection and the proportionate division of fees paid among various copyright owners shall cover the 5-year period beginning on January 1 of the second year following the year in which the petition is filed. The parties to each negotiation proceeding shall bear their own costs.

(4) In the absence of license agreements negotiated under paragraph (2) or (3), the Copyright Royalty Judges shall, pursuant to chapter 8, conduct a proceeding to determine and publish in the Federal Register a schedule of rates and terms which, subject to paragraph (2), shall be binding on all owners of copyright in works specified by this subsection and public broadcasting entities, regardless of whether such copyright owners have submitted proposals to the Copyright Royalty Judges. In establishing such rates and terms the Copyright Royalty Judges may consider the rates for comparable circumstances under voluntary license agreements negotiated as provided in paragraph (2) or (3). The Copyright Royalty Judges shall also establish requirements by which copyright owners may receive reasonable notice of the use of their works under this section, and under which records of such use shall be kept by public broadcasting entities.

(c) Subject to the terms of any voluntary license agreements that have been negotiated as provided by subsection (b)(2) or (3), a public broadcasting entity may, upon compliance with the provisions of this section, including the rates and terms established by the Copyright Royalty Judges under subsection (b)(4), engage in the following activities with respect to published nondramatic musical works and published pictorial, graphic, and sculptural works:

(1) performance or display of work by or in the course of a transmission made by a noncommercial educational broadcast station referred to in subsection (f); and

(2) production of a transmission program, reproduction of copies or phonorecords of such a transmission program, and distribution of such copies or phonorecords, where such production, reproduction, or distribution is made by a nonprofit institution or organization solely for the purpose of transmissions specified in paragraph (1); and

(3) the making of reproductions by a governmental body or a nonprofit institution of a transmission program simultaneously with its transmission as specified in paragraph (1), and the performance or display of the contents of such program under the conditions specified by paragraph (1) of section 110 [17 USCS § 110], but only if the reproductions are used for performances or displays for a period of no more than seven days from the date of the transmission specified in paragraph (1), and are destroyed

before or at the end of such period. No person supplying, in accordance with paragraph (2), a reproduction of a transmission program to governmental bodies or nonprofit institutions under this paragraph shall have any liability as a result of failure of such body or institution to destroy such reproduction: Provided, That it shall have notified such body or institution of the requirement for such destruction pursuant to this paragraph: And provided further, That if such body or institution itself fails to destroy such reproduction it shall be deemed to have infringed.

(d) Except as expressly provided in this subsection, this section shall have no applicability to works other than those specified in subsection (b). Owners of copyright in nondramatic literary works and public broadcasting entities may, during the course of voluntary negotiations, agree among themselves, respectively, as to the terms and rates of royalty payments without liability under the antitrust laws. Any such terms and rates of royalty payments shall be effective upon filing with the Copyright Royalty Judges, in accordance with regulations that the Copyright Royalty Judges shall prescribe as provided in section 803(b)(6).

(e) Nothing in this section shall be construed to permit, beyond the limits of fair use as provided by section 107 [17 USCS § 107], the unauthorized dramatization of a nondramatic musical work, the production of a transmission program drawn to any substantial extent from a published compilation of pictorial, graphic, or sculptural works, or the unauthorized use of any portion of an audiovisual work.

(f) As used in this section, the term "public broadcasting entity" means a noncommercial educational broadcast station as defined in section 397 of title 47 and any nonprofit institution or organization engaged in the activities described in paragraph (2) of subsection (c).

(Oct. 19, 1976, P. L. 94-553, Title I, § 101, 90 Stat. 2565; Dec. 17, 1993, P. L. 103-198, § 4, 107 Stat. 2309; Aug. 5, 1999, P. L. 106-44, § 1(g)(3), 113 Stat. 222; Nov. 2, 2002, P. L. 107-273, Div C, Title III, Subtitle B, § 13210(7), 116 Stat. 1909; Nov. 30, 2004, P. L. 108-419, § 5(f), 118 Stat. 2365; Oct. 6, 2006, P.L. 109-303, § 4(d), 120 Stat. 1478.)

§ 119 Limitations on exclusive rights: Secondary transmissions of superstations and network stations for private home viewing

(a) **Secondary Transmissions by Satellite Carriers.**

(1) *Superstations.* Subject to the provisions of paragraphs (5), (6), and (8) of this subsection and section 114(d) [17 USCS § 114(d)], secondary transmissions of a performance or display of a work embodied in a primary transmission made by a superstation shall be subject to statutory licensing under this section if the secondary transmission is made by a satellite carrier to the public for private home viewing or for viewing in

a commercial establishment, with regard to secondary transmissions the satellite carrier is in compliance with the rules, regulations, or authorizations of the Federal Communications Commission governing the carriage of television broadcast station signals, and the carrier makes a direct or indirect charge for each retransmission service to each subscriber receiving the secondary transmission or to a distributor that has contracted with the carrier for direct or indirect delivery of the secondary transmission to the public for private home viewing or for viewing in a commercial establishment.

(2) *Network stations.*

(A) In general. Subject to the provisions of subparagraphs (B) and (C) of this paragraph and paragraphs (5), (6), (7), and (8) of this subsection and section 114(d) [17 USCS § 114(d)], secondary transmissions of a performance or display of a work embodied in a primary transmission made by a network station shall be subject to statutory licensing under this section if the secondary transmission is made by a satellite carrier to the public for private home viewing, with regard to secondary transmissions the satellite carrier is in compliance with the rules, regulations, or authorizations of the Federal Communications Commission governing the carriage of television broadcast station signals, and the carrier makes a direct or indirect charge for such retransmission service to each subscriber receiving the secondary transmission.

(B) Secondary transmissions to unserved households.

(i) In general. The statutory license provided for in subparagraph (A) shall be limited to secondary transmissions of the signals of no more than two network stations in a single day for each television network to persons who reside in unserved households. The limitation in this clause shall not apply to secondary transmissions under paragraph (3).

(ii) Accurate determinations of eligibility.

(I) Accurate predictive model. In determining presumptively whether a person resides in an unserved household under subsection (d)(10)(A), a court shall rely on the Individual Location Longley-Rice model set forth by the Federal Communications Commission in Docket No. 98-201, as that model may be amended by the Commission over time under section 339(c)(3) of the Communications Act of 1934 [47 USCS § 339(c)(3)] to increase the accuracy of that model.

(II) Accurate measurements. For purposes of site measurements to determine whether a person resides in an unserved household under subsection (d)(10)(A), a court shall rely on section 339(c)(4) of the Communications Act of 1934 [47 USCS § 339(c)(4)].

(iii) C-band exemption to unserved households.—

(I) In general. The limitations of clause (i) shall not apply to any secondary transmissions by C-band services of network stations that a subscriber to C-band service received before any termination of such secondary transmissions before October 31, 1999.

(II) Definition. In this clause the term "C-band service" means a service that is licensed by the Federal Communications Commission and operates in the Fixed Satellite Service under part 25 of title 47 of the Code of Federal Regulations.

(C) Exceptions.

(i) States with single full-power network station. In a State in which there is licensed by the Federal Communications Commission a single full-power station that was a network station on January 1, 1995, the statutory license provided for in subparagraph (A) shall apply to the secondary transmission by a satellite carrier of the primary transmission of that station to any subscriber in a community that is located within that State and that is not within the first 50 television markets as listed in the regulations of the Commission as in effect on such date (47 CFR 76.51).

(ii) States with all network stations and superstations in same local market. In a State in which all network stations and superstations licensed by the Federal Communications Commission within that State as of January 1, 1995, are assigned to the same local market and that local market does not encompass all counties of that State, the statutory license provided under subparagraph (A) shall apply to the secondary transmission by a satellite carrier of the primary transmissions of such station to all subscribers in the State who reside in a local market that is within the first 50 major television markets as listed in the regulations of the Commission as in effect on such date (section 76.51 of title 47 of the Code of Federal Regulations).

(iii) Additional stations. In the case of that State in which are located 4 counties that—

(I) on January 1, 2004, were in local markets principally comprised of counties in another State, and

(II) had a combined total of 41,340 television households, according to the U.S. Television Household Estimates by Nielsen Media Research for 2004, the statutory license provided under subparagraph (A) shall apply to secondary transmissions by a satellite carrier to subscribers in any such county of the primary transmissions of any network station located in that State, if the satellite carrier was making such secondary transmissions to any subscribers in that county on January 1, 2004.

(iv) Certain additional stations. If 2 adjacent counties in a single State are in a local market comprised principally of counties located in another State, the statutory license provided for in subparagraph (A) shall apply to the secondary transmission by a satellite carrier to subscribers in those 2 counties of the primary transmissions of any network station located in the capital of the State in which such 2 counties are located, if—

(I) the 2 counties are located in a local market that is in the top 100 markets for the year 2003 according to Nielsen Media Research; and

(II) the total number of television households in the 2 counties combined did not exceed 10,000 for the year 2003 according to Nielsen Media Research.

(v) Applicability of royalty rates. The royalty rates under subsection (b)(1)(B) apply to the secondary transmissions to which the statutory license under subparagraph (A) applies under clauses (i), (ii), (iii), and (iv).

(D) Submission of subscriber lists to networks.—

(i) Initial lists. A satellite carrier that makes secondary transmissions of a primary transmission made by a network station pursuant to subparagraph (A) shall, 90 days after commencing such secondary transmissions, submit to the network that owns or is affiliated with the network station—

(I) a list identifying (by name and address, including street or rural route number, city, State, and zip code) all subscribers to which the satellite carrier makes secondary transmissions of that primary transmission to subscribers in unserved households; and

(II) a separate list, aggregated by designated market area (as defined in section 122(j) [17 USCS § 122(j)]) (by name and address, including street or rural route number, city, State, and zip code), which shall indicate those subscribers being served pursuant to paragraph (3), relating to significantly viewed stations.

(ii) Monthly lists. After the submission of the initial lists under clause (i), on the 15th of each month, the satellite carrier shall submit to the network—

(I) a list identifying (by name and address, including street or rural route number, city, State, and zip code) any persons who have been added or dropped as subscribers under clause (i)(I) since the last submission under clause (i); and

(II) a separate list, aggregated by designated market area (by name and street address, including street or rural route number, city, State, and zip code), identifying those subscribers whose service pursuant to paragraph (3), relating to significantly viewed stations, has been added or dropped.

(iii) Use of subscriber information. Subscriber information submitted by a satellite carrier under this subparagraph may be used only for purposes of monitoring compliance by the satellite carrier with this subsection.

(iv) Applicability. The submission requirements of this subparagraph shall apply to a satellite carrier only if the network to which the submissions are to be made places on file with the Register of Copyrights a document identifying the name and address of the person to whom such submissions are to be made. The Register shall maintain for public inspection a file of all such documents.

(3) *Secondary transmissions of significantly viewed signals*—

(A) In general. Notwithstanding the provisions of paragraph (2)(B), and subject to subparagraph (B) of this paragraph, the statutory license provided for in paragraphs (1) and (2) shall apply to the secondary transmission of the primary transmission of a network station or a superstation to a subscriber who resides outside the station's local market (as defined in section 122(j) [17 USCS § 122(j)]) but within a community in which the signal has been determined by the Federal Communications Commission, to be significantly viewed in such community, pursuant to the rules, regulations, and authorizations of the Federal Communications Commission in effect on April 15, 1976, applicable to determining with respect to a cable system whether signals are significantly viewed in a community.

(B) Limitation. Subparagraph (A) shall apply only to secondary transmissions of the primary transmissions of network stations and superstations to subscribers who receive secondary transmissions from a satellite carrier pursuant to the statutory license under section 122 [17 USCS § 122].

(C) Waiver.—

(i) In general. A subscriber who is denied the secondary transmission of the primary transmission of a network station under subparagraph (B) may request a waiver from such denial by submitting a request, through the subscriber's satellite carrier, to the network station in the local market affiliated with the same network where the subscriber is located. The network station shall accept or reject the subscriber's request for a waiver within 30 days after receipt of the request. If the network station fails to accept or reject the subscriber's request for a waiver within that 30-day period, that network station shall be deemed to agree to the waiver request. Unless specifically stated by the network station, a waiver that was granted before the date of the enactment of the Satellite Home Viewer Extension and Reauthorization Act of 2004 [enacted Dec. 8, 2004] under section 339(c)(2) of the Communications Act of 1934 [47 USCS § 339(c)(2)] shall not constitute a waiver for purposes of this subparagraph.

(ii) Sunset. The authority under clause (i) to grant waivers shall terminate on December 31, 2008, and any such waiver in effect shall terminate on that date.

(4) *Statutory license where retransmissions into local market available.*

(A) Rules for subscribers to analog signals under subsection (e).—

(i) For those receiving distant analog signals. In the case of a subscriber of a satellite carrier who is eligible to receive the secondary transmission of the primary analog transmission of a network station solely by reason of subsection (e) (in this subparagraph referred to as a "distant analog signal"), and who, as of October 1, 2004, is receiving the distant analog signal of that network station, the following shall apply:

(I) In a case in which the satellite carrier makes available to the subscriber the secondary transmission of the primary analog transmission of a local network station affiliated with the same television network pursuant to the statutory license under section 122 [17 USCS § 122], the statutory license under paragraph (2) shall apply only to secondary transmissions by that satellite carrier to that subscriber of the distant analog signal of a station affiliated with the same television network—

(aa) if, within 60 days after receiving the notice of the satellite carrier under section 338(h)(1) of the Communications Act of 1934 [47 USCS § 338(h)(1)], the subscriber elects to retain the distant analog signal; but (bb) only until such time as the subscriber elects to receive such local analog signal.

(II) Notwithstanding subclause (I), the statutory license under paragraph (2) shall not apply with respect to any subscriber who is eligible to receive the distant analog signal of a television network station solely by reason of subsection (e), unless the satellite carrier, within 60 days after the date of the enactment of the Satellite Home Viewer Extension and Reauthorization Act of 2004 [enacted Dec. 8, 2004], submits to that television network a list, aggregated by designated market area (as defined in section 122(j)(2)(C) [17 USCS § 122(j)(2)(C)]), that—

(aa) identifies that subscriber by name and address (street or rural route number, city, State, and zip code) and specifies the distant analog signals received by the subscriber; and

(bb) states, to the best of the satellite carrier's knowledge and belief, after having made diligent and good faith inquiries, that the subscriber is eligible under subsection (e) to receive the distant analog signals.

(ii) For those not receiving distant analog signals. In the case of any subscriber of a satellite carrier who is eligible to receive the distant analog signal of a network station solely by reason of subsection (e) and who did not receive a distant analog signal of a station affiliated with the same network on October 1, 2004, the statutory license under paragraph (2) shall not apply to secondary transmissions by that satellite carrier to that subscriber of the distant analog signal of a station affiliated with the same network.

(B) Rules for other subscribers. In the case of a subscriber of a satellite carrier who is eligible to receive the secondary transmission of the primary analog transmission of a network station under the statutory license under paragraph (2) (in this subparagraph referred to as a "distant analog signal"), other than subscribers to whom subparagraph (A) applies, the following shall apply:

(i) In a case in which the satellite carrier makes available to that subscriber, on January 1, 2005, the secondary transmission of the primary analog transmission of a local network station affiliated with the same television network pursuant to the statutory license under section 122 [17 USCS § 122], the statutory license under paragraph (2) shall apply only to secondary transmissions by that satellite carrier to that subscriber of the distant analog signal of a station affiliated with the same television network if the subscriber's satellite carrier, not later than March 1, 2005, submits to that television network a list, aggregated by designated market area (as defined in section 122(j)(2)(C) [17 USCS § 122(j)(2)(C)]), that identifies that subscriber by name and address (street or rural route number, city, State, and zip code) and specifies the distant analog signals received by the subscriber.

(ii) In a case in which the satellite carrier does not make available to that subscriber, on January 1, 2005, the secondary transmission of the primary analog transmission of a local network station affiliated with the same television network pursuant to the statutory license under section 122 [17 USCS § 122], the statutory license under paragraph (2) shall apply only to secondary transmissions by that satellite carrier of the distant analog signal of a station affiliated with the same network to that subscriber if—

(I) that subscriber seeks to subscribe to such distant analog signal before the date on which such carrier commences to provide pursuant to the statutory license under section 122 [17 USCS § 122] the secondary transmissions of the primary analog transmission of stations from the local market of such local network station; and

(II) the satellite carrier, within 60 days after such date, submits to each television network a list that identifies each subscriber in that local market provided such an analog signal by name and address (street or rural route number, city, State, and zip code) and specifies the distant analog signals received by the subscriber.

(C) Future applicability. The statutory license under paragraph (2) shall not apply to the secondary transmission by a satellite carrier of a primary analog transmission of a network station to a person who—

(i) is not a subscriber lawfully receiving such secondary transmission as of the date of the enactment of the Satellite Home Viewer Extension and Reauthorization Act of 2004 [enacted Dec. 8, 2004]; and

(ii) at the time such person seeks to subscribe to receive such secondary transmission, resides in a local market where the satellite carrier makes available to that person the secondary transmission of the primary analog transmission of a local network station affiliated with the same television network pursuant to the statutory license under section 122 [17 USCS § 122], and such secondary transmission of such primary transmission can reach such person.

(D) Special rules for distant digital signals. The statutory license under paragraph (2) shall apply to secondary transmissions by a satellite carrier to a subscriber of primary digital transmissions of network stations if such secondary transmissions to such subscriber are permitted under section 339(a)(2)(D) of the Communications Act of 1934 [47 USCS § 339(a)(2)(D)], as in effect on the day after the date of the enactment of the Satellite Home Viewer Extension and Reauthorization Act of 2004 [enacted Dec. 8, 2004], except that the reference to section 73.683(a) of title 47, Code of Federal Regulations, referred to in section 339(a)(2)(D)(i)(I) [47 USCS § 339(a)(2)(D)(i)(I)] shall refer to such section as in effect on the date of the enactment of the Satellite Home Viewer Extension and Reauthorization Act of 2004 [enacted Dec. 8, 2004].

(E) Other provisions not affected. This paragraph shall not affect the applicability of the statutory license to secondary transmissions under paragraph (3) or to unserved households included under paragraph (12).

(F) Waiver. A subscriber who is denied the secondary transmission of a network station under subparagraph (C) or (D) may request a waiver from such denial by submitting a request, through the subscriber's satellite carrier, to the network station in the local market affiliated with the same network where the subscriber is located. The network station shall accept or reject the subscriber's request for a waiver within 30 days after receipt of the request. If the network station fails to accept or reject the subscriber's request for a waiver within that 30-day period, that network station shall be deemed to agree to the waiver request. Unless specifically stated by the network station, a waiver that was granted before the date of the enactment of the Satellite Home Viewer Extension and Reauthorization Act of 2004 [enacted Dec. 8, 2004] under section 339(c)(2) of the Communications Act of 1934 [47 USCS § 339(c)(2)] shall not constitute a waiver for purposes of this subparagraph.

(G) Available defined. For purposes of this paragraph, a satellite carrier makes available a secondary transmission of the primary transmission of a local station to a subscriber or person if the satellite carrier offers that secondary transmission to other subscribers who reside in the same zip code as that subscriber or person.

(5) *Noncompliance with reporting and payment requirements.* Notwithstanding the provisions of paragraphs (1) and (2), the willful or repeated secondary transmission to the public by a satellite carrier of a primary transmission made by a superstation or a network station and embodying a performance or display of a work is actionable as an act of infringement under section 501 [17 USCS § 501], and is fully subject to the remedies provided by sections 502 through 506 and 509 [17 USCS §§ 502–506 and 509], where the satellite carrier has not deposited the

statement of account and royalty fee required by subsection (b), or has failed to make the submissions to networks required by paragraph (2) C).

(6) *Willful alterations.* Notwithstanding the provisions of paragraphs (1) and (2), the secondary transmission to the public by a satellite carrier of a performance or display of a work embodied in a primary transmission made by a superstation or a network station is actionable as an act of infringement under section 501 [17 USCS § 501], and is fully subject to the remedies provided by sections 502 through 506 [17 USCS §§ 502–506] and section 510 [17 USCS § 510], if the content of the particular program in which the performance or display is embodied, or any commercial advertising or station announcement transmitted by the primary transmitter during, or immediately before or after, the transmission of such program, is in any way willfully altered by the satellite carrier through changes, deletions, or additions, or is combined with programming from any other broadcast signal.

(7) *Violation of territorial restrictions on statutory license for network stations.*—

(A) Individual violations. The willful or repeated secondary transmission by a satellite carrier of a primary transmission made by a network station and embodying a performance or display of a work to a subscriber who is not eligible to receive the transmission under this section is actionable as an act of infringement under section 501 [17 USCS § 501] and is fully subject to the remedies provided by sections 502 through 506 [17 USCS §§ 502–506], except that—

(i) no damages shall be awarded for such act of infringement if the satellite carrier took corrective action by promptly withdrawing service from the ineligible subscriber, and

(ii) any statutory damages shall not exceed $5 for such subscriber for each month during which the violation occurred.

(B) Pattern of violations. If a satellite carrier engages in a willful or repeated pattern or practice of delivering a primary transmission made by a network station and embodying a performance or display of a work to subscribers who are not eligible to receive the transmission under this section, then in addition to the remedies set forth in subparagraph (A)—

(i) if the pattern or practice has been carried out on a substantially nationwide basis, the court shall order a permanent injunction barring the secondary transmission by the satellite carrier, for private home viewing, of the primary transmissions of any primary network station affiliated with the same network, and the court may order statutory damages of not to exceed $250,000 for each 6-month period during which the pattern or practice was carried out; and

(ii) if the pattern or practice has been carried out on a local or regional basis, the court shall order a permanent injunction barring the secondary transmission, for private home viewing in that locality or region, by the satellite carrier of the primary transmissions of any primary network station affiliated with the same network, and the court may order statutory damages of not to exceed $250,000 for each 6-month period during which the pattern or practice was carried out.

(C) Previous subscribers excluded. Subparagraphs (A) and (B) do not apply to secondary transmissions by a satellite carrier to persons who subscribed to receive such secondary transmissions from the satellite carrier or a distributor before November 16, 1988.

(D) Burden of proof. In any action brought under this paragraph, the satellite carrier shall have the burden of proving that its secondary transmission of a primary transmission by a network station is to a subscriber who is eligible to receive the secondary transmission under this section.

(E) Exception. The secondary transmission by a satellite carrier of a performance or display of a work embodied in a primary transmission made by a network station to subscribers who do not reside in unserved households shall not be an act of infringement if—

(i) the station on May 1, 1991, was retransmitted by a satellite carrier and was not on that date owned or operated by or affiliated with a television network that offered interconnected program service on a regular basis for 15 or more hours per week to at least 25 affiliated television licensees in 10 or more States;

(ii) as of July 1, 1998, such station was retransmitted by a satellite carrier under the statutory license of this section; and

(iii) the station is not owned or operated by or affiliated with a television network that, as of January 1, 1995, offered interconnected program service on a regular basis for 15 or more hours per week to at least 25 affiliated television licensees in 10 or more States.

(8) *Discrimination by a satellite carrier.* Notwithstanding the provisions of paragraph (1), the willful or repeated secondary transmission to the public by a satellite carrier of a performance or display of a work embodied in a primary transmission made by a superstation or a network station is actionable as an act of infringement under section 501 [17 USCS § 501], and is fully subject to the remedies provided by sections 502 through 506 [17 USCS §§ 502–506], if the satellite carrier unlawfully discriminates against a distributor.

(9) *Geographic limitation on secondary transmissions.* The statutory license created by this section shall apply only to secondary transmissions to households located in the United States.

(10) *Loser pays for signal intensity measurement; recovery of measurement costs in a civil action.* In any civil action filed relating to the eligibility of subscribing households as unserved households—

(A) a network station challenging such eligibility shall, within 60 days after receipt of the measurement results and a statement of such costs, reimburse the satellite carrier for any signal intensity measurement that is conducted by that carrier in response to a challenge by the network station and that establishes the household is an unserved household; and

(B) a satellite carrier shall, within 60 days after receipt of the measurement results and a statement of such costs, reimburse the network station challenging such eligibility for any signal intensity measurement that is conducted by that station and that establishes the household is not an unserved household.

(11) *Inability to conduct measurement.* If a network station makes a reasonable attempt to conduct a site measurement of its signal at a subscriber's household and is denied access for the purpose of conducting the measurement, and is otherwise unable to conduct a measurement, the satellite carrier shall within 60 days notice thereof, terminate service of the station's network to that household.

(12) *Service to recreational vehicles and commercial trucks.*—

(A) Exemption.—

(i) In general. For purposes of this subsection, and subject to clauses (ii) and (iii), the term "unserved household" shall include—

(I) recreational vehicles as defined in regulations of the Secretary of Housing and Urban Development under section 3282.8 of title 24 of the Code of Federal Regulations; and

(II) commercial trucks that qualify as commercial motor vehicles under regulations of the Secretary of Transportation under section 383.5 of title 49 of the Code of Federal Regulations.

(ii) Limitation. Clause (i) shall apply only to a recreational vehicle or commercial truck if any satellite carrier that proposes to make a secondary transmission of a network station to the operator of such a recreational vehicle or commercial truck complies with the documentation requirements under subparagraphs (B) and (C).

(iii) Exclusion. For purposes of this subparagraph, the terms "recreational vehicle" and "commercial truck" shall not include any fixed dwelling, whether a mobile home or otherwise.

(B) Documentation requirements. A recreational vehicle or commercial truck shall be deemed to be an unserved household beginning 10 days after the relevant satellite carrier provides to the network that owns or is affiliated with the network station that will be secondarily transmitted to the recreational vehicle or commercial truck the following documents:

(i) Declaration. A signed declaration by the operator of the recreational vehicle or commercial truck that the satellite dish is permanently attached to the recreational vehicle or commercial truck, and will not be used to receive satellite programming at any fixed dwelling.

(ii) Registration. In the case of a recreational vehicle, a copy of the current State vehicle registration for the recreational vehicle.

(iii) Registration and license. In the case of a commercial truck, a copy of—

(I) the current State vehicle registration for the truck; and

(II) a copy of a valid, current commercial driver's license, as defined in regulations of the Secretary of Transportation under section 383 of title 49 of the Code of Federal Regulations, issued to the operator.

(C) Updated documentation requirements. If a satellite carrier wishes to continue to make secondary transmissions to a recreational vehicle or commercial truck for more than a 2-year period, that carrier shall provide each network, upon request, with updated documentation in the form described under subparagraph (B) during the 90 days before expiration of that 2-year period.

(13) *Statutory license contingent on compliance with FCC rules and remedial steps.* Notwithstanding any other provision of this section, the willful or repeated secondary transmission to the public by a satellite carrier of a primary transmission embodying a performance or display of a work made by a broadcast station licensed by the Federal Communications Commission is actionable as an act of infringement under section 501 [17 USCS § 501], and is fully subject to the remedies provided by sections 502 through 506 [17 USCS §§ 502–506], if, at the time of such transmission, the satellite carrier is not in compliance with the rules, regulations, and authorizations of the Federal Communications Commission concerning the carriage of television broadcast station signals.

(14) *Waivers.* A subscriber who is denied the secondary transmission of a signal of a network station under subsection (a)(2)(B) may request a waiver from such denial by submitting a request, through the subscriber's satellite carrier, to the network station asserting that the secondary transmission is prohibited. The network station shall accept or reject a subscriber's request for a waiver within 30 days after receipt of the request. If a television network station fails to accept or reject a subscriber's request for a waiver within the 30-day period after receipt of the request, that station shall be deemed to agree to the waiver request and have filed such written waiver. Unless specifically stated by the network station, a waiver that was granted before the date of the enactment of the Satellite Home Viewer Extension and Reauthorization Act of 2004 [enacted Dec. 8, 2004] under section 339(c)(2) of the Communications Act of 1934 [47 USCS § 339(c)(2)], and that was in effect on such date of enactment, shall constitute a waiver for purposes of this paragraph.

(15) *Carriage of low power television stations.*—

(A) In general. Notwithstanding paragraph (2)(B), and subject to subparagraphs (B) through (F) of this paragraph, the statutory license provided for in paragraphs (1) and (2) shall apply to the secondary transmission of the primary transmission of a network station or a superstation that is licensed as a low power television station, to a subscriber who resides within the same local market.

(B) Geographic limitation.

(i) Network stations. With respect to network stations, secondary transmissions provided for in subparagraph (A) shall be limited to secondary transmissions to subscribers who—

(I) reside in the same local market as the station originating the signal; and

(II) reside within 35 miles of the transmitter site of such station, except that in the case of such a station located in a standard metropolitan statistical area which has 1 of the 50 largest populations of all standard metropolitan statistical areas (based on the 1980 decennial census of population taken by the Secretary of Commerce), the number of miles shall be 20.

(ii) Superstations. With respect to superstations, secondary transmissions provided for in subparagraph (A) shall be limited to secondary transmissions to subscribers who reside in the same local market as the station originating the signal.

(C) No applicability to repeaters and translators. Secondary transmissions provided for in subparagraph (A) shall not apply to any low power television station that retransmits the programs and signals of another television station for more than 2 hours each day.

(D) Royalty fees. Notwithstanding subsection (b)(1)(B), a satellite carrier whose secondary transmissions of the primary transmissions of a low power television station are subject to statutory licensing under this section shall have no royalty obligation for secondary transmissions to a subscriber who resides within 35 miles of the transmitter site of such station, except that in the case of such a station located in a standard metropolitan statistical area which has 1 of the 50 largest populations of all standard metropolitan statistical areas (based on the 1980 decennial census of population taken by the Secretary of Commerce), the number of miles shall be 20. Carriage of a superstation that is a low power television station within the station's local market, but outside of the 35-mile or 20-mile radius described in the preceding sentence, shall be subject to royalty payments under subsection (b)(1)(B).

(E) Limitation to subscribers taking local-into-local service. Secondary transmissions provided for in subparagraph (A) may be made only to subscribers who receive secondary transmissions of primary transmissions from that satellite carrier pursuant to the statutory license under section 122 [47 USCS § 122], and only in conformity with the requirements under 340(b) of the Communications Act of 1934 [47 USCS § 340(b)], as in effect on the date of the enactment of the Satellite Home Viewer Extension and Reauthorization Act of 2004 [enacted Dec. 8, 2004].

(16) *Restricted transmission of out-of-State distant network signals into certain markets.*—

(A) Out-of-State network affiliates. Notwithstanding any other provision of this title, the statutory license in this subsection and subsection (b) shall not apply to any secondary transmission of the primary transmission of a network station located outside of the State of Alaska to any subscriber in that State to whom the secondary transmission of the primary transmission of a television station located in that State is made available by the satellite carrier pursuant to section 122 [17 USCS § 122].

(B) Exception. The limitation in subparagraph (A) shall not apply to the secondary transmission of the primary transmission of a digital signal of a network station located outside of the State of Alaska if at the time that the secondary transmission is made, no television station licensed to a community in the State and affiliated with the same network makes primary transmissions of a digital signal.

(b) **Statutory License for Secondary Transmissions.**—

(1) *Deposits with the Register of Copyrights.* A satellite carrier whose secondary transmissions are subject to statutory licensing under subsection (a) shall, on a semiannual basis, deposit with the Register of

Copyrights, in accordance with requirements that the Register shall prescribe by regulation—

(A) a statement of account, covering the preceding 6-month period, specifying the names and locations of all superstations and network stations whose signals were retransmitted, at any time during that period, to subscribers as described in subsections (a)(1) and (a)(2), the total number of subscribers that received such retransmissions, and such other data as the Register of Copyrights may from time to time prescribe by regulation; and

(B) a royalty fee for that 6-month period, computed by multiplying the total number of subscribers receiving each secondary transmission of each superstation or network station during each calendar month by the appropriate rate in effect under this section.

Notwithstanding the provisions of subparagraph (B), a satellite carrier whose secondary transmissions are subject to statutory licensing under paragraph (1) or (2) of subsection (a) shall have no royalty obligation for secondary transmissions to a subscriber under paragraph (3) of such subsection.

(2) *Investment of fees.* The Register of Copyrights shall receive all fees deposited under this section and, after deducting the reasonable costs incurred by the Copyright Office under this section (other than the costs deducted under paragraph (4)), shall deposit the balance in the Treasury of the United States, in such manner as the Secretary of the Treasury directs. All funds held by the Secretary of the Treasury shall be invested in interest-bearing securities of the United States for later distribution with interest by the Librarian of Congress as provided by this title.

(3) *Persons to whom fees are distributed.* The royalty fees deposited under paragraph (2) shall, in accordance with the procedures provided by paragraph (4), be distributed to those copyright owners whose works were included in a secondary transmission made by a satellite carrier during the applicable 6-month accounting period and who file a claim with the Copyright Royalty Judges under paragraph (4).

(4) *Procedures for distribution.* The royalty fees deposited under paragraph (2) shall be distributed in accordance with the following procedures:

(A) Filing of claims for fees. During the month of July in each year, each person claiming to be entitled to statutory license fees for secondary transmissions shall file a claim with the Copyright Royalty Judges, in accordance with requirements that the Copyright Royalty Judges shall prescribe by regulation. For purposes of this paragraph, any claimants may agree among themselves as to the proportionate division of statutory license fees among them, may lump their claims together and file them jointly or as a single claim, or may designate a common agent to receive payment on their behalf.

(B) Determination of controversy; distributions. After the first day of August of each year, the Copyright Royalty Judges shall determine whether there exists a controversy concerning the distribution of royalty fees. If the Copyright Royalty Judges determine that no such controversy exists, the Copyright Royalty Judges shall authorize the Librarian of Congress to proceed to distribute such fees to the copyright owners entitled to receive them, or to their designated agents, subject to the deduction of reasonable administrative costs under this section. If the Copyright Royalty Judges find the existence of a controversy, the Copyright Royalty Judges shall, pursuant to chapter 8 of this title [17 USCS §§ 801 et seq.], conduct a proceeding to determine the distribution of royalty fees.

(C) Withholding of fees during controversy. During the pendency of any proceeding under this subsection, the Copyright Royalty Judges shall have the discretion to authorize the Librarian of Congress to proceed to distribute any amounts that are not in controversy.

(c) **Adjustment of Royalty Fees.**

(1) *Applicability and determination of royalty fees for analog signals.—*

(A) Initial fee. The appropriate fee for purposes of determining the royalty fee under subsection (b)(1)(B) for the secondary transmission of the primary analog transmissions of network stations and superstations shall be the appropriate fee set forth in part 258 of title 37, Code of Federal Regulations, as in effect on July 1, 2004, as modified under this paragraph.

(B) Fee set by voluntary negotiation. On or before January 2, 2005, the Librarian of Congress shall cause to be published in the Federal Register of the initiation of voluntary negotiation proceedings for the purpose of determining the royalty fee to be paid by satellite carriers for the secondary transmission of the primary analog transmission of network stations and superstations under subsection (b)(1)(B).

(C) Negotiations. Satellite carriers, distributors, and copyright owners entitled to royalty fees under this section shall negotiate in good faith in an effort to reach a voluntary agreement or agreements for the payment of royalty fees. Any such satellite carriers, distributors and copyright owners may at any time negotiate and agree to the royalty fee, and may designate common agents to negotiate, agree to, or pay such fees. If the parties fail to identify common agents, the Librarian of Congress shall do so, after requesting recommendations from the parties to the negotiation proceeding. The parties to each negotiation proceeding shall bear the cost thereof.

(D) Agreements binding on parties; filing of agreements; public notice.—

(i) Voluntary agreements negotiated at any time in accordance with this paragraph shall be binding upon all satellite carriers, distributors, and copyright owners that a parties thereto. Copies of such agreements shall be filed with the Copyright Office within 30 days after execution in accordance with regulations that the Register of Copyrights shall prescribe.

(ii) (I) Within 10 days after publication in the Federal Register of a notice of the initiation of voluntary negotiation proceedings, parties who have reached a voluntary agreement may request that the royalty fees in that agreement be applied to all satellite carriers, distributors, and copyright owners without convening an arbitration proceeding pursuant to subparagraph (E).

(II) Upon receiving a request under subclause (I), the Librarian of Congress shall immediately provide public notice of the royalty fees from the voluntary agreement and afford parties an opportunity to state that they object to those fees.

(III) The Librarian shall adopt the royalty fees from the voluntary agreement for all satellite carriers, distributors, and copyright owners without convening an arbitration proceeding unless a party with an intent to participate in the arbitration proceeding and a significant interest in the outcome of that proceeding objects under subclause (II).

(E) Period agreement is in effect. The obligation to pay the royalty fees established under a voluntary agreement which has been filed with the Copyright Office in accordance with this paragraph shall become effective on the date specified in the agreement, and shall remain in effect until December 31, 2009, or in accordance with the terms of the agreement, whichever is later.

(F) Fee set by compulsory arbitration.—

(i) Notice of initiation of proceedings. On or before May 1, 2005, the Librarian of Congress shall cause notice to be published in the Federal Register of the initiation of arbitration proceedings for the purpose of determining the royalty fee to be paid for the secondary transmission of primary analog transmission of network stations and superstations under subsection (b)(1)(B) by satellite carriers and distributors

(I) in the absence of a voluntary agreement filed in accordance with subparagraph (D) that establishes royalty fees to be paid by all satellite carriers and distributors; or

(II) if an objection to the fees from a voluntary agreement submitted for adoption by the Librarian of Congress to apply to all satellite carriers, distributors, and copyright owners is received under subparagraph (D) from a party with an intent to participate in the arbitration proceeding and a significant interest in the outcome of that proceeding.

Such arbitration proceeding shall be conducted under chapter 8 [17 USCS §§ 801 et seq.] as in effect on the day before the date of the enactment of the Copyright Royalty and Distribution Act of 2004 [enacted Dec. 8, 2004].

(ii) Establishment of royalty fees. In determining royalty fees under this subparagraph, the copyright arbitration royalty panel appointed under chapter 8, as in effect on the day before the date of the enactment of the Copyright Royalty and Distribution Act of 2004 [enacted Dec. 8, 2004] shall establish fees for the secondary transmissions of the primary analog transmission of network stations and superstations that most clearly represent the fair market value of secondary transmissions, except that the Librarian of Congress and any copyright arbitration royalty panel shall adjust those fees to account for the obligations of the parties under any applicable voluntary agreement filed with the Copyright Office pursuant to subparagraph (D). In determining the fair market value, the panel shall base its decision on economic, competitive, and programming information presented by the parties, including—

(I) the competitive environment in which such programming is distributed, the cost of similar signals in similar private and compulsory license marketplaces, and any special features and conditions of the retransmission marketplace;

(II) the economic impact of such fees on copyright owners and satellite carriers; and

(III) the impact on the continued availability of secondary transmissions to the public.

(iii) Period during which decision of arbitration panel or order of librarian effective. The obligation to pay the royalty fee established under a determination which—

(I) is made by a copyright arbitration royalty panel in an arbitration proceeding under this paragraph and is adopted by the Librarian of Congress under section 802(f) [17 USCS § 802(f)], as in effect on the day before the date of the enactment of the Copyright Royalty and Distribution Act of 2004 [enacted Dec. 8, 2004]; or

(II) is established by the Librarian under section 802(f) [17 USCS § 802(f)] as in effect on the day before such date of enactment shall be effective as of January 1, 2005.

(iv) Persons subject to royalty fee. The royalty fee referred to in (iii) shall be binding on all satellite carriers, distributors and copyright owners, who are not party to a voluntary agreement filed with the Copyright Office under subparagraph (D).

(2) *Applicability and determination of royalty fees for digital signals.* The process and requirements for establishing the royalty fee payable under subsection (b)(1)(B) for the secondary transmission of the primary digital transmissions of network stations and superstations shall be the same as that set forth in paragraph (1) for the secondary transmission of the primary analog transmission of network stations and superstations, except that—

(A) the initial fee under paragraph (1)(A) shall be the rates set forth in section 298.3(b)(1) and (2) of title 37, Code of Federal Regulations, as in effect on the date of the enactment of the Satellite Home Viewer Extension and Reauthorization Act of 2004 [enacted Dec. 8, 2004], reduced by 22.5 percent;

(B) the notice of initiation of arbitration proceedings required in paragraph (1)(F)(i) shall be published on or before December 31, 2005;

(C) the royalty fees that are established for the secondary transmission of the primary digital transmission of network stations and superstations in accordance with to the procedures set forth in paragraph (1)(F)(iii) and are payable under subsection (b)(1)(B)—

(i) shall be reduced by 22.5 percent; and

(ii) shall be adjusted by the Librarian of Congress on January 1, 2007, and on January 1 of each year thereafter, to reflect any changes occurring during the preceding 12 months in the cost of living as determined by the most recent Consumer Price Index (for all consumers and items) published by the Secretary of Labor.

(d) **Definitions. As used in this section—**

(1) *Distributor.* The term "distributor" means an entity which contracts to distribute secondary transmissions from a satellite carrier and, either as a single channel or in a package with other programming, provides the secondary transmission either directly to individual subscribers or indirectly through other program distribution entities in accordance with the provisions of this section.

(2) *Network station.* The term "network station" means—

(A) a television station licensed by the Federal Communications Commission, including any translator station or terrestrial satellite station that rebroadcasts all or substantially all of the programming broadcast by a network station, that is owned or operated by, or affiliated with, one or more of the television networks in the United States which offer an interconnected program service on a regular basis for 15 or more hours per week to at least 25 of its affiliated television licensees in 10 or more States; or

(B) a noncommercial educational broadcast station (as defined in section 397 of the Communications Act of 1934 [47 USCS § 397]); except that the term does not include the signal of the Alaska Rural Communications Service, or any successor entity to that service.

(3) *Primary network station.* The term "primary network station" means a network station that broadcasts or rebroadcasts the basic programming service of a particular national network.

(4) *Primary transmission.* The term "primary transmission" has the meaning given that term in section 111(f) of this title [17 USCS § 111(f)].

(5) *Private home viewing.* The term "private home viewing" means the viewing, for private use in a household by means of satellite reception equipment which is operated by an individual in that household and which serves only such household, of a secondary transmission delivered by a satellite carrier of a primary transmission of a television station licensed by the Federal Communications Commission.

(6) *Satellite carrier.* The term "satellite carrier" means an entity that uses the facilities of a satellite or satellite service licensed by the Federal Communications Commission and operates in the Fixed-Satellite Service under part 25 of title 47 of the Code of Federal Regulations or the Direct Broadcast Satellite Service under part 100 of title 47 of the Code of Federal Regulations, to establish and operate a channel of communications for point-to-multipoint distribution of television station signals, and that owns or leases a capacity or service on a satellite in order to provide such point-to-multipoint distribution, except to the extent that such entity provides such distribution pursuant to tariff under the Communications Act of 1934, other than for private home viewing pursuant to this section.

(7) *Secondary transmission.* The term "secondary transmission" has the meaning given that term in section 111(f) of this title [17 USCS § 111(f)].

(8) *Subscriber.* The term "subscriber" means an individual or entity that receives a secondary transmission service by means of a secondary transmission from a satellite carrier and pays a fee for the

service, directly or indirectly, to the satellite carrier or to a distributor in accordance with the provisions of this section.

(9) *Superstation.* The term "superstation" means a television station, other than a network station, licensed by the Federal Communications Commission, that is secondarily transmitted by a satellite carrier.

(10) *Unserved household.* The term "unserved household", with respect to a particular television network, means a household that—

(A) cannot receive, through the use of a conventional, stationary, outdoor rooftop receiving antenna, an over-the-air signal of a primary network station affiliated with that network of Grade B intensity as defined by the Federal Communications Commission under section 73.683(a) of title 47 of the Code of Federal Regulations, as in effect on January 1, 1999;

(B) is subject to a waiver that meets the standards of subsection (a)(14) whether or not the waiver was granted before the date of the enactment of the Satellite Home Viewer Extension and Reauthorization Act of 2004;

(C) is a subscriber to whom subsection (e) applies;

(D) is a subscriber to whom subsection (a)(12) applies; or

(E) is a subscriber to whom the exemption under subsection (a)(2)(B)(iii) applies.

(11) *Local market.* The term "local market" has the meaning given such term under section 122(j) [17 USCS § 122(j)], except that with respect to a low power television station, the term "local market" means the designated market area in which the station is located.

(12) *Low power television station.* The term "low power television station" means a low power television as defined under section 74.701(f) of title 47, Code of Federal Regulations, as in effect on June 1, 2004. For purposes of this paragraph, the term "low power television station" includes a low power television station that has been accorded primary status as a Class A television licensee under section 73.6001(a) of title 47, Code of Federal Regulations.

(13) *Commercial establishment.* The term "commercial establishment"—

(A) means an establishment used for commercial purposes, such as a bar, restaurant, private office, fitness club, oil rig, retail store, bank or other financial institution, supermarket, automobile or boat dealership, or any other establishment with a common business area; and

(B) does not include a multi-unit permanent or temporary dwelling where private home viewing occurs, such as a hotel, dormitory, hospital, apartment, condominium, or prison.

(e) Moratorium on copyright liability. Until February 28, 2010, a subscriber who does not receive a signal of Grade A intensity (as defined in the regulations of the Federal Communications Commission under section 73.683(a) of title 47 of the Code of Federal Regulations, as in effect on January 1, 1999, or predicted by the Federal Communications Commission using the Individual Location Longley-Rice methodology described by the Federal Communications Commission in Docket No. 98-201) of a local network television broadcast station shall remain eligible to receive signals of network stations affiliated with the same network, if that subscriber had satellite service of such network signal terminated after July 11, 1998, and before October 31, 1999, as required by this section, or received such service on October 31, 1999.

(f) Expedited consideration by Justice Department of voluntary agreements to provide satellite secondary transmissions to local markets.

(1) *In general.* In a case in which no satellite carrier makes available, to subscribers located in a local market, as defined in section 122(j)(2) [17 USCS § 122(j)(2)], the secondary transmission into that market of a primary transmission of one or more television broadcast stations licensed by the Federal Communications Commission, and two or more satellite carriers request a business review letter in accordance with section 50.6 of title 28, Code of Federal Regulations (as in effect on July 7, 2004), in order to assess the legality under the antitrust laws of proposed business conduct to make or carry out an agreement to provide such secondary transmission into such local market, the appropriate official of the Department of Justice shall respond to the request no later than 90 days after the date on which the request is received.

(2) *Definition.* For purposes of this subsection, the term "antitrust laws"—

(A) has the meaning given that term in subsection (a) of the first section of the Clayton Act (15 U.S.C. 12(a)), except that such term includes section 5 of the Federal Trade Commission Act (15 U.S.C. 45) to the extent such section 5 applies to unfair methods of competition; and

(B) includes any State law similar to the laws referred to in paragraph (1).

(Added Nov. 16, 1988, P. L. 100-667, Title II, § 202(2), 102 Stat. 3949; Dec. 17, 1993, P. L. 103-198, § 5, 107 Stat. 2310; Oct. 18, 1994, P. L. 103-369, § 2, 108 Stat. 3477; Nov. 1, 1995, P. L. 104-39, § 5(c), 109 Stat. 348; Nov. 13, 1997, P. L. 105-80, §§ 1, 12(a)(8), 111 Stat. 1529, 1535; Aug. 5, 1999, P. L. 106-44, § 1(g)(4), 113 Stat. 222; Nov. 29, 1999, P. L. 106-113, Div B, § 1000(a)(9), 113 Stat. 1536; Nov. 2, 2002, P. L. 107-273, Div C, Title III, Subtitle B, §§ 13209, 13210(1), (8), 116 Stat. 1908, 1909; Nov. 30, 2004, P.L. 108-419, § 5(g), (h), 118 Stat. 2367; Dec. 8, 2004, P.L. 108-447, Div J, Title IX, Title I, §§ 101(b), 102-105, 107(a), 108, 111(a), 118 Stat. 3394, 3407, 3408; October 6, 2006, P.L. 109-303, § 4(e), 120 Stat. 1478; October 13, 2008, P.L. 110-403, § 209(a)(4), 122 Stat. 4260; Dec. 19, 2009, P.L. 111-118, § 1003(a), 123 Stat. 3409.)

§ 120 Scope of exclusive rights in architectural works

(a) **Pictorial Representations Permitted.** The copyright in an architectural work that has been constructed does not include the right to prevent the making, distributing, or public display of pictures, paintings, photographs, or other pictorial representations of the work, if the building in which the work is embodied is located in or ordinarily visible from a public place.

(b) **Alterations to and Destruction of Buildings.** Notwithstanding the provisions of section 106(2), the owners of a building embodying an architectural work may, without the consent of the author or copyright owner of the architectural work, make or authorize the making of alterations to such building, and destroy or authorize the destruction of such building.

(Added Dec. 1, 1990, P. L. 101-650, Title VII, § 704(a), 104 Stat. 5133.)

§ 121 Limitations on exclusive rights: Reproduction for blind or other people with disabilities

(a) Notwithstanding the provisions of section 106, it is not an infringement of copyright for an authorized entity to reproduce or to distribute copies or phonorecords of a previously published, nondramatic literary work if such copies or phonorecords are reproduced or distributed in specialized formats exclusively for use by blind or other persons with disabilities.

(b) (1) Copies or phonorecords to which this section applies shall—

(A) not be reproduced or distributed in a format other than a specialized format exclusively for use by blind or other persons with disabilities;

(B) bear a notice that any further reproduction or distribution in a format other than a specialized format is an infringement; and

(C) include a copyright notice identifying the copyright owner and the date of the original publication.

(2) The provisions of this subsection shall not apply to standardized, secure, or norm-referenced tests and related testing material, or to computer programs, except the portions thereof that are in conventional human language (including descriptions of pictorial works) and displayed to users in the ordinary course of using the computer programs.

(c) Notwithstanding the provisions of section 106, it is not an infringement of copyright for a publisher of print instructional materials for use in elementary or secondary schools to create and distribute to the National Instructional Materials Access Center copies of the electronic files described in sections 612(a)(23)(C), 613(a)(6), and section 674(e) of the Individuals with Disabilities Education Act that contain the contents of print instructional materials using the National Instructional Material Accessibility Standard (as defined in section 674(e)(3) of that Act) if—

(1) the inclusion of the contents of such print instructional materials is required by any State educational agency or local educational agency;

(2) the publisher had the right to publish such print instructional materials in print formats; and

(3) such copies are used solely for reproduction or distribution of the contents of such print instructional materials in specialized formats.

(d) For purposes of this section, the term—

(1) "authorized entity" means a nonprofit organization or a governmental agency that has a primary mission to provide specialized services relating to training, education, or adaptive reading or information access needs of blind or other persons with disabilities;

(2) "blind or other persons with disabilities" means individuals who are eligible or who may qualify in accordance with the Act entitled "An Act to provide books for the adult blind", approved March 3, 1931 (2 U.S.C. 135a; 46 Stat. 1487) to receive books and other publications produced in specialized formats;

(3) "print instructional materials" has the meaning given under section 674(e)(3)(C) of the Individuals with Disabilities Education Act; and

(4) "specialized formats" means—

(A) braille, audio, or digital text which is exclusively for use by blind or other persons with disabilities; and

(B) with respect to print instructional materials, includes large print formats when such materials are distributed exclusively for use by blind or other persons with disabilities.

(Added Sept. 16, 1996, P. L. 104-197, Title III, § 316(a), 110 Stat. 2416; Oct. 27, 2000, P. L. 106-379, § 3(b), 114 Stat. 1445; Nov. 2, 2002, P. L. 107-273, Div C, Title III, Subtitle B, § 13210(3)(A), 116 Stat. 1909; Dec. 3, 2004, P. L. 108-446, Title III, § 306, 118 Stat. 2807.)

§ 122 Limitations on exclusive rights: Secondary transmissions by satellite carriers within local markets

(a) **Secondary Transmissions of Television Broadcast Stations by Satellite Carriers.** A secondary transmission of a performance or display of a work embodied in a primary transmission of a television broadcast station into the station's local market shall be subject to statutory licensing under this section if—

(1) the secondary transmission is made by a satellite carrier to the public;

(2) with regard to secondary transmissions, the satellite carrier is in compliance with the rules, regulations, or authorizations of the Federal Communications Commission governing the carriage of television broadcast station signals; and

(3) the satellite carrier makes a direct or indirect charge for the secondary transmission to—

(A) each subscriber receiving the secondary transmission; or

(B) a distributor that has contracted with the satellite carrier for direct or indirect delivery of the secondary transmission to the public.

(b) **Reporting Requirements.**

(1) *Initial lists.* A satellite carrier that makes secondary transmissions of a primary transmission made by a network station under subsection (a) shall, within 90 days after commencing such secondary transmissions, submit to the network that owns or is affiliated with the network station a list identifying (by name in alphabetical order and street address, including county and zip code) all subscribers to which the satellite carrier makes secondary transmissions of that primary transmission under subsection (a).

(2) *Subsequent lists.* After the list is submitted under paragraph (1), the satellite carrier shall, on the 15th of each month, submit to the network a list identifying (by name in alphabetical order and street address, including county and zip code) any subscribers who have been added or dropped as subscribers since the last submission under this subsection.

(3) *Use of subscriber information.* Subscriber information submitted by a satellite carrier under this subsection may be used only for the purposes of monitoring compliance by the satellite carrier with this section.

(4) *Requirements of networks.* The submission requirements of this subsection shall apply to a satellite carrier only if the network to which the submissions are to be made places on file with the Register of Copyrights a document identifying the name and address of the person to whom such submissions are to be made. The Register of Copyrights shall maintain for public inspection a file of all such documents.

(c) **No Royalty Fee Required.** A satellite carrier whose secondary transmissions are subject to statutory licensing under subsection (a) shall have no royalty obligation for such secondary transmissions.

(d) **Noncompliance with Reporting and Regulatory Requirements.** Notwithstanding subsection (a), the willful or repeated secondary transmission to the public by a satellite carrier into the local market of a television broadcast station of a primary transmission embodying a performance or display of a work made by that television broadcast station is actionable as an act of infringement under section 501 [17 USCS § 501], and is fully subject to the remedies provided under sections 502 through 506 [17 USCS §§ 502–506], if the satellite carrier has not complied with the reporting requirements of subsection (b) or with the rules, regulations, and authorizations of the Federal Communications Commission concerning the carriage of television broadcast signals.

(e) **Willful Alterations.** Notwithstanding subsection (a), the secondary transmission to the public by a satellite carrier into the local market of a television broadcast station of a performance or display of a work embodied in a primary transmission made by that television broadcast station is actionable as an act of infringement under section 501 [17 USCS § 501], and is fully subject to the remedies provided by sections 502 through 506 [17 USCS §§ 502–506] and section 510 [17 USCS § 510], if the content of the particular program in which the performance or display is embodied, or any commercial advertising or station announcement transmitted by the primary transmitter during, or immediately before or after, the transmission of such program, is in any way willfully altered by the satellite carrier through changes, deletions, or additions, or is combined with programming from any other broadcast signal.

(f) **Violation of Territorial Restrictions on Statutory License for Television Broadcast Stations.**

(1) *Individual violations.* The willful or repeated secondary transmission to the public by a satellite carrier of a primary transmission embodying a performance or display of a work made by a television broadcast station to a subscriber who does not reside in that station's local market, and is not subject to statutory licensing under section 119 [17 USCS § 119] or a private licensing agreement, is actionable as an act of infringement under section 501 [17 USCS § 501] and is fully subject to the remedies provided by sections 502 through 506 [17 USCS §§ 502–506], except that—

(A) no damages shall be awarded for such act of infringement if the satellite carrier took corrective action by promptly withdrawing service from the ineligible subscriber; and

(B) any statutory damages shall not exceed $ 5 for such subscriber for each month during which the violation occurred.

(2) *Pattern of violations.* If a satellite carrier engages in a willful or repeated pattern or practice of secondarily transmitting to the public a primary transmission embodying a performance or display of a work made by a television broadcast station to subscribers who do not reside in that station's local market, and are not subject to statutory licensing under section 119 [17 USCS § 119] or a private licensing agreement, then in addition to the remedies under paragraph (1)—

(A) if the pattern or practice has been carried out on a substantially nationwide basis, the court—

(i) shall order a permanent injunction barring the secondary transmission by the satellite carrier of the primary transmissions of that television broadcast station (and if such television broadcast station is a network station, all other television broadcast stations affiliated with such network); and

(ii) may order statutory damages not exceeding $250,000 for each 6-month period during which the pattern or practice was carried out; and

(B) if the pattern or practice has been carried out on a local or regional basis with respect to more than one television broadcast station, the court—

(i) shall order a permanent injunction barring the secondary transmission in that locality or region by the satellite carrier of the primary transmissions of any television broadcast station; and

(ii) may order statutory damages not exceeding $ 250,000 for each 6-month period during which the pattern or practice was carried out.

(g) **Burden of Proof.** In any action brought under subsection (f), the satellite carrier shall have the burden of proving that its secondary transmission of a primary transmission by a television broadcast station is made only to subscribers located within that station's local market or subscribers being served in compliance with section 119 [17 USCS § 119] or a private licensing agreement.

(h) **Geographic Limitations on Secondary Transmissions.** The statutory license created by this section shall apply to secondary transmissions to locations in the United States.

(i) **Exclusivity with Respect to Secondary Transmissions of Broadcast Stations by Satellite to Members of the Public.** No provision of section 111 [17 USCS § 111] or any other law (other than this section and section 119 [17 USCS § 119]) shall be construed to contain any authorization, exemption, or license through which secondary transmissions by satellite carriers of programming contained in a primary transmission made by a television broadcast station may be made without obtaining the consent of the copyright owner.

(j) **Definitions.** In this section—

(1) *Distributor.* The term "distributor" means an entity which contracts to distribute secondary transmissions from a satellite carrier and, either as a single channel or in a package with other programming, provides the secondary transmission either directly to individual subscribers or indirectly through other program distribution entities.

(2) *Local market.*

(A) In general. The term "local market",in the case of both commercial and noncommercial television broadcast stations, means the designated market area in which a station is located, and—

(i) in the case of a commercial television broadcast station, all commercial television broadcast stations licensed to a community within the same designated market area are within the same local market; and

(ii) in the case of a noncommercial educational television broadcast station, the market includes any station that is licensed to a community within the same designated market area as the noncommercial educational television broadcast station.

(B) County of license. In addition to the area described in subparagraph (A), a station's local market includes the county in which the station's community of license is located.

(C) Designated market area. For purposes of subparagraph (A), the term "designated market area" means a designated market area, as determined by Nielsen Media Research and published in the 1999–2000 Nielsen Station Index Directory and Nielsen Station Index United States Television Household Estimates or any successor publication.

(D) Certain areas outside of any designated market area. Any census area, borough, or other area in the State of Alaska that is outside of a designated market area, as determined by Nielsen Media Research, shall be deemed to be part of one of the local markets in the State of Alaska. A satellite carrier may determine which local market in the State of Alaska will be deemed to be the relevant local market in connection with each subscriber in such census area, borough, or other area.

(3) *Network station; satellite carrier; secondary transmission.* The terms "network station", "satellite carrier", and "secondary transmission" have the meanings given such terms under section 119(d) [17 USCS § 119(d)].

(4) *Subscriber.* The term "subscriber" means a person who receives a secondary transmission service from a satellite carrier and pays a fee for the service, directly or indirectly, to the satellite carrier or to a distributor.

(5) *Television broadcast station.* The term "television broadcast station"—

(A) means an over-the-air, commercial or noncommercial television broadcast station licensed by the Federal Communications Commission under subpart E of part 73 of title 47, Code of Federal Regulations, except that such term does not include a low-power or translator television station; and

(B) includes a television broadcast station licensed by an appropriate governmental authority of Canada or Mexico if the station broadcasts primarily in the English language and is a network station as defined in section 119(d)(2)(A) [17 USCS § 119(d)(2)(A)].

(Added Nov. 29, 1999, P. L. 106-113, Div B, § 1000(a)(9), 113 Stat. 1536; Nov. 2, 2002, P. L. 107-273, Div C, Title III, Subtitle B, § 13210(2)(A), 116 Stat. 1909; Dec. 8, 2004, P. L. 108-447, Div J, Title IX, Title I, § 111(b), 118 Stat. 3409; October 13, 2008, P. L. 110-403, § 209(a)(5), 122 Stat. 4260.)

CHAPTER 2—COPYRIGHT OWNERSHIP AND TRANSFER

Section

§ 201 Ownership of copyright

(a) **Initial Ownership.** Copyright in a work protected under this title vests initially in the author or authors of the work. The authors of a joint work are co-owners of copyright in the work.

(b) **Works Made for Hire.** In the case of a work made for hire, the employer or other person for whom the work was prepared is considered the author for purposes of this title, and, unless the parties have expressly agreed otherwise in a written instrument signed by them, owns all of the rights comprised in the copyright.

(c) **Contributions to Collective Works.** Copyright in each separate contribution to a collective work is distinct from copyright in the collective work as a whole, and vests initially in the author of the contribution. In the absence of an express transfer of the copyright or of any rights under it, the owner of copyright in the collective work is presumed to have acquired only the privilege of reproducing and distributing the contribution as part of that particular collective work, any revision of that collective work, and any later collective work in the same series.

(d) **Transfer of Ownership.**

(1) The ownership of a copyright may be transferred in whole or in part by any means of conveyance or by operation of law, and may be bequeathed by will or pass as personal property by the applicable laws of intestate succession.

(2) Any of the exclusive rights comprised in a copyright, including any subdivision of any of the rights specified by section 106, may be transferred as provided by clause (1) and owned separately. The owner of any particular exclusive right is entitled, to the extent of that right, to all of the protection and remedies accorded to the copyright owner by this title.

(e) **Involuntary Transfer.** When an individual author's ownership of a copyright, or of any of the exclusive rights under a copyright, has not previously been transferred voluntarily by that individual author, no action by any governmental body or other official or organization purporting to seize, expropriate, transfer, or exercise rights of ownership with respect to the copyright, or any of the exclusive rights under a copyright, shall be given effect under this title, except as provided under title 11.

(Oct. 19, 1976, P. L. 94-553, Title I, § 101, 90 Stat. 2568; Nov. 6, 1978, P. L. 95-598, Title III, § 313, 92 Stat. 2676.)

§ 202 Ownership of copyright as distinct from ownership of material object

Ownership of a copyright, or of any of the exclusive rights under a copyright, is distinct from ownership of any material object in which the work is embodied. Transfer of ownership of any material object, including the copy or phonorecord in which the work is first fixed, does not of itself convey any rights in the copyrighted work embodied in the object; nor, in the absence of an agreement, does transfer of ownership of a copyright or of any exclusive rights under a copyright convey property rights in any material object.

(Oct. 19, 1976, P. L. 94-553, Title I, § 101, 90 Stat. 2568.)

§ 203 Termination of transfers and licenses granted by the author

(a) **Conditions for Termination.** In the case of any work other than a work made for hire, the exclusive or nonexclusive grant of a transfer or license of copyright or of any right under a copyright, executed by the author on or after January 1, 1978, otherwise than by will, is subject to termination under the following conditions:

(1) In the case of a grant executed by one author, termination of the grant may be effected by that author or, if the author is dead, by the person or persons who, under clause (2) of this subsection, own and are entitled to exercise a total of more than one-half of that author's termination interest. In the case of a grant executed by two or more authors of a joint work, termination of the grant may be effected by a majority of the authors who executed it; if any of such authors is dead, the termination interest of any such author may be exercised as a unit by the person or persons who, under clause (2) of this subsection, own and are entitled to exercise a total of more than one-half of that author's interest.

(2) Where an author is dead, his or her termination interest is owned, and may be exercised, as follows:

(A) The widow or widower owns the author's entire termination interest unless there are any surviving children or grandchildren of the author, in which case the widow or widower owns one-half of the author's interest.

(B) The author's surviving children, and the surviving children of any dead child of the author, own the author's entire termination interest unless there is a widow or widower, in which case the ownership of one-half of the author's interest is divided among them.

(C) The rights of the author's children and grandchildren are in all cases divided among them and exercised on a per stirpes basis according to the number of such author's children represented; the share of the children of a dead child in a termination interest can be exercised only by the action of a majority of them.

(D) In So in original. Probably should not be capitalized. [Editor's Note: This footnote from the Government Printing Office's version of the United States Code is included because, unlike many of the other footnotes in that version, this footnote points to a needed correction rather than to extraneous notes that follow the statute in that version but that are not reproduced here. There is no footnote 1 here.] the event that the author's widow or widower, children, and grandchildren are not living, the author's executor, administrator, personal representative, or trustee shall own the author's entire termination interest.

(3) Termination of the grant may be effected at any time during a period of five years beginning at the end of thirty-five years from the date of execution of the grant; or, if the grant covers the right of publication of the work, the period begins at the end of thirty-five years from the date of publication of the work under the grant or at the end of forty years from the date of execution of the grant, whichever term ends earlier.

(4) The termination shall be effected by serving an advance notice in writing, signed by the number and proportion of owners of termination interests required under clauses (1) and (2) of this subsection, or by their duly authorized agents, upon the grantee or the grantee's successor in title.

(A) The notice shall state the effective date of the termination, which shall fall within the five-year period specified by clause (3) of this subsection, and the notice shall be served not less than two or more than ten years before that date. A copy of the notice shall be recorded in the Copyright Office before the effective date of termination, as a condition to its taking effect.

(B) The notice shall comply, in form, content, and manner of service, with requirements that the Register of Copyrights shall prescribe by regulation.

(5) Termination of the grant may be effected notwithstanding any agreement to the contrary, including an agreement to make a will or to make any future grant.

(b) **Effect of Termination.** Upon the effective date of termination, all rights under this title that were covered by the terminated grants revert to the author, authors, and other persons owning termination interests under clauses (1) and (2) of subsection (a), including those owners who did not join in signing the notice of termination under clause (4) of subsection (a), but with the following limitations:

(1) A derivative work prepared under authority of the grant before its termination may continue to be utilized under the terms of the grant after its termination, but this privilege does not extend to the preparation after the termination of other derivative works based upon the copyrighted work covered by the terminated grant.

(2) The future rights that will revert upon termination of the grant become vested on the date the notice of termination has been served as provided by clause (4) of subsection (a). The rights vest in the author, authors, and other persons named in, and in the proportionate shares provided by, clauses (1) and (2) of subsection (a).

(3) Subject to the provisions of clause (4) of this subsection, a further grant, or agreement to make a further grant, of any right covered by a terminated grant is valid only if it is signed by the same number and proportion of the owners, in whom the right has vested under clause (2) of this subsection, as are required to terminate the grant under clauses (1) and (2) of subsection (a). Such further grant or agreement is effective with respect to all of the persons in whom the right it covers has vested under clause (2) of this subsection, including those who did not join in signing it. If any person dies after rights under a terminated grant have vested in him or her, that person's legal representatives, legatees, or heirs at law represent him or her for purposes of this clause.

(4) A further grant, or agreement to make a further grant, of any right covered by a terminated grant is valid only if it is made after the effective date of the termination. As an exception, however, an agreement for such a further grant may be made between the persons provided by clause (3) of this subsection and the original grantee or such grantee's successor in title, after the notice of termination has been served as provided by clause (4) of subsection (a).

(5) Termination of a grant under this section affects only those rights covered by the grants that arise under this title, and in no way affects rights arising under any other Federal, State, or foreign laws.

(6) Unless and until termination is effected under this section, the grant, if it does not provide otherwise, continues in effect for the term of copyright provided by this title.

(Oct. 19, 1976, P. L. 94-553, Title I, § 101, 90 Stat. 2569; Oct. 27, 1998, P. L. 105-298, Title I, § 103, 112 Stat. 2829; Nov. 2, 2002, P. L. 107-273, Div C, Title III, Subtitle B, § 13210(9), 116 Stat. 1909.)

§ 204 Execution of transfers of copyright ownership

(a) A transfer of copyright ownership, other than by operation of law, is not valid unless an instrument of conveyance, or a note or memorandum of the transfer, is in writing and signed by the owner of the rights conveyed or such owner's duly authorized agent.

(b) A certificate of acknowledgement is not required for the validity of a transfer, but is prima facie evidence of the execution of the transfer if—

(1) in the case of a transfer executed in the United States, the certificate is issued by a person authorized to administer oaths within the United States; or

(2) in the case of a transfer executed in a foreign country, the certificate is issued by a diplomatic or consular officer of the United States, or by a person authorized to administer oaths whose authority is proved by a certificate of such an officer.

(Oct. 19, 1976, P. L. 94-553, Title I, § 101, 90 Stat. 2570.)

§ 205 Recordation of transfers and other documents

(a) **Conditions for Recordation.** Any transfer of copyright ownership or other document pertaining to a copyright may be recorded in the Copyright Office if the document filed for recordation bears the actual signature of the person who executed it, or if it is accompanied by a sworn or official certification that it is a true copy of the original, signed document.

(b) **Certificate of Recordation.** The Register of Copyrights shall, upon receipt of a document as provided by subsection (a) and of the fee provided by section 708, record the document and return it with a certificate of recordation.

(c) **Recordation as Constructive Notice.** Recordation of a document in the Copyright Office gives all persons constructive notice of the facts stated in the recorded document, but only if—

(1) the document, or material attached to it, specifically identifies the work to which it pertains so that, after the document is indexed by the

Register of Copyrights, it would be revealed by a reasonable search under the title or registration number of the work; and

(2) registration has been made for the work.

(d) **Priority Between Conflicting Transfers.** As between two conflicting transfers, the one executed first prevails if it is recorded, in the manner required to give constructive notice under subsection (c), within one month after its execution in the United States or within two months after its execution outside the United States, or at any time before recordation in such manner of the later transfer. Otherwise the later transfer prevails if recorded first in such manner, and if taken in good faith, for valuable consideration or on the basis of a binding promise to pay royalties, and without notice of the earlier transfer.

(e) **Priority Between Conflicting Transfer of Ownership and Nonexclusive License.** A nonexclusive license, whether recorded or not, prevails over a conflicting transfer of copyright ownership if the license is evidenced by a written instrument signed by the owner of the rights licensed or such owner's duly authorized agent, and if—

(1) the license was taken before execution of the transfer; or

(2) the license was taken in good faith before recordation of the transfer and without notice of it.

[Redesignated] (Oct. 19, 1976, P. L. 94-553, Title I, § 101, 90 Stat. 2571; Oct. 31, 1988, P. L. 100-568, § 5, 102 Stat. 2857.)

CHAPTER 3—DURATION OF COPYRIGHT

§ 301 Preemption with respect to other laws

(a) On and after January 1, 1978, all legal or equitable rights that are equivalent to any of the exclusive rights within the general scope of copyright as specified by section 106 in works of authorship that are fixed in a tangible medium of expression and come within the subject matter of copyright as specified by sections 102 and 103, whether created before or after that date and whether published or unpublished, are governed exclusively by this title. Thereafter, no person is entitled to any such right or equivalent right in any such work under the common law or statutes of any State.

(b) Nothing in this title annuls or limits any rights or remedies under the common law or statutes of any State with respect to—

(1) subject matter that does not come within the subject matter of copyright as specified by sections 102 and 103, including works of authorship not fixed in any tangible medium of expression; or

(2) any cause of action arising from undertakings commenced before January 1, 1978;

(3) activities violating legal or equitable rights that are not equivalent to any of the exclusive rights within the general scope of copyright as specified by section 106 or

(4) State and local landmarks, historic preservation, zoning, or building codes, relating to architectural works protected under section 102(a)(8).

(c) With respect to sound recordings fixed before February 15, 1972, any rights or remedies under the common law or statutes of any State shall not be annulled or limited by this title until February 15, 2067. The preemptive provisions of subsection (a) shall apply to any such rights and remedies pertaining to any cause of action arising from undertakings commenced on and after February 15, 2067. Notwithstanding the provisions of section 303, no sound recording fixed before February 15, 1972, shall be subject to copyright under this title before, on, or after February 15, 2067.

(d) Nothing in this title annuls or limits any rights or remedies under any other Federal statute.

(e) The scope of Federal preemption under this section is not affected by the adherence of the United States to the Berne Convention or the satisfaction of obligations of the United States thereunder.

(f) (1) On or after the effective date set forth in section 610(a) of the Visual Artists Rights Act of 1990 [17 USCS § 106A note], all legal or equitable rights that are equivalent to any of the rights conferred by section 106A with respect to works of visual art to which the rights conferred by section 106A apply are governed exclusively by section 106A and section 113(d) and the provisions of this title relating to such sections. Thereafter, no person is entitled to any such right or equivalent right in any work of visual art under the common law or statutes of any State.

(2) Nothing in paragraph (1) annuls or limits any rights or remedies under the common law or statutes of any State with respect to—

(A) any cause of action from undertakings commenced before the effective date set forth in section 610(a) of the Visual Artists Rights Act of 1990 [17 USCS § 106A note];

(B) activities violating legal or equitable rights that are not equivalent to any of the rights conferred by section 106A with respect to works of visual art; or

(C) activities violating legal or equitable rights which extend beyond the life of the author.

(Oct. 19, 1976, P. L. 94-553, Title I, § 101, 90 Stat. 2572; Oct. 31, 1988, P. L. 100-568, § 6, 102 Stat. 2857; Dec. 1, 1990, P. L. 101-650, Title VI, § 605, Title VII, § 705, 104 Stat. 5131, 5134; Oct. 27, 1998, P. L. 105-298, Title I, § 102(a), 112 Stat. 2827.)

§ 302 Duration of copyright: Works created on or after January 1, 1978

(a) **In General.** Copyright in a work created on or after January 1, 1978, subsists from its creation and, except as provided by the following subsections, endures for a term consisting of the life of the author and 70 years after the author's death.

(b) **Joint Works.** In the case of a joint work prepared by two or more authors who did not work for hire, the copyright endures for a term consisting of the life of the last surviving author and 70 years after such last surviving author's death.

(c) **Anonymous Works, Pseudonymous Works, and Works Made for Hire.** In the case of an anonymous work, a pseudonymous work, or a work made for hire, the copyright endures for a term of 95 years from the year of its first publication, or a term of 120 years from the year of its creation, whichever expires first. If, before the end of such term, the identity of one or more of the authors of an anonymous or pseudonymous work is revealed in the records of a registration made for that work under subsections (a) or (d) of section 408, or in the records provided by this subsection, the copyright in the work endures for the term specified by subsection (a) or (b), based on the life of the author or authors whose identity has been revealed. Any person having an interest in the copyright in an anonymous or pseudonymous work may at any time record, in records to be maintained by the Copyright Office for that purpose, a statement identifying one or more authors of the work; the statement shall also identify the person filing it, the nature of that person's interest, the source of the information recorded, and the particular work affected, and shall comply in form and content with requirements that the Register of Copyrights shall prescribe by regulation.

(d) **Records Relating to Death of Authors.** Any person having an interest in a copyright may at any time record in the Copyright Office a statement of the date of death of the author of the copyrighted work, or a statement that the author is still living on a particular date. The statement shall identify the person filing it, the nature of that person's interest, and the source of the information recorded, and shall comply in form and content with requirements that the Register of Copyrights shall prescribe by regulation. The Register shall maintain current records of information relating to the death of authors of copyrighted works, based on such recorded statements and, to the extent the Register considers practicable, on data contained in any of the records of the Copyright Office or in other reference sources.

(e) **Presumption as to Author's Death.** After a period of 95 years from the year of first publication of a work, or a period of 120 years from the year of its creation, whichever expires first, any person who obtains from the Copyright Office a certified report that the records provided by subsection (d) disclose nothing to indicate that the author of the work is living, or died less than 70 years before, is entitled to the benefit of a presumption that the author has been dead for at least 70 years. Reliance in good faith upon this presumption shall be a complete defense to any action for infringement under this title.

(Oct. 19, 1976, P. L. 94-553, Title I, § 101, 90 Stat. 2572; Oct. 27, 1998, P.L. 105-298, Title I, § 102(b), 112 Stat. 2827.)

§ 303 Duration of copyright: Works created but not published or copyrighted before January 1, 1978

(a) Copyright in a work created before January 1, 1978, but not theretofore in the public domain or copyrighted, subsists from January 1, 1978, and endures for the term provided by section 302. In no case, however, shall the term of copyright in such a work expire before December 31, 2002; and, if the work is published on or before December 31, 2002, the term of copyright shall not expire before December 31, 2047.

(b) The distribution before January 1, 1978, of a phonorecord shall not for any purpose constitute a publication of the musical work embodied therein.

(Oct. 19, 1976, P. L. 94-553, Title I, § 101, 90 Stat. 2573; Nov. 13, 1997, P. L. 105-80, § 11, 111 Stat. 1534; Oct. 27, 1998, P. L. 105-298, Title I, § 102(c), 112 Stat. 2827.)

§ 304 Duration of copyright: Subsisting copyrights

(a) **Copyrights in their First Term on January 1, 1978.***

(1) (A) Any copyright, the first term of which is subsisting on January 1, 1978, shall endure for 28 years from the date it was originally secured.

(B) In the case of—

(i) any posthumous work or of any periodical, cyclopedic, or other composite work upon which the copyright was originally secured by the proprietor thereof, or

* Before the enactment of the Copyright Renewal Act of 1992 (effective June 26, 1992), § 304(a) read:

(a) **Copyrights in their first term on January 1, 1978.** Any copyright, the first term of which is subsisting on January 1, 1978, shall endure for twenty-eight years from the date it was originally secured: Provided, That in the case of any posthumous work or of any periodical, cyclopedic, or other composite work upon which the copyright was originally secured by the proprietor thereof, or of any work copyrighted by a corporate body (otherwise than as assignee or licensee of the individual author) or by an employer for whom such work is made for hire, the proprietor of such copyright shall be entitled to a renewal and extension of the copyright

(ii) any work copyrighted by a corporate body (otherwise than as assignee or licensee of the individual author) or by an employer for whom such work is made for hire,

the proprietor of such copyright shall be entitled to a renewal and extension of the copyright in such work for the further term of 67 years.

(C) In the case of any other copyrighted work, including a contribution by an individual author to a periodical or to a cyclopedic or other composite work—

(i) the author of such work, if the author is still living,

(ii) the widow, widower, or children of the author, if the author is not living,

(iii) the author's executors, if such author, widow, widower, or children are not living, or

(iv) the author's next of kin, in the absence of a will of the author,

shall be entitled to a renewal and extension of the copyright in such work for a further term of 67 years.

---

in such work for the further term of forty-seven years when application for such renewal and extension shall have been made to the Copyright Office and duly registered therein within one year prior to the expiration of the original term of copyright: And provided further, That in the case of any other copyrighted work, including a contribution by an individual author to a periodical or to a cyclopedic or other composite work, the author of such work, if still living, or the widow, widower, or children of the author, if the author be not living, or if such author, widow, widower, or children be not living, then the author's executors, or in the absence of a will, his or her next of kin shall be entitled to a renewal and extension of the copyright in such work for a further term of forty-seven years when application for such renewal and extension shall have been made to the Copyright Office and duly registered therein within one year prior to the expiration of the original term of copyright: And provided further, That in default of the registration of such application for renewal and extension, the copyright in any work shall terminate at the expiration of twenty-eight years from the date copyright was originally secured.

The Copyright Renewal Act of 1992 provided in § 102 thereof:

Legal Effect of Renewal of Copyright Unchanged. The renewal and extension of a copyright for a further term of 47 years provided for under paragraphs (1) and (2) of section 304(a) . . . (as amended . . .) shall have the same effect with respect to any grant, before the effective date of this section, of a transfer or license of the further term as did the renewal of a copyright before the effective date of this section under the law in effect at the time of such grant.

. . .

Effective Date; Copyrights Affected by Amendment. (1) Subject to paragraphs (2) and (3), this section and the amendments made by this section shall take effect on the date of the enactment of this Act [i.e., June 26, 1992].

(2) The amendments made by this section shall apply only to those copyrights secured between January 1, 1964, and December 31, 1977. Copyrights secured before January 1, 1964, shall be governed by the provisions of section 304(a) . . . in effect on the day before the effective date of this section.

(3) This section and the amendments made by this section shall not affect any court proceedings pending on the effective date of this section.—*Eds.*

(2) (A) At the expiration of the original term of copyright in a work specified in paragraph (1)(B) of this subsection, the copyright shall endure for a renewed and extended further term of 67 years, which—

(i) if an application to register a claim to such further term has been made to the Copyright Office within 1 year before the expiration of the original term of copyright, and the claim is registered, shall vest, upon the beginning of such further term, in the proprietor of the copyright who is entitled to claim the renewal of copyright at the time the application is made; or

(ii) if no such application is made or the claim pursuant to such application is not registered, shall vest, upon the beginning of such further term, in the person or entity that was the proprietor of the copyright as of the last day of the original term of copyright.

(B) At the expiration of the original term of copyright in a work specified in paragraph (1)(C) of this subsection, the copyright shall endure for a renewed and extended further term of 67 years, which—

(i) if an application to register a claim to such further term has been made to the Copyright Office within 1 year before the expiration of the original term of copyright, and the claim is registered, shall vest, upon the beginning of such further term, in any person who is entitled under paragraph (1)(C) to the renewal and extension of the copyright at the time the application is made; or

(ii) if no such application is made or the claim pursuant to such application is not registered, shall vest, upon the beginning of such further term, in any person entitled under paragraph (1)(C), as of the last day of the original term of copyright, to the renewal and extension of the copyright.

(3) (A) An application to register a claim to the renewed and extended term of copyright in a work may be made to the Copyright Office—

(i) within 1 year before the expiration of the original term of copyright by any person entitled under paragraph (1)(B) or (C) to such further term of 67 years; and

(ii) at any time during the renewed and extended term by any person in whom such further term vested, under paragraph (2) (A) or (B), or by any successor or assign of such person, if the application is made in the name of such person.

(B) Such an application is not a condition of the renewal and extension of the copyright in a work for a further term of 67 years.

(4) (A) If an application to register a claim to the renewed and extended term of copyright in a work is not made within 1 year before the expiration of the original term of copyright in a work, or if the claim pursuant to such application is not registered, then a derivative work prepared under authority of a grant of a transfer or license of the copyright that is made before the expiration of the original term of copyright may continue to be used under the terms of the grant during the renewed and extended term of copyright without infringing the copyright, except that such use does not extend to the preparation during such renewed and extended term of other derivative works based upon the copyrighted work covered by such grant.

(B) If an application to register a claim to the renewed and extended term of copyright in a work is made within 1 year before its expiration, and the claim is registered, the certificate of such registration shall constitute prima facie evidence as to the validity of the copyright during its renewed and extended term and of the facts stated in the certificate. The evidentiary weight to be accorded the certificates of a registration of a renewed and extended term of copyright made after the end of that 1-year period shall be within the discretion of the court.

(b) **Copyrights in their Renewal Term at the Time of the Effective Date of the Sonny Bono Copyright Term Extension Act.*** Any copyright still in its renewal term at the time that the Sonny Bono Copyright Term Extension Act becomes effective [effective Oct. 27, 1998] shall have a copyright term of 95 years from the date copyright was originally secured.

(c) **Termination of Transfers and Licenses Covering Extended Renewal Term.** In the case of any copyright subsisting in either its first or renewal term on January 1, 1978, other than a copyright in a work made for hire, the exclusive or nonexclusive grant of a transfer or license of the renewal copyright or any right under it, executed before January 1, 1978, by any of the persons designated by subsection (a)(1)(C) of this section, otherwise than by will, is subject to termination under the following conditions:

(1) In the case of a grant executed by a person or persons other than the author, termination of the grant may be effected by the surviving person or persons who executed it. In the case of a grant executed by one or more of the authors of the work, termination of the grant may be

* Before the enactment of the Copyright Term Extension Act (effective October 27, 1998), § 304(b) read:

The duration of any copyright, the renewal term of which is subsisting at any time between December 31, 1976, and December 31, 1977, inclusive, or for which renewal registration is made between December 31, 1976, and December 31, 1977, inclusive, is extended to endure for a term of seventy-five years from the date copyright was originally secured.—*Eds.*

effected, to the extent of a particular author's share in the ownership of the renewal copyright, by the author who executed it or, if such author is dead, by the person or persons who, under clause (2) of this subsection, own and are entitled to exercise a total of more than one-half of that author's termination interest.

(2) Where an author is dead, his or her termination interest is owned, and may be exercised, as follows:

(A) The widow or widower owns the author's entire termination interest unless there are any surviving children or grandchildren of the author, in which case the widow or widower owns one-half of the author's interest.

(B) The author's surviving children, and the surviving children of any dead child of the author, own the author's entire termination interest unless there is a widow or widower, in which case the ownership of one-half of the author's interest is divided among them.

(C) The rights of the author's children and grandchildren are in all cases divided among them and exercised on a per stirpes basis according to the number of such author's children represented; the share of the children of a dead child in a termination interest can be exercised only by the action of a majority of them.

(D) In So in original. Probably should not be capitalized. [Editor's Note: This footnote from the Government Printing Office's version of the United States Code is included because, unlike many of the other footnotes in that version, this footnote points to a needed correction rather than to extraneous notes that follow the statute in that version but that are not reproduced here. There is no footnote 1 here.] the event that the author's widow or widower, children, and grandchildren are not living, the author's executor, administrator, personal representative, or trustee shall own the author's entire termination interest.

(3) Termination of the grant may be effected at any time during a period of five years beginning at the end of fifty-six years from the date copyright was originally secured, or beginning on January 1, 1978, whichever is later.

(4) The termination shall be effected by serving an advance notice in writing upon the grantee or the grantee's successor in title. In the case of a grant executed by a person or persons other than the author, the notice shall be signed by all of those entitled to terminate the grant under clause (1) of this subsection, or by their duly authorized agents. In the case of a grant executed by one or more of the authors of the work, the notice as to any one author's share shall be signed by that author or his or her duly authorized agent or, if that author is dead, by the number and proportion of the owners of his or her termination interest required under clauses (1) and (2) of this subsection, or by their duly authorized agents.

(A) The notice shall state the effective date of the termination, which shall fall within the five-year period specified by clause (3) of this subsection, or, in the case of a termination under subsection (d), within the five-year period specified by subsection (d)(2), and the notice shall be served not less than two or more than ten years before that date. A copy of the notice shall be recorded in the Copyright Office before the effective date of termination, as a condition to its taking effect.

(B) The notice shall comply, in form, content, and manner of service, with requirements that the Register of Copyrights shall prescribe by regulation.

(5) Termination of the grant may be effected notwithstanding any agreement to the contrary, including an agreement to make a will or to make any future grant.

(6) In the case of a grant executed by a person or persons other than the author, all rights under this title that were covered by the terminated grant revert, upon the effective date of termination, to all of those entitled to terminate the grant under clause (1) of this subsection. In the case of a grant executed by one or more of the authors of the work, all of a particular author's rights under this title that were covered by the terminated grant revert, upon the effective date of termination, to that author or, if that author is dead, to the persons owning his or her termination interest under clause (2) of this subsection, including those owners who did not join in signing the notice of termination under clause (4) of this subsection. In all cases the reversion of rights is subject to the following limitations:

(A) A derivative work prepared under authority of the grant before its termination may continue to be utilized under the terms of the grant after its termination, but this privilege does not extend to the preparation after the termination of other derivative works based upon the copyrighted work covered by the terminated grant.

(B) The future rights that will revert upon termination of the grant become vested on the date the notice of termination has been served as provided by clause (4) of this subsection.

(C) Where the author's rights revert to two or more persons under clause (2) of this subsection, they shall vest in those persons in the proportionate shares provided by that clause. In such a case, and subject to the provisions of subclause (D) of this clause, a further grant, or agreement to make a further grant, of a particular author's share with respect to any right covered by a terminated grant is valid only if it is signed by the same number and proportion of the owners, in whom the right has vested under this clause, as are required to terminate the grant under clause (2) of this subsection. Such further grant or agreement is effective with respect to all of the persons in whom the right it covers has vested under this subclause, including those who did not join in signing it. If any person dies after rights under a terminated grant have vested in him or her, that person's legal representatives, legatees, or heirs at law represent him or her for purposes of this subclause.

(D) A further grant, or agreement to make a further grant, of any right covered by a terminated grant is valid only if it is made after the effective date of the termination. As an exception, however, an agreement for such a further grant may be made between the author or any of the persons provided by the first sentence of clause (6) of this subsection, or between the persons provided by subclause (C) of this clause, and the original grantee or such grantee's successor in title, after the notice of termination has been served as provided by clause (4) of this subsection.

(E) Termination of a grant under this subsection affects only those rights covered by the grant that arise under this title, and in no way affects rights arising under any other Federal, State, or foreign laws.

(F) Unless and until termination is effected under this subsection, the grant, if it does not provide otherwise, continues in effect for the remainder of the extended renewal term.

(d) **Termination Rights Provided in Subsection (C) Which Have Expired on or Before the Effective Date of the Sonny Bono Copyright Term Extension Act.** In the case of any copyright other than a work made for hire, subsisting in its renewal term on the effective date of the Sonny Bono Copyright Term Extension Act [effective October 27, 1998] for which the termination right provided in subsection (c) has expired by such date, where the author or owner of the termination right has not previously exercised such termination right, the exclusive or nonexclusive grant of a transfer or license of the renewal copyright or any right under it, executed before January 1, 1978, by any of the persons designated in subsection (a)(1)(C) of this section, other than by will, is subject to termination under the following conditions:

(1) The conditions specified in subsections (c)(1), (2), (4), (5), and (6) of this section apply to terminations of the last 20 years of copyright term as provided by the amendments made by the Sonny Bono Copyright Term Extension Act.

(2) Termination of the grant may be effected at any time during a period of 5 years beginning at the end of 75 years from the date copyright was originally secured.

(Oct. 19, 1976, P. L. 94-553, Title I, § 101, 90 Stat. 2573; June 26, 1992, P. L. 102-307, Title I, § 102(a), (d), 106 Stat. 264, 266; Nov. 13, 1997, P.L. 105-80, § 12(a)(9), 111 Stat. 1535; Oct. 27, 1998, P. L. 105-298, Title I, §§ 102(d)(1), 103, 112 Stat. 2827, 2829; Nov. 2, 2002, P. L. 107-273, Div C, Title III, Subtitle B, § 13210(10), 116 Stat. 1910.)

§ 305 Duration of copyright: Terminal date

All terms of copyright provided by sections 302 through 304 run to the end of the calendar year in which they would otherwise expire.

(Oct. 19, 1976, P.L. 94-553, Title I, § 101, 90 Stat. 2576.)

CHAPTER 4—COPYRIGHT NOTICE, DEPOSIT, AND REGISTRATION

Section

§ 401 Notice of copyright: Visually perceptible copies

(a) **General Provisions.** Whenever a work protected under this title is published in the United States or elsewhere by authority of the copyright owner, a notice of copyright as provided by this section may be placed on publicly distributed copies from which the work can be visually perceived, either directly or with the aid of a machine or device.

(b) **Form of Notice.** If a notice appears on the copies, it shall consist of the following three elements:

(1) the symbol © (the letter C in a circle), or the word "Copyright", or the abbreviation "Copr."; and

(2) the year of first publication of the work; in the case of compilations or derivative works incorporating previously published material, the year date of first publication of the compilation or derivative work is sufficient. The year date may be omitted where a pictorial, graphic, or sculptural work, with accompanying text matter, if any, is reproduced in or on greeting cards, postcards, stationery, jewelry, dolls, toys, or any useful articles; and

(3) the name of the owner of copyright in the work, or an abbreviation by which the name can be recognized, or a generally known alternative designation of the owner.

(c) **Position of Notice.** The notice shall be affixed to the copies in such manner and location as to give reasonable notice of the claim of copyright. The Register of Copyrights shall prescribe by regulation, as examples, specific methods of affixation and positions of the notice on various types of works that will satisfy this requirement, but these specifications shall not be considered exhaustive.

(d) **Evidentiary Weight of Notice.** If a notice of copyright in the form and position specified by this section appears on the published copy or copies to which a defendant in a copyright infringement suit had access, then no weight shall be given to such a defendant's interposition of a defense based on innocent infringement in mitigation of actual or statutory damages, except as provided in the last sentence of section 504(c)(2).

(Oct. 19, 1976, P. L. 94-553, Title I, § 101, 90 Stat. 2576; Oct. 31, 1988, P. L. 100-568, § 7(a), 102 Stat. 2857.)

§ 402 Notice of copyright: Phonorecords of sound recordings

(a) **General Provisions.** Whenever a sound recording protected under this title is published in the United States or elsewhere by authority of the copyright owner, a notice of copyright as provided by this section may be placed on publicly distributed phonorecords of the sound recording.

(b) **Form of Notice.** If a notice appears on the phonorecords, it shall consist of the following three elements:

(1) the symbol ℗ (the letter P in a circle); and

(2) the year of first publication of the sound recording; and

(3) the name of the owner of copyright in the sound recording, or an abbreviation by which the name can be recognized, or a generally known alternative designation of the owner; if the producer of the sound recording is named on the phonorecord labels or containers, and if no other name appears in conjunction with the notice, the producer's name shall be considered a part of the notice.

(c) **Position of Notice.** The notice shall be placed on the surface of the phonorecord, or on the phonorecord label or container, in such manner and location as to give reasonable notice of the claim of copyright.

(d) **Evidentiary Weight of Notice.** If a notice of copyright in the form and position specified by this section appears on the published phonorecord or phonorecords to which a defendant in a copyright infringement suit had access, then no weight shall be given to such a defendant's interposition of a defense based on innocent infringement in mitigation of actual or statutory damages, except as provided in the last sentence of section 504(c)(2)

(Oct. 19, 1976, P.L. 94-553, Title I, § 101, 90 Stat. 2577; Oct. 31, 1988, P.L. 100-568, § 7(b), 102 Stat. 2857.)

§ 403 Notice of copyright: Publications incorporating United States Government works

Sections 401(d) and 402(d) shall not apply to a work published in copies or phonorecords consisting predominantly of one or more works of the United States Government unless the notice of copyright appearing on the published copies or phonorecords to which a defendant in the copyright infringement suit had access includes a statement identifying, either affirmatively or negatively, those portions of the copies or phonorecords embodying any work or works protected under this title.

(Oct. 19, 1976, P.L. 94-553, Title I, § 101, 90 Stat. 2577; Oct. 31, 1988, P.L. 100-568, § 7(c), 102 Stat. 2858.)

§ 404 Notice of copyright: Contributions to collective works

(a) A separate contribution to a collective work may bear its own notice of copyright, as provided by sections 401 through 403. However, a single notice applicable to the collective work as a whole is sufficient to invoke the provisions of section 401(d) or 402(d), as applicable with respect to the separate contributions it contains (not including advertisements inserted on behalf of persons other than the owner of copyright in the collective work), regardless of the ownership of copyright in the contributions and whether or not they have been previously published.

(b) With respect to copies and phonorecords publicly distributed by authority of the copyright owner before the effective date of the Berne Convention Implementation Act of 1988, where the person named in a single notice applicable to a collective work as a whole is not the owner of copyright in a separate contribution that does not bear its own notice, the case is governed by the provisions of section 406(a).

(Oct. 19, 1976, P. L. 94-553, Title I, § 101, 90 Stat. 2577; Oct. 31, 1988, P. L. 100-568, § 7(d), 102 Stat. 2858.)

§ 405 Notice of copyright: Omission of notice on certain copies and phonorecords

(a) **Effect of Omission on Copyright.** With respect to copies and phonorecords publicly distributed by authority of the copyright owner before the effective date of the Berne Convention Implementation Act of 1988, the omission of the copyright notice described in sections 401 through 403 from copies or phonorecords publicly distributed by authority of the copyright owner does not invalidate the copyright in a work if—

(1) the notice has been omitted from no more than a relatively small number of copies or phonorecords distributed to the public; or

(2) registration for the work has been made before or is made within five years after the publication without notice, and a reasonable effort is made to add notice to all copies or phonorecords that are distributed to the public in the United States after the omission has been discovered; or

(3) the notice has been omitted in violation of an express requirement in writing that, as a condition of the copyright owner's authorization of the public distribution of copies or phonorecords, they bear the prescribed notice.

(b) **Effect of Omission on Innocent Infringers.** Any person who innocently infringes a copyright, in reliance upon an authorized copy or phonorecord from which the copyright notice has been omitted and which was publicly distributed by authority of the copyright owner before the effective date of the Berne Convention Implementation Act of 1988, incurs no liability for actual or statutory damages under section 504 for any infringing acts committed before receiving actual notice that registration for the work has been made under section 408, if such person proves that he or she was misled by the omission of notice. In a suit for infringement in such a case the court may allow or disallow recovery of any of the infringer's profits attributable to the infringement, and may enjoin the continuation of the infringing undertaking or may require, as a condition for permitting the continuation of the infringing undertaking, that the infringer pay the copyright owner a reasonable license fee in an amount and on terms fixed by the court.

(c) **Removal of Notice.** Protection under this title is not affected by the removal, destruction, or obliteration of the notice, without the authorization of the copyright owner, from any publicly distributed copies or phonorecords.

(Oct. 19, 1976, P. L. 94-553, Title I, § 101, 90 Stat. 2578; Oct. 31, 1988, P. L. 100-568, § 7(e), 102 Stat. 2858; Nov. 13, 1997, P. L. 105-80, § 12(a)(10), 111 Stat. 1535.)

§ 406 Notice of copyright: Error in name or date on certain copies and phonorecords

(a) **Error in Name.** With respect to copies and phonorecords publicly distributed by authority of the copyright owner before the effective date of the Berne Convention Implementation Act of 1988, where the person named in the copyright notice on copies or phonorecords publicly distributed by authority of the copyright owner is not the owner of copyright, the validity and ownership of the copyright are not affected. In such a case, however, any person who innocently begins an undertaking that infringes the copyright has a complete defense to any action for such infringement if such person proves that he or she was misled by the notice and began the undertaking in good faith under a purported transfer or license from the person named therein, unless before the undertaking was begun—

(1) registration for the work had been made in the name of the owner of copyright; or

(2) a document executed by the person named in the notice and showing the ownership of the copyright had been recorded.

The person named in the notice is liable to account to the copyright owner for all receipts from transfers or licenses purportedly made under the copyright by the person named in the notice.

(b) **Error in Date.** When the year date in the notice on copies or phonorecords distributed before the effective date of the Berne Convention Implementation Act of 1988 by authority of the copyright owner is earlier than the year in which publication first occurred, any period computed from the year of first publication under section 302 is to be computed from the year in the notice. Where the year date is more than one year later than the year in which publication first occurred, the work is considered to have been published without any notice and is governed by the provisions of section 405.

(c) **Omission of Name or Date.** Where copies or phonorecords publicly distributed before the effective date of the Berne Convention Implementation Act of 1988 by authority of the copyright owner contain no name or no date that could reasonably be considered a part of the notice, the work is considered to have been published without any notice and is governed by the provisions of section 405 as in effect on the day before the effective date of the Berne Convention Implementation Act of 1988.

(Oct. 19, 1976, P. L. 94-553, Title I, § 101, 90 Stat. 2578; Oct. 31, 1988, P.L. 100-568, § 7(f), 102 Stat. 2858.)

§ 407 Deposit of copies or phonorecords for Library of Congress

(a) Except as provided by subsection (c), and subject to the provisions of subsection (e), the owner of copyright or of the exclusive right of publication in a work published in the United States shall deposit, within three months after the date of such publication—

(1) two complete copies of the best edition; or

(2) if the work is a sound recording, two complete phonorecords of the best edition, together with any printed or other visually perceptible material published with such phonorecords.

Neither the deposit requirements of this subsection nor the acquisition provisions of subsection (e) are conditions of copyright protection.

(b) The required copies or phonorecords shall be deposited in the Copyright Office for the use or disposition of the Library of Congress. The Register of Copyrights shall, when requested by the depositor and upon payment of the fee prescribed by section 708, issue a receipt for the deposit.

(c) The Register of Copyrights may be regulation exempt any categories of material from the deposit requirements of this section, or require deposit of only one copy or phonorecord with respect to any categories. Such regulations shall provide either for complete exemption from the deposit requirements of this section, or for alternative forms of deposit aimed at providing a satisfactory archival record of a work without imposing practical or financial hardships on the depositor, where the individual author is the owner of copyright in a pictorial, graphic, or sculptural work and (i) less than five copies of the work have been published, or (ii) the work has been published in a limited edition consisting of numbered copies, the monetary value of which would make the mandatory deposit of two copies of the best edition of the work burdensome, unfair, or unreasonable.

(d) At any time after publication of a work as provided by subsection (a), the Register of Copyrights may make written demand for the required deposit on any of the persons obligated to make the deposit under subsection (a). Unless deposit is made within three months after the demand is received, the person or persons on whom the demand was made are liable—

(1) to a fine of not more than $250 for each work; and

(2) to pay into a specially designated fund in the Library of Congress the total retail price of the copies or phonorecords demanded, or, if no retail price has been fixed, the reasonable cost to the Library of Congress of acquiring them; and

(3) to pay a fine of $2,500, in addition to any fine or liability imposed under clauses (1) and (2), if such person willfully or repeatedly fails or refuses to comply with such a demand.

(e) With respect to transmission programs that have been fixed and transmitted to the public in the United States but have not been published, the Register of Copyrights shall, after consulting with the Librarian of Congress and other interested organizations and officials, establish regulations governing the acquisition, through deposit or otherwise, of copies or phonorecords of such programs for the collections of the Library of Congress.

(1) The Librarian of Congress shall be permitted, under the standards and conditions set forth in such regulations, to make a fixation of a transmission program directly from a transmission to the public, and to reproduce one copy or phonorecord from such fixation for archival purposes.

(2) Such regulations shall also provide standards and procedures by which the Register of Copyrights may make written demand, upon the owner of the right of transmission in the United States, for the deposit of a copy or phonorecord of a specific transmission program. Such deposit may, at the option of the owner of the right of transmission in the United States, be accomplished by gift, by loan for purposes of reproduction, or by sale at a price not to exceed the cost of reproducing and supplying the copy or phonorecord. The regulations established under this clause shall provide reasonable periods of not less than three months for compliance with a demand, and shall allow for extensions of such periods and adjustments in the scope of the demand or the methods for fulfilling it, as reasonably warranted by the circumstances. Willful failure or refusal to comply with the conditions prescribed by such regulations shall subject the owner of the right of transmission in the United States to liability for an amount, not to exceed the cost of reproducing and supplying the copy or phonorecord in question, to be paid into a specially designated fund in the Library of Congress.

(3) Nothing in this subsection shall be construed to require the making or retention, for purposes of deposit, of any copy or phonorecord of an unpublished transmission program, the transmission of which occurs before the receipt of a specific written demand as provided by clause (2).

(4) No activity undertaken in compliance with regulations prescribed under clauses (1) or (2) of this subsection shall result in liability if intended solely to assist in the acquisition of copies or phonorecords under this subsection.

(Oct. 19, 1976, P.L. 94-553, Title I, § 101, 90 Stat. 2579; Oct. 31, 1988, P.L. 100-568, § 8, 102 Stat. 2859; Nov. 13, 1997, P. L. 105-80, § 12(a)(11), 111 Stat. 1535.)

§ 408 Copyright registration in general

(a) **Registration Permissive.** At any time during the subsistence of the first term of copyright in any published or unpublished work in which the copyright was secured before January 1, 1978, and during the subsistence of any copyright secured on or after that date, the owner of copyright or of any exclusive right in the work may obtain registration of the copyright claim by delivering to the Copyright Office the deposit specified by this section, together with the application and fee specified by sections 409 and 708. Such registration is not a condition of copyright protection.

(b) **Deposit for Copyright Registration.** Except as provided by subsection (c), the material deposited for registration shall include—

(1) in the case of an unpublished work, one complete copy or phonorecord;

(2) in the case of a published work, two complete copies or phonorecords of the best edition;

(3) in the case of a work first published outside the United States, one complete copy or phonorecord as so published;

(4) in the case of a contribution to a collective work, one complete copy or phonorecord of the best edition of the collective work.

Copies or phonorecords deposited for the Library of Congress under section 407 may be used to satisfy the deposit provisions of this section, if they are accompanied by the prescribed application and fee, and by any additional identifying material that the Register may, by regulation, require. The Register shall also prescribe regulations establishing requirements under which copies or phonorecords acquired for the Library of Congress under subsection (e) of section 407, otherwise than by deposit, may be used to satisfy the deposit provisions of this section.

(c) **Administrative Classification and Optional Deposit.**

(1) The Register of Copyrights is authorized to specify by regulation the administrative classes into which works are to be placed for purposes of deposit and registration, and the nature of the copies or phonorecords to be deposited in the various classes specified. The regulations may require or permit, for particular classes, the deposit of identifying material instead of copies or phonorecords, the deposit of only one copy or phonorecord where two would normally be required, or a single registration for a group of related works. This administrative classification of works has no significance with respect to the subject matter of copyright or the exclusive rights provided by this title.

(2) Without prejudice to the general authority provided under clause (1), the Register of Copyrights shall establish regulations specifically permitting a single registration for a group of works by the same individual author, all first published as contributions to periodicals, including newspapers, within a twelve-month period, on the basis of a single deposit, application, and registration fee, under the following conditions:

(A) if the deposit consists of one copy of the entire issue of the periodical, or of the entire section in the case of a newspaper, in which each contribution was first published; and

(B) if the application identifies each work separately, including the periodical containing it and its date of first publication.

(C) [Redesignated].

(3) As an alternative to separate renewal registrations under subsection (a) of section 304, a single renewal registration may be made for a group of works by the same individual author, all first published as contributions to periodicals, including newspapers, upon the filing of a single application and fee, under all of the following conditions:

(A) the renewal claimant or claimants, and the basis of claim or claims under section 304(a), is the same for each of the works; and

(B) the works were all copyrighted upon their first publication, either through separate copyright notice and registration or by virtue of a general copyright notice in the periodical issue as a whole; and

(C) the renewal application and fee are received not more than twenty-eight or less than twenty-seven years after the thirty-first day of December of the calendar year in which all of the works were first published; and

(D) the renewal application identifies each work separately, including the periodical containing it and its date of first publication.

(d) **Corrections and Amplifications.** The Register may also establish, by regulation, formal procedures for the filing of an application for supplementary registration, to correct an error in a copyright registration or to amplify the information given in a registration. Such application shall be accompanied by the fee provided by section 708, and shall clearly identify the registration to be corrected or amplified. The information contained in a supplementary registration augments but does not supersede that contained in the earlier registration.

(e) **Published Edition of Previously Registered Work.** Registration for the first published edition of a work previously registered in unpublished form may be made even though the work as published is substantially the same as the unpublished version.

(f) **Preregistration of Works Being Prepared for Commercial Distribution.**

(1) *Rulemaking.* Not later than 180 days after the date of enactment of this subsection, the Register of Copyrights shall issue regulations to establish procedures for preregistration of a work that is being prepared for commercial distribution and has not been published.

(2) *Class of works.* The regulations established under paragraph (1) shall permit preregistration for any work that is in a class of works that the Register determines has had a history of infringement prior to authorized commercial distribution.

(3) *Application for registration.* Not later than 3 months after the first publication of a work preregistered under this subsection, the applicant shall submit to the Copyright Office—

(A) an application for registration of the work;

(B) a deposit; and

(C) the applicable fee.

(4) *Effect of untimely application.* An action under this chapter for infringement of a work preregistered under this subsection, in a case in which the infringement commenced no later than 2 months after the first publication of the work, shall be dismissed if the items described in paragraph (3) are not submitted to the Copyright Office in proper form within the earlier of—

(A) 3 months after the first publication of the work; or

(B) 1 month after the copyright owner has learned of the infringement.

(Oct. 19, 1976, P. L. 94-553, Title I, § 101, 90 Stat. 2580; Oct. 31, 1988, P. L. 100-568, § 9(a), 102 Stat. 2859; June 26, 1992, P. L. 102-307, Title I, § 102(e), 106 Stat. 266; April 27, 2005, P. L. 109-9, Title I, § 104(a), 119 Stat. 221.)

§ 409 Application for copyright registration

The application for copyright registration shall be made on a form prescribed by the Register of Copyrights and shall include—

(1) the name and address of the copyright claimant;

(2) in the case of a work other than an anonymous or pseudonymous work, the name and nationality or domicile of the author or authors, and, if one or more of the authors is dead, the dates of their deaths;

(3) if the work is anonymous or pseudonymous, the nationality or domicile of the author or authors;

(4) in the case of a work made for hire, a statement to this effect;

(5) if the copyright claimant is not the author, a brief statement of how the claimant obtained ownership of the copyright;

(6) the title of the work, together with any previous or alternative titles under which the work can be identified;

(7) the year in which creation of the work was completed;

(8) if the work has been published, the date and nation of its first publication;

(9) in the case of a compilation or derivative work, an identification of any preexisting work or works that it is based on or incorporates, and a brief, general statement of the additional material covered by the copyright claim being registered;

(10) in the case of a published work containing material of which copies are required by section 601 to be manufactured in the United States, the names of the persons or organizations who performed the processes specified by subsection (c) of section 601 with respect to that material, and the places where those processes were performed; and

(11) any other information regarded by the Register of Copyrights as bearing upon the preparation or identification of the work or the existence, ownership, or duration of the copyright.

If an application is submitted for the renewed and extended term provided for in section 304(a)(3)(A) and an original term registration has not been made, the Register may request information with respect to the existence, ownership, or duration of the copyright for the original term.

(Oct. 19, 1976, P. L. 94-553, Title I, § 101, 90 Stat. 2582; June 26, 1992, P.L. 102-307, Title I, § 102(b)(1), 106 Stat. 266.)

§ 410 Registration of claim and issuance of certificate

(a) When, after examination, the Register of Copyrights determines that, in accordance with the provisions of this title, the material deposited constitutes copyrightable subject matter and that the other legal and formal requirements of this title have been met, the Register shall register the claim and issue to the applicant a certificate of registration under the seal of the Copyright Office. The certificate shall contain the information given in the application, together with the number and effective date of the registration.

(b) In any case in which the Register of Copyrights determines that, in accordance with the provisions of this title, the material deposited does not constitute copyrightable subject matter or that the claim is invalid for any other reason, the Register shall refuse registration and shall notify the applicant in writing of the reasons for such refusal.

(c) In any judicial proceedings the certificate of a registration made before or within five years after first publication of the work shall constitute prima facie evidence of the validity of the copyright and of the facts stated in the certificate. The evidentiary weight to be accorded the certificate of a registration made thereafter shall be within the discretion of the court.

(d) The effective date of a copyright registration is the day on which an application, deposit, and fee, which are later determined by the Register of Copyrights or by a court of competent jurisdiction to be acceptable for registration, have all been received in the Copyright Office.

(Oct. 19, 1976, P. L. 94-553, Title I, § 101, 90 Stat. 2582.)

§ 411 Registration and civil infringement actions

(a) Except for an action brought for a violation of the rights of the author under section 106A(a), and subject to the provisions of subsection (b), no civil action for infringement of the copyright in any United States work shall be instituted until preregistration or registration of the copyright claim has been made in accordance with this title. In any case, however, where the deposit, application, and fee required for registration have been delivered to the Copyright Office in proper form and registration has been refused, the applicant is entitled to institute a civil action for infringement if notice thereof, with a copy of the complaint, is served on the Register of Copyrights. The Register may, at his or her option, become a party to the action with respect to the issue of registrability of the copyright claim by entering an appearance within sixty days after such service, but the Register's failure to become a party shall not deprive the court of jurisdiction to determine that issue.

(b) (1) A certificate of registration satisfies the requirements of this section and section 412 [17 USCS § 412], regardless of whether the certificate contains any inaccurate information, unless—

(A) the inaccurate information was included on the application for copyright registration with knowledge that it was inaccurate; and

(B) the inaccuracy of the information, if known, would have caused the Register of Copyrights to refuse registration.

(2) In any case in which inaccurate information described under paragraph (1) is alleged, the court shall request the Register of Copyrights to advise the court whether the inaccurate information, if known, would have caused the Register of Copyrights to refuse registration.

(3) Nothing in this subsection shall affect any rights, obligations, or requirements of a person related to information contained in a registration certificate, except for the institution of and remedies in infringement actions under this section and section 412 [17 USCS § 412].

(c) In the case of a work consisting of sounds, images, or both, the first fixation of which is made simultaneously with its transmission, the copyright owner may, either before or after such fixation takes place, institute an action for infringement under section 501, fully subject to the remedies provided by sections 502 through 505 [17 USCS §§ 502 through 505] and section 510 [17 USCS § 510], if, in accordance with requirements that the Register of Copyrights shall prescribe by regulation, the copyright owner—

(1) serves notice upon the infringer, not less than 48 hours before such fixation, identifying the work and the specific time and source of its first transmission, and declaring an intention to secure copyright in the work; and

(2) makes registration for the work, if required by subsection (a), within three months after its first transmission.

(Oct. 19, 1976, P. L. 94-553, Title I, § 101, 90 Stat. 2583; Oct. 31, 1988, P. L. 100-568, § 9(b)(1), 102 Stat. 2859; Dec. 1, 1990, P. L. 101-650, Title VI, § 606(c)(1), 104 Stat. 5131; Nov. 13, 1997, P. L. 105-80, § 6, 111 Stat. 1532; Oct. 28, 1998, P. L. 105-304, Title I, § 102(d), 112 Stat. 2863; April 27, 2005, P. L. 109-9, Title I, § 104(b), 119 Stat. 222; Oct. 13, 2008, P. L. 110-403, § 101(a), (b)(2) 209(a)(6), 122 Stat. 4260.)

§ 412 Registration as prerequisite to certain remedies for infringement

In any action under this title, other than an action brought for a violation of the rights of the author under section 106A(a) [17 USCS § 106A(a)], an action for infringement of the copyright of a work that has been preregistered under section 408(f) [17 USCS § 408(f)] before the commencement of the infringement and that has an effective date of registration not later than the earlier of 3 months after the first publication of the work or 1 month after the copyright owner has learned of the infringement, or an action instituted under section 411(c) [17 USCS § 411(c)], no award of statutory damages or of attorney's fees, as provided by sections 504 and 505 [17 USCS §§ 504 and 505], shall be made for—

(1) any infringement of copyright in an unpublished work commenced before the effective date of its registration; or

(2) any infringement of copyright commenced after first publication of the work and before the effective date of its registration, unless such registration is made within three months after the first publication of the work.

(Oct. 19, 1976, P. L. 94-553, Title I, § 101, 90 Stat. 2583; Dec. 1, 1990, P. L. 101-650, Title VI, § 606(c)(2), 104 Stat. 5131; April 27, 2005, P. L. 109-9, Title I, § 104(c), 119 Stat. 222; Oct. 13, 2008, P. L. 110-403, Title I, § 101(b)(1), 122 Stat. 4260.)

CHAPTER 5—COPYRIGHT INFRINGEMENT AND REMEDIES

Section

§ 501 Infringement of copyright

(a) Anyone who violates any of the exclusive rights of the copyright owner as provided by sections 106 through 122 or of the author as provided in section 106A(a), or who imports copies or phonorecords into the United States in violation of section 602, is an infringer of the copyright or right of the author, as the case may be. For purposes of this chapter [17 USCS §§ 501 et seq.] (other than section 506), any reference to copyright shall be deemed to include the rights conferred by section 106A(a). As used in this subsection, the term "anyone" includes any State, any instrumentality of a State, and any officer or employee of a State or instrumentality of a State acting in his or her official capacity. Any State, and any such instrumentality, officer, or employee, shall be subject to the provisions of this title in the same manner and to the same extent as any nongovernmental entity.

(b) The legal or beneficial owner of an exclusive right under a copyright is entitled, subject to the requirements of section 411, to institute an action for any infringement of that particular right committed while he or she is the owner of it. The court may require such owner to serve written notice of the action with a copy of the complaint upon any person shown, by the records of the Copyright Office or otherwise, to have or claim an interest in the copyright, and shall require that such notice be served upon any person whose interest is likely to be affected by a decision in the case. The court may require the joinder, and shall permit the intervention, of any person having or claiming an interest in the copyright.

(c) For any secondary transmission by a cable system that embodies a performance or a display of a work which is actionable as an act of infringement under subsection (c) of section 111, a television broadcast station holding a copyright or other license to transmit or perform the same version of that work shall, for purposes of subsection (b) of this section, be treated as a legal or beneficial owner if such secondary transmission occurs within the local service area of that television station.

(d) For any secondary transmission by a cable system that is actionable as an act of infringement pursuant to section 111(c)(3), the following shall also have standing to sue: (i) the primary transmitter whose transmission has been altered by the cable system; and (ii) any broadcast station within whose local service area the secondary transmission occurs.

(e) With respect to any secondary transmission that is made by a satellite carrier of a performance or display of a work embodied in a primary transmission and is actionable as an act of infringement under section 119(a)(5)], a network station holding a copyright or other license to transmit or perform the same version of that work shall, for purposes of subsection (b) of this section, be treated as a legal or beneficial owner if such secondary transmission occurs within the local service area of that station.

(f) (1) With respect to any secondary transmission that is made by a satellite carrier of a performance or display of a work embodied in a primary transmission and is actionable as an act of infringement under section 122, a television broadcast station holding a copyright or other license to transmit or perform the same version of that work shall, for purposes of subsection (b) of this section, be treated as a legal or beneficial owner if such secondary transmission occurs within the local market of that station.

(2) A television broadcast station may file a civil action against any satellite carrier that has refused to carry television broadcast signals, as required under section 122(a)(2), to enforce that television broadcast station's rights under section 338(a) of the Communications Act of 1934 [47 USCS § 338(a)].

(Oct. 19, 1976, P. L. 94-553, Title I, § 101, 90 Stat. 2584; Oct. 31, 1988, P. L. 100-568, § 10(a), 102 Stat. 2860; Nov. 16, 1988, P. L. 100-667, Title II, § 202(3), 102 Stat. 3957; Nov. 15, 1990, P. L. 101-553, § 2(a)(1), 104 Stat. 2749; Dec. 1, 1990, P. L. 101-650, Title VI, § 606(a), 104 Stat. 5131; Aug. 5, 1999, P. L. 106-44, § 1(g)(5), 113 Stat. 222; Nov. 29, 1999, P. L. 106-113, Div B, § 1000(a)(9), 113 Stat. 1536; Nov. 2, 2002, P. L. 107-273, Div C, Title III, Subtitle B, § 13210(4)(B), 116 Stat. 1909.)

§ 502 Remedies for infringement: Injunctions

(a) Any court having jurisdiction of a civil action arising under this title may, subject to the provisions of section 1498 of title 28, grant temporary and final injunctions on such terms as it may deem reasonable to prevent or restrain infringement of a copyright.

(b) Any such injunction may be served anywhere in the United States on the person enjoined; it shall be operative throughout the United States and shall be enforceable, by proceedings in contempt or otherwise, by any United States court having jurisdiction of that person. The clerk of the court granting the injunction shall, when requested by any other court in which enforcement of the injunction is sought, transmit promptly to the other court a certified copy of all the papers in the case on file in such clerk's office.

(Oct. 19, 1976, P. L. 94-553, Title I, § 101, 90 Stat. 2584.)

§ 503 Remedies for infringement: Impounding and disposition of infringing articles

(a) (1) At any time while an action under this title is pending, the court may order the impounding, on such terms as it may deem reasonable—

(A) of all copies or phonorecords claimed to have been made or used in violation of the exclusive right of the copyright owner;

(B) of all plates, molds, matrices, masters, tapes, film negatives, or other articles by means of which such copies of phonorecords may be reproduced;

(C) of records documenting the manufacture, sale, or receipt of things involved in any such violation, provided that any records seized under this subparagraph shall be taken into the custody of the court.

(2) For impoundments of records ordered under paragraph (1)(C), the court shall enter an appropriate protective order with respect to discovery and use of any records or information that has been impounded. The protective order shall provide for appropriate procedures to ensure that confidential, private, proprietary, or privileged information contained in such records is not improperly disclosed or used.

(3) The relevant provisions of paragraphs (2) through (11) of section 34(d) of the Trademark Act (15 U.S.C. 1116(d)(2) through (11)) shall extend to any impoundment of records ordered under paragraph (1)(C) that is based upon an ex parte application, notwithstanding the provisions of rule 65 of the Federal Rules of Civil Procedure. Any references in paragraphs (2) through (11) of section 34(d) of the Trademark Act to section 32 of such Act [15 USCS § 1114] shall be read as references to section 501 of this title [17 USCS § 501], and references to use of a counterfeit mark in connection with the sale, offering for sale, or distribution of goods or services shall be read as references to infringement of a copyright.

(b) As part of a final judgment or decree, the court may order the destruction or other reasonable disposition of all copies or phonorecords found to have been made or used in violation of the copyright owner's exclusive rights, and of all plates, molds, matrices, masters, tapes, film negatives, or other articles by means of which such copies or phonorecords may be reproduced.

(Oct. 19, 1976, P. L. 94-553, Title I, § 101, 90 Stat. 2585; Oct. 13, 2008, P. L. 110-403, § 102(a), 122 Stat. 4260.)

§ 504 Remedies for infringement: Damages and profits

(a) **In General.** Except as otherwise provided by this title, an infringer of copyright is liable for either—

(1) the copyright owner's actual damages and any additional profits of the infringer, as provided by subsection (b); or

(2) statutory damages, as provided by subsection (c).

(b) **Actual Damages and Profits.** The copyright owner is entitled to recover the actual damages suffered by him or her as a result of the infringement, and any profits of the infringer that are attributable to the infringement and are not taken into account in computing the actual damages. In establishing the infringer's profits, the copyright owner is required to present of the infringer's gross revenue, and the infringer is required to prove deductible expenses and the elements of profit attributable to facto than the copyrighted work.

(c) **Statutory Damages.**

(1) Except as provided by clause (2) of this subsection, the copyright owner may elect, at any time before final judgment is rendered, to recover, instead of actual damages and profits, an award of statutory damages for all infringements involved in the action, with respect to any one work, for which any one infringer is liable individually, or for which any two or more infringers are liable jointly and severally, in a sum of not less than $750 or more than $30,000 as the court considers just. For the purposes of this subsection, all the parts of a compilation or derivative work constitute one work.

(2) In a case where the copyright owner sustains the burden of proving, and the court finds, that infringement was committed willfully, the court in its discretion may increase the award of statutory damages to a sum of not more than $150,000. In a case where the infringer sustains the burden of proving, and the court finds, that such infringer was not aware and had no reason to believe that his or her acts constituted an infringement of copyright, the court in its discretion may reduce the award of statutory damages to a sum of not less than $200. The court shall remit statutory damages in any case where an infringer believed and had reasonable grounds for believing that his or her use of the copyrighted work was a fair use under section 107 [17 USCS § 107], if the infringer was: (i) an employee or agent of a nonprofit educational institution, library, or archives acting within the scope of his or her employment who, or such institution, library, or archives itself, which infringed by reproducing the work in copies or phonorecords; or (ii) a public broadcasting entity which or a person who, as a regular part of the nonprofit activities of a public broadcasting entity (as defined in subsection (g) of section 118 [17 USCS § 118]) infringed by performing a published nondramatic literary work or by reproducing a transmission program embodying a performance of such a work.

(3) (A) In a case of infringement, it shall be a rebuttable presumption that the infringement was committed willfully for purposes of determining relief if the violator, or a person acting in concert with the violator, knowingly provided or knowingly caused to be provided materially false contact information to a domain name registrar, domain name registry, or other domain name registration authority in registering, maintaining, or renewing a domain name used in connection with the infringement.

(B) Nothing in this paragraph limits what may be considered willful infringement under this subsection.

(C) For purposes of this paragraph, the term "domain name" has the meaning given that term in section 45 of the Act entitled "An Act to provide for the registration and protection of trademarks used in commerce, to carry out the provisions of certain international conventions, and for other purposes" approved July 5, 1946 (commonly referred to as the "Trademark Act of 1946"; 15 U.S.C. 1127).

(d) **Additional Damages in Certain Cases.** In any case in which the court finds that a defendant proprietor of an establishment who claims as a defense that its activities were exempt under section 110(5) [17 USCS § 110(5)] did not have reasonable grounds to believe that its use of a copyrighted work was exempt under such section, the plaintiff shall be entitled to, in addition to any award of damages under this section, an additional award of two times the amount of the license fee that the proprietor of the establishment concerned should have paid the plaintiff for such use during the preceding period of up to 3 years.

(Oct. 19, 1976, P. L. 94-553, Title I, § 101, 90 Stat. 2585; Oct. 31, 1988, P. L. 100-568, § 10(b), 102 Stat. 2860; Nov. 13, 1997, P. L. 105-80, § 12(a)(13), 111 Stat. 1535; Oct. 27, 1998, P. L. 105-298, Title II, § 204, 112 Stat. 2833; Dec. 9, 1999, P. L. 106-160, § 2, 113 Stat. 1774; Dec. 23, 2004, P. L. 108-482, Title II, § 203, 118 Stat. 3916.)

§ 505 Remedies for infringement: Costs and attorney's fees

In any civil action under this title, the court in its discretion may allow the recovery of full costs by or against any party other than the United States or an officer thereof. Except as otherwise provided by this title, the court may also award a reasonable attorney's fee to the prevailing party as part of the costs.

(Oct. 19, 1976, P. L. 94-553, Title I, § 101, 90 Stat. 2586.)

§ 506 Criminal offenses

(a) **Criminal Infringement.**

(1) *In general.* Any person who willfully infringes a copyright shall be punished as provided under section 2319 of title 18, if the infringement was committed—

(A) for purposes of commercial advantage or private financial gain;

(B) by the reproduction or distribution, including by electronic means, during any 180-day period, of 1 or more copies or phonorecords of 1 or more copyrighted works, which have a total retail value of more than $1,000; or

(C) by the distribution of a work being prepared for commercial distribution, by making it available on a computer network accessible to members of the public, if such person knew or should have known that the work was intended for commercial distribution.

(2) *Evidence.* For purposes of this subsection, evidence of reproduction or distribution of a copyrighted work, by itself, shall not be sufficient to establish willful infringement of a copyright.

(3) *Definition.* In this subsection, the term "work being prepared for commercial distribution" means—

(A) a computer program, a musical work, a motion picture or other audiovisual work, or a sound recording, if, at the time of unauthorized distribution—

(i) the copyright owner has a reasonable expectation of commercial distribution; and

(ii) the copies or phonorecords of the work have not been commercially distributed; or

(B) a motion picture, if, at the time of unauthorized distribution, the motion picture—

(i) has been made available for viewing in a motion picture exhibition facility; and

(ii) has not been made available in copies for sale to the general public in the United States in a format intended to permit viewing outside a motion picture exhibition facility.

(b) **Forfeiture, Destruction, and Restitution.** Forfeiture, destruction, and restitution relating to this section shall be subject to section 2323 of title 18 [18 USCS § 2323], to the extent provided in that section, in addition to any other similar remedies provided by law.

(c) **Fraudulent Copyright Notice.** Any person who, with fraudulent intent, places on any article a notice of copyright or words of the same purport that such person knows to be false, or who, with fraudulent intent, publicly distributes or imports for public distribution any article bearing such notice or words that such person knows to be false, shall be fined not more than $2,500.

(d) **Fraudulent Removal of Copyright Notice.** Any person who, with fraudulent intent, removes or alters any notice of copyright appearing on a copy of a copyrighted work shall be fined not more than $2,500.

(e) **False Representation.** Any person who knowingly makes a false representation of a material fact in the application for copyright registration provided for by section 409, or in any written statement filed in connection with the application, shall be fined not more than $2,500.

(f) **Rights of Attribution and Integrity.** Nothing in this section applies to infringement of the rights conferred by section 106A(a) § 106A(a).

(Oct. 19, 1976, P. L. 94-553, Title I, § 101, 90 Stat. 2586; May 24, 1982, P. L. 97-180, § 5, 96 Stat. 93; Dec. 1, 1990, P. L. 101-650, Title VI, § 606(b), 104 Stat. 5131; Dec. 16, 1997, P. L. 105-147, § 2(b), 111 Stat. 2678; April 27, 2005, P. L. 109-9, Title I, § 103(a), 119 Stat. 220; October 13, 2008, P. L. 110-403, Title II, § 201(a), 122 Stat. 4260.)

§ 507 Limitations on actions

(a) **Criminal Proceedings.** Except as expressly provided otherwise in this title, no criminal proceeding shall be maintained under the provisions of this title unless it is commenced within 5 years after the cause of action arose.

(b) **Civil Actions.** No civil action shall be maintained under the provisions of this title unless it is commenced within three years after the claim accrued.

(Oct. 19, 1976, P. L. 94-553, Title I, § 101, 90 Stat. 2586; Dec. 16, 1997, P. L. 105-147, § 2(c), 111 Stat. 2678; Oct. 28, 1998, P. L. 105-304, Title I, § 102(e), 112 Stat. 2863.)

§ 508 Notification of filing and determination of actions

(a) Within one month after the filing of any action under this title, the clerks of the courts of the United States shall send written notification to the Register of Copyrights setting forth, as far as is shown by the papers filed in the court, the names and addresses of the parties and the title, author, and registration number of each work involved in the action. If any other copyrighted work is later included in the action by amendment, answer, or other pleading, the clerk shall also send a notification concerning it to the Register within one month after the pleading is filed.

(b) Within one month after any final order or judgment is issued in the case, the clerk of the court shall notify the Register of it, sending with the notification a copy of the order or judgment together with the written opinion, if any, of the court.

(c) Upon receiving the notifications specified in this section, the Register shall make them a part of the public records of the Copyright Office.

(Oct. 19, 1976, P. L. 94-553, Title I, § 101, 90 Stat. 2586.)

§ 509 [Repealed]

(Oct. 19, 1976, P. L. 94-553, Title I, § 101, 90 Stat. 2587; Nov. 13, 1997, P.L. 105-80, § 12(a)(14), 111 Stat. 1535. Repealed October 13, 2008, P.L. 110-403, § 201(b), 122 Stat. 4260.)

§ 510 Remedies for alteration of programming by cable systems

(a) In any action filed pursuant to section 111(c)(3), the following remedies shall be available:

(1) Where an action is brought by a party identified in subsections (b) or (c) of section 501, the remedies provided by sections 502 through 505, and the remedy provided by subsection (b) of this section; and

(2) When an action is brought by a party identified in subsection (d) of section 501, the remedies provided by sections 502 and 505, together with any actual damages suffered by such party as a result of the infringement, and the remedy provided by subsection (b) of this section.

(b) In any action filed pursuant to section 111(c)(3), the court may decree that, for a period not to exceed thirty days, the cable system shall be deprived of the benefit of a statutory license for one or more distant signals carried by such cable system.

(Oct. 19, 1976, P. L. 94-553, Title I, § 101, 90 Stat. 2587; Nov. 29, 1999, P. L. 106-113, Div B, § 1000(a)(9), 113 Stat. 1536.)

§ 511 Liability of States, instrumentalities of States, and State officials for infringement of copyright

(a) **In General.** Any State, any instrumentality of a State, and any officer or employee of a State or instrumentality of a State acting in his or her official capacity, shall not be immune, under the Eleventh Amendment of the Constitution of the United States or under any other doctrine of sovereign immunity, from suit in Federal Court by any person, including any governmental or nongovernmental entity, for a violation of any of the exclusive rights of a copyright owner provided by sections 106 through 122, for importing copies of phonorecords in violation of section 602, or for any other violation under this title.

(b) **Remedies.** In a suit described in subsection (a) for a violation described in that subsection, remedies (including remedies both at law and in equity) are available for the violation to the same extent as such remedies are available for such a violation in a suit against any public or private entity other than a State, instrumentality of a State, or officer or employee of a State acting in his or her official capacity. Such remedies include impounding and disposition of infringing articles under section 503, actual damages and profits and statutory damages under section 504, costs and attorney's fees under section 505, and the remedies provided in section 510.

(Added Nov. 15, 1990, P. L. 101-553, § 2(a)(2), 104 Stat. 2749; Aug. 5, 1999, P. L 106-44, § 1(g)(6), 113 Stat. 222; Nov. 2, 2002, P. L. 107-273, Div C, Title III, Subtitle B, § 13210(4)(C), 116 Stat. 1909.)

§ 512 Limitations on liability relating to material online*

(a) **Transitory Digital Network Communications.** A service provider shall not be liable for monetary relief, or, except as provided in subsection (j), for injunctive or other equitable relief, for infringement of copyright by reason of the provider's transmitting, routing, or providing connections for, material through a system or network controlled or operated by or for the service provider, or by reason of the intermediate and transient storage of that material in the course of such transmitting, routing, or providing connections, if—

(1) the transmission of the material was initiated by or at the direction of a person other than the service provider;

(2) the transmission, routing, provision of connections, or storage is carried out through an automatic technical process without selection of the material by the service provider;

(3) the service provider does not select the recipients of the material except as an automatic response to the request of another person;

(4) no copy of the material made by the service provider in the course of such intermediate or transient storage is maintained on the system or network in a manner ordinarily accessible to anyone other than anticipated recipients, and no such copy is maintained on the system or network in a manner ordinarily accessible to such anticipated recipients for a longer period than is reasonably necessary for the transmission, routing, or provision of connections; and

(5) the material is transmitted through the system or network without modification of its content.

(b) **System Caching.**

(1) *Limitation on liability.* A service provider shall not be liable for monetary relief, or, except as provided in subsection (j), for injunctive or other equitable relief, for infringement of copyright by reason of the intermediate and temporary storage of material on a system or network controlled or operated by or for the service provider in a case in which—

(A) the material is made available online by a person other than the service provider;

(B) the material is transmitted from the person described in subparagraph (A) through the system or network to a person other than the person described in subparagraph (A) at the direction of that other person; and

---

* Effective date of section: This section took effect on October 28, 1998, pursuant to §203 of the Act of Oct. 28, 1998, Pub. L. 105-304.—*Eds.*

(C) the storage is carried out through an automatic technical process for the purpose of making the material available to users of the system or network who, after the material is transmitted as described in subparagraph (B), request access to the material from the person described in subparagraph (A),

if the conditions set forth in paragraph (2) are met.

(2) *Conditions.* The conditions referred to in paragraph (1) are that—

(A) the material described in paragraph (1) is transmitted to the subsequent users described in paragraph (1)(C) without modification to its content from the manner in which the material was transmitted from the person described in paragraph (1)(A);

(B) the service provider described in paragraph (1) complies with rules concerning the refreshing, reloading, or other updating of the material when specified by the person making the material available online in accordance with a generally accepted industry standard data communications protocol for the system or network through which that person makes the material available, except that this subparagraph applies only if those rules are not used by the person described in paragraph (1)(A) to prevent or unreasonably impair the intermediate storage to which this subsection applies;

(C) the service provider does not interfere with the ability of technology associated with the material to return to the person described in paragraph (1)(A) the information that would have been available to that person if the material had been obtained by the subsequent users described in paragraph (1)(C) directly from that person, except that this subparagraph applies only if that technology—

(i) does not significantly interfere with the performance of the provider's system or network or with the intermediate storage of the material;

(ii) is consistent with generally accepted industry standard communications protocols; and

(iii) does not extract information from the provider's system or network other than the information that would have been available to the person described in paragraph (1)(A) if the subsequent users had gained access to the material directly from that person;

(D) if the person described in paragraph (1)(A) has in effect a condition that a person must meet prior to having access to the material, such as a condition based on payment of a fee or provision of a password or other information, the service provider permits access to the stored material in significant part only to users of its system or network that have met those conditions and only in accordance with those conditions; and

(E) if the person described in paragraph (1)(A) makes that material available online without the authorization of the copyright owner of the material, the service provider responds expeditiously to remove, or disable access to, the material that is claimed to be infringing upon notification of claimed infringement as described in subsection (c)(3), except that this subparagraph applies only if—

(i) the material has previously been removed from the originating site or access to it has been disabled, or a court has ordered that the material be removed from the originating site or that access to the material on the originating site be disabled; and

(ii) the party giving the notification includes in the notification a statement confirming that the material has been removed from the originating site or access to it has been disabled or that a court has ordered that the material be removed from the originating site or that access to the material on the originating site be disabled.

(c) **Information Residing on Systems or Networks at Direction of Users.**

(1) *In general.* A service provider shall not be liable for monetary relief, or, except as provided in subsection (j), for injunctive or other equitable relief, for infringement of copyright by reason of the storage at the direction of a user of material that resides on a system or network controlled or operated by or for the service provider, if the service provider—

(A) (i) does not have actual knowledge that the material or an activity using the material on the system or network is infringing;

(ii) in the absence of such actual knowledge, is not aware of facts or circumstances from which infringing activity is apparent; or

(iii) upon obtaining such knowledge or awareness, acts expeditiously to remove, or disable access to, the material;

(B) does not receive a financial benefit directly attributable to the infringing activity, in a case in which the service provider has the right and ability to control such activity; and

(C) upon notification of claimed infringement as described in paragraph (3), responds expeditiously to remove, or disable access to, the material that is claimed to be infringing or to be the subject of infringing activity.

(2) *Designated agent.* The limitations on liability established in this subsection apply to a service provider only if the service provider

has designated an agent to receive notifications of claimed infringement described in paragraph (3), by making available through its service, including on its website in a location accessible to the public, and by providing to the Copyright Office, substantially the following information:

(A) the name, address, phone number, and electronic mail address of the agent.

(B) other contact information which the Register of Copyrights may deem appropriate.

The Register of Copyrights shall maintain a current directory of agents available to the public for inspection, including through the Internet, in both electronic and hard copy formats, and may require payment of a fee by service providers to cover the costs of maintaining the directory.

(3) *Elements of notification.*

(A) To be effective under this subsection, a notification of claimed infringement must be a written communication provided to the designated agent of a service provider that includes substantially the following:

(i) A physical or electronic signature of a person authorized to act on behalf of the owner of an exclusive right that is allegedly infringed.

(ii) Identification of the copyrighted work claimed to have been infringed, or, if multiple copyrighted works at a single online site are covered by a single notification, a representative list of such works at that site.

(iii) Identification of the material that is claimed to be infringing or to be the subject of infringing activity and that is to be removed or access to which is to be disabled, and information reasonably sufficient to permit the service provider to locate the material.

(iv) Information reasonably sufficient to permit the service provider to contact the complaining party, such as an address, telephone number, and, if available, an electronic mail address at which the complaining party may be contacted.

(v) A statement that the complaining party has a good faith belief that use of the material in the manner complained of is not authorized by the copyright owner, its agent, or the law.

(vi) A statement that the information in the notification is accurate, and under penalty of perjury, that the complaining party is authorized to act on behalf of the owner of an exclusive right that is allegedly infringed.

(B) (i) Subject to clause (ii), a notification from a copyright owner or from a person authorized to act on behalf of the copyright owner that fails to comply substantially with the provisions of subparagraph (A) shall not be considered under paragraph (1)(A) in determining whether a service provider has actual knowledge or is aware of facts or circumstances from which infringing activity is apparent.

(ii) In a case in which the notification that is provided to the service provider's designated agent fails to comply substantially with all the provisions of subparagraph (A) but substantially complies with clauses (ii), (iii), and (iv) of subparagraph (A), clause (i) of this subparagraph applies only if the service provider promptly attempts to contact the person making the notification or takes other reasonable steps to assist in the receipt of notification that substantially complies with all the provisions of subparagraph (A).

(d) **Information Location Tools.** A service provider shall not be liable for monetary relief, or, except as provided in subsection (j), for injunctive or other equitable relief, for infringement of copyright by reason of the provider referring or linking users to an online location containing infringing material or infringing activity, by using information location tools, including a directory, index, reference, pointer, or hypertext link, if the service provider—

(1) (A) does not have actual knowledge that the material or activity is infringing;

(B) in the absence of such actual knowledge, is not aware of facts or circumstances from which infringing activity is apparent; or

(C) upon obtaining such knowledge or awareness, acts expeditiously to remove, or disable access to, the material;

(2) does not receive a financial benefit directly attributable to the infringing activity, in a case in which the service provider has the right and ability to control such activity; and

(3) upon notification of claimed infringement as described in subsection (c)(3), responds expeditiously to remove, or disable access to, the material that is claimed to be infringing or to be the subject of infringing activity, except that, for purposes of this paragraph, the information described in subsection (c)(3)(A)(iii) shall be identification of the reference or link, to material or activity claimed to be infringing, that is to be removed or access to which is to be disabled, and information reasonably sufficient to permit the service provider to locate that reference or link.

(e) **Limitation on Liability of Nonprofit Educational Institutions.**

(1) When a public or other nonprofit institution of higher education is a service provider, and when a faculty member or graduate student who is an employee of such institution is performing a teaching or research function, for the purposes of subsections (a) and (b) such fac-

ulty member or graduate student shall be considered to be a person other than the institution, and for the purposes of subsections (c) and (d) such faculty member's or graduate student's knowledge or awareness of his or her infringing activities shall not be attributed to the institution, if—

(A) such faculty member's or graduate student's infringing activities do not involve the provision of online access to instructional materials that are or were required or recommended, within the preceding 3-year period, for a course taught at the institution by such faculty member or graduate student;

(B) the institution has not, within the preceding 3-year period, received more than two notifications described in subsection (c)(3) of claimed infringement by such faculty member or graduate student, and such notifications of claimed infringement were not actionable under subsection (f); and

(C) the institution provides to all users of its system or network informational materials that accurately describe, and promote compliance with, the laws of the United States relating to copyright.

(2) For the purposes of this subsection, the limitations on injunctive relief contained in subsections (j)(2) and (j)(3), but not those in (j)(1), shall apply.

(f) **Misrepresentations.** Any person who knowingly materially misrepresents under this section—

(1) that material or activity is infringing, or

(2) that material or activity was removed or disabled by mistake or misidentification,

shall be liable for any damages, including costs and attorneys' fees, incurred by the alleged infringer, by any copyright owner or copyright owner's authorized licensee, or by a service provider, who is injured by such misrepresentation, as the result of the service provider relying upon such misrepresentation in removing or disabling access to the material or activity claimed to be infringing, or in replacing the removed material or ceasing to disable access to it.

(g) **Replacement of Removed or Disabled Material and Limitation on Other Liability.**

(1) *No liability for taking down generally.* Subject to paragraph (2), a service provider shall not be liable to any person for any claim based on the service provider's good faith disabling of access to, or removal of, material or activity claimed to be infringing or based on facts or circumstances from which infringing activity is apparent, regardless of whether the material or activity is ultimately determined to be infringing.

(2) *Exception.* Paragraph (1) shall not apply with respect to material residing at the direction of a subscriber of the service provider on a system or network controlled or operated by or for the service provider that is removed, or to which access is disabled by the service provider, pursuant to a notice provided under subsection (c)(1)(C), unless the service provider—

(A) takes reasonable steps promptly to notify the subscriber that it has removed or disabled access to the material;

(B) upon receipt of a counter notification described in paragraph (3), promptly provides the person who provided the notification under subsection (c)(1)(C) with a copy of the counter notification, and informs that person that it will replace the removed material or cease disabling access to it in 10 business days; and

(C) replaces the removed material and ceases disabling access to it not less than 10, nor more than 14, business days following receipt of the counter notice, unless its designated agent first receives notice from the person who submitted the notification under subsection (c)(1)(C) that such person has filed an action seeking a court order to restrain the subscriber from engaging in infringing activity relating to the material on the service provider's system or network.

(3) *Contents of counter notification.* To be effective under this subsection, a counter notification must be a written communication provided to the service provider's designated agent that includes substantially the following:

(A) A physical or electronic signature of the subscriber.

(B) Identification of the material that has been removed or to which access has been disabled and the location at which the material appeared before it was removed or access to it was disabled.

(C) A statement under penalty of perjury that the subscriber has a good faith belief that the material was removed or disabled as a result of mistake or misidentification of the material to be removed or disabled.

(D) The subscriber's name, address, and telephone number, and a statement that the subscriber consents to the jurisdiction of Federal District Court for the judicial district in which the address is located, or if the subscriber's address is outside of the United States, for any judicial district in which the service provider may be found, and that the subscriber will accept service of process from the person who provided notification under subsection (c)(1)(C) or an agent of such person.

(4) *Limitation on other liability.* A service provider's compliance with paragraph (2) shall not subject the service provider to liability for copyright infringement with respect to the material identified in the notice provided under subsection (c)(1)(C).

(h) **Subpoena to Identify Infringer.**

(1) *Request.* A copyright owner or a person authorized to act on the owner's behalf may request the clerk of any United States district court to issue a subpoena to a service provider for identification of an alleged infringer in accordance with this subsection.

(2) *Contents of request.* The request may be made by filing with the clerk—

(A) a copy of a notification described in subsection (c)(3)(A);

(B) a proposed subpoena; and

(C) a sworn declaration to the effect that the purpose for which the subpoena is sought is to obtain the identity of an alleged infringer and that such information will only be used for the purpose of protecting rights under this title.

(3) *Contents of subpoena.* The subpoena shall authorize and order the service provider receiving the notification and the subpoena to expeditiously disclose to the copyright owner or person authorized by the copyright owner information sufficient to identify the alleged infringer of the material described in the notification to the extent such information is available to the service provider.

(4) *Basis for granting subpoena.* If the notification filed satisfies the provisions of subsection (c)(3)(A), the proposed subpoena is in proper form, and the accompanying declaration is properly executed, the clerk shall expeditiously issue and sign the proposed subpoena and return it to the requester for delivery to the service provider.

(5) *Actions of service provider receiving subpoena.* Upon receipt of the issued subpoena, either accompanying or subsequent to the receipt of a notification described in subsection (c)(3)(A), the service provider shall expeditiously disclose to the copyright owner or person authorized by the copyright owner the information required by the subpoena, notwithstanding any other provision of law and regardless of whether the service provider responds to the notification.

(6) *Rules applicable to subpoena.* Unless otherwise provided by this section or by applicable rules of the court, the procedure for issuance and delivery of the subpoena, and the remedies for noncompliance with the subpoena, shall be governed to the greatest extent practicable by those provisions of the Federal Rules of Civil Procedure governing the issuance, service, and enforcement of a subpoena duces tecum.

(i) **Conditions for Eligibility.**

(1) *Accommodation of technology.* The limitations on liability established by this section shall apply to a service provider only if the service provider—

(A) has adopted and reasonably implemented, and informs subscribers and account holders of the service provider's system or network of, a policy that provides for the termination in appropriate circumstances of subscribers and account holders of the service provider's system or network who are repeat infringers; and

(B) accommodates and does not interfere with standard technical measures.

(2) *Definition.* As used in this subsection, the term "standard technical measures" means technical measures that are used by copyright owners to identify or protect copyrighted works and—

(A) have been developed pursuant to a broad consensus of copyright owners and service providers in an open, fair, voluntary, multi-industry standards process;

(B) are available to any person on reasonable and nondiscriminatory terms; and

(C) do not impose substantial costs on service providers or substantial burdens on their systems or networks.

(j) **Injunctions.** The following rules shall apply in the case of any application for an injunction under section 502 against a service provider that is not subject to monetary remedies under this section:

(1) *Scope of relief.*

(A) With respect to conduct other than that which qualifies for the limitation on remedies set forth in subsection (a), the court may grant injunctive relief with respect to a service provider only in one or more of the following forms:

(i) An order restraining the service provider from providing access to infringing material or activity residing at a particular online site on the provider's system or network.

(ii) An order restraining the service provider from providing access to a subscriber or account holder of the service provider's system or network who is engaging in infringing activity and is identified in the order, by terminating the accounts of the subscriber or account holder that are specified in the order.

(iii) Such other injunctive relief as the court may consider necessary to prevent or restrain infringement of copyrighted material specified in the order of the court at a particular online location, if such relief is the least burdensome to the service provider among the forms of relief comparably effective for that purpose.

(B) If the service provider qualifies for the limitation on remedies described in subsection (a), the court may only grant injunctive relief in one or both of the following forms:

(i) An order restraining the service provider from providing access to a subscriber or account holder of the service provider's system or network who is using the provider's service to engage in infringing activity and is identified in the order, by terminating the accounts of the subscriber or account holder that are specified in the order.

(ii) An order restraining the service provider from providing access, by taking reasonable steps specified in the order to block access, to a specific, identified, online location outside the United States.

(2) *Considerations.* The court, in considering the relevant criteria for injunctive relief under applicable law, shall consider—

(A) whether such an injunction, either alone or in combination with other such injunctions issued against the same service provider under this subsection, would significantly burden either the provider or the operation of the provider's system or network;

(B) the magnitude of the harm likely to be suffered by the copyright owner in the digital network environment if steps are not taken to prevent or restrain the infringement;

(C) whether implementation of such an injunction would be technically feasible and effective, and would not interfere with access to noninfringing material at other online locations; and

(D) whether other less burdensome and comparably effective means of preventing or restraining access to the infringing material are available.

(3) *Notice and ex parte orders.* Injunctive relief under this subsection shall be available only after notice to the service provider and an opportunity for the service provider to appear are provided, except for orders ensuring the preservation of evidence or other orders having no material adverse effect on the operation of the service provider's communications network.

(k) **Definitions.**

(1) *Service provider.*

(A) As used in subsection (a), the term "service provider" means an entity offering the transmission, routing, or providing of connections for digital online communications, between or among points specified by a user, of material of the user's choosing, without modification to the content of the material as sent or received.

(B) As used in this section, other than subsection (a), the term "service provider" means a provider of online services or network access, or the operator of facilities therefor, and includes an entity described in subparagraph (A).

(2) *Monetary relief.* As used in this section, the term "monetary relief" means damages, costs, attorneys' fees, and any other form of monetary payment.

(l) **Other Defenses not Affected.** The failure of a service provider's conduct to qualify for limitation of liability under this section shall not bear adversely upon the consideration of a defense by the service provider that the service provider's conduct is not infringing under this title or any other defense.

(m) **Protection of Privacy.** Nothing in this section shall be construed to condition the applicability of subsections (a) through (d) on—

(1) a service provider monitoring its service or affirmatively seeking facts indicating infringing activity, except to the extent consistent with a standard technical measure complying with the provisions of subsection (i); or

(2) a service provider gaining access to, removing, or disabling access to material in cases in which such conduct is prohibited by law.

(n) **Construction.** Subsections (a), (b), (c), and (d) describe separate and distinct functions for purposes of applying this section. Whether a service provider qualifies for the limitation on liability in any one of those subsections shall be based solely on the criteria in that subsection, and shall not affect a determination of whether that service provider qualifies for the limitations on liability under any other such subsection.

(Added Oct. 28, 1998, P. L. 105-304, Title II, § 202(a), 112 Stat. 2877; Aug. 5, 1999, P. L. 106-44, § 1(d), 113 Stat. 222.)

§ 513 Determination of reasonable license fees for individual proprietors*

In the case of any performing rights society subject to a consent decree which provides for the determination of reasonable license rates or fees to be charged by the performing rights society, notwithstanding the provisions of that consent decree, an individual proprietor who owns or operates fewer than 7 non-publicly traded establishments in which nondramatic musical works are performed publicly and who claims that any license agreement offered by that performing rights society is unreasonable in its license rate or fee as to that individual proprietor, shall be entitled to determination of a reasonable license rate or fee as follows:

(1) The individual proprietor may commence such proceeding for determination of a reasonable license rate or fee by filing an application in the applicable district court under paragraph (2) that a rate disagreement

* Effective date of section: This section took effect 90 days after enactment, pursuant to § 207 of the Act of Oct. 27, 1998, P. L. 105-298.—*Eds.*

exists and by serving a copy of the application on the performing rights society. Such proceeding shall commence in the applicable district court within 90 days after the service of such copy, except that such 90-day requirement shall be subject to the administrative requirements of the court.

(2) The proceeding under paragraph (1) shall be held, at the individual proprietor's election, in the judicial district of the district court with jurisdiction over the applicable consent decree or in that place of holding court of a district court that is the seat of the Federal circuit (other than the Court of Appeals for the Federal Circuit) in which the proprietor's establishment is located.

(3) Such proceeding shall be held before the judge of the court with jurisdiction over the consent decree governing the performing rights society. At the discretion of the court, the proceeding shall be held before a special master or magistrate judge appointed by such judge. Should that consent decree provide for the appointment of an advisor or advisors to the court for any purpose, any such advisor shall be the special master so named by the court.

(4) In any such proceeding, the industry rate shall be presumed to have been reasonable at the time it was agreed to or determined by the court. Such presumption shall in no way affect a determination of whether the rate is being correctly applied to the individual proprietor.

(5) Pending the completion of such proceeding, the individual proprietor shall have the right to perform publicly the copyrighted musical compositions in the repertoire of the performing rights society by paying an interim license rate or fee into an interest bearing escrow account with the clerk of the court, subject to retroactive adjustment when a final rate or fee has been determined, in an amount equal to the industry rate, or, in the absence of an industry rate, the amount of the most recent license rate or fee agreed to by the parties.

(6) Any decision rendered in such proceeding by a special master or magistrate judge named under paragraph (3) shall be reviewed by the judge of the court with jurisdiction over the consent decree governing the performing rights society. Such proceeding, including such review, shall be concluded within 6 months after its commencement.

(7) Any such final determination shall be binding only as to the individual proprietor commencing the proceeding, and shall not be applicable to any other proprietor or any other performing rights society, and the performing rights society shall be relieved of any obligation of nondiscrimination among similarly situated music users that may be imposed by the consent decree governing its operations.

(8) An individual proprietor may not bring more than one proceeding provided for in this section for the determination of a reasonable license rate or fee under any license agreement with respect to any one performing rights society.

(9) For purposes of this section, the term "industry rate" means the license fee a performing rights society has agreed to with, or which has been determined by the court for, a significant segment of the music user industry to which the individual proprietor belongs.

(Added Oct. 27, 1998, P. L. 105-298, Title II, § 203(a), 112 Stat. 2831; Aug. 5, 1999, P. L. 106-44, § 1(c)(1), 113 Stat. 221.)

CHAPTER 6—MANUFACTURING REQUIREMENTS, IMPORTATION, AND EXPORTATION

Section

§ 601 Manufacture, importation and public distribution of certain copies

(a) Prior to July 1, 1986, and except as provided by subsection (b), the importation into or public distribution in the United States of copies of a work consisting preponderantly of nondramatic literary material that is in the English language and is protected under this title is prohibited unless the portions consisting of such material have been manufactured in the United States or Canada.

(b) The provisions of subsection (a) do not apply—

(1) where, on the date when importation is sought or public distribution in the United States is made, the author of any substantial part of such material is neither a national nor a domiciliary of the United States or, if such author is a national of the United States, he or she has been domiciled outside the United States for a continuous period of at least one year immediately preceding that date; in the case of a work made for hire, the exemption provided by this clause does not apply unless a substantial part of the work was prepared for an employer or other person who is not a national or domiciliary of the United States or a domestic corporation or enterprise;

(2) where United States Customs and Border Protection is presented with an import statement issued under the seal of the Copyright Office, in which case a total of no more than two thousand copies of any one such work shall be allowed entry; the import statement shall be issued upon request to the copyright owner or to a person designated by such owner at the time of registration for the work under section 408 or at any time thereafter;

(3) where importation is sought under the authority or for the use, other than in schools, of the Government of the United States or of any State or political subdivision of a State;

(4) where importation, for use and not for sale, is sought—

(A) by any person with respect to no more than one copy of any work at any one time;

(B) by any person arriving from outside the United States, with respect to copies forming part of such person's personal baggage; or

(C) by an organization operated for scholarly, educational, or religious purposes and not for private gain, with respect to copies intended to form a part of its library;

(5) where the copies are reproduced in raised characters for the use of the blind; or

(6) where, in addition to copies imported under clauses (3) and (4) of this subsection, no more than two thousand copies of any one such work, which have not been manufactured in the United States or Canada, are publicly distributed in the United States; or

(7) where, on the date when importation is sought or public distribution in the United States is made—

(A) the author of any substantial part of such material is an individual and receives compensation for the transfer or license of the right to distribute the work in the United States; and

(B) the first publication of the work has previously taken place outside the United States under a transfer or license granted by such author to a transferee or licensee who was not a national or domiciliary of the United States or a domestic corporation or enterprise; and

(C) there has been no publication of an authorized edition of the work of which the copies were manufactured in the United States; and

(D) the copies were reproduced under a transfer or license granted by such author or by the transferee or licensee of the right of first publication as mentioned in subclause (B), and the transferee or the licensee of the right of reproduction was not a national or domiciliary of the United States or a domestic corporation or enterprise.

(c) The requirement of this section that copies be manufactured in the United States or Canada is satisfied if—

(1) in the case where the copies are printed directly from type that has been set, or directly from plates made from such type, the setting of the type and the making of the plates have been performed in the United States or Canada; or

(2) in the case where the making of plates by a lithographic or photoengraving process is a final or intermediate step preceding the printing of the copies, the making of the plates has been performed in the United States or Canada; and

(3) in any case, the printing or other final process of producing multiple copies and any binding of the copies have been performed in the United States or Canada.

(d) Importation or public distribution of copies in violation of this section does not invalidate protection for a work under this title. However, in any civil action or criminal proceeding for infringement of the exclusive rights to reproduce and distribute copies of the work, the infringer has a complete defense with respect to all of the nondramatic literary material comprised in the work and any other parts of the work in which the exclusive rights to reproduce and distribute copies are owned by the same person who owns such exclusive rights in the nondramatic literary material, if the infringer proves—

(1) that copies of the work have been imported into or publicly distributed in the United States in violation of this section by or with the authority of the owner of such exclusive rights; and

(2) that the infringing copies were manufactured in the United States or Canada in accordance with the provisions of subsection (c); and

(3) that the infringement was commenced before the effective date of registration for an authorized edition of the work, the copies of which have been manufactured in the United States or Canada in accordance with the provisions of subsection (c).

(e) In any action for infringement of the exclusive rights to reproduce and distribute copies of a work containing material required by this section to be manufactured in the United States or Canada, the copyright owner shall set forth in the complaint the names of the persons or organizations who performed the processes specified by subsection (c) with respect to that material, and the places where those processes were performed.

(Oct. 19, 1976, P. L. 94-553, Title I, § 101, 90 Stat. 2588; July 13, 1982, P.L. 97-215, 96 Stat. 178; Nov. 13, 1997, P. L. 105-80, § 12(a)(15), (16), 111 Stat. 1535; October 13, 2008, P. L. 110-403, § 105(c)(2), 122 Stat. 4260.)

§ 602 Infringing importation or exportation of copies or phonorecords

(a) **Infringing Importation or Exportation.**

(1) *Importation.* Importation into the United States, without the authority of the owner of copyright under this title, of copies or phonorecords of a work that have been acquired outside the United States is an infringement of the exclusive right to distribute copies or phonorecords under section 106, actionable under section 501.

(2) *Importation or exportation of infringing items.* Importation into the United States or exportation from the United States, without the authority of the owner of copyright under this title, of copies or phonorecords, the making of which either constituted an infringement of copyright, or which would have constituted an infringement of copyright if

this title had been applicable, is an infringement of the exclusive right to distribute copies or phonorecords under section 106 [17 USCS § 106], actionable under sections 501 and 506 [17 USCS §§ 501 and 506].

(3) *Exceptions.* This subsection does not apply to—

(A) importation or exportation of copies or phonorecords under the authority or for the use of the Government of the United States or of any State or political subdivision of a State, but not including copies or phonorecords for use in schools, or copies of any audiovisual work imported for purposes other than archival use;

(B) importation or exportation, for the private use of the importer or exporter, and not for distribution, by any person with respect to no more than one copy or phonorecord of any one work at any one time, or by any person arriving from outside the United States or departing from the United States with respect to copies or phonorecords forming part of such person's personal baggage; or

(C) importation by or for an organization operated for scholarly, educational, or religious purposes and not for private gain, with respect to no more than one copy of an audiovisual work solely for its archival purposes, and no more than five copies or phonorecords of any other work for its library lending or archival purposes, unless the importation of such copies or phonorecords is part of an activity consisting of systematic reproduction or distribution, engaged in by such organization in violation of the provisions of section 108(g)(2).

(b) **Import Prohibition.** In a case where the making of the copies or phonorecords would have constituted an infringement of copyright if this title had been applicable, their importation is prohibited. In a case where the copies or phonorecords were lawfully made, United States Customs and Border Protection has no authority to prevent their importation unless the provisions of section 601 are applicable. In either case, the Secretary of the Treasury is authorized to prescribe, by regulation, a procedure under which any person claiming an interest in the copyright in a particular work may, upon payment of a specified fee, be entitled to notification by United States Customs and Border Protection of the importation of articles that appear to be copies or phonorecords of the work.

(Oct. 19, 1976, P. L. 94-553, Title I, § 101, 90 Stat. 2589; October 13, 2008, P. L. 110-403, § 105(c)(1), 122 Stat. 4260.)

§ 603 Importation prohibitions: Enforcement and disposition of excluded articles

(a) The Secretary of the Treasury and the United States Postal Service shall separately or jointly make regulations for the enforcement of the provisions of this title prohibiting importation.

(b) These regulations may require, as a condition for the exclusion of articles under section 602—

(1) that the person seeking exclusion obtain a court order enjoining importation of the articles; or

(2) that the person seeking exclusion furnish proof, of a specified nature and in accordance with prescribed procedures, that the copyright in which such person claims an interest is valid and that the importation would violate the prohibition in section 602; the person seeking exclusion may also be required to post a surety bond for any injury that may result if the detention or exclusion of the articles proves to be unjustified.

(c) Articles imported in violation of the importation prohibitions of this title are subject to seizure and forfeiture in the same manner as property imported in violation of the customs revenue laws. Forfeited articles shall be destroyed as directed by the Secretary of the Treasury or the court, as the case may be.

(Oct. 19, 1976, P. L. 94-553, Title I, § 101, 90 Stat. 2590.)

CHAPTER 7—COPYRIGHT OFFICE

Section

§ 701 The Copyright Office: General responsibilities and organization

(a) All administrative functions and duties under this title, except as otherwise specified, are the responsibility of the Register of Copyrights as director of the Copyright Office of the Library of Congress. The Register of Copyrights, together with the subordinate officers and employees of the Copyright Office, shall be appointed by the Librarian of Congress, and shall act under the Librarian's general direction and supervision.

(b) In addition to the functions and duties set out elsewhere in this chapter [17 USCS §§ 701 et seq.], the Register of Copyrights shall perform the following functions:

(1) Advise Congress on national and international issues relating to copyright, other matters arising under this title, and related matters.

(2) Provide information and assistance to Federal departments and agencies and the Judiciary on national and international issues relating to copyright, other matters arising under this title, and related matters.

(3) Participate in meetings of international intergovernmental organizations and meetings with foreign government officials relating to copyright, other matters arising under this title, and related matters, including as a member of United States delegations as authorized by the appropriate Executive branch authority.

(4) Conduct studies and programs regarding copyright, other matters arising under this title, and related matters, the administration of the Copyright Office, or any function vested in the Copyright Office by law, including educational programs conducted cooperatively with foreign intellectual property offices and international intergovernmental organizations.

(5) Perform such other functions as Congress may direct, or as may be appropriate in furtherance of the functions and duties specifically set forth in this title.

(c) The Register of Copyrights shall adopt a seal to be used on and after January 1, 1978, to authenticate all certified documents issued by the Copyright Office.

(d) The Register of Copyrights shall make an annual report to the Librarian of Congress of the work and accomplishments of the Copyright Office during the previous fiscal year. The annual report of the Register of Copyrights shall be published separately and as a part of the annual report of the Librarian of Congress.

(e) Except as provided by section 706(b) and the regulations issued thereunder, all actions taken by the Register of Copyrights under this title are subject to the provisions of the Administrative Procedure Act of June 11, 1946, as amended (c. 324, 60 Stat. 237, Title 5, United States Code, Chapter 5, Subchapter II and Chapter 7).

(f) The Register of Copyrights shall be compensated at the rate of pay in effect for level III of the Executive Schedule under section 5314 of title 5. The Librarian of Congress shall establish not more than four positions for Associate Registers of Copyrights, in accordance with the recommendations of the Register of Copyrights. The Librarian shall make appointments to such positions after consultation with the Register of Copyrights. Each Associate Register of Copyrights shall be paid at a rate not to exceed the maximum annual rate of basic pay payable for GS-18 of the General Schedule under section 5332 of title 5.

(Oct. 19, 1976, P. L. 94-553, Title I, § 101, 90 Stat. 2591; July 3, 1990, P.L. 101-319, § 2(b), 104 Stat. 290; Oct. 28, 1998, P. L. 105-304, Title IV, § 401(a)(2), (b), 112 Stat. 2887.)

§ 702 Copyright Office regulations

The Register of Copyrights is authorized to establish regulations not inconsistent with law for the administration of the functions and duties made the responsibility of the Register under this title. All regulations established by the Register under this title are subject to the approval of the Librarian of Congress.

(Oct. 19, 1976, P. L. 94-553, Title I, § 101, 90 Stat. 2591.)

§ 703 Effective date of actions in Copyright Office

In any case in which time limits are prescribed under this title for the performance of an action in the Copyright Office, and in which the last day of the prescribed period falls on a Saturday, Sunday, holiday, or other nonbusiness day within the District of Columbia or the Federal Government, the action may be taken on the next succeeding business day, and is effective as of the date when the period expired.

(Oct. 19, 1976, P. L. 94-553, Title I, § 101, 90 Stat. 2591.)

§ 704 Retention and disposition of articles deposited in Copyright Office

(a) Upon their deposit in the Copyright Office under sections 407 and 408, all copies, phonorecords, and identifying material, including those deposited in connection with claims that have been refused registration, are the property of the United States Government.

(b) In the case of published works, all copies, phonorecords, and identifying material deposited are available to the Library of Congress for its collections, or for exchange or transfer to any other library. In the case of unpublished works, the Library is entitled, under regulations that the Register of Copyrights shall prescribe, to select any deposits for its collections or for transfer to the National Archives of the United States or to a Federal records center, as defined in section 2901 of title 44.

(c) The Register of Copyrights is authorized, for specific or general categories of works, to make a facsimile reproduction of all or any part of the material deposited under section 408, and to make such reproduction a part of the Copyright Office records of the registration, before transferring such material to the Library of Congress as provided by subsection (b), or before destroying or otherwise disposing of such material as provided by subsection (d).

(d) Deposits not selected by the Library under subsection (b), or identifying portions or reproductions of them, shall be retained under the control of the Copyright Office, including retention in Government storage facilities, for the longest period considered practicable and desirable by the Register of Copyrights and the Librarian of Congress. After that period it is within the joint discretion of the Register and the Librarian to order their destruction or other disposition; but, in the case of unpublished works, no deposit shall be knowingly or intentionally destroyed or otherwise disposed of during its term of copyright unless a facsimile reproduction of the entire deposit has been made a part of the Copyright Office records as provided by subsection (c).

(e) The depositor of copies, phonorecords, or identifying material under section 408, or the copyright owner of record, may request retention, under the control of the Copyright Office, of one or more of such articles for the full term of copyright in the work. The Register of Copyrights shall prescribe, by regulation, the conditions under which such requests are to be made and granted, and shall fix the fee to be charged under section 708(a)(10) if the request is granted.

(Oct. 19, 1976, P. L. 94-553, Title I, § 101, 90 Stat. 2591; July 3, 1990, P. L. 101-318, § 2(c), 104 Stat. 288.)

§ 705 Copyright Office records: Preparation, maintenance, public inspection, and searching

(a) The Register of Copyrights shall ensure that records of deposits, registrations, recordations, and other actions taken under this title are maintained, and that indexes of such records are prepared.

(b) Such records and indexes, as well as the articles deposited in connection with completed copyright registrations and retained under the control of the Copyright Office, shall be open to public inspection.

(c) Upon request and payment of the fee specified by section 708, the Copyright Office shall make a search of its public records, indexes, and deposits, and shall furnish a report of the information they disclose with respect to any particular deposits, registrations, or recorded documents.

(Oct. 19, 1976, P. L. 94-553, Title I, § 101, 90 Stat. 2592; Oct. 27, 2000, P. L. 106-379, § 3(a)(2), 114 Stat. 1445.)

§ 706 Copies of Copyright Office records

(a) Copies may be made of any public records or indexes of the Copyright Office; additional certificates of copyright registration and copies of any public records or indexes may be furnished upon request and payment of the fees specified by section 708.

(b) Copies or reproductions of deposited articles retained under the control of the Copyright Office shall be authorized or furnished only under the conditions specified by the Copyright Office regulations.

(Oct. 19, 1976, P. L. 94-553, Title I, § 101, 90 Stat. 2592.)

§ 707 Copyright Office forms and publications

(a) **Catalog of Copyright Entries.** The Register of Copyrights shall compile and publish at periodic intervals catalogs of all copyright registrations. These catalogs shall be divided into parts in accordance with the various classes of works, and the Register has discretion to determine, on the basis of practicability and usefulness, the form and frequency of publication of each particular part.

(b) **Other Publications.** The Register shall furnish, free of charge upon request, application forms for copyright registration and general informational material in connection with the functions of the Copyright Office. The Register also has the authority to publish compilations of information, bibliographies, and other material he or she considers to be of value to the public.

(c) **Distribution of Publications.** All publications of the Copyright Office shall be furnished to depository libraries as specified under section 1905 of title 44, and, aside from those furnished free of charge, shall be offered for sale to the public at prices based on the cost of reproduction and distribution.

(Oct. 19, 1976, P. L. 94-553, Title I, § 101, 90 Stat. 2592.)

§ 708 Copyright Office fees

(a) **Fees.** Fees shall be paid to the Register of Copyrights—

(1) on filing each application under section 408 for registration of a copyright claim or for a supplementary registration, including the issuance of a certificate of registration if registration is made;

(2) on filing each application for registration of a claim for renewal of a subsisting copyright under section 304(a), including the issuance of a certificate of registration if registration is made;

(3) for the issuance of a receipt for a deposit under section 407;

(4) for the recordation, as provided by section 205, of a transfer of copyright ownership or other document;

(5) for the filing, under section 115(b), of a notice of intention to obtain a compulsory license;

(6) for the recordation, under section 302(c), of a statement revealing the identity of an author of an anonymous or pseudonymous work, or for the recordation, under section 302(d), of a statement relating to the death of an author;

(7) for the issuance, under section 706, of an additional certificate of registration;

(8) for the issuance of any other certification; and

(9) for the making and reporting of a search as provided by section 705, and for any related services.

The Register is authorized to fix fees for other services, including the cost of preparing copies of Copyright Office records, whether or not such copies are certified, based on the cost of providing the service.

(b) **Adjustment of Fees.** The Register of Copyrights may, by regulation, adjust the fees for the services specified in paragraphs (1) through (9) of subsection (a) in the following manner:

(1) The Register shall conduct a study of the costs incurred by the Copyright Office for the registration of claims, the recordation of documents, and the provision of services. The study shall also consider the timing of any adjustment in fees and the authority to use such fees consistent with the budget.

(2) The Register may, on the basis of the study under paragraph (1), and subject to paragraph (5), adjust fees to not more than that necessary to cover the reasonable costs incurred by the Copyright Office for the services described in paragraph (1), plus a reasonable inflation adjustment to account for any estimated increase in costs.

(3) Any fee established under paragraph (2) shall be rounded off to the nearest dollar, or for a fee less than $ 12, rounded off to the nearest 50 cents.

(4) Fees established under this subsection shall be fair and equitable and give due consideration to the objectives of the copyright system.

(5) If the Register determines under paragraph (2) that fees should be adjusted, the Register shall prepare a proposed fee schedule and submit the schedule with the accompanying economic analysis to the Congress. The fees proposed by the Register may be instituted after the end of 120 days after the schedule is submitted to the Congress unless, within that 120-day period, a law is enacted stating in substance that the Congress does not approve the schedule.

(c) The fees prescribed by or under this section are applicable to the United States Government and any of its agencies, employees, or officers, but the Register of Copyrights has discretion to waive the requirement of this subsection in occasional or isolated cases involving relatively small amounts.

(d) (1) Except as provided in paragraph (2), all fees received under this section shall be deposited by the Register of Copyrights in the Treasury of the United States and shall be credited to the appropriations for necessary expenses of the Copyright Office. Such fees that are collected shall remain available until expended. The Register may, in accordance with regulations that he or she shall prescribe, refund any sum paid by mistake or in excess of the fee required by this section.

(2) In the case of fees deposited against future services, the Register of Copyrights shall request the Secretary of the Treasury to invest in interest-bearing securities in the United States Treasury any portion of the fees that, as determined by the Register, is not required to meet current deposit account demands. Funds from such portion of fees shall be invested in securities that permit funds to be available to the Copyright Office at all times if they are determined to be necessary to meet current deposit account demands. Such investments shall be in public debt securities with maturities suitable to the needs of the Copyright Office, as determined by the Register of Copyrights, and bearing interest at rates determined by the Secretary of the Treasury, taking into consideration current market yields on outstanding marketable obligations of the United States of comparable maturities.

(3) The income on such investments shall be deposited in the Treasury of the United States and shall be credited to the appropriations for necessary expenses of the Copyright Office.

(Oct. 19, 1976, P. L. 94-553, Title I, § 101, 90 Stat. 2593; Aug. 5, 1977, P. L. 95-94, § 406(b), 91 Stat. 682; Oct. 15, 1982, P. L. 97-366, § 1, 96 Stat. 1759; July 3, 1990, P. L. 101-318, § 2, 104 Stat. 287; June 26, 1992, P. L. 102-307, Title I, § 102(f), 106 Stat. 266; Nov. 13, 1997, P. L. 105-80, § 7, 111 Stat. 1532; Oct. 27, 2000, P.L. 106-379, § 3(a)(3), 114 Stat. 1445.)

§ 709 Delay in delivery caused by disruption of postal or other services

In any case in which the Register of Copyrights determines, on the basis of such evidence as the Register may by regulation require, that a deposit, application, fee, or any other material to be delivered to the Copyright Office by a particular date, would have been received in the Copyright Office in due time except for a general disruption or suspension of postal or other transportation or communications services, the actual receipt of such material in the Copyright Office within one month after the date on which the Register determines that the disruption or suspension of such services has terminated, shall be considered timely.

(Oct. 19, 1976, P. L. 94-553, Title I, § 101, 90 Stat. 2594.)

§ 710 [Repealed]

[Editor's Note: This section (Act Oct. 19, 1976, P.L. 94-553, Title I, § 101, 90 Stat. 2594) was repealed by Act Oct. 27. 2000, P.L. 106-379, § 3(a)(1), 114 Stat. 1445 (effective on enactment, as provided by § 3(c)(1) of such Act). Prior to being repealed this section read as follows:§ 710. Reproduction for use of the blind and physically handicapped: Voluntary licensing forms and procedures

The Register of Copyrights shall, after consultation with the Chief of the Division for the Blind and Physically Handicapped and other appropriate officials of the Library of Congress, established by regulation standardized forms and procedures by which, at the time applications covering certain specified categories of nondramatic literary works are submitted for registration under section 408 of this title, the copyright owner may voluntarily grant to the Library of Congress a license to reproduce the copyrighted work by means of Braille or similar tactile symbols, or by fixation of a reading of the work in a phonorecord, or both, and to distribute the resulting copies or phonorecords solely for the use of the blind and physically handicapped and under limited conditions to be specified in the standardized forms.]

CHAPTER 8—PROCEEDINGS BY COPYRIGHT ROYALTY JUDGES

Section

§ 801 Copyright Royalty Judges; appointment and functions

(a) **Appointment.** The Librarian of Congress shall appoint 3 full-time Copyright Royalty Judges, and shall appoint 1 of the 3 as the Chief Copyright Royalty Judge. The Librarian shall make appointments to such positions after consultation with the Register of Copyrights.

(b) **Functions.** Subject to the provisions of this chapter [17 USCS §§ 801 et seq.], the functions of the Copyright Royalty Judges shall be as follows:

(1) To make determinations and adjustments of reasonable terms and rates of royalty payments as provided in sections 112(e), 114, 115, 116, 118, 119, and 1004 [17 USCS §§ 112(e), 114, 115, 116, 118, 119, and 1004]. The rates applicable under sections 114(f)(1)(B), 115, and 116 [17 USCS §§ 114(f)(1)(B), 115, and 116] shall be calculated to achieve the following objectives:

(A) To maximize the availability of creative works to the public.

(B) To afford the copyright owner a fair return for his or her creative work and the copyright user a fair income under existing economic conditions.

(C) To reflect the relative roles of the copyright owner and the copyright user in the product made available to the public with respect to relative creative contribution, technological contribution, capital investment, cost, risk, and contribution to the opening of new markets for creative expression and media for their communication.

(D) To minimize any disruptive impact on the structure of the industries involved and on generally prevailing industry practices.

(2) To make determinations concerning the adjustment of the copyright royalty rates under section 111 [17 USCS § 111] solely in accordance with the following provisions:

(A) The rates established by section 111(d)(1)(B) [17 USCS § 111(d)(1)(B)] may be adjusted to reflect—

(i) national monetary inflation or deflation; or

(ii) changes in the average rates charged cable subscribers for the basic service of providing secondary transmissions to maintain the real constant dollar level of the royalty fee per subscriber which existed as of the date of October 19, 1976, except that—

(I) if the average rates charged cable system subscribers for the basic service of providing secondary transmissions are changed so that the average rates exceed national monetary inflation, no change in the rates established by section 111(d)(1)(B) [17 USCS § 111(d)(1)(B)] shall be permitted; and

(II) no increase in the royalty fee shall be permitted based on any reduction in the average number of distant signal equivalents per subscriber.

The Copyright Royalty Judges may consider all factors relating to the maintenance of such level of payments, including, as an extenuating factor, whether the industry has been restrained by subscriber rate regulating authorities from increasing the rates for the basic service of providing secondary transmissions.

(B) In the event that the rules and regulations of the Federal Communications Commission are amended at any time after April 15, 1976, to permit the carriage by cable systems of additional television broadcast signals beyond the local service area of the primary transmitters of such signals, the royalty rates established by section 111(d)(1)(B) [17 USCS § 111(d)(1)(B)] may be adjusted to ensure that the rates for the additional distant signal equivalents resulting from such carriage are reasonable in the light of the changes effected by the amendment to such rules and regulations. In determining the reasonableness of rates proposed following an amendment of Federal Communications Commission rules and regulations, the Copyright Royalty Judges shall consider, among other factors, the economic impact on copyright owners and users; except that no adjustment in royalty rates shall be made under this subparagraph with respect to any distant signal equivalent or fraction thereof represented by—

(i) carriage of any signal permitted under the rules and regulations of the Federal Communications Commission in effect on April 15, 1976, or the carriage of a signal of the same type (that is, independent, network, or noncommercial educational) substituted for such permitted signal; or

(ii) a television broadcast signal first carried after April 15, 1976, pursuant to an individual waiver of the rules and regulations of the Federal Communications Commission, as such rules and regulations were in effect on April 15, 1976.

(C) In the event of any change in the rules and regulations of the Federal Communications Commission with respect to syndicated and sports program exclusivity after April 15, 1976, the rates established by section 111(d)(1)(B) [17 USCS § 111(d)(1)(B)] may be adjusted to assure that such rates are reasonable in light of the changes to such rules and regulations, but any such adjustment shall apply only to the affected television broadcast signals carried on those systems affected by the change.

(D) The gross receipts limitations established by section 111(d)(1)(C) and (D) [17 USCS § 111(d)(1)(C) and (D)] shall be adjusted to reflect national monetary inflation or deflation or changes in the average rates charged cable system subscribers for the basic service of providing secondary transmissions to maintain the real constant dollar value of the exemption provided by such section, and the royalty rate specified therein shall not be subject to adjustment.

(3) (A) To authorize the distribution, under sections 111, 119, and 1007 [17 USCS §§ 111, 119, and 1007], of those royalty fees collected under sections 111, 119, and 1005 [17 USCS §§ 111, 119, and 1005], as the case may be, to the extent that the Copyright Royalty Judges have found that the distribution of such fees is not subject to controversy.

(B) In cases where the Copyright Royalty Judges determine that controversy exists, the Copyright Royalty Judges shall determine the distribution of such fees, including partial distributions, in accordance with section 111, 119, or 1007 [17 USCS § 111, 119, or 1007], as the case may be.

(C) Notwithstanding section 804(b)(8) [17 USCS § 804(b)(8)], the Copyright Royalty Judges, at any time after the filing of claims under section 111, 119, or 1007 [17 USCS § 111, 119, or 1007], may, upon motion of one or more of the claimants and after publication in the Federal Register of a request for responses to the motion from interested claimants, make a partial distribution of such fees, if, based upon all responses received during the 30-day period beginning on the date of such publication, the Copyright Royalty Judges conclude that no claimant entitled to receive such fees has stated a reasonable objection to the partial distribution, and all such claimants—

(i) agree to the partial distribution;

(ii) sign an agreement obligating them to return any excess amounts to the extent necessary to comply with the final determination on the distribution of the fees made under subparagraph (B);

(iii) file the agreement with the Copyright Royalty Judges; and

(iv) agree that such funds are available for distribution.

(D) The Copyright Royalty Judges and any other officer or employee acting in good faith in distributing funds under subparagraph (C) shall not be held liable for the payment of any excess fees under subparagraph (C). The Copyright Royalty Judges shall, at the time the final determination is made, calculate any such excess amounts.

(4) To accept or reject royalty claims filed under sections 111, 119, and 1007 [17 USCS §§ 111, 119, and 1007], on the basis of timeliness or the failure to establish the basis for a claim.

(5) To accept or reject rate adjustment petitions as provided in section 804 [17 USCS § 804] and petitions to participate as provided in section 803(b)(1) and (2) [17 USCS § 803(b)(1) and (2)].

(6) To determine the status of a digital audio recording device or a digital audio interface device under sections 1002 and 1003 [17 USCS §§ 1002 and 1003], as provided in section 1010 [17 USCS § 1010].

(7) (A) To adopt as a basis for statutory terms and rates or as a basis for the distribution of statutory royalty payments, an agreement concerning such matters reached among some or all of the participants in a proceeding at any time during the proceeding, except that—

(i) the Copyright Royalty Judges shall provide to those that would be bound by the terms, rates, or other determination set by any agreement in a proceeding to determine royalty rates an opportunity to comment on the agreement and shall provide to participants in the proceeding under section 803(b)(2) [17 USCS § 803(b)(2)] that would be bound by the terms, rates, or other determination set by the agreement an opportunity to comment on the agreement and object to its adoption as a basis for statutory terms and rates; and

(ii) the Copyright Royalty Judges may decline to adopt the agreement as a basis for statutory terms and rates for participants that are not parties to the agreement, if any participant described in clause (i) objects to the agreement and the Copyright Royalty Judges conclude, based on the record before them if one exists, that the agreement does not provide a reasonable basis for setting statutory terms or rates.

(B) License agreements voluntarily negotiated pursuant to section 112(e)(5), 114(f)(3), 115(c)(3)(E)(i), 116(c), or 118(b)(2) [17 USCS § 112(e)(5), 114(f)(3), 115(c)(3)(E)(i), 116(c), or 118(b)(2)] that do not result in statutory terms and rates shall not be subject to clauses (i) and (ii) of subparagraph (A).

(C) Interested parties may negotiate and agree to, and the Copyright Royalty Judges may adopt, an agreement that specifies as terms notice and recordkeeping requirements that apply in lieu of those that would otherwise apply under regulations.

(8) To perform other duties, as assigned by the Register of Copyrights within the Library of Congress, except as provided in section 802(g) [17 USCS § 802(g)], at times when Copyright Royalty Judges are not engaged in performing the other duties set forth in this section.

(c) **Rulings.** The Copyright Royalty Judges may make any necessary procedural or evidentiary rulings in any proceeding under this chapter [17 USCS §§ 801 et seq.] and may, before commencing a proceeding under this chapter [17 USCS §§ 801 et seq.], make any such rulings that would apply to the proceedings conducted by the Copyright Royalty Judges.

(d) **Administrative Support.** The Librarian of Congress shall provide the Copyright Royalty Judges with the necessary administrative services related to proceedings under this chapter [17 USCS §§ 801 et seq.].

(e) **Location in Library of Congress.** The offices of the Copyright Royalty Judges and staff shall be in the Library of Congress.

(f) **Effective Date of Actions.** On and after the date of the enactment of the Copyright Royalty and Distribution Reform Act of 2004 [enacted Nov. 30, 2004], in any case in which time limits are prescribed under this title for performance of an action with or by the Copyright Royalty Judges, and in which the last day of the prescribed period falls on a Saturday, Sunday, holiday, or other nonbusiness day within the District of Columbia or the Federal Government, the action may be taken on the next succeeding business day, and is effective as of the date when the period expired.

(Added Act Nov. 30, 2004, P. L. 108-419, § 3(a), 118 Stat. 2341; This section took effect six months after enactment, pursuant to § 6(a) of Act Nov. 30, 2004, P.L. 108-419; October 6, 2006, P.L. 109-303, §§ 3, 5, 120 Stat. 1478.)

§ 802 Copyright Royalty Judgeships; staff

(a) **Qualifications of Copyright Royalty Judges.**

(1) *In general.* Each Copyright Royalty Judge shall be an attorney who has at least 7 years of legal experience. The Chief Copyright Royalty Judge shall have at least 5 years of experience in adjudications, arbitrations, or court trials. Of the other 2 Copyright Royalty Judges, 1 shall have significant knowledge of copyright law, and the other shall have significant knowledge of economics. An individual may serve as a Copyright Royalty Judge only if the individual is free of any financial conflict of interest under subsection (h).

(2) *Definition.* In this subsection, the term "adjudication" has the meaning given that term in section 551 of title 5 [5 USCS § 551], but does not include mediation.

(b) **Staff.** The Chief Copyright Royalty Judge shall hire 3 full-time staff members to assist the Copyright Royalty Judges in performing their functions.

(c) **Terms.** The individual first appointed as the Chief Copyright Royalty Judge shall be appointed to a term of 6 years, and of the remaining individuals first appointed as Copyright Royalty Judges, 1 shall be appointed to a term of 4 years, and the other shall be appointed to a term of 2 years. Thereafter, the terms of succeeding Copyright Royalty Judges shall each be 6 years. An individual serving as a Copyright Royalty Judge may be reappointed to subsequent terms. The term of a Copyright Royalty Judge shall begin when the term of the predecessor of that Copyright Royalty Judge ends. When the term of office of a Copyright Royalty Judge ends, the individual serving that term may continue to serve until a successor is selected.

(d) **Vacancies or Incapacity.**

(1) *Vacancies.* If a vacancy should occur in the position of Copyright Royalty Judge, the Librarian of Congress shall act expeditiously to fill the vacancy, and may appoint an interim Copyright Royalty Judge to serve until another Copyright Royalty Judge is appointed under this section. An individual appointed to fill the vacancy occurring before the expiration of the term for which the predecessor of that individual was appointed shall be appointed for the remainder of that term.

(2) *Incapacity.* In the case in which a Copyright Royalty Judge is temporarily unable to perform his or her duties, the Librarian of Congress may appoint an interim Copyright Royalty Judge to perform such duties during the period of such incapacity.

(e) **Compensation.**

(1) *Judges.* The Chief Copyright Royalty Judge shall receive compensation at the rate of basic pay payable for level AL-1 for administrative law judges pursuant to section 5372(b) of title 5, and each of the other two Copyright Royalty Judges shall receive compensation at the rate of basic

pay payable for level AL-2 for administrative law judges pursuant to such section. The compensation of the Copyright Royalty Judges shall not be subject to any regulations adopted by the Office of Personnel Management pursuant to its authority under section 5376(b)(1) of title 5.

(2) *Staff members.* Of the staff members appointed under subsection (b)—

(A) the rate of pay of 1 staff member shall be not more than the basic rate of pay payable for level 10 of GS-15 of the General Schedule;

(B) the rate of pay of 1 staff member shall be not less than the basic rate of pay payable for GS-13 of the General Schedule and not more than the basic rate of pay payable for level 10 of GS-14 of such Schedule; and

(C) the rate of pay for the third staff member shall be not less than the basic rate of pay payable for GS-8 of the General Schedule and not more than the basic rate of pay payable for level 10 of GS-11 of such Schedule.

(3) *Locality pay.* All rates of pay referred to under this subsection shall include locality pay.

(f) **Independence of Copyright Royalty Judge.**

(1) *In making determinations.*

(A) In general.

(i) Subject to subparagraph (B) and clause (ii) of this subparagraph, the Copyright Royalty Judges shall have full independence in making determinations concerning adjustments and determinations of copyright royalty rates and terms, the distribution of copyright royalties, the acceptance or rejection of royalty claims, rate adjustment petitions, and petitions to participate, and in issuing other rulings under this title, except that the Copyright Royalty Judges may consult with the Register of Copyrights on any matter other than a question of fact.

(ii) One or more Copyright Royalty Judges may, or by motion to the Copyright Royalty Judges, any participant in a proceeding may, request from the Register of Copyrights an interpretation of any material questions of substantive law that relate to the construction of provisions of this title and arise in the course of the proceeding. Any request for a written interpretation shall be in writing and on the record, and reasonable provision shall be made to permit participants in the proceeding to comment on the material questions of substantive law in a manner that minimizes duplication and delay. Except as provided in subparagraph (B), the Register of Copyrights shall deliver to the Copyright

Royalty Judges a written response within 14 days after the receipt of all briefs and comments from the participants. The Copyright Royalty Judges shall apply the legal interpretation embodied in the response of the Register of Copyrights if it is timely delivered, and the response shall be included in the record that accompanies the final determination. The authority under this clause shall not be construed to authorize the Register of Copyrights to provide an interpretation of questions of procedure before the Copyright Royalty Judges, the ultimate adjustments and determinations of copyright royalty rates and terms, the ultimate distribution of copyright royalties, or the acceptance or rejection of royalty claims, rate adjustment petitions, or petitions to participate in a proceeding.

(B) Novel questions.

(i) In any case in which a novel material question of substantive law concerning an interpretation of those provisions of this title that are the subject of the proceeding is presented, the Copyright Royalty Judges shall request a decision of the Register of Copyrights, in writing, to resolve such novel question. Reasonable provision shall be made for comment on such request by the participants in the proceeding, in such a wayas to minimize duplication and delay. The Register of Copyrights shall transmit his or her decision to the Copyright Royalty Judges within 30 days after the Register of Copyrights receives all of the briefs or comments of the participants. Such decision shall be in writing and included by the Copyright Royalty Judges in the record that accompanies their final determination. If such a decision is timely delivered to the Copyright Royalty Judges, the Copyright Royalty Judges shall apply the legal determinations embodied in the decision of the Register of Copyrights in resolving material questions of substantive law.

(ii) In clause (i), a 'novel question of law' is a question of law that has not been determined in prior decisions, determinations, and rulings described in section 803(a) [17 USCS § 803(a)].

(C) Consultation. Notwithstanding the provisions of subparagraph (A), the Copyright Royalty Judges shall consult with the Register of Copyrights with respect to any determination or ruling that would require that any act be performed by the Copyright Office, and any such determination or ruling shall not be binding upon the Register of Copyrights.

(D) Review of legal conclusions by the Register of Copyrights. The Register of Copyrights may review for legal error the resolution by the Copyright Royalty Judges of a material question of substantive law under this title that underlies or is contained in a final determination of the Copyright Royalty Judges. If the Register of Copyrights concludes, after taking into consideration the views of the participants in the proceeding, that any resolution reached by the Copyright Royalty Judges was in material error, the Register of Copyrights shall issue a written decision correcting such legal error, which shall be made part of the record of the proceeding. The Register of Copyrights shall issue such written decision not later than 60 days after the date on which the final determination by the Copyright Royalty Judges is issued. Additionally, the Register of Copyrights shall cause to be published in the Federal Register such written decision, together with a specific identification of the legal conclusion of the Copyright Royalty Judges that is determined to be erroneous. As to conclusions of substantive law involving an interpretation of the statutory provisions of this title, the decision of the Register of Copyrights shall be binding as precedent upon the Copyright Royalty Judges in subsequent proceedings under this chapter [17 USCS §§ 801 et seq.]. When a decision has been rendered pursuant to this subparagraph, the Register of Copyrights may, on the basis of and in accordance with such decision, intervene as of right in any appeal of a final determination of the Copyright Royalty Judges pursuant to section 803(d) [17 USCS § 803(d)] in the United States Court of Appeals for the District of Columbia Circuit. If, prior to intervening in such an appeal, the Register of Copyrights gives notification to, and undertakes to consult with, the Attorney General with respect to such intervention, and the Attorney General fails, within a reasonable period after receiving such notification, to intervene in such appeal, the Register of Copyrights may intervene in such appeal in his or her own name by any attorney designated by the Register of Copyrights for such purpose. Intervention by the Register of Copyrights in his or her own name shall not preclude the Attorney General from intervening on behalf of the United States in such an appeal as may be otherwise provided or required by law.

(E) Effect on judicial review. Nothing in this section shall be interpreted to alter the standard applied by a court in reviewing legal determinations involving an interpretation or construction of the provisions of this title or to affect the extent to which any construction or interpretation of the provisions of this title shall be accorded deference by a reviewing court.

(2) *Performance appraisals.*

(A) In general. Notwithstanding any other provision of law or any regulation of the Library of Congress, and subject to subparagraph (B), the Copyright Royalty Judges shall not receive performance appraisals.

(B) Relating to sanction or removal. To the extent that the Librarian of Congress adopts regulations under subsection (h) relating to the sanction or removal of a Copyright Royalty Judge and such regulations require documentation to establish the cause of such sanction or removal, the Copyright Royalty Judge may receive an appraisal related specifically to the cause of the sanction or removal.

(g) **Inconsistent Duties Barred.** No Copyright Royalty Judge may undertake duties that conflict with his or her duties and responsibilities as a Copyright Royalty Judge.

(h) **Standards of Conduct.** The Librarian of Congress shall adopt regulations regarding the standards of conduct, including financial conflict of interest and restrictions against ex parte communications, which shall govern the Copyright Royalty Judges and the proceedings under this chapter [17 USCS §§ 801 et seq.].

(i) **Removal or Sanction.** The Librarian of Congress may sanction or remove a Copyright Royalty Judge for violation of the standards of conduct adopted under subsection (h), misconduct, neglect of duty, or any disqualifying physical or mental disability. Any such sanction or removal may be made only after notice and opportunity for a hearing, but the Librarian of Congress may suspend the Copyright Royalty Judge during the pendency of such hearing. The Librarian shall appoint an interim Copyright Royalty Judge during the period of any such suspension.

(Added Act Nov. 30, 2004, P.L. 108-419, § 3(a), 118 Stat. 2345; October 6, 2006, P.L. 109-303, § 3, 120 Stat. 1478. This section took effect six months after enactment, pursuant to § 6(a) of Act Nov. 30, 2004, P.L. 108-419, which appears as 17 USCS § 801 note.)

§ 803 Proceedings of Copyright Royalty Judges

(a) **Proceedings.**

(1) *In general.* The Copyright Royalty Judges shall act in accordance with this title, and to the extent not inconsistent with this title, in accordance with subchapter II of chapter 5 of title 5 [5 USCS §§ 551 et seq.], in carrying out the purposes set forth in section 801 [17 USCS § 801]. The Copyright Royalty Judges shall act in accordance with regulations issued by the Copyright Royalty Judges and the Librarian of Congress, and on the basis of a written record, prior determinations and interpretations of the Copyright Royalty Tribunal, Librarian of Congress, the Register of Copyrights, copyright arbitration royalty panels (to the extent those determinations are not inconsistent with a decision of the Librarian of Congress or the Register of Copyrights), and the Copyright Royalty Judges (to the extent those determinations are not inconsistent with a decision of the Register of Copyrights that was timely delivered to the Copyright Royalty Judges pursuant to section 802(f)(1)(A) or

(B) [17 USCS § 802(f)(1)(A) or (B)], or with a decision of the Register of Copyrights pursuant to section 802(f)(1)(D) [17 USCS § 802(f)(1)(D)]), under this chapter [17 USCS §§ 801 et seq.], and decisions of the court of appeals under this chapter [17 USCS §§ 801 et seq.] before, on, or after the effective date of the Copyright Royalty and Distribution Reform Act of 2004 [effective May 30, 2005].

(2) *Judges acting as panel and individually.* The Copyright Royalty Judges shall preside over hearings in proceedings under this chapter [17 USCS §§ 801 et seq.] en banc. The Chief Copyright Royalty Judge may designate a Copyright Royalty Judge to preside individually over such collateral and administrative proceedings, and over such proceedings under paragraphs (1) through (5) of subsection (b), as the Chief Judge considers appropriate.

(3) *Determinations.* Final determinations of the Copyright Royalty Judges in proceedings under this chapter [17 USCS §§ 801 et seq.] shall be made by majority vote. A Copyright Royalty Judge dissenting from the majority on any determination under this chapter [17 USCS §§ 801 et seq.] may issue his or her dissenting opinion, which shall be included with the determination.

(b) **Procedures.**

(1) *Initiation.*

(A) Call for petitions to participate.

(i) The Copyright Royalty Judges shall cause to be published in the Federal Register notice of commencement of proceedings under this chapter [17 USCS §§ 801 et seq.], calling for the filing of petitions to participate in a proceeding under this chapter [17 USCS §§ 801 et seq.] for the purpose of making the relevant determination under section 111, 112, 114, 115, 116, 118, 119, 1004, or 1007 [17 USCS § 111, 112, 114, 115, 116, 118, 119, 1004, or 1007], as the case may be—

(I) promptly upon a determination made under section 804(a) [17 USCS § 804(a)];

(II) by no later than January 5 of a year specified in paragraph (2) of section 804(b) [17 USCS § 804(b)] for the commencement of proceedings;

(III) by no later than January 5 of a year specified in subparagraph (A) or (B) of paragraph (3) of section 804(b) [17 USCS § 804(b)] for the commencement of proceedings, or as otherwise provided in subparagraph (A) or (C) of such paragraph for the commencement of proceedings;

(IV) as provided under section 804(b)(8) [17 USCS § 804(b)(8)]; or

(V) by no later than January 5 of a year specified in any other provision of section 804(b) [17 USCS § 804(b)] for the filing of petitions for the commencement of proceedings, if a petition has not been filed by that date, except that the publication of notice requirement shall not apply in the case of proceedings under section 111 [17 USCS § 111] that are scheduled to commence in 2005.

(ii) Petitions to participate shall be filed by no later than 30 days after publication of notice of commencement of a proceeding under clause (i), except that the Copyright Royalty Judges may, for substantial good cause shown and if there is no prejudice to the participants that have already filed petitions, accept late petitions to participate at any time up to the date that is 90 days before the date on which participants in the proceeding are to file their written direct statements. Notwithstanding the preceding sentence, petitioners whose petitions are filed more than 30 days after publication of notice of commencement of a proceeding are not eligible to object to a settlement reached during the voluntary negotiation period under paragraph (3), and any objection filed by such a petitioner shall not be taken into account by the Copyright Royalty Judges.

(B) Petitions to participate. Each petition to participate in a proceeding shall describe the petitioner's interest in the subject matter of the proceeding. Parties with similar interests may file a single petition to participate.

(2) *Participation in general.* Subject to paragraph (4), a person may participate in a proceeding under this chapter [17 USCS §§ 801 et seq.], including through the submission of briefs or other information, only if—

(A) that person has filed a petition to participate in accordance with paragraph (1) (either individually or as a group under paragraph (1)(B));

(B) the Copyright Royalty Judges have not determined that the petition to participate is facially invalid;

(C) the Copyright Royalty Judges have not determined, sua sponte or on the motion of another participant in the proceeding, that the person lacks a significant interest in the proceeding; and

(D) the petition to participate is accompanied by either—

(i) in a proceeding to determine royalty rates, a filing fee of $150; or

(ii) in a proceeding to determine distribution of royalty fees—

(I) a filing fee of $150; or

(II) a statement that the petitioner (individually or as a group) will not seek a distribution of more than $1000, in which case the amount distributed to the petitioner shall not exceed $1000.

(3) *Voluntary negotiation period.*

(A) Commencement of proceedings.

(i) Rate adjustment proceeding. Promptly after the date for filing of petitions to participate in a proceeding, the Copyright Royalty Judges shall make available to all participants in the proceeding a list of such participants and shall initiate a voluntary negotiation period among the participants.

(ii) Distribution proceeding. Promptly after the date for filing of petitions to participate in a proceeding to determine the distribution of royalties, the Copyright Royalty Judges shall make available to all participants in the proceeding a list of such participants. The initiation of a voluntary negotiation period among the participants shall be set at a time determined by the Copyright Royalty Judges.

(B) Length of proceedings. The voluntary negotiation period initiated under subparagraph (A) shall be 3 months.

(C) Determination of subsequent proceedings. At the close of the voluntary negotiation proceedings, the Copyright Royalty Judges shall, if further proceedings under this chapter [17 USCS §§ 801 et seq.] are necessary, determine whether and to what extent paragraphs (4) and (5) will apply to the parties.

(4) *Small claims procedure in distribution proceedings.*

(A) In general. If, in a proceeding under this chapter [17 USCS §§ 801 et seq.] to determine the distribution of royalties, the contested amount of a claim is $10,000 or less, the Copyright Royalty Judges shall decide the controversy on the basis of the filing of the written direct statement by the participant, the response by any opposing participant, and 1 additional response by each such party.

(B) Bad faith inflation of claim. If the Copyright Royalty Judges determine that a participant asserts in bad faith an amount in controversy in excess of $10,000 for the purpose of avoiding a determination under the procedure set forth in subparagraph (A), the Copyright Royalty Judges shall impose a fine on that participant in an amount not to exceed the difference between the actual amount distributed and the amount asserted by the participant.

(5) *Paper proceedings.* The Copyright Royalty Judges in proceedings under this chapter [17 USCS §§ 801 et seq.] may decide, sua sponte or upon motion of a participant, to determine issues on the basis of the filing of the written direct statement by the participant, the response by any opposing participant, and one additional response by each such participant. Prior to making such decision to proceed on such a paper record only, the Copyright Royalty Judges shall offer to all parties to the proceeding the opportunity to comment on the decision. The procedure under this paragraph—

(A) shall be applied in cases in which there is no genuine issue of material fact, there is no need for evidentiary hearings, and all participants in the proceeding agree in writing to the procedure; and

(B) may be applied under such other circumstances as the Copyright Royalty Judges consider appropriate.

(6) *Regulations.*

(A) In general. The Copyright Royalty Judges may issue regulations to carry out their functions under this title. All regulations issued by the Copyright Royalty Judges are subject to the approval of the Librarian of Congress. Not later than 120 days after Copyright Royalty Judges or interim Copyright Royalty Judges, as the case may be, are first appointed after the enactment of the Copyright Royalty and Distribution Reform Act of 2004 (enacted Nov. 30, 2004), such judges shall issue regulations to govern proceedings under this chapter [17 USCS §§ 801 et seq.].

(B) Interim regulations. Until regulations are adopted under subparagraph (A), the Copyright Royalty Judges shall apply the regulations in effect under this chapter [17 USCS §§ 801 et seq.] on the day before the effective date of the Copyright Royalty and Distribution Reform Act of 2004 [effective May 30, 2005], to the extent such regulations are not inconsistent with this chapter [17 USCS §§ 801 et seq.], except that functions carried out under such regulations by the Librarian of Congress, the Register of Copyrights, or copyright arbitration royalty panels that, as of such date of enactment, are to be carried out by the Copyright Royalty Judges under this chapter [17 USCS §§ 801 et seq.], shall be carried out by the Copyright Royalty Judges under such regulations.

(C) Requirements. Regulations issued under subparagraph (A) shall include the following:

(i) The written direct statements and written rebuttal statements of all participants in a proceeding under paragraph (2) shall be filed by a date specified by the Copyright Royalty Judges, which, in the case of written direct statements, may be not earlier than 4 months, and not later than

5 months, after the end of the voluntary negotiation period under paragraph (3). Notwithstanding the preceding sentence, the Copyright Royalty Judges may allow a participant in a proceeding to file an amended written direct statement based on new information received during the discovery process, within 15 days after the end of the discovery period specified in clause (iv).

(ii) (I) Following the submission to the Copyright Royalty Judges of written direct statements and written rebuttal statements by the participants in a proceeding under paragraph (2), the Copyright Royalty Judges, after taking into consideration the views of the participants in the proceeding, shall determine a schedule for conducting and completing discovery.

(II) In this chapter [17 USCS §§ 801 et seq.], the term "written direct statements" means witness statements, testimony, and exhibits to be presented in the proceedings, and such other information that is necessary to establish terms and rates, or the distribution of royalty payments, as the case may be, as set forth in regulations issued by the Copyright Royalty Judges.

(iii) Hearsay may be admitted in proceedings under this chapter [17 USCS §§ 801 et seq.] to the extent deemed appropriate by the Copyright Royalty Judges.

(iv) Discovery in connection with written direct statements shall be permitted for a period of 60 days, except for discovery ordered by the Copyright Royalty Judges in connection with the resolution of motions, orders, and disputes pending at the end of such period. The Copyright Royalty Judges may order a discovery schedule in connection with written rebuttal statements.

(v) Any participant under paragraph (2) in a proceeding under this chapter [17 USCS §§ 801 et seq.] to determine royalty rates may request of an opposing participant nonprivileged documents directly related to the written direct statement or written rebuttal statement of that participant. Any objection to such a request shall be resolved by a motion or request to compel production made to the Copyright Royalty Judges in accordance with regulations adopted by the Copyright Royalty Judges. Each motion or request to compel discovery shall be determined by the Copyright Royalty Judges, or by a Copyright Royalty Judge when permitted under subsection (a)(2). Upon such motion, the Copyright Royalty Judges may order discovery pursuant to regulations established under this paragraph.

(vi) (I) Any participant under paragraph (2) in a proceeding under this chapter [17 USCS §§ 801 et seq.] to determine royalty rates may, by means of written motion or on the record, request of an opposing participant or witness other relevant information and materials if, absent the discovery sought, the Copyright Royalty Judges' resolution of the proceeding would be substantially impaired. In determining whether discovery will be granted under this clause, the Copyright Royalty Judges may consider—

(aa) whether the burden or expense of producing the requested information or materials outweighs the likely benefit, taking into account the needs and resources of the participants, the importance of the issues at stake, and the probative value of the requested information or materials in resolving such issues;

(bb) whether the requested information or materials would be unreasonably cumulative or duplicative, or are obtainable from another source that is more convenient, less burdensome, or less expensive; and

(cc) whether the participant seeking discovery has had ample opportunity by discovery in the proceeding or by other means to obtain the information sought.

(II) This clause shall not apply to any proceeding scheduled to commence after December 31, 2010.

(vii) In a proceeding under this chapter [17 USCS §§ 801 et seq.] to determine royalty rates, the participants entitled to receive royalties shall collectively be permitted to take no more than 10 depositions and secure responses to no more than 25 interrogatories, and the participants obligated to pay royalties shall collectively be permitted to take no more than 10 depositions and secure responses to no more than 25 interrogatories. The Copyright Royalty Judges shall resolve any disputes among similarly aligned participants to allocate the number of depositions or interrogatories permitted under this clause.

(viii) The rules and practices in effect on the day before the effective date of the Copyright Royalty and Distribution Reform Act of 2004 [effective May 30, 2005], relating to discovery in proceedings under this chapter [17 USCS §§ 801 et seq.] to determine the distribution of royalty fees, shall continue to apply to such proceedings on and after such effective date.

(ix) In proceedings to determine royalty rates, the Copyright Royalty Judges may issue a subpoena commanding a participant or witness to appear and give testimony, or to produce and permit inspection of documents or tangible things, if the Copyright Royalty Judges' resolution of the proceeding would be substantially impaired by the absence of such testimony or production of documents or tangible things. Such subpoena shall specify with reasonable particularity the materials to be produced or the scope and nature of the required testimony. Nothing in this clause shall preclude the Copyright Royalty Judges from requesting the production by a nonparticipant of information or materials relevant to the resolution by the Copyright Royalty Judges of a material issue of fact.

(x) The Copyright Royalty Judges shall order a settlement conference among the participants in the proceeding to facilitate the presentation of offers of settlement among the participants. The settlement conference shall be held during a 21-day period following the 60-day discovery period specified in clause (iv) and shall take place outside the presence of the Copyright Royalty Judges.

(xi) No evidence, including exhibits, may be submitted in the written direct statement or written rebuttal statement of a participant without a sponsoring witness, except where the Copyright Royalty Judges have taken official notice, or in the case of incorporation by reference of past records, or for good cause shown.

(c) **Determination of Copyright Royalty Judges.**

(1) *Timing.* The Copyright Royalty Judges shall issue their determination in a proceeding not later than 11 months after the conclusion of the 21-day settlement conference period under subsection (b)(6)(C)(x), but, in the case of a proceeding to determine successors to rates or terms that expire on a specified date, in no event later than 15 days before the expiration of the then current statutory rates and terms.

(2) *Rehearings.*

(A) In general The Copyright Royalty Judges may, in exceptional cases, upon motion of a participant in a proceeding under subsection (b)(2), order a rehearing, after the determination in the proceeding is issued under paragraph (1), on such matters as the Copyright Royalty Judges determine to be appropriate.

(B) Timing for filing motion. Any motion for a rehearing under subparagraph (A) may only be filed within 15 days after the date on which the Copyright Royalty Judges deliver to the participants in the proceeding their initial determination.

(C) Participation by opposing party not required. In any case in which a rehearing is ordered, any opposing party shall not be required to participate in the rehearing, except that nonparticipation may give rise to the limitations with respect to judicial review provided for in subsection (d)(1).

(D) No negative inference. No negative inference shall be drawn from lack of participation in a rehearing.

(E) Continuity of rates and terms.

(i) If the decision of the Copyright Royalty Judges on any motion for a rehearing is not rendered before the expiration of the statutory rates and terms that were previously in effect, in the case of a proceeding to determine successors to rates and terms that expire on a specified date, then—

(I) the initial determination of the Copyright Royalty Judges that is the subject of the rehearing motion shall be effective as of the day following the date on which the rates and terms that were previously in effect expire; and

(II) in the case of a proceeding under section 114(f)(1)(C) or 114(f)(2)(C) [17 USCS § 114(f)(1)(C) or 114(f)(2)(C)], royalty rates and terms shall, for purposes of section 114(f)(4)(B) [17 USCS § 114(f)(4)(B)], be deemed to have been set at those rates and terms contained in the initial determination of the Copyright Royalty Judges that is the subject of the rehearing motion, as of the date of that determination.

(ii) The pendency of a motion for a rehearing under this paragraph shall not relieve persons obligated to make royalty payments who would be affected by the determination on that motion from providing the statements of account and any reports of use, to the extent required, and paying the royalties required under the relevant determination or regulations.

(iii) Notwithstanding clause (ii), whenever royalties described in clause (ii) are paid to a person other than the Copyright Office, the entity designated by the Copyright Royalty Judges to which such royalties are paid by the copyright user (and any successor thereto) shall, within 60 days after the motion for rehearing is resolved or, if the motion is granted, within 60 days after the rehearing is concluded, return any excess amounts previously paid to the extent necessary to comply with the final determination of royalty rates by the Copyright Royalty Judges. Any underpayment of royalties resulting from a rehearing shall be paid within the same period.

(3) *Contents of determination.* A determination of the Copyright Royalty Judges shall be supported by the written record and shall set forth the findings of fact relied on by the Copyright Royalty Judges. Among other terms adopted in a determination, the Copyright Royalty Judges may specify notice and recordkeeping requirements of users of the copyrights at issue that apply in lieu of those that would otherwise apply under regulations.

(4) *Continuing jurisdiction.* The Copyright Royalty Judges may issue an amendment to a written determination to correct any technical or clerical errors in the determination or to modify the terms, but not the rates, of royalty payments in response to unforeseen circumstances that would frustrate the proper implementation of such determination. Such amendment shall be set forth in a written addendum to the determination that shall be distributed to the participants of the proceeding and shall be published in the Federal Register.

(5) *Protective order.* The Copyright Royalty Judges may issue such orders as may be appropriate to protect confidential information, including orders excluding confidential information from the record of the determination that is published or made available to the public, except that any terms or rates of royalty payments or distributions may not be excluded.

(6) *Publication of determination.* By no later than the end of the 60-day period provided in section 802(f)(1)(D) [17 USCS § 802(f)(1)(D)], the Librarian of Congress shall cause the determination, and any corrections thereto, to be published in the Federal Register. The Librarian of Congress shall also publicize the determination and corrections in such other manner as the Librarian considers appropriate, including, but not limited to, publication on the Internet. The Librarian of Congress shall also make the determination, corrections, and the accompanying record available for public inspection and copying.

(7) *Late payment.* A determination of the Copyright Royalty Judges may include terms with respect to late payment, but in no way shall such terms prevent the copyright holder from asserting other rights or remedies provided under this title.

(d) **Judicial Review.**

(1) *Appeal.* Any determination of the Copyright Royalty Judges under subsection (c) may, within 30 days after the publication of the determination in the Federal Register, be appealed, to the United States Court of Appeals for the District of Columbia Circuit, by any aggrieved participant in the proceeding under subsection (b)(2) who fully participated in the proceeding and who would be bound by the determination. Any participant that did not participate in a rehearing may not raise any issue that was the subject of that rehearing at any stage of judicial review of the hearing determination. If no appeal is brought within that 30-day

period, the determination of the Copyright Royalty Judges shall be final, and the royalty fee or determination with respect to the distribution of fees, as the case may be, shall take effect as set forth in paragraph (2).

(2) *Effect of rates.*

(A) Expiration on specified date. When this title provides that the royalty rates and terms that were previously in effect are to expire on a specified date, any adjustment or determination by the Copyright Royalty Judges of successor rates and terms for an ensuing statutory license period shall be effective as of the day following the date of expiration of the rates and terms that were previously in effect, even if the determination of the Copyright Royalty Judges is rendered on a later date. A licensee shall be obligated to continue making payments under the rates and terms previously in effect until such time as rates and terms for the successor period are established. Whenever royalties pursuant to this section are paid to a person other than the Copyright Office, the entity designated by the Copyright Royalty Judges to which such royalties are paid by the copyright user (and any successor thereto) shall, within 60 days after the final determination of the Copyright Royalty Judges establishing rates and terms for a successor period or the exhaustion of all rehearings or appeals of such determination, if any, return any excess amounts previously paid to the extent necessary to comply with the final determination of royalty rates. Any underpayment of royalties by a copyright user shall be paid to the entity designated by the Copyright Royalty Judges within the same period.

(B) Other cases. In cases where rates and terms have not, prior to the inception of an activity, been established for that particular activity under the relevant license, such rates and terms shall be retroactive to the inception of activity under the relevant license covered by such rates and terms. In other cases where rates and terms do not expire on a specified date, successor rates and terms shall take effect on the first day of the second month that begins after the publication of the determination of the Copyright Royalty Judges in the Federal Register, except as otherwise provided in this title, or by the Copyright Royalty Judges, or as agreed by the participants in a proceeding that would be bound by the rates and terms. Except as otherwise provided in this title, the rates and terms, to the extent applicable, shall remain in effect until such successor rates and terms become effective.

(C) Obligation to make payments.

(i) The pendency of an appeal under this subsection shall not relieve persons obligated to make royalty payments under section 111, 112, 114, 115, 116, 118, 119, or 1003

[17 USCS § 111, 112, 114, 115, 116, 118, 119, or 1003], who would be affected by the determination on appeal, from—

(I) providing the applicable statements of account and reports of use; and

(II) paying the royalties required under the relevant determination or regulations.

(ii) Notwithstanding clause (i), whenever royalties described in clause (i) are paid to a person other than the Copyright Office, the entity designated by the Copyright Royalty Judges to which such royalties are paid by the copyright user (and any successor thereto) shall, within 60 days after the final resolution of the appeal, return any excess amounts previously paid (and interest thereon, if ordered pursuant to paragraph (3)) to the extent necessary to comply with the final determination of royalty rates on appeal. Any underpayment of royalties resulting from an appeal (and interest thereon, if ordered pursuant to paragraph (3)) shall be paid within the same period.

(3) *Jurisdiction of court.* Section 706 of title 5 shall apply with respect to review by the court of appeals under this subsection. If the court modifies or vacates a determination of the Copyright Royalty Judges, the court may enter its own determination with respect to the amount or distribution of royalty fees and costs, and order the repayment of any excess fees, the payment of any underpaid fees, and the payment of interest pertaining respectively thereto, in accordance with its final judgment. The court may also vacate the determination of the Copyright Royalty Judges and remand the case to the Copyright Royalty Judges for further proceedings in accordance with subsection (a).

(e) **Administrative Matters.**

(1) *Deduction of costs of Library of Congress and Copyright Office from filing fees.*

(A) Deduction from filing fees. The Librarian of Congress may, to the extent not otherwise provided under this title, deduct from the filing fees collected under subsection (b) for a particular proceeding under this chapter [17 USCS §§ 801 et seq.] the reasonable costs incurred by the Librarian of Congress, the Copyright Office, and the Copyright Royalty Judges in conducting that proceeding, other than the salaries of the Copyright Royalty Judges and the 3 staff members appointed under section 802(b) [17 USCS § 802(b)].

(B) Authorization of appropriations. There are authorized to be appropriated such sums as may be necessary to pay the costs incurred under this chapter [17 USCS §§ 801 et seq.] not covered by the filing fees collected under subsection (b). All funds made available pursuant to this subparagraph shall remain available until expended.

(2) *Positions required for administration of compulsory licensing.* Section 307 of the Legislative Branch Appropriations Act, 1994 [2 USCS § 60-1 note], shall not apply to employee positions in the Library of Congress that are required to be filled in order to carry out section 111, 112, 114, 115, 116, 118, or 119 [17 USCS § 111, 112, 114, 115, 116, 118, or 119] or chapter 10 [17 USCS §§ 1001 et seq.].

(Added Nov. 30, 2004, P.L. 108-419, § 3(a), 118 Stat. 2348; Dec. 8, 2004, P.L. 108-447, Div J, Title IX, Title I, § 112, 118 Stat. 3409; October 6, 2006, P.L. 109-303, § 3, 120 Stat. 1478. This section took effect six months after enactment, pursuant to § 6(a) of Act Nov. 30, 2004, P.L. 108-419, which appears as 17 USCS § 801 note.)

§ 804 Institution of proceedings

(a) **Filing of Petition.** With respect to proceedings referred to in paragraphs (1) and (2) of section 801(b) [17 USCS § 801(b)] concerning the determination or adjustment of royalty rates as provided in sections 111, 112, 114, 115, 116, 118, 119, and 1004 [17 USCS §§ 111, 112, 114, 115, 116, 118, 119, and 1004], during the calendar years specified in the schedule set forth in subsection (b), any owner or user of a copyrighted work whose royalty rates are specified by this title, or are established under this chapter [17 USCS §§ 801 et seq.] before or after the enactment of the Copyright Royalty and Distribution Reform Act of 2004 [enacted Nov. 30, 2004], may file a petition with the Copyright Royalty Judges declaring that the petitioner requests a determination or adjustment of the rate. The Copyright Royalty Judges shall make a determination as to whether the petitioner has such a significant interest in the royalty rate in which a determination or adjustment is requested. If the Copyright Royalty Judges determine that the petitioner has such a significant interest, the Copyright Royalty Judges shall cause notice of this determination, with the reasons for such determination, to be published in the Federal Register, together with the notice of commencement of proceedings under this chapter [17 USCS §§ 801 et seq.]. With respect to proceedings under paragraph (1) of section 801(b) [17 USCS § 801(b)] concerning the determination or adjustment of royalty rates as provided in sections 112 and 114, during the calendar years specified in the schedule set forth in subsection (b), the Copyright Royalty Judges shall cause notice of commencement of proceedings under this chapter [17 USCS §§ 801 et seq.] to be published in the Federal Register as provided in section 803(b)(1)(A) [17 USCS § 803(b)(1)(A)].

(b) **Timing of Proceedings.**

(1) *Section 111 proceedings.*

(A) A petition described in subsection (a) to initiate proceedings under section 801(b)(2) [17 USCS § 801(b)(2)] concerning the adjustment of royalty rates under section 111 to which subparagraph (A) or (D) of section 801(b)(2) [17 USCS § 801(b)(2)] applies may be filed during the year 2005 and in each subsequent fifth calendar year.

(B) In order to initiate proceedings under section 801(b)(2) [17 USCS § 801(b)(2)] concerning the adjustment of royalty rates under section 111 [17 USCS § 111] to which subparagraph (B) or (C) of section 801(b)(2) [17 USCS § 801(b)(2)] applies, within 12 months after an event described in either of those subsections, any owner or user of a copyrighted work whose royalty rates are specified by section 111 [17 USCS § 111], or by a rate established under this chapter before or after the enactment of the Copyright Royalty and Distribution Reform Act of 2004 [enacted November 30, 2004], may file a petition with the Copyright Royalty Judges declaring that the petitioner requests an adjustment of the rate. The Copyright Royalty Judges shall then proceed as set forth in subsection (a) of this section. Any change in royalty rates made under this chapter [17 USCS §§ 801 et seq.] pursuant to this subparagraph may be reconsidered in the year 2005, and each fifth calendar year thereafter, in accordance with the provisions in section 801(b)(2) (B) or (C) [17 USCS § 801(b)(2)(B) or (C)], as the case may be. A petition for adjustment of rates established by section 111(d)(1)(B) [17 USCS § 111(d)(1)(B)] as a result of a change in the rules and regulations of the Federal Communications Commission shall set forth the change on which the petition is based.

(C) Any adjustment of royalty rates under section 111 [17 USCS § 111] shall take effect as of the first accounting period commencing after the publication of the determination of the Copyright Royalty Judges in the Federal Register, or on such other date as is specified in that determination.

(2) *Certain section 112 proceedings.* Proceedings under this chapter shall be commenced in the year 2007 to determine reasonable terms and rates of royalty payments for the activities described in section 112(e)(1) [17 USCS § 112(e)(1)] relating to the limitation on exclusive rights specified by section 114(d)(1)(C)(iv) [17 USCS § 114(d)(1)(C)(iv)], to become effective on January 1, 2009. Such proceedings shall be repeated in each subsequent fifth calendar year.

(3) *Section 114 and corresponding 112 proceedings.*

(A) For eligible nonsubscription services and new subscription services. Proceedings under this chapter [17 USCS §§ 801 et seq.] shall be commenced as soon as practicable after the date of enactment of the Copyright Royalty and Distribution Reform Act of 2004 [effective May 30, 2005] to determine reasonable terms and rates of royalty payments under sections 114 and 112 [17 USCS §§ 114 and 112] for the activities of eligible nonsubscription transmission services and new subscription services, to be effective for the period beginning on January 1, 2006, and ending on December 31, 2010. Such proceedings shall next be commenced in January 2009 to determine reasonable terms and rates of royalty payments, to become effective on January 1, 2011. Thereafter, such proceedings shall be repeated in each subsequent fifth calendar year.

(B) For preexisting subscription and satellite digital audio radio services. Proceedings under this chapter [17 USCS §§ 801 et seq.] shall be commenced in January 2006 to determine reasonable terms and rates of royalty payments under sections 114 and 112 [17 USCS §§ 114 and 112] for the activities of preexisting subscription services, to be effective during the period beginning on January 1, 2008, and ending on December 31, 2012, and preexisting satellite digital audio radio services, to be effective during the period beginning on January 1, 2007, and ending on December 31, 2012. Such proceedings shall next be commenced in 2011 to determine reasonable terms and rates of royalty payments, to become effective on January 1, 2013. Thereafter, such proceedings shall be repeated in each subsequent fifth calendar year.

(C) (i) Notwithstanding any other provision of this chapter [17 USCS §§ 801 et seq.], this subparagraph shall govern proceedings commenced pursuant to section 114(f)(1)(C) and 114(f)(2)(C), [17 USCS §§ 114(f)(1)(c) and 114(f)(2)(c)] concerning new types of services.

(ii) Not later than 30 days after a petition to determine rates and terms for a new type of service is filed by any copyright owner of sound recordings, or such new type of service, indicating that such new type of service is or is about to become operational, the Copyright Royalty Judges shall issue a notice for a proceeding to determine rates and terms for such service.

(iii) The proceeding shall follow the schedule set forth in subsections (b), (c), and (d) of section 803 [17 USCS § 803], except that—

(I) the determination shall be issued by not later than 24 months after the publication of the notice under clause (ii); and

(II) the decision shall take effect as provided in subsections (c)(2) and (d)(2) of section 803 [17 USCS § 803] and section 114(f)(4)(B)(ii) and (C) [17 USCS § 114(f)(4)(B)(ii) and (C)].

(iv) The rates and terms shall remain in effect for the period set forth in section 114(f)(1)(C) or 114(f)(2)(C), as the case may be.

(4) *Section 115 proceedings.* A petition described in subsection (a) to initiate proceedings under section 801(b)(1) [17 USCS § 801(b)(1)] concerning the adjustment or determination of royalty rates as provided in section 115 [17 USCS § 115] may be filed in the year 2006 and in each

subsequent fifth calendar year, or at such other times as the parties have agreed under section 115(c)(3) (B) and (C) [17 USCS § 115(c)(3)(B) and (C)].

(5) *Section 116 proceedings.*

(A) A petition described in subsection (a) to initiate proceedings under section 801(b) [17 USCS § 801(b)] concerning the determination of royalty rates and terms as provided in section 116 [17 USCS § 116] may be filed at any time within 1 year after negotiated licenses authorized by section 116 [17 USCS § 116] are terminated or expire and are not replaced by subsequent agreements.

(B) If a negotiated license authorized by section 116 [17 USCS § 116] is terminated or expires and is not replaced by another such license agreement which provides permission to use a quantity of musical works not substantially smaller than the quantity of such works performed on coin-operated phonorecord players during the 1-year period ending March 1, 1989, the Copyright Royalty Judges shall, upon petition filed under paragraph (1) within 1 year after such termination or expiration, commence a proceeding to promptly establish an interim royalty rate or rates for the public performance by means of a coin-operated phonorecord player of nondramatic musical works embodied in phonorecords which had been subject to the terminated or expired negotiated license agreement. Such rate or rates shall be the same as the last such rate or rates and shall remain in force until the conclusion of proceedings by the Copyright Royalty Judges, in accordance with section 803 [17 USCS § 803], to adjust the royalty rates applicable to such works, or until superseded by a new negotiated license agreement, as provided in section 116(b) [17 USCS § 116(b)].

(6) *Section 118 proceedings.* A petition described in subsection (a) to initiate proceedings under section 801(b)(1) [17 USCS § 801(b)(1)] concerning the determination of reasonable terms and rates of royalty payments as provided in section 118 [17 USCS § 118] may be filed in the year 2006 and in each subsequent fifth calendar year.

(7) *Section 1004 proceedings.* A petition described in subsection (a) to initiate proceedings under section 801(b)(1) [17 USCS § 801(b)(1)] concerning the adjustment of reasonable royalty rates under section 1004 [17 USCS § 1004] may be filed as provided in section 1004(a)(3) [17 USCS § 1004(a)(3)].

(8) *Proceedings concerning distribution of royalty fees.* With respect to proceedings under section 801(b)(3) [17 USCS § 801(b)(3)] concerning the distribution of royalty fees in certain circumstances under section 111, 119, or 1007 [17 USCS § 111, 119, or 1007], the Copyright Royalty Judges shall, upon a determination that a controversy exists concerning such distribution, cause to be published in the Federal Register notice of commencement of proceedings under this chapter [17 USCS §§ 801 et seq.].

(Added Act Nov. 30, 2004, P. L. 108-419, § 3(a), 118 Stat. 2357; October 6, 2006, P.L. 109-303, § 3, 120 Stat. 1478. This section took effect six months after enactment, pursuant to § 6(a) of Act Nov. 30, 2004, P.L. 108-419, which appears as 17 USCS § 801 note.)

§ 805 General rule for voluntarily negotiated agreements

Any rates or terms under this title that—

(1) are agreed to by participants to a proceeding under section 803(b)(3) [17 USCS § 803(b)(3)],

(2) are adopted by the Copyright Royalty Judges as part of a determination under this chapter [17 USCS §§ 801 et seq.], and

(3) are in effect for a period shorter than would otherwise apply under a determination pursuant to this chapter [17 USCS §§ 801 et seq.], shall remain in effect for such period of time as would otherwise apply under such determination, except that the Copyright Royalty Judges shall adjust the rates pursuant to the voluntary negotiations to reflect national monetary inflation during the additional period the rates remain in effect.

(Added Act Nov. 30, 2004, P. L. 108-419, § 3(a), 118 Stat. 2360. This section took effect six months after enactment, pursuant to § 6(a) of Act Nov. 30, 2004, P.L. 108-419, which appears as 17 USCS § 801 note).

TRANSITIONAL AND SUPPLEMENTARY PROVISIONS

SEC. 102. This Act becomes effective on January 1, 1978, except as otherwise expressly provided by this Act, including provisions of the first section of this Act. The provisions of sections 118, 304(b), and chapter 8 of title 17, as amended by the first section of this Act, take effect upon enactment of this Act.

SEC. 103. This Act does not provide copyright protection for any work that goes into the public domain before January 1, 1978. The exclusive rights, as provided by section 106 of title 17 as amended by the first section of this Act, to reproduce a work in phonorecords and to distribute phonorecords of the work, do not extend to any nondramatic musical work copyrighted before July 1, 1909.

SEC. 104. All proclamations issued by the President under section 1(e) or 9(b) of title 17 as it existed on December 31, 1977, or under previous copyright statutes of the United States, shall continue in force until terminated, suspended, or revised by the President.

SEC. 105. (a) (1) Section 505 of title 44 is amended to read as follows:

"505. Sale of Duplicate Plates

"The Public Printer shall sell, under regulations of the Joint Committee on Printing to persons who may apply, additional or duplicate stereotype or electrotype plates from which a Government publication is printed, at a price not to exceed the cost of composition, the metal, and making to the Government, plus 10 per centum, and the full amount of the price shall be paid when the order is filed."

(2) The item relating to section 505 in the sectional analysis at the beginning of chapter 5 of title 44, is amended to read as follows: "505. Sale of duplicate plates."

(b) Section 2113 of title 44 is amended to read as follows:

"2113. Limitation on Liability

"When letters and other intellectual productions (exclusive of patented material, published works under copyright protection, and unpublished works for which copyright registration has been made) come into the custody or possession of the Administrator of General Services, the United States or its agents are not liable for infringement of copyright or analogous rights arising out of use of the materials for display, inspection, research, reproduction, or other purposes."

(c) In section 1498(b) of title 28, the phrase "section 101(b) of title 17" is amended to read "section 504(c) of title 17".

(d) Section 543(a)(4) of the Internal Revenue Code of 1954, as amended, is amended by striking out "(other than by reason of section 2 or 6 thereof)".

(e) Section 3202(a) of title 39 is amended by striking out clause (5). Section 3206 of title 39 is amended by deleting the words "subsections (b) and (c)" and inserting "subsection (b)" in subsection (a), and by deleting subsection (c). Section 3206(d) is renumbered (c).

(f) Subsection (a) of section 290(e) of title 15 is amended by deleting the phrase "section 8" and inserting in lieu thereof the phrase "section 105".

(g) Section 131 of title 2 is amended by deleting the phrase "deposit to secure copyright," and inserting in lieu thereof the phrase "acquisition of material under the copyright law."

SEC. 106. In any case where, before January 1, 1978, a person has lawfully made parts of instruments serving to reproduce mechanically a copyrighted work under the compulsory license provisions of section 1(e) of title 17 as it existed on December 31, 1977, such person may continue to make and distribute such parts embodying the same mechanical reproduction without obtaining a new compulsory license under the terms of section 115 of title 17 as amended by the first section of this Act. However, such parts made on or after January 1, 1978, constitute phonorecords and are otherwise subject to the provisions of said section 115.

SEC. 107. In the case of any work in which an ad interim copyright is subsisting or is capable of being secured on December 31, 1977, under section 22 of title 17 as it existed on that date, copyright protection is hereby extended to endure for the term or terms provided by section 304 of title 17 as amended by the first section of this Act.

SEC. 108. The notice provisions of sections 401 through 403 of title 17 as amended by the first section of this Act apply to all copies or phonorecords publicly distributed on or after January 1, 1978. However, in the case of a work published before January 1, 1978, compliance with the notice provisions of title 17 either as it existed on December 31, 1977, or as amended by the first section of this Act, is adequate with respect to copies publicly distributed after December 31, 1977.

SEC. 109. The registration of claims to copyright for which the required deposit, application, and fee were received in the Copyright Office before January 1, 1978, and the recordation of assignments of copyright or other instruments received in the Copyright Office before January 1, 1978, shall be made in accordance with title 17 as it existed on December 31, 1977.

SEC. 110. The demand and penalty provisions of section 14 of title 17 as it existed on December 31, 1977, apply to any work in which copyright has been secured by publication with notice of copyright on or before that date, but any deposit and registration made after that date in response to a demand under that section shall be made in accordance with the provisions of title 17 as amended by the first section of this Act.

SEC. 111. Section 2318 of title 18 of the United States Code is amended to read as follows:

"§ 2318. Transportation, sale or receipt of phonograph records bearing forged or counterfeit labels

"(a) Whoever knowingly and with fraudulent intent transports, causes to be transported, receives, sells, or offers for sale in interstate or foreign commerce any phonograph record, disk, wire, tape, film, or other article on which sounds are recorded, to which or upon which is stamped, pasted, or affixed any forged or counterfeited label, knowing the label to have been falsely made, forged, or counterfeited shall be fined not more than $10,000 or imprisoned for not more than one year, or both, for the first such offense and shall be fined not more than $25,000 or imprisoned for not more than two years, or both, for any subsequent offense."

"(b) When any person is convicted of any violation of subsection (a), the court in its judgment of conviction shall, in addition to the penalty therein prescribed, order the forfeiture and destruction or other disposition of all counterfeit labels and all articles to which counterfeit labels have been affixed or which were intended to have had such labels affixed."

"(c) Except to the extent they are inconsistent with the provisions of this title, all provisions of section 509, title 17, United States Code, are applicable to violations of subsection (a)."

SEC. 112. All causes of action that arose under title 17 before January 1, 1978, shall be governed by title 17 as it existed when the cause of action arose.

SEC. 113. (a) The Librarian of Congress (hereinafter referred to as the "Librarian") shall establish and maintain in the Library of Congress a library to be known as the American Television and Radio Archives (hereinafter referred to as the "Archives"). The purpose of the Archives shall be to preserve a permanent record of the television and radio programs which are the heritage of the people of the United States and to provide access to such programs to historians and scholars without encouraging or causing copyright infringement.

(1) The Librarian, after consultation with interested organizations and individuals, shall determine and place in the Archives such copies and phonorecords of television and radio programs transmitted to the public in the United States and in other countries which are of present or potential public or cultural interest, historical significance, cognitive value, or otherwise worthy of preservation, including copies and phonorecords of published and unpublished transmission programs—

(A) acquired in accordance with sections 407 and 408 of title 17 as amended by the first section of this Act; and

(B) transferred from the existing collections of the Library of Congress; and

(C) given to or exchanged with the Archives by other libraries, archives, organizations, and individuals; and

(D) purchased from the owner thereof.

(2) The Librarian shall maintain and publish appropriate catalogs and indexes of the collections of the Archives, and shall make such collections available for study and research under the conditions prescribed under this section.

(b) Notwithstanding the provisions of section 106 of title 17 as amended by the first section of this Act, the Librarian is authorized with respect to a transmission program which consists of a regularly scheduled newscast or on-the-spot coverage of news events and, under standards and conditions that the Librarian shall prescribe by regulation—

(1) to reproduce a fixation of such a program, in the same or another tangible form, for the purposes of preservation or security or for distribution under the conditions of clause (3) of this subsection; and

(2) to compile, without abridgment or any other editing, portions of such fixations according to subject matter, and to reproduce such compilations for the purpose of clause (1) of this subsection; and

(3) to distribute a reproduction made under clause (1) or (2) of this subsection—

(A) by loan to a person engaged in research; and

(B) for deposit in a library or archives which meets the requirements of section 108(a) of title 17 as amended by the first section of this Act, in either case for use only in research and not for further reproduction or performance.

(c) The Librarian or any employee of the Library who is acting under the authority of this section shall not be liable in any action for copyright infringement committed by any other person unless the Librarian or such employee knowingly participated in the act of infringement committed by such person. Nothing in this section shall be construed to excuse or limit liability under title 17 as amended by the first section of this Act for any act not authorized by that title or this section, or for any act performed by a person not authorized to act under that title or this section.

(d) This section may be cited as the "American Television and Radio Archives Act".

SEC. 114. There are hereby authorized to be appropriated such funds as may be necessary to carry out the purposes of this Act.

SEC. 115. If any provision of title 17, as amended by the first section of this Act, is declared unconstitutional, the validity of the remainder of this title is not affected.

ADDITIONAL PROVISIONS

U.S. CODE: TITLE 17

17 U.S.C. §§ 901–1332
(AS AMENDED THROUGH DECEMBER 19, 2009)

CHAPTER 9—PROTECTION OF SEMICONDUCTOR CHIP PRODUCTS

§ 901 Definitions

(a) As used in this chapter [17 USCS §§ 901 et seq.]—

(1) a "semiconductor chip product" is the final or intermediate form of any product—

(A) having two or more layers of metallic, insulating, or semiconductor material, deposited or otherwise placed on, or etched away or otherwise removed from, a piece of semiconductor material in accordance with a predetermined pattern; and

(B) intended to perform electronic circuitry functions;

(2) a "mask work" is a series of related images, however fixed or encoded—

(A) having or representing the predetermined, three-dimensional pattern of metallic, insulating, or semiconductor material present or removed from the layers of a semiconductor chip product; and

(B) in which series the relation of the images to one another is that each image has the pattern of the surface of one form of the semiconductor chip product;

(3) a mask work is "fixed" in a semiconductor chip product when its embodiment in the product is sufficiently permanent or stable to permit the mask work to be perceived or reproduced from the product for a period of more than transitory duration;

(4) to "distribute" means to sell, or to lease, bail, or otherwise transfer, or to offer to sell, lease, bail, or otherwise transfer;

(5) to "commercially exploit" a mask work is to distribute to the public for commercial purposes a semiconductor chip product embodying the mask work; except that such term includes an offer to sell or transfer a semiconductor chip product only when the offer is in writing and occurs after the mask work is fixed in the semiconductor chip product;

(6) the "owner" of a mask work is the person who created the mask work, the legal representative of that person if that person is deceased or under a legal incapacity, or a party to whom all the rights under this chapter [17 USCS §§ 901 et seq.] of such person or representative are transferred in accordance with section 903(b); except that, in the case of a work made within the scope of a person's employment, the owner is the employer for whom the person created the mask work or a party to whom all the rights under this chapter [17 USCS §§ 901 et seq.] of the employer are transferred in accordance with section 903(b).

(7) an "innocent purchaser" is a person who purchases a semiconductor chip product in good faith and without having notice of protection with respect to the semiconductor chip product;

(8) having "notice of protection" means having actual knowledge that, or reasonable grounds to believe that, a mask work is protected under this chapter [17 USCS §§ 901 et seq.]; and

(9) an "infringing semiconductor chip product" is a semiconductor chip product which is made, imported, or distributed in violation of the exclusive rights of the owner of a mask work under this chapter [17 USCS §§ 901 et seq.].

(b) For purposes of this chapter [17 USCS §§ 901 et seq.], the distribution or importation of a product incorporating a semiconductor chip product as a part thereof is a distribution or importation of that semiconductor chip product.

(Added Nov. 8, 1984, P. L. 98-620, Title III, § 302, 98 Stat. 3347.)

§ 902 Subject matter of protection

(a) (1) Subject to the provisions of subsection (b), a mask work fixed in a semiconductor chip product, by or under the authority of the owner of the mask work, is eligible for protection under this chapter [17 USCS §§ 901 et seq.] if—

(A) on the date on which the mask work is registered under section 908, or is first commercially exploited anywhere in the world, whichever occurs first, the owner of the mask work is (i) a national or domiciliary of the United States, (ii) a national, domiciliary, or sovereign authority of a foreign nation that is a party to a treaty affording protection to mask works to which the United States is also a party, or (iii) a stateless person, wherever that person may be domiciled;

(B) the mask work is first commercially exploited in the United States; or

(C) the mask work comes within the scope of a Presidential proclamation issued under paragraph (2).

(2) Whenever the President finds that a foreign nation extends, to mask works of owners who are nationals or domiciliaries of the United States protection (A) on substantially the same basis as that on which the foreign nation extends protection to mask works of its own nationals and domiciliaries and mask works first commercially exploited in that nation, or (B) on substantially the same basis as provided in this chapter [17 USCS §§ 901 et seq.], the President may by proclamation extend protection under this chapter [17 USCS §§ 901 et seq.] to mask works (i) of owners who are, on the date on which the mask works are registered under section 908, or the date on which the mask works are first commercially exploited anywhere in the world, whichever occurs first, nationals, domiciliaries, or sovereign authorities of that nation, or (ii) which are first commercially exploited in that nation. The President may revise, suspend, or revoke any such proclamation or impose any conditions or limitations on protection extended under any such proclamation.

(b) Protection under this chapter [17 USCS §§ 901 et seq.] shall not be available for a mask work that—

(1) is not original; or

(2) consists of designs that are staple, commonplace, or familiar in the semiconductor industry, or variations of such designs, combined in a way that, considered as a whole, is not original.

(c) In no case does protection under this chapter [17 USCS §§ 901 et seq.] for a mask work extend to any idea, procedure, process, system, method of operation, concept, principle, or discovery, regardless of the form in which it is described, explained, illustrated, or embodied in such work.

(Added Nov. 8, 1984, P. L. 98-620, Title III, § 302, 98 Stat. 3348; Nov. 9, 1987, P. L. 100-159, § 3, 101 Stat. 900.)

§ 903 Ownership, transfer, licensing, and recordation

(a) The exclusive rights in a mask work subject to protection under this chapter [17 USCS §§ 901 et seq.] belong to the owner of the mask work.

(b) The owner of the exclusive rights in a mask work may transfer all of those rights, or license all or less than all of those rights, by any written instrument signed by such owner or a duly authorized agent of the owner. Such rights may be transferred or licensed by operation of law, may be bequeathed by will, and may pass as personal property by the applicable laws of intestate succession.

(c) (1) Any document pertaining to a mask work may be recorded in the Copyright Office if the document filed for recordation bears the actual signature of the person who executed it, or if it is accompanied by a sworn or official certification that it is a true copy of the original, signed document. The Register of Copyrights shall, upon receipt of the document and the fee specified pursuant to section 908(d), record the document and return it with a certificate of recordation. The recordation of any transfer or license under this paragraph gives all persons constructive notice of the facts stated in the recorded document concerning the transfer or license.

(2) In any case in which conflicting transfers of the exclusive rights in a mask work are made, the transfer first executed shall be void as against a subsequent transfer which is made for a valuable consideration and without notice of the first transfer, unless the first transfer is recorded in accordance with paragraph (1) within three months after the date on which it is executed, but in no case later than the day before the date of such subsequent transfer.

(d) Mask works prepared by an officer or employee of the United States Government as part of that person's official duties are not protected under this chapter [17 USCS §§ 901 et seq.], but the United States Government is not precluded from receiving and holding exclusive rights in mask works transferred to the Government under subsection (b).

(Added Nov. 8, 1984, P. L. 98-620, Title III, § 302, 98 Stat. 3349.)

§ 904 Duration of protection

(a) The protection provided for a mask work under this chapter [17 USCS §§ 901 et seq.] shall commence on the date on which the mask work is registered under section 908, or the date on which the mask work is first commercially exploited anywhere in the world, whichever occurs first.

(b) Subject to subsection (c) and the provisions of this chapter [17 USCS §§ 901 et seq.], the protection provided under this chapter [17 USCS §§ 901 et seq.] to a mask work shall end ten years after the date on which such protection commences under subsection (a).

(c) All terms of protection provided in this section shall run to the end of the calendar year in which they would otherwise expire.

(Added Nov. 8, 1984, P. L. 98-620, Title III § 302, 98 Stat. 3349.)

§ 905 Exclusive rights in mask works

The owner of a mask work provided protection under this chapter [17 USCS §§ 901 et seq.] has the exclusive rights to do and to authorize any of the following:

(1) to reproduce the mask work by optical, electronic, or any other means;

(2) to import or distribute a semiconductor chip product in which the mask work is embodied; and

(3) to induce or knowingly to cause another person to do any of the acts described in paragraphs (1) and (2).

(Added Nov. 8, 1984, P. L. 98-620, Title III, § 302, 98 Stat. 3350.)

§ 906 Limitation on exclusive rights: reverse engineering; first sale

(a) Notwithstanding the provisions of section 905, it is not an infringement of the exclusive rights of the owner of a mask work for—

(1) a person to reproduce the mask work solely for the purpose of teaching, analyzing, or evaluating the concepts or techniques embodied in the mask work or the circuitry, logic flow, or organization of components used in the mask work; or

(2) a person who performs the analysis or evaluation described in paragraph (1) to incorporate the results of such conduct in an original mask work which is made to be distributed.

(b) Notwithstanding the provisions of section 905(2), the owner of a particular semiconductor chip product made by the owner of the mask work, or by any person authorized by the owner of the mask work, may import, distribute, or otherwise dispose of or use, but not reproduce, that particular semiconductor chip product without the authority of the owner of the mask work.

(Added Nov. 8, 1984, P. L. 98-620, Title III, § 302, 98 Stat. 3350.)

§ 907 Limitation on exclusive rights: innocent infringement

(a) Notwithstanding any other provision of this chapter [17 USCS §§ 901 et seq.], an innocent purchaser of an infringing semiconductor chip product—

(1) shall incur no liability under this chapter [17 USCS §§ 901 et seq.] with respect to the importation or distribution of units of the infringing semiconductor chip product that occurs before the innocent purchaser has notice of protection with respect to the mask work embodied in the semiconductor chip product; and

(2) shall be liable only for a reasonable royalty on each unit of the infringing semiconductor chip product that the innocent purchaser imports or distributes after having notice of protection with respect to the mask work embodied in the semiconductor chip product.

(b) The amount of the royalty referred to in subsection (a)(2) shall be determined by the court in a civil action for infringement unless the parties resolve the issue by voluntary negotiation, mediation, or binding arbitration.

(c) The immunity of an innocent purchaser from liability referred to in subsection (a)(1) and the limitation of remedies with respect to an innocent purchaser referred to in subsection (a)(2) shall extend to any person who directly or indirectly purchases an infringing semiconductor chip product from an innocent purchaser.

(d) The provisions of subsections (a), (b), and (c) apply only with respect to those units of an infringing semiconductor chip product that an innocent purchaser purchased before having notice of protection with respect to the mask work embodied in the semiconductor chip product.

(Added Nov. 8, 1984, P. L. 98-620, Title III, § 302, 98 Stat. 3350.)

§ 908 Registration of claims of protection

(a) The owner of a mask work may apply to the Register of Copyrights for registration of a claim of protection in a mask work. Protection of a mask work under this chapter [17 USCS §§ 901 et seq.] shall terminate if application for registration of a claim of protection in the mask work is not made as provided in this chapter [17 USCS §§ 901 et seq.] within two years after the date on which the mask work is first commercially exploited anywhere in the world.

(b) The Register of Copyrights shall be responsible for all administrative functions and duties under this chapter [17 USCS §§ 901 et seq.]. Except for section 708, the provisions of chapter 7 of this title [17 USCS §§ 701 et seq.] relating to the general responsibilities, organization, regulatory authority, actions, records, and publications of the Copyright Office shall apply to this chapter [17 USCS §§ 901 et seq.], except that the Register of Copyrights may make such changes as may be necessary in applying those provisions to this chapter [17 USCS §§ 901 et seq.].

(c) The application for registration of a mask work shall be made on a form prescribed by the Register of Copyrights. Such form may require any information regarded by the Register as bearing upon the preparation or identification of the mask work, the existence or duration of protection of the mask work under this chapter [17 USCS §§ 901 et seq.], or ownership of the mask work. The application shall be accompanied by the fee set pursuant to subsection (d) and the identifying material specified pursuant to such subsection.

(d) The Register of Copyrights shall by regulation set reasonable fees for the filing of applications to register claims of protection in mask works under this chapter, and for other services relating to the administration of this chapter [17 USCS §§ 901 et seq.] or the rights under this chapter [17 USCS §§ 901 et seq.], taking into consideration the cost of providing those services, the benefits of a public record, and statutory fee schedules under this title. The Register shall also specify the identifying material to be deposited in connection with the claim for registration.

(e) If the Register of Copyrights, after examining an application for registration, determines, in accordance with the provisions of this chapter [17 USCS §§ 901 et seq.], that the application relates to a mask work which is entitled to protection under this chapter [17 USCS §§ 901 et seq.], then the Register shall register the claim of protection and issue to the applicant a certificate of registration of the claim of protection under the seal of the Copyright Office. The effective date of registration of a claim of protection shall be the date on which an application, deposit of identifying material, and fee, which are determined by the Register of Copyrights or by a court of competent jurisdiction to be acceptable for registration of the claim, have all been received in the Copyright Office.

(f) In any action for infringement under this chapter [17 USCS §§ 901 et seq.], the certificate of registration of a mask work shall constitute prima facie evidence (1) of the facts stated in the certificate, and (2) that the applicant issued the certificate has met the requirements of this chapter [17 USCS §§ 901 et seq.], and the regulations issued under this chapter [17 USCS §§ 901 et seq.], with respect to the registration of claims.

(g) Any applicant for registration under this section who is dissatisfied with the refusal of the Register of Copyrights to issue a certificate of registration under this section may seek judicial review of that refusal by bringing an action for such review in an appropriate United States district court not later than sixty days after the refusal. The provisions of chapter 7 of title 5 [5 USCS §§ 701 et seq.] shall apply to such judicial review. The failure of the Register of Copyrights to issue a certificate of registration within four months after an application for registration is filed shall be deemed to be a refusal to issue a certificate of registration for purposes of this subsection and section 910(b)(2), except that, upon a showing of good cause, the district court may shorten such four-month period.

(Added Nov. 8, 1984, P. L. 98-620, Title III, § 302, 98 Stat. 3351.)

§ 909 Mask work notice

(a) The owner of a mask work provided protection under this chapter [17 USCS §§ 901 et seq.] may affix notice to the mask work, and to masks and semiconductor chip products embodying the mask work, in such manner and location as to give reasonable notice of such protection. The Register of Copyrights shall prescribe by regulation, as examples, specific methods of affixation and positions of notice for purposes of this section, but these specifications shall not be considered exhaustive. The affixation of such notice is not a condition of protection under this chapter [17 USCS §§ 901 et seq.], but shall constitute prima facie evidence of notice of protection.

(b) The notice referred to in subsection (a) shall consist of—

(1) the words "mask work", the symbol *M*, or the symbol Ⓜ (the letter M in a circle); and

(2) the name of the owner or owners of the mask work or an abbreviation by which the name is recognized or is generally known.

(Added Nov. 8, 1984, P. L. 98-620, Title III, § 302, 98 Stat. 3352; Nov. 13, 1997, P. L. 105-80, § 12(a)(22), 111 Stat. 1535.)

§ 910 Enforcement of exclusive rights

(a) Except as otherwise provided in this chapter [17 USCS §§ 901 et seq.], any person who violates any of the exclusive rights of the owner of a mask work under this chapter [17 USCS §§ 901 et seq.], by conduct in or affecting commerce, shall be liable as an infringer of such rights. As used in this subsection, the term "any person" includes any State, any instrumentality of a State, and any officer or employee of a State or instrumentality of a State acting in his or her official capacity. Any State, and any such instrumentality, officer, or employee, shall be subject to the provisions of this chapter in the same manner and to the same extent as any nongovernmental entity.

(b) (1) The owner of a mask work protected under this chapter [17 USCS §§ 901 et seq.], or the exclusive licensee of all rights under this chapter [17 USCS §§ 901 et seq.], with respect to the mask work, shall, after a certificate of registration of a claim of protection in that mask work has been issued under section 908, be entitled to institute a civil action for any infringement with respect to the mask work which is committed after the commencement of protection of the mask work under section 904(a).

(2) In any case in which an application for registration of a claim of protection in a mask work and the required deposit of identifying material and fee have been received in the Copyright Office in proper

form and registration of the mask work has been refused, the applicant is entitled to institute a civil action for infringement under this chapter [17 USCS §§ 901 et seq.] with respect to the mask work if notice of the action, together with a copy of the complaint, is served on the Register of Copyrights, in accordance with the Federal Rules of Civil Procedure. The Register may, at his or her option, become a party to the action with respect to the issue of whether the claim of protection is eligible for registration by entering an appearance within sixty days after such service, but the failure of the Register to become a party to the action shall not deprive the court of jurisdiction to determine that issue.

(c) (1) The Secretary of the Treasury and the United States Postal Service shall separately or jointly issue regulations for the enforcement of the rights set forth in section 905 with respect to importation. These regulations may require, as a condition for the exclusion of articles from the United States, that the person seeking exclusion take any one or more of the following actions:

(A) Obtain a court order enjoining, or an order of the International Trade Commission under section 337 of the Tariff Act of 1930 [19 USCS § 1337] excluding, importation of the articles.

(B) Furnish proof that the mask work involved is protected under this chapter [17 USCS §§ 901 et seq.] and that the importation of the articles would infringe the rights in the mask work under this chapter [17 USCS §§ 901 et seq.].

(C) Post a surety bond for any injury that may result if the detention or exclusion of the articles proves to be unjustified.

(2) Articles imported in violation of the rights set forth in section 905 [17 USCS § 905] are subject to seizure and forfeiture in the same manner as property imported in violation of the customs laws. Any such forfeited articles shall be destroyed as directed by the Secretary of the Treasury or the court, as the case may be, except that the articles may be returned to the country of export whenever it is shown to the satisfaction of the Secretary of the Treasury that the importer had no reasonable grounds for believing that his or her acts constituted a violation of the law.

(Added Nov. 8, 1984, P. L. 98-620, Title III, § 302, 98 Stat. 3352; Nov. 15, 1990, P. L. 101-553, § 2(b)(1), 104 Stat. 2750; Nov. 13, 1997, P. L. 105-80, § 12(a)(23), 111 Stat. 1535.)

§ 911 Civil actions

(a) Any court having jurisdiction of a civil action arising under this chapter [17 USCS §§ 901 et seq.] may grant temporary restraining orders, preliminary injunctions, and permanent injunctions on such terms as the court may deem reasonable to prevent or restrain infringement of the exclusive rights in a mask work under this chapter [17 USCS §§ 901 et seq.].

(b) Upon finding an infringer liable, to a person entitled under section 910(b)(1) to institute a civil action, for an infringement of any exclusive right under this chapter [17 USCS §§ 901 et seq.], the court shall award such person actual damages suffered by the person as a result of the infringement. The court shall also award such person the infringer's profits that are attributable to the infringement and are not taken into account in computing the award of actual damages. In establishing the infringer's profits, such person is required to present proof only of the infringer's gross revenue, and the infringer is required to prove his or her deductible expenses and the elements of profit attributable to factors other than the mask work.

(c) At any time before final judgment is rendered, a person entitled to institute a civil action for infringement may elect, instead of actual damages and profits as provided by subsection (b), an award of statutory damages for all infringements involved in the action, with respect to any one mask work for which any one infringer is liable individually, or for which any two or more infringers are liable jointly and severally, in an amount not more than $ 250,000 as the court considers just.

(d) An action for infringement under this chapter [17 USCS §§ 901 et seq.] shall be barred unless the action is commenced within three years after the claim accrues.

(e) (1) At any time while an action for infringement of the exclusive rights in a mask work under this chapter [17 USCS §§ 901 et seq.] is pending, the court may order the impounding, on such terms as it may deem reasonable, of all semiconductor chip products, and any drawings, tapes, masks, or other products by means of which such products may be reproduced, that are claimed to have been made, imported, or used in violation of those exclusive rights. Insofar as practicable, applications for orders under this paragraph shall be heard and determined in the same manner as an application for a temporary restraining order or preliminary injunction.

(2) As part of a final judgment or decree, the court may order the destruction or other disposition of any infringing semiconductor chip products, and any masks, tapes, or other articles by means of which such products may be reproduced.

(f) In any civil action arising under this chapter [17 USCS §§ 901 et seq.], the court in its discretion may allow the recovery of full costs, including reasonable attorneys' fees, to the prevailing party.

(g) (1) Any State, any instrumentality of a State, and any officer or employee of a State or instrumentality of a State acting in his or her official capacity, shall not be immune, under the Eleventh Amendment of the Constitution of the United States or under any other doctrine of sovereign immunity, from suit in Federal court by any person, including any governmental or nongovernmental entity, for a violation of any of the exclusive rights of the owner of a mask work under this chapter [17 USCS §§ 901 et seq.], or for any other violation under this chapter [17 USCS §§ 901 et seq.].

(2) In a suit described in paragraph (1) for a violation described in that paragraph, remedies (including remedies both at law and in equity) are available for the violation to the same extent as such remedies are available for such a violation in a suit against any public or private entity other than a State, instrumentality of a State, or officer or employee of a State acting in his or her official capacity. Such remedies include actual damages and profits under subsection (b), statutory damages under subsection (c), impounding and disposition of infringing articles under subsection (e), and costs and attorney's fees under subsection (f).

(Added Nov. 8, 1984, P. L. 98-620, Title III, § 302, 98 Stat. 3353; Nov. 15, 1990, P. L. 101-553, § 2(b)(2), 104 Stat. 2750.)

§ 912 Relation to other laws

(a) Nothing in this chapter [17 USCS §§ 901 et seq.] shall affect any right or remedy held by any person under chapters 1 through 8 or 10 of this title [17 USCS §§ 101 et seq. through 801 et seq. or 1001 et seq.], or under title 35.

(b) Except as provided in section 908(b) of this title, references to "this title" or "title 17" in chapters 1 through 8 or 10 of this title [17 USCS §§ 101 et seq. through 801 et seq. or 1001 et seq.] shall be deemed not to apply to this chapter [17 USCS §§ 901 et seq.].

(c) The provisions of this chapter [17 USCS §§ 901 et seq.] shall preempt the laws of any State to the extent those laws provide any rights or remedies with respect to a mask work which are equivalent to those rights or remedies provided by this chapter [17 USCS §§ 901 et seq.], except that such preemption shall be effective only with respect to actions filed on or after January 1, 1986.

(d) Notwithstanding subsection (c), nothing in this chapter [17 USCS §§ 901 et seq.] shall detract from any rights of a mask work owner, whether under Federal law (exclusive of this chapter [17 USCS §§ 901 et seq.]) or under the common law or the statutes of a State, heretofore or hereafter declared or enacted, with respect to any mask work first commercially exploited before July 1, 1983.

(Added Nov. 8, 1984, P. L. 98-620, Title III, § 302, 98 Stat. 3354; Nov. 19, 1988, P. L. 100-702, Title X, § 1020(b), 102 Stat. 4672; Oct. 28, 1992, P. L. 102-563, § 3(c), 106 Stat. 4248.)

§ 913 Transitional provisions

(a) No application for registration under section 908 may be filed, and no civil action under section 910 or other enforcement proceeding under this chapter [17 USCS §§ 901 et seq.] may be instituted, until sixty days after the date of the enactment of this chapter [Nov. 8, 1984].

(b) No monetary relief under section 911 may be granted with respect to any conduct that occurred before the date of the enactment of this chapter [Nov. 8, 1984], except as provided in subsection (d).

(c) Subject to subsection (a), the provisions of this chapter [17 USCS §§ 901 et seq.] apply to all mask works that are first commercially exploited or are registered under this chapter [17 USCS §§ 901 et seq.], or both, on or after the date of the enactment of this chapter [Nov. 8, 1984].

(d) (1) Subject to subsection (a), protection is available under this chapter [17 USCS §§ 901 et seq.] to any mask work that was first commercially exploited on or after July 1, 1983, and before the date of the enactment of this chapter [Nov. 8, 1984], if a claim of protection in the mask work is registered in the Copyright Office before July 1, 1985, under section 908.

(2) In the case of any mask work described in paragraph (1) that is provided protection under this chapter [17 USCS §§ 901 et seq.], infringing semiconductor chip product units manufactured before the date of the enactment of this chapter [Nov. 8, 1984] may, without liability under sections 910 and 911, be imported into or distributed in the United States, or both, until two years after the date of registration of the mask work under section 908, but only if the importer or distributor, as the case may be, first pays or offers to pay the reasonable royalty referred to in section 907(a)(2) to the mask work owner, on all such units imported or distributed, or both, after the date of the enactment of this chapter [Nov. 8, 1984].

(3) In the event that a person imports or distributes infringing semiconductor chip product units described in paragraph (2) of this subsection without first paying or offering to pay the reasonable royalty specified in such paragraph, or if the person refuses or fails to make such payment, the mask work owner shall be entitled to the relief provided in sections 910 and 911.

(Added Nov. 8, 1984, P. L. 98-620, Title III, § 302, 98 Stat. 3354.)

§ 914 International transitional provisions

(a) Notwithstanding the conditions set forth in subparagraphs (A) and (C) of section 902(a)(1) with respect to the availability of protection under this chapter [17 USCS §§ 901 et seq.] to nationals, domiciliaries, and sovereign authorities of a foreign nation, the Secretary of Commerce may, upon the petition of any person, or upon the Secretary's own motion, issue an order extending protection under this chapter [17 USCS §§ 901 et seq.] to such foreign nationals, domiciliaries, and sovereign authorities if the Secretary finds—

(1) that the foreign nation is making good faith efforts and reasonable progress toward—

(A) entering into a treaty described in section 902(a)(1)(A); or

(B) enacting or implementing legislation that would be in compliance with subparagraph (A) or (B) or section 902(a)(2) and

(2) that the nationals, domiciliaries, and sovereign authorities of the foreign nation, and persons controlled by them, are not engaged in the misappropriation, or unauthorized distribution or commercial exploitation, of mask works; and

(3) that issuing the order would promote the purposes of this chapter [17 USCS §§ 901 et seq.] and international comity with respect to the protection of mask works.

(b) While an order under subsection (a) is in effect with respect to a foreign nation, no application for registration of a claim for protection in a mask work under this chapter [17 USCS §§ 901 et seq.] may be denied solely because the owner of the mask work is a national, domiciliary, or sovereign authority of that foreign nation, or solely because the mask work was first commercially exploited in that foreign nation.

(c) Any order issued by the Secretary of Commerce under subsection (a) shall be effective for such period as the Secretary designates in the order, except that no such order may be effective after the date on which the authority of the Secretary of Commerce terminates under subsection (e). The effective date of any such order shall also be designated in the order. In the case of an order issued upon the petition of a person, such effective date may be no earlier than the date on which the Secretary receives such petition.

(d) (1) Any order issued under this section shall terminate if—

(A) the Secretary of Commerce finds that any of the conditions set forth in paragraphs (1), (2), and (3) of subsection (a) no longer exist; or

(B) mask works of nationals, domiciliaries, and sovereign authorities of that foreign nation or mask works first commercially exploited in that foreign nation become eligible for protection under subparagraphs (A) or (C) of section 902(a)(1).

(2) Upon the termination or expiration of an order issued under this section, registrations of claims of protection in mask works made pursuant to that order shall remain valid for the period specified in section 904.

(e) The authority of the Secretary of Commerce under this section shall commence on the date of the enactment of this chapter [enacted Nov. 8, 1984], and shall terminate on July 1, 1995.

(f) (1) The Secretary of Commerce shall promptly notify the Register of Copyrights and the Committees on the Judiciary of the Senate and the House of Representatives of the issuance or termination of any order under this section, together with a statement of the reasons for such action. The Secretary shall also publish such notification and statement of reasons in the Federal Register.

(2) Two years after the date of the enactment of this chapter [enacted Nov. 8, 1984], the Secretary of Commerce, in consultation with the Register of Copyrights, shall transmit to the Committees on the Judiciary of the Senate and the House of Representatives a report on the actions taken under this section and on the current status of international recognition of mask work protection. The report shall include such recommendations for modifications of the protection accorded under this chapter to mask works owned by nationals, domiciliaries, or sovereign authorities of foreign nations as the Secretary, in consultation with the Register of Copyrights, considers would promote the purposes of this chapter [17 USCS §§ 901 et seq.] and international comity with respect to mask work protection. Not later than July 1, 1994, the Secretary of Commerce, in consultation with the Register of Copyrights, shall transmit to the Committees on the Judiciary of the Senate and the House of Representatives a report updating the matters contained in the report transmitted under the preceding sentence.

(Added Nov. 8, 1984, P. L. 98-620, Title III, § 302, 98 Stat. 3355; Nov. 9, 1987, P. L. 100-159, §§ 2, 4, 101 Stat. 899, 900; June 28, 1991, P. L. 102-64, §§ 3, 4, 105 Stat. 520, 521.)

CHAPTER 10—DIGITAL AUDIO RECORDING DEVICES AND MEDIA

SUBCHAPTER A—DEFINITIONS

§ 1001 Definitions

As used in this chapter [17 USCS §§ 1001 et seq.], the following terms have the following meanings:

(1) A "digital audio copied recording" is a reproduction in a digital recording format of a digital musical recording, whether that reproduction is made directly from another digital musical recording or indirectly from a transmission.

(2) A "digital audio interface device" is any machine or device that is designed specifically to communicate digital audio information and related interface data to a digital audio recording device through a nonprofessional interface.

(3) A "digital audio recording device" is any machine or device of a type commonly distributed to individuals for use by individuals, whether or not included with or as part of some other machine or device, the digital recording function of which is designed or marketed for the primary purpose of, and that is capable of, making a digital audio copied recording for private use, except for—

(A) professional model products, and

(B) dictation machines, answering machines, and other audio recording equipment that is designed and marketed primarily for the creation of sound recordings resulting from the fixation of nonmusical sounds.

(4) (A) A "digital audio recording medium" is any material object in a form commonly distributed for use by individuals, that is primarily marketed or most commonly used by consumers for the purpose of making digital audio copied recordings by use of a digital audio recording device.

(B) Such term does not include any material object—

(i) that embodies a sound recording at the time it is first distributed by the importer or manufacturer; or

(ii) that is primarily marketed and most commonly used by consumers either for the purpose of making copies of motion pictures or other audiovisual works or for the purpose of making copies of nonmusical literary works, including computer programs or data bases.

(5) (A) A "digital musical recording" is a material object—

(i) in which are fixed, in a digital recording format, only sounds, and material, statements, or instructions incidental to those fixed sounds, if any, and

(ii) from which the sounds and material can be perceived, reproduced, or otherwise communicated, either directly or with the aid of a machine or device.

(B) A "digital musical recording" does not include a material object—

(i) in which the fixed sounds consist entirely of spoken word recordings, or

(ii) in which one or more computer programs are fixed, except that a digital musical recording may contain statements or instructions constituting the fixed sounds and incidental material, and statements or instructions to be used directly or indirectly in order to bring about the perception, reproduction, or communication of the fixed sounds and incidental material.

(C) For purposes of this paragraph—

(i) a "spoken word recording" is a sound recording in which are fixed only a series of spoken words, except that the spoken words may be accompanied by incidental musical or other sounds, and

(ii) the term "incidental" means related to and relatively minor by comparison.

(6) "Distribute" means to sell, lease, or assign a product to consumers in the United States, or to sell, lease, or assign a product in the United States for ultimate transfer to consumers in the United States.

(7) An "interested copyright party" is—

(A) the owner of the exclusive right under section 106(1) of this title to reproduce a sound recording of a musical work that has been embodied in a digital musical recording or analog musical recording lawfully made under this title that has been distributed;

(B) the legal or beneficial owner of, or the person that controls, the right to reproduce in a digital musical recording or analog musical recording a musical work that has been embodied in a digital musical recording or analog musical recording lawfully made under this title that has been distributed;

(C) a featured recording artist who performs on a sound recording that has been distributed; or

(D) any association or other organization—

(i) representing persons specified in subparagraph (A), (B), or (C), or

(ii) engaged in licensing rights in musical works to music users on behalf of writers and publishers.

(8) To "manufacture" means to produce or assemble a product in the United States. A "manufacturer" is a person who manufactures.

(9) A "music publisher" is a person that is authorized to license the reproduction of a particular musical work in a sound recording.

(10) A "professional model product" is an audio recording device that is designed, manufactured, marketed, and intended for use by recording professionals in the ordinary course of a lawful business, in accordance with such requirements as the Secretary of Commerce shall establish by regulation.

(11) The term "serial copying" means the duplication in a digital format of a copyrighted musical work or sound recording from a digital reproduction of a digital musical recording. The term "digital reproduction of a digital musical recording" does not include a digital musical recording as distributed, by authority of the copyright owner, for ultimate sale to consumers.

(12) The "transfer price" of a digital audio recording device or a digital audio recording medium—

(A) is, subject to subparagraph (B)—

(i) in the case of an imported product, the actual entered value at United States Customs (exclusive of any freight, insurance, and applicable duty), and

(ii) in the case of a domestic product, the manufacturer's transfer price (FOB the manufacturer, and exclusive of any direct sales taxes or excise taxes incurred in connection with the sale); and

(B) shall, in a case in which the transferor and transferee are related entities or within a single entity, not be less than a reasonable arms-length price under the principles of the regulations adopted pursuant to section 482 of the Internal Revenue Code of 1986 [26 USCS § 482], or any successor provision to such section.

(13) A "writer" is the composer or lyricist of a particular musical work.

(Added Oct. 28, 1992, P. L. 102-563, § 2, 106 Stat. 4237.)

SUBCHAPTER B—COPYING CONTROLS

§ 1002 Incorporation of copying controls

(a) **Prohibition on Importation, Manufacture, and Distribution.** No person shall import, manufacture, or distribute any digital audio recording device or digital audio interface device that does not conform to—

(1) the Serial Copy Management System;

(2) a system that has the same functional characteristics as the Serial Copy Management System and requires that copyright and generation status information be accurately sent, received, and acted upon between devices using the system's method of serial copying regulation and devices using the Serial Copy Management System; or

(3) any other system certified by the Secretary of Commerce as prohibiting unauthorized serial copying.

(b) **Development of Verification Procedure.** The Secretary of Commerce shall establish a procedure to verify, upon the petition of an interested party, that a system meets the standards set forth in subsection (a)(2).

(c) **Prohibition on Circumvention of the System.** No person shall import, manufacture, or distribute any device, or offer or perform any service, the primary purpose or effect of which is to avoid, bypass, remove, deactivate, or otherwise circumvent any program or circuit which implements, in whole or in part, a system described in subsection (a).

(d) **Encoding of Information on Digital Musical Recordings.**

(1) *Prohibition on encoding inaccurate information.* No person shall encode a digital musical recording of a sound recording with inaccurate information relating to the category code, copyright status, or generation status of the source material for the recording.

(2) *Encoding of copyright status not required.* Nothing in this chapter [17 USCS §§ 1001 et seq.] requires any person engaged in the importation or manufacture of digital musical recordings to encode any such digital musical recording with respect to its copyright status.

(e) **Information Accompanying Transmissions in Digital Format.** Any person who transmits or otherwise communicates to the public any sound recording in digital format is not required under this chapter [17 USCS §§ 1001 et seq.] to transmit or otherwise communicate the information relating to the copyright status of the sound recording. Any such person who does transmit or otherwise communicate such copyright status information shall transmit or communicate such information accurately.

(Added Oct. 28, 1992, P. L. 102-563, § 2, 106 Stat. 4240.)

SUBCHAPTER C—ROYALTY PAYMENTS

§ 1003 Obligation to make royalty payments

(a) **Prohibition on Importation and Manufacture.** No person shall import into and distribute, or manufacture and distribute, any digital audio recording device or digital audio recording medium unless such person records the notice specified by this section and subsequently deposits the statements of account and applicable royalty payments for such device or medium specified in section 1004.

(b) **Filing of Notice.** The importer or manufacturer of any digital audio recording device or digital audio recording medium, within a product category or utilizing a technology with respect to which such manufacturer or importer has not previously filed a notice under this subsection, shall file with the Register of Copyrights a notice with respect to such device or medium, in such form and content as the Register shall prescribe by regulation.

(c) **Filing of Quarterly and Annual Statements of Account.**

(1) *Generally.* Any importer or manufacturer that distributes any digital audio recording device or digital audio recording medium that it manufactured or imported shall file with the Register of Copyrights, in such form and content as the Register shall prescribe by regulation, such quarterly and annual statements of account with respect to such distribution as the Register shall prescribe by regulation.

(2) *Certification, verification, and confidentiality.* Each such statement shall be certified as accurate by an authorized officer or principal of the importer or manufacturer. The Register shall issue regulations to provide for the verification and audit of such statements and to protect the confidentiality of the information contained in such statements. Such regulations shall provide for the disclosure, in confidence, of such statements to interested copyright parties.

(3) *Royalty payments.* Each such statement shall be accompanied by the royalty payments specified in section 1004.

(Added Oct. 28, 1992, P. L. 102-563, § 2, 106 Stat. 4240.)

§ 1004 Royalty payments

(a) **Digital Audio Recording Devices.**

(1) *Amount of payment.* The royalty payment due under section 1003 [17 USCS § 1003] for each digital audio recording device imported into and distributed in the United States, or manufactured and distributed in the United States, shall be 2 percent of the transfer price. Only

the first person to manufacture and distribute or import and distribute such device shall be required to pay the royalty with respect to such device.

(2) *Calculation for devices distributed with other devices.* With respect to a digital audio recording device first distributed in combination with one or more devices, either as a physically integrated unit or as separate components, the royalty payment shall be calculated as follows:

(A) If the digital audio recording device and such other devices are part of a physically integrated unit, the royalty payment shall be based on the transfer price of the unit, but shall be reduced by any royalty payment made on any digital audio recording device included within the unit that was not first distributed in combination with the unit.

(B) If the digital audio recording device is not part of a physically integrated unit and substantially similar devices have been distributed separately at any time during the preceding 4 calendar quarters, the royalty payment shall be based on the average transfer price of such devices during those 4 quarters.

(C) If the digital audio recording device is not part of a physically integrated unit and substantially similar devices have not been distributed separately at any time during the preceding 4 calendar quarters, the royalty payment shall be based on a constructed price reflecting the proportional value of such device to the combination as a whole.

(3) *Limits on royalties.* Notwithstanding paragraph (1) or (2), the amount of the royalty payment for each digital audio recording device shall not be less than $1 nor more than the royalty maximum. The royalty maximum shall be $8 per device, except that in the case of a physically integrated unit containing more than 1 digital audio recording device, the royalty maximum for such unit shall be $12. During the 6th year after the effective date of this chapter [Oct. 28, 1992], and not more than once each year thereafter, any interested copyright party may petition the Copyright Royalty Judges to increase the royalty maximum and, if more than 20 percent of the royalty payments are at the relevant royalty maximum, the Copyright Royalty Judges shall prospectively increase such royalty maximum with the goal of having no more than 10 percent of such payments at the new royalty maximum; however the amount of any such increase as a percentage of the royalty maximum shall in no event exceed the percentage increase in the Consumer Price Index during the period under review.

(b) *Digital audio recording media.* The royalty payment due under section 1003 [17 USCS § 1003] for each digital audio recording medium imported into and distributed in the United States, or manufactured and distributed in the United States, shall be 3 percent of the transfer price. Only the first person to manufacture and distribute or import and distribute such medium shall be required to pay the royalty with respect to such medium.

(Added Oct. 28, 1992, P. L. 102-563, § 2, 106 Stat. 4241; Dec. 17, 1993, P. L. 103-198, § 6(b)(1), 107 Stat. 2312; Nov. 30, 2004, P. L. 108-419, § 5(i)(1), 118 Stat. 2368.)

§ 1005 Deposit of royalty payments and deduction of expenses

The Register of Copyrights shall receive all royalty payments deposited under this chapter [17 USCS §§ 1001 et seq.] and, after deducting the reasonable costs incurred by the Copyright Office under this chapter [17 USCS §§ 1001 et seq.], shall deposit the balance in the Treasury of the United States as offsetting receipts, in such manner as the Secretary of the Treasury directs. All funds held by the Secretary of the Treasury shall be invested in interest-bearing United States securities for later distribution with interest under section 1007. The Register may, in the Register's discretion, 4 years after the close of any calendar year, close out the royalty payments account for that calendar year, and may treat any funds remaining in such account and any subsequent deposits that would otherwise be attributable to that calendar year as attributable to the succeeding calendar year.

(Added Oct. 28, 1992, P. L. 102-563, § 2, 106 Stat. 4242; Dec. 17, 1993, P.L. 103-198, § 6(b)(2), 107 Stat. 2312.)

§ 1006 Entitlement to royalty payments

(a) **Interested Copyright Parties.** The royalty payments deposited pursuant to section 1005 [17 USCS § 1005] shall, in accordance with the procedures specified in section 1007 [17 USCS § 1007], be distributed to any interested copyright party—

(1) whose musical work or sound recording has been—

(A) embodied in a digital musical recording or an analog musical recording lawfully made under this title that has been distributed, and

(B) distributed in the form of digital musical recordings or analog musical recordings or disseminated to the public in transmissions, during the period to which such payments pertain; and

(2) who has filed a claim under section 1007 [17 USCS § 1007].

(b) **Allocation of Royalty Payments to Groups.** The royalty payments shall be divided into 2 funds as follows:

(1) *The sound recordings fund.* 66 ⅔ percent of the royalty payments shall be allocated to the Sound Recordings Fund. 2 ⅝ percent of the

royalty payments allocated to the Sound Recordings Fund shall be placed in an escrow account managed by an independent administrator jointly appointed by the interested copyright parties described in section 1001(7)(A) [17 USCS § 1001(7)(A)] and the American Federation of Musicians (or any successor entity) to be distributed to nonfeatured musicians (whether or not members of the American Federation of Musicians or any successor entity) who have performed on sound recordings distributed in the United States. 1 3/8 percent of the royalty payments allocated to the Sound Recordings Fund shall be placed in an escrow account managed by an independent administrator jointly appointed by the interested copyright parties described in section 1001(7)(A) [17 USCS § 1001(7)(A)] and the American Federation of Television and Radio Artists (or any successor entity) to be distributed to nonfeatured vocalists (whether or not members of the American Federation of Television and Radio Artists or any successor entity) who have performed on sound recordings distributed in the United States. 40 percent of the remaining royalty payments in the Sound Recordings Fund shall be distributed to the interested copyright parties described in section 1001(7)(C) [17 USCS § 1001(7)(C)], and 60 percent of such remaining royalty payments shall be distributed to the interested copyright parties described in section 1001(7)(A) [17 USCS § 1001(7)(A)].

(2) *The musical works fund.*

(A) 33 1/3 percent of the royalty payments shall be allocated to the Musical Works Fund for distribution to interested copyright parties described in section 1001(7)(B).

(B) (i) Music publishers shall be entitled to 50 percent of the royalty payments allocated to the Musical Works Fund.

(ii) Writers shall be entitled to the other 50 percent of the royalty payments allocated to the Musical Works Fund.

(c) **Allocation of Royalty Payments Within Groups.** If all interested copyright parties within a group specified in subsection (b) do not agree on a voluntary proposal for the distribution of the royalty payments within each group, the Copyright Royalty Judges shall, pursuant to the procedures specified under section 1007(c) [17 USCS § 1007(c)], allocate royalty payments under this section based on the extent to which, during the relevant period—

(1) for the Sound Recordings Fund, each sound recording was distributed in the form of digital musical recordings or analog musical recordings; and

(2) for the Musical Works Fund, each musical work was distributed in the form of digital musical recordings or analog musical recordings or disseminated to the public in transmissions.

(Added Oct. 28, 1992, P. L. 102-563, § 2, 106 Stat. 4242; Dec. 17, 1993, P. L. 103-198, § 6(b)(3), 107 Stat. 2312; Nov. 13, 1997, P. L. 105-80, § 12(a)(24), 111 Stat. 1535; Nov. 30, 2004, P. L. 108-419, § 5(i)(2), 118 Stat. 2368.)

§ 1007 Procedures for distributing royalty payments

(a) **Filing of Claims and Negotiations.**

(1) *Filing of claims.* During the first 2 months of each calendar year, every interested copyright party seeking to receive royalty payments to which such party is entitled under section 1006 [17 USCS § 1006] shall file with the Copyright Royalty Judges a claim for payments collected during the preceding year in such form and manner as the Copyright Royalty Judges shall prescribe by regulation.

(2) *Negotiations.* Notwithstanding any provision of the antitrust laws, for purposes of this section interested copyright parties within each group specified in section 1006(b) [17 USCS § 1006(b)] may agree among themselves to the proportionate division of royalty payments, may lump their claims together and file them jointly or as a single claim, or may designate a common agent, including any organization described in section 1001(7)(D) [17 USCS § 1001(7)(D)], to negotiate or receive payment on their behalf; except that no agreement under this subsection may modify the allocation of royalties specified in section 1006(b) [17 USCS § 1006(b)].

(b) **Distribution of Payments in the Absence of a Dispute.** After the period established for the filing of claims under subsection (a), in each year, the Copyright Royalty Judges shall determine whether there exists a controversy concerning the distribution of royalty payments under section 1006(c) [17 USCS § 1006(c)]. If the Copyright Royalty Judges determine that no such controversy exists, the Copyright Royalty Judges shall, within 30 days after such determination, authorize the distribution of the royalty payments as set forth in the agreements regarding the distribution of royalty payments entered into pursuant to subsection (a). The Librarian of Congress shall, before such royalty payments are distributed, deduct the reasonable administrative costs incurred under this section.

(c) **Resolution of Disputes.** If the Copyright Royalty Judges find the existence of a controversy, the Copyright Royalty Judges shall, pursuant to chapter 8 of this title [17 USCS §§ 801 et seq.], conduct a proceeding to determine the distribution of royalty payments. During the pendency of such a proceeding, the Copyright Royalty Judges shall withhold from distribution an amount sufficient to satisfy all claims with respect to which a controversy exists, but shall, to the extent feasible, authorize the distribution of any amounts that are not in controversy. The Librarian of Congress shall, before such royalty payments are distributed, deduct the reasonable administrative costs incurred under this section.

(Added Oct. 28, 1992, P. L. 102-563, § 2, 106 Stat. 4244; Dec. 17, 1993, P. L. 103-198, § 6(b)(4), 107 Stat. 2312; Nov. 13, 1997, P. L. 105-80, §§ 9, 12(25), 111 Stat. 1534, 1535; Nov. 30, 2004, P. L. 108-419, § 5(i)(3), 118 Stat. 2368; October 6, 2006, P.L. 109-303, § 4(f), 120 Stat. 1478.)

SUBCHAPTER D—PROHIBITON ON CERTAIN INFRINGEMENT ACTIONS, REMEDIES, AND ARBITRATION

§ 1008 Prohibition on certain infringement actions

No action may be brought under this title alleging infringement of copyright based on the manufacture, importation, or distribution of a digital audio recording device, a digital audio recording medium, an analog recording device, or an analog recording medium, or based on the noncommercial use by a consumer of such a device or medium for making digital musical recordings or analog musical recordings.

(Added Oct. 28, 1992, P. L. 102-563, § 2, 106 Stat. 4244.)

§ 1009 Civil remedies

(a) **Civil Actions.** Any interested copyright party injured by a violation of section 1002 or 1003 may bring a civil action in an appropriate United States district court against any person for such violation.

(b) **Other Civil Actions.** Any person injured by a violation of this chapter [17 USCS §§ 1001 et seq.] may bring a civil action in an appropriate United States district court for actual damages incurred as a result of such violation.

(c) **Powers of the Court.** In an action brought under subsection (a), the court—

(1) may grant temporary and permanent injunctions on such terms as it deems reasonable to prevent or restrain such violation;

(2) in the case of a violation of section 1002, or in the case of an injury resulting from a failure to make royalty payments required by section 1003, shall award damages under subsection (d);

(3) in its discretion may allow the recovery of costs by or against any party other than the United States or an officer thereof; and

(4) in its discretion may award a reasonable attorney's fee to the prevailing party.

(d) **Award of Damages.**

(1) *Damages for section 1002 or 1003 violations.*

(A) Actual damages.

(i) In an action brought under subsection (a), if the court finds that a violation of section 1002 or 1003 has occurred, the court shall award to the complaining party its actual damages if the complaining party elects such damages at any time before final judgment is entered.

(ii) In the case of section 1003, actual damages shall constitute the royalty payments that should have been paid under section 1004 and deposited under section 1005. In such a case, the court, in its discretion, may award an additional amount of not to exceed 50 percent of the actual damages.

(B) Statutory damages for section 1002 violations.

(i) *Device.* A complaining party may recover an award of statutory damages for each violation of section 1002 (a) or (c) in the sum of not more than $2,500 per device involved in such violation or per device on which a service prohibited by section 1002(c) has been performed, as the court considers just.

(ii) *Digital musical recording.* A complaining party may recover an award of statutory damages for each violation of section 1002(d) in the sum of not more than $25 per digital musical recording involved in such violation, as the court considers just.

(iii) *Transmission.* A complaining party may recover an award of damages for each transmission or communication that violates section 1002(e) in the sum of not more than $10,000, as the court considers just.

(2) *Repeated violations.* In any case in which the court finds that a person has violated section 1002 or 1003 within 3 years after a final judgment against that person for another such violation was entered, the court may increase the award of damages to not more than double the amounts that would otherwise be awarded under paragraph (1), as the court considers just.

(3) *Innocent violations of section 1002.* The court in its discretion may reduce the total award of damages against a person violating section 1002 to a sum of not less than $250 in any case in which the court finds that the violator was not aware and had no reason to believe that its acts constituted a violation of section 1002.

(e) **Payment of Damages.** Any award of damages under subsection (d) shall be deposited with the Register pursuant to section 1005 for distribution to interested copyright parties as though such funds were royalty payments made pursuant to section 1003.

(f) **Impounding of Articles.** At any time while an action under subsection (a) is pending, the court may order the impounding, on such terms as it deems reasonable, of any digital audio recording device, digital musical recording, or device specified in section 1002(c) that is in the custody or control of the alleged violator and that the court has reasonable cause to believe does not comply with, or was involved in a violation of, section 1002.

(g) **Remedial Modification and Destruction of Articles.** In an action brought under subsection (a), the court may, as part of a final judgment or decree finding a violation of section 1002, order the remedial modification or the destruction of any digital audio recording device, digital musical recording, or device specified in section 1002(c) that—

(1) does not comply with, or was involved in a violation of, section 1002, and

(2) is in the custody or control of the violator or has been impounded under subsection (f).

(Added Oct. 28, 1992, P. L. 102-563, § 2, 106 Stat. 4245.)

§ 1010 Determination of certain disputes

(a) **Scope of Determination.** Before the date of first distribution in the United States of a digital audio recording device or a digital audio interface device,any party manufacturing, importing, or distributing such device, and any interested copyright party may mutually agree to petition the Copyright Royalty Judges to determine whether such device is subject to section 1002 [17 USCS § 1002], or the basis on which royalty payments for such device are to be made under section 1003 [17 USCS § 1003].

(b) **Initiation of Proceedings.** The parties under subsection (a) shall file the petition with the Copyright Royalty Judges requesting the commencement of a proceeding. Within 2 weeks after receiving such a petition, the Chief Copyright Royalty Judge shall cause notice to be published in the Federal Register of the initiation of the proceeding.

(c) **Stay of Judicial Proceedings.** Any civil action brought under section 1009 [17 USCS § 1009] against a party to a proceeding under this section shall, on application of one of the parties to the proceeding, be stayed until completion of the proceeding.

(d) **Proceeding.** The Copyright Royalty Judges shall conduct a proceeding with respect to the matter concerned, in accordance with such procedures as the Copyright Royalty Judges may adopt. The Copyright Royalty Judges shall act on the basis of a fully documented written record. Any party to the proceeding may submit relevant information and proposals to the Copyright Royalty Judges. The parties to the proceeding shall each bear their respective costs of participation.

(e) **Judicial Review.** Any determination of the Copyright Royalty Judges under subsection (d) may be appealed, by a party to the proceeding, in accordance with section 803(d) of this title [17 USCS § 803(d)]. The pendency of an appeal under this subsection shall not stay the determination of the Copyright Royalty Judges. If the court modifies the determination of the Copyright Royalty Judges, the court shall have jurisdiction to enter its own decision in accordance with its final judgment. The court may further vacate the determination of the Copyright Royalty Judges and remand the case for proceedings as provided in this section.

(Added Oct. 28, 1992, P. L. 102-563, § 2, 106 Stat. 4246; Dec. 17, 1993, P. L. 103-198, § 6(b)(5), 107 Stat. 2312; Nov. 30, 2004, P. L. 108-419, § 5(i)(4)(A), 118 Stat. 2368.)

CHAPTER 11—SOUND RECORDINGS AND MUSIC VIDEOS

Section

§ 1101 Unauthorized fixation and trafficking in sound recordings and music videos

(a) **Unauthorized Acts.** Anyone who, without the consent of the performer or performers involved—

(1) fixes the sounds or sounds and images of a live musical performance in a copy or phonorecord, or reproduces copies or phonorecords of such a performance from an unauthorized fixation,

(2) transmits or otherwise communicates to the public the sounds or sounds and images of a live musical performance, or

(3) distributes or offers to distribute, sells or offers to sell, rents or offers to rent, or traffics in any copy or phonorecord fixed as described in paragraph (1), regardless of whether the fixations occurred in the United States, shall be subject to the remedies provided in sections 502 through 505, to the same extent as an infringer of copyright.

(b) **Definition.** In this section, the term "traffic" has the same meaning as in section 2320(e) of title 18 [18 USCS § 2320(e)].

(c) **Applicability.** This section shall apply to any act or acts that occur on or after the date of the enactment of the Uruguay Round Agreements Act [enacted Dec. 8, 1994].

(d) **State Law not Preempted.** Nothing in this section may be construed to annul or limit any rights or remedies under the common law or statutes of any State.

(Added Dec. 8, 1994, P. L. 103-465, Title V, Subtitle A, § 512(a), 108 Stat. 4974; March 16, 2006, P. L. 109-181, § 2(c)(3), 120 Stat. 288.)

CHAPTER 12—COPYRIGHT PROTECTION AND MANAGEMENT SYSTEMS

Section

§ 1201 Circumvention of copyright protection systems

(a) **Violations Regarding Circumvention of Technological Measures.**

(1) (A) No person shall circumvent a technological measure that effectively controls access to a work protected under this title. The prohibition contained in the preceding sentence shall take effect at the end of the 2-year period beginning on the date of the enactment of this chapter [enacted Oct. 28, 1998].

(B) The prohibition contained in subparagraph (A) shall not apply to persons who are users of a copyrighted work which is in a particular class of works, if such persons are, or are likely to be in the succeeding 3-year period, adversely affected by virtue of such prohibition in their ability to make noninfringing uses of that particular class of works under this title, as determined under subparagraph (C).

(C) During the 2-year period described in subparagraph (A), and during each succeeding 3-year period, the Librarian of Congress, upon the recommendation of the Register of Copyrights, who shall consult with the Assistant Secretary for Communications and Information of the Department of Commerce and report and comment on his or her views in making such recommendation, shall make the determination in a rulemaking proceeding for purposes of subparagraph (B) of whether persons who are users of a copyrighted work are, or are likely to be in the succeeding 3-year period, adversely affected by the prohibition under subparagraph (A) in their ability to make noninfringing uses under this title of a particular class of copyrighted works. In conducting such rulemaking, the Librarian shall examine—

(i) the availability for use of copyrighted works;

(ii) the availability for use of works for nonprofit archival, preservation, and educational purposes;

(iii) the impact that the prohibition on the circumvention of technological measures applied to copyrighted works has on criticism, comment, news reporting, teaching, scholarship, or research;

(iv) the effect of circumvention of technological measures on the market for or value of copyrighted works; and

(v) such other factors as the Librarian considers appropriate.

(D) The Librarian shall publish any class of copyrighted works for which the Librarian has determined, pursuant to the rulemaking conducted under subparagraph (C), that noninfringing uses by persons who are users of a copyrighted work are, or are likely to be, adversely affected, and the prohibition contained in subparagraph (A) shall not apply to such users with respect to such class of works for the ensuing 3-year period.

(E) Neither the exception under subparagraph (B) from the applicability of the prohibition contained in subparagraph (A), nor any determination made in a rulemaking conducted under subparagraph (C), may be used as a defense in any action to enforce any provision of this title other than this paragraph.

(2) No person shall manufacture, import, offer to the public, provide, or otherwise traffic in any technology, product, service, device, component, or part thereof, that—

(A) is primarily designed or produced for the purpose of circumventing a technological measure that effectively controls access to a work protected under this title;

(B) has only limited commercially significant purpose or use other than to circumvent a technological measure that effectively controls access to a work protected under this title; or

(C) is marketed by that person or another acting in concert with that person with that person's knowledge for use in circumventing a technological measure that effectively controls access to a work protected under this title.

(3) As used in this subsection—

(A) to "circumvent a technological measure" means to descramble a scrambled work, to decrypt an encrypted work, or otherwise to avoid, bypass, remove, deactivate, or impair a technological measure, without the authority of the copyright owner; and

(B) a technological measure "effectively controls access to a work" if the measure, in the ordinary course of its operation, requires the application of information, or a process or a treatment, with the authority of the copyright owner, to gain access to the work.

(b) **Additional Violations.**

(1) No person shall manufacture, import, offer to the public, provide, or otherwise traffic in any technology, product, service, device, component, or part thereof, that—

(A) is primarily designed or produced for the purpose of circumventing protection afforded by a technological measure that effectively protects a right of a copyright owner under this title in a work or a portion thereof;

(B) has only limited commercially significant purpose or use other than to circumvent protection afforded by a technological measure that effectively protects a right of a copyright owner under this title in a work or a portion thereof; or

(C) is marketed by that person or another acting in concert with that person with that person's knowledge for use in circumventing protection afforded by a technological measure that effectively protects a right of a copyright owner under this title in a work or a portion thereof.

(2) As used in this subsection—

(A) to "circumvent protection afforded by a technological measure" means avoiding, bypassing, removing, deactivating, or otherwise impairing a technological measure; and

(B) a technological measure "effectively protects a right of a copyright owner under this title" if the measure, in the ordinary course of its operation, prevents, restricts, or otherwise limits the exercise of a right of a copyright owner under this title.

(c) **Other Rights, etc., not Affected.**

(1) Nothing in this section shall affect rights, remedies, limitations, or defenses to copyright infringement, including fair use, under this title.

(2) Nothing in this section shall enlarge or diminish vicarious or contributory liability for copyright infringement in connection with any technology, product, service, device, component, or part thereof.

(3) Nothing in this section shall require that the design of, or design and selection of parts and components for, a consumer electronics, telecommunications, or computing product provide for a response to any particular technological measure, so long as such part or component, or the product in which such part or component is integrated, does not otherwise fall within the prohibitions of subsection (a)(2) or (b)(1).

(4) Nothing in this section shall enlarge or diminish any rights of free speech or the press for activities using consumer electronics, telecommunications, or computing products.

(d) **Exemption for Nonprofit Libraries, Archives, and Educational Institutions.**

(1) A nonprofit library, archives, or educational institution which gains access to a commercially exploited copyrighted work solely in order to make a good faith determination of whether to acquire a copy of that work for the sole purpose of engaging in conduct permitted under this title shall not be in violation of subsection (a)(1)(A). A copy of a work to which access has been gained under this paragraph—

(A) may not be retained longer than necessary to make such good faith determination; and

(B) may not be used for any other purpose.

(2) The exemption made available under paragraph (1) shall only apply with respect to a work when an identical copy of that work is not reasonably available in another form.

(3) A nonprofit library, archives, or educational institution that willfully for the purpose of commercial advantage or financial gain violates paragraph (1)—

(A) shall, for the first offense, be subject to the civil remedies under section 1203; and

(B) shall, for repeated or subsequent offenses, in addition to the civil remedies under section 1203, forfeit the exemption provided under paragraph (1).

(4) This subsection may not be used as a defense to a claim under subsection (a)(2) or (b), nor may this subsection permit a nonprofit library, archives, or educational institution to manufacture, import, offer to the public, provide, or otherwise traffic in any technology, product, service, component, or part thereof, which circumvents a technological measure.

(5) In order for a library or archives to qualify for the exemption under this subsection, the collections of that library or archives shall be—

(A) open to the public; or

(B) available not only to researchers affiliated with the library or archives or with the institution of which it is a part, but also to other persons doing research in a specialized field.

(e) **Law enforcement, Intelligence, and Other Government Activities.** This section does not prohibit any lawfully authorized investigative, protective, information security, or intelligence activity of an officer, agent, or employee of the United States, a State, or a political subdivision of a State, or a person acting pursuant to a contract with the United States, a State, or a political subdivision of a State. For purposes of this subsection, the term "information security" means activities carried out in order to identify and address the vulnerabilities of a government computer, computer system, or computer network.

(f) **Reverse Engineering.**

(1) Notwithstanding the provisions of subsection (a)(1)(A), a person who has lawfully obtained the right to use a copy of a computer program may circumvent a technological measure that effectively controls access to a particular portion of that program for the sole purpose of identifying and analyzing those elements of the program that are necessary to achieve interoperability of an independently created computer program with other programs, and that have not previously been readily available to the person engaging in the circumvention, to the extent any such acts of identification and analysis do not constitute infringement under this title.

(2) Notwithstanding the provisions of subsections (a)(2) and (b), a person may develop and employ technological means to circumvent a technological measure, or to circumvent protection afforded by a technological measure, in order to enable the identification and analysis under paragraph (1), or for the purpose of enabling interoperability of an independently created computer program with other programs, if such means are necessary to achieve such interoperability, to the extent that doing so does not constitute infringement under this title.

(3) The information acquired through the acts permitted under paragraph (1), and the means permitted under paragraph (2), may be made available to others if the person referred to in paragraph (1) or (2), as the case may be, provides such information or means solely for the purpose of enabling interoperability of an independently created computer program with other programs, and to the extent that doing so does not constitute infringement under this title or violate applicable law other than this section.

(4) For purposes of this subsection, the term "interoperability" means the ability of computer programs to exchange information, and of such programs mutually to use the information which has been exchanged.

(g) **Encryption Research.**

(1) *Definitions.* For purposes of this subsection—

(A) the term "encryption research" means activities necessary to identify and analyze flaws and vulnerabilities of encryption technologies applied to copyrighted works, if these activities are conducted to advance the state of knowledge in the field of encryption technology or to assist in the development of encryption products; and

(B) the term "encryption technology" means the scrambling and descrambling of information using mathematical formulas or algorithms.

(2) *Permissible acts of encryption research.* Notwithstanding the provisions of subsection (a)(1)(A), it is not a violation of that subsection

for a person to circumvent a technological measure as applied to a copy, phonorecord, performance, or display of a published work in the course of an act of good faith encryption research if—

(A) the person lawfully obtained the encrypted copy, phonorecord, performance, or display of the published work;

(B) such act is necessary to conduct such encryption research;

(C) the person made a good faith effort to obtain authorization before the circumvention; and

(D) such act does not constitute infringement under this title or a violation of applicable law other than this section, including section 1030 of title 18 and those provisions of title 18 amended by the Computer Fraud and Abuse Act of 1986 [18 USCS § 1030(a)–(c), (e), (f)].

(3) *Factors in determining exemption.* In determining whether a person qualifies for the exemption under paragraph (2), the factors to be considered shall include—

(A) whether the information derived from the encryption research was disseminated, and if so, whether it was disseminated in a manner reasonably calculated to advance the state of knowledge or development of encryption technology, versus whether it was disseminated in a manner that facilitates infringement under this title or a violation of applicable law other than this section, including a violation of privacy or breach of security;

(B) whether the person is engaged in a legitimate course of study, is employed, or is appropriately trained or experienced, in the field of encryption technology; and

(C) whether the person provides the copyright owner of the work to which the technological measure is applied with notice of the findings and documentation of the research, and the time when such notice is provided.

(4) *Use of technological means for research activities.* Notwithstanding the provisions of subsection (a)(2), it is not a violation of that subsection for a person to—

(A) develop and employ technological means to circumvent a te-chnological measure for the sole purpose of that person performing the acts of good faith encryption research described in paragraph (2); and

(B) provide the technological means to another person with whom he or she is working collaboratively for the purpose of conducting the acts of good faith encryption research described in paragraph (2) or for the purpose of having that other person verify his or her acts of good faith encryption research described in paragraph (2).

(5) *Report to Congress.* Not later than 1 year after the date of the enactment of this chapter [enacted Oct. 28, 1998], the Register of Copyrights and the Assistant Secretary for Communications and Information of the Department of Commerce shall jointly report to the Congress on the effect this subsection has had on—

(A) encryption research and the development of encryption technology;

(B) the adequacy and effectiveness of technological measures designed to protect copyrighted works; and

(C) protection of copyright owners against the unauthorized access to their encrypted copyrighted works.

The report shall include legislative recommendations, if any.

(h) **Exceptions Regarding Minors.** In applying subsection (a) to a component or part, the court may consider the necessity for its intended and actual incorporation in a technology, product, service, or device, which—

(1) does not itself violate the provisions of this title; and

(2) has the sole purpose to prevent the access of minors to material on the Internet.

(i) **Protection of Personally Identifying Information.**

(1) *Circumvention permitted.* Notwithstanding the provisions of subsection (a)(1)(A), it is not a violation of that subsection for a person to circumvent a technological measure that effectively controls access to a work protected under this title, if—

(A) the technological measure, or the work it protects, contains the capability of collecting or disseminating personally identifying information reflecting the online activities of a natural person who seeks to gain access to the work protected;

(B) in the normal course of its operation, the technological measure, or the work it protects, collects or disseminates personally identifying information about the person who seeks to gain access to the work protected, without providing conspicuous notice of such collection or dissemination to such person, and without providing such person with the capability to prevent or restrict such collection or dissemination;

(C) the act of circumvention has the sole effect of identifying and disabling the capability described in subparagraph (A), and has no other effect on the ability of any person to gain access to any work; and

(D) the act of circumvention is carried out solely for the purpose of preventing the collection or dissemination of personally identifying information about a natural person who seeks to gain access to the work protected, and is not in violation of any other law.

(2) *Inapplicability to certain technological measures.* This subsection does not apply to a technological measure, or a work it protects, that does not collect or disseminate personally identifying information and that is disclosed to a user as not having or using such capability.

(j) **Security Testing.**

(1) *Definition.* For purposes of this subsection, the term "security testing" means accessing a computer, computer system, or computer network, solely for the purpose of good faith testing, investigating, or correcting, a security flaw or vulnerability, with the authorization of the owner or operator of such computer, computer system, or computer network.

(2) *Permissible acts of security testing.* Notwithstanding the provisions of subsection (a)(1)(A), it is not a violation of that subsection for a person to engage in an act of security testing, if such act does not constitute infringement under this title or a violation of applicable law other than this section, including section 1030 of title 18 and those provisions of title 18 amended by the Computer Fraud and Abuse Act of 1986.

(3) *Factors in determining exemption.* In determining whether a person qualifies for the exemption under paragraph (2), the factors to be considered shall include—

(A) whether the information derived from the security testing was used solely to promote the security of the owner or operator of such computer, computer system or computer network, or shared directly with the developer of such computer, computer system, or computer network; and

(B) whether the information derived from the security testing was used or maintained in a manner that does not facilitate infringement under this title or a violation of applicable law other than this section, including a violation of privacy or breach of security.

(4) *Use of technological means for security testing.* Notwithstanding the provisions of subsection (a)(2), it is not a violation of that subsection for a person to develop, produce, distribute or employ technological means for the sole purpose of performing the acts of security testing described in subsection (2), provided such technological means does not otherwise violate section (a)(2).

(k) **Certain Analog Devices and Certain Technological Measures.**

(1) *Certain analog devices.*

(A) Effective 18 months after the date of the enactment of this chapter [enacted Oct. 28, 1998], no person shall manufacture, import, offer to the public, provide or otherwise traffic in any—

(i) VHS format analog video cassette recorder unless such recorder conforms to the automatic gain control copy control technology;

(ii) 8mm format analog video cassette camcorder unless such camcorder conforms to the automatic gain control technology;

(iii) Beta format analog video cassette recorder, unless such recorder conforms to the automatic gain control copy control technology, except that this requirement shall not apply until there are 1,000 Beta format analog video cassette recorders sold in the United States in any one calendar year after the date of the enactment of this chapter [enacted Oct. 28, 1998];

(iv) 8mm format analog video cassette recorder that is not an analog video cassette camcorder, unless such recorder conforms to the automatic gain control copy control technology, except that this requirement shall not apply until there are 20,000 such recorders sold in the United States in any one calendar year after the date of the enactment of this chapter [enacted Oct. 28, 1998]; or

(v) analog video cassette recorder that records using an NTSC format video input and that is not otherwise covered under clauses (i) through (iv), unless such device conforms to the automatic gain control copy control technology.

(B) Effective on the date of the enactment of this chapter [enacted Oct. 28, 1998], no person shall manufacture, import, offer to the public, provide or otherwise traffic in—

(i) any VHS format analog video cassette recorder or any 8mm format analog video cassette recorder if the design of the model of such recorder has been modified after such date of enactment so that a model of recorder that previously conformed to the automatic gain control copy control technology no longer conforms to such technology; or

(ii) any VHS format analog video cassette recorder, or any 8mm format analog video cassette recorder that is not an 8mm analog video cassette camcorder, if the design of the model of such recorder has been modified after such date of enactment so that a model of recorder that previously conformed to the four-line colorstripe copy control technology no longer conforms to such technology.

Manufacturers that have not previously manufactured or sold a VHS format analog video cassette recorder, or an 8mm format analog cassette recorder, shall be required to conform to the four-line colorstripe copy control technology in the initial model of any such recorder manufactured after the date of the enactment of this chapter [enacted Oct. 28, 1998], and thereafter to continue conforming to the four-line colorstripe copy control technology. For purposes of this subparagraph, an analog video cassette recorder "conforms to" the four-line colorstripe copy control technology if it records a signal that, when played back by the playback function of that recorder in the normal viewing mode, exhibits, on a reference display device, a display containing distracting visible lines through portions of the viewable picture.

(2) *Certain encoding restrictions.* No person shall apply the automatic gain control copy control technology or colorstripe copy control technology to prevent or limit consumer copying except such copying—

(A) of a single transmission, or specified group of transmissions, of live events or of audiovisual works for which a member of the public has exercised choice in selecting the transmissions, including the content of the transmissions or the time of receipt of such transmissions, or both, and as to which such member is charged a separate fee for each such transmission or specified group of transmissions;

(B) from a copy of a transmission of a live event or an audiovisual work if such transmission is provided by a channel or service where payment is made by a member of the public for such channel or service in the form of a subscription fee that entitles the member of the public to receive all of the programming contained in such channel or service;

(C) from a physical medium containing one or more prerecorded audiovisual works; or

(D) from a copy of a transmission described in subparagraph (A) or from a copy made from a physical medium described in subparagraph (C).

In the event that a transmission meets both the conditions set forth in subparagraph (A) and those set forth in subparagraph (B), the transmission shall be treated as a transmission described in subparagraph (A).

(3) *Inapplicability.* This subsection shall not—

(A) require any analog video cassette camcorder to conform to the automatic gain control copy control technology with respect to any video signal received through a camera lens;

(B) apply to the manufacture, importation, offer for sale, provision of, or other trafficking in, any professional analog video cassette recorder; or

(C) apply to the offer for sale or provision of, or other trafficking in, any previously owned analog video cassette recorder, if such recorder was legally manufactured and sold when new and not subsequently modified in violation of paragraph (1)(B).

(4) *Definitions.* For purposes of this subsection:

(A) An "analog video cassette recorder" means a device that records, or a device that includes a function that records, on electromagnetic tape in an analog format the electronic impulses produced by the video and audio portions of a television program, motion picture, or other form of audiovisual work.

(B) An "analog video cassette camcorder" means an analog video cassette recorder that contains a recording function that operates through a camera lens and through a video input that may be connected with a television or other video playback device.

(C) An analog video cassette recorder "conforms" to the automatic gain control copy control technology if it—

(i) detects one or more of the elements of such technology and does not record the motion picture or transmission protected by such technology; or

(ii) records a signal that, when played back, exhibits a meaningfully distorted or degraded display.

(D) The term "professional analog video cassette recorder" means an analog video cassette recorder that is designed, manufactured, marketed, and intended for use by a person who regularly employs such a device for a lawful business or industrial use, including making, performing, displaying, distributing, or transmitting copies of motion pictures on a commercial scale.

(E) The terms " VHS format", "8mm format", "Beta format", "automatic gain control copy control technology", "colorstripe copy control technology", "four-line version of the colorstripe copy control technology", and "NTSC" have the meanings that are commonly understood in the consumer electronics and motion picture industries as of the date of the enactment of this chapter [enacted Oct. 28, 1998].

(5) *Violations.* Any violation of paragraph (1) of this subsection shall be treated as a violation of subsection (b)(1) of this section. Any violation of paragraph (2) of this subsection shall be deemed an "act of circumvention" for the purposes of section 1203(c)(3)(A) of this chapter.

(Added Oct. 28, 1998, P. L. 105-304, Title I, § 103(a), 112 Stat. 2863; Nov. 29, 1999, P. L. 106-113, Div B, § 1000(a)(9), 113 Stat. 1536.)

§ 1202 Integrity of copyright management information

(a) **False Copyright Management Information.** No person shall knowingly and with the intent to induce, enable, facilitate, or conceal infringement—

(1) provide copyright management information that is false, or

(2) distribute or import for distribution copyright management information that is false.

(b) **Removal or Alteration of Copyright Management Information.** No person shall, without the authority of the copyright owner or the law—

(1) intentionally remove or alter any copyright management information,

(2) distribute or import for distribution copyright management information knowing that the copyright management information has been removed or altered without authority of the copyright owner or the law, or

(3) distribute, import for distribution, or publicly perform works, copies of works, or phonorecords,

knowing that copyright management information has been removed or altered without authority of the copyright owner or the law, knowing, or, with respect to civil remedies under section 1203, having reasonable grounds to know, that it will induce, enable, facilitate, or conceal an infringement of any right under this title.

(c) **Definition.** As used in this section, the term "copyright management information" means any of the following information conveyed in connection with copies or phonorecords of a work or performances or displays of a work, including in digital form, except that such term does not include any personally identifying information about a user of a work or of a copy, phonorecord, performance, or display of a work:

(1) The title and other information identifying the work, including the information set forth on a notice of copyright.

(2) The name of, and other identifying information about, the author of a work.

(3) The name of, and other identifying information about, the copyright owner of the work, including the information set forth in a notice of copyright.

(4) With the exception of public performances of works by radio and television broadcast stations, the name of, and other identifying information about, a performer whose performance is fixed in a work other than an audiovisual work.

(5) With the exception of public performances of works by radio and television broadcast stations, in the case of an audiovisual work, the name of, and other identifying information about, a writer, performer, or director who is credited in the audiovisual work.

(6) Terms and conditions for use of the work.

(7) Identifying numbers or symbols referring to such information or links to such information.

(8) Such other information as the Register of Copyrights may prescribe by regulation, except that the Register of Copyrights may not require the provision of any information concerning the user of a copyrighted work.

(d) **Law Enforcement, Intelligence, and Other Government Activities.** This section does not prohibit any lawfully authorized investigative, protective, information security, or intelligence activity of an officer, agent, or employee of the United States, a State, or a political subdivision of a State, or a person acting pursuant to a contract with the United States, a State, or a political subdivision of a State. For purposes of this subsection, the term "information security" means activities carried out in order to identify and address the vulnerabilities of a government computer, computer system, or computer network.

(e) **Limitations on Liability.**

(1) *Analog transmissions.* In the case of an analog transmission, a person who is making transmissions in its capacity as a broadcast station, or as a cable system, or someone who provides programming to such station or system, shall not be liable for a violation of subsection (b) if—

(A) avoiding the activity that constitutes such violation is not technically feasible or would create an undue financial hardship on such person; and

(B) such person did not intend, by engaging in such activity, to induce, enable, facilitate, or conceal infringement of a right under this title.

(2) *Digital transmissions.*

(A) If a digital transmission standard for the placement of copyright management information for a category of works is set in a voluntary, consensus standard-setting process involving a representative cross-section of broadcast stations or cable systems and copyright owners of a category of works that are intended for public performance by such stations or systems, a person identified in paragraph (1) shall not be liable for a violation of subsection (b) with respect to the particular copyright management information addressed by such standard if—

(i) the placement of such information by someone other than such person is not in accordance with such standard; and

(ii) the activity that constitutes such violation is not intended to induce, enable, facilitate, or conceal infringement of a right under this title.

(B) Until a digital transmission standard has been set pursuant to subparagraph (A) with respect to the placement of copyright management information for a category of works, a person identified in paragraph (1) shall not be liable for a violation of subsection (b) with respect to such copyright management information, if the activity that constitutes such violation is not intended to induce, enable, facilitate, or conceal infringement of a right under this title, and if—

(i) the transmission of such information by such person would result in a perceptible visual or aural degradation of the digital signal; or

(ii) the transmission of such information by such person would conflict with—

(I) an applicable government regulation relating to transmission of information in a digital signal;

(II) an applicable industry-wide standard relating to the transmission of information in a digital signal that was adopted by a voluntary consensus standards body prior to the effective date of this chapter; or

(III) an applicable industry-wide standard relating to the transmission of information in a digital signal that was adopted in a voluntary, consensus standards-setting process open to participation by a representative cross-section of broadcast stations or cable systems and copyright owners of a category of works that are intended for public performance by such stations or systems.

(3) *Definitions.* As used in this subsection—

(A) the term "broadcast station" has the meaning given that term in section 3 of the Communications Act of 1934 (47 U.S.C. 153); and

(B) the term "cable system" has the meaning given that term in section 602 of the Communications Act of 1934 (47 U.S.C. 522).

(Added Oct. 28, 1998, P. L. 105-304, Title I, § 103(a), 112 Stat. 2872; Aug. 5, 1999, P. L. 106-44, § 1(e), 113 Stat. 222.)

§ 1203 Civil remedies

(a) **Civil Actions.** Any person injured by a violation of section 1201 or 1202 may bring a civil action in an appropriate United States district court for such violation.

(b) Powers of the court. In an action brought under subsection (a), the court—

(1) may grant temporary and permanent injunctions on such terms as it deems reasonable to prevent or restrain a violation, but in no event shall impose a prior restraint on free speech or the press protected under the 1st amendment to the Constitution;

(2) at any time while an action is pending, may order the impounding, on such terms as it deems reasonable, of any device or product that is in the custody or control of the alleged violator and that the court has reasonable cause to believe was involved in a violation;

(3) may award damages under subsection (c);

(4) in its discretion may allow the recovery of costs by or against any party other than the United States or an officer thereof;

(5) in its discretion may award reasonable attorney's fees to the prevailing party; and

(6) may, as part of a final judgment or decree finding a violation, order the remedial modification or the destruction of any device or product involved in the violation that is in the custody or control of the violator or has been impounded under paragraph (2).

(c) **Award of Damages.**

(1) *In general.* Except as otherwise provided in this title, a person committing a violation of section 1201 or 1202 is liable for either—

(A) the actual damages and any additional profits of the violator, as provided in paragraph (2), or

(B) statutory damages, as provided in paragraph (3).

(2) *Actual damages.* The court shall award to the complaining party the actual damages suffered by the party as a result of the violation, and any profits of the violator that are attributable to the violation and are not taken into account in computing the actual damages, if the complaining party elects such damages at any time before final judgment is entered.

(3) *Statutory damages.*

(A) At any time before final judgment is entered, a complaining party may elect to recover an award of statutory damages for each violation of section 1201 in the sum of not less than $200 or more than $2,500 per act of circumvention, device, product, component, offer, or performance of service, as the court considers just.

(B) At any time before final judgment is entered, a complaining party may elect to recover an award of statutory damages for each violation of section 1202 in the sum of not less than $2,500 or more than $25,000.

(4) *Repeated violations.* In any case in which the injured party sustains the burden of proving, and the court finds, that a person has violated section 1201 or 1202 within 3 years after a final judgment was entered against the person for another such violation, the court may

increase the award of damages up to triple the amount that would otherwise be awarded, as the court considers just.

(5) *Innocent violations.*

(A) *In general.* The court in its discretion may reduce or remit the total award of damages in any case in which the violator sustains the burden of proving, and the court finds, that the violator was not aware and had no reason to believe that its acts constituted a violation.

(B) *Nonprofit library, archives, educational institutions, or public broadcasting entities.*

(i) *Definition.* In this subparagraph, the term "public broadcasting entity" has the meaning given such term under section 118(g).

(ii) *In general.* In the case of a nonprofit library, archives, educational institution, or public broadcasting entity, the court shall remit damages in any case in which the library, archives, educational institution, or public broadcasting entity sustains the burden of proving, and the court finds, that the library, archives, educational institution, or public broadcasting entity was not aware and had no reason to believe that its acts constituted a violation.

(Added Oct. 28, 1998, P.L. 105-304, Title I, § 103(a), 112 Stat. 2874; Nov. 29, 1999, P.L. 106-113, Div B, § 1000(a)(9), 113 Stat. 1536.)

§ 1204 Criminal offenses and penalties

(a) *In general.* Any person who violates section 1201 or 1202 willfully and for purposes of commercial advantage or private financial gain—

(1) shall be fined not more than $ 500,000 or imprisoned for not more than 5 years, or both, for the first offense; and

(2) shall be fined not more than $ 1,000,000 or imprisoned for not more than 10 years, or both, for any subsequent offense.

(b) *Limitation for nonprofit library, archives, educational institution, or public broadcasting entity.* Subsection (a) shall not apply to a nonprofit library, archives, educational institution, or public broadcasting entity (as defined under section 118(g).

(c) *Statute of limitations.* No criminal proceeding shall be brought under this section unless such proceeding is commenced within 5 years after the cause of action arose.

(Added Oct. 28, 1998, P.L. 105-304, Title I, § 103(a), 112 Stat. 2876; Nov. 29, 1999, P.L. 106-113, Div B, § 1000(a)(9), 113 Stat. 1536.)

§ 1205 Savings clause

Nothing in this chapter [17 USCS §§ 1201 et seq.] abrogates, diminishes, or weakens the provisions of, nor provides any defense or element of mitigation in a criminal prosecution or civil action under, any Federal or State law that prevents the violation of the privacy of an individual in connection with the individual's use of the Internet.

(Added Oct. 28, 1998, P. L. 105-304, Title I, § 103(a), 112 Stat. 2876.)

CHAPTER 13—PROTECTION OF ORIGINAL DESIGNS

Section

§ 1301 Designs protected

(a) **Designs Protected.**

(1) *In general.* The designer or other owner of an original design of a useful article which makes the article attractive or distinctive in appearance to the purchasing or using public may secure the protection provided by this chapter [17 USCS §§ 1301 et seq.] upon complying with and subject to this chapter [17 USCS §§ 1301 et seq.].

(2) *Vessel features.* The design of a vessel hull, deck, or combination of a hull and deck, including a plug or mold, is subject to protection under this chapter, notwithstanding section 1302(4) [17 USCS § 1302(4)].

(3) *Exceptions.* Department of Defense rights in a registered design under this chapter, including the right to build to such registered design, shall be determined solely by operation of section 2320 of title 10 [10 USCS § 2320] or by the instrument under which the design was developed for the United States Government.

(b) **Definitions.** For the purpose of this chapter [17 USCS §§ 1301 et seq.], the following terms have the following meanings:

(1) A design is "original" if it is the result of the designer's creative endeavor that provides a distinguishable variation over prior work pertaining to similar articles which is more than merely trivial and has not been copied from another source.

(2) A "useful article" is a vessel hull or deck, including a plug or mold, which in normal use has an intrinsic utilitarian function that is not merely to portray the appearance of the article or to convey information. An article which normally is part of a useful article shall be deemed to be a useful article.

(3) A "vessel" is a craft—

(A) that is designed and capable of independently steering a course on or through water through its own means of propulsion; and

(B) that is designed and capable of carrying and transporting one or more passengers.

(4) A "hull" is the exterior frame or body of a vessel, exclusive of the deck, superstructure, masts, sails, yards, rigging, hardware, fixtures, and other attachments.

(5) A "plug" means a device or model used to make a mold for the purpose of exact duplication, regardless of whether the device or model has an intrinsic utilitarian function that is not only to portray the appearance of the product or to convey information.

(6) A "mold" means a matrix or form in which a substance for material is used, regardless of whether the matrix or form has an intrinsic utilitarian function that is not only to portray the appearance of the product or to convey information.

(7) A "deck" is the horizontal surface of a vessel that covers the hull, including exterior cabin and cockpit surfaces, and exclusive of masts, sails, yards, rigging, hardware, fixtures, and other attachments.

(Added Oct. 28, 1998, P. L. 105-304, Title V, § 502, 112 Stat. 2905; Nov. 29, 1999, P. L. 106-113, Div B, § 1000(a)(9), 113 Stat. 1536; October 16, 2008, P. L. 110-434, § 1(b), 122 Stat. 4972.)

§ 1302 Designs not subject to protection

Protection under this chapter [17 USCS §§ 1301 et seq.] shall not be available for a design that is—

(1) not original;

(2) staple or commonplace, such as a standard geometric figure, a familiar symbol, an emblem, or a motif, or another shape, pattern, or configuration which has become standard, common, prevalent, or ordinary;

(3) different from a design excluded by paragraph (2) only in insignificant details or in elements which are variants commonly used in the relevant trades;

(4) dictated solely by a utilitarian function of the article that embodies it; or

(5) embodied in a useful article that was made public by the designer or owner in the United States or a foreign country more than 2 years before the date of the application for registration under this chapter [17 USCS §§ 1301 et seq.].

(Added Oct. 28, 1998, P. L. 105-304, Title V, § 502, 112 Stat. 2906; Aug. 5, 1999, P. L. 106-44, § 1(f)(1), 113 Stat. 222.)

§ 1303 Revisions, adaptations, and rearrangements

Protection for a design under this chapter [17 USCS §§ 1301 et seq.] shall be available notwithstanding the employment in the design of subject matter excluded from protection under section 1302 if the design is a substantial revision, adaptation, or rearrangement of such subject matter. Such protection shall be independent of any subsisting protection in subject matter employed in the design, and shall not be construed as securing any right to subject matter excluded from protection under this chapter [17 USCS §§ 1301 et seq.] or as extending any subsisting protection under this chapter [17 USCS §§ 1301 et seq.].

(Added Oct. 28, 1998, P. L. 105-304, Title V, § 502, 112 Stat. 2906.)

1304 Commencement of protection

The protection provided for a design under this chapter [17 USCS §§ 1301 et seq.] shall commence upon the earlier of the date of publication of the registration under section 1313(a) or the date the design is first made public as defined by section 1310(b).

(Added Oct. 28, 1998, P. L. 105-304, Title V, § 502, 112 Stat. 2907.)

§ 1305 Term of protection

(a) **In General.** Subject to subsection (b), the protection provided under this chapter [17 USCS §§ 1301 et seq.] for a design shall continue for a term of 10 years beginning on the date of the commencement of protection under section 1304.

(b) **Expiration.** All terms of protection provided in this section shall run to the end of the calendar year in which they would otherwise expire.

(c) **Termination of Rights.** Upon expiration or termination of protection in a particular design under this chapter [17 USCS §§ 1301 et seq.], all rights under this chapter [17 USCS §§ 1301 et seq.] in the design shall terminate, regardless of the number of different articles in which the design may have been used during the term of its protection.

(Added Oct. 28, 1998, P. L. 105-304, Title V, § 502, 112 Stat. 2907.)

§ 1306 Design notice

(a) **Contents of Design Notice.**

(1) Whenever any design for which protection is sought under this chapter [17 USCS §§ 1301 et seq.] is made public under section 1310(b), the owner of the design shall, subject to the provisions of section 1307, mark it or have it marked legibly with a design notice consisting of—

(A) the words "Protected Design", the abbreviation "Prot'd Des.", or the letter "D" with a circle, or the symbol "*D*";

(B) the year of the date on which protection for the design commenced; and

(C) the name of the owner, an abbreviation by which the name can be recognized, or a generally accepted alternative designation of the owner.

Any distinctive identification of the owner may be used for purposes of subparagraph (C) if it has been recorded by the Administrator before the design marked with such identification is registered.

(2) After registration, the registration number may be used instead of the elements specified in subparagraphs (B) and (C) of paragraph (1).

(b) **Location of Notice.** The design notice shall be so located and applied as to give reasonable notice of design protection while the useful article embodying the design is passing through its normal channels of commerce.

(c) **Subsequent Removal of Notice.** When the owner of a design has complied with the provisions of this section, protection under this chapter [17 USCS §§ 1301 et seq.] shall not be affected by the removal, destruction, or obliteration by others of the design notice on an article.

(Added Oct. 28, 1998, P. L. 105-304, Title V, § 502, 112 Stat. 2907.)

§ 1307 Effect of omission of notice

(a) **Actions with Notice.** Except as provided in subsection (b), the omission of the notice prescribed in section 1306 shall not cause loss of the protection under this chapter [17 USCS §§ 1301 et seq.] or prevent recovery for infringement under this chapter [17 USCS §§ 1301 et seq.] against any person who, after receiving written notice of the design protection, begins an undertaking leading to infringement under this chapter [17 USCS §§ 1301 et seq.].

(b) **Actions Without Notice.** The omission of the notice prescribed in section 1306 shall prevent any recovery under section 1323 against a person who began an undertaking leading to infringement under this chapter [17 USCS §§ 1301 et seq.] before receiving written notice of the design protection. No injunction shall be issued under this chapter [17 USCS §§ 1301 et seq.] with respect to such undertaking unless the owner of the design reimburses that person for any reasonable expenditure or contractual obligation in connection with such undertaking that was incurred before receiving written notice of the design protection, as the court in its discretion directs. The burden of providing written notice of design protection shall be on the owner of the design.

(Added Oct. 28, 1998, P. L. 105-304, Title V, § 502, 112 Stat. 2907.)

§ 1308 Exclusive rights

The owner of a design protected under this chapter [17 USCS §§ 1301 et seq.] has the exclusive right to—

(1) make, have made, or import, for sale or for use in trade, any useful article embodying that design; and

(2) sell or distribute for sale or for use in trade any useful article embodying that design.

(Added Oct. 28, 1998, P. L. 105-304, Title V, § 502, 112 Stat. 2908.)

§ 1309 Infringement

(a) **Acts of Infringement.** Except as provided in subsection (b), it shall be infringement of the exclusive rights in a design protected under this chapter [17 USCS §§ 1301 et seq.] for any person, without the consent of the owner of the design, within the United States and during the term of such protection, to—

(1) make, have made, or import, for sale or for use in trade, any infringing article as defined in subsection (e); or

(2) sell or distribute for sale or for use in trade any such infringing article.

(b) **Acts of Sellers and Distributors.** A seller or distributor of an infringing article who did not make or import the article shall be deemed to have infringed on a design protected under this chapter [17 USCS §§ 1301 et seq.] only if that person—

(1) induced or acted in collusion with a manufacturer to make, or an importer to import such article, except that merely purchasing or giving an order to purchase such article in the ordinary course of business shall not of itself constitute such inducement or collusion; or

(2) refused or failed, upon the request of the owner of the design, to make a prompt and full disclosure of that person's source of such article, and that person orders or reorders such article after receiving notice by registered or certified mail of the protection subsisting in the design.

(c) **Acts Without Knowledge.** It shall not be infringement under this section to make, have made, import, sell, or distribute, any article embodying a design which was created without knowledge that a design was protected under this chapter [17 USCS §§ 1301 et seq.] and was copied from such protected design.

(d) **Acts in Ordinary Course of Business.** A person who incorporates into that person's product of manufacture an infringing article acquired from others in the ordinary course of business, or who, without knowledge of the protected design embodied in an infringing article, makes or processes the infringing article for the account of another person in the ordinary course of business, shall not be deemed to have infringed the rights in that design under this chapter [17 USCS §§ 1301 et seq.] except under a condition contained in paragraph (1) or (2) of subsection (b). Accepting an order or reorder from the source of the infringing article shall be deemed ordering or reordering within the meaning of subsection (b)(2).

(e) **Infringing Article Defined.** As used in this section, an "infringing article" is any article the design of which has been copied from a design protected under this chapter [17 USCS §§ 1301 et seq.], without the consent of the owner of the protected design. An infringing article is not an illustration or picture of a protected design in an advertisement, book, periodical, newspaper, photograph, broadcast, motion picture, or similar medium. A design shall not be deemed to have been copied from a protected design if it is original and not substantially similar in appearance to a protected design.

(f) **Establishing Originality.** The party to any action or proceeding under this chapter [17 USCS §§ 1301 et seq.] who alleges rights under this chapter [17 USCS §§ 1301 et seq.] in a design shall have the burden of establishing the design's originality whenever the opposing party introduces an earlier work which is identical to such design, or so similar as to make prima facie showing that such design was copied from such work.

(g) **Reproduction for Teaching or Analysis.** It is not an infringement of the exclusive rights of a design owner for a person to reproduce the design in a useful article or in any other form solely for the purpose of teaching, analyzing, or evaluating the appearance, concepts, or techniques embodied in the design, or the function of the useful article embodying the design.

(Added Oct. 28, 1998, P. L. 105-304, Title V, § 502, 112 Stat. 2908.)

§ 1310 Application for registration

(a) **Time Limit for Application for Registration.** Protection under this chapter [17 USCS §§ 1301 et seq.] shall be lost if application for registration of the design is not made within 2 years after the date on which the design is first made public.

(b) **When Design is Made Public.** A design is made public when an existing useful article embodying the design is anywhere publicly exhibited, publicly distributed, or offered for sale or sold to the public by the owner of the design or with the owner's consent.

(c) **Application by Owner of Design.** Application for registration may be made by the owner of the design.

(d) **Contents of Application.** The application for registration shall be made to the Administrator and shall state—

(1) the name and address of the designer or designers of the design;

(2) the name and address of the owner if different from the designer;

(3) the specific name of the useful article embodying the design;

(4) the date, if any, that the design was first made public, if such date was earlier than the date of the application;

(5) affirmation that the design has been fixed in a useful article; and

(6) such other information as may be required by the Administrator. The application for registration may include a description setting forth the salient features of the design, but the absence of such a description shall not prevent registration under this chapter [17 USCS §§ 1301 et seq.].

(e) **Sworn Statement.** The application for registration shall be accompanied by a statement under oath by the applicant or the applicant's duly authorized agent or representative, setting forth, to the best of the applicant's knowledge and belief—

(1) that the design is original and was created by the designer or designers named in the application;

(2) that the design has not previously been registered on behalf of the applicant or the applicant's predecessor in title; and

(3) that the applicant is the person entitled to protection and to registration under this chapter [17 USCS §§ 1301 et seq.].

If the design has been made public with the design notice prescribed in section 1306 [17 USCS § 1306], the statement shall also describe the exact form and position of the design notice.

(f) **Effect of Errors.**

(1) Error in any statement or assertion as to the utility of the useful article named in the application under this section, the design of which is sought to be registered, shall not affect the protection secured under this chapter [17 USCS §§ 1301 et seq.].

(2) Errors in omitting a joint designer or in naming an alleged joint designer shall not affect the validity of the registration, or the actual ownership or the protection of the design, unless it is shown that the error occurred with deceptive intent.

(g) **Design Made in Scope of Employment.** In a case in which the design was made within the regular scope of the designer's employment and individual authorship of the design is difficult or impossible to ascribe and the application so states, the name and address of the employer for whom the design was made may be stated instead of that of the individual designer.

(h) **Pictorial Representation of Design.** The application for registration shall be accompanied by two copies of a drawing or other pictorial representation of the useful article embodying the design, having one or more views, adequate to show the design, in a form and style suitable for reproduction, which shall be deemed a part of the application.

(i) **Design in More Than One Useful Article.** If the distinguishing elements of a design are in substantially the same form in different useful articles, the design shall be protected as to all such useful articles when protected as to one of them, but not more than one registration shall be required for the design.

(j) **Application for More Than One Design.** More than one design may be included in the same application under such conditions as may be prescribed by the Administrator. For each design included in an application the fee prescribed for a single design shall be paid.

(Added Oct. 28, 1998, P. L. 105-304, Title V, § 502, 112 Stat. 2909.)

§ 1311 Benefit of earlier filing date in foreign country

An application for registration of a design filed in the United States by any person who has, or whose legal representative or predecessor or successor in title has, previously filed an application for registration of the same design in a foreign country which extends to designs of owners who are citizens of the United States, or to applications filed under this chapter [17 USCS §§ 1301 et seq.], similar protection to that provided under this chapter [17 USCS §§ 1301 et seq.] shall have that same effect as if filed in the United States on the date on which the application was first filed in such foreign country, if the application in the United States is filed within 6 months after the earliest date on which any such foreign application was filed.

(Added Oct. 28, 1998, P. L. 105-304, Title V, § 502, 112 Stat. 2910.)

§ 1312 Oaths and acknowledgments

(a) **In General.** Oaths and acknowledgments required by this chapter [17 USCS §§ 1301 et seq.]—

(1) may be made—

(A) before any person in the United States authorized by law to administer oaths; or

(B) when made in a foreign country, before any diplomatic or consular officer of the United States authorized to administer oaths, or before any official authorized to administer oaths in the foreign country concerned, whose authority shall be proved by a certificate of a diplomatic or consular officer of the United States; and

(2) shall be valid if they comply with the laws of the State or country where made.

(b) **Written Declaration in Lieu of Oath.**

(1) The Administrator may by rule prescribe that any document which is to be filed under this chapter [17 USCS §§ 1301 et seq.] in the Office of the Administrator and which is required by any law, rule, or other regulation to be under oath, may be subscribed to by a written declaration in such form as the Administrator may prescribe, and such declaration shall be in lieu of the oath otherwise required.

(2) Whenever a written declaration under paragraph (1) is used, the document containing the declaration shall state that willful false statements are punishable by fine or imprisonment, or both, pursuant to section 1001 of title 18, and may jeopardize the validity of the application or document or a registration resulting therefrom.

(Added Oct. 28, 1998, P. L. 105-304, Title V, § 502, 112 Stat. 2911.)

§ 1313 Examination of application and issue or refusal of registration

(a) **Determination of Registrability of Design; Registration.** Upon the filing of an application for registration in proper form under section 1310, and upon payment of the fee prescribed under section 1316, the Administrator shall determine whether or not the application relates to a design which on its face appears to be subject to protection under this chapter [17 USCS §§ 1301 et seq.], and, if so, the Register shall register the design. Registration under this subsection shall be announced by publication. The date of registration shall be the date of publication.

(b) **Refusal to Register; Reconsideration.** If, in the judgment of the Administrator, the application for registration relates to a design which on its face is not subject to protection under this chapter [17 USCS §§ 1301 et seq.], the Administrator shall send to the applicant a notice of refusal to register and the grounds for the refusal. Within 3 months after the date on which the notice of refusal is sent, the applicant may, by written request, seek reconsideration of the application. After consideration of such a request, the Administrator shall either register the design or send to the applicant a notice of final refusal to register.

(c) **Application to Cancel Registration.** Any person who believes he or she is or will be damaged by a registration under this chapter [17 USCS §§ 1301 et seq.] may, upon payment of the prescribed fee, apply to the Administrator at any time to cancel the registration on the ground that the design is not subject to protection under this chapter [17 USCS §§ 1301 et seq.], stating the reasons for the request. Upon receipt of an application for cancellation, the Administrator shall send to the owner of the design, as shown in the records of the Office of the Administrator, a notice of the application, and the owner shall have a period of 3 months after the date on which such notice is mailed in which to present arguments to the Administrator for support of the validity of the registration. The Administrator shall also have the authority to establish, by regulation, conditions under which the opposing parties may appear and be heard in support of their arguments. If, after the periods provided for the presentation of arguments have expired, the Administrator determines that the applicant for cancellation has established that the design is not subject to protection under this chapter [17 USCS §§ 1301 et seq.], the Administrator shall order the registration stricken from the record. Cancellation under this subsection shall be announced by publication, and notice of the Administrator's final determination with respect to any application for cancellation shall be sent to the applicant and to the owner of record. Costs of the cancellation procedure under this subsection shall be borne by the nonprevailing party or parties, and the Administrator shall have the authority to assess and collect such costs.

(Added Oct. 28, 1998, P. L. 105-304, Title V, § 502, 112 Stat. 2911; Nov. 29, 1999, P. L. 106-113, Div B, § 1000(a)(9), 113 Stat. 1536.)

§ 1314 Certification of registration

Certificates of registration shall be issued in the name of the United States under the seal of the Office of the Administrator and shall be recorded in the official records of the Office. The certificate shall state the name of the useful article, the date of filing of the application, the date of registration, and the date the design was made public, if earlier than the date of filing of the application, and shall contain a reproduction of the drawing or other pictorial representation of the design. If a description of the salient features of the design appears in the application, the description shall also appear in the certificate. A certificate of registration shall be admitted in any court as prima facie evidence of the facts stated in the certificate.

(Added Oct. 28, 1998, P. L. 105-304, Title V, § 502, 112 Stat. 2912.)

§ 1315 Publication of announcements and indexes

(a) **Publications of the Administrator.** The Administrator shall publish lists and indexes of registered designs and cancellations of designs and may also publish the drawings or other pictorial representations of registered designs for sale or other distribution.

(b) **File of Representatives of Registered Designs.** The Administrator shall establish and maintain a file of the drawings or other pictorial representations of registered designs. The file shall be available for use by the public under such conditions as the Administrator may prescribe.

(Added Oct. 28, 1998, P. L. 105-304, Title V, § 502, 112 Stat. 2912.)

§ 1316 Fees

The Administrator shall by regulation set reasonable fees for the filing of applications to register designs under this chapter [17 USCS §§ 1301 et seq.] and for other services relating to the administration of this chapter [17 USCS §§ 1301 et seq.], taking into consideration the cost of providing these services and the benefit of a public record.

(Added Oct. 28, 1998, P. L. 105-304, Title V, § 502, 112 Stat. 2912.)

§ 1317 Regulations

The Administrator may establish regulations for the administration of this chapter [17 USCS §§ 1301 et seq.].

(Added Oct. 28, 1998, P. L. 105-304, Title V, § 502, 112 Stat. 2912.)

§ 1318 Copies of records

Upon payment of the prescribed fee, any person may obtain a certified copy of any official record of the Office of the Administrator that relates to this chapter [17 USCS §§ 1301 et seq.]. That copy shall be admissible in evidence with the same effect as the original.

(Added Oct. 28, 1998, P. L. 105-304, Title V, § 502, 112 Stat. 2913.)

§ 1319 Correction of errors in certificates

The Administrator may, by a certificate of correction under seal, correct any error in a registration incurred through the fault of the Office, or, upon payment of the required fee, any error of a clerical or typographical nature occurring in good faith but not through the fault of the Office. Such registration, together with the certificate, shall thereafter have the same effect as if it had been originally issued in such corrected form.

(Added Oct. 28, 1998, P. L. 105-304, Title V, § 502, 112 Stat. 2913.)

§ 1320 Ownership and transfer

(a) **Property Right in Design.** The property right in a design subject to protection under this chapter [17 USCS §§ 1301 et seq.] shall vest in the designer, the legal representatives of a deceased designer or of one under legal incapacity, the employer for whom the designer created the design in the case of a design made within the regular scope of the designer's employment, or a person to whom the rights of the designer or of such employer have been transferred. The person in whom the property right is vested shall be considered the owner of the design.

(b) **Transfer of Property Right.** The property right in a registered design, or a design for which an application for registration has been or may be filed, may be assigned, granted, conveyed, or mortgaged by an instrument in writing, signed by the owner, or may be bequeathed by will.

(c) **Oath or Acknowledgment of Transfer.** An oath or acknowledgment under section 1312 [17 USCS § 1312] shall be prima facie evidence of the execution of an assignment, grant, conveyance, or mortgage under subsection (b).

(d) **Recordation of Transfer.** An assignment, grant, conveyance, or mortgage under subsection (b) shall be void as against any subsequent purchaser or mortgagee for a valuable consideration, unless it is recorded in the Office of the Administrator within 3 months after its date of execution or before the date of such subsequent purchase or mortgage.

(Added Oct. 28, 1998, P. L. 105-304, Title V, § 502, 112 Stat. 2913; Aug. 5, 1999, P. L. 106-44, § 1(f)(2), 113 Stat. 222.)

§ 1321 Remedy for infringement

(a) **In General.** The owner of a design is entitled, after issuance of a certificate of registration of the design under this chapter [17 USCS §§ 1301 et seq.], to institute an action for any infringement of the design.

(b) **Review of Refusal to Register.**

(1) Subject to paragraph (2), the owner of a design may seek judicial review of a final refusal of the Administrator to register the design under this chapter [17 USCS §§ 1301 et seq.] by bringing a civil action, and may in the same action, if the court adjudges the design subject to protection under this chapter [17 USCS §§ 1301 et seq.], enforce the rights in that design under this chapter [17 USCS §§ 1301 et seq.].

(2) The owner of a design may seek judicial review under this section if—

(A) the owner has previously duly filed and prosecuted to final refusal an application in proper form for registration of the design;

(B) the owner causes a copy of the complaint in the action to be delivered to the Administrator within 10 days after the commencement of the action; and

(C) the defendant has committed acts in respect to the design which would constitute infringement with respect to a design protected under this chapter [17 USCS §§ 1301 et seq.].

(c) **Administrator as Party to Action.** The Administrator may, at the Administrator's option, become a party to the action with respect to the issue of registrability of the design claim by entering an appearance within

60 days after being served with the complaint, but the failure of the Administrator to become a party shall not deprive the court of jurisdiction to determine that issue.

(d) **Use of Arbitration to Resolve Dispute.** The parties to an infringement dispute under this chapter [17 USCS §§ 1301 et seq.], within such time as may be specified by the Administrator by regulation, may determine the dispute, or any aspect of the dispute, by arbitration. Arbitration shall be governed by title 9. The parties shall give notice of any arbitration award to the Administrator, and such award shall, as between the parties to the arbitration, be dispositive of the issues to which it relates. The arbitration award shall be unenforceable until such notice is given. Nothing in this subsection shall preclude the Administrator from determining whether a design is subject to registration in a cancellation proceeding under section 1313(c).

(Added Oct. 28, 1998, P. L. 105-304, Title V, § 502, 112 Stat. 2913.)

§ 1322 Injunctions

(a) **In General.** A court having jurisdiction over actions under this chapter [17 USCS §§ 1301 et seq.] may grant injunctions in accordance with the principles of equity to prevent infringement of a design under this chapter [17 USCS §§ 1301 et seq.], including, in its discretion, prompt relief by temporary restraining orders and preliminary injunctions.

(b) **Damages for Injunctive Relief Wrongfully Obtained.** A seller or distributor who suffers damage by reason of injunctive relief wrongfully obtained under this section has a cause of action against the applicant for such injunctive relief and may recover such relief as may be appropriate, including damages for lost profits, cost of materials, loss of good will, and punitive damages in instances where the injunctive relief was sought in bad faith, and, unless the court finds extenuating circumstances, reasonable attorney's fees.

(Added Oct. 28, 1998, P. L. 105-304, Title V, § 502, 112 Stat. 2914.)

§ 1323 Recovery for infringement

(a) **Damages.** Upon a finding for the claimant in an action for infringement under this chapter [17 USCS §§ 1301 et seq.], the court shall award the claimant damages adequate to compensate for the infringement. In addition, the court may increase the damages to such amount, not exceeding $50,000 or $1 per copy, whichever is greater, as the court determines to be just. The damages awarded shall constitute compensation and not a penalty. The court may receive expert testimony as an aid to the determination of damages.

(b) **Infringer's Profits.** As an alternative to the remedies provided in subsection (a), the court may award the claimant the infringer's profits resulting from the sale of the copies if the court finds that the infringer's sales are reasonably related to the use of the claimant's design. In such a case, the claimant shall be required to prove only the amount of the infringer's sales and the infringer shall be required to prove its expenses against such sales.

(c) **Statute of Limitations.** No recovery under subsection (a) or (b) shall be had for any infringement committed more than 3 years before the date on which the complaint is filed.

(d) **Attorney's Fees.** In an action for infringement under this chapter [17 USCS §§ 1301 et seq.], the court may award reasonable attorney's fees to the prevailing party.

(e) **Disposition of Infringing and Other Articles.** The court may order that all infringing articles, and any plates, molds, patterns, models, or other means specifically adapted for making the articles, be delivered up for destruction or other disposition as the court may direct.

(Added Oct. 28, 1998, P. L. 105-304, Title V, § 502, 112 Stat. 2914.)

§ 1324 Power of court over registration

In any action involving the protection of a design under this chapter [17 USCS §§1301 et seq.], the court, when appropriate, may order registration of a design under this chapter [17 USCS §§ 1301 et seq.] or the cancellation of such a registration. Any such order shall be certified by the court to the Administrator, who shall make an appropriate entry upon the record.

(Added Oct. 28, 1998, P. L. 105-304, Title V, § 502, 112 Stat. 2915.)

§ 1325 Liability for action on registration fraudulently obtained

Any person who brings an action for infringement knowing that registration of the design was obtained by a false or fraudulent representation materially affecting the rights under this chapter [17 USCS §§ 1301 et seq.], shall be liable in the sum of $10,000, or such part of that amount as the court may determine. That amount shall be to compensate the defendant and shall be charged against the plaintiff and paid to the defendant, in addition to such costs and attorney's fees of the defendant as may be assessed by the court.

(Added Oct. 28, 1998, P. L. 105-304, Title V, § 502, 112 Stat. 2915.)

§ 1326 Penalty for false marking

(a) **In General.** Whoever, for the purpose of deceiving the public, marks upon, applies to, or uses in advertising in connection with an article made, used, distributed, or sold, a design which is not protected under this chapter [17 USCS §§ 1301 et seq.], a design notice specified in section 1306 [17 USCS § 1306], or any other words or symbols importing that the design is protected under this chapter [17 USCS §§ 1301 et seq.], knowing that the design is not so protected, shall pay a civil fine of not more than $500 for each such offense.

(b) **Suit by Private Persons.** Any person may sue for the penalty established by subsection (a), in which event one-half of the penalty shall be awarded to the person suing and the remainder shall be awarded to the United States.

(Added Oct. 28, 1998, P. L. 105-304, Title V, § 502, 112 Stat. 2915.)

§ 1327 Penalty for false representation

Whoever knowingly makes a false representation materially affecting the rights obtainable under this chapter [17 USCS §§1301 et seq.] for the purpose of obtaining registration of a design under this chapter [17 USCS §§ 1301 et seq.] shall pay a penalty of not less than $500 and not more than $1,000, and any rights or privileges that individual may have in the design under this chapter [17 USCS §§ 1301 et seq.] shall be forfeited.

(Added Oct. 28, 1998, P. L. 105-304, Title V, § 502, 112 Stat. 2915.)

§ 1328 Enforcement by Treasury and Postal Service

(a) **Regulations.** The Secretary of the Treasury and the United States Postal Service shall separately or jointly issue regulations for the enforcement of the rights set forth in section 1308 with respect to importation. Such regulations may require, as a condition for the exclusion of articles from the United States, that the person seeking exclusion take any one or more of the following actions:

(1) Obtain a court order enjoining, or an order of the International Trade Commission under section 337 of the Tariff Act of 1930 [19 USCS § 1337] excluding, importation of the articles.

(2) Furnish proof that the design involved is protected under this chapter [17 USCS §§ 1301 et seq.] and that the importation of the articles would infringe the rights in the design under this chapter [17 USCS §§ 1301 et seq.].

(3) Post a surety bond for any injury that may result if the detention or exclusion of the articles proves to be unjustified.

(b) **Seizure and Forfeiture.** Articles imported in violation of the rights set forth in section 1308 are subject to seizure and forfeiture in the same manner as property imported in violation of the customs laws. Any such forfeited articles shall be destroyed as directed by the Secretary of the Treasury or the court, as the case may be, except that the articles may be returned to the country of export whenever it is shown to the satisfaction of the Secretary of the Treasury that the importer had no reasonable grounds for believing that his or her acts constituted a violation of the law.

(Added Oct. 28, 1998, P. L. 105-304, Title V, § 502, 112 Stat. 2916.)

§ 1329 Relation to design patent law

The issuance of a design patent under title 35, United States Code, for an original design for an article of manufacture shall terminate any protection of the original design under this chapter [17 USCS §§ 1301 et seq.].

(Added Oct. 28, 1998, P. L. 105-304, Title V, § 502, 112 Stat. 2916.)

§ 1330 Common law and other rights unaffected

Nothing in this chapter [17 USCS §§ 1301 et seq.] shall annul or limit—

(1) common law or other rights or remedies, if any, available to or held by any person with respect to a design which has not been registered under this chapter [17 USCS §§ 1301 et seq.]; or

(2) any right under the trademark laws or any right protected against unfair competition.

(Added Oct. 28, 1998, P. L. 105-304, Title V, § 502, 112 Stat. 2916.)

§ 1331 Administrator; Office of the Administrator

In this chapter [17 USCS §§ 1301 et seq.], the "Administrator" is the Register of Copyrights, and the "Office of the Administrator" and the "Office" refer to the Copyright Office of the Library of Congress.

(Added Oct. 28, 1998, P. L. 105-304, Title V, § 502, 112 Stat. 2916.)

§ 1332 No retroactive effect

Protection under this chapter [17 USCS §§ 1301 et seq.] shall not be available for any design that has been made public under section 1310(b) before the effective date of this chapter [17 USCS §§ 1301 et seq.].

(Added Oct. 28, 1998, P. L. 105-304, Title V, § 502, 112 Stat. 2916.)

COPYRIGHT ACT OF 1909

17 U.S.C. §§ 1–216
(AS AMENDED TO DECEMBER 31, 1977)

CHAPTER 1—REGISTRATION OF COPYRIGHTS

Section

1. Exclusive rights as to copyrighted works
2. Rights of author or proprietor of unpublished work
3. Protection of component parts of work copyrighted; composite works or periodicals
4. All writings of author included
5. Classification of works for registration
6. Registration of prints and labels
7. Copyright on compilations of works in public domain or of copyrighted works; subsisting copyrights not affected
8. Copyright not to subsist in works in public domain, or published prior to July 1, 1909, and not already copyrighted, or Government publications; publication by Government of copyrighted material
9. Authors or proprietors, entitled; aliens
10. Publication of work with notice
11. Registration of claim and issuance of certificate
12. Works not reproduced for sale
13. Deposit of copies after publication; action or proceeding for infringement
14. Same; failure to deposit; demand; penalty
15. Same; postmaster's receipt; transmission by mail without cost
16. Mechanical work to be done in United States
17. Affidavit to accompany copies
18. Making false affidavit
19. Notice; form
20. Same; place of application of; one notice in each volume or number of newspaper or periodical
21. Same; effect of accidental omission from copy or copies
22. Ad interim protection of book or periodical published abroad
23. Same; extension to full term
24. Duration, renewal and extension
25. Renewal of copyrights registered in Patent Office under repealed law
26. Terms defined
27. Copyright distinct from property in object copyrighted; effect of sale of object, and of assignment of copyright

28. Assignments and bequests
29. Same; executed in foreign country; acknowledgment and certificate
30. Same; record
31. Same; certificate of record
32. Same; use of name of assignee in notice

§1 Exclusive rights as to copyrighted works

Any person entitled thereto, upon complying with the provisions of this title, shall have the exclusive right:

(a) To print, reprint, publish, copy, and vend the copyrighted work;

(b) To translate the copyrighted work into other languages or dialects, or make any other version thereof, if it be a literary work; to dramatize it if it be a nondramatic work; to convert it into a novel or other nondramatic work if it be a drama; to arrange or adapt it if it be a musical work; to complete, execute, and finish it if it be a model or design for a work of art;

(c) To deliver, authorize the delivery of, read, or present the copyrighted work in public for profit if it be a lecture, sermon, address or similar production, or other nondramatic literary work; to make or procure the making of any transcription or record thereof by or from which, in whole or in part, it may in any manner or by any method be exhibited, delivered, presented, produced, or reproduced; and to play or perform it in public for profit, and to exhibit, represent, produce, or reproduce it in any manner or by any method whatsoever. The damages for the infringement by broadcast of any work referred to in this subsection shall not exceed the sum of $100 where the infringing broadcaster shows that he was not aware that he was infringing and that such infringement could not have been reasonably foreseen; and

(d) To perform or represent the copyrighted work publicly if it be a drama or, if it be a dramatic work and not reproduced in copies for sale, to vend any manuscript or any record whatsoever thereof; to make or to procure the making of any transcription or record thereof by or from which, in whole or in part, it may in any manner or by any method be exhibited, performed, represented, produced, or reproduced; and to exhibit, perform, represent, produce, or reproduce it in any manner or by any method whatsoever; and

(e) To perform the copyrighted work publicly for profit if it be a musical composition; and for the purpose of public performance for profit, and for the purposes set forth in subsection (a) hereof, to make any arrangement or setting of it or of the melody of it in any system of notation or any form of record in which the thought of an author may be recorded and from which it may be read or reproduced: *Provided,* That the provisions of this title, so far as they secure copyright controlling the parts of instruments serving to reproduce mechanically the musical work, shall include only compositions published and copyrighted after July 1, 1909, and shall not include the works of a foreign author or composer unless the foreign state or nation of which such author or composer is a citizen or subject grants, either by treaty, convention, agreement, or law, to citizens of the United States similar rights. And as a condition of extending the copyrighted control to such mechanical reproductions, that whenever the owner of a musical copyright has used or permitted or knowingly acquiesced in the use of the copyrighted work upon the parts of instruments serving to reproduce mechanically the musical work, any other person may make similar use of the copyrighted work upon the payment to the copyright proprietor of a royalty of 2 cents on each such part manufactured, to be paid by the manufacturer thereof; and the copyright proprietor may require, and if so the manufacturer shall furnish, a report under oath on the 20th day of each month on the number of parts of instruments manufactured during the previous month serving to reproduce mechanically said musical work, and royalties shall be due on the parts manufactured during any month upon the 20th of the next succeeding month. The payment of the royalty provided for by this section shall free the articles or devices for which such royalty has been paid from further contribution to the copyright except in case of public performance for profit. It shall be the duty of the copyright owner, if he uses the musical composition himself for the manufacture of parts of instruments serving to reproduce mechanically the musical work, or licenses others to do so, to file notice thereof, accompanied by a recording fee, in the Copyright Office, and any failure to file such notice shall be a complete defense to any suit, action, or proceeding for any infringement of such copyright.

In case of failure of such manufacturer to pay to the copyright proprietor within thirty days after demand in writing the full sum of royalties due at said rate at the date of such demand, the court may award taxable costs to the plaintiff and a reasonable counsel fee, and the court may, in its discretion, enter judgment therein for any sum in addition over the amount found to be due as royalty in accordance with the terms of this title, not exceeding three times such amount.

The reproduction or rendition of a musical composition by or upon coin-operated machines shall not be deemed a public performance for profit unless a fee is charged for admission to the place where such reproduction or rendition occurs.

(f) To reproduce and distribute to the public by sale or other transfer of ownership, or by rental, lease, or lending, reproductions of the copyrighted work if it be a sound recording: *Provided,* That the exclusive right of the owner of a copyright in a sound recording to reproduce it is limited to the right to duplicate the sound recording in a tangible form that directly or indirectly recaptures the actual sounds fixed in the recording: *Provided further,* That this right does not extend to the making or duplication of another sound recording that is an independent fixation of other sounds, even though such sounds imitate or simulate those in the copyrighted sound recording; or to reproductions made by transmitting organizations exclusively for their own use. July 30, 1947, c. 391, 61 Stat. 652; July 17, 1952, c. 923, § 1, 66 Stat. 752; Oct. 15, 1971, Pub. L. 92-140, § 1(a), 85 Stat. 391.

§2 Rights of author or proprietor of unpublished work

Nothing in this title shall be construed to annul or limit the right of the author or proprietor of an unpublished work, at common law or in equity, to prevent the copying, publication, or use of such unpublished work without his consent, and to obtain damages therefor. July 30, 1947, c. 391, 61 Stat. 654.

§3 Protection of component parts of work copyrighted; composite works or periodicals

The copyright provided by this title shall protect all the copyrightable component parts of the work copyrighted, and all matter therein in which copyright is already subsisting, but without extending the duration or scope of such copyright. The copyright upon composite works or periodicals shall give to the proprietor thereof all the rights in respect thereto which he would have if each part were individually copyrighted under this title. July 30, 1947, c. 391, 61 Stat. 654; Oct. 31, 1951, c. 655, §16(a), 65 Stat. 716.

§4 All writings of author included

The works for which copyright may be secured under this title shall include all the writings of an author. July 30, 1947, c. 391, 61 Stat. 654.

§5 Classification of works for registration

The application for registration shall specify to which of the following classes the work in which copyright is claimed belongs:

(a) Books, including composite and cyclopedic works, directories, gazetteers, and other compilations.

(b) Periodicals, including newspapers.

(c) Lectures, sermons, addresses (prepared for oral delivery).

(d) Dramatic or dramatico-musical compositions.

(e) Musical compositions.

(f) Maps.

(g) Works of art; models or designs for works of art.

(h) Reproductions of a work of art.

(i) Drawings or plastic works of a scientific or technical character.

(j) Photographs.

(k) Prints and pictorial illustrations including prints or labels used for articles of merchandise.

(l) Motion-picture photoplays.

(m) Motion pictures other than photoplays.

(n) Sound recordings.

The above specifications shall not be held to limit the subject matter of copyright as defined in section 4 of this title, nor shall any error in classification invalidate or impair the copyright protection secured under this title. July 30, 1947, c. 391, 61 Stat. 654; Oct. 15, 1971, Pub. L. 92-140, § 1(b), 85 Stat. 391.

§ 6 Registration of prints and labels

Commencing July 1, 1940, the Register of Copyrights is charged with the registration of claims to copyright properly presented, in all prints and labels published in connection with the sale or advertisement of articles of merchandise, including all claims to copyright in prints and labels pending in the Patent Office and uncleared at the close of business June 30, 1940. There shall be paid for registering a claim of copyright in any such print or label not a trade-mark $6, which sum shall cover the expense of furnishing a certificate of such registration, under the seal of the Copyright Office, to the claimant of copyright. July 30, 1947, c. 391, 61 Stat. 654.

§ 7 Copyright on compilations of works in public domain or of copyrighted works; subsisting copyrights not affected

Compilations or abridgments, adaptations, arrangements, dramatizations, translations, or other versions of works in the public domain or of copyrighted works when produced with the consent of the proprietor of the copyright in such works, or works republished with new matter, shall be regarded as new works subject to copyright under the provisions of this title; but the publication of any such new works shall not affect the force or validity of any subsisting copyright upon the matter employed or any part thereof, or be construed to imply an exclusive right to such use of the original works, or to secure or extend copyright in such original works. July 30, 1947, c. 391, 61 Stat. 655.

§ 8 Copyright not to subsist in works in public domain, or published prior to July 1, 1909, and not already copyrighted, or Government publications; publication by Government of copyrighted material

No copyright shall subsist in the original text of any work which is in the public domain, or in any work which was published in this country or any foreign country prior to July 1, 1909, and has not been already copyrighted in the United States, or in any publication of the United States Government, or any reprint, in whole or in part, thereof, except that the United States Postal Service may secure copyright on behalf of the United States in the whole or any part of the publications authorized by section 405 of title 39.

The publication or republication by the Government, either separately or in a public document, of any material in which copyright is subsisting shall not be taken to cause any abridgment or annulment of the copyright or to authorize any use or appropriation of such material without the consent of the copyright proprietor. July 30, 1947, c. 391, 61 Stat. 655; Oct. 31, 1951, c. 655, §16(b), 65 Stat. 716; Sept. 7, 1962, Pub. L. 87-646, §21, 76 Stat. 446; Aug. 12, 1970, Pub. L. 91-375, § 6(i), 84 Stat. 777.

§9 Authors or proprietors, entitled; aliens

The author or proprietor of any work made the subject of copyright by this title, or his executors, administrators, or assigns, shall have copyright for such work under the conditions and for the terms specified in this title: *Provided, however,* That the copyright secured by this title shall extend to the work of an author or proprietor who is a citizen or subject of a foreign state or nation only under the conditions described in subsections (a), (b), or (c) below:

(a) When an alien author or proprietor shall be domiciled within the United States at the time of the first publication of his work; or

(b) When the foreign state or nation of which such author or proprietor is a citizen or subject grants, either by treaty, convention, agreement, or law, to citizens of the United States the benefit of copyright on substantially the same basis as to its own citizens, or copyright protection, substantially equal to the protection secured to such foreign author under this title or by treaty; or when such foreign state or nation is a party to an international agreement which provides for reciprocity in the granting of copyright, by the terms of which agreement the United States may, at its pleasure, become a party thereto.

The existence of the reciprocal conditions aforesaid shall be determined by the President of the United States, by proclamation made from time to time, as the purposes of this title may require: *Provided*, That whenever the President shall find that the authors, copyright owners, or proprietors of works first produced or published abroad and subject to copyright or to renewal of copyright under the laws of the United States, including works subject to ad interim copyright, are or may have been temporarily unable to comply with the conditions and formalities prescribed with respect to such works by the copyright laws of the United States, because of the disruption or suspension of facilities essential for such compliance, he may by proclamation grant such extension of time as he may deem appropriate for the fulfillment of such conditions or formalities by authors, copyright owners, or proprietors who are citizens of the United States or who are nationals of countries which accord substantially equal treatment in this respect to authors, copyright owners, or proprietors who are citizens of the United States: *Provided further,* That no liability shall attach under this title for lawful uses made or acts done prior to the effective date of such proclamation in connection with such works, or in respect to the continuance for one year subsequent to such date of any business undertaking or enterprise lawfully undertaken prior to such date involving expenditure or contractual obligation in connection with the exploitation, production, reproduction, circulation, or performance of any such work.

The President may at any time terminate any proclamation authorized herein or any part thereof or suspend or extend its operation for such period or periods of time as in his judgment the interests of the United States may require.

(c) When the Universal Copyright Convention, signed at Geneva on September 6, 1952, shall be in force between the United States of America and the foreign state or nation of which such author is a citizen or subject, or in which the work was first published. Any work to which copyright is extended pursuant to this subsection shall be exempt from the following provisions of this title: (1) The requirement in section 1(e) that a foreign state or nation must grant to United States citizens mechanical reproduction rights similar to those specified therein; (2) the obligatory deposit requirements of the first sentence of section 13; (3) the provisions of sections 14, 16, 17, and 18; (4) the import prohibitions of section 107, to the extent that they are related to the manufacturing requirements of section 16; and (5) the requirements of sections 19 and 20: *Provided, however,* That such exemptions shall apply only if from the time of first publication all the copies of the work published with the authority of the author or other copyright proprietor shall bear the symbol © accompanied by the name of the copyright proprietor and the year of first publication placed in such manner and location as to give reasonable notice of claim of copyright.

Upon the coming into force of the Universal Copyright Convention in a foreign state or nation as hereinbefore provided, every book or periodical of a citizen or subject thereof in which ad interim copyright was subsisting on the effective date of said coming into force shall have copyright for twenty-eight years from the date of first publication abroad without the necessity of complying with the further formalities specified in section 23 of this title.

The provisions of this subsection shall not be extended to works of an author who is a citizen of, or domiciled in the United States of America regardless of place of first publication, or to works first published in the United States. July 30, 1947, c. 391, 61 Stat. 655; Aug. 31, 1954, c. 1161, § 1, 68 Stat. 1030.

§10 Publication of work with notice

Any person entitled thereto by this title may secure copyright for his work by publication thereof with the notice of copyright required by this title; and such notice shall be affixed to each copy thereof published or offered for sale in the United States by authority of the copyright proprietor, except in the case of books seeking ad interim protection under section 22 of this title. July 30, 1947, c. 391, 61 Stat. 656.

§11 Registration of claim and issuance of certificate

Such person may obtain registration of his claim to copyright by complying with the provisions of this title, including the deposit of copies, and upon such compliance the Register of Copyrights shall issue to him the certificates provided for in section 209 of this title. July 30, 1947, c. 391, 61 Stat. 656.

§12 Works not reproduced for sale

Copyright may also be had of the works of an author, of which copies are not reproduced for sale, by the deposit, with claim of copyright, of one complete copy of such work if it be a lecture or similar production or a dramatic, musical, or dramatico-musical composition; of a title and description, with one print taken from each scene or act, if the work be a motion-picture photoplay; of a photographic print if the work be a photograph; of a title and description, with not less than two prints taken from different sections of a complete motion picture, if the work be a motion picture other than a photoplay; or of a photograph or other identifying reproduction thereof, if it be a work of art or a plastic work or drawing. But the privilege of registration of copyright secured hereunder shall not exempt the copyright proprietor from the deposit of copies, under sections 13 and 14 of this title, where the work is later reproduced in copies for sale. July 30, 1947, c. 391, 61 Stat. 656.

§13 Deposit of copies after publication; action or proceeding for infringement

After copyright has been secured by publication of the work with the notice of copyright as provided in section 10 of this title, there shall be promptly deposited in the Copyright Office or in the mail addressed to the Register of Copyrights, Washington, District of Columbia, two complete copies of the best edition thereof then published, or if the work is by an author who is a citizen or subject of a foreign state or nation and has been published in a foreign country, one complete copy of the best edition then published in such foreign country, which copies or copy, if the work be a book or periodical, shall have been produced in accordance with the manufacturing provisions specified in section 16 of this title; or if such work be a contribution to a periodical, for which contribution special registration is requested, one copy of the issue or issues containing such contribution; or if the work belongs to a class specified in subsections (g), (h), (i) or (k) of section 5 of this title, and if the Register of Copyrights determines that it is impracticable to deposit copies because of their size, weight, fragility, or monetary value he may permit the deposit of photographs or other identifying reproductions in lieu of copies of the work as published under such rules and regulations as he may prescribe with the approval of the Librarian of Congress; or if the work is not reproduced in copies for sale there shall be deposited the copy, print, photograph, or other identifying reproduction provided by section 12 of this title, such copies or copy, print, photograph, or other reproduction to be accompanied in each case by a claim of copyright. No action or proceeding shall be maintained for infringement of copyright in any work until the provisions of this title with respect to the deposit of copies and registration of such work shall have been complied with. July 30, 1947, c. 391, 61 Stat. 656; Mar. 29, 1956, c. 109, 70 Stat. 63.

§14 Same; failure to deposit; demand; penalty

Should the copies called for by section 13 of this title not be promptly deposited as provided in this title, the Register of Copyrights may at any time after the publication of the work, upon actual notice, require the proprietor of the copyright to deposit them, and after the said demand shall have been made, in default of the deposit of copies of the work within three months from any part of the United States, except an outlying territorial possession of the United States, or within six months from any outlying territorial possession of the United States, or from any foreign country, the proprietor of the copyright shall be liable to a fine of $100 and to pay to the Library of Congress twice the amount of the retail price of the best edition of the work, and the copyright shall become void. July 30, 1947, c. 391, 61 Stat. 657.

§15 Same; postmaster's receipt; transmission by mail without cost

The postmaster to whom are delivered the articles deposited as provided in sections 12 and 13 of this title shall, if requested, give a receipt therefor and shall mail them to their destination without cost to the copyright claimant. July 30, 1947, c. 391, 61 Stat. 657.

§16 Mechanical work to be done in United States

Of the printed book or periodical specified in section 5, subsections (a) and (b), of this title, except the original text of a book or periodical of foreign origin in a language or languages other than English, the text of all copies accorded protection under this title, except as below provided, shall be printed from type set within the limits of the United States, either by hand or by the aid of any kind of typesetting machine, or from plates made within the limits of the United States from type set therein, or, if the text be produced by lithographic process, or photoengraving process, then by a process wholly performed within the limits of the United States, and the printing of the text and binding of the said book shall be performed within the limits of the United States; which requirements shall extend also to the illustrations within a book consisting of printed text and illustrations produced by lithographic process, or photoengraving process, and also to separate lithographs or photoengravings, except where in either case the subjects represented are located in a foreign country and illustrate a scientific work or reproduce a work of art: *Provided, however,* That said requirements shall not apply to works in raised characters for the use of the blind, or to books or periodicals of foreign origin in a language or languages other than English, or to works printed or produced in the United States by any other process than those above specified in this section, or to copies of books or periodicals, first published abroad in the English language, imported into the United States within five years after first publication in a foreign state or nation up to the number of fifteen hundred copies of each such book or periodical if said copies shall contain notice of copyright in accordance with sections 10, 19, and 20 of this title and if ad interim copyright in said work shall have been obtained pursuant to section 22 of this title prior to the importation into the United States of any copy except those permitted by the provisions of section 107 of this title: *Provided further,* That the provisions of this section shall not affect the right of importation under the provisions of section 107 of this title. July 30, 1947, c. 391, 61 Stat. 657; June 3, 1949, c. 171, § 1, 63 Stat. 153; Aug. 31, 1954, c. 1161, § 2, 68 Stat. 1031.

§ 17 Affidavit to accompany copies

In the case of the book the copies so deposited shall be accompanied by an affidavit under the official seal of any officer authorized to administer oaths within the United States, duly made by the person claiming copyright or by his duly authorized agent or representative residing in the United States, or by the printer who has printed the book, setting forth that the copies deposited have been printed from type set within the limits of the United States or from plates made within the limits of the United States from type set therein; or, if the text be produced by lithographic process, or photoengraving process, that such process was wholly performed within the limits of the United States and that the printing of the text and binding of the said book have also been performed within the limits of the United States. Such affidavit shall state also the place where and the establishment or establishments in which such type was set or plates were made or lithographic process, or photoengraving process or printing and binding were performed and the date of the completion of the printing of the book or the date of publication. July 30, 1947, c. 391, 61 Stat. 657.

§ 18 Making false affidavit

Any person who, for the purpose of obtaining registration of a claim to copyright, shall knowingly make a false affidavit as to his having complied with the above conditions shall be deemed guilty of a misdemeanor, and upon conviction thereof shall be punished by a fine of not more than $1,000, and all of his rights and privileges under said copyright shall thereafter be forfeited. July 30, 1947, c. 391, 61 Stat. 658.

§ 19 Notice; form

The notice of copyright required by section 10 of this title shall consist either of the word "Copyright," the abbreviation "Copr.," or the symbol ©, accompanied by the name of the copyright proprietor, and if the work be a printed literary, musical, or dramatic work, the notice shall include also the year in which the copyright was secured by publication. In the case, however, of copies of works specified in subsections (f) to (k), inclusive, of section 5 of this title, the notice may consist of the letter C enclosed within a circle, thus ©, accompanied by the initials, monogram, mark, or symbol of the copyright proprietor: *Provided,* That on some accessible portion of such copies or of the margin, back, permanent base, or pedestal, or of the substance on which such copies shall be mounted, his name shall appear. But in the case of works in which copyright was subsisting on July 1, 1909, the notice of copyright may be either in one of the forms prescribed herein or may consist of the following words: "Entered according to Act of Congress, in the year 0000, by A.B., and in the office of the Librarian of Congress, at Washington, D.C.," or, at his option, the word "Copyright," together with the year the copyright was entered and the name of the party by whom it was taken out; thus, "Copyright, 1900, by A.B."

In the case of reproductions of works specified in subsection (n) of section 5 of this title, the notice shall consist of the symbol Ⓟ (the letter P in a circle), the year of first publication of the sound recording, and the name of the owner of copyright in the sound recording, or an abbreviation by which the name can be recognized, or a generally known alternative designation of the owner: *Provided,* That if the producer of the sound recording is named on the labels or containers of the reproduction, and if no other name appears in conjunction with the notice, his name shall be considered a part of the notice. July 30, 1947, c. 391, 61 Stat. 658; Aug. 31, 1954, c. 1161, §3, 68 Stat. 1032; Oct. 15, 1971, Pub. L. 92-140, §1(c), 85 Stat. 391.

§20 Same; place of application of; one notice in each volume or number of newspaper or periodical

The notice of copyright shall be applied, in the case of a book or other printed publication, upon its title page or the page immediately following, or if a periodical either upon the title page or upon the first page of text of each separate number or under the title heading, or if a musical work either upon its title page or the first page of music, or if a sound recording on the surface of reproductions thereof or on the label or container in such manner and location as to give reasonable notice of the claim of copyright. One notice of copyright in each volume or in each number of a newspaper or periodical published shall suffice. July 30, 1947, c. 391, 61 Stat. 658; Oct. 15, 1971, Pub. L. 92-140, §1(d), 85 Stat. 391.

§21 Same; effect of accidental omission from copy or copies

Where the copyright proprietor has sought to comply with the provisions of this title with respect to notice, the omission by accident or mistake of the prescribed notice from a particular copy or copies shall not invalidate the copyright or prevent recovery for infringement against any person who, after actual notice of the copyright, begins an undertaking to infringe it, but shall prevent the recovery of damages against an innocent infringer who has been misled by the omission of the notice; and in a suit for infringement no permanent injunction shall be had unless the copyright proprietor shall reimburse to the innocent infringer his reasonable outlay innocently incurred if the court, in its discretion, shall so direct. July 30, 1947, c. 391, 61 Stat. 658.

§22 Ad interim protection of book or periodical published abroad

In the case of a book or periodical first published abroad in the English language the deposit in the Copyright Office, not later than six months after its publication abroad, of one complete copy of the foreign edition, with a request for the reservation of the copyright and a statement of the name and nationality of the author and of the copyright proprietor and of the date of publication of the said book or periodical, shall secure to the author or proprietor an ad interim copyright therein, which shall have all the force and effect given to copyright by this title, and shall endure until the expiration of five years after the date of first publication abroad. July 30, 1947, c. 391, 61 Stat. 659; June 3, 1949, c. 171, §2, 63 Stat. 154.

§23 Same; extension to full term

Whenever within the period of such ad interim protection an authorized edition of such books or periodicals shall be published within the United States, in accordance with the manufacturing provisions specified in section 16 of this title, and whenever the provisions of this title as to deposit of copies, registration, filing of affidavits, and the printing of the copyright notice shall have been duly complied with, the copyright shall be extended to endure in such book or periodical for the term provided in this title. July 30, 1947, c. 391, 61 Stat. 659; June 3, 1949, c. 171, §3, 63 Stat. 154.

§24 Duration, renewal and extension

The copyright secured by this title shall endure for twenty-eight years from the date of first publication, whether the copyrighted work bears the author's true name or is published anonymously or under an assumed name: *Provided,* That in the case of any posthumous work or of any periodical, cyclopedic, or other composite work upon which the copyright was originally secured by the proprietor thereof, or of any work copyrighted by a corporate body (otherwise than as assignee or licensee of the individual author) or by an employer for whom such work is made for hire, the proprietor of such copyright shall be entitled to a renewal and extension of the copyright in such work for the further term of twenty-eight years when application for such renewal and extension shall have been made to the Copyright Office and duly registered therein within one year prior to the expiration of the original term of copyright: *And provided further,* That in the case of any other copyrighted work, including a contribution by an individual author to a periodical or to a cyclopedic or other composite work, the author of such work, if still living, or the widow, widower, or children of the author, if the author be not living, or if such author, widow, widower or children be not living, then the author's executors, or in the absence of a will, his next of kin shall be entitled to a renewal and extension of the copyright in such work for a further term of twenty-eight years when application for such renewal and extension shall have been made to the Copyright Office and duly registered therein within one year prior to the expiration of the original term of copyright: *And provided further,* That in default of the registration of such application for renewal and extension, the copyright in any work shall determine at the expiration of twenty-eight years from first publication. July 30, 1947, c. 391, 61 Stat. 659.

§25 Renewal of copyrights registered in Patent Office under repealed law

Subsisting copyrights originally registered in the Patent Office prior to July 1, 1940, under section 3 of the act of June 18, 1874, shall be subject to renewal in behalf of the proprietor upon application made to the Register of Copyrights within one year prior to the expiration of the original term of twenty-eight years. July 30, 1947, c. 391, 61 Stat. 659.

§26 Terms defined

In the interpretation and construction of this title "the date of publication" shall in the case of a work of which copies are reproduced for sale or distribution be held to be the earliest date when copies of the first authorized edition were placed on sale, sold, or publicly distributed by the proprietor of the copyright or under his authority, and the word "author" shall include an employer in the case of works made for hire.

For the purposes of this section and sections 10, 11, 13, 14, 21, 101, 106, 109, 209, 215, but not for any other purpose, a reproduction of a work described in subsection 5(n) shall be considered to be a copy thereof. "Sound recordings" are works that result from the fixation of a series of musical, spoken, or other sounds, but not including the sounds accompanying a motion picture. "Reproductions of sound recordings" are material objects in which sounds other than those accompanying a motion picture are fixed by any method now known or later developed, and from which the sounds can be perceived, reproduced, or otherwise communicated, either directly or with the aid of a machine or device, and include the "parts of instruments serving to reproduce mechanically the musical work," "mechanical reproductions," and "interchangeable parts, such as discs or tapes for use in mechanical music-producing machines" referred to in sections 1(e) and 101(e) of this title. July 30, 1947, c. 391, 61 Stat. 659; Oct. 15, 1971, Pub. L. 92-140, §1(e), 85 Stat. 391.

§27 Copyright distinct from property in object copyrighted; effect of sale of object, and of assignment of copyright

The copyright is distinct from the property in the material object copyrighted, and the sale or conveyance, by gift or otherwise, of the material object shall not of itself constitute a transfer of the copyright, nor shall the assignment of the copyright constitute a transfer of the title to the material object; but nothing in this title shall be deemed to forbid, prevent, or restrict the transfer of any copy of a copyrighted work the possession of which has been lawfully obtained. July 30, 1947, c. 391, 61 Stat. 660.

§28 Assignments and bequests

Copyright secured under this title or previous copyright laws of the United States may be assigned, granted, or mortgaged by an instrument in writing signed by the proprietor of the copyright, or may be bequeathed by will. July 30, 1947, c. 391, 61 Stat. 660.

§29 Same; executed in foreign country; acknowledgment and certificate

Every assignment of copyright executed in a foreign country shall be acknowledged by the assignor before a consular officer or secretary of legation of the United States authorized by law to administer oaths or perform notarial acts. The certificate of such acknowledgment under the hand and official seal of such consular officer or secretary of legation shall be prima facie evidence of the execution of the instrument. July 30, 1947, c. 391, 61 Stat. 660.

§30 Same; record

Every assignment of copyright shall be recorded in the Copyright Office within three calendar months after its execution in the United States or within six calendar months after its execution without the limits of the United States, in default of which it shall be void as against any subsequent purchaser or mortgagee for a valuable consideration, without notice, whose assignment has been duly recorded. July 30, 1947, c. 391, 61 Stat. 660.

§31 Same; certificate of record

The Register of Copyrights shall, upon payment of the prescribed fee, record such assignment, and shall return it to the sender with a certificate of record attached under seal of the Copyright Office, and upon the payment of the fee prescribed by this title he shall furnish to any person requesting the same a certified copy thereof under the said seal. July 30, 1947, c. 391, 61 Stat. 660.

§32 Same; use of name of assignee in notice

When an assignment of the copyright in a specified book or other work has been recorded the assignee may substitute his name for that of the assignor in the statutory notice of copyright prescribed by this title. July 30, 1947, c. 391, 61 Stat. 660.

CHAPTER 2—INFRINGEMENT PROCEEDINGS

§ 101 Infringement

If any person shall infringe the copyright in any work protected under the copyright laws of the United States such person shall be liable:

(a) Injunction

To an injunction restraining such infringement;

(b) Damages and profits; amounts; other remedies

To pay to the copyright proprietor such damages as the copyright proprietor may have suffered due to the infringement, as well as all the profits which the infringer shall have made from such infringement, and in proving profits the plaintiff shall be required to prove sales only, and the defendant shall be required to prove every element of cost which he claims, or in lieu of actual damages and profits, such damages as to the court shall appear to be just, and in assessing such damages the court may, in its discretion, allow the amounts as hereinafter stated, but in case of a newspaper reproduction of a copyrighted photograph, such damages shall not exceed the sum of $200 nor be less than the sum of $50, and in the case of the infringement of an undramatized or non-dramatic work by means of motion pictures, where the infringer shall show that he was not aware that he was infringing, and that such infringement could not have been reasonably foreseen, such damages shall not exceed the sum of $100; and in the case of an infringement of a copyrighted dramatic or dramatico-musical work by a maker of motion pictures and his agencies for distribution thereof to exhibitors, where such infringer shows that he was not aware that he was infringing a copyrighted work, and that such infringements could not reasonably have been foreseen, the entire sum of such damages recoverable by the copyright proprietor from such infringing maker and his agencies for the distribution to exhibitors of such infringing motion picture shall not exceed the sum of $5,000 nor be less than $250, and such damages shall in no other case exceed the sum of $5,000 nor be less than the sum of $250, and shall not be regarded as a penalty. But the foregoing exceptions shall not deprive the copyright proprietor of any other remedy given him under this law, nor shall the limitation as to the amount of recovery apply to infringements occurring after the actual notice to a defendant, either by service of process in a suit or other written notice served upon him.

First. In the case of a painting, statue, or sculpture, $10 for every infringing copy made or sold by or found in the possession of the infringer or his agents or employees.

Second. In the case of any work enumerated in section 5 of this title, except a painting, statue, or sculpture, $1 for every infringing copy made or sold by or found in the possession of the infringer or his agents or employees.

Third. In the case of a lecture, sermon, or address, $50 for every infringing delivery.

Fourth. In the case of a dramatic or dramatico-musical or a choral or orchestral composition, $100 for the first and $50 for every subsequent infringing performance; in the case of other musical compositions $10 for every infringing performance;

(c) Impounding during action

To deliver up on oath, to be impounded during the pendency of the action, upon such terms and conditions as the court may prescribe, all articles alleged to infringe a copyright;

(d) Destruction of infringing copies and plates

To deliver up on oath for destruction all the infringing copies or devices, as well as all plates, molds, matrices, or other means for making such infringing copies as the court may order.

(e) Interchangeable parts for use in mechanical music-producing machines

Interchangeable parts, such as discs or tapes for use in mechanical music-producing machines adapted to reproduce copyrighted musical works, shall be considered copies of the copyrighted musical works which they serve to reproduce mechanically for the purposes of this section 101 and sections 106 and 109 of this title, and the unauthorized manufacture, use, or sale of such interchangeable parts shall constitute an infringement of the copyrighted work rendering the infringer liable in accordance with all provisions of this title dealing with infringements of copyright and, in a case of willful infringement for profit, to criminal prosecution pursuant to section 104 of this title. Whenever any person, in the absence of a license agreement, intends to use a copyrighted musical composition upon the parts of instruments serving to reproduce mechanically the musical work, relying upon the compulsory license provision of this title, he shall serve notice of such intention, by registered mail, upon the copyright proprietor at his last address disclosed by the records of the Copyright Office, sending to the Copyright Office a duplicate of such notice. July 30, 1947, c. 391, 61 Stat. 661; June 25, 1948, c. 646, §39, 62 Stat. 992; Oct. 15, 1971, Pub. L. 92-140, §2, 85 Stat. 392.

§§102, 103. Repealed. June 25, 1948, c. 646, §39, 62 Stat. 992

§104 Willful infringement for profit

(a) Except as provided in subsection (b), any person who willfully and for profit shall infringe any copyright secured by this title, or who shall knowingly and willfully aid or abet such infringement, shall be deemed guilty of a misdemeanor, and upon conviction thereof shall be punished by imprisonment for not exceeding one year or by a fine of not less than $100 nor more than $1,000, or both, in the discretion of the court: *Provided, however,* That nothing in this title shall be so construed as to prevent the performance of religious or secular works such as oratorios, cantatas, masses, or octavo choruses by public schools, church choirs, or vocal societies, rented, borrowed, or obtained from some public library, public school, church choir, school choir, or vocal society, provided the performance is given for charitable or educational purposes and not for profit.

(b) Any person who willfully and for profit shall infringe any copyright provided by section 1(f) of this title, or who should knowingly and willfully aid or abet such infringement, shall be fined not more than $25,000 or imprisoned not more than one year, or both, for the first offense and shall be fined not more than $50,000 or imprisoned not more than two years, or both for any subsequent offense. July 30, 1947, c. 391, 61 Stat. 662; Dec. 31, 1974, Pub. L. 93-573, Title I, §102, 88 Stat. 1873.

§ 105 Fraudulent notice of copyright, or removal or alteration of notice

Any person who, with fraudulent intent, shall insert or impress any notice of copyright required by this title, or words of the same purport, in or upon any uncopyrighted article or with fraudulent intent shall remove or alter the copyright notice upon any article duly copyrighted shall be guilty of a misdemeanor, punishable by a fine of not less than $100 and not more than $1,000. Any person who shall knowingly issue or sell any article bearing a notice of United States copyright which has not been copyrighted in this country, or who shall knowingly import any article bearing such notice or words of the same purport, which has not been copyrighted in this country, shall be liable [for] a fine of $100. July 30, 1947, c. 391, 61 Stat. 662.

§ 106 Importation of article bearing false notice or piratical copies of copyrighted work

The importation into the United States of any article bearing a false notice of copyright when there is no existing copyright thereon in the United States, or of any piratical copies of any work copyrighted in the United States, is prohibited. July 30, 1947, c. 391, 61 Stat. 663.

§ 107 Importation, during existence of copyright, of piratical copies, or of copies not produced in accordance with Section 16 of this title

During the existence of the American copyright in any book, the importation into the United States of any piratical copies thereof or of any copies thereof (although authorized by the author or proprietor) which have not been produced in accordance with the manufacturing provisions specified in section 16 of this title, or any plates of the same not made from type set within the limits of the United States, or any copies thereof produced by lithographic or photoengraving process not performed within the limits of the United States, in accordance with the provisions of section 16 of this title, is prohibited: *Provided, however,* That, except as regards piratical copies, such prohibition shall not apply:

(a) To works in raised characters for the use of the blind.

(b) To a foreign newspaper or magazine, although containing matter copyrighted in the United States printed or reprinted by authority of the copyright proprietor, unless such newspaper or magazine contains also copyright matter printed or reprinted without such authorization.

(c) To the authorized edition of a book in a foreign language or languages of which only a translation into English has been copyrighted in this country.

(d) To any book published abroad with the authorization of the author or copyright proprietor when imported under the circumstances stated in one of the four subdivisions following, that is to say:

First. When imported, not more than one copy at one time, for individual use and not for sale; but such privilege of importation shall not extend to a foreign reprint of a book by an American author copyrighted in the United States.

Second. When imported by the authority or for the use of the United States.

Third. When imported, for use and not for sale, not more than one copy of any such book in any one invoice, in good faith by or for any society or institution incorporated for educational, literary, philosophical, scientific, or religious purposes, or for the encouragement of the fine arts, or for any college, academy, school, or seminary of learning, or for any State, school, college, university, or free public library in the United States.

Fourth. When such books form parts of libraries or collections purchased en bloc for the use of societies, institutions, or libraries designated in the foregoing paragraph, or form parts of the libraries or personal baggage belonging to persons or families arriving from foreign countries and are not intended for sale: *Provided,* That copies imported as above may not lawfully be used in any way to violate the rights of the proprietor of the American copyright or annul or limit the copyright protection secured by this title, and such unlawful use shall be deemed an infringement of copyright. July 30, 1947, c. 391, 61 Stat. 663.

§ 108 Forfeiture and destruction of articles prohibited importation

Any and all articles prohibited importation by this title which are brought into the United States from any foreign country (except in the mails) shall be seized and forfeited by like proceedings as those provided by law for the seizure and condemnation of property imported into the United States in violation of the customs revenue laws. Such articles when forfeited shall be destroyed in such manner as the Secretary of the Treasury or the court, as the case may be, shall direct: *Provided, however,* That all copies of authorized editions of copyright books imported in the mails or otherwise in violation of the provisions of this title may be exported and returned to the country of export whenever it is shown to the satisfaction of the Secretary of the Treasury, in a written application, that such importation does not involve willful negligence or fraud. July 30, 1947, c. 391, 61 Stat. 664.

§ 109 Importation of prohibited articles; regulations; proof of deposit of copies by complainants

The Secretary of the Treasury and the Postmaster General are hereby empowered and required to make and enforce individually or jointly such rules and regulations as shall prevent the importation into the United States of articles prohibited importation by this title, and may require, as conditions precedent to exclusion of any work in which copyright is claimed, the copyright proprietor or any person claiming actual or potential injury by reason of actual or contemplated importations of copies of such work to file with the Post Office Department or the Treasury Department a certificate of the Register of Copyrights that the provisions of section 13 of this title have been fully complied with, and to give notice of such compliance to postmasters or to customs officers at the ports of entry into the United States in such form and accompanied by such exhibits as may be deemed necessary for the practical and efficient administration and enforcement of the provisions of sections 106 and 107 of this title. July 30, 1947, c. 391, 61 Stat. 664.

§§110, 111. Repealed. June 25, 1948, c. 646, §39, 62 Stat. 992

§112 Injunctions; service and enforcement

Any court mentioned in section 1338 of Title 28 or judge thereof shall have power, upon complaint filed by any party aggrieved, to grant injunctions to prevent and restrain the violation of any right secured by this title, according to the course and principles of courts of equity, on such terms as said court or judge may deem reasonable. Any injunction that may be granted restraining and enjoining the doing of anything forbidden by this title may be served on the parties against whom such injunction may be granted anywhere in the United States, and shall be operative throughout the United States and be enforceable by proceedings in contempt or otherwise by any other court or judge possessing jurisdiction of the defendants. July 30, 1947, c. 391, 61 Stat. 664; Oct. 31, 1951, c. 655, §16(c), 65 Stat. 716.

§113 Transmission of certified copies of papers for enforcement of injunction by other court

The clerk of the court, or judge granting the injunction, shall, when required so to do by the court hearing the application to enforce said injunction, transmit without delay to said court a certified copy of all the papers in said cause that are on file in his office. July 30, 1947, c. 391, 61 Stat. 664.

§114 Review of orders, judgments, or decrees

The orders, judgments, or decrees of any court mentioned in section 1338 of Title 28 arising under the copyright laws of the United States may be reviewed on appeal in the manner and to the extent now provided by law for the review of cases determined in said courts, respectively. July 30, 1947, c. 391, 61 Stat. 665; Oct. 31, 1951, c. 655, §17, 65 Stat. 717.

§115 Limitations

(a) Criminal proceedings

No criminal proceedings shall be maintained under the provisions of this title unless the same is commenced within three years after the cause of action arose.

(b) Civil actions

No civil action shall be maintained under the provisions of this title unless the same is commenced within three years after the claim accrued. July 30, 1947, c. 391, 61 Stat. 665; Sept. 7, 1957, Pub. L. 85-313, §1, 71 Stat. 633.

§116 Costs; attorney's fees

In all actions, suits, or proceedings under this title, except when brought by or against the United States or any officer thereof, full costs shall be allowed, and the court may award to the prevailing party a reasonable attorney's fee as part of the costs. July 30, 1947, c. 391, 61 Stat. 665.

CHAPTER 3—COPYRIGHT OFFICE

Section

201. Copyright Office; preservation of records
202. Register, Assistant Register, and subordinates
203. Same; deposit of moneys received; reports
204. [Repealed.]
205. Same; annual report
206. Seal of Copyright Office
207. Rules for registration of claims
208. Record books in Copyright Office
209. Certificates of registration; effect as evidence; receipt for copies deposited
210. Catalog of copyright entries; effect as evidence
211. Same; distribution and sale; disposal of proceeds
212. Records and works deposited in Copyright Office open to public inspection; taking copies of entries
213. Disposition of articles deposited in Office
214. Destruction of articles deposited in Office remaining undisposed of; removal of by author or proprietor; manuscripts of unpublished works
215. Fees
216. When the day for taking action falls on Saturday, Sunday, or a holiday

§201 Copyright Office; preservation of records

All records and other things relating to copyrights required by law to be preserved shall be kept and preserved in the Copyright Office, Library of Congress, District of Columbia, and shall be under the control of the Register of Copyrights, who shall under the direction and supervision of the Librarian of Congress, perform all the duties relating to the registration of copyrights. July 30, 1947, c. 391, 61 Stat. 665.

§202 Register, Assistant Register, and subordinates

There shall be appointed by the Librarian of Congress a Register of Copyrights, and one Assistant Register of Copyrights, who shall have authority during the absence of the Register of Copyrights to attach the Copyright Office seal to all papers issued from the said office and to sign such certificates and other papers as may be necessary. There shall also be appointed by the Librarian such subordinate assistants to the Register as may from time to time be authorized by law. July 30, 1947, c. 391, 61 Stat. 665.

§203 Same; deposit of moneys received; reports

The Register of Copyrights shall make daily deposits in some bank in the District of Columbia, designated for this purpose by the Secretary of the Treasury as a national depository, of all moneys received to be applied as copyright fees, and shall make weekly deposits with the Secretary of the Treasury, in such manner as the latter shall direct, of all copyright fees actually applied under the provisions of this title, and annual deposits of sums received which it has not been possible to apply as copyright fees or to return to the remitters, and shall also make monthly reports to the Secretary of the Treasury and to the Librarian of Congress of the applied copyright fees for each calendar month, together with a statement of all remittances received, trust funds on hand, moneys refunded, and unapplied balances. All moneys deposited with the Secretary of the Treasury under this section shall be credited to the appropriation for necessary expenses of the Copyright Office. July 30, 1947, c. 391, 61 Stat. 665; Aug. 5, 1977, Pub. L. 95-94, §406, 91 Stat. 682.

§204 Repealed. Pub. L. 92-310, Title II, §205(a), June 6, 1972, 86 Stat. 203

§205 Same; annual report

The Register of Copyrights shall make an annual report to the Librarian of Congress, to be printed in the annual report on the Library of Congress, of all copyright business for the previous fiscal year, including the number and kind of works which have been deposited in the [C]opyright [O]ffice during the fiscal year, under the provisions of this title. July 30, 1947, c. 391, 61 Stat. 666.

§206 Seal of Copyright Office

The seal used in the Copyright Office on July 1, 1909, shall be the seal of the Copyright Office, and by it all papers issued from the Copyright Office requiring authentication shall be authenticated. July 30, 1947, c. 391, 61 Stat. 666.

§207 Rules for registration of claims

Subject to the approval of the Librarian of Congress, the Register of Copyrights shall be authorized to make rules and regulations for the registration of claims to copyright as provided by this title. July 30, 1947, c. 391, 61 Stat. 666.

§208 Record books in Copyright Office

The Register of Copyrights shall provide and keep such record books in the Copyright Office as are required to carry out the provisions of this title, and whenever deposit has been made in the Copyright Office of a copy of any work under the provisions of this title he shall make entry thereof. July 30, 1947, c. 391, 61 Stat. 666.

§209 Certificate of registration; effect as evidence; receipt for copies deposited

In the case of each entry the person recorded as the claimant of the copyright shall be entitled to a certificate of registration under seal of the Copyright Office, to contain the name and address of said claimant, the name of the country of which the author of the work is a citizen or subject, and when an alien author domiciled in the United States at the time of said registration, then a statement of that fact, including his place of domicile, the name of the author (when the records of the Copyright Office shall show the same), the title of the work which is registered for which copyright is claimed, the date of the deposit of the copies of such work, the date of publication if the work has been reproduced in copies for sale, or publicly distributed, and such marks as to class designation and entry number as shall fully identify the entry. In the case of a book, the certificate shall also state the receipt of the affidavit, as provided by section 17 of this title, and the date of the completion of the printing, or the date of the publication of the book, as stated in the said affidavit. The Register of Copyrights shall prepare a printed form for the said certificate, to be filled out in each case as above provided for in the case of all registrations made after July 1, 1909, and in the case of all previous registrations so far as the Copyright Office record books shall show such facts, which certificate, sealed with the seal of the Copyright Office, shall, upon payment of the prescribed fee, be given to any person making application for the same. Said certificate shall be admitted in any court as prima facie evidence of the facts stated therein. In addition to such certificate the Register of Copyrights shall furnish, upon request, without additional fee, a receipt for the copies of the work deposited to complete the registration. July 30, 1947, c. 391, 61 Stat. 666.

§210 Catalog of copyright entries; effect as evidence

The Register of Copyrights shall fully index all copyright registrations and assignments and shall print at periodic intervals a catalog of the titles of articles deposited and registered for copyright, together with suitable indexes, and at stated intervals shall print complete and indexed catalog for each class of copyright entries, and may thereupon, if expedient, destroy the original manuscript catalog cards containing the titles included in such printed volumes and representing the entries made during such intervals. The current catalog of copyright entries and the index volumes herein provided for shall be admitted in any court as prima facie evidence of the facts stated therein as regards any copyright registration. July 30, 1947, c. 391, 61 Stat. 666.

§211 Same; distribution and sale; disposal of proceeds

The said printed current catalogs as they are issued shall be promptly distributed by the Superintendent of Documents to the collectors of customs of the United States and to the postmasters of all exchange offices of receipt of foreign mails, in accordance with revised list of such collectors of customs and postmasters prepared by the Secretary of the Treasury and the Postmaster General, and they shall also be furnished in whole or in part to all parties desiring them at a price to be determined by the Register of Copyrights for each part of the catalog not exceeding $75 for the complete yearly catalog of copyright entries. The consolidated catalogs and indexes shall also be supplied to all persons ordering them at such prices as may be fixed by the Register of Copyrights, and all subscriptions for the catalogs shall be received by the Superintendent of Documents, who shall forward the said publications; and the moneys thus received shall be paid into the Treasury of the United States and accounted for under such laws and Treasury regulations as shall be in force at the time. July 30, 1947, c. 391, 61 Stat. 667; Apr. 27, 1948, c. 236, §1, 62 Stat. 202; Oct. 27, 1965, Pub. L. 89-297, §1, 79 Stat. 1072.

§212 Records and works deposited in Copyright Office open to public inspection; taking copies of entries

The record books of the Copyright Office, together with the indexes to such record books, and all works deposited and retained in the Copyright Office, shall be open to public inspection; and copies may be taken of the copyright entries actually made in such record books, subject to such safeguards and regulations as shall be prescribed by the Register of Copyrights and approved by the Librarian of Congress. July 30, 1947, c. 391, 61 Stat. 667.

§213 Disposition of articles deposited in Office

Of the articles deposited in the Copyright Office under the provisions of the copyright laws of the United States, the Librarian of Congress shall determine what books and other articles shall be transferred to the permanent collections of the Library of Congress, including the law library, and what other books or articles shall be placed in the reserve collections of the Library of Congress for sale or exchange, or be transferred to other governmental libraries in the District of Columbia for use therein. July 30, 1947, c. 391, 61 Stat. 667.

§214 Destruction of articles deposited in Office remaining undisposed of; removal of by author or proprietor; manuscripts of unpublished works

Of any articles undisposed of as above provided, together with all titles and correspondence relating thereto, the Librarian of Congress and the Register of Copyrights jointly shall, at suitable intervals, determine [which] of th[o]se received during any period of years it is desirable or useful to preserve in the permanent files of the Copyright Office, and, after due notice as hereinafter provided, may within their discretion cause the remaining articles and other things to be destroyed: *Provided, That* there shall be printed in the Catalog of Copyright Entries from February to November, inclusive, a statement of the years of receipt of such articles and a notice to permit any author, copyright proprietor, or other lawful claimant to claim and remove before the expiration of the month of December of that year anything found which relates to any of his productions deposited or registered for copyright within the period of years stated, not reserved or disposed of as provided for in this title. No manuscript of an unpublished work shall be destroyed during its term of copyright without specific notice to the copyright proprietor of record, permitting him to claim and remove it. July 30, 1947, c. 391, 61 Stat. 667.

§215 Fees

The Register of Copyrights shall receive, and the persons to whom the services designated are rendered shall pay, the following fees:

For the registration of a claim to copyright in any work, including a print or label used for articles of merchandise, $6; for the registration of a claim to renewal of copyright, $4; which fees shall include a certificate for each registration: *Provided*, that only one registration fee shall be required in the case of several volumes of the same book published and deposited at the same time: *And provided further,* That with respect to works of foreign origin, in lieu of payment of the copyright fee of $6 together with one copy of the work and application, the foreign author or proprietor may at any time within six months from the date of first publication abroad deposit in the Copyright Office an application for registration and two copies of the work which shall be accompanied by a catalog card in form and content satisfactory to the Register of Copyrights.

For every additional certificate of registration, $2.

For certifying a copy of an application for registration of copyright, and for all other certifications, $3.

For recording every assignment, agreement, power of attorney or other paper not exceeding six pages, $5; for each additional page or less, 50 cents; for each title over one in the paper recorded, 50 cents additional.

For recording a notice of use, or notice of intention to use, $3, for each notice of not more than five titles; and 50 cents for each additional title.

For any requested search of Copyright Office records, works deposited, or other available material, or services rendered in connection therewith, $5, for each hour of time consumed. July 30, 1947, c. 391, 61 Stat. 668; Apr. 27, 1948, c. 236, §2, 62 Stat. 202; June 3, 1949, c. 171, §4, 63 Stat. 154; Oct. 27, 1965, Pub. L. 89-297, §2, 79 Stat. 1072.

§216 When the day for taking action falls on Saturday, Sunday, or a holiday

When the last day for making any deposit or application, or for paying any fee, or for delivering any other material to the Copyright Office falls on Saturday, Sunday, or a holiday within the District of Columbia, such action may be taken on the next succeeding business day. Added Apr. 13, 1954, c. 137, §1, 68 Stat. 52.

CURRENT LEGISLATIVE MATERIALS

111th CONGRESS
1st Session
S. 379
(Performance Rights Act)

To provide fair compensation to artists for use of their sound recordings.

IN THE SENATE OF THE UNITED STATES

February 4, 2009

Mr. LEAHY (for himself, Mr. HATCH, Mrs. FEINSTEIN, Mr. CORKER, Mrs. BOXER, Mr. ALEXANDER, and Mr. SCHUMER) introduced the following bill; which was read twice and referred to the Committee on the Judiciary

October 15, 2009

Reported by Mr. LEAHY, with amendments

[Omit the part struck through and insert the part printed in italic]

A BILL

To provide fair compensation to artists for use of their sound recordings.

Be it enacted by the Senate and House of Representatives of the United States of America in Congress assembled,

SECTION 1. SHORT TITLE.

This Act may be cited as the 'Performance Rights Act'.

SECTION 2. ~~EQUITABLE TREATMENT FOR TERRESTRIAL BROADCASTS~~ *ESTABLISHING EQUITABLE TREATMENT FOR TERRESTRIAL, CABLE, SATELLITE, AND INTERNET SERVICES*.

(a) Performance Right Applicable to Radio Transmissions Generally— Section 106(6) of title 17, United States Code, is amended to read as follows:

'(6) in the case of sound recordings, to perform the copyrighted work publicly by means of an audio transmission.'.

(b) Inclusion of Terrestrial Broadcasts in Existing Performance Right— Section 114(d)(1) of title 17, United States Code, is amended—

(1) in the matter preceding subparagraph (A), by striking 'a digital' and inserting 'an'; and

(2) by striking subparagraph (A).

(c) Inclusion of Terrestrial Broadcasts in Existing Statutory License System— Section 114(j)(6) of title 17, United States Code, is amended by striking 'digital'.

(d) Eliminating Regulatory Burdens for Terrestrial Broadcast Stations— Section 114(d)(2) of title 17, United States Code, is amended in the matter preceding subparagraph (A) by striking 'subsection (f) if' and inserting 'subsection (f) if, other than for a nonsubscription and noninteractive broadcast transmission,'.

(e) Ensuring Platform Parity— Section 114(f) of title 17, United States Code, is amended—

(1) by striking paragraph (1);

(2) by redesignating paragraphs (2), (3), (4), and (5) as paragraphs (1), (2), (3), and (4), respectively; and

(3) in paragraph (1), as redesignated—

(A) in subparagraph (A), by striking 'under chapter 8' and all that follows through the end of the third sentence and inserting 'under chapter 8 shall determine reasonable rates and terms of royalty payments for transmissions subject to statutory licensing under subsection (d)(2) during 5-year periods beginning on January 1 of the second year following the year in which the proceedings are to be commenced, except in the case of a different transitional period provided under section 6(b)(3) of the Copyright Royalty and Distribution Reform Act of 2004, or such other period as the parties may agree.';

(B) in subparagraph (B)—

(i) in the second sentence, by striking 'eligible nonsubscription transmission'; and

(ii) in the third sentence, by striking 'eligible nonsubscription services and new subscription' and all that follows through 'subparagraph (A)' and inserting 'services, in addition to the objectives set forth in subparagraphs (A), (B), and (C) of section 801(b)(1), the Copyright Royalty Judges may consider the rates and terms for comparable types of services and comparable circumstances under voluntary license agreements. Notwithstanding section 801(b)(1), the provisions of section 801(b)(1)(D) shall not be taken into account by the Copyright Royalty Judges in any proceeding under this section'; and

(C) by striking subparagraph (C) and inserting the following:

'(C) The procedures under subparagraphs (A) and (B) shall also be initiated pursuant to a petition filed by any copyright owner

of sound recordings or any transmitting entity indicating that a new type of service on which sound recordings are performed is or is about to become operational, for the purpose of determining reasonable terms and rates of royalty payments with respect to such new type of service for the period beginning with the inception of such new type of service and ending on the date on which the royalty rates and terms for preexisting services most recently determined under subparagraph (A) or (B) and chapter 8 expire, or such other period as the parties may agree.'.

(f) Technical and Conforming Amendments—

(1) SECTION 114(F)— Section 114(f) of title 17, United States Code (as amended by subsection (e)), is further amended—

(A) in paragraph (1)(B), in the first sentence, by striking 'paragraph (3)' and inserting 'paragraph (2)'; and

(B) in paragraph (4)(C), by striking 'under paragraph (4)' and inserting 'under paragraph (3)'.

(2) SECTION 114(J)— Section 114(j)(6) of title 17, United States Code, is amended by striking 'retransmissions of broadcast transmissions' and inserting 'broadcast transmissions and retransmissions of broadcast transmissions'.

(3) SECTION 804— Section 804(b)(3)(C) of title 17, United States Code, is amended—

(A) in clause (i), by striking 'and 114(f)(2)(C)';

(B) in clause (iii)(II), by striking '114(f)(4)(B)(ii)' and inserting '114(f)(3)(B)(ii)'; and

(C) in clause (iv), by striking 'or 114(f)(2)(C), as the case may be'.

~~SECTION 3. SPECIAL TREATMENT FOR SMALL, NONCOMMERCIAL, EDUCATIONAL, AND RELIGIOUS STATIONS AND CERTAIN USES.~~

~~(a) Small, Noncommercial, Educational, and Religious Radio Stations—~~

~~(1) IN GENERAL— Section 114(f)(2) of title 17, United States Code, is amended by adding at the end the following:~~

~~'(D) Notwithstanding the provisions of subparagraphs (A) through (C), each individual terrestrial broadcast station that has gross revenues in any calendar year of less than $1,250,000 may elect to pay for its over-the-air nonsubscription broadcast transmissions a royalty fee of $5,000 per year, in lieu of the amount such station would otherwise be required to pay under this~~

~~paragraph. Such royalty fee shall not be taken into account in determining royalty rates in a proceeding under chapter 8, or in any other administrative, judicial, or other Federal Government proceeding.~~

~~'(E) Notwithstanding the provisions of subparagraphs (A) through (C), each individual terrestrial broadcast station that is a public broadcasting entity as defined in section 118(f) may elect to pay for its over-the-air nonsubscription broadcast transmissions a royalty fee of $1,000 per year, in lieu of the amount such station would otherwise be required to pay under this paragraph. Such royalty fee shall not be taken into account in determining royalty rates in a proceeding under chapter 8, or in any other administrative, judicial, or other Federal Government proceeding.'.~~

SECTION 3. SPECIAL TREATMENT FOR SMALL, NONCOMMERCIAL, EDUCATIONAL, AND RELIGIOUS STATIONS AND CERTAIN USES.

(a) Small, Noncommercial, Educational, and Religious Radio Stations—

(1) IN GENERAL— Section 114(f)(1) of title 17, United States Code, as redesignated by section 2(e), is amended by adding at the end the following:

'(D)(i) Notwithstanding the provisions of subparagraphs (A) through (C), each individual terrestrial broadcast station that has gross revenues within a range specified in clause (ii) may elect to pay for its over-the-air nonsubscription broadcast transmissions a royalty fee as provided in clause (ii), in lieu of the amount such station would otherwise be required to pay under this paragraph. Such royalty fee shall not be taken into account in determining royalty rates in a proceeding under chapter 8, or in any other administrative, judicial, or other Federal Government proceeding.

'(ii) As provided in clause (i), each individual terrestrial broadcast station that has gross revenues in any calendar year of—

'(I) less than $50,000 may elect to pay for its over-the-air nonsubscription broadcast transmissions a royalty fee of $100 per year;

'(II) at least $50,000 but less than $100,000 may elect to pay for its over-the-air nonsubscription broadcast transmissions a royalty fee of $500 per year;

'(III) at least $100,000 but less than $500,000 may elect to pay for its over-the-air nonsubscription broadcast transmissions a royalty fee of $2,500 per year; and

'(IV) at least $500,000 but less than $1,250,000 may elect to pay for its over-the-air nonsubscription broadcast transmissions a royalty fee of $5,000 per year.

'(E)(i) Notwithstanding the provisions of subparagraphs (A) through (C), each individual terrestrial broadcast station that is a public broadcasting entity as defined in section 118(f) and that has gross revenues within a range specified in clause (ii) may elect to pay for its over-the-air nonsubscription broadcast transmissions a royalty fee as provided in clause (ii), in lieu of the amount such station would otherwise be required to pay under this paragraph. Such royalty fee shall not be taken into account in determining royalty rates in a proceeding under chapter 8, or in any other administrative, judicial, or other Federal Government proceeding.

'(ii) As provided in clause (i), each individual terrestrial broadcast station that is a public broadcasting entity as defined in section 118(f) and has gross receipts in any calendar year of—

'(I) less than $50,000 may elect to pay for its over-the-air nonsubscription broadcast transmissions a royalty fee of $100 per year;

'(II) at least $50,000 but less than $100,000 may elect to pay for its over-the-air nonsubscription broadcast transmissions a royalty fee of $500 per year; and

'(III) $100,000 or more may elect to pay for its over-the-air nonsubscription broadcast transmissions a royalty fee of $1,000 per year.

'(F) Notwithstanding the provisions of subparagraphs (A) through (E), each individual terrestrial broadcast station that had total gross revenues during the 4 full calendar quarters immediately preceding the date of enactment of the Performance Rights Act of—

'(i) less than $5,000,000 shall not be required to pay a royalty under this paragraph during the 3 years immediately following the date of enactment of the Performance Rights Act; and

'(ii) $5,000,000 or more shall not be required to pay a royalty under this paragraph during the 1 year immediately following the date of enactment of the Performance Rights Act.

The provisions of this subparagraph shall not be taken into account in determining royalty rates in a proceeding under chapter 8, or in any other administrative, judicial, or other Federal Government proceeding.'.

(2) PAYMENT DATE— A payment under subparagraph (D) or (E) of section ~~114(f)(2)~~ *114(f)(1)* of title 17, United States Code, as added by

paragraph (1), shall not be due until the due date of the first royalty payments for nonsubscription broadcast transmissions that are determined, after the date of the enactment of this Act, under such section ~~114(f)(2)~~ *114(f)(1)* by reason of the amendment made by section 2(b)(2) of this Act.

(b) Transmission of Religious Services; Incidental Uses of Music— Section 114(d)(1) of title 17, United States Code, as amended by section 2(b), is further amended by inserting the following before subparagraph (B):

'(A) an eligible nonsubscription transmission of—

'(i) services at a place of worship or other religious assembly; ~~and~~ *or*

'(ii) an incidental use of a musical sound recording;'.

SECTION 4. AVAILABILITY OF PER PROGRAM LICENSE.

Section ~~114(f)(2)(B) of title 17, United States Code~~ *114(f)(1)(B) of title 17, United States Code, as redesignated by section 2(e)*, is amended by inserting after the second sentence the following new sentence: 'Such rates and terms shall include a per program license option for terrestrial broadcast stations that make limited feature uses of sound recordings.'.

~~SECTION 5. NO HARMFUL EFFECTS ON SONGWRITERS.~~

~~(a) Preservation of Royalties on Underlying Works— Section 114(i) of title 17, United States Code, is amended in the second sentence by striking 'It is the intent of Congress that royalties' and inserting 'Royalties'.~~

~~(b) Public Performance Rights and Royalties— Nothing in this Act shall adversely affect in any respect the public performance rights of or royalties payable to songwriters or copyright owners of musical works.~~

SECTION 5. NO HARMFUL EFFECTS ON SONGWRITERS.

(a) No Adverse Affect on License Fees for Underlying Musical Works; Necessity for Other Licenses—

(1) IN GENERAL— Section 114(i) of title 17, United States Code, is amended to read as follows:

'(i) No Adverse Affect on License Fees for Underlying Musical Works; Necessity for Other Licenses—

'(1) NO ADVERSE AFFECT ON LICENSE FEES FOR UNDERLYING MUSICAL WORKS— License fees payable for the public performance of sound recordings under section 106(6) shall not be cited, taken into account, or otherwise used in any administrative, judicial, or other governmental forum or proceeding, or otherwise, to set or adjust the license fees payable to copyright owners of musical works or their

representatives for the public performance of their works, for the purpose of reducing or adversely affecting such license fees. License fees payable to copyright owners for the public performance of their musical works shall not be reduced or adversely affected in any respect as a result of the rights granted by section 106(6).

'(2) NECESSITY FOR OTHER LICENSES— Notwithstanding the grant by an owner of copyright in a sound recording of an exclusive or nonexclusive license of the right under section 106(6) to perform the work publicly, a licensee of that sound recording may not publicly perform such sound recording unless a license has been granted for the public performance of any copyrighted musical work contained in the sound recording. Such license to publicly perform the copyrighted musical work may be granted either by a performing rights society representing the copyright owner or by the copyright owner.'.

(2) CONFORMING AMENDMENT— Section 114(d)(3)(C) of title 17, United States Code, is hereby repealed.

(b) Public Performance Rights and Royalties— Nothing in this Act or the amendments made by this Act shall adversely affect in any respect the public performance rights of or royalties payable to songwriters or copyright owners of musical works.

(c) Preservation of Royalties on Underlying Works Publicly Performed by Terrestrial Broadcast Stations— Section 114(f) of title 17, United States Code, is amended by adding at the end the following new paragraph:

'(5) Notwithstanding any other provision of this section, under no circumstances shall the rates established by the Copyright Royalty Judges for the public performance of sound recordings be cited, taken into account, or otherwise used in any administrative, judicial, or other governmental forum or proceeding, or otherwise, to reduce or adversely affect the license fees payable to copyright owners of musical works or their representatives for the public performance of their works by terrestrial broadcast stations, and such license fees for the public performance of musical works shall be independent of license fees paid for the public performance of sound recordings.'.

SECTION 6. PAYMENT OF CERTAIN ROYALTIES.

Section 114(g) of title 17, United States Code, is amended—

(1) by amending paragraph (1) to read as follows:

'(1) Except in the case of a transmission to which paragraph (5) applies or a transmission licensed under a statutory license in accordance with subsection (f) of this section, the following shall apply:

'(A) A featured recording artist who performs on a sound recording that has been licensed for public performance by means of

an audio transmission shall be entitled to receive payments from the copyright owner of the sound recording in accordance with the terms of the artist's contract.

'(B) (i) In a case in which the copyright owner of a sound recording has licensed the sound recording for the public performance of the sound recording by means of an audio transmission, the copyright owner shall deposit 1 percent of the receipts from the license with the American Federation of Musicians and American Federation of Television and Radio Artists Intellectual Property Rights Distribution Fund (or any successor entity) (in this subparagraph referred to as the 'Fund') to be distributed to nonfeatured performers who have performed on sound recordings. The sound recording copyright owner shall make such deposits for receipts received during the first half of a calendar year by August 15 and for receipts received during the second half of a calendar year by February 15 of the following calendar year.

'(ii) A sound recording copyright owner shall include with deposits under clause (i) information regarding the amount of such deposits attributable to each licensee and, subject to obtaining consent, if necessary, from such licensee, for each sound recording performed by means of an audio transmission by such licensee during the applicable time period, and to the extent included in the accounting reports provided by the licensee to the sound recording copyright owner—

'(I) the identity of the artist;

'(II) the International Standard Recording Code of the sound recording;

'(III) the title of the sound recording;

'(IV) the number of times the sound recording was transmitted; and

'(V) the total amount of receipts collected from that licensee.

'(iii) The Fund shall make the distributions described in clause (i) as follows: 50 percent shall be paid to nonfeatured musicians (whether or not members of the American Federation of Musicians) and 50 percent shall be paid to nonfeatured vocalists (whether or not members of the American Federation of Television and Radio Artists). The Fund may, prior to making such distributions, deduct the reasonable costs related to making such distributions.

'(iv) The sound recording copyright owner shall not be required to provide any additional information to the Fund

other than what is required under this subparagraph. Sound recording copyright owners shall use reasonable good faith efforts to include in all relevant licenses a requirement to report the information identified in subclauses (I) through (V) of clause (ii). Amounts required under clause (i) that are not paid by the date specified in such clause shall be subject to interest at the rate of 6 percent per annum for each day of nonpayment after the date the payment was due.';

(2) in paragraph (2)(A), by striking 'digital'; and

(3) by adding at the end the following new paragraph:

'(5) Notwithstanding paragraph (1), to the extent that a license granted by the copyright owner of a sound recording to a transmitting entity eligible for a statutory license as specified by subsection (d)(2) extends to such entity's transmissions otherwise licensable under a statutory license in accordance with subsection (f), such entity shall pay to the agent designated to distribute statutory licensing receipts from the licensing of transmissions in accordance with subsection (f), 50 percent of the total royalties that such entity is required, pursuant to the applicable license agreement, to pay for such transmissions otherwise licensable under a statutory license in accordance with subsection (f). That agent shall distribute such payments in proportion to the distributions provided in subparagraphs (B) through (D) of paragraph (2), and such payments shall be the sole payments to which featured and nonfeatured artists are entitled by virtue of such transmissions under the direct license with such entity.'.

SECTION 7. EPHEMERAL RECORDINGS ROYALTY.

Section 112(e)(4) of title 17, United States Code, is amended to read as follows:

'(4)(A) The schedule of reasonable rates and terms determined by the Copyright Royalty Judges shall, subject to paragraph (5), be binding on all copyright owners of sound recordings and transmitting organizations entitled to a statutory license under this subsection during the 5-year period specified in paragraph (3), or such other period as the parties may agree. Such rates shall include a minimum fee for each type of service offered by transmitting organizations.

'(B) With respect to phonorecords made pursuant to this subsection to facilitate transmissions of public performances under the limitation on exclusive rights specified by section 114(d)(1)(C)(iv), the Copyright Royalty Judges shall establish rates that most clearly represent the fees that would have been negotiated in the marketplace between a willing buyer and a willing seller. In determining such rates and terms, the Copyright Royalty Judges shall base their decision on economic, competitive, and programming information presented by the parties, including—

'(i) whether use of the service may substitute for or may promote the sales of phonorecords or otherwise interferes with or enhances the copyright owner's traditional streams of revenue;

'(ii) the relative roles of the copyright owner and the transmitting organization in the copyrighted work and the service made available to the public with respect to relative creative contribution, technological contribution, capital investment, cost, and risk; and

'(iii) rates and terms under voluntary license agreements described in paragraphs (2) and (3).

'(C) With respect to phonorecords made pursuant to this subsection to facilitate transmissions of public performances under a statutory license in accordance with section 114(f)—

'(i) the Copyright Royalty Judges shall establish rates and terms by application of the applicable standard in section 114(f) covering both the applicable public performances, and the making of phonorecords pursuant to this subsection solely to facilitate such public performances, together; and

'(ii) the royalty payable under this subsection for the making of phonorecords used by the transmitting organization solely to facilitate transmissions for which it pays royalties established as provided in clause (i) shall constitute 5 percent of such payments.

'(D) The Copyright Royalty Judges shall also establish requirements by which copyright owners may receive reasonable notice of the use of their sound recordings under this section, and under which records of such use shall be kept and made available by transmitting organizations entitled to obtain a statutory license under this subsection.'.

111th CONGRESS
1st Session
H. R. 2196
(Design Piracy Prohibition Act)

To amend title 17, United States Code, to extend protection to fashion design, and for other purposes.

IN THE HOUSE OF REPRESENTATIVES

April 30, 2009

Mr. DELAHUNT (for himself, Mr. GOODLATTE, Mr. NADLER of New York, Mr. ISSA, Ms. JACKSON-LEE of Texas, Mrs. BONO MACK, Mr. SENSENBRENNER, Ms. WASSERMAN SCHULTZ, Mr. COBLE, Mr. MAFFEI, Mr. WEINER, Mr. RANGEL, Mr. WEXLER, Ms. WATERS, Mr. COHEN, Mrs. MALONEY, Mr. GEORGE MILLER of California, and Ms. DELAURO) introduced the following bill; which was referred to the Committee on the Judiciary

A BILL

To amend title 17, United States Code, to extend protection to fashion design, and for other purposes.

Be it enacted by the Senate and House of Representatives of the United States of America in Congress assembled,

SECTION 1. SHORT TITLE.

This Act may be cited as the 'Design Piracy Prohibition Act'.

SECTION 2. AMENDMENTS TO TITLE 17, UNITED STATES CODE.

(a) Designs Protected— Section 1301 of title 17, United States Code, is amended—

(1) in subsection (a), by adding at the end the following:

'(3) FASHION DESIGN— A fashion design is subject to protection under this chapter.'; and

(2) in subsection (b)—

(A) in paragraph (2), by inserting ', or an article of apparel,' after 'plug or mold'; and

(B) by adding at the end the following:

'(7) A 'fashion design'—

'(A) is the appearance as a whole of an article of apparel, including its ornamentation; and

'(B) includes original elements of the article of apparel or the original arrangement or placement of original or non-original elements as incorporated in the overall appearance of the article of apparel.

'(8) The term 'design' includes fashion design, except to the extent expressly limited to the design of a vessel.

'(9) The term 'apparel' means—

'(A) an article of men's, women's, or children's clothing, including undergarments, outerwear, gloves, footwear, and headgear;

'(B) handbags, purses, wallets, duffel bags, suitcases, tote bags, and belts; and

'(C) eyeglass frames.

'(10) In the case of a fashion design, the term 'trend' means a newly popular concept, idea, or principle expressed in, or as part of, a wide variety of designs of articles of apparel that create an immediate amplified demand for articles of apparel embodying that concept, idea, or principle.'.

(b) Designs Not Subject to Protection— Section 1302(5) of title 17, United States Code, is amended—

(1) by striking '(5)' and inserting '(5)(A) in the case of a design of a vessel hull,';

(2) by striking the period and inserting '; or'; and

(3) by adding at the end the following:

'(B) in the case of a fashion design, embodied in a useful article that was made public by the designer or owner in the United States or a foreign country more than 6 months before the date of the application for registration under this chapter.'.

(c) Revisions, Adaptations, and Rearrangements— Section 1303 of title 17, United States Code, is amended by adding at the end the following: 'The presence or absence of a particular color or colors or of a pictorial or graphic work imprinted on fabric shall not be considered in determining the originality of a fashion design under section 1301 or 1302 or this section or the similarity or absence of similarity of fashion designs in determining infringement under section 1309.'.

(d) Term of Protection— Section 1305(a) of title 17, United States Code, is amended to read as follows:

'(a) In General— Subject to subsection (b), the protection provided under this chapter—

'(1) for a design of a vessel hull, shall continue for a term of 10 years beginning on the date of the commencement of protection under section 1304; and

'(2) for a fashion design, shall continue for a term of 3 years beginning on the date of the commencement of protection under section 1304.'.

(e) Infringement— Section 1309 of title 17, United States Code, is amended—

(1) in subsection (c), by striking 'that a design was protected' and inserting 'or reasonable grounds to know that protection for the design is claimed';

(2) by amending subsection (e) to read as follows:

'(e) Infringing Article Defined—

'(1) IN GENERAL— As used in this section, an 'infringing article' is any article the design of which has been copied from a design protected under this chapter, or from an image thereof, without the consent of the owner of the protected design. An infringing article is not an illustration or picture of a protected design in an advertisement, book, periodical, newspaper, photograph, broadcast, motion picture, or similar medium.

'(2) VESSEL HULL DESIGN— In the case of a design of a vessel hull, a design shall not be deemed to have been copied from a protected design if it is original and not substantially similar in appearance to a protected design.

'(3) FASHION DESIGN— In the case of a fashion design, a design shall not be deemed to have been copied from a protected design if it is original and not closely and substantially similar in overall visual appearance to a protected design, if it merely reflects a trend, or if it is the result of independent creation. This paragraph shall not be construed to permit the copying of a discrete design protected by this chapter.'; and

(3) by adding at the end the following:

'(h) Secondary Liability— The doctrines of secondary infringement or secondary liability that are applied in actions under chapter 5 of this title apply to the same extent to actions under this chapter. Any person who is liable under either such doctrine under this chapter is subject to all the remedies provided under this chapter, including those attributable to any underlying or resulting infringement.'.

(f) Application for Registration— Section 1310 of title 17, United States Code, is amended—

(1) by amending subsection (a) to read as follows:

'(a) Time Limit for Application for Registration—

'(1) VESSEL HULL DESIGN— In the case of a design of a vessel hull, protection under this chapter shall be lost if application for registration of the design is not made within 2 years after the date on which the design is first made public.

'(2) FASHION DESIGN— In the case of a fashion design, protection under this chapter shall be lost if application for registration of the design is not made within 6 months after the date on which the design is first made public by the designer or owner in the United States or a foreign country.';

(2) in subsection (b), by striking 'offered for sale' and inserting 'offered for individual or public sale'; and

(3) in subsection (d)—

(A) by redesignating paragraphs (1) through (6) as subparagraphs (A) through (F), respectively, and moving such subparagraphs 2 ems to the right;

(B) by striking 'The application for registration shall be made to the Administrator and shall state—' and inserting the following:

'(1) IN GENERAL— The application for registration shall be made to the Administrator and shall state—'; and

(C) by adding at the end the following:

'(2) VESSEL HULL DESIGNS— In the case of a design of a vessel hull, the application for registration may include a description setting forth the salient features of the design, but the absence of such a description shall not prevent registration under this chapter.

'(3) FASHION DESIGNS— In the case of a fashion design, the Administrator shall require a brief description of the design for purposes of matching the search criteria of the searchable database established under section 1333, except that such brief descriptions shall in no way limit the protection granted to the design or the subject matter of the registration under this chapter.'.

(g) Recovery for Infringement— Section 1323 of title 17, United States Code, is amended by striking '$50,000 or $1 per copy' and inserting '250,000 or $5 per copy'.

(h) Penalty for False Representation— Section 1327 of title 17, United States Code, is amended—

(1) by striking '$500' and inserting '5,000'; and

(2) by striking '$1,000' and inserting '$10,000'.

(i) Common Law and Other Rights Unaffected— Section 1330 of title 17, United States Code, is amended—

(1) in paragraph (1), by striking 'or' after the semicolon;

(2) in paragraph (2), by striking the period and inserting '; or'; and

(3) by adding at the end the following:

'(3) any rights that may exist under provisions of this title other than this chapter.'.

(j) Searchable Database for Fashion Design—

(1) IN GENERAL— Chapter 13 of title 17, United States Code, is amended by adding at the end the following:

'Sec. 1333. Searchable database for fashion design

'(a) In General— The Administrator shall establish and maintain a computerized database of fashion designs protected under this chapter. The database—

'(1) shall be searchable electronically, by general apparel and accessory categories;

'(2) shall include the information required by subparagraphs (A), (B), (C), (D), and (F) of paragraph (1), and paragraph (3), or section 1310(d); and

'(3) shall be available to the public without a fee or other access charge.

'(b) Additional Requirements— The database under subsection (a) shall contain a substantially complete visual representation of all fashion designs that have been submitted for registration under this chapter, and shall include information as to the status of those designs, such as whether such designs are—

'(1) registered under section 1313(a);

'(2) denied registration under section 1313 (b);

'(3) cancelled under section 1313(c); or

'(4) expired under section 1305.'.

(2) CONFORMING AMENDMENT— The table of sections for chapter 13 of title 17, United States Code, is amended by adding at the end the following:

'1333. Searchable database for fashion design.'.

(3) AUTHORIZATION OF APPROPRIATIONS— There are authorized to be appropriated such sums as may be necessary to carry out the amendments made by this subsection.

SECTION 3. EFFECTIVE DATE.

This Act and the amendments made by this Act shall take effect on the date of the enactment of this Act.

PART TWO

INTERNATIONAL PROTECTIONS AND THE NETWORKED INFORMATION ENVIRONMENT

SYNOPSIS

BERNE CONVENTION

The Berne Convention for the Protection of Literary and Artistic Works

Paris Text — July 24, 1971

TABLE OF CONTENTS[1]

---

[1] Prepared by World Intellectual Property Organization. Not part of original text.—*Eds.*

APPENDIX

[*Special Provisions Regarding Developing Countries*]

Scope of Chapter

Signed on September 9, 1886, completed at Paris on May 4, 1896, revised at Berlin on November 13, 1908, completed at Berne on March 20, 1914, and revised at Rome on June 2, 1928, at Brussels on June 26, 1948, at Stockholm on July 14, 1967, and at Paris on July 24, 1971.

The countries of the Union, being equally animated by the desire to protect, in as effective and uniform a manner as possible, the rights of authors in their literary and artistic works,

Recognizing the importance of the work of the Revision Conference held at Stockholm in 1967,

Have resolved to revise the Act adopted by the Stockholm Conference, while maintaining without change Articles 1 to 20 and 22 to 26 of that Act.

Consequently, the undersigned Plenipotentiaries, having presented their full power, recognized as in good and due form, have agreed as follows:

Article 1

The countries to which this Convention applies constitute a Union for the protection of the rights of authors in their literary and artistic works.

Article 2

(1) The expression "literary and artistic works" shall include every production in the literary, scientific and artistic domain, whatever may be the mode or form of its expression, such as books, pamphlets and other writings; lectures, addresses, sermons and other works of the same nature; dramatic or dramatico-musical works; choreographic works and entertainments in dumb

show; musical compositions with or without words; cinematographic works to which are assimilated works expressed by a process analogous to cinematography; works of drawing, painting, architecture, sculpture, engraving and lithography; photographic works to which are assimilated works expressed by a process analogous to photography; works of applied art; illustrations, maps, plans, sketches and three-dimensional works relative to geography, topography, architecture or science.

(2) It shall, however, be a matter for legislation in the countries of the Union to prescribe that works in general or any specified categories of works shall not be protected unless they have been fixed in some material form.

(3) Translations, adaptations, arrangements of music and other alterations of a literary or artistic work shall be protected as original works without prejudice to the copyright in the original work.

(4) It shall be a matter for legislation in the countries of the Union to determine the protection to be granted to official texts of a legislative, administrative and legal nature, and to official translations of such texts.

(5) Collections of literary or artistic works such as encyclopedias and anthologies which, by reason of the selection and arrangement of their contents, constitute intellectual creations shall be protected as such, without prejudice to the copyright in each of the works forming part of such collections.

(6) The works mentioned in this Article shall enjoy protection in all countries of the Union. This protection shall operate for the benefit of the author and his successors in title.

(7) Subject to the provisions of Article 7(4) of this Convention, it shall be a matter for legislation in the countries of the Union to determine the extent of the application of their laws to works of applied art and industrial designs and models, as well as the conditions under which such works, designs and models shall be protected. Works protected in the country of origin solely as designs and models shall be entitled in another country of the Union only to such special protection as is granted in that country to designs and models; however, if no such special protection is granted in that country, such works shall be protected as artistic works.

(8) The protection of this Convention shall not apply to news of the day or to miscellaneous facts having the character of mere items of press information.

Article 2*bis*

(1) It shall be a matter for legislation in the countries of the Union to exclude, wholly or in part, from the protection provided by the preceding Article political speeches and speeches delivered in the course of legal proceedings.

(2) It shall also be a matter for legislation in the countries of the Union to determine the conditions under which lectures, addresses and other works of the same nature which are delivered in public may be reproduced by the press, broadcast, communicated to the public by wire and made the subject of public

communication as envisaged in Article 11bis (1) of this Convention, when such use is justified by the informatory purpose.

(3) Nevertheless, the author shall enjoy the exclusive right of making a collection of his works mentioned in the preceding paragraphs.

Article 3

(1) The protection of this Convention shall apply to:

(a) authors who are nationals of one of the countries of the Union, for their works, whether published or not;

(b) authors who are not nationals of one of the countries of the Union, for their works first published in one of those countries, or simultaneously in a country outside the Union and in a country of the Union.

(2) Authors who are not nationals of one of the countries of the Union but who have their habitual residence in one of them shall, for the purpose of this Convention, be assimilated to nationals of that country.

(3) The expression "published works" means works published with the consent of their authors, whatever may be the means of manufacture of the copies, provided that the availability of such copies has been such as to satisfy the reasonable requirements of the public, having regard to the nature of the work. The performance of a dramatic, dramatico-musical, cinematographic or musical work, the public recitation of a literary work, the communication by wire or the broadcasting of literary or artistic works, the exhibition of a work of art and the construction of a work of architecture shall not constitute publication.

(4) A work shall be considered as having been published simultaneously in several countries if it has been published in two or more countries within thirty days of its first publication.

Article 4

The protection of this Convention shall apply, even if the conditions of Article 3 are not fulfilled, to:

(a) authors of cinematographic works the maker of which has his headquarters or habitual residence in one of the countries of the Union;

(b) authors of works of architecture erected in a country of the Union or of other artistic works incorporated in a building or other structure located in a country of the Union.

Article 5

(1) Authors shall enjoy, in respect of works for which they are protected under this Convention, in countries of the Union other than the country of origin, the rights which their respective laws do now or may hereafter grant to their nationals, as well as the rights specially granted by this Convention.

(2) The enjoyment and the exercise of these rights shall not be subject to any formality; such enjoyment and such exercise shall be independent of the existence of protection in the country of origin of the work. Consequently, apart

from the provisions of the Convention, the extent of protection, as well as the means of redress afforded to the author to protect his rights, shall be governed exclusively by the laws of the country where protection is claimed.

(3) Protection in the country of origin is governed by domestic law. However, when the author is not a national of the country of origin of the work for which he is protected under this Convention, he shall enjoy in that country the same rights as national authors.

(4) The country of origin shall be considered to be:

(a) in the case of works first published in a country of the Union, that country; in the case of works published simultaneously in several countries of the Union which grant different terms of protection, the country whose legislation grants the shortest term of protection;

(b) in the case of works published simultaneously in a country outside the Union and in a country of the Union, the latter country;

(c) in the case of unpublished works or of works first published in a country outside the Union, without simultaneous publication in a country of the Union, the country of the Union of which the author is a national, provided that:

(i) when these are cinematographic works the maker of which has his headquarters or his habitual residence in a country of the Union, the country of origin shall be that country, and

(ii) when these are works of architecture erected in a country of the Union or other artistic works incorporated in a building or other structure located in a country of the Union, the country of origin shall be that country.

Article 6

(1) Where any country outside the Union Fails to protect in an adequate manner the works of authors who are nationals of one of the countries of the Union, the latter country may restrict the protection given to the works of authors who are, at the date of the first publication thereof, nationals of the other country and are not habitually resident in one of the countries of the Union. If the country of first publication avails itself of this right, the other countries of the Union shall not be required to grant to works thus subjected to special treatment a wider protection than that granted to them in the country of first publication.

(2) No restrictions introduced by virtue of the preceding paragraph shall affect the rights which an author may have acquired in respect of a work published in a country of the Union before such restrictions were put into force.

(3) The countries of the Union which restrict the grant of copyright in accordance with this Article shall give notice thereof to the Director General of the World Intellectual Property Organization (hereinafter designated as "the Director General") by a written declaration specifying the countries in

regard to which protection is restricted, and the restrictions to which rights of authors who are nationals of those countries are subjected. The Director General shall immediately communicate this declaration to all the countries of the Union.

Article 6*bis*

(1) Independently of the author's economic rights, and even after the transfer of the said rights, the author shall have the right to claim authorship of the work and to object to any distortion, mutilation, or other modification of, or other derogatory action in relation to, the said work, which would be prejudicial to his honor or reputation.

(2) The rights granted to the author in accordance with the preceding paragraph shall, after his death, be maintained, at least until the expiry of the economic rights, and shall be exercisable by the persons or institutions authorized by the legislation of the country where protection is claimed. However, those countries whose legislation, at the moment of their ratification of or accession to this Act, does not provide for the protection after the death of the author of all the rights set out in the preceding paragraph may provide that some of these rights may, after his death, cease to be maintained.

(3) The means of redress for safeguarding the rights granted by this Article shall be governed by the legislation of the country where protection is claimed.

Article 7

(1) The term of protection granted by this Convention shall be the life of the author and fifty years after his death.

(2) However, in the case of cinematographic works, the countries of the Union may provide that the term of protection shall expire fifty years after the work has been made available to the public with the consent of the author, or, failing such an event within fifty years from the making of such a work, fifty years after the making.

(3) In the case of anonymous or pseudonymous works, the term of protection granted by this Convention shall expire fifty years after the work has been lawfully made available to the public. However, when the pseudonym adopted by the author leaves no doubt as to his identity, the term of protection shall be that provided in paragraph (1). If the author of an anonymous or pseudonymous work discloses his identity during the above-mentioned period, the term of protection applicable shall be that provided in paragraph (1). The countries of the Union shall not be required to protect anonymous or pseudonymous works in respect of which it is reasonable to presume that their author has been dead for fifty years.

(4) It shall be a matter for legislation in the countries of the Union to determine the term of protection of photographic works and that of works of applied art in so far as they are protected as artistic works; however, this term shall last at least until the end of a period of twenty-five years from the making of such a work.

(5) The term of protection subsequent to the death of the author and the terms provided by paragraphs (2), (3) and (4) shall run from the date of death or of the event referred to in those paragraphs, but such terms shall always be deemed to begin on the first of January of the year following the death or such event.

(6) The countries of the Union may grant a term of protection in excess of those provided by the preceding paragraphs.

(7) Those countries of the Union bound by the Rome Act of this Convention which grant, in their national legislation in force at the time of signature of the present Act, shorter terms of protection than those provided for in the preceding paragraphs shall have the right to maintain such terms when ratifying or acceding to the present Act.

(8) In any case, the term shall be governed by the legislation of the country where protection is claimed; however, unless the legislation of that country otherwise provides, the term shall not exceed the term fixed in the country of origin of the work.

Article 7*bis*

The provisions of the preceding Article shall also apply in the case of a work of joint authorship, provided that the terms measured from the death of the author shall be calculated from the death of the last surviving author.

Article 8

Authors of literary and artistic works protected by this Convention shall enjoy the exclusive right of making and of authorizing the translation of their works throughout the term of protection of their rights in the original works.

Article 9

(1) Authors of literary and artistic works protected by this Convention shall have the exclusive right of authorizing the reproduction of these works, in any manner or form.

(2) It shall be a matter for legislation in the countries of the Union to permit the reproduction of such works in certain special cases, provided that such reproduction does not conflict with a normal exploitation of the work and does not unreasonably prejudice the legitimate interests of the author.

(3) Any sound or visual recording shall be considered as a reproduction for the purposes of this Convention.

Article 10

(1) It shall be permissible to make quotations from a work which has already been lawfully made available to the public, provided that their making is compatible with fair practice, and their extent does not exceed that justified by the purpose, including quotations from newspaper articles and periodicals in the form of press summaries.

(2) It shall be a matter for legislation in the countries of the Union, and for special agreements existing or to be concluded between them, to permit the utilization, to the extent justified by the purpose, of literary or artistic works by way of illustration in publications, broadcasts or sound or visual recordings for teaching, provided such utilization is compatible with fair practice.

(3) Where use is made of works in accordance with the preceding paragraphs of this Article, mention shall be made of the source, and of the name of the author if it appears thereon.

Article 10*bis*

(1) It shall be a matter for legislation in the countries of the Union to permit the reproduction by the press, the broadcasting or the communication to the public by wire of articles published in newspapers or periodicals on current economic, political or religious topics, and of broadcast works of the same character, in cases in which the reproduction, broadcasting or such communication thereof is not expressly reserved. Nevertheless, the source must always be clearly indicated; the legal consequences of a breach of this obligation shall be determined by the legislation of the country where protection is claimed.

(2) It shall also be a matter for legislation in the countries of the Union to determine the conditions under which, for the purpose of reporting current events by means of photography, cinematography, broadcasting or communication to the public by wire, literary or artistic works seen or heard in the course of the event may, to the extent justified by the informatory purpose, be reproduced and made available to the public.

Article 11

(1) Authors of dramatic, dramatico-musical and musical works shall enjoy the exclusive right of authorizing:

(i) the public performance of their works, including such public performance by any means or process;

(ii) any communication to the public of the performance of their works.

(2) Authors of dramatic or dramatico-musical works shall enjoy, during the full term of their rights in the original works, the same rights with respect to translations thereof.

Article 11*bis*

(1) Authors of literary and artistic works shall enjoy the exclusive right of authorizing:

(i) the broadcasting of their works or the communication thereof to the public by any other means of wireless diffusion of signs, sounds or images;

(ii) any communication to the public by wire or by rebroadcasting of the broadcast of the work, when this communication is made by an organization other than the original one;

(iii) the public communication by loudspeaker or any other analogous instrument transmitting, by signs, sounds or images, the broadcast of the work.

(2) It shall be a matter for legislation in the countries of the Union to determine the conditions under which the rights mentioned in the preceding paragraph may be exercised, but these conditions shall apply only in the countries where they have been prescribed. They shall not in any circumstances be

prejudicial to the moral rights of the author, nor to his right to obtain equitable remuneration which, in the absence of agreement, shall be fixed by competent authority.

(3) In the absence of any contrary stipulation, permission granted in accordance with paragraph (1) of this Article shall not imply permission to record, by means of instruments recording sounds or images, the work broadcast. It shall, however, be a matter for legislation in the countries of the Union to determine the regulations for ephemeral recordings made by a broadcasting organization by means of its own facilities and used for its own broadcasts. The preservation of these recordings in official archives may, on the ground, of their exceptional documentary character, be authorized by such legislation.

Article 11*ter*

(1) Authors of literary works shall enjoy the exclusive right of authorizing:

(i) the public recitation of their works, including such public recitation by any means or process;

(ii) any communication to the public of the recitation of their works.

(2) Authors of literary works shall enjoy, during the full term of their rights in the original works, the same rights with respect to translations thereof.

Article 12

Authors of literary or artistic works shall enjoy the exclusive right of authorizing adaptations, arrangements and other alterations of their works.

Article 13

(1) Each country of the Union may impose for itself reservations and conditions on the exclusive right granted to the author of a musical work and to the author of any words, the recording of which together with the musical work has already been authorized by the latter, to authorize the sound recording of that musical work, together with such words, if any; but all such reservations and conditions shall apply only in the countries which have imposed them and shall not, in any circumstances, be prejudicial to the rights of these authors to obtain equitable remuneration which, in the absence of agreement, shall be fixed by competent authority.

(2) Recordings of musical works made in a country of the Union in accordance with Article 13(3) of the Conventions signed at Rome on June 2, 1928, and at Brussels on June 26, 1948, may be reproduced in that country without the permission of the author of the musical work until a date two years after that country becomes bound by this Act.

(3) Recordings made in accordance with paragraphs (1) and (2) of this Article and imported without permission from the parties concerned into a country where they are treated as infringing recordings shall be liable to seizure.

Article 14

(1) Authors of literary or artistic works shall have the exclusive right of authorizing:

(i) the cinematographic adaptation and reproduction of these works, and the distribution of the works thus adapted or reproduced;

(ii) the public performance and communication to the public by wire of the works thus adapted or reproduced.

(2) The adaptation into any other artistic form of a cinematographic production derived from literary or artistic works shall, without prejudice to the authorization of the author of the cinematographic production, remain subject to the authorization of the authors of the original works.

(3) The provisions of Article 13(1) shall not apply.

Article 14bis

(1) Without prejudice to the copyright in any work which may have been adapted or reproduced, a cinematographic work shall be protected as an original work. The owner of copyright in a cinematographic work shall enjoy the same rights as the author of an original work, including the rights referred to in the preceding Article.

(2) *(a)* Ownership of copyright in a cinematographic work shall be a matter for legislation in the country where protection is claimed.

(b) However, in the countries of the Union which, by legislation, include among the owners of copyright in a cinematographic work authors who have brought contributions to the making of the work, such authors, if they have undertaken to bring such contributions, may not, in the absence of any contrary or special stipulation, object to the reproduction, distribution, public performance, communication to the public by wire, broadcasting or any other communication to the public, or to the subtitling or dubbing of texts, of the work.

(c) The question whether or not the form of the undertaking referred to above should, for the application of the preceding subparagraph *(b)*, be in a written agreement or a written act of the same effect shall be a matter for the legislation of the country where the maker of the cinematographic work has his headquarters or habitual residence. However, it shall be a matter for the legislation of the country of the Union where protection is claimed to provide that the said undertaking shall be in a written agreement or a written act of the same effect. The countries whose legislation so provides shall notify the Director General by means of a written declaration, which will be immediately communicated by him to all the other countries of the Union.

(d) By "contrary or special stipulation" is meant any restrictive condition which is relevant to the aforesaid undertaking.

(3) Unless the national legislation provides to the contrary, the provisions of paragraph (2)*(b)* above shall not be applicable to authors of scenarios, dialogues and musical works created for the making of the cinematographic work, or to the principal director thereof. However, those countries of the Union whose legislation does not contain rules providing for the application of the said paragraph (2)*(b)* to such director shall notify the Director General

by means of a written declaration, which will be immediately communicated by him to all the other countries of the Union.

Article 14[ter]

(1) The author, or after his death the persons or institutions authorized by national legislation, shall, with respect to original works of art and original manuscripts of writers and composers, enjoy the inalienable right to an interest in any sale of the work subsequent to the first transfer by the author of the work.

(2) The protection provided by the preceding paragraph may be claimed in a country of the Union only if legislation in the country to which the author belongs so permits, and to the extent permitted by the country where this protection is claimed.

(3) The procedure for collection and the amounts shall be matters for determination by national legislation.

Article 15

(1) In order that the author of a literary or artistic work protected by this Convention shall, in the absence of proof to the contrary, be regarded as such, and consequently be entitled to institute infringement proceedings in the countries of the Union, it shall be sufficient for his name to appear on the work in the usual manner. This paragraph shall be applicable even if this name is a pseudonym, where the pseudonym adopted by the author leaves no doubt as to his identity.

(2) The person or body corporate whose name appears on a cinematographic work in the usual manner shall, in the absence of proof to the contrary, be presumed to be the maker of the said work.

(3) In the case of anonymous and pseudonymous works, other than those referred to in paragraph (1) above, the publisher whose name appears on the work shall, in the absence of proof to the contrary, be deemed to represent the author, and in this capacity he shall be entitled to protect and enforce the author's rights. The provisions of this paragraph shall cease to apply when the author reveals his identity and establishes his claim to authorship of the work.

(4) *(a)* In the case of unpublished works where the identity of the author is unknown, but where there is every ground to presume that he is a national of a country of the Union, it shall be a matter for legislation in that country to designate the competent authority which shall represent the author and shall be entitled to protect and enforce his rights in the countries of the Union.

(b) Countries of the Union which make such designation under the terms of this provision shall notify the Director General by means of a written declaration giving full information concerning the authority thus designated. The Director General shall at once communicate this declaration to all other countries of the Union.

Article 16

(1) Infringing copies of a work shall be liable to seizure in any country of the Union where the work enjoys legal protection.

(2) The provisions of the preceding paragraph shall also apply to reproductions coming from a country where the work is not protected, or has ceased to be protected.

(3) The seizure shall take place in accordance with the legislation of each country.

Article 17

The provisions of this Convention cannot in any way affect the right of the Government of each country of the Union to permit, to control, or to prohibit, by legislation or regulation, the circulation, presentation, or exhibition of any work or production in regard to which the competent authority may find it necessary to exercise that right.

Article 18

(1) This Convention shall apply to all works which, at the moment of its coming into force, have not yet fallen into the public domain in the country of origin through the expiry of the term of protection.

(2) If, however, through the expiry of the term of protection which was previously granted, a work has fallen into the public domain of the country where protection is claimed, that work shall not be protected anew.

(3) The application of this principle shall be subject to any provisions contained in special conventions to that effect existing or to be concluded between countries of the Union. In the absence of such provisions, the respective countries shall determine, each in so far as it is concerned, the conditions of application of this principle.

(4) The preceding provisions shall also apply in the case of new accessions to the Union and to cases in which protection is extended by the application of Article 7 or by the abandonment of reservations.

Article 19

The provisions of this Convention shall not preclude the making of a claim to the benefit of any greater protection which may be granted by legislation in a country of the Union.

Article 20

The Governments of the countries of the Union reserve the right to enter into special agreements among themselves, in so far as such agreements grant to authors more extensive rights than those granted by the Convention, or contain other provisions not contrary to this Convention. The provisions of existing agreements which satisfy these conditions shall remain applicable.

Article 21

(1) Special provisions regarding developing countries are included in the Appendix.

(2) Subject to the provisions of Article 28(1)*(b)*, the Appendix forms an integral part of this Act.

Article 22

(1) *(a)* The Union shall have an Assembly consisting of those countries of the Union which are bound by Articles 22 to 26.

(b) The Government of each country shall be represented by one delegate, who may be assisted by alternate delegates, advisors, and experts.

(c) The expenses of each delegation shall be borne by the Government which has appointed it.

(2) *(a)* The Assembly shall:

(i) deal with all matters concerning the maintenance and development of the Union and the implementation of this Convention;

(ii) give directions concerning the preparation for conferences of revision to the International Bureau of Intellectual Property (hereinafter designated as "the International Bureau"8) referred to in the Convention Establishing the World Intellectual Property Organization (hereinafter designated as "the Organization"), due account being taken of any comments made by those countries of the Union which are not bound by Articles 22 to 26;

(iii) review and approve the reports and activities of the Director General of the Organization concerning the Union, and give him all necessary instructions concerning matters within the competence of the Union;

(iv) elect the members of the Executive Committee of the Assembly;

(v) review and approve the reports and activities of its Executive Committee, and give instructions to such Committee;

(vi) determine the program and adopt the triennial budget[2] of the Union, and approve its final accounts;

(vii) adopt the financial regulations of the Union;

(viii) establish such committees of experts and working groups as may be necessary for the work of the Union;

(ix) determine which countries not members of the Union and which intergovernmental and international nongovernmental organizations shall be admitted to its meetings as observers;

(xx) adopt amendments to Articles 22 to 26;

---

[2] By amendment adopted in 1979 (entered into force November 19, 1984), Art. 22(2)(a)(vi), "triennial" is replaced by "biennial".—*Eds.*

(xxi) take any other appropriate action designed to further the objectives of the Union;

(xxii) exercise such other functions as are appropriate under this Convention;

(xxiii) subject to its acceptance, exercise such rights as are given to it in the Convention establishing the Organization.

(b) With respect to matters which are of interest also to other Unions administered by the Organization, the Assembly shall make its decisions after having heard the advice of the Coordination Committee of the Organization.

(3) *(a)* Each country member of the Assembly shall have one vote.

(b) One-half of the countries members of the Assembly shall constitute a quorum.

(c) Notwithstanding the provisions of subparagraph *(b)*, if, in any session, the number of countries represented is less than one-half but equal to or more than one-third of the countries members of the Assembly, the Assembly may make decisions but, with the exception of decisions concerning its own procedure, all such decisions shall take effect only if the following conditions are fulfilled. The International Bureau shall communicate the said decisions to the countries members of the Assembly which were not represented and shall invite them to express in writing their vote or abstention within a period of three months from the date of the communication. If, at the expiration of this period, the number of countries having thus expressed their vote or abstention attains the number of countries which was lacking for attaining the quorum in the session itself, such decisions shall take effect provided that at the same time the required majority still obtains.

(d) Subject to the provisions of Article 26(2), the decisions of the Assembly shall require two-thirds of the votes cast.

(e) Abstentions shall not be considered as votes.

(f) A delegate may represent, and vote in the name of, one country only.

(g) Countries of the Union not members of the Assembly shall be admitted to its meetings as observers.

(4) *(a)* The Assembly shall meet once in every third calendar year[3] in ordinary session upon convocation by the Director General and, in the absence of exceptional circumstances, during the same period and at the same place as the General Assembly of the Organization.

---

[3] By amendment adopted in 1979 (entered into force November 19, 1984), Art. 22 (4)(a), "third" is replaced by "second".—*Eds.*

(b) The Assembly shall meet in extraordinary session upon convocation by the Director General, at the request of the Executive Committee or at the request of one-fourth of the countries members of the Assembly.

(5) The Assembly shall adopt its own rules of procedure.

Article 23

(1) The Assembly shall have an Executive Committee.

(2) *(a)* The Executive Committee shall consist of countries elected by the Assembly from among countries members of the Assembly. Furthermore, the country on whose territory the Organization has its headquarters shall, subject to the provisions of Article 25(7)*(b)*, have an *ex officio* seat on the Committee.

(b) The Government of each country member of the Executive Committee shall be represented by one delegate, who may be assisted by alternate delegates, advisors, and experts.

(c) The expenses of each delegation shall be borne by the Government which has appointed it.

(3) The number of countries members of the Executive Committee shall correspond to one-fourth of the number of countries members of the Assembly. In establishing the number of seats to be filled, remainders after division by four shall be disregarded.

(4) In electing the members of the Executive Committee, the Assembly shall have due regard to an equitable geographical distribution and to the need for countries party to the Special Agreements which might be established in relation with the Union to be among the countries constituting the Executive Committee.

(5) *(a)* Each member of the Executive Committee shall serve from the close of the session of the Assembly which elected it to the close of the next ordinary session of the Assembly.

(b) Members of the Executive Committee may be reelected, but not more than two-thirds of them.

(c) The Assembly shall establish the details of the rules governing the election and possible re-election of the members of the Executive Committee.

(6) *(a)* The Executive Committee shall:

(i) prepare the draft agenda of the Assembly;

(ii) submit proposals to the Assembly respecting the draft program and triennial[4] budget of the Union prepared by the Director General;

[4] By amendments adopted in 1979 (entered into force November 19, 1984, Art. 23(6)(a)(ii), "triennial" is replaced by "biennial" and Art. 23(6)(a), item (iii) is deleted.—*Eds.*

(iii) approve, within the limits of the program and the triennial[5] budget, the specific yearly budgets and programs prepared by the Director General;

(iv) submit, with appropriate comments, to the Assembly the periodical reports of the Director General and the yearly audit reports on the accounts;

(v) in accordance with the decisions of the Assembly and having regard to circumstances arising between two ordinary sessions of the Assembly, take all necessary measures to ensure the execution of the program of the Union by the Director General;

(vi) perform such other functions as are allocated to it under this Convention.

(b) With respect to matters which are of interest also to other Unions administered by the Organization, the Executive Committee shall make its decisions after having heard the advice of the Coordination Committee of the Organization.

(7) *(a)* The Executive Committee shall meet once a year in ordinary session upon convocation by the Director General, preferably during the same period and at the same place as the Coordination Committee of the Organization.

(b) The Executive Committee shall meet in extraordinary session upon convocation by the Director General, either on his own initiative, or at the request of its Chairman or one-fourth of its members.

(8) *(a)* Each country member of the Executive Committee shall have one vote.

(b) One-half of the members of the Executive Committee shall constitute a quorum.

(c) Decisions shall be made by a simple majority of the votes cast.

(d) Abstentions shall not be considered as votes.

(e) A delegate may represent, and vote in the name of, one country only.

(9) Countries of the Union not members of the Executive Committee shall be admitted to its meetings as observers.

(10) The Executive Committee shall adopt its own rules of procedure.

Article 24

(1) *(a)* The administrative tasks with respect to the Union shall be performed by the International Bureau, which is a continuation of the Bureau of

---

[5] By amendments adopted in 1979 (entered into force November 19, 1984, Art. 23(6)(a)(ii), "triennial" is replaced by "biennial" and Art. 23(6)(a), item (iii) is deleted.—*Eds.*

the Union united with the Bureau of the Union established by the International Convention for the Protection of Industrial Property.

(b) In particular, the International Bureau shall provide the secretariat of the various organs of the Union.

(c) The Director General of the Organization shall be the chief executive of the Union and shall represent the Union.

(2) The International Bureau shall assemble and publish information concerning the protection of copyright. Each country of the Union shall promptly communicate to the International Bureau all new laws and official texts concerning the protection of copyright.

(3) The International Bureau shall publish a monthly periodical.

(4) The International Bureau shall, on request, furnish information to any country of the Union on matters concerning the protection of copyright.

(5) The International Bureau shall conduct studies, and shall provide services, designed to facilitate the protection of copyright.

(6) The Director General and any staff member designated by him shall participate, without the right to vote, in all meetings of the Assembly, the Executive Committee and any other committee of experts or working group. The Director General, or a staff member designated by him, shall be *ex officio* secretary of these bodies.

(7) *(a)* The International Bureau shall, in accordance with the directions of the Assembly and in cooperation with the Executive Committee, make the preparations for the conferences of revision of the provisions of the Convention other than Articles 22 to 26.

(b) The International Bureau may consult with intergovernmental and international non-governmental organizations concerning preparations for conferences of revision.

(c) The Director General and persons designated by him shall take part, without the right to vote, in the discussions at these conferences.

(8) The International Bureau shall carry out any other tasks assigned to it.

Article 25

(1) *(a)* The Union shall have a budget.

(b) The budget of the Union shall include the income and expenses proper to the Union, its contribution to the budget of expenses common to the Unions, and, where applicable, the sum made available to the budget of the Conference of the Organization.

(c) Expenses not attributable exclusively to the Union but also to one or more other Unions administered by the Organization shall be considered as expenses common to the Unions. The share of the Union in such common expenses shall be in proportion to the interest the Union has in them.

(2) The budget of the Union shall be established with due regard to the requirements of coordination with the budgets of the other Unions administered by the Organization.

(3) The budget of the Union shall be financed from the following sources:

(i) contributions of the countries of the Union;

(ii) fees and charges due for services performed by the International Bureau in relation to the Union;

(iii) sale of, or royalties on, the publications of the International Bureau concerning the Union;

(iv) gifts, bequests, and subventions;

(v) rents, interests, and other miscellaneous income.

(4) *(a)* For the purpose of establishing its contribution towards the budget, each country of the Union shall belong to a class, and shall pay its annual contributions on the basis of a number of units fixed as follows:

Class I	25
Class II	20
Class III	15
Class IV	10
Class V	5
Class VI	3
Class VII	1

(b) Unless it has already done so, each country shall indicate, concurrently with depositing its instrument of ratification or accession, the class to which it wishes to belong. Any country may change class. If it chooses a lower class, the country must announce it to the Assembly at one of its ordinary sessions. Any such change shall take effect at the beginning of the calendar year following the session.

(c) The annual contribution of each country shall be an amount in the same proportion to the total sum to be contributed to the annual budget of the Union by all countries as the number of its units is to the total of the units of all contributing countries.

(d) Contributions shall become due on the first of January of each year.

(e) A country which is in arrears in the payment of its contributions shall have no vote in any of the organs of the Union of which it is a member if the amount of its arrears equals or exceeds the amount of the contributions due from it for the preceding two full years. However, any organ of the Union may allow such a country to continue to exercise its vote in that organ if, and as long as, it is satisfied that the delay in payment is due to exceptional and unavoidable circumstances.

(f) If the budget is not adopted before the beginning of a new financial period, it shall be at the same level as the budget of the previous year, in accordance with the financial regulations.

(5) The amount of the fees and charges due for services rendered by the International Bureau in relation to the Union shall be established, and shall be reported to the Assembly and the Executive Committee, by the Director General.

(6) *(a)* The Union shall have a working capital fund which shall be constituted by a single payment made by each country of the Union. If the fund becomes insufficient, an increase shall be decided by the Assembly.

(b) The amount of the initial payment of each country to the said fund or of its participation in the increase thereof shall be a proportion of the contribution of that country for the year in which the fund is established or the increase decided.

(c) The proportion and the terms of payment shall be fixed by the Assembly on the proposal of the Director General and after it has heard the advice of the Coordination Committee of the Organization.

(7) *(a)* In the headquarters agreement concluded with the country on the territory of which the Organization has its headquarters, it shall be provided that, whenever the working capital fund is insufficient, such country shall grant advances. The amount of these advances and the conditions on which they are granted shall be the subject of separate agreements, in each case, between such country and the Organization. As long as it remains under the obligation to grant advances, such country shall have an *ex officio* seat on the Executive Committee.

(b) The country referred to in subparagraph *(a)* and the Organization shall each have the right to denounce the obligation to grant advances, by written notification. Denunciation shall take effect three years after the end of the year in which it has been notified.

(8) The auditing of the accounts shall be effected by one or more of the countries of the Union or by external auditors, as provided in the financial regulations. They shall be designated, with their agreement, by the Assembly.

Article 26

(1) Proposals for the amendment of Articles 22, 23, 24, 25, and the present Article, may be initiated by any country member of the Assembly, by the Executive Committee, or by the Director General. Such proposals shall be communicated by the Director General to the member countries of the Assembly at least six months in advance of their consideration by the Assembly.

(2) Amendments to the Articles referred to in paragraph (1) shall be adopted by the Assembly. Adoption shall require three-fourths of the votes cast, provided that any amendment of Article 22, and of the present paragraph, shall require four-fifths of the votes cast.

(3) Any amendment to the Articles referred to in paragraph (1) shall enter into force one month after written notifications of acceptance, effected in accordance with their respective constitutional processes, have been received by the Director General from three-fourths of the countries members of the Assembly at the time it adopted the amendment. Any amendment to the said Articles thus accepted shall bind all the countries which are members of the Assembly at the time the amendment enters into force, or which become

members thereof at a subsequent date, provided that any amendment increasing the financial obligations of countries of the Union shall bind only those countries which have notified their acceptance of such amendment.

Article 27

(1) This Convention shall be submitted to revision with a view to the introduction of amendments designed to improve the system of the Union.

(2) For this purpose, conferences shall be held successively in one of the countries of the Union among the delegates of the said countries.

(3) Subject to the provisions of Article 26 which apply to the amendment of Articles 22 to 26, any revision of this Act, including the Appendix, shall require the unanimity of the votes cast.

Article 28

(1) *(a)* Any country of the Union which has signed this Act may ratify it, and, if it has not signed it, may accede to it. Instruments of ratification or accession shall be deposited with the Director General.

(b) Any country of the Union may declare in its instrument of ratification or accession that its ratification or accession shall not apply to Articles 1 to 21 and the Appendix, provided that, if such country has previously made a declaration under Article VI(1) of the Appendix, then it may declare in the said instrument only that its ratification or accession shall not apply to Articles 1 to 20.

(c) Any country of the Union which, in accordance with subparagraph *(b)*, has excluded provisions therein referred to from the effects of its ratification or accession may at any later time declare that it extends the effects of its ratification or accession to those provisions. Such declaration shall be deposited with the Director General.

(2) *(a)* Articles 1 to 21 and the Appendix shall enter into force three months after both of the following two conditions are fulfilled:

(i) at least five countries of the Union have ratified or acceded to this Act without making a declaration under paragraph (1)*(b)*,

(ii) France, Spain, the United Kingdom of Great Britain and Northern Ireland, and the United States of America, have become bound by the Universal Copyright Convention as revised at Paris on July 24, 1971.

(b) The entry into force referred to in subparagraph *(a)* shall apply to those countries of the Union which, at least three months before the said entry into force, have deposited instruments of ratification or accession not containing a declaration under paragraph (1)*(b)*.

(c) With respect to any country of the Union not covered by subparagraph *(b)* and which ratifies or accedes to this Act without making a declaration under paragraph (1)*(b)*, Articles 1 to 21 and the Appendix shall enter into force three months after the date on which the Director General has notified the deposit of the relevant instrument of ratification or accession, unless a subsequent date has been indicated in the instrument

deposited. In the latter case, Articles 1 to 21 and the Appendix shall enter into force with respect to that country on the date thus indicated.

(d) The provisions of subparagraphs *(a)* to *(c)* do not affect the application of Article VI of the Appendix.

(3) With respect to any country of the Union which ratifies or accedes to this Act with or without a declaration made under paragraph (1)*(b)*, Articles 22 to 38 shall enter into force three months after the date on which the Director General has notified the deposit of the relevant instrument of ratification or accession, unless a subsequent date has been indicated in the instrument deposited. In the latter case, Articles 22 to 38 shall enter into force with respect to that country on the date thus indicated.

Article 29

(1) Any country outside the Union may accede to this Act and thereby become party to this Convention and a member of the Union. Instruments of accession shall be deposited with the Director General.

(2) *(a)* Subject to subparagraph *(b)*, this Convention shall enter into force with respect to any country outside the Union three months after the date on which the Director General has notified the deposit of its instrument of accession, unless a subsequent date has been indicated in the instrument deposited. In the latter case, this Convention shall enter into force with respect to that country on the date thus indicated.

(b) If the entry into force according to subparagraph *(a)* precedes the entry into force of Articles 1 to 21 and the Appendix according to Article 28(2)*(a)*, the said country shall, in the meantime, be bound, instead of by Articles 1 to 21 and the Appendix, by Articles 1 to 20 of the Brussels Act of this Convention.

Article 29*bis*

Ratification of or accession to this Act by any country not bound by Articles 22 to 38 of the Stockholm Act of this Convention shall, for the sole purposes of Article 14(2) of the Convention establishing the Organization, amount to ratification of or accession to the said Stockholm Act with the limitation set forth in Article 28(1)*(b)*(i) thereof.

Article 30

(1) Subject to the exceptions permitted by paragraph (2) of this Article, by Article 28(1)*(b)*, by Article 33(2), and by the Appendix, ratification or accession shall automatically entail acceptance of all the provisions and admission to all the advantages of this Convention.

(2) *(a)* Any country of the Union ratifying or acceding to this Act may, subject to Article V(2) of the Appendix, retain the benefit of the reservations it has previously formulated on condition that it makes a declaration to that effect at the time of the deposit of its instrument of ratification or accession.

(b) Any country outside the Union may declare, in acceding to this Convention and subject to Article V(2) of the Appendix, that it intends to

substitute, temporarily at least, for Article 8 of this Act concerning the right of translation, the provisions of Article 5 of the Union Convention of 1886, as completed at Paris in 1896, on the clear understanding that the said provisions are applicable only to translations into a language in general use in the said country. Subject to Article I(6)*(b)* of the Appendix, any country has the right to apply, in relation to the right of translation of works whose country of origin is a country availing itself of such a reservation, a protection which is equivalent to the protection granted by the latter country.

(c) Any country may withdraw such reservations at any time by notification addressed to the Director General.

Article 31

(1) Any country may declare in its instrument of ratification or accession, or may inform the Director General by written notification at any time thereafter, that this Convention shall be applicable to all or part of those territories, designated in the declaration or notification, for the external relations of which it is responsible.

(2) Any country which has made such a declaration or given such a notification may, at any time, notify the Director General that this Convention shall cease to be applicable to all or part of such territories.

(3) *(a)* Any declaration made under paragraph (1) shall take effect on the same date as the ratification or accession in which it was included, and any notification given under that paragraph shall take effect three months after its notification by the Director General.

(b) Any notification given under paragraph (2) shall take effect twelve months after its receipt by the Director General.

(4) This Article shall in no way be understood as implying the recognition or tacit acceptance by a country of the Union of the factual situation concerning a territory to which this Convention is made applicable by another country of the Union by virtue of a declaration under paragraph (1).

Article 32

(1) This Act shall, as regards relations between the countries of the Union, and to the extent that it applies, replace the Berne Convention of September 9, 1886, and the subsequent Acts of revision. The Acts previously in force shall continue to be applicable, in their entirety or to the extent that this Act does not replace them by virtue of the preceding sentence, in relations with countries of the Union which do not ratify or accede to this Act.

(2) Countries outside the Union which become party to this Act shall, subject to paragraph (3), apply it with respect to any country of the Union not bound by this Act or which, although bound by this Act, has made a declaration pursuant to Article 28(1)*(b)*. Such countries recognize that the said country of the Union, in its relations with them:

(i) may apply the provisions of the most recent Act by which it is bound, and

(ii) subject to Article I(6) of the Appendix, has the right to adapt the protection to the level provided for by this Act.

(3) Any country which has availed itself of any of the faculties provided for in the Appendix may apply the provisions of the Appendix relating to the faculty or faculties of which it has availed itself in its relations with any other country of the Union which is not bound by this Act, provided that the latter country has accepted the application of the said provisions.

Article 33

(1) Any dispute between two or more countries of the Union concerning the interpretation or application of this Convention, not settled by negotiation, may, by any one of the countries concerned, be brought before the International Court of Justice by application in conformity with the Statute of the Court, unless the countries concerned agree on some other method of settlement. The country bringing the dispute before the Court shall inform the International Bureau; the International Bureau shall bring the matter to the attention of the other countries of the Union.

(2) Each country may, at the time it signs this Act or deposits its instrument of ratification or accession, declare that it does not consider itself bound by the provisions of paragraph (1). With regard to any dispute between such country and any other country of the Union, the provisions of paragraph (1) shall not apply.

(3) Any country having made a declaration in accordance with the provisions of paragraph (2) may, at any time, withdraw its declaration by notification addressed to the Director General.

Article 34

(1) Subject to Article 29*bis*, no country may ratify or accede to earlier Acts of this Convention once Articles 1 to 21 and the Appendix have entered into force.

(2) Once Articles 1 to 21 and the Appendix have entered into force, no country may make a declaration under Article 5 of the Protocol Regarding Developing Countries attached to the Stockholm Act.

Article 35

(1) This Convention shall remain in force without limitation as to time.

(2) Any country may denounce this Act by notification addressed to the Director General. Such denunciation shall constitute also denunciation of all earlier Acts and shall affect only the country making it, the Convention remaining in full force and effect as regards the other countries of the Union.

(3) Denunciation shall take effect one year after the day on which the Director General has received the notification.

(4) The right of denunciation provided by this Article shall not be exercised by any country before the expiration of five years from the date upon which it becomes a member of the Union.

Article 36

(1) Any country party to this Convention undertakes to adopt, in accordance with its constitution, the measures necessary to ensure the application of this Convention.

(2) It is understood that, at the time a country becomes bound by this Convention, it will be in a position under its domestic law to give effect to the provisions of this Convention.

Article 37

(1) *(a)* This Act shall be signed in a single copy in the French and English languages and, subject to paragraph (2), shall be deposited with the Director General.

(b) Official texts shall be established by the Director General, after consultation with the interested Governments, in the Arabic, German, Italian, Portuguese and Spanish languages, and such other languages as the Assembly may designate.

(c) In case of differences of opinion on the interpretation of the various texts, the French text shall prevail.

(2) This Act shall remain open for signature until January 31, 1972. Until that date, the copy referred to in paragraph (1)*(a)* shall be deposited with the Government of the French Republic.

(3) The Director General shall certify and transmit two copies of the signed text of this Act to the Governments of all countries of the Union and, on request, to the Government of any other country.

(4) The Director General shall register this Act with the Secretariat of the United Nations.

(5) The Director General shall notify the Governments of all countries of the Union of signatures, deposits of instruments of ratification or accession and any declarations included in such instruments or made pursuant to Articles 28(1)*(c)*, 30(2)*(a)* and *(b)*, and 33(2), entry into force of any provisions of this Act, notifications of denunciation, and notifications pursuant to Articles 30(2)*(c)*, 31(1) and (2), 33(3), and 38(1), as well as the Appendix.

Article 38

(1) Countries of the Union which have not ratified or acceded to this Act and which are not bound by Articles 22 to 26 of the Stockholm Act of this Convention may, until April 26, 1975, exercise, if they so desire, the rights provided under the said Articles as if they were bound by them. Any country desiring to exercise such rights shall give written notification to this effect to the Director

General; this notification shall be effective on the date of its receipt. Such countries shall be deemed to be members of the Assembly until the said date.

(2) As long as all the countries of the Union have not become Members of the Organization, the International Bureau of the Organization shall also function as the Bureau of the Union, and the Director General as the Director of the said Bureau.

(3) Once all the countries of the Union have become Members of the Organization, the rights, obligations, and property, of the Bureau of the Union shall devolve on the International Bureau of the Organization.

APPENDIX

[Special Provisions Regarding Developing Countries]

Article I

(1) Any country regarded as a developing country in conformity with the established practice of the General Assembly of the United Nations which ratifies or accedes to this Act, of which this Appendix forms an integral part, and which, having regard to its economic situation and its social or cultural needs, does not consider itself immediately in a position to make provision for the protection of all the rights as provided for in this Act, may, by a notification deposited with the Director General at the time of depositing its instrument of ratification or accession or, subject to Article V(1)*(c)*, at any time thereafter, declare that it will avail itself of the faculty provided for in Article II, or of the faculty provided for in Article III, or of both of those faculties. It may, instead of availing itself of the faculty provided for in Article II, make a declaration according to Article V(1)*(a)*.

(2) *(a)* Any declaration under paragraph (1) notified before the expiration of the period of ten years from the entry into force of Articles 1 to 21 and this Appendix according to Article 28(2) shall be effective until the expiration of the said period. Any such declaration may be renewed in whole or in part for periods of ten years each by a notification deposited with the Director General not more than fifteen months and not less than three months before the expiration of the ten-year period then running.

(b) Any declaration under paragraph (1) notified after the expiration of the period of ten years from the entry into force of Articles 1 to 21 and this Appendix according to Article 28(2) shall be effective until the expiration of the ten-year period then running. Any such declaration may be renewed as provided for in the second sentence of subparagraph *(a)*.

(3) Any country of the Union which has ceased to be regarded as a developing country as referred to in paragraph (1) shall no longer be entitled to renew its declaration as provided in paragraph (2), and, whether or not it formally withdraws its declaration, such country shall be precluded from availing itself of the faculties referred to in paragraph (1) from the expiration of the ten-year period then running or from the expiration of a period of three years after it has ceased to be regarded as a developing country, whichever period expires later.

(4) Where, at the time when the declaration made under paragraph (1) or (2) ceases to be effective, there are copies in stock which were made under a license granted by virtue of this Appendix, such copies may continue to be distributed until their stock is exhausted.

(5) Any country which is bound by the provisions of this Act and which has deposited a declaration or a notification in accordance with Article 31(1) with respect to the application of this Act to a particular territory, the situation of which can be regarded as analogous to that of the countries referred to in paragraph (1), may, in respect of such territory, make the declaration referred to in paragraph (1) and the notification of renewal referred to in paragraph (2). As long as such declaration or notification remains in effect, the provisions of this Appendix shall be applicable to the territory in respect of which it was made.

(6) *(a)* The fact that a country avails itself of any of the faculties referred to in paragraph (1) does not permit another country to give less protection to works of which the country of origin is the former country than it is obliged to grant under Articles 1 to 20.

(b) The right to apply reciprocal treatment provided for in Article 30(2)*(b)*, second sentence, shall not, until the date on which the period applicable under Article I(3) expires, be exercised in respect of works the country of origin of which is a country which has made a declaration according to Article V(1)*(a)*.

Article II

(1) Any country which has declared that it will avail itself of the faculty provided for in this Article shall be entitled, so far as works published in printed or analogous forms of reproduction are concerned, to substitute for the exclusive right of translation provided for in Article 8 a system of non-exclusive and non-transferable licenses, granted by the competent authority under the following conditions and subject to Article IV.

(2) *(a)* Subject to paragraph (3), if, after the expiration of a period of three years, or of any longer period determined by the national legislation of the said country, commencing on the date of the first publication of the work, a translation of such work has not been published in a language in general use in that country by the owner of the right of translation, or with his authorization, any national of such country may obtain a license to make a translation of the work in the said language and publish the translation in printed or analogous forms of reproduction.

(b) A license under the conditions provided for in this Article may also be granted if all the editions of the translation published in the language concerned are out of print.

(3) *(a)* In the case of translations into a language which is not in general use in one or more developed countries which are members of the Union, a period of one year shall be substituted for the period of three years referred to in paragraph (2)*(a)*.

(b) Any country referred to in paragraph (1) may, with the unanimous agreement of the developed countries which are members of the Union and in which the same language is in general use, substitute, in the case of translations into that language, for the period of three years referred to in paragraph (2)*(a)* a shorter period as determined by such agreement but not less than one year. However, the provisions of the foregoing sentence shall not apply where the language in question is English, French or Spanish. The Director General shall be notified of any such agreement by the Governments which have concluded it.

(4) *(a)* No license obtainable after three years shall be granted under this Article until a further period of six months has elapsed, and no license obtainable after one year shall be granted under this Article until a further period of nine months has elapsed

(i) from the date on which the applicant complies with the requirements mentioned in Article IV(1), or

(ii) where the identity or the address of the owner of the right of translation is unknown, from the date on which the applicant sends, as provided for in Article IV(2), copies of his application submitted to the authority competent to grant the license.

(b) If, during the said period of six or nine months, a translation in the language in respect of which the application was made is published by the owner of the right of translation or with his authorization, no license under this Article shall be granted.

(5) Any license under this Article shall be granted only for the purpose of teaching, scholarship or research.

(6) If a translation of a work is published by the owner of the right of translation or with his authorization at a price reasonably related to that normally charged in the country for comparable works, any license granted under this Article shall terminate if such translation is in the same language and with substantially the same content as the translation published under the license. Any copies already made before the license terminates may continue to be distributed until their stock is exhausted.

(7) For works which are composed mainly of illustrations, a license to make and publish a translation of the text and to reproduce and publish the illustrations may be granted only if the conditions of Article III are also fulfilled.

(8) No license shall be granted under this Article when the author has withdrawn from circulation all copies of his work.

(9) *(a)* A license to make a translation of a work which has been published in printed or analogous forms of reproduction may also be granted to any broadcasting organization having its headquarters in a country referred to in paragraph (1), upon an application made to the competent authority of that country by the said organization, provided that all of the following conditions are met:

(i) the translation is made from a copy made and acquired in accordance with the laws of the said country;

(ii) the translation is only for use in broadcasts intended exclusively for teaching or for the dissemination of the results of specialized technical or scientific research to experts in a particular profession;

(iii) the translation is used exclusively for the purposes referred to in condition (ii) through broadcasts made lawfully and intended for recipients on the territory of the said country, including broadcasts made through the medium of sound or visual recordings lawfully and exclusively made for the purpose of such broadcasts;

(iv) all uses made of the translation are without any commercial purpose.

(b) Sound or visual recordings of a translation which was made by a broadcasting organization under a license granted by virtue of this paragraph may, for the purposes subject to the conditions referred to in subparagraph *(a)* and with the agreement of that organization, also be used by any other broadcasting organization having its headquarters in the country whose competent authority granted the license in question.

(c) Provided that all of the criteria and conditions set out in subparagraph *(a)* are met, a license may also be granted to a broadcasting organization to translate any text incorporated in an audio-visual fixation where such fixation was itself prepared and published for the sole purpose of being used in connection with systematic instructional activities.

(d) Subject to subparagraphs *(a)* to *(c)*, the provisions of the preceding paragraphs shall apply to the grant and exercise of any license granted under this paragraph.

Article III

(1) Any country which has declared that it will avail itself of the faculty provided for in this Article shall be entitled to substitute for the exclusive right of reproduction provided for in Article 9 a system of non-exclusive and non-transferable licenses, granted by the competent authority under the following conditions and subject to Article IV.

(2) *(a)* If, in relation to a work to which this Article applies by virtue of paragraph (7), after the expiration of

(i) the relevant period specified in paragraph (3), commencing on the date of first publication of a particular edition of the work, or

(ii) any longer period determined by national legislation of the country referred to in paragraph (1), commencing on the same date,copies of such edition have not been distributed in that country to the general public or in connection with systematic instructional activities, by the owner of the right of reproduction or with his authorization, at a price reasonably related to that normally charged in the country for comparable works, any national of such country may obtain a license to reproduce and publish such edition at that or a lower price for use in connection with systematic instructional activities.

(b) A license to reproduce and publish an edition which has been distributed as described in subparagraph *(a)* may also be granted under the conditions provided for in this Article if, after the expiration of the applicable period, no authorized copies of that edition have been on sale for a period of six months in the country concerned to the general public or in connection with systematic instructional activities at a price reasonably related to that normally charged in the country for comparable works.

(3) The period referred to in paragraph (2)*(a)*(i) shall be five years, except that

(i) for works of the natural and physical sciences, including mathematics, and of technology, the period shall be three years;

(ii) for works of fiction, poetry, drama and music, and for art books, the period shall be seven years.

(4) *(a)* No license obtainable after three years shall be granted under this Article until a period of six months has elapsed

(i) from the date on which the applicant complies with the requirements mentioned in Article IV(1), or

(ii) where the identity or the address of the owner of the right of reproduction is unknown, from the date on which the applicant sends, as provided for in Article IV(2), copies of his application submitted to the authority competent to grant the license.

(b) Where licenses are obtainable after other periods and Article IV(2) is applicable, no license shall be granted until a period of three months has elapsed from the date of the dispatch of the copies of the application.

(c) If, during the period of six or three months referred to in subparagraphs *(a)* and *(b)*, a distribution as described in paragraph (2)*(a)* has taken place, no license shall be granted under this Article.

(d) No license shall be granted if the author has withdrawn from circulation all copies of the edition for the reproduction and publication of which the license has been applied for.

(5) A license to reproduce and publish a translation of a work shall not be granted under this Article in the following cases:

(i) where the translation was not published by the owner of the right of translation or with his authorization, or

(ii) where the translation is not in a language in general use in the country in which the license is applied for.

(6) If copies of an edition of a work are distributed in the country referred to in paragraph (1) to the general public or in connection with systematic instructional activities, by the owner of the right of reproduction or with his authorization, at a price reasonably related to that normally charged in the country for comparable works, any license granted under this Article shall terminate if such edition is in the same language and with substantially the same content as the edition which was published under the said license. Any copies already made before the license terminates may continue to be distributed until their stock is exhausted.

(7) *(a)* Subject to subparagraph *(b)*, the works to which this Article applies shall be limited to works published in printed or analogous forms of reproduction.

(b) This Article shall also apply to the reproduction in audio-visual form of lawfully made audio-visual fixations including any protected works incorporated therein and to the translation of any incorporated text into a language in general use in the country in which the license is applied for, always provided that the audio-visual fixations in question were prepared and published for the sole purpose of being used in connection with systematic instructional activities.

Article IV

(1) A license under Article II or Article III may be granted only if the applicant, in accordance with the procedure of the country concerned, establishes either that he has requested, and has been denied, authorization by the owner of the right to make and publish the translation or to reproduce and publish the edition, as the case may be, or that, after due diligence on his part, he was unable to find the owner of the right. At the same time as making the request, the applicant shall inform any national or international information center referred to in paragraph (2).

(2) If the owner of the right cannot be found, the applicant for a license shall send, by registered airmail, copies of his application, submitted to the authority competent to grant the license, to the publisher whose name appears on the work and to any national or international information center which may have been designated, in a notification to that effect deposited with the Director General, by the Government of the country in which the publisher is believed to have his principal place of business.

(3) The name of the author shall be indicated on all copies of the translation or reproduction published under a license granted under Article II or Article III. The title of the work shall appear on all such copies. In the case of a translation, the original title of the work shall appear in any case on all the said copies.

(4) *(a)* No license granted under Article II or Article III shall extend to the export of copies, and any such license shall be valid only for publication of the translation or of the reproduction, as the case may be, in the territory of the country in which it has been applied for.

(b) For the purposes of subparagraph *(a)*, the notion of export shall include the sending of copies from any territory to the country which, in respect of that territory, has made a declaration under Article I(5).

(c) Where a governmental or other public entity of a country which has granted a license to make a translation under Article II into a language other than English, French or Spanish sends copies of a translation published under such license to another country, such sending of copies shall not, for the purposes of subparagraph *(a)*, be considered to constitute export if all of the following conditions are met:

(i) the recipients are individuals who are nationals of the country whose competent authority has granted the license, or organizations grouping such individuals;

(ii) the copies are to be used only for the purpose of teaching, scholarship or research;

(iii) the sending of the copies and their subsequent distribution to recipients is without any commercial purpose; and

(iv) the country to which the copies have been sent has agreed with the country whose competent authority has granted the license to allow the receipt, or distribution, or both, and the Director General has been notified of the agreement by the Government of the country in which the license has been granted.

(5) All copies published under a license granted by virtue of Article II or Article III shall bear a notice in the appropriate language that the copies are available for distribution only in the country or territory to which the said license applies.

(6) *(a)* Due provision shall be made at the national level to ensure

(i) that the license provides, in favour of the owner of the right of translation or of reproduction, as the case may be, for just compensation that is consistent with standards of royalties normally operating on licenses freely negotiated between persons in the two countries concerned, and

(ii) payment and transmittal of the compensation: should national currency regulations intervene, the competent authority shall make all efforts, by the use of international machinery, to ensure transmittal in internationally convertible currency or its equivalent.

(b) Due provision shall be made by national legislation to ensure a correct translation of the work, or an accurate reproduction of the particular edition, as the case may be.

Article V

(1) *(a)* Any country entitled to make a declaration that it will avail itself of the faculty provided for in Article II may, instead, at the time of ratifying or acceding to this Act:

(i) if it is a country to which Article 30(2)*(a)* applies, make a declaration under that provision as far as the right of translation is concerned;

(ii) if it is a country to which Article 30(2)*(a)* does not apply, and even if it is not a country outside the Union, make a declaration as provided for in Article 30(2)*(b)*, first sentence.

(b) In the case of a country which ceases to be regarded as a developing country as referred to in Article I(1), a declaration made according to this paragraph shall be effective until the date on which the period applicable under Article I(3) expires.

(c) Any country which has made a declaration according to this paragraph may not subsequently avail itself of the faculty provided for in Article I even if it withdraws the said declaration.

(2) Subject to paragraph (3), any country which has availed itself of the faculty provided for in Article II may not subsequently make a declaration according to paragraph (1).

(3) Any country which has ceased to be regarded as a developing country as referred to in Article I(1) may, not later than two years prior to the expiration of the period applicable under Article I(3), make a declaration to the effect provided for in Article 30(2)*(b)*, first sentence, notwithstanding the fact that it is not a country outside the Union. Such declaration shall take effect at the date on which the period applicable under Article I(3) expires.

Article VI

(1) Any country of the Union may declare, as from the date of this Act, and at any time before becoming bound by Articles 1 to 21 and this Appendix:

(i) if it is a country which, were it bound by Articles 1 to 21 and this Appendix, would be entitled to avail itself of the faculties referred to in Article I(1), that it will apply the provisions of Article II or of Article III or of both to works whose country of origin is a country which, pursuant to (ii) below, admits the application of those Articles to such works, or which is bound by Articles 1 to 21 and this Appendix; such declaration may, instead of referring to Article II, refer to Article V;

(ii) that it admits the application of this Appendix to works of which it is the country of origin by countries which have made a declaration under (i) above or a notification under Article I.

(2) Any declaration made under paragraph (1) shall be in writing and shall be deposited with the Director General. The declaration shall become effective from the date of its deposit.

IN WITNESS WHEREOF, the undersigned, being duly authorized thereto, have signed this Act.[6]

DONE at Paris on July 24, 1971.

[6] On July 24, 1971, the Act was signed by the Plenipotentiaries of the 28 following countries; Brazil, Cameroon, Ceylon, Cyprus, Denmark, France, Germany (Federal Republic), Holy See, Hungary, India, Israel, Italy, Ivory Coast, Lebanon, Liechtenstein, Luxembourg, Mexico, Monaco, Morocco, Netherlands, People's Republic of the Congo, Senegal, Spain, Sweden, Switzerland, Tunisia, United Kingdom, Yugoslavia.

In accordance with Article 37, the Convention remained open for signature until January 31, 1972.—*Eds.*

BERNE CONVENTION IMPLEMENTATION ACT OF 1988

Summary Overview of the Berne Convention Implementation Act of 1988

Effective March 1, 1989, the United States officially became the 80th adherent to the Berne Convention for the Protection of Literary and Artistic Works (the "Convention" or "Berne"). U.S. adherence was the product of two separate but coordinated acts: Senate ratification of the Convention (Oct. 20, 1988); and the signing by President Reagan of enabling legislation entitled the "Berne Convention Implementation Act of 1988" (Pub. L. 100-568, 102 Stat. 2853, Oct. 31, 1988) (the "Implementation Act" or "BCIA").

The Convention consists of the original treaty signed in Berne, Switzerland on September 9, 1886, and several revisions thereto (the most recent being the Paris Text of July 24, 1971, reproduced earlier). As between any two member nations, the latest version or "Text" of the Convention adopted by each controls within that country. In connection with U.S. adherence, Congress determined that the Paris Text should not be self-executing in this country. Rather, Congress decided that the United States would apply to so-called "Berne Convention works" its domestic law, the provisions of which, under the terms of the Convention, must in theory be compatible with the minimum standards of the Paris Text. Thus, to achieve minimal compatibility for U.S. adherence, Congress passed the Implementation Act, which is reproduced immediately following this overview.

Internationally, Berne Convention adherence provided several benefits to the United States. For one thing, the Convention is superior to existing multilateral means of protecting American creativity abroad, *e.g.*, the Universal Copyright Convention (the "U.C.C."). While both the Berne Convention and the U.C.C. require each member state to accord to nationals of other member states the same protection accorded to the member state's own nationals, Berne provides a higher, more detailed set of minimum standards and broader subject matter coverage. In addition to those advantages, Berne also provides a means of managing copyright relations with approximately two dozen countries with which the United States previously lacked even bilateral agreements. Taken together, these effects enhance this country's ability to combat international copyright piracy and protect its leading position in the world intellectual property marketplace. Finally, adherence to the Berne Convention transformed the United States from an observer into an active participant in the development of international copyright policy, as evidenced subsequently by GATT/TRIPS agreement in 1994 and the two new WIPO treaties in 1996.

Domestically, Berne Convention adherence effected significant changes in U.S. law. Precisely because the Convention is not self-executing, however, an understanding of those changes can be gleaned only from an examination of the amendments to existing copyright law mandated by the Berne Convention Implementation Act of 1988. Therefore, the remainder of this summary is devoted to a section-by-section overview of that legislation. To explore in more detail the effects of the Implementation Act on U.S. law, see the texts of the BCIA and the Convention, William F. Patry's COPYRIGHT LAW AND PRACTICE from BNA, and the latest edition of NIMMER ON COPYRIGHT from Matthew Bender & Co., Inc.

SECTION 1 SHORT TITLE

The Act may be cited as the "Berne Convention Implementation Act of 1988."

SECTION 2 DECLARATIONS

Paragraph 1 declares that the Berne Convention is not self-executing under the Constitution and laws of the United States.

Paragraph 2 states that the obligations of the United States under Berne may be performed only pursuant to appropriate domestic law.

Paragraph 3 declares that the amendments made by the Implementation Act to Title 17 of the U.S. Code (the Copyright Act) satisfy the United States' obligations in adhering to Berne, and that no further rights or interests shall be recognized or created for the purpose of adherence.

SECTION 3 CONSTRUCTION OF THE BERNE CONVENTION

By providing that the Convention's provisions are not enforceable under Berne itself, subsection 3(a) reinforces § 2. The subsection adds, however, that, besides Title 17, the Convention's provisions may be given effect under "any other relevant provision of Federal or State law, including common law." Subsection 3(b) makes explicit, however, that certain rights — specifically, the rights "to claim authorship of [a] work" or "to object to any distortion, mutilation, or other modification of, or other derogatory action in relation to, [a] work, that would prejudice the author's honor or reputation" — are not expanded or reduced by the Convention itself, by U. S. adherence thereto, or by satisfaction of U.S. obligations thereunder.

In other words, Congress in § 3 chose not to include within U.S. domestic law the *droit moral, i.e.,* noneconomic, moral rights, recognized by article 6*bis* of the Berne Convention, except insofar as rights consistent with the *droit moral* exist already under federal or state statutes, or common law. Whether in this respect the Implementation Act complies with article 5(1) of the Convention, requiring member states to provide to all authors coming within Berne's protection the rights "specially granted" by the Convention, seems debatable.

SECTION 4 SUBJECT MATTER AND SCOPE OF COPYRIGHTS

Subsection (a)(1)(A) amended the definition of "pictorial, graphic, and sculptural works" in § 101 of the Copyright Act to include architectural plans (but not architectural structures), thereby clarifying the application of American copyright law to such works, which are mentioned specifically in the Convention.

Subsection (a)(1)(B) further amended § 101 to identify works eligible for protection under the Implementation Act. In addition to defining "Berne Convention," the subsection particularized what constitutes a "Berne Convention work":

— The term comprehends an *unpublished* work if one or more of the authors is "a national of a nation adhering to the Berne Convention" (*i.e.,* is domiciled in or has his or her habitual residence in a nation adhering to the Convention). A *published* work is a "Berne Convention work" if one or more of the authors is such a national on the date of the first publication of the work.

— In order to qualify, the work must have been first published in a Berne Convention member state, or published in a member state and a nonadhering foreign country "simultaneously" (*i.e.,* the publications occurred within 30 days of one another).

— Also qualifying as a "Berne Convention work" are: audiovisual works, where one or more of a work's authors is a legal entity with its headquarters in a Berne member state or is an individual whose domicile or habitual residence is in such a state; and pictorial, graphic, or sculptural works, where the work is "incorporated in a building or other structure ... located" in a member state.

Subsection 4(a)(1)(C) added to § 101 of the Copyright Act a definition of "country of origin" solely for purposes of § 411 (which, as revised by the Implementation Act, makes registration a prerequisite to infringement actions, except for Berne Convention works "whose country of origin is not the United States"):

— A work's "country of origin" *is* the United States, in the case of a published work, where the work is first published in the United States, or is first published "simultaneously" either in the U.S. and another Berne member state with the same or a longer term of protection, or in the U.S. and a non-Berne nation. The country of origin for a published work may be the United States even when the work is first published only in a non-Berne nation, provided that *all* of the authors are nationals, domiciliaries or habitual residents of, or, in the case of an audiovisual work, legal entities with their headquarters in, the United States.

— Likewise, in the case of an *un*published work, the United States is the country of origin where all of the authors are nationals, domiciliaries or habitual residents of, or, in the case of an audiovisual work, legal entities headquartered in, this country.

— In the case of a pictorial, graphic, or sculptural work incorporated in a building or structure, the United States is the country of origin if the building or structure is located here.

— In all other instances, the United States is *not* the "country of origin" for § 411 purposes.

Like §§2 and 3, §4 contains a provision declaring that no rights or interests may be claimed under the Convention directly, but rather solely under Title 17, other federal or state statutes, or common law.

Finally, §4 of the Implementation Act added to Title 17 a new §116A, designed to encourage negotiated jukebox licenses for the performance of nondramatic musical works embodied in phonorecords. The provision was amended — and renumbered as §116 — in 1993. New §116 (replacing the compulsory licensing scheme under old §116) permits owners of copyrights and operators of jukeboxes to negotiate voluntary licensing agreements (or have them arbitrated), thereby creating maximum flexibility as to terms and rates of royalty payments, etc. Negotiations that result in such voluntary agreements are to be given effect "in lieu of any otherwise applicable determination by a copyright arbitration royalty panel."

SECTION 5 RECORDATION

Section 205(d) of the Copyright Act, which prior to the effective date of the Implementation Act required recordation of the instrument of transfer as a prerequisite to the institution of an infringement action by a transferee, was stricken by §5.

SECTION 6 PREEMPTION WITH RESPECT TO OTHER LAWS NOT AFFECTED

Section 301 of Title 17 was amended by adding a new subsection (e), providing that the scope of federal preemption "is not affected by the adherence of the United States to the Berne Convention or the satisfaction of the obligations of the United States thereunder."

SECTION 7 NOTICE OF COPYRIGHT

The mandatory notice requirements of former §§401 and 402 of the Copyright Act were made permissive for works publicly distributed by authority of the copyright owner on or after March 1, 1989. New subsections (d) were added to §§401 and 402, stating that, except as provided in the last sentence of 17 U.S.C. §504(c)(2) (concerning certain nonprofit institutions), an innocent infringer defense asserted in mitigation of actual or statutory damages shall be given no weight where the defendant had access to a copy of a work bearing the specified notice. By amendment to §403, however, the new subsections of §§401 and 402 are inapplicable to works consisting predominantly of one or more works of the United States Government unless "a statement identifying, either affirmatively or negatively, those portions" embodying protected material is included.

Section 404 (notice for contributions to collective works) also was tied to the revised innocent infringer provisions of new subsections 401(d) and 402(d).

The provisions in §§405 and 406 regarding curative steps for omission of notice, and for errors in name or date, were amended to apply solely to distributions before the effective date of the Act.

SECTION 8 DEPOSIT OF COPIES OR PHONORECORDS FOR LIBRARY OF CONGRESS

17 U.S.C. § 407(a), which formerly required deposit of copies of a work published in the United States "with notice of copyright," was amended by deleting the language just quoted. The effect was to expand the deposit requirement to apply to all published works, whether or not publication occurred with notice. Country of origin is irrelevant.

SECTION 9 COPYRIGHT REGISTRATION

Section 411, which as enacted in 1976 required registration (or a refusal of registration by the Copyright Office) before institution of an infringement actions, was substantially revised by establishing a two-tiered system. Under this system, a "Berne Convention work" whose "country of origin" is the United States still has to comply with the registration procedures. A Berne Convention work whose country of origin is not the United States is, however, exempt from the requirements of revised § 411. The incentives for registration found in § 412 (statutory damages and attorneys' fees) remain applicable to all works.

SECTION 10 COPYRIGHT INFRINGEMENT AND REMEDIES

In a measure logically unconnected with Berne Convention adherence, 17 U.S.C. § 504(c) was amended by doubling the minimum statutory damages from $250 to $500, the maximum nonwillful statutory damages from $10,000 to $20,000, the maximum willful statutory damages from $50,000 to $100,000, and the floor for innocent infringer remission from $100 to $200.

SECTION 11 COPYRIGHT ROYALTY TRIBUNAL

This section provided guidance for the Tribunal (now replaced by copyright arbitration royalty panels) in administering new § 116A (now amended and renumbered as § 116) (negotiated jukebox licenses).

SECTION 12 WORKS IN THE PUBLIC DOMAIN

This section, evidently the product of abundant caution on the part of Congress, made explicit that the Implementation Act "does not provide copyright protection for any work that is in the public domain in the United States" prior to the effective date of the Act.

SECTION 13 EFFECTIVE DATE; EFFECT ON PENDING CASES

Subsection (a) provided that the Implementation Act would take effect on the day on which the Berne Convention entered into force with respect to the United States (March 1, 1989). Subsection (b) provided that any action arising under Title 17 before the effective date of the legislation was to be governed by the provisions of Title 17 in effect when the cause of action arose.

BERNE CONVENTION IMPLEMENTATION ACT OF 1988

(Pub. L. 100-568, 102 Stat. 2853)

Sec. 1 Short Title and References to Title 17, United States Code

(a) Short title. This Act may be cited as the "Berne Convention Implementation Act of 1988."

(b) References to Title 17, United States Code. Whenever in this Act an amendment or repeal is expressed in terms of an amendment to or a repeal of a section or other provision, the reference shall be considered to be made to a section or other provision of title 17, United States Code.

Sec. 2 Declarations

The Congress makes the following declarations:

(1) The Convention for the Protection of Literary and Artistic Works, signed at Berne, Switzerland, on September 9, 1886, and all acts, protocols, and revisions thereto (hereafter in this Act referred to as the "Berne Convention") are not self-executing under the Constitution and laws of the United States.

(2) The obligations of the United States under the Berne Convention may be performed only pursuant to appropriate domestic law.

(3) The amendments made by this Act, together with the law as it exists on the date of the enactment of this Act, satisfy the obligations of the United States in adhering to the Berne Convention and no further rights or interests shall be recognized or created for that purpose.

Sec. 3 Construction of the Berne Convention

(a) Relationship with Domestic Law. The provisions of the Berne Convention—

(1) shall be given effect under title 17, as amended by this Act, and any other relevant provision of Federal or State law, including the common law; and

(2) shall not be enforceable in any action brought pursuant to the provisions of the Berne Convention itself.

(b) Certain Rights Not Affected. The provisions of the Berne Convention, the adherence of the United States thereto, and satisfaction of United States obligations thereunder, do not expand or reduce any right of an author of a work, whether claimed under Federal, State, or the common law —

(1) to claim authorship of the work; or

(2) to object to any distortion, mutilation, or other modification of, or other derogatory action in relation to, the work, that would prejudice the author's honor or reputation.

Sec. 4 Subject Matter and Scope of Copyrights

(a) Subject and Scope. Chapter 1 is amended —

(1) in section 101 —

(A) in the definition of "Pictorial, graphic, and sculptural works" by striking out in the first sentence "technical drawings, diagrams and models" and inserting in lieu thereof "diagrams, models, and technical drawings, including architectural plans";

(B) by inserting after the definition of "Audiovisual works" the following:

The "Berne Convention" is the Convention for the Protection of Literary and Artistic Works, signed at Berne, Switzerland, on September 9, 1886, and all acts protocols and revisions thereto.

A work is a "Berne Convention work" if —

(1) in the case of an unpublished work, one or more of the authors is a national of a nation adhering to the Berne Convention, or in the case of a published work, one or more of the authors is a national of a nation adhering to Berne Convention on the date of first publication;

(2) the work was first published in a nation adhering to the Berne Convention, or was simultaneously first published in a nation adhering to the Berne Convention and in a foreign nation that does not adhere to the Berne Convention;

(3) in the case of an audiovisual work —

(A) if one or more of the authors is a legal entity, that author has its headquarters in a nation adhering to the Berne Convention; or

(B) if one or more of the authors is an individual, that author is domiciled [in], or has his or her habitual residence in, a nation adhering to the Berne Convention; or

(4) in the case of a pictorial, graphic, or sculptural work that is incorporated in a building or other structure, the building or structure is located in a nation adhering to the Berne Convention.

For purposes of paragraph (1), an author who is domiciled in[,] or has his or her habitual residence in, a nation adhering to the Berne Convention is considered to be a national of that nation. For purposes of paragraph (2), a work is considered to have been simultaneously published in two or more nations if its dates of publication are within 30 days of one another"; and

(C) by inserting after the definition of "Copyright owner" the following:

The "country of origin" of a Berne Convention work, for purposes of section 411, is the United States if—

(1) in the case of a published work, the work is first published—

(A) in the United States;

(B) simultaneously in the United States and another nation or nations adhering to the Berne Convention, whose law grants a term of copyright protection that is the same as or longer than the term provided in the United States;

(C) simultaneously in the United States and a foreign nation that does not adhere to the Berne Convention; or

(D) in a foreign nation that does not adhere to the Berne Convention, and all of the authors of the work are nationals, domiciliaries, or habitual residents of, or in the case of an audiovisual work legal entities with headquarters in, the United States;

(2) in the case of an unpublished work, all the authors of the work are nationals, domiciliaries, or habitual residents of the United States, or, in the case of an unpublished audiovisual work, all the authors are legal entities with headquarters in the United States; or

(3) in the case of a pictorial, graphic, or sculptural work incorporated in a building or structure, the building or sculpture is located in the United States.For the purposes of section 411, the "country of origin" of any other Berne Convention work is not in the United States;

(2) in section 104(b) —

(A) by redesignating paragraph (4) as paragraph (5); and

(B) by inserting after paragraph (3) the following new paragraph:

(4) the work is a Berne Convention work or;

(3) in section 104 by adding at the end thereof the following:

(C) Effect of Berne Convention. No right or interest in a work eligible for protection under this title may be claimed by virtue of, or in reliance upon, the provisions of the Berne Convention, or the adherence of the United States thereto. Any rights in a work eligible for protection under this title that derive from this title, other Federal or State statutes, or the common law, shall not be expanded or reduced by virtue of, or in reliance upon, the provisions of the Berne Convention, or the adherence of the United States thereto"; and

(4) by inserting after section 116 the following new section:

§ 116A. Negotiated licenses for public performances by means of coin-operated phonorecord players

(a) Applicability of Section. This section applies to any nondramatic musical work embodied in a phonorecord.

(b) Limitation on Exclusive Right if Licenses Not Negotiated

(1) Applicability. In the case of a work to which this section applies, the exclusive right under clause (4) of section 106 to perform the work publicly by means of a coin-operated phonorecord player is limited by section 116 to the extend provided in this section.

(2) Determination by Copyright Royalty Tribunal. The Copyright Royalty Tribunal, at the end of the 1-year period beginning on the effective date of the Berne Convention Implementation Act of 1988, and periodically thereafter to the extent necessary to carry out subsection (f), shall determine whether or not negotiated licenses authorized by subsection (c) are in effect so as to provide permission to use a quantity of musical works not substantially smaller than the quantity of such works performed on coin-operated phonorecord players during the 1-year period ending on the effective date of that Act. If the Copyright Royalty Tribunal determines that such negotiated licenses are not so in effect, the Tribunal shall, upon making the determination, publish the determination in the Federal Register. Upon such publication, section 116 shall apply with respect to musical works that are not the subject of such negotiated licenses.

(c) Negotiated Licenses

(1) Authority for Negotiations. Any owners of copyright in works to which this section applies and any operators of coin-operated phonorecord players may negotiate and agree upon the terms and rates of royalty payments for the performance of such works, and the proportionate division of fees paid among copyright owners, and may designate common agents to negotiate, agree to, pay, or receive such royalty payments.

(2) Arbitration. Parties to such a negotiation, within such time as may be specified by the Copyright Royalty Tribunal by regulation, may determine the result of the negotiation by arbitration. Such arbitration shall be governed by the provisions of title 9, to the extent such title is not inconsistent with this section. The parties shall give notice to the Copyright Royalty Tribunal of any determination reached by arbitration and any such determination shall, as between the parties to the arbitration, be dispositive of the issues to which it relates.

(d) License Agreements Superior to Copyright Royalty Tribunal Determinations. License agreements between one or more copyright owners and one or more operators of coin-operated phonorecord players, which are negotiated in accordance with subsection (c), shall be given effect in lieu of any otherwise applicable determination by the Copyright Royalty Tribunal.

(e) Negotiation Schedule. Not later than 60 days after the effective date of the Berne Convention Implementation Act of 1988, if the Chairman of the Copyright Royalty Tribunal has not received notice, from copyright owners and operators of coin-operated phonorecord players referred to in subsection (c)(1), of the date and location of the first meeting between such copyright owners and such operators to commence negotiations authorized by subsection (c), the Chairman shall announce the date and location of such meeting. Such meeting may not be held more than 90 days after the effective date of such Act.

(f) Copyright Royalty Tribunal to Suspend Various Activities. The Copyright Royalty Tribunal shall not conduct any ratemaking activity with respect to coin-operated phonorecord players unless, at any time more than one year after the effective date of the Berne Convention Implementation Act of 1988, the negotiated licenses adopted by the parties under this section do not provide permission to use a quantity of musical works not substantially smaller than the quantity of such works performed on coin-operated phonorecord players during the one-year period ending on the effective date of such Act.

(g) Transition Provisions; Retention of Copyright Royalty Tribunal Jurisdiction. Until such time as licensing provisions are determined by the parties under this section, the terms of the compulsory license under section 116, with respect to the public performance of nondramatic musical works by means of coin-operated phonorecord players, which is in effect on the day before the effective date of the Berne Convention Implementation Act of 1988, shall remain in force. If a negotiated license authorized by this section comes into force so as to supersede previous determinations of the Copyright Royalty Tribunal, as provided in subsection (d), but thereafter is terminated or expires and is not replaced by another licensing agreement, then section 116 shall be effective with respect to musical works that were the subject of such terminated or expired licenses.

(b) **Technical Amendments** —

(1) Section 116 is amended —

(A) by amending the section heading to read as follows:

§ 116. Scope of exclusive rights in nondramatic musical works: compulsory licenses for public performances by means of coin-operated phonorecord players;

(B) in subsection (a) in the matter preceding paragraph (1), by inserting after "in a phonorecord," the following: "the performance of which is subject to this section as provided in section 116A,"; and

(C) in subsection (e), by inserting "and section 116A" after "As used in this section."

(2) The table of section at the beginning of chapter 1 is amended by striking out the item relating to section 116, and inserting in lieu thereof the following:

§116. Scope of exclusive rights in nondramatic musical works: Compulsory licenses for public performances by means of coin-operated phonorecord players.

§116A. Negotiated licenses for public performances by means of coin-operated phonorecord players.

Sec. 5 Recordation

Section 205 is amended —

(1) by striking out subsection (d); and

(2) by redesignating subsections (e) and (f) as subsections (d) and (e), respectively.

Sec. 6 Preemption with Respect to Other Laws Not Affected

Section 301 is amended by adding at the end thereof the following:

(e) The scope of Federal preemption under this section is not affected by the adherence of the United States to the Berne Convention or the satisfaction of obligations of the United States thereunder.

Sec. 7 Notice of Copyright

(a) Visually Perceptible Copies. Section 401 is amended —

(1) in subsection (a), by amending the subsection heading to read as follows:

(a) General Provisions.;

(2) in subsection (a), by striking out "shall be placed on all" and inserting in lieu thereof "may be placed on";

(3) in subsection (b), by striking out "The notice appearing on the copies" and inserting in lieu thereof "If a notice appears on the copies, it"; and

(4) by adding at thc end the following:

(d) Evidentiary Weight of Notice. If a notice of copyright in the form and position specified by this section appears on the published copy or copies to which a defendant in a copyright infringement suit had access, then no weight shall be given to such a defendant's interposition of a defense based on innocent infringement in mitigation of actual or statutory damages, except as provided in the last sentence of section 504(c)(2).

(b) Phonorecords of Sound Recordings. Section 402 is amended —

(1) in subsection (a), by amending the subsection heading to read as follows:

(a) General Provisions.;

(2) in subsection (a), by striking out "shall be placed on all" and inserting in lieu thereof "may be placed on";

(3) in subsection (b), by striking out "The notice appearing on the phonorecords" and inserting in lieu thereof "If a notice appears on the phonorecords, it"; and

(4) by adding at the end thereof the following new subsection:

(d) Evidentiary Weight of Notice. If a notice of copyright in the form and position specified by this section appears on the published phonorecord or phonorecords to which a defendant in a copyright infringement suit had access, then no weight shall be given to such a defendant's interposition of a defense based on innocent infringement in mitigation of actual or statutory damages, except as provided in the last sentence of section 504(c)(2).

(c) Publications Incorporating United States Government Works. Section 403 is amended to read as follows:

Sections 401(d) and 402(d) shall not apply to a work published in copies or phonorecords consisting predominantly of one or more works of the United States Government unless the notice of copyright appearing on the published copies or phonorecords to which a defendant in the copyright infringement suit had access includes a statement identifying, either affirmatively or negatively, those portions of the copies or phonorecords embodying any work or works protected under this title.

(d) Notice of Copyright: Contributions to Collective Works. Section 404 is amended —

(1) in subsection (a), by striking out "to satisfy the requirements of sections 401 through 403," and inserting in lieu thereof "to invoke the provisions of section 401(d) or 402(d), as applicable"; and

(2) in subsection (b), by striking out "Where" and inserting in lieu thereof "With respect to copies and phonorecords publicly distributed by authority of the copyright owner before the effective date of the Berne Convention Implementation Act of 1988, where".

(e) Omission of Notice. Section 405 is amended —

(1) in subsection (a), by striking out "The omission of the copyright notice prescribed by" and inserting in lieu thereof "With respect to copies and phonorecords publicly distributed by authority of the copyright owner before the effective date of the Berne Convention Implementation Act of 1988, the omission of the copyright notice described in";

(2) in subsection (b), by striking out "omitted," in the first sentence and inserting in lieu thereof, "omitted and which was publicly distributed by authority of the copyright owner before the effective date of the Berne Convention Implementation Act of 1988,"; and

(3) by amending the section heading to read as follows:

§405. Notice of copyright: Omission of notice on certain copies and phonorecords

(f) Error in Name or Date. Section 406 is amended —

(1) in subsection (a) by striking out "Where" and inserting in lieu thereof "With respect to copies and phonorecords publicly distributed by authority of the copyright owner before the effective date of the Berne Convention Implementation Act of 1988, where";

(2) in subsection (b) by inserting "before the effective date of the Berne Convention Implementation Act of 1988" after "distribution";

(3) in subsection (c) —

(A) by inserting "before the effective date of the Berne Convention Implementation Act of 1988" after "publicly distributed"; and

(B) by inserting after "405" the following: "as in effect on the day before the effective date of the Berne Convention Implementation Act of 1988"; and

(4) by amending the section heading to read as follows:

Sec. 406. Notice of copyright: Error in name or date on certain copies and phonorecords.

(g) Clerical Amendment. The table of sections at the beginning of chapter 4 is amended by striking out the items relating to sections 405 and 406 and inserting in lieu thereof the following:

405. Notice of copyright: Omission of notice on certain copies and phonorecords.

406. Notice of copyright: Error in name or date on certain copies and phonorecords.

Sec. 8 Deposit of Copies or Phonorecords for Library of Congress

Section 407(a) is amended by striking out "with notice of copyright."

Sec. 9 Copyright Registration

(a) Registration in General. Section 408 is amended —

(1) in subsection (a), by striking out "Subject to the provisions of section 405(a), such" in the second sentence and inserting in lieu thereof "Such";

(2) in subsection (c)(2) —

(A) by striking out "all of the following conditions —" and inserting in lieu thereof "the following conditions";

(B) by striking out subparagraph (A); and

(C) by redesignating subparagraphs (B) and (C) as subparagraphs (A) and (B), respectively.

(b) Infringement Actions

(1) Registration as a Prerequisite. Section 411 is amended —

(A) by amending the section heading to read as follows:

§411. Registration and infringement actions;

(B) in subsection (a) by striking out "Subject" and inserting in lieu thereof "Except for actions for infringement of copyright in Berne Conventions works whose country of origin is not the United States, and subject"; and

(C) in subsection (b)(2) by inserting "if required by subsection (a)," after "work".

(2) Table of Sections. The table of sections at the beginning of chapter 4 is amended by striking out the item relating to section 411 and inserting in lieu thereof the following:

§411. Registration and infringement actions

Sec. 10 Copyright Infringement and Remedies

(a) Infringement. Section 501(b) is amended by striking out "sections 205(d) and 411," and inserting in lieu thereof "section 411."

(b) Damages and Profits. Section 504(c) is amended —

(1) in paragraph (1) —

(A) by striking out "$250," and inserting in lieu thereof "$500"; and

(B) by striking out "$10,000," and inserting in lieu thereof "$20,000"; and

(2) in paragraph (2) —

(A) by striking out "$50,000," and inserting in lieu thereof "100,000"; and

(B) by striking out "$100," and inserting in lieu thereof "$200."

Sec. 11 Copyright Royalty Tribunal

Chapter 8 is amended —

(1) in section 801, by adding at the end of subsection (b) the following:

In determining whether a return to a copyright owner under section 116 is fair, appropriate weight shall be given to —

(i) the rates previously determined by the Tribunal to provide a fair return to the copyright owner, and

(ii) the rates contained in any license negotiated pursuant to section 116A of this title; and

(2) by amending section 804(a)(2)(C) to read as follows:

(C) (i) In proceedings under section 801(b)(1) concerning the adjustment of royalty rates as provided in section 11[6], such petition may be filed in 1990 and in each subsequent tenth calendar year, and at any time within 1 year after negotiated licenses authorized by section 116A are terminated or expire and are not replaced by subsequent agreements.

(ii) If negotiated licenses authorized by section 116A come into force so as to supersede previous determinations of the Tribunal, as provided in section 116A(d), but thereafter are terminated or expire and are not replaced by subsequent agreements, the Tribunal shall, upon petition of any party to such terminated or expired negotiated license agreement, promptly establish an interim royalty rate or rates for the public performance by means of a coin-operated phonorecord player of nondramatic musical works embodied in phonorecords which had been subject to the terminated or expired negotiated license agreement. Such interim royalty rate or rates shall be the same as the last such rate or rates and shall remain in force until the conclusion of proceedings to adjust the royalty rates applicable to such works, or until superseded by a new negotiated license agreement, as provided in section 116A(d).

Sec. 12 Works in the Public Domain

Title 17, United States Code, as amended by this Act, does not provide copyright protection for any work that is in the public domain in the United States.

Sec. 13 Effective Date; Effect on Pending Cases

(a) Effective Date. This Act and the amendments made by this Act take effect on the date on which the Berne Convention (as defined in section 101 of title 17, United States Code) enters into force with respect to the United States.

(b) Effect on Pending Cases. Any cause of action arising under title 17, United States Code, before the effective date of this Act shall be governed by the provisions of such title as in effect when the cause of action arose.

GATT/TRIPS AND NAFTA

Summary Overview of GATT/TRIPS and NAFTA[1]

INTRODUCTION

As copyright became a trade issue (first seen in the Caribbean Basin Economic Initiative of 1983 and the General System of Preferences renewal of 1984), the next logical step was to include intellectual property provisions in multilateral trade agreements.

NAFTA

The first trade agreement entered into by the United States to extend retroactive protection to foreign works was the North American Free Trade Agreement ("NAFTA") of January 1, 1994. This protection, limited to Canadian and Mexican motion pictures and works first published in motion pictures, was codified in §104A of Title 17. Statements of intent to claim a restored copyright were required to be filed with the U.S. Copyright Office by December 31, 1995, else no protection could be claimed. Restored protection was granted for the term of protection the work would otherwise have been granted, but was limited to works that fell into the public domain for failure to comply with the 1976 Act's notice provisions.

The Copyright Office filed its list of those claiming protection under NAFTA §104A on February 13, 1995. 60 Fed. Reg. 8252. The Office's final regulations establishing procedures for filing Statements of Intent for restoration were not published until November 15, 1994, 59 Fed. Reg. 1994, almost one year after NAFTA was signed, and only six weeks before the one-year window for filing such statements closed. Interim regulations were published on March 16, 1994. 59 Fed. Reg. 12162. Only four comments were received on the interim regulations, including one from the Mexican government, requesting that works published before January 1, 1978 without notice be included. The request was denied.

GATT/TRIPS

The GATT Implementing Legislation

The biggest accomplishment of the 103d Congress in the field of copyright was, without question, passage of Public Law No. 103-465, legislation implementing the United States' obligations — and then some — under the Uruguay Round of the General Agreement on Tariffs and Trade ("GATT").

---

[1] Abbreviated, adapted and updated from an address by William F. Patry to the State Bar of Texas Section on Intellectual Property on June 3, 1995. For fuller discussion, see William F. Patry, Copyright And The GATT: an Interpretation and Legislative History of the Uruguay Round Agreements Act (BNA 1995).—*Eds.*

The United States' lack of success in solving serious disputes with the European Union over national treatment for audiovisual works and sound recordings, content quotas on broadcasts and television, and market access for audiovisual works threatened completion of the Uruguay Round. Nevertheless, the component of the Uruguay Round agreements concerning Trade-Related Aspects of Intellectual Property Rights ("TRIPS") contains a number of provisions that are beneficial for U.S. copyright owners, including (1) a requirement that GATT contracting parties comply with Articles 1 through 21 of the Berne Convention (with the important exception of Article 6*bis*); (2) protection for computer programs as literary works under Berne; (3) protection for data bases; (4) a rental right for computer programs and phonorecords; (5) restrictions on countries' ability to provide extensive exceptions to protection; (6) protection for sound recordings; and (7) strong enforcement of rights requirements.

Two principles of the Uruguay Round Agreements must be mentioned. First, with respect to the United States at least, the Agreements are not self-executing. They must be implemented in our domestic laws. Second, the Agreements are not a treaty. The Senate did not give its advice and consent. The only action by the U.S. Congress was passage of the implementing legislation that became Public Law No. 103-465. Thus, as with the Berne Convention Implementation Act of 1988, the only law that matters is domestic U.S. law: actions cannot be brought in U.S. courts directly under the TRIPS Agreement, nor can that Agreement form the basis of U.S. law.

Enactment of the Uruguay Round Agreements Act

Shortly after the United States and its trading partners signed the Uruguay Round Agreements on April 15, 1994 in Marrakesh, informal discussions about the content of the implementing legislation began between the Clinton Administration, represented principally by the Office of the U.S. Trade Representative ("USTR"), and the Congressional copyright subcommittees. The USTR divided possible legislative initiatives into two categories: (1) necessary and (2) appropriate (or better, "discretionary"). According to the USTR, in the copyright field only, repeal of the October 1997 computer program rental sunset was necessary to satisfy the United States' TRIPS obligations. The Congressional copyright subcommittees expressed an interest, however, in including federal anti-bootlegging provisions and a provision to implement the retroactivity requirements of Article 18 of the Berne Convention.

On August 3, 1994, Rep. William J. Hughes, chair of the House Subcommittee on Intellectual Property and Judicial Administration, introduced for discussion purposes a bill containing a repeal of the computer program rental sunset, a civil federal anti-bootlegging statute, and retroactive protection for foreign works from Berne and WTO countries in the public domain in the United States. On August 5, 1994, Sen. Dennis DeConcini, chair of the Senate Subcommittee on Patents, Copyrights, and Trademarks, introduced, also for discussion purposes, the USTR's draft bill. The introduction of the bills was timed to coincide with a joint hearing held by the subcommittees on

August 12, 1994. After the hearings, the subcommittees and the USTR jointly drafted compromise intellectual property provisions, which were included in the final text of the bill submitted by the Administration and introduced in both houses on September 27, 1994.

That bill, H.R. 5110, was passed by the House on November 29, 1994. The Senate debated H.R. 5110 on November 30 and December 1, 1994, passing it on December 1. On December 8, 1994, President Clinton signed the bill into law as the Uruguay Round Agreements Act ("URAA").

The Copyright Components of the URAA

Title V of the URAA contains a number of amendments to U.S. intellectual property laws. Subtitle A includes the provisions on copyright and related rights; Subtitle B, trademark; and Subtitle C, patents.

The copyright subtitle has four components:

1. Section 511 makes permanent the ban enacted by Congress in 1990, Act. of Dec. 1, 1990, Pub. L. No. 101-650, Title VIII, 101st Cong., 2d Sess., 104 Stat. 5089, 5134–37, on the rental of computer programs for purposes of direct or indirect commercial advantage. The legislation was scheduled to "sunset" on October 1, 1997. URAA § 511 strikes the sunset provision of the 1990 Act. No substantive amendment to the Copyright Act itself was required;

2. Section 512 adds to Title 17, United States Code, a new Chapter 11. Chapter 11 provides a new civil cause of action for performers to prevent the unauthorized fixation or communication to the public of the sound or sounds and images of their live musical performances, as well as the unauthorized reproduction, distribution, sale, rental, or "trafficking in" of copies or phonorecords made from such unauthorized fixations. New Chapter 11 — which contains a single section, § 1101 — is *not* a part of the Copyright Act;

3. Section 513 concerns the same activities as section 512 (i.e., "bootlegs" of live musical performances). Section 513, however, provides new criminal penalties for such activities by adding to Title 18, United States Code, new § 2319A, applicable where the bootlegging occurs "knowingly, and for purposes of commercial advantage or private financial gain"; and

4. Section 514, the most far-reaching of the URAA provisions concerning copyright and related rights, provides retroactive protection for works whose source country is a member of the Berne Convention or the World Trade Organization or is the subject of a presidential proclamation, if the subject works are in the public domain in the United States through failure to comply with U.S. formalities, lack of national eligibility, or, in the case of pre-1972 sound recordings, lack of subject matter protection. URAA § 514 also amends the Copyright Act's § 109(a) first sale doctrine to provide that copies or phonorecords of *restored works* made or manufactured before the date of restoration — or, in the case of reliance parties, before notice — may be disposed of for "direct or indirect commercial advantage" *only* during the one-year sell-off period allowed for reliance parties.

Section 511[2]: Computer Program Rental

In 1990, Congress banned the rental of computer programs for purposes of direct or indirect commercial advantage. The legislation was scheduled to "sunset" (expire) on October 1, 1997. Section 511 of the URAA fulfills the United States' obligation under Article 11 of the TRIPS Agreement with respect to computer programs by striking the sunset provision in the 1990 Act, thereby making the rental ban permanent. No substantive changes were required or made to § 109 of the Copyright Act.

Sections 512 and 513: "Bootlegs" of Live Musical Performances

Section 512: Civil Cause of Action

1. The Right Granted

Section 512 of the URAA creates a new Chapter 11 in Title 17, United States Code. Chapter 11 contains one section, § 1101, the operative portion of which is subsection (a):

(a) Unauthorized acts. Anyone who, without the consent of the performer or performers involved—

> (1) fixes the sounds or sounds and images of a live musical performance in a copy or phonorecord, or reproduces copies or phonorecords of such a performance from an unauthorized fixation,
>
> (2) transmits or otherwise communicates to the public the sounds or sounds and images of a live musical performance, or
>
> (3) distributes or offers to distribute, sells or offers to sell, rents or offers to rent, or traffics in any copy or phonorecord fixed as described in paragraph (1), regardless of whether the fixations occurred in the United States,shall be subject to the remedies provided in §§ 502 through 505, to the same extent as an infringer of copyright.

2. Constitutional Basis of the Right

Although § 1101 is part of Title 17, it is not a copyright right, but instead an independent right based on the Commerce Clause, placed in Title 17 for purposes of administrative convenience, such as use of the definitions in § 101 (*e.g.*, "fixed," "copy," or "phonorecord").

3. Ownership of the Right

Section 1101(a) grants rights to the "performer or performers" of a "live musical performance." The term "performer" is not defined. In order to ensure that the § 1101(a) right can not be defeated by incidental or pick-up musicians, the term "or performers" was included so that the consent of *all* performers must be obtained. This rule of unanimity is absolute.

---

[2] The section numbers in this and the following headings refer to the relevant section of the implementing legislation, not to a section of the Copyright Act.—*Eds.*

4. "Live Musical Performance"

Another important undefined term is "live musical performance." One interpretation of the term is to construe it in relation to its opposite: a prerecorded musical performance. Another interpretation of "live musical performance" would limit it to its colloquial meaning: performances in front of public audiences. This latter interpretation is, however, inconsistent another aspect of the § 1101 right that may easily be overlooked by copyright lawyers: the right is not limited to "public" live musical performances; *any* live musical performance is within the scope of the right.

5. National Eligibility Requirements

There is no national eligibility requirement in § 1101 since the section simply extends rights to a "performer or performers." Thus, all performers throughout the world are entitled to the rights granted in § 1101.

6. Remedies

Actions for violation of § 1101(a)(1) must be brought in federal district court by the performer or performers whose rights have been violated or by their heirs or assignees. Because there are no registration requirements or other formalities, actions are brought merely by filing a complaint, with the full remedies provided in §§ 502 through 505 of Title 17 being available, so long as the violation occurred within the three-year statute of limitations set forth in § 507(b).

7. Duration of the Right

There is no limitation on the duration of the § 1101 right, and the right is thus perpetual.

8. Protection of Preexisting Live Musical Performances

Section 1101 applies both to unauthorized fixations of live musical performances that occur on or after the date of enactment (December 8, 1994, which is also the effective date) and to unauthorized fixations and reproductions of such fixations that occurred before that date, although there is liability only for acts that occur after the date of enactment.

Section 513: Criminal Provisions for Bootlegs

Section 513 of the URAA makes it a criminal offense in new 18 U.S.C. § 2319A(a) to engage in the same activities covered by § 512 provided those activities are done "knowingly, and for purposes of commercial advantage or private financial gain." The quoted language is taken from the 1992 omnibus revision of the criminal copyright provisions, as are the penalties: five years and/or a fine for a first violation, and 10 years and/or a fine for a second or subsequent offense.

Section 514: Retroactivity

Article 9 of the TRIPS Agreement obligates WTO members to comply with Articles 1 through 21 of the 1971 text of the Berne Convention for the protection of Literary and Artistic Works, with the exception of Article 6*bis* (which provides for *droit moral*). Article 18 of the Berne Convention requires a country newly adhering to the Berne Union to provide protection to the preexisting works of already adhering members unless those works are in the public domain either in their country of origin or in the newly adhering country as a result of the expiration of their term of protection.

Article 18 of the Berne Convention has particular significance for the United States, because the U.S. is virtually the only country to have imposed formalities on the enjoyment and exercise of copyright, including at various times requirements of affixing a notice to copies of the work, filing a renewal application, mandatory deposit, and domestic manufacture.

Retroactivity Under the URAA

Nature of Protection and Effective Date

Retroactivity under NAFTA was conditioned on compliance with a formality (filing with the Copyright Office). By contrast, retroactivity as set forth in § 104A(a) as amended by the URAA is automatic: "Copyright subsists, in accordance with this section, and vests automatically on the date of restoration."

Effective Date

The date on which protection is granted for preexisting works under § 514 of the URAA is determined by reference to the "date of restoration." That term is defined in § 104A(h)(2) as the later of:

> (A) the date on which the Agreement on Trade-Related Aspects of Intellectual Property referred to in § 101(d)(15) of the Uruguay Round Agreements Act enters into force with respect to the United States, if the source country of the restored work is a nation adhering to the Berne Convention or a WTO member country on such date; or
>
> (B) the date of adherence or proclamation, in the case of any other source country of the restored work.

The Agreement on Trade-Related Aspects of Intellectual Property entered into force with respect to the United States according to § 101(b) of the URAA on the date the President determined that "a sufficient number of foreign countries are accepting the obligations of the Uruguay Round Agreements ... to ensure the effective operation of, and adequate benefits for the United States" under, those agreements.

On December 23, 1994, by proclamation, President Clinton directed the United States Trade Representative to publish in the Federal Register a memorandum declaring, pursuant to § 101(b), that a sufficient number of countries had accepted the obligations of the Uruguay Round Agreements, and that the United States would, as of January 1, 1995, accept those agreements. The Agreement on the Trade-Related Aspects of Intellectual Property thus entered into force on January 1, 1995. From this, one might have concluded that, pursuant to § 104A(h)(2)(A), the "date of restoration" was January 1, 1995 for works whose source country was a nation that adhered either to the Berne Convention or was a WTO member as of that date.

Nevertheless, on March 23, 1995, President Clinton issued a second proclamation setting January 1, 1996 as the effective date for § 104A(h)(A). For elaboration, see 60 Fed. Reg. 15845 (Mar. 27, 1995).

In addition, the Copyright Office issued a policy decision specifying January 1, 1996 as the initial effective date, 60 Fed. Reg. 7793–95 (Feb. 9, 1995). And finally, in a technical corrections act, Pub. L. No. 105-80, 111 Stat. 1529, signed by President Clinton on November 5, 1997, Congress itself declared January 1, 1996 to have been the effective date of the restoration provisions. The matter, thus, appears to be settled.

Automatic Restoration

If the source country of the restored work was a Berne or WTO member, copyright in all preexisting original works of authorship from that country were automatically restored. No filing with the Copyright Office or other formality is required to obtain protection.

Ownership of the Restored Copyright: § 104A(b)

Section 104A(b) generally follows the principle of § 201(a): copyright in a restored work vests initially in the author of the work. Section 104A(b), however, adds to this basic principle the vesting of restored copyright in the "initial rightholder" to take into account the fact that in many countries sound recordings are protected under neighboring rights regimes, not under copyright. In such countries, there is no "author" of "copyright" in a sound recording; instead, there is an "initial rightholder." The term "initial rightholder" does *not* include other types of subject matter, such as motion pictures, nor more generally work-for-hire situations. "Initial rightholder" is strictly limited to sound recordings.

Transferees are *not* initial authors or rightholders. Instead, transferees of the initial author or rightholder are left to state court contract actions to secure whatever rights they have by virtue of their contract with the author or rightholder.

Under § 104A(b), the question of who is the initial author or rightholder is determined in federal court according to the law of the source country of the work. This statutory conflict of laws provision requires U.S. courts to decide the issue of initial ownership of the restored copyright not by looking at the U.S. Copyright Act, but by looking to the law of foreign source country, a task that may include examination not only of foreign statutes, but also foreign regulations and foreign case law.

Duration of Protection in Restored Works

Section 104A(1)(B) states that copyright in restored works will subsist "for the remainder of the term of copyright that the work would have otherwise been granted in the United States if the work never entered the public domain in the United States." Unlike ownership of restored works, which is determined by the law of the foreign source country, the term of protection is governed solely by U.S. law. That law will be either the 1909 or the 1976 Act, depending upon the date of first publication or creation of the work.

Remedies: § 104A(d)

For purposes of remedies only, the URAA distinguishes between two categories of persons: "reliance parties" and others (non-reliance parties). This distinction takes into account the interests of persons who before restoration (that is, while the work was in the public domain in the United States) either acquired copies or phonorecords of a restored work or created derivative works based on a restored work. Where a person is not a reliance party, all of the remedies granted in Chapter 5 of Title 17, United States Code, are available with respect to any act of infringement that commenced on or after the date of restoration (usually, January 1, 1995). All of the conditions applicable to the awarding of the Chapter 5 remedies also apply, such as registration with the Copyright Act before infringement in order to collect statutory damages and attorney's fees (§ 412), and in the case of works whose country of origin is not a member of the Berne Convention (or is the United States), registration before an infringement suit is instituted (§ 411(a)).

1. Remedies Against Reliance Parties: §§ 104A(d)(2)–(4)

"Reliance party" is defined in § 104A(h)(4) as any person who,

> (A) with respect to a particular work, engages in acts, before the source country of that work becomes an eligible country, which would have violated section 106 if the restored work had been subject to copyright protection, and who, after the source country becomes an eligible country, continues to engage in such acts;
>
> (B) before the source country of a particular work becomes an eligible country, makes or acquires one or more copies or phonorecords of that work; or
>
> (C) as the result of the sale or other disposition of a derivative work covered under subsection(d)(3), or significant assets of a person described in subparagraph (A) or (B), is a successor, assignee, or licensee of that person.Reliance status must be established for each individual work for which it is claimed: one does not gain such status for more than one work by establishing reliance party status for one work.

2. Notices of Intent and the Cut-Off of Reliance Party Immunity

Although the availability of reliance party status was generally cut off on January 1, 1996 (the general date of restoration), the remedies available against reliance parties are governed separately by § 104A(d)(2). Subparagraphs (A) and (B) of that section give the restored copyright owner two options for securing the maximum possible remedies. Under § 104A(d)(2)(A)(i), the restored copyright owner may, during the two-year period beginning on the date of restoration, file with the Copyright Office a notice of intent to enforce the restored copyright as provided by § 104A(e)(1). If such a notice is filed, it is effective, once published in the Federal Register, as to all reliance parties. Alternatively, at any time during the term of protection of the restored copyright, the restored copyright owner may serve directly on the reliance party a notice of intent to enforce the restored copyright as provided by § 104A(e)(2).

When a notice of intent to enforce a restored copyright has been filed either with the Copyright Office or directly on a reliance party, § 104A(d)(2)(A) & (B), with its backwards phrasing, creates the following results with respect to remedies: until the restored copyright owner either files a notice of intent to enforce its restored copyright with the Copyright Office (and that notice is published in the Federal Register) or serves actual notice on the reliance party, the reliance party may continue to exploit the work without liability even though such exploitation technically constitutes infringement. Once the notice has been published in the Federal Register or served on the reliance party, no further copies or phonorecords may be made; if they are made, full liability results. For conduct that would otherwise be infringing (except for reproduction), a reliance party may during the 12-month period after publication of the notice in the Federal Register or service of actual notice engage in that conduct (such as selling off existing stock). Full liability arises for infringing conduct that arises after the 12-month period expires.

The Copyright Office's Final Regulations

On September 29, 1995, the Copyright Office issued final regulations to implement the URAA, effective January 1, 1996. 60 Fed. Reg. 50414. With one exception,[3] the regulations are fairly unremarkable. The Office will permit an owner of multiple restored works to file a single notice of intent if each work is identified by title, has the same author, is owned by the same copyright owner, and the rights owned are the same. Acknowledgments of notices will be filed and records of notices filed will be stored in the Library of Congress's computer COPICS database and published in the Federal Register. Helpfully, the Office has created a suggested form for notices of intent, available also over the Internet.

For information concerning all of these matters, including forms for registering restored works (GATT, GATT/GRP, and GATT/CON) and current fees ($30 for a single work, effective July 1, 2002), consult the Copyright Office website at www.loc.gov/copyright. Incidentally, in a "first" for the Office, credit cards are acceptable for filings but only under the URAA!

[3] Based on its belief that it "seems essential to retain the concept of claimant since the authors may no longer be alive," the Copyright Office will permit the "owner of an exclusive right" to file simultaneously for registration of a restored copyright (not to be confused with a notice of intent to enforce the restored copyright against reliance parties). The statute, however, in specifying who may file for simultaneous registration, refers in § 104A(e)(1)(D)(ii) to "owners of restored copyrights"; and § 104A(b) provides that ownership of a restored copyright "vests initially in the author or initial rightholder of the work as determined by the law of the source country of the work." Thus, the Office will accept multiple, and possibly adverse, registrations (and notices) for the same work. Congress appears to have distinguished, clearly and deliberately, between who may file a simultaneous registration for a restored work (the author) and who may file a notice of intent (the owner of the restored copyright or the owner of an exclusive right therein)—in short, to have limited the restoration right itself to the author, and not to assignees. By also permitting the owner of an exclusive right to file for registration, the regulations seem to defeat that Congressional purpose.—*Eds.*

TRIPS AGREEMENT

AGREEMENT ON TRADE-RELATED ASPECTS OF INTELLECTUAL PROPERTY RIGHTS

Members,

Desiring to reduce distortions and impediments to international trade, and taking into account the need to promote effective and adequate protection of intellectual property rights, and to ensure that measures and procedures to enforce intellectual property rights do not themselves become barriers to legitimate trade;

Recognizing, to this end, the need for new rules and disciplines concerning:

(a) the applicability of the basic principles of GATT 1994 and of relevant international intellectual property agreements or conventions;

(b) the provision of adequate standards and principles concerning the availability, scope and use of trade-related intellectual property rights;

(c) the provision of effective and appropriate means for the enforcement of trade-related intellectual property rights, taking into account differences in national legal systems;

(d) the provision of effective and expeditious procedures for the multilateral prevention and settlement of disputes between governments; and

(e) transitional arrangements aiming at the fullest participation in the results of the negotiations;

Recognizing the need for a multilateral framework of principles, rules and disciplines dealing with international trade in counterfeit goods;

Recognizing that intellectual property rights are private rights;

Recognizing the underlying public policy objectives of national systems for the protection of intellectual property, including developmental and technological objectives;

Recognizing also the special needs of the least-developed country Members in respect of maximum flexibility in the domestic implementation of laws and regulations in order to enable them to create a sound and viable technological base;

Emphasizing the importance of reducing tensions by reaching strengthened commitments to resolve disputes on trade-related intellectual property issues through multilateral procedures;

Desiring to establish a mutually supportive relationship between the WTO and the World Intellectual Property Organization (referred to in this Agreement as "WIPO") as well as other relevant international organizations;

Hereby agree as follows:

PART I. GENERAL PROVISIONS AND BASIC PRINCIPLES

Article 1 Nature and Scope of Obligations

1. Members shall give effect to the provisions of this Agreement. Members may, but shall not be obliged to, implement in their law more extensive protection than is required by this Agreement, provided that such protection does not contravene the provisions of this Agreement. Members shall be free to determine the appropriate method of implementing the provisions of this Agreement within their own legal system and practice.

2. For the purposes of this Agreement, the term "intellectual property" refers to all categories of intellectual property that are the subject of Sections 1 through 7 of Part II.

3. Members shall accord the treatment provided for in this Agreement to the nationals of other Members.[1] In respect of the relevant intellectual

[1] When "nationals" are referred to in this Agreement, they shall be deemed, in the case of a separate customs territory Member of the WTO, to mean persons, natural or legal, who are domiciled or who have a real and effective industrial or commercial establishment in that customs territory.—*Eds.*

property right, the nationals of other Members shall be understood as those natural or legal persons that would meet the criteria for eligibility for protection provided for in the Paris Convention (1967), the Berne Convention (1971), the Rome Convention and the Treaty on Intellectual Property in Respect of Integrated Circuits, were all Members of the WTO members of those conventions.[2] Any Member availing itself of the possibilities provided in paragraph 3 of Article 5 or paragraph 2 of Article 6 of the Rome Convention shall make a notification as foreseen in those provisions to the Council for Trade-Related Aspects of Intellectual Property Rights (the "Council for TRIPS").

Article 2
Intellectual Property Conventions

1. In respect of Parts II, III and IV of this Agreement, Members shall comply with Articles 1 through 12, and Article 19, of the Paris Convention (1967).

2. Nothing in Parts I to IV of this Agreement shall derogate from existing obligations that Members may have to each other under the Paris Convention, the Berne Convention, the Rome Convention and the Treaty on Intellectual Property in Respect of Integrated Circuits.

Article 3
National Treatment

1. Each Member shall accord to the nationals of other Members treatment no less favourable than that it accords to its own nationals with regard to the protection[3] of intellectual property, subject to the exceptions already provided in, respectively, the Paris Convention (1967), the Berne Convention (1971), the Rome Convention or the Treaty on Intellectual Property in Respect of Integrated Circuits. In respect of performers, producers of phonograms and broadcasting organizations, this obligation only applies in respect of the rights provided under this Agreement. Any Member availing itself of the possibilities provided in Article 6 of the Berne Convention (1971) or paragraph 1(b) of Article 16 of the Rome Convention shall make a notification as foreseen in those provisions to the Council for TRIPS.

---

[2] In this Agreement, "Paris Convention" refers to the Paris Convention for the Protection of Industrial Property; "Paris Convention (1967)" refers to the Stockholm Act of this Convention of 14 July 1967. "Berne Convention" refers to the Berne Convention for the Protection of Literary and Artistic Works; "Berne Convention (1971)" refers to the Paris Act of this Convention of 24 July 1971. "Rome Convention" refers to the International Convention for the Protection of Performers, Producers of Phonograms and Broadcasting Organizations, adopted at Rome on 26 October 1961. "Treaty on Intellectual Property in Respect of Integrated Circuits" (IPIC Treaty) refers to the Treaty on Intellectual Property in Respect of Integrated Circuits, adopted at Washington on 26 May 1989. "WTO Agreement" refers to the Agreement Establishing the WTO.—Eds.

[3] For the purposes of Articles 3 and 4, "protection" shall include matters affecting the availability, acquisition, scope, maintenance and enforcement of intellectual property rights as well as those matters affecting the use of intellectual property rights specifically addressed in this Agreement.—*Eds.*

2. Members may avail themselves of the exceptions permitted under paragraph 1 in relation to judicial and administrative procedures, including the designation of an address for service or the appointment of an agent within the jurisdiction of a Member, only where such exceptions are necessary to secure compliance with laws and regulations which are not inconsistent with the provisions of this Agreement and where such practices are not applied in a manner which would constitute a disguised restriction on trade.

Article 4
Most-Favoured-Nation Treatment

With regard to the protection of intellectual property, any advantage, favour, privilege or immunity granted by a Member to the nationals of any other country shall be accorded immediately and unconditionally to the nationals of all other Members. Exempted from this obligation are any advantage, favour, privilege or immunity accorded by a Member:

(a) deriving from international agreements on judicial assistance or law enforcement of a general nature and not particularly confined to the protection of intellectual property;

(b) granted in accordance with the provisions of the Berne Convention (1971) or the Rome Convention authorizing that the treatment accorded be a function not of national treatment but of the treatment accorded in another country;

(c) in respect of the rights of performers, producers of phonograms and broadcasting organizations not provided under this Agreement;

(d) deriving from international agreements related to the protection of intellectual property which entered into force prior to the entry into force of the WTO Agreement, provided that such agreements are notified to the Council for TRIPS and do not constitute an arbitrary or unjustifiable discrimination against nationals of other Members.

Article 5
Multilateral Agreements on Acquisition or Maintenance of Protection

The obligations under Articles 3 and 4 do not apply to procedures provided in multilateral agreements concluded under the auspices of WIPO relating to the acquisition or maintenance of intellectual property rights.

Article 6
Exhaustion

For the purposes of dispute settlement under this Agreement, subject to the provisions of Articles 3 and 4 nothing in this Agreement shall be used to address the issue of the exhaustion of intellectual property rights.

Article 7
Objectives

The protection and enforcement of intellectual property rights should contribute to the promotion of technological innovation and to the transfer and dissemination of technology, to the mutual advantage of producers and users of technological knowledge and in a manner conducive to social and economic welfare, and to a balance of rights and obligations.

Article 8
Principles

1. Members may, in formulating or amending their laws and regulations, adopt measures necessary to protect public health and nutrition, and to promote the public interest in sectors of vital importance to their socio-economic and technological development, provided that such measures are consistent with the provisions of this Agreement.

2. Appropriate measures, provided that they are consistent with the provisions of this Agreement, may be needed to prevent the abuse of intellectual property rights by right holders or the resort to practices which unreasonably restrain trade or adversely affect the international transfer of technology.

PART II.
STANDARDS CONCERNING THE AVAILABILITY, SCOPE AND USE OF INTELLECTUAL PROPERTY RIGHTS

SECTION 1: COPYRIGHT AND RELATED RIGHTS

Article 9
Relation to the Berne Convention

1. Members shall comply with Articles 1 through 21 of the Berne Convention (1971) and the Appendix thereto. However, Members shall not have rights or obligations under this Agreement in respect of the rights conferred under Article 6*bis* of that Convention or of the rights derived therefrom.

2. Copyright protection shall extend to expressions and not to ideas, procedures, methods of operation or mathematical concepts as such.

Article 10
Computer Programs and Compilations of Data

1. Computer programs, whether in source or object code, shall be protected as literary works under the Berne Convention (1971).

2. Compilations of data or other material, whether in machine readable or other form, which by reason of the selection or arrangement of their contents constitute intellectual creations shall be protected as such. Such protection,

which shall not extend to the data or material itself, shall be without prejudice to any copyright subsisting in the data or material itself.

Article 11
Rental Rights

In respect of at least computer programs and cinematographic works, a Member shall provide authors and their successors in title the right to authorize or to prohibit the commercial rental to the public of originals or copies of their copyright works. A Member shall be excepted from this obligation in respect of cinematographic works unless such rental has led to widespread copying of such works which is materially impairing the exclusive right of reproduction conferred in that Member on authors and their successors in title. In respect of computer programs, this obligation does not apply to rentals where the program itself is not the essential object of the rental.

Article 12
Term of Protection

Whenever the term of protection of a work, other than a photographic work or a work of applied art, is calculated on a basis other than the life of a natural person, such term shall be no less than 50 years from the end of the calendar year of authorized publication, or, failing such authorized publication within 50 years from the making of the work, 50 years from the end of the calendar year of making.

Article 13
Limitations and Exceptions

Members shall confine limitations or exceptions to exclusive rights to certain special cases which do not conflict with a normal exploitation of the work and do not unreasonably prejudice the legitimate interests of the right holder.

Article 14
Protection of Performers, Producers of Phonograms (Sound Recordings) and Broadcasting Organizations

1. In respect of a fixation of their performance on a phonogram, performers shall have the possibility of preventing the following acts when undertaken without their authorization: the fixation of their unfixed performance and the reproduction of such fixation. Performers shall also have the possibility of preventing the following acts when undertaken without their authorization: the broadcasting by wireless means and the communication to the public of their live performance.

2. Producers of phonograms shall enjoy the right to authorize or prohibit the direct or indirect reproduction of their phonograms.

3. Broadcasting organizations shall have the right to prohibit the following acts when undertaken without their authorization: the fixation, the reproduction of fixations, and the rebroadcasting by wireless means of

broadcasts, as well as the communication to the public of television broadcasts of the same. Where Members do not grant such rights to broadcasting organizations, they shall provide owners of copyright in the subject matter of broadcasts with the possibility of preventing the above acts, subject to the provisions of the Berne Convention (1971).

4. The provisions of Article 11 in respect of computer programs shall apply *mutatis mutandis* to producers of phonograms and any other right holders in phonograms as determined in a Member's law. If on 15 April 1994 a Member has in force a system of equitable remuneration of right holders in respect of the rental of phonograms, it may maintain such system provided that the commercial rental of phonograms is not giving rise to the material impairment of the exclusive rights of reproduction of right holders.

5. The term of the protection available under this Agreement to performers and producers of phonograms shall last at least until the end of a period of 50 years computed from the end of the calendar year in which the fixation was made or the performance took place. The term of protection granted pursuant to paragraph 3 shall last for at least 20 years from the end of the calendar year in which the broadcast took place.

6. Any Member may, in relation to the rights conferred under paragraphs 1, 2 and 3, provide for conditions, limitations, exceptions and reservations to the extent permitted by the Rome Convention. However, the provisions of Article 18 of the Berne Convention (1971) shall also apply, *mutatis mutandis,* to the rights of performers and producers of phonograms in phonograms.

SECTION 2: TRADEMARKS

Article 15
Protectable Subject Matter

1. Any sign, or any combination of signs, capable of distinguishing the goods or services of one undertaking from those of other undertakings, shall be capable of constituting a trademark. Such signs, in particular words including personal names, letters, numerals, figurative elements and combinations of colours as well as any combination of such signs, shall be eligible for registration as trademarks. Where signs are not inherently capable of distinguishing the relevant goods or services, Members may make registrability depend on distinctiveness acquired through use. Members may require, as a condition of registration, that signs be visually perceptible.

2. Paragraph 1 shall not be understood to prevent a Member from denying registration of a trademark on other grounds, provided that they do not derogate from the provisions of the Paris Convention (1967).

3. Members may make registrability depend on use. However, actual use of a trademark shall not be a condition for filing an application for registration. An application shall not be refused solely on the ground that intended use has not taken place before the expiry of a period of three years from the date of application.

4. The nature of the goods or services to which a trademark is to be applied shall in no case form an obstacle to registration of the trademark.

5. Members shall publish each trademark either before it is registered or promptly after it is registered and shall afford a reasonable opportunity for petitions to cancel the registration. In addition, Members may afford an opportunity for the registration of a trademark to be opposed.

Article 16
Rights Conferred

1. The owner of a registered trademark shall have the exclusive right to prevent all third parties not having the owner's consent from using in the course of trade identical or similar signs for goods or services which are identical or similar to those in respect of which the trademark is registered where such use would result in a likelihood of confusion. In case of the use of an identical sign for identical goods or services, a likelihood of confusion shall be presumed. The rights described above shall not prejudice any existing prior rights, nor shall they affect the possibility of Members making rights available on the basis of use.

2. Article 6bis of the Paris Convention (1967) shall apply, *mutatis mutandis,* to services. In determining whether a trademark is well-known, Members shall take account of the knowledge of the trademark in the relevant sector of the public, including knowledge in the Member concerned which has been obtained as a result of the promotion of the trademark.

3. Article 6bis of the Paris Convention (1967) shall apply, *mutatis mutandis,* to goods or services which are not similar to those in respect of which a trademark is registered, provided that use of that trademark in relation to those goods or services would indicate a connection between those goods or services and the owner of the registered trademark and provided that the interests of the owner of the registered trademark are likely to be damaged by such use.

Article 17
Exceptions

Members may provide limited exceptions to the rights conferred by a trademark, such as fair use of descriptive terms, provided that such exceptions take account of the legitimate interests of the owner of the trademark and of third parties.

Article 18
Term of Protection

Initial registration, and each renewal of registration, of a trademark shall be for a term of no less than seven years. The registration of a trademark shall be renewable indefinitely.

Article 19
Requirement of Use

1. If use is required to maintain a registration, the registration may be cancelled only after an uninterrupted period of at least three years of non-use, unless valid reasons based on the existence of obstacles to such use are shown by the trademark owner. Circumstances arising independently of the will of the owner of the trademark which constitute an obstacle to the use of the trademark, such as import restrictions on or other government requirements for goods or services protected by the trademark, shall be recognized as valid reasons for non-use.

2. When subject to the control of its owner, use of a trademark by another person shall be recognized as use of the trademark for the purpose of maintaining the registration.

Article 20
Other Requirements

The use of a trademark in the course of trade shall not be unjustifiably encumbered by special requirements, such as use with another trademark, use in a special form or use in a manner detrimental to its capability to distinguish the goods or services of one undertaking from those of other undertakings. This will not preclude a requirement prescribing the use of the trademark identifying the undertaking producing the goods or services along with, but without linking it to, the trademark distinguishing the specific goods or services in question of that undertaking.

Article 21
Licensing and Assignment

Members may determine conditions on the licensing and assignment of trademarks, it being understood that the compulsory licensing of trademarks shall not be permitted and that the owner of a registered trademark shall have the right to assign the trademark with or without the transfer of the business to which the trademark belongs.

SECTION 3: GEOGRAPHICAL INDICATIONS

Article 22
Protection of Geographical Indications

1. Geographical indications are, for the purposes of this Agreement, indications which identify a good as originating in the territory of a Member, or a region or locality in that territory, where a given quality, reputation or other characteristic of the good is essentially attributable to its geographical origin.

2. In respect of geographical indications, Members shall provide the legal means for interested parties to prevent:

(a) the use of any means in the designation or presentation of a good that indicates or suggests that the good in question originates in a geographical area other than the true place of origin in a manner which misleads the public as to the geographical origin of the good;

(b) any use which constitutes an act of unfair competition within the meaning of Article 10bis of the Paris Convention (1967).

3. A Member shall, *ex officio* if its legislation so permits or at the request of an interested party, refuse or invalidate the registration of a trademark which contains or consists of a geographical indication with respect to goods not originating in the territory indicated, if use of the indication in the trademark for such goods in that Member is of such a nature as to mislead the public as to the true place of origin.

4. The protection under paragraphs 1, 2 and 3 shall be applicable against a geographical indication which, although literally true as to the territory, region or locality in which the goods originate, falsely represents to the public that the goods originate in another territory.

Article 23
Additional Protection for Geographical Indications for Wines and Spirits

1. Each Member shall provide the legal means for interested parties to prevent use of a geographical indication identifying wines for wines not originating in the place indicated by the geographical indication in question or identifying spirits for spirits not originating in the place indicated by the geographical indication in question, even where the true origin of the goods is indicated or the geographical indication is used in translation or accompanied by expressions such as "kind," "type," "style," "imitation" or the like.[4]

2. The registration of a trademark for wines which contains or consists of a geographical indication identifying wines or for spirits which contains or consists of a geographical indication identifying spirits shall be refused or invalidated, *ex officio* if a Member's legislation so permits or at the request of an interested party, with respect to such wines or spirits not having this origin.

3. In the case of homonymous geographical indications for wines, protection shall be accorded to each indication, subject to the provisions of paragraph 4 of Article 22. Each Member shall determine the practical conditions under which the homonymous indications in question will be differentiated from each other, taking into account the need to ensure equitable treatment of the producers concerned and that consumers are not misled.

[4] Notwithstanding the first sentence of Article 42, Members may, with respect to these obligations, instead provide for enforcement by administrative action.—*Eds.*

4. In order to facilitate the protection of geographical indications for wines, negotiations shall be undertaken in the Council for TRIPS concerning the establishment of a multilateral system of notification and registration of geographical indications for wines eligible for protection in those Members participating in the system.

Article 24
International Negotiations; Exceptions

1. Members agree to enter into negotiations aimed at increasing the protection of individual geographical indications under Article 23. The provisions of paragraphs 4 through 8 below shall not be used by a Member to refuse to conduct negotiations or to conclude bilateral or multilateral agreements. In the context of such negotiations, Members shall be willing to consider the continued applicability of these provisions to individual geographical indications whose use was the subject of such negotiations.

2. The Council for TRIPS shall keep under review the application of the provisions of this Section; the first such review shall take place within two years of the entry into force of the WTO Agreement. Any matter affecting the compliance with the obligations under these provisions may be drawn to the attention of the Council, which, at the request of a Member, shall consult with any Member or Members in respect of such matter in respect of which it has not been possible to find a satisfactory solution through bilateral or plurilateral consultations between the Members concerned. The Council shall take such action as may be agreed to facilitate the operation and further the objectives of this Section.

3. In implementing this Section, a Member shall not diminish the protection of geographical indications that existed in that Member immediately prior to the date of entry into force of the WTO Agreement.

4. Nothing in this Section shall require a Member to prevent continued and similar use of a particular geographical indication of another Member identifying wines or spirits in connection with goods or services by any of its nationals or domiciliaries who have used that geographical indication in a continuous manner with regard to the same or related goods or services in the territory of that Member either (*a*) for at least 10 years preceding 15 April 1994 or (*b*) in good faith preceding that date.

5. Where a trademark has been applied for or registered in good faith, or where rights to a trademark have been acquired through use in good faith either:

(a) before the date of application of these provisions in that Member as defined in Part VI; or

(b) before the geographical indication is protected in its country of origin; measures adopted to implement this Section shall not prejudice eligibility for or the validity of the registration of a trademark, or the right to use a trademark, on the basis that such a trademark is identical with, or similar to, a geographical indication.

6. Nothing in this Section shall require a Member to apply its provisions in respect of a geographical indication of any other Member with respect to goods or services for which the relevant indication is identical with the term customary in common language as the common name for such goods or services in the territory of that Member. Nothing in this Section shall require a Member to apply its provisions in respect of a geographical indication of any other Member with respect to products of the vine for which the relevant indication is identical with the customary name of a grape variety existing in the territory of that Member as of the date of entry into force of the WTO Agreement.

7. A Member may provide that any request made under this Section in connection with the use or registration of a trademark must be presented within five years after the adverse use of the protected indication has become generally known in that Member or after the date of registration of the trademark in that Member provided that the trademark has been published by that date, if such date is earlier than the date on which the adverse use became generally known in that Member, provided that the geographical indication is not used or registered in bad faith.

8. The provisions of this Section shall in no way prejudice the right of any person to use, in the course of trade, that person's name or the name of that person's predecessor in business, except where such name is used in such a manner as to mislead the public.

9. There shall be no obligation under this Agreement to protect geographical indications which are not or cease to be protected in their country of origin, or which have fallen into disuse in that country.

SECTION 4: INDUSTRIAL DESIGNS

Article 25
Requirements for Protection

1. Members shall provide for the protection of independently created industrial designs that are new or original. Members may provide that designs are not new or original if they do not significantly differ from known designs or combinations of known design features. Members may provide that such protection shall not extend to designs dictated essentially by technical or functional considerations.

2. Each Member shall ensure that requirements for securing protection for textile designs, in particular in regard to any cost, examination or publication, do not unreasonably impair the opportunity to seek and obtain such protection. Members shall be free to meet this obligation through industrial design law or through copyright law.

Article 26
Protection

1. The owner of a protected industrial design shall have the right to prevent third parties not having the owner's consent from making, selling or importing articles bearing or embodying a design which is a copy, or substantially a copy, of the protected design, when such acts are undertaken for commercial purposes.

2. Members may provide limited exceptions to the protection of industrial designs, provided that such exceptions do not unreasonably conflict with the normal exploitation of protected industrial designs and do not unreasonably prejudice the legitimate interests of the owner of the protected design, taking account of the legitimate interests of third parties.

3. The duration of protection available shall amount to at least 10 years.

SECTION 5: PATENTS

Article 27
Patentable Subject Matter

1. Subject to the provisions of paragraphs 2 and 3, patents shall be available for any inventions, whether products or processes, in all fields of technology, provided that they are new, involve an inventive step and are capable of industrial application.[5] Subject to paragraph 4 of Article 65, paragraph 8 of Article 70 and paragraph 3 of this Article, patents shall be available and patent rights enjoyable without discrimination as to the place of invention, the field of technology and whether products are imported or locally produced.

2. Members may exclude from patentability inventions, the prevention within their territory of the commercial exploitation of which is necessary to protect *ordre public* or morality, including to protect human, animal or plant life or health or to avoid serious prejudice to the environment, provided that such exclusion is not made merely because the exploitation is prohibited by their law.

3. Members may also exclude from patentability:

(a) diagnostic, therapeutic and surgical methods for the treatment of humans or animals;

(b) plants and animals other than micro-organisms, and essentially biological processes for the production of plants or animals other

[5] For the purposes of the Article, the terms "inventive step" and "capable of industrial application" may be deemed by a Member to be synonymous with the terms "non-obvious" and "useful" respectively.—*Eds.*

than non-biological and microbiological processes. However, Members shall provide for the protection of plant varieties either by patents or by an effective *sui generis* system or by any combination thereof. The provisions of this subparagraph shall be reviewed four years after the date of entry into force of the WTO Agreement.

Article 28
Rights Conferred

1. A patent shall confer on its owner the following exclusive rights:

(a) where the subject matter of a patent is a product, to prevent third parties not having the owner's consent from the acts of: making, using, offering for sale, selling, or importing[6] for these purposes that product;

(b) where the subject matter of a patent is a process, to prevent third parties not having the owner's consent from the act of using the process, and from the acts of: using, offering for sale, selling, or importing for these purposes at least the product obtained directly by that process.

2. Patent owners shall also have the right to assign, or transfer by succession, the patent and to conclude licensing contracts.

Article 29
Conditions on Patent Applicants

1. Members shall require that an applicant for a patent shall disclose the invention in a manner sufficiently clear and complete for the invention to be carried out by a person skilled in the art and may require the applicant to indicate the best mode for carrying out the invention known to the inventor at the filing date or, where priority is claimed, at the priority date of the application.

2. Members may require an applicant for a patent to provide information concerning the applicant's corresponding foreign applications and grants.

Article 30
Exceptions to Rights Conferred

Members may provide limited exceptions to the exclusive rights conferred by a patent, provided that such exceptions do not unreasonably conflict with a normal exploitation of the patent and do not unreasonably prejudice the legitimate interests of the patent owner, taking account of the legitimate interests of third parties.

---

[6] This right, like all other rights conferred under this Agreement in respect of the use, sale, importation or other distribution of goods, is subject to the provisions of Article 6.—*Eds.*

Article 31
Other Use Without Authorization of the Right Holder

Where the law of a Member allows for other use[7] of the subject matter of a patent without the authorization of the right holder, including use by the government or third parties authorized by the government, the following provisions shall be respected:

(a) authorization of such use shall be considered on its individual merits;

(b) such use may only be permitted if, prior to such use, the proposed user has made efforts to obtain authorization from the right holder on reasonable commercial terms and conditions and that such efforts have not been successful within a reasonable period of time. This requirement may be waived by a Member in the case of a national emergency or other circumstances of extreme urgency or in cases of public non-commercial use. In situations of national emergency or other circumstances of extreme urgency, the right holder shall, nevertheless, be notified as soon as reasonably practicable. In the case of public non-commercial use, where the government or contractor, without making a patent search, knows or has demonstrable grounds to know that a valid patent is or will be used by or for the government, the right holder shall be informed promptly;

(c) the scope and duration of such use shall be limited to the purpose for which it was authorized, and in the case of semi-conductor technology shall only be for public non-commercial use or to remedy a practice determined after judicial or administrative process to be anti-competitive;

(d) such use shall be non-exclusive;

(e) such use shall be non-assignable, except with that part of the enterprise or goodwill which enjoys such use;

(f) any such use shall be authorized predominantly for the supply of the domestic market of the Member authorizing such use;

(g) authorization for such use shall be liable, subject to adequate protection of the legitimate interests of the persons so authorized, to be terminated if and when the circumstances which led to it cease to exist and are unlikely to recur. The competent authority shall have the authority to review, upon motivated request, the continued existence of these circumstances;

(h) the right holder shall be paid adequate remuneration in the circumstances of each case, taking into account the economic value of the authorization;

---

[7] "Other use" refers to use other than that allowed under Article 30.—*Eds.*

(i) the legal validity of any decision relating to the authorization of such use shall be subject to judicial review or other independent review by a distinct higher authority in that Member;

(j) any decision relating to the remuneration provided in respect of such use shall be subject to judicial review or other independent review by a distinct higher authority in that Member;

(k) Members are not obliged to apply the conditions set forth in subparagraphs (b) and (f) where such use is permitted to remedy a practice determined after judicial or administrative process to be anti-competitive. The need to correct anti-competitive practices may be taken into account in determining the amount of remuneration in such cases. Competent authorities shall have the authority to refuse termination of authorization if and when the conditions which led to such authorization are likely to recur;

(l) where such use is authorized to permit the exploitation of a patent ("the second patent") which cannot be exploited without infringing another patent ("the first patent"), the following additional conditions shall apply:

(i) the invention claimed in the second patent shall involve an important technical advance of considerable economic significance in relation to the invention claimed in the first patent;

(ii) the owner of the first patent shall be entitled to a cross-licence on reasonable terms to use the invention claimed in the second patent; and

(iii) the use authorized in respect of the first patent shall be non-assignable except with the assignment of the second patent.

Article 32
Revocation/Forfeiture

An opportunity for judicial review of any decision to revoke or forfeit a patent shall be available.

Article 33
Term of Protection

The term of protection available shall not end before the expiration of a period of twenty years counted from the filing date.[8]

Article 34
Process Patents: Burden of Proof

1. For the purposes of civil proceedings in respect of the infringement of the rights of the owner referred to in paragraph 1(b) of Article 28, if the subject

[8] It is understood that those Members which do not have a system of original grant may provide that the term of protection shall be computed from the filing date in the system of original grant.—*Eds.*

matter of a patent is a process for obtaining a product, the judicial authorities shall have the authority to order the defendant to prove that the process to obtain an identical product is different from the patented process. Therefore, Members shall provide, in at least one of the following circumstances, that any identical product when produced without the consent of the patent owner shall, in the absence of proof to the contrary, be deemed to have been obtained by the patented process:

(a) if the product obtained by the patented process is new;

(b) if there is a substantial likelihood that the identical product was made by the process and the owner of the patent has been unable through reasonable efforts to determine the process actually used.

2. Any Member shall be free to provide that the burden of proof indicated in paragraph 1 shall be on the alleged infringer only if the condition referred to in subparagraph (a) is fulfilled or only if the condition referred to in subparagraph (b) is fulfilled.

3. In the adduction of proof to the contrary, the legitimate interests of defendants in protecting their manufacturing and business secrets shall be taken into account.

SECTION 6: LAYOUT-DESIGNS (TOPOGRAPHIES) OF INTEGRATED CIRCUITS

Article 35
Relation to the IPIC Treaty

Members agree to provide protection to the layout-designs (topographies) of integrated circuits (referred to in this Agreement as "layout-designs") in accordance with Articles 2 through 7 (other than paragraph 3 of Article 6), Article 12 and paragraph 3 of Article 16 of the Treaty on Intellectual Property in Respect of Integrated Circuits and, in addition, to comply with the following provisions.

Article 36
Scope of the Protection

Subject to the provisions of paragraph 1 of Article 37, Members shall consider unlawful the following acts if performed without the authorization of the right holder:[9] importing, selling, or otherwise distributing for commercial purposes a protected layout-design, an integrated circuit in which a protected layout-design is incorporated, or an article incorporating such an integrated circuit only in so far as it continues to contain an unlawfully reproduced layout-design.

[9] The term "right holder" in this Section shall be understood as having the same meaning as the term "holder of the right" in the IPIC Treaty.—*Eds.*

Article 37
Acts Not Requiring the Authorization of the Right Holder

1. Notwithstanding Article 36, no Member shall consider unlawful the performance of any of the acts referred to in that Article in respect of an integrated circuit incorporating an unlawfully reproduced layout-design or any article incorporating such an integrated circuit where the person performing or ordering such acts did not know and had no reasonable ground to know, when acquiring the integrated circuit or article incorporating such an integrated circuit, that it incorporated an unlawfully reproduced layout-design. Members shall provide that, after the time that such person has received sufficient notice that the layout-design was unlawfully reproduced, that person may perform any of the acts with respect to the stock on hand or ordered before such time, but shall be liable to pay to the right holder a sum equivalent to a reasonable royalty such as would be payable under a freely negotiated licence in respect of such a layout-design.

2. The conditions set out in subparagraphs (a) through (k) of Article 31 shall apply *mutatis mutandis* in the event of any non-voluntary licensing of a layout-design or of its use by or for the government without the authorization of the right holder.

Article 38
Term of Protection

1. In Members requiring registration as a condition of protection, the term of protection of layout-designs shall not end before the expiration of a period of 10 years counted from the date of filing an application for registration or from the first commercial exploitation wherever in the world it occurs.

2. In Members not requiring registration as a condition for protection, layout-designs shall be protected for a term of no less than 10 years from the date of the first commercial exploitation wherever in the world it occurs.

3. Notwithstanding paragraphs 1 and 2, a Member may provide that protection shall lapse 15 years after the creation of the layout-design.

SECTION 7: PROTECTION OF UNDISCLOSED INFORMATION

Article 39

1. In the course of ensuring effective protection against unfair competition as provided in Article 10*bis* of the Paris Convention (1967), Members shall protect undisclosed information in accordance with paragraph 2 and data submitted to governments or governmental agencies in accordance with paragraph 3.

2. Natural and legal persons shall have the possibility of preventing information lawfully within their control from being disclosed to, acquired by,

or used by others without their consent in a manner contrary to honest commercial practices[10] so long as such information:

(a) is secret in the sense that it is not, as a body or in the precise configuration and assembly of its components, generally known among or readily accessible to persons within the circles that normally deal with the kind of information in question;

(b) has commercial value because it is secret; and

(c) has been subject to reasonable steps under the circumstances, by the person lawfully in control of the information, to keep it secret.

3. Members, when requiring, as a condition of approving the marketing of pharmaceutical or of agricultural chemical products which utilize new chemical entities, the submission of undisclosed test or other data, the origination of which involves a considerable effort, shall protect such data against unfair commercial use. In addition, Members shall protect such data against disclosure, except where necessary to protect the public, or unless steps are taken to ensure that the data are protected against unfair commercial use.

SECTION 8: CONTROL OF ANTI-COMPETITIVE PRACTICES IN CONTRACTUAL LICENSES

Article 40

1. Members agree that some licensing practices or conditions pertaining to intellectual property rights which restrain competition may have adverse effects on trade and may impede the transfer and dissemination of technology.

2. Nothing in this Agreement shall prevent Members from specifying in their legislation licensing practices or conditions that may in particular cases constitute an abuse of intellectual property rights having an adverse effect on competition in the relevant market. As provided above, a Member may adopt, consistently with the other provisions of this Agreement, appropriate measures to prevent or control such practices, which may include for example exclusive grantback conditions, conditions preventing challenges to validity and coercive package licensing, in the light of the relevant laws and regulations of that Member.

3. Each Member shall enter, upon request, into consultations with any other Member which has cause to believe that an intellectual property right owner that is a national or domiciliary of the Member to which the request for consultations has been addressed is undertaking practices in violation of the requesting Member's laws and regulations on the subject matter of this Section,

[10] For the purpose of this provision, "a manner contrary to honest commercial practices" shall mean at least practices such as breach of contract, breach of confidence and inducement to breach, and includes the acquisition of undisclosed information by third parties who knew, or were grossly negligent in failing to know, that such practices were involved in the acquisition.—*Eds.*

and which wishes to secure compliance with such legislation, without prejudice to any action under the law and to the full freedom of an ultimate decision of either Member. The Member addressed shall accord full and sympathetic consideration to, and shall afford adequate opportunity for, consultations with the requesting Member, and shall cooperate through supply of publicly available non-confidential information of relevance to the matter in question and of other information available to the Member, subject to domestic law and to the conclusion of mutually satisfactory agreements concerning the safeguarding of its confidentiality by the requesting Member.

4. A Member whose nationals or domiciliaries are subject to proceedings in another Member concerning alleged violation of that other Member's laws and regulations on the subject matter of this Section shall, upon request, be granted an opportunity for consultations by the other Member under the same conditions as those foreseen in paragraph 3.

PART III
ENFORCEMENT OF INTELLECTUAL PROPERTY RIGHTS

SECTION 1: GENERAL OBLIGATIONS

Article 41

1. Members shall ensure that enforcement procedures as specified in this Part are available under their law so as to permit effective action against any act of infringement of intellectual property rights covered by this Agreement, including expeditious remedies to prevent infringements and remedies which constitute a deterrent to further infringements. These procedures shall be applied in such a manner as to avoid the creation of barriers to legitimate trade and to provide for safeguards against their abuse.

2. Procedures concerning the enforcement of intellectual property rights shall be fair and equitable. They shall not be unnecessarily complicated or costly, or entail unreasonable time-limits or unwarranted delays.

3. Decisions on the merits of a case shall preferably be in writing and reasoned. They shall be made available at least to the parties to the proceeding without undue delay. Decisions on the merits of a case shall be based only on evidence in respect of which parties were offered the opportunity to be heard.

4. Parties to a proceeding shall have an opportunity for review by a judicial authority of final administrative decisions and, subject to jurisdictional provisions in a Member's law concerning the importance of a case, of at least the legal aspects of initial judicial decisions on the merits of a case. However, there shall be no obligation to provide an opportunity for review of acquittals in criminal cases.

5. It is understood that this Part does not create any obligation to put in place a judicial system for the enforcement of intellectual property rights distinct from that for the enforcement of law in general, nor does it affect the capacity of Members to enforce their law in general. Nothing in this Part creates any obligation with respect to the distribution of resources as between enforcement of intellectual property rights and the enforcement of law in general.

SECTION 2: CIVIL AND ADMINISTRATIVE PROCEDURES AND REMEDIES

Article 42
Fair and Equitable Procedures

Members shall make available to right holders[11] civil judicial procedures concerning the enforcement of any intellectual property right covered by this Agreement. Defendants shall have the right to written notice which is timely and contains sufficient detail, including the basis of the claims. Parties shall be allowed to be represented by independent legal counsel, and procedures shall not impose overly burdensome requirements concerning mandatory personal appearances. All parties to such procedures shall be duly entitled to substantiate their claims and to present all relevant evidence. The procedure shall provide a means to identify and protect confidential information, unless this would be contrary to existing constitutional requirements.

Article 43
Evidence

1. The judicial authorities shall have the authority, where a party has presented reasonably available evidence sufficient to support its claims and has specified evidence relevant to substantiation of its claims which lies in the control of the opposing party, to order that this evidence be produced by the opposing party, subject in appropriate cases to conditions which ensure the protection of confidential information.

2. In cases in which a party to a proceeding voluntarily and without good reason refuses access to, or otherwise does not provide necessary information within a reasonable period, or significantly impedes a procedure relating to an enforcement action, a Member may accord judicial authorities the authority to make preliminary and final determinations, affirmative or negative, on the basis of the information presented to them, including the complaint or the allegation presented by the party adversely affected by the denial of access to information, subject to providing the parties an opportunity to be heard on the allegations or evidence.

Article 44
Injunctions

1. The judicial authorities shall have the authority to order a party to desist from an infringement, *inter alia* to prevent the entry into the channels of commerce in their jurisdiction of imported goods that involve the infringement of an intellectual property right, immediately after customs clearance of such goods. Members are not obliged to accord such authority in respect of protected subject matter acquired or ordered by a person prior to knowing or

---

[11] For the purpose of this Part, the term "right holder" includes federations and associations having legal standing to assert such rights.—*Eds.*

having reasonable grounds to know that dealing in such subject matter would entail the infringement of an intellectual property right.

2. Notwithstanding the other provisions of this Part and provided that the provisions of Part II specifically addressing use by governments, or by third parties authorized by a government, without the authorization of the right holder are complied with, Members may limit the remedies available against such use to payment of remuneration in accordance with subparagraph (h) of Article 31. In other cases, the remedies under this Part shall apply or, where these remedies are inconsistent with a Member's law, declaratory judgments and adequate compensation shall be available.

Article 45
Damages

1. The judicial authorities shall have the authority to order the infringer to pay the right holder damages adequate to compensate for the injury the right holder has suffered because of an infringement of that person's intellectual property right by an infringer who knowingly, or with reasonable grounds to know, engaged in infringing activity.

2. The judicial authorities shall also have the authority to order the infringer to pay the right holder expenses, which may include appropriate attorney's fees. In appropriate cases, Members may authorize the judicial authorities to order recovery of profits and/or payment of pre-established damages even where the infringer did not knowingly, or with reasonable grounds to know, engage in infringing activity.

Article 46
Other Remedies

In order to create an effective deterrent to infringement, the judicial authorities shall have the authority to order that goods that they have found to be infringing be, without compensation of any sort, disposed of outside the channels of commerce in such a manner as to avoid any harm caused to the right holder, or, unless this would be contrary to existing constitutional requirements, destroyed. The judicial authorities shall also have the authority to order that materials and implements the predominant use of which has been in the creation of the infringing goods be, without compensation of any sort, disposed of outside the channels of commerce in such a manner as to minimize the risks of further infringements. In considering such requests, the need for proportionality between the seriousness of the infringement and the remedies ordered as well as the interests of third parties shall be taken into account. In regard to counterfeit trademark goods, the simple removal of the trademark unlawfully affixed shall not be sufficient, other than in exceptional cases, to permit release of the goods into the channels of commerce.

Article 47
Right of Information

Members may provide that the judicial authorities shall have the authority, unless this would be out of proportion to the seriousness of the infringement, to order the infringer to inform the right holder of the identity of third persons involved in the production and distribution of the infringing goods or services and of their channels of distribution.

Article 48
Indemnification of the Defendant

1. The judicial authorities shall have the authority to order a party at whose request measures were taken and who has abused enforcement procedures to provide to a party wrongfully enjoined or restrained adequate compensation for the injury suffered because of such abuse. The judicial authorities shall also have the authority to order the applicant to pay the defendant expenses, which may include appropriate attorney's fees.

2. In respect of the administration of any law pertaining to the protection or enforcement of intellectual property rights, Members shall only exempt both public authorities and officials from liability to appropriate remedial measures where actions are taken or intended in good faith in the course of the administration of that law.

Article 49
Administrative Procedures

To the extent that any civil remedy can be ordered as a result of administrative procedures on the merits of a case, such procedures shall conform to principles equivalent in substance to those set forth in this Section.

SECTION 3: PROVISIONAL MEASURES

Article 50

1. The judicial authorities shall have the authority to order prompt and effective provisional measures:

(a) to prevent an infringement of any intellectual property right from occurring, and in particular to prevent the entry into the channels of commerce in their jurisdiction of goods, including imported goods immediately after customs clearance;

(b) to preserve relevant evidence in regard to the alleged infringement.

2. The judicial authorities shall have the authority to adopt provisional measures *inaudita altera parte* where appropriate, in particular where any delay is likely to cause irreparable harm to the right holder, or where there is a demonstrable risk of evidence being destroyed.

3. The judicial authorities shall have the authority to require the applicant to provide any reasonably available evidence in order to satisfy themselves with a sufficient degree of certainty that the applicant is the right holder and that the applicant's right is being infringed or that such infringement is imminent, and to order the applicant to provide a security or equivalent assurance sufficient to protect the defendant and to prevent abuse.

4. Where provisional measures have been adopted *inaudita altera parte,* the parties affected shall be given notice, without delay after the execution of the measures at the latest. A review, including a right to be heard, shall take place upon request of the defendant with a view to deciding, within a reasonable period after the notification of the measures, whether these measures shall be modified, revoked or confirmed.

5. The applicant may be required to supply other information necessary for the identification of the goods concerned by the authority that will execute the provisional measures.

6. Without prejudice to paragraph 4, provisional measures taken on the basis of paragraphs 1 and 2 shall, upon request by the defendant, be revoked or otherwise cease to have effect, if proceedings leading to a decision on the merits of the case are not initiated within a reasonable period, to be determined by the judicial authority ordering the measures where a Member's law so permits or, in the absence of such a determination, not to exceed 20 working days or 31 calendar days, whichever is the longer.

7. Where the provisional measures are revoked or where they lapse due to any act or omission by the applicant, or where it is subsequently found that there has been no infringement or threat of infringement of an intellectual property right, the judicial authorities shall have the authority to order the applicant, upon request of the defendant, to provide the defendant appropriate compensation for any injury caused by these measures.

8. To the extent that any provisional measure can be ordered as a result of administrative procedures, such procedures shall conform to principles equivalent in substance to those set forth in this Section.

SECTION 4: SPECIAL REQUIREMENTS RELATED TO BORDER MEASURES[12]

Article 51
Suspension of Release by Customs Authorities

Members shall, in conformity with the provisions set out below, adopt procedures[13] to enable a right holder, who has valid grounds for suspecting that the importation of counterfeit trademark or pirated copyright goods[14] may take place, to lodge an application in writing with competent authorities,

[12] For the purpose of this Part, the term "right holder" includes federations and associations having legal standing to assert such rights.—*Eds.*

[13] It is understood that there shall be no obligation to apply such procedures to imports of goods put on the market in another country by or with the consent of the right holder, or to goods in transit.—*Eds.*

[14] For the purposes of this Agreement:

(a) "counterfeit trademark goods" shall mean any goods, including packaging, bearing without authorization a trademark which is identical to the trademark validly registered in respect of such

administrative or judicial, for the suspension by the customs authorities of the release into free circulation of such goods. Members may enable such an application to be made in respect of goods which involve other infringements of intellectual property rights, provided that the requirements of this Section are met. Members may also provide for corresponding procedures concerning the suspension by the customs authorities of the release of infringing goods destined for exportation from their territories.

Article 52
Application

Any right holder initiating the procedures under Article 51 shall be required to provide adequate evidence to satisfy the competent authorities that, under the laws of the country of importation, there is *prima facie* an infringement of the right holder's intellectual property right and to supply a sufficiently detailed description of the goods to make them readily recognizable by the customs authorities. The competent authorities shall inform the applicant within a reasonable period whether they have accepted the application and, where determined by the competent authorities, the period for which the customs authorities will take action.

Article 53
Security or Equivalent Assurance

1. The competent authorities shall have the authority to require an applicant to provide a security or equivalent assurance sufficient to protect the defendant and the competent authorities and to prevent abuse. Such security or equivalent assurance shall not unreasonably deter recourse to these procedures.

2. Where pursuant to an application under this Section the release of goods involving industrial designs, patents, layout-designs or undisclosed information into free circulation has been suspended by customs authorities on the basis of a decision other than by a judicial or other independent authority, and the period provided for in Article 55 has expired without the granting of provisional relief by the duly empowered authority, and provided that all other conditions for importation have been complied with, the owner, importer, or consignee of such goods shall be entitled to their release on the posting of a security in an amount sufficient to protect the right holder for any infringement. Payment of such security shall not prejudice any other remedy available

---

goods, or which cannot be distinguished in its essential aspects from such a trademark, and which thereby infringes the rights of the owner of the trademark in question under the law of the country of importation;

(b) "pirated copyright goods" shall mean any goods which are copies made without the consent of the right holder or person duly authorized by the right holder in the country of production and which are made directly or indirectly from an article where the making of that copy would have constituted an infringement of a copyright or a related right under the law of the country of importation.—*Eds.*

to the right holder, it being understood that the security shall be released if the right holder fails to pursue the right of action within a reasonable period of time.

Article 54
Notice of Suspension

The importer and the applicant shall be promptly notified of the suspension of the release of goods according to Article 51.

Article 55
Duration of Suspension

If, within a period not exceeding 10 working days after the applicant has been served notice of the suspension, the customs authorities have not been informed that proceedings leading to a decision on the merits of the case have been initiated by a party other than the defendant, or that the duly empowered authority has taken provisional measures prolonging the suspension of the release of the goods, the goods shall be released, provided that all other conditions for importation or exportation have been complied with; in appropriate cases, this time-limit may be extended by another 10 working days. If proceedings leading to a decision on the merits of the case have been initiated, a review, including a right to be heard, shall take place upon request of the defendant with a view to deciding, within a reasonable period, whether these measures shall be modified, revoked or confirmed. Notwithstanding the above, where the suspension of the release of goods is carried out or continued in accordance with a provisional judicial measure, the provisions of paragraph 6 of Article 50 shall apply.

Article 56
Indemnification of the Importer and of the Owner of the Goods

Relevant authorities shall have the authority to order the applicant to pay the importer, the consignee and the owner of the goods appropriate compensation for any injury caused to them through the wrongful detention of goods or through the detention of goods released pursuant to Article 55.

Article 57
Right of Inspection and Information

Without prejudice to the protection of confidential information, Members shall provide the competent authorities the authority to give the right holder sufficient opportunity to have any goods detained by the customs authorities inspected in order to substantiate the right holder's claims. The competent authorities shall also have authority to give the importer an equivalent opportunity to have any such goods inspected. Where a positive determination has been made on the merits of a case, Members may provide the competent authorities the authority to inform the right holder of the names and addresses of the consignor, the importer and the consignee and of the quantity of the goods in question.

Article 58
Ex Officio Action

Where Members require competent authorities to act upon their own initiative and to suspend the release of goods in respect of which they have acquired *prima facie* evidence that an intellectual property right is being infringed:

(a) the competent authorities may at any time seek from the right holder any information that may assist them to exercise these powers;

(b) the importer and the right holder shall be promptly notified of the suspension. Where the importer has lodged an appeal against the suspension with the competent authorities, the suspension shall be subject to the conditions, *mutatis mutandis,* set out at Article 55;

(c) Members shall only exempt both public authorities and officials from liability to appropriate remedial measures where actions are taken or intended in good faith.

Article 59
Remedies

Without prejudice to other rights of action open to the right holder and subject to the right of the defendant to seek review by a judicial authority, competent authorities shall have the authority to order the destruction or disposal of infringing goods in accordance with the principles set out in Article 46. In regard to counterfeit trademark goods, the authorities shall not allow the re-exportation of the infringing goods in an unaltered state or subject them to a different customs procedure, other than in exceptional circumstances.

Article 60
De Minimis Imports

Members may exclude from the application of the above provisions small quantities of goods of a non-commercial nature contained in travellers' personal luggage or sent in small consignments.

SECTION 5: CRIMINAL PROCEDURES

Article 61

Members shall provide for criminal procedures and penalties to be applied at least in cases of wilful trademark counterfeiting or copyright piracy on a commercial scale. Remedies available shall include imprisonment and/or monetary fines sufficient to provide a deterrent, consistently with the level of penalties applied for crimes of a corresponding gravity. In appropriate cases, remedies available shall also include the seizure, forfeiture and destruction of the infringing goods and of any materials and implements the predominant use of which has been in the commission of the offence. Members may provide for criminal procedures and penalties to be applied in other cases of infringement of intellectual property rights, in particular where they are committed wilfully and on a commercial scale.

PART IV
ACQUISITION AND MAINTENANCE OF INTELLECTUAL PROPERTY RIGHTS AND RELATED INTER-PARTES PROCEDURES

Article 62

1. Members may require, as a condition of the acquisition or maintenance of the intellectual property rights provided for under Sections 2 through 6 of Part II, compliance with reasonable procedures and formalities. Such procedures and formalities shall be consistent with the provisions of this Agreement.

2. Where the acquisition of an intellectual property right is subject to the right being granted or registered, Members shall ensure that the procedures for grant or registration, subject to compliance with the substantive conditions for acquisition of the right, permit the granting or registration of the right within a reasonable period of time so as to avoid unwarranted curtailment of the period of protection.

3. Article 4 of the Paris Convention (1967) shall apply *mutatis mutandis* to service marks.

4. Procedures concerning the acquisition or maintenance of intellectual property rights and, where a Member's law provides for such procedures, administrative revocation and *inter partes* procedures such as opposition, revocation and cancellation, shall be governed by the general principles set out in paragraphs 2 and 3 of Article 41.

5. Final administrative decisions in any of the procedures referred to under paragraph 4 shall be subject to review by a judicial or quasi-judicial authority. However, there shall be no obligation to provide an opportunity for such review of decisions in cases of unsuccessful opposition or administrative revocation, provided that the grounds for such procedures can be the subject of invalidation procedures.

PART V
DISPUTE PREVENTION AND SETTLEMENT

Article 63
Transparency

1. Laws and regulations, and final judicial decisions and administrative rulings of general application, made effective by a Member pertaining to the subject matter of this Agreement (the availability, scope, acquisition,

enforcement and prevention of the abuse of intellectual property rights) shall be published, or where such publication is not practicable made publicly available, in a national language, in such a manner as to enable governments and right holders to become acquainted with them. Agreements concerning the subject matter of this Agreement which are in force between the government or a governmental agency of a Member and the government or a governmental agency of another Member shall also be published.

2. Members shall notify the laws and regulations referred to in paragraph 1 to the Council for TRIPS in order to assist that Council in its review of the operation of this Agreement. The Council shall attempt to minimize the burden on Members in carrying out this obligation and may decide to waive the obligation to notify such laws and regulations directly to the Council if consultations with WIPO on the establishment of a common register containing these laws and regulations are successful. The Council shall also consider in this connection any action required regarding notifications pursuant to the obligations under this Agreement stemming from the provisions of Article 6ter of the Paris Convention (1967).

3. Each Member shall be prepared to supply, in response to a written request from another Member, information of the sort referred to in paragraph 1. A Member, having reason to believe that a specific judicial decision or administrative ruling or bilateral agreement in the area of intellectual property rights affects its rights under this Agreement, may also request in writing to be given access to or be informed in sufficient detail of such specific judicial decisions or administrative rulings or bilateral agreements.

4. Nothing in paragraphs 1, 2 and 3 shall require Members to disclose confidential information which would impede law enforcement or otherwise be contrary to the public interest or would prejudice the legitimate commercial interests of particular enterprises, public or private.

Article 64
Dispute Settlement

1. The provisions of Articles XXII and XXIII of GATT 1994 as elaborated and applied by the Dispute Settlement Understanding shall apply to consultations and the settlement of disputes under this Agreement except as otherwise specifically provided herein.

2. Subparagraphs 1(b) and 1(c) of Article XXIII of GATT 1994 shall not apply to the settlement of disputes under this Agreement for a period of five years from the date of entry into force of the WTO Agreement.

3. During the time period referred to in paragraph 2, the Council for TRIPS shall examine the scope and modalities for complaints of the type provided for under subparagraphs 1(b) and 1(c) of Article XXIII of GATT 1994 made pursuant to this Agreement, and submit its recommendations to the Ministerial Conference for approval. Any decision of the Ministerial Conference to approve such recommendations or to extend the period in paragraph 2 shall

be made only by consensus, and approved recommendations shall be effective for all Members without further formal acceptance process.

PART VI
TRANSITIONAL ARRANGEMENTS

Article 65
Transitional Arrangements

1. Subject to the provisions of paragraphs 2, 3 and 4, no Member shall be obliged to apply the provisions of this Agreement before the expiry of a general period of one year following the date of entry into force of the WTO Agreement.

2. A developing country Member is entitled to delay for a further period of four years the date of application, as defined in paragraph 1, of the provisions of this Agreement other than Articles 3, 4 and 5.

3. Any other Member which is in the process of transformation from a centrally-planned into a market, free-enterprise economy and which is undertaking structural reform of its intellectual property system and facing special problems in the preparation and implementation of intellectual property laws and regulations, may also benefit from a period of delay as foreseen in paragraph 2.

4. To the extent that a developing country Member is obliged by this Agreement to extend product patent protection to areas of technology not so protectable in its territory on the general date of application of this Agreement for that Member, as defined in paragraph 2, it may delay the application of the provisions on product patents of Section 5 of Part II to such areas of technology for an additional period of five years.

5. A Member availing itself of a transitional period under paragraphs 1, 2, 3 or 4 shall ensure that any changes in its laws, regulations and practice made during that period do not result in a lesser degree of consistency with the provisions of this Agreement.

Article 66
Least-Developed Country Members

1. In view of the special needs and requirements of least-developed country Members, their economic, financial and administrative constraints, and their need for flexibility to create a viable technological base, such Members shall not be required to apply the provisions of this Agreement, other than Articles 3, 4 and 5, for a period of 10 years from the date of application as defined under paragraph 1 of Article 65. The Council for TRIPS shall, upon duly motivated request by a least-developed country Member, accord extensions of this period.

2. Developed country Members shall provide incentives to enterprises and institutions in their territories for the purpose of promoting and encouraging technology transfer to least-developed country Members in order to enable them to create a sound and viable technological base.

Article 67
Technical Cooperation

In order to facilitate the implementation of this Agreement, developed country Members shall provide, on request and on mutually agreed terms and conditions, technical and financial cooperation in favour of developing and least-developed country Members. Such cooperation shall include assistance in the preparation of laws and regulations on the protection and enforcement of intellectual property rights as well as on the prevention of their abuse, and shall include support regarding the establishment or reinforcement of domestic offices and agencies relevant to these matters, including the training of personnel.

PART VII
INSTITUTIONAL ARRANGEMENTS; FINAL PROVISIONS

Article 68
Council for Trade-Related Aspects of Intellectual Property Rights

The Council for TRIPS shall monitor the operation of this Agreement and, in particular, Members' compliance with their obligations hereunder, and shall afford Members the opportunity of consulting on matters relating to the trade-related aspects of intellectual property rights. It shall carry out such other responsibilities as assigned to it by the Members, and it shall, in particular, provide any assistance requested by them in the context of dispute settlement procedures. In carrying out its functions, the Council for TRIPS may consult with and seek information from any source it deems appropriate. In consultation with WIPO, the Council shall seek to establish, within one year of its first meeting, appropriate arrangements for cooperation with bodies of that Organization.

Article 69
International Cooperation

Members agree to cooperate with each other with a view to eliminating international trade in goods infringing intellectual property rights. For this purpose, they shall establish and notify contact points in their administrations and be ready to exchange information on trade in infringing goods. They shall, in particular, promote the exchange of information and cooperation between customs authorities with regard to trade in counterfeit trademark goods and pirated copyright goods.

Article 70
Protection of Existing Subject Matter

1. This Agreement does not give rise to obligations in respect of acts which occurred before the date of application of the Agreement for the Member in question.

2. Except as otherwise provided for in this Agreement, this Agreement gives rise to obligations in respect of all subject matter existing at the date of

application of this Agreement for the Member in question, and which is protected in that Member on the said date, or which meets or comes subsequently to meet the criteria for protection under the terms of this Agreement. In respect of this paragraph and paragraphs 3 and 4, copyright obligations with respect to existing works shall be solely determined under Article 18 of the Berne Convention (1971), and obligations with respect to the rights of producers of phonograms and performers in existing phonograms shall be determined solely under Article 18 of the Berne Convention (1971) as made applicable under paragraph 6 of Article 14 of this Agreement.

3. There shall be no obligation to restore protection to subject matter which on the date of application of this Agreement for the Member in question has fallen into the public domain.

4. In respect of any acts in respect of specific objects embodying protected subject matter which become infringing under the terms of legislation in conformity with this Agreement, and which were commenced, or in respect of which a significant investment was made, before the date of acceptance of the WTO Agreement by that Member, any Member may provide for a limitation of the remedies available to the right holder as to the continued performance of such acts after the date of application of this Agreement for that Member. In such cases the Member shall, however, at least provide for the payment of equitable remuneration.

5. A Member is not obliged to apply the provisions of Article 11 and of paragraph 4 of Article 14 with respect to originals or copies purchased prior to the date of application of this Agreement for that Member.

6. Members shall not be required to apply Article 31, or the requirement in paragraph 1 of Article 27 that patent rights shall be enjoyable without discrimination as to the field of technology, to use without the authorization of the right holder where authorization for such use was granted by the government before the date this Agreement became known.

7. In the case of intellectual property rights for which protection is conditional upon registration, applications for protection which are pending on the date of application of this Agreement for the Member in question shall be permitted to be amended to claim any enhanced protection provided under the provisions of this Agreement. Such amendments shall not include new matter.

8. Where a Member does not make available as of the date of entry into force of the WTO Agreement patent protection for pharmaceutical and agricultural chemical products commensurate with its obligations under Article 27, that Member shall:

(a) notwithstanding the provisions of Part VI, provide as from the date of entry into force of the WTO Agreement a means by which applications for patents for such inventions can be filed;

(b) apply to these applications, as of the date of application of this Agreement, the criteria for patentability as laid down in this Agreement as if those criteria were being applied on the date of filing in that Member or, where priority is available and claimed, the priority date of the application; and

(c) provide patent protection in accordance with this Agreement as from the grant of the patent and for the remainder of the patent term, counted from the filing date in accordance with Article 33 of this Agreement, for those of these applications that meet the criteria for protection referred to in subparagraph (b).

9. Where a product is the subject of a patent application in a Member in accordance with paragraph 8(a), exclusive marketing rights shall be granted, notwithstanding the provisions of Part VI, for a period of five years after obtaining marketing approval in that Member or until a product patent is granted or rejected in that Member, whichever period is shorter, provided that, subsequent to the entry into force of the WTO Agreement, a patent application has been filed and a patent granted for that product in another Member and marketing approval obtained in such other Member.

Article 71
Review and Amendment

1. The Council for TRIPS shall review the implementation of this Agreement after the expiration of the transitional period referred to in paragraph 2 of Article 65. The Council shall, having regard to the experience gained in its implementation, review it two years after that date, and at identical intervals thereafter. The Council may also undertake reviews in the light of any relevant new developments which might warrant modification or amendment of this Agreement.

2. Amendments merely serving the purpose of adjusting to higher levels of protection of intellectual property rights achieved, and in force, in other multilateral agreements and accepted under those agreements by all Members of the WTO may be referred to the Ministerial Conference for action in accordance with paragraph 6 of Article X of the WTO Agreement on the basis of a consensus proposal from the Council for TRIPS.

Article 72
Reservations

Reservations may not be entered in respect of any of the provisions of this Agreement without the consent of the other Members.

Article 73
Security Exceptions

Nothing in this Agreement shall be construed:

(a) to require a Member to furnish any information the disclosure of which it considers contrary to its essential security interests; or

(b) to prevent a Member from taking any action which it considers necessary for the protection of its essential security interests:

(i) relating to fissionable materials or the materials from which they are derived;

(ii) relating to the traffic in arms, ammunition and implements of war and to such traffic in other goods and materials as is carried on directly or indirectly for the purpose of supplying a military establishment;

(iii) taken in time of war or other emergency in international relations; or

(c) to prevent a Member from taking any action in pursuance of its obligations under the United Nations Charter for the maintenance of international peace and security.

THE 1996 W.I.P.O. TREATIES

Summary Overview of the 1996 Treaties[1]

As the casebook explains, from its inception in 1886 to the Paris Act of 1971, the Berne Convention for the Protection of Literary and Artistic Works was revised six times, with each revision the result of a consensus on new proposals arrived at in the course of an international diplomatic conference attended by all the member states of the Berne Union. By the early 1990s, however, it was clear that the stakes in international copyright had become so great, and the differences between Berne Union members on some issues so considerable, that another general revision of the treaty text was unlikely. At about the same time, however, the injection of copyright (and other intellectual property) issues into the agenda of the Uruguay Round of the General Agreement on Tariffs and Trade, which eventually would produce the GATT/ TRIPS agreement, had begun to pose a challenge to position of Berne as the dominant international agreement relating to literary and artistic property — and, even, more specifically, to the position of W.I.P.O. as the preeminent international organization in the field.

W.I.P.O.'s response was to announce a program to update the Berne Convention by developing one or more new agreements, or "protocols," which would supplement but not displace the 1971 Act. Such agreements, and the enhanced international norms they would contain, would be binding only on those Berne Union countries which signed and ratified them. By the same token, however, they could be concluded by something less than the whole membership of the Union — thus offering a chance to avoid the likely stalemate which would result from any effort to achieve a general revision of the treaty itself.

In furtherance of this scheme, the International Bureau of W.I.P.O. convened a series of preparatory meetings, beginning in November, 1991, to discuss proposals to upgrade the kind and quality of protection available under Berne. Issues as to which there was a perceived lack of international uniformity, and which were discussed as possible topics of new treaty language at the early meetings of what was called the "Committee of Experts on a Possible Protocol to the Berne Convention," included: protection of computer programs; database protection; the position of artificial intelligence and computer-generated works; the scope of the right of reproduction (including personal and library photocopying); the future of compulsory licensing; the rights of distribution, display, rental, public lending, and importation; broadcasting rights; the term of protection for photographic works; the proper application of the principle of national treatment; and copyright enforcement.

In addition, the delegations representing various governments at these meetings in Geneva agreed that protection for sound recordings was a likely topic for new treaty language, given the failures of the Rome Convention and the Geneva Phonogram Convention to attract sufficient numbers of adherents. But they also agreed that such language would be better contained in a new treaty separate from any "Berne Protocol," rather than as part of it.

---

[1] By Peter Jaszi. Copyright 1997. Used with permission.

Thereafter, the "Committee of Experts" became the "Committees of Experts" — one to prepare for the "Protocol" and another for the so-called "New Instrument for the Protection of the Producers and Performers of Phonograms" — though their membership was substantially overlapping and their meetings generally occurred back-to-back.

As the deliberations of the Committees of Experts proceeded from year to year, many of these issues proved too controversial to be considered ripe for inclusion in a new treaty or treaties, and thus dropped out of the agenda. Moreover, since many of topics that remained were covered in the GATT/TRIPS agreement concluded in April 1994, questions arose as to the continued relevance of the W.I.P.O. exercise. At the first post-TRIPS meeting of the Committees of Experts, in December 1994, the head of the U.S. delegation, Commissioner Bruce Lehman of the Patent and Trademark Office, offered an answer to those questions: The Committees of Experts, he urged, should shift their work program away from traditional copyright issues to those implicated by the emerging "global information infrastructure" — issues which, incidentally, had not been (at least for the most part) addressed in TRIPS!

On September 5, 1995, a government task force chaired by Commissioner Lehman released its "White Paper" on copyright and the networked digital environment simultaneously in Washington and at a meeting of the W.I.P.O. Committees of Experts in Geneva. The U.S. soon followed with proposals for specific language to implement what came to be called the "digital agenda" in the "Berne Protocol" and the "New Instrument" — language closely paralleling the "White Paper"'s draft for U.S. domestic legislation and variants on those proposals proffered by the European Union.

In February 1996, the dates of the Diplomatic Conference to consider the work product of the Committees of Experts were set for December of that year. In May, at the final meeting of the Committees of Experts, the U.S. and Europe rounded out the "digital agenda" by submitting competing versions of yet another new treaty, designed to require adhering countries to enact domestic legislation to provide sui generis protection for non-original databases (including but not limited to those in digital formats). Back in March, the European Parliament and the Council of the European Union had adopted a final "Directive on the Legal Protection of Databases" (96/9/EC), requiring countries of the Union to recognize a new right to protection to investment of time, money and effort by the maker of a database, irrespective of whether the database is in itself innovative, if there has been a "substantial investment," in qualitative or quantitative terms, in obtaining, verifying or presenting its contents. And legislation with the same general thrust, although proposing a 25-year term of protection rather than the 15 years provided for in the Directive, also had been introduced in the U.S. Congress. These initiatives provided the basis for the sui generis proposals in Geneva.

The "Basic Proposals" for three new intellectual property agreements were released in late August 1996 (and, like the other W.I.P.O. documents referred to in this note, can be found at http://www.wipo.org). These documents, synthesized by the chairperson of the Committees of Experts from the treaty language on various issues submitted by various government delegations and designed to be the basis for discussion at the December Diplomatic Conference, dealt with both traditional copyright issues and those which constituted the "digital agenda." They included: creation of a strong new "right of communication to the public" (the functional equivalent of the digital "transmission right" which had been proposed in the "White Paper"), extension (or, in the view of some, a clarification) of the reproduction right to cover all temporary and ephemeral digital reproductions (such as those in RAM and cache), restriction of the applicability of "limitations and exceptions" to copyright (such as "fair use") in cyberspace; prohibitions against the manufacture and sale of technologies (or the provision of services) which can be employed to circumvent technological protection measures employed to safeguard copyrighted works in the network environment; and further prohibitions against unauthorized tampering with digital records of so-called "copyright management information" — along with (in the third of the "Basic Proposals") a scheme of sui generis database protection.

At the Conference itself, these issues proved the most controversial. Some governments, particularly those of developing countries, already were skeptical about the merits of the "digital agenda" prior to arrival in Geneva. In addition, however, a wide range of groups and organizations (from telecommunications companies and electronics manufacturers to libraries and cultural associations) were on hand there to lobby the national delegations against adoption of these components of the "Basic Proposals" — and to demand that the Conference take up other related issues, such as the limitation of the liability of on-line Internet service providers (OSP/ISPs) for acts of infringement actually committed by the customers or subscribers to whom they provide network access. (An extremely useful summary of the events of the Diplomatic Conference, "Big Media Beaten Back" by Professor Pamela Samuelson can be found in the March 1997 issue of Wired magazine, at p. 61. In the same issue, there is a related article, "Africa 1, Hollywood 0," by John Browning.)

On December 20, 1996, when the Conference concluded, delegates had agreed on the texts of two new treaties: the "W.I.P.O. Copyright Treaty" (formerly known as the "Berne Protocol") and the "W.I.P.O. Performances and Phonograms Treaty" (the one-time "New Instrument"). No database treaty emerged from the Conference, at least in part because of the insistence of the delegates of developing countries that the development of international norms for the sui generis protection of non-original compilations should be closely linked to an issue that had not been on the agenda of the Conference — the development of a new international legal regime for the protection of folkloric works and other cultural property. In all likelihood, it will now be several years, at the very least, before W.I.P.O. puts forward a new proposal for a database treaty. Otherwise, the two treaties which did emerge were shorn of their most controversial provisions.

Where traditional copyright issues are concerned, the new Copyright Treaty provides for the protection of computer programs as literary works, and for copyright in original (as distinct from non-original) compilations of data. It obligates ratifying states to recognize a general right of distribution and a rental right limited to computer programs, movies and "works embodied in phonograms," and is itself subject to a number of significant exceptions. It also bars ratifying states from taking advantage of Berne Convention provisions which, standing alone, would permit them to allow lesser terms of protection to photographs than to other copyrighted works.

By contrast, the Performances and Phonograms Treaty breaks some significant new ground. Though to an extent it restates the obligations to provide significant protection for sound recordings, whether by means of copyright or by means of neighboring rights, already contained in the GATT/TRIPS agreement (which are derivative, in turn, of the Rome Convention), it goes further. In addition to a right to control reproduction and a limited commercial rental right, it provides record producers with a distribution right, and a right of remuneration in connection with broadcasting and communication to the public (the latter being qualified so as to permit countries such as the United States to continue to afford remuneration only in connection with digital broadcasts of sound recordings). Performers also fare better under the new treaty than under GATT/TRIPS: not only are they afforded more extensive economic rights, but (significantly) the text provides explicitly for the basic moral rights of the performer "as regards ... live aural performances fixed in phonograms."

With respect to the digital agenda, the relevant provisions of the two treaties approved in December 1996 are substantially identical. Their preambles recognize explicitly the need to "maintain a balance between" the interests of right holders and "the larger public interest, particularly education, research, and access to information" — novel language that directly reflects the lobbying efforts of various "user" groups before and during the Diplomatic Conference. In their final forms, the treaty texts make no mention of the status of temporary and ephemeral reproduction. Among the obligations the final acts of the treaties do entail is a duty to recognize a right of "communication to the public," along with a limited mandate for the protection of "copyright management information" against tampering, and another relating to "anti-circumvention" technology. The last, however, is far less stringent than the version originally proposed. In effect, it requires ratifying signatories to do no more than adopt legislation specifically addressing the problem of "black boxes" — devices or systems specifically designed to break technological security systems — as such. And the clarifying "agreed statements" that accompany the text address some of the most difficult issues not resolved by the text, in terms that can only be called moderate and constructive. (These statements are important because, under Article 31 of the Vienna Convention on the Law of Treaties, such a consensus document has special status as a guide to interpretation of otherwise ambiguous treaty provisions.)

On the issue of the applicability of "fair use" and other limitations or exemptions to the digital networked environment, for example, the relevant "agreed statements" provide that:

> It is understood that the provision of [these treaties] permit Contracting Parties to carry forward and appropriately extend into the digital

environment limitations and exceptions in their national laws which have been considered acceptable under the Berne Convention. Similarly, these provisions should be understood to permit Contracting Parties to devise new exceptions and limitations that are appropriate in the digital network environment.

Likewise, the treaties also are accompanied by helpful "agreed statements" clarifying the applicability of the new "right of communication to the public" in connection with OSP/ISP liability:

> It is understood that the mere provision of physical facilities for enabling or making a communication does not in itself amount to communication within the meaning of [these treaties] or the Berne Convention.

In addition, the Conference also produced an "agreed statement" relating to the issue of temporary and ephemeral reproduction, the significance of which is somewhat clouded by its particular history. In the final hours of the Conference, after debates during which a proposed sentence that would explicitly have identified temporary ephemeral reproductions as copyright-relevant "copies" was deleted, the following text emerged:

> The reproduction right, as set out in … the Berne Convention, and the exceptions thereto, fully apply in the digital environment, in particular to the use of works in digital form. It is understood that the storage of a protected work in digital form in an electronic medium constitutes a reproduction within the meaning of the Berne Convention.

The first sentence represents an "agreed statement" in the classic sense in which that term is understood in international law, but (by contrast) the second was adopted only by a majority vote and over substantial objections. In light of this, efforts to portray it as a victory for the "digital agenda," snatched from the jaws of defeat, are open to question. Not only is the authority of the sentence doubtful in light of its procedural history, but there is a real question as to whether the reference to "storage" (a term with a specific, and limited, meaning in international copyright discourse) can fairly be understood to reach anything more than the making of permanent, stable, digital records.

In the United States, consideration of the treaties necessarily involved two formally independent (although functionally linked) Congressional processes: ratification by the Senate, and enactment of implementing legislation by the House and Senate together. These processes have been duly accomplished. See Title I of the Digital Millennium Copyright Act, Pub. L. No. 105-394, 112 Stat. 2860 (Oct. 28, 1998), for the final form of the implementing legislation signed into law by President Clinton.

Internationally, both the Copyright Treaty and the Performances and Phonograms Treaty entered into force in 2002 upon deposit with W.I.P.O.'s Director General of "instruments of ratification or accession" by 30 members states. For discussion of the issues posed by the treaties, see especially §§ 1.04, 7.01 and 10.05 in the casebook.

THE W.I.P.O. COPYRIGHT TREATY (CRNR/DC/94)

Adopted by the Diplomatic Conference on December 20, 1996

Contents

Preamble

The Contracting Parties,

Desiring to develop and maintain the protection of the rights of authors in their literary and artistic works in a manner as effective and uniform as possible,

Recognizing the need to introduce new international rules and clarify the interpretation of certain existing rules in order to provide adequate solutions to the questions raised by new economic, social, cultural and technological developments,

Recognizing the profound impact of the development and convergence of information and communication technologies on the creation and use of literary and artistic works,

Emphasizing the outstanding significance of copyright protection as an incentive for literary and artistic creation,

Recognizing the need to maintain a balance between the rights of authors and the larger public interest, particularly education, research and access to information, as reflected in the Berne Convention,

Have agreed as follows:

Article 1
Relation to the Berne Convention

(1) This Treaty is a special agreement within the meaning of Article 20 of the Berne Convention for the Protection of Literary and Artistic Works, as regards Contracting Parties that are countries of the Union established by that Convention. This Treaty shall not have any connection with treaties other than the Berne Convention, nor shall it prejudice any rights and obligations under any other treaties.

(2) Nothing in this Treaty shall derogate from existing obligations that Contracting Parties have to each other under the Berne Convention for the Protection of Literary and Artistic Works.

(3) Hereinafter, "Berne Convention" shall refer to the Paris Act of July 24, 1971 of the Berne Convention for the Protection of Literary and Artistic Works.

(4) Contracting Parties shall comply with Articles 1 to 21 and the Appendix of the Berne Convention.

Article 2
Scope of Copyright Protection

Copyright protection extends to expressions and not to ideas, procedures, methods of operation or mathematical concepts as such.

Article 3
Application of Articles 2 to 6 of the Berne Convention

Contracting Parties shall apply mutatis mutandis the provisions of Articles 2 to 6 of the Berne Convention in respect of the protection provided for in this Treaty.

Article 4
Computer Programs

Computer programs are protected as literary works within the meaning of Article 2 of the Berne Convention. Such protection applies to computer programs, whatever may be the mode or form of their expression.

Article 5
Compilations of Data (Databases)

Compilations of data or other material, in any form, which by reason of the selection or arrangement of their contents constitute intellectual creations, are protected as such. This protection does not extend to the data or the material itself and is without prejudice to any copyright subsisting in the data or material contained in the compilation.

Article 6
Right of Distribution

(1) Authors of literary and artistic works shall enjoy the exclusive right of authorizing the making available to the public of the original and copies of their works through sale or other transfer of ownership.

(2) Nothing in this Treaty shall affect the freedom of Contracting Parties to determine the conditions, if any, under which the exhaustion of the right in paragraph (1) applies after the first sale or other transfer of ownership of the original or a copy of the work with the authorization of the author.

Article 7
Right of Rental

(1) Authors of:

(i) computer programs;

(ii) cinematographic works; and

(iii) works embodied in phonograms as determined in the national law of Contracting Parties, shall enjoy the exclusive right of authorizing commercial rental to the public of the originals or copies of their works.

(2) Paragraph (1) shall not apply:

(i) in the case of computer programs where the program itself is not the essential object of the rental; and

(ii) in the case of cinematographic works, unless such commercial rental has led to widespread copying of such works materially impairing the exclusive right of reproduction.

(3) Notwithstanding the provisions of paragraph (1), a Contracting Party that, on April 15, 1994, had and continues to have in force a system of equitable remuneration of authors for the rental of copies of their works embodied in phonograms may maintain that system provided that the commercial rental of works embodied in phonograms is not giving rise to the material impairment of the exclusive rights of reproduction of authors.

Article 8
Right of Communication to the Public

Without prejudice to the provisions of Articles 11(1)(ii), 11bis(1)(i) and (ii), 11ter(1)(ii), 14(1)(ii) and 14bis(1) of the Berne Convention, authors of literary and artistic works shall enjoy the exclusive right of authorizing any communication to the public of their works, by wire or wireless means, including the making available to the public of their works in such a way that members of the public may access these works from a place and at a time individually chosen by them.

Article 9
Duration of the Protection of Photographic Works

In respect of photographic works, the Contracting Parties shall not apply the provisions of Article 7(4) of the Berne Convention.

Article 10
Limitations and Exceptions

(1) Contracting Parties may, in their national legislation, provide for limitations of or exceptions to the rights granted to authors of literary and artistic works under this Treaty in certain special cases that do not conflict with a normal exploitation of the work and do not unreasonably prejudice the legitimate interests of the author.

(2) Contracting Parties shall, when applying the Berne Convention, confine any limitations of or exceptions to rights provided for therein to certain special cases that do not conflict with a normal exploitation of the work and do not unreasonably prejudice the legitimate interests of the author.

Article 11
Obligations concerning Technological Measures

Contracting Parties shall provide adequate legal protection and effective legal remedies against the circumvention of effective technological measures that are used by authors in connection with the exercise of their rights under this Treaty or the Berne Convention and that restrict acts, in respect of their works, which are not authorized by the authors concerned or permitted by law.

Article 12
Obligations concerning Rights Management Information

(1) Contracting Parties shall provide adequate and effective legal remedies against any person knowingly performing any of the following acts knowing or, with respect to civil remedies having reasonable grounds to know, that it will induce, enable, facilitate or conceal an infringement of any right covered by this Treaty or the Berne Convention:

(i) to remove or alter any electronic rights management information without authority;

(ii) to distribute, import for distribution, broadcast or communicate to the public, without authority, works or copies of works knowing that electronic rights management information has been removed or altered without authority.

(2) As used in this Article, "rights management information" means information which identifies the work, the author of the work, the owner of any

right in the work, or information about the terms and conditions of use of the work, and any numbers or codes that represent such information, when any of these items of information is attached to a copy of a work or appears in connection with the communication of a work to the public.

Article 13
Application in Time

Contracting Parties shall apply the provisions of Article 18 of the Berne Convention to all protection provided for in this Treaty.

Article 14
Provisions on Enforcement of Rights

(1) Contracting Parties undertake to adopt, in accordance with their legal systems, the measures necessary to ensure the application of this Treaty.

(2) Contracting Parties shall ensure that enforcement procedures are available under their law so as to permit effective action against any act of infringement of rights covered by this Treaty, including expeditious remedies to prevent infringements and remedies which constitute a deterrent to further infringements.

Article 15
Assembly

(1) (a) The Contracting Parties shall have an Assembly.

(b) Each Contracting Party shall be represented by one delegate who may be assisted by alternate delegates, advisors and experts.

(c) The expenses of each delegation shall be borne by the Contracting Party that has appointed the delegation. The Assembly may ask the World Intellectual Property Organization (hereinafter referred to as "WIPO") to grant financial assistance to facilitate the participation of delegations of Contracting Parties that are regarded as developing countries in conformity with the established practice of the General Assembly of the United Nations or that are countries in transition to a market economy.

(2) (a) The Assembly shall deal with matters concerning the maintenance and development of this Treaty and the application and operation of this Treaty.

(b) The Assembly shall perform the function allocated to it under Article 17(2) in respect of the admission of certain intergovernmental organizations to become party to this Treaty.

(c) The Assembly shall decide the convocation of any diplomatic conference for the revision of this Treaty and give the necessary instructions to the Director General of WIPO for the preparation of such diplomatic conference.

(3) (a) Each Contracting Party that is a State shall have one vote and shall vote only in its own name.

(b) Any Contracting Party that is an intergovernmental organization may participate in the vote, in place of its Member States, with a number of votes equal to the number of its Member States which are party to this Treaty. No such intergovernmental organization shall participate in the vote if any one of its Member States exercises its right to vote and vice versa.

(4) The Assembly shall meet in ordinary session once every two years upon convocation by the Director General of WIPO.

(5) The Assembly shall establish its own rules of procedure, including the convocation of extraordinary sessions, the requirements of a quorum and, subject to the provisions of this Treaty, the required majority for various kinds of decisions.

Article 16
International Bureau

The International Bureau of WIPO shall perform the administrative tasks concerning the Treaty.

Article 17
Eligibility for Becoming Party to the Treaty

(1) Any Member State of WIPO may become party to this Treaty.

(2) The Assembly may decide to admit any intergovernmental organization to become party to this Treaty which declares that it is competent in respect of, and has its own legislation binding on all its Member States on, matters covered by this Treaty and that it has been duly authorized, in accordance with its internal procedures, to become party to this Treaty.

(3) The European Community, having made the declaration referred to in the preceding paragraph in the Diplomatic Conference that has adopted this Treaty, may become party to this Treaty.

Article 18
Rights and Obligations under the Treaty

Subject to any specific provisions to the contrary in this Treaty, each Contracting Party shall enjoy all of the rights and assume all of the obligations under this Treaty.

Article 19
Signature of the Treaty

This Treaty shall be open for signature until December 31, 1997, by any Member State of WIPO and by the European Community.

Article 20
Entry into Force of the Treaty

This Treaty shall enter into force three months after 30 instruments of ratification or accession by States have been deposited with the Director General of WIPO.

Article 21
Effective Date of Becoming Party to the Treaty

This Treaty shall bind

(i) the 30 States referred to in Article 20, from the date on which this Treaty has entered into force;

(ii) each other State from the expiration of three months from the date on which the State has deposited its instrument with the Director General of WIPO;

(iii) the European Community, from the expiration of three months after the deposit of its instrument of ratification or accession if such instrument has been deposited after the entry into force of this Treaty according to Article 20, or, three months after the entry into force of this Treaty if such instrument has been deposited before the entry into force of this Treaty;

(iv) any other intergovernmental organization that is admitted to become party to this Treaty, from the expiration of three months after the deposit of its instrument of accession.

Article 22
No Reservation to the Treaty

No reservation to this Treaty shall be admitted.

Article 23
Denunciation of the Treaty

This Treaty may be denounced by any Contracting Party by notification addressed to the Director General of WIPO. Any denunciation shall take effect one year from the date on which the Director General of WIPO received the notification.

Article 24
Languages of the Treaty

(1) This Treaty is signed in a single original in English, Arabic, Chinese, French, Russian and Spanish languages, the versions in all these languages being equally authentic.

(2) An official text in any language other than those referred to in paragraph (1) shall be established by the Director General of WIPO on the request of an interested party, after consultation with all the interested parties. For the purposes of this paragraph, "interested party" means any Member State of WIPO whose official language, or one of whose official languages, is involved and the European Community, and any other intergovernmental organization that may become party to this Treaty, if one of its official languages is involved.

Article 25
Depositary

The Director General of WIPO is the depositary of this Treaty.

THE W.I.P.O. PERFORMANCES AND PHONOGRAMS TREATY (CRNR/DC/95)

Adopted by the Diplomatic Conference on December 20, 1996

Contents

Preamble

The Contracting Parties,

Desiring to develop and maintain the protection of the rights of performers and producers of phonograms in a manner as effective and uniform as possible,

Recognizing the need to introduce new international rules in order to provide adequate solutions to the questions raised by economic, social, cultural and technological developments,

Recognizing the profound impact of the development and convergence of information and communication technologies on the production and use of performances and phonograms,

Recognizing the need to maintain a balance between the rights of the performers and producers of phonograms and the larger public interest, particularly education, research and access to information,

Have agreed as follows:

CHAPTER I

GENERAL PROVISIONS

Article 1
Relation to Other Conventions

(1) Nothing in this Treaty shall derogate from existing obligations that Contracting Parties have to each other under the International Convention for the Protection of Performers, Producers of Phonograms and Broadcasting Organizations done in Rome, October 26, 1961 (hereinafter the "Rome Convention").

(2) Protection granted under this Treaty shall leave intact and shall in no way affect the protection of copyright in literary and artistic works. Consequently, no provision of this Treaty may be interpreted as prejudicing such protection.

(3) This Treaty shall not have any connection with, nor shall it prejudice any rights and obligations under, any other treaties.

Article 2
Definitions

For the purposes of this Treaty:

(a) "performers" are actors, singers, musicians, dancers, and other persons who act, sing, deliver, declaim, play in, interpret, or otherwise perform literary or artistic works or expressions of folklore;

(b) "phonogram" means the fixation of the sounds of a performance or of other sounds, or of a representation of sounds other than in the form of a fixation incorporated in a cinematographic or other audiovisual work;

(c) "fixation" means the embodiment of sounds, or of the representations thereof, from which they can be perceived, reproduced or communicated through a device;

(d) "producer of a phonogram" means the person, or the legal entity, who or which takes the initiative and has the responsibility for the first fixation of the sounds of a performance or other sounds, or the representations of sounds;

(e) "publication" of a fixed performance or a phonogram means the offering of copies of the fixed performance or the phonogram to the public, with the consent of the rightholder, and provided that copies are offered to the public in reasonable quantity;

(f) "broadcasting" means the transmission by wireless means for public reception of sounds or of images and sounds or of the representations thereof; such transmission by satellite is also "broadcasting"; transmission of encrypted signals is "broadcasting" where the means for decrypting are provided to the public by the broadcasting organization or with its consent;

(g) "communication to the public" of a performance or a phonogram means the transmission to the public by any medium, otherwise than by broadcasting, of sounds of a performance or the sounds or the representations of sounds fixed in a phonogram. For the purposes of Article 15, "communication to the public" includes making the sounds or representations of sounds fixed in a phonogram audible to the public.

Article 3
Beneficiaries of Protection under this Treaty

(1) Contracting Parties shall accord the protection provided under this Treaty to the performers and producers of phonograms who are nationals of other Contracting Parties.

(2) The nationals of other Contracting Parties shall be understood to be those performers or producers of phonograms who would meet the criteria for eligibility for protection provided under the Rome Convention, were all the Contracting Parties to this Treaty Contracting States of that Convention. In respect of these criteria of eligibility, Contracting Parties shall apply the relevant definitions in Article 2 of this Treaty.

(3) Any Contracting Party availing itself of the possibilities provided in Article 5(3) of the Rome Conventions or, for the purposes of Article 5 of the same Convention, Article 17 thereof shall make a notification as foreseen in those provisions to the Director General of the World Intellectual Property Organization (WIPO).

Article 4
National Treatment

(1) Each Contracting Party shall accord to nationals of other Contracting Parties, as defined in Article 3(2), the treatment it accords to its own nationals with regard to the exclusive rights specifically granted in this Treaty and to the right to equitable remuneration provided for in Article 15 of this Treaty.

(2) The obligation provided for in paragraph (1) does not apply to the extent that another Contracting Party makes use of the reservations permitted by Article 15(3) of this Treaty.

CHAPTER II

RIGHTS OF PERFORMERS

Article 5
Moral Rights of Performers

(1) Independently of a performer's economic rights, and even after the transfer of those rights, the performer shall, as regards his live aural performances or perfomances fixed in phonograms have the right to claim to be identified as the performer of his performances, except where omission is dictated by the manner of the use of the performance, and to object to any distortion, mutilation or other modification of his performances that would be prejudicial to his reputation.

(2) The rights granted to a performer in accordance with paragraph (1) shall, after his death, be maintained, at least until the expiry of the economic rights, and shall be exercisable by the persons or institutions authorized by the legislation of the Contracting Party where protection is claimed. However, those Contracting Parties whose legislation, at the moment of their ratification of or accession to this Treaty, does not provide for protection after the death of the performer of all rights set out in the preceding paragraph may provide that some of these rights will, after his death, cease to be maintained.

(3) The means of redress for safeguarding the rights granted under this Article shall be governed by the legislation of the Contracting Party where protection is claimed.

Article 6
Economic Rights of Performers in their Unfixed Performances

Performers shall enjoy the exclusive right of authorizing, as regards their performances:

(i) the broadcasting and communication to the public of their unfixed performances except where the performance is already a broadcast performance; and

(ii) the fixation of their unfixed performances.

Article 7
Right of Reproduction

Performers shall enjoy the exclusive right of authorizing the direct or indirect reproduction of their performances fixed in phonograms, in any manner or form.

Article 8
Right of Distribution

(1) Performers shall enjoy the exclusive right of authorizing the making available to the public of the original and copies of their performances fixed in phonograms through sale or other transfer of ownership.

(2) Nothing in this Treaty shall affect the freedom of Contracting Parties to determine the conditions, if any, under which the exhaustion of the right in paragraph (1) applies after the first sale or other transfer of ownership of the original or a copy of the fixed performance with the authorization of the performer.

Article 9
Right of Rental

(1) Performers shall enjoy the exclusive right of authorizing the commercial rental to the public of the original and copies of their performances fixed in phonograms as determined in the national law of Contracting Parties, even after distribution of them by, or pursuant to, authorization by the performer.

(2) Notwithstanding the provisions of paragraph (1), a Contracting Party that, on April 15, 1994, had and continues to have in force a system of equitable remuneration of performers for the rental of copies of their performances fixed in phonograms, may maintain that system provided that the commercial rental of phonograms is not giving rise to the material impairment of the exclusive rights of reproduction of performers.

Article 10
Right of Making Available of Fixed Performances

Performers shall enjoy the exclusive right of authorizing the making available to the public of their performances fixed in phonograms, by wire or wireless means, in such a way that members of the public may access them from a place and at a time individually chosen by them.

CHAPTER III

RIGHTS OF PRODUCERS OF PHONOGRAMS

Article 11
Right of Reproduction

Producers of phonograms shall enjoy the exclusive right of authorizing the direct or indirect reproduction of their phonograms, in any manner or form.

Article 12
Right of Distribution

(1) Producers of phonograms shall enjoy the exclusive right of authorizing the making available to the public of the original and copies of their phonograms through sale or other transfer of ownership.

(2) Nothing in this Treaty shall affect the freedom of Contracting Parties to determine the conditions, if any, under which the exhaustion of the right in paragraph (1) applies after the first sale or transfer of ownership of the original or a copy of the phonogram with the authorization of the producer of phonograms.

Article 13
Right of Rental

(1) Producers of phonograms shall enjoy the exclusive right of authorizing the commercial rental to the public of the original and copies of their phonograms, even after distribution of them by or pursuant to authorization by the producer.

(2) Notwithstanding the provisions of paragraph (1), a Contracting Party that, on April 15, 1994, had and continues to have in force a system of equitable remuneration of producers of phonograms for the rental of copies of their phonograms, may maintain that system provided that the commercial rental of phonograms is not giving rise to the material impairment of the exclusive rights of reproduction of producers of phonograms.

Article 14
Right of Making Available of Phonograms

Producers of phonograms shall enjoy the exclusive right of authorizing the making available to the public of their phonograms, by wire or wireless means, in such a way that members of the public may access them from a place and at a time individually chosen by them.

CHAPTER IV

COMMON PROVISIONS

Article 15
Right to Remuneration for Broadcasting and Communication to the Public

(1) Performers and producers of phonograms shall enjoy the right to a single equitable remuneration for the direct or indirect use of phonograms published for commercial purposes for broadcasting or for any communication to the public.

(2) Contracting Parties may establish in their national legislation that the single equitable remuneration shall be claimed from the user by the performer or by the producer of a phonogram or by both. Contracting Parties may enact national legislation that, in the absence of an agreement between the performer and the producer of a phonogram, sets the terms according to which performers and producers of phonograms shall share the single equitable remuneration.

(3) Any Contracting Party may in a notification deposited with the Director General of WIPO, declare that it will apply the provisions of paragraph (1) only in respect of certain uses, or that it will limit their application in some other way, or that it will not apply these provisions at all.

(4) For the purposes of this Article, phonograms made available to the to the public by wire or wireless means in such a way that members of the public may access them from a place and at a time individually chosen by them shall be considered as if they had been published for commercial purposes.

Article 16
Limitations and Exceptions

(1) Contracting Parties may, in their national legislation, provide for the same kinds of limitations or exceptions with regard to the protection of performers and producers of phonograms as they provide for, in their national legislation, in connection with the protection of copyright in literary and artistic works.

(2) Contracting Parties shall confine any limitations of or exceptions to rights provided for in this Treaty to certain special cases which do not conflict with a normal exploitation of the performance or phonogram and do not unreasonably prejudice the legitimate interests of the performer or of the producer of phonograms.

Article 17
Term of Protection

(1) The term of protection to be granted to performers under this Treaty shall last, at least, until the end of a period of 50 years computed from the end of the year in which the performance was fixed in a phonogram.

(2) The term of protection to be granted to producers of phonograms under this Treaty shall last, at least, until the end of a period of 50 years computed from the end of the year in which the phonogram was published, or failing such publication within 50 years from fixation of the phonogram, 50 years from the end of the year in which the fixation was made.

Article 18
Obligations concerning Technological Measures

Contracting Parties shall provide adequate legal protection and effective legal remedies against the circumvention of effective technological measures that are used by performers or producers of phonograms in connection with the exercise of their rights under this Treaty and that restrict acts, in respect of their performances or phonograms, which are not authorized by the performers or the producers of phonograms concerned or permitted by law.

Article 19
Obligations concerning Rights Management Information

(1) Contracting Parties shall provide adequate and effective legal remedies against any person knowingly performing any of the following acts knowing or, with respect to civil remedies, having reasonable grounds to know that it will induce, enable, facilitate or conceal an infringement of any right covered by this Treaty:

(i) to remove or alter any electronic rights management information without authority;

(ii) to distribute, import for distribution, broadcast, communicate or make available to the public, without authority, performances, copies of fixed performances or phonograms knowing that electronic rights management information has been removed or altered without authority.

(2) As used in this Article, "rights management information" means information which identifies the performer, the performance of the performer, the producer of the phonogram, the phonogram, the owner of any right in the performance or phonogram, or information about the terms and conditions of use of the performance or phonogram, and any numbers or codes that represent such information, when any of these items of information is attached to a copy of a fixed performance or a phonogram or appears in connection with the communication or making available of a fixed performance or a phonogram to the public.

Article 20
Formalities

The enjoyment and exercise of the rights provided for in this Treaty shall not be subject to any formality.

Article 21
Reservations

Subject to the provisions of Article 15(3), no reservations to this Treaty shall be permitted.

Article 22
Application in Time

(1) Contracting Parties shall apply the provisions of Article 18 of the Berne Convention, mutatis mutandis, to the rights of performers and producers of phonograms provided for in this Treaty.

(2) Notwithstanding paragraph (1), a Contracting Party may limit the application of Article 5 of this Treaty to performances which occurred after the entry into force of this Treaty for that Party.

Article 23
Provisions on Enforcement of Rights

(1) Contracting Parties undertake to adopt, in accordance with their legal systems, the measures necessary to ensure the application of this Treaty.

(2) Contracting Parties shall ensure that enforcement procedures are available under their law so as to permit effective action against any act of infringement of rights covered by this Treaty, including expeditious remedies to prevent infringements and remedies which constitute a deterrent to further infringements.

CHAPTER V

ADMINISTRATIVE AND FINAL CLAUSES

Article 24
Assembly

(1) (a) The Contracting Parties shall have an Assembly.

(b) Each Contracting Party shall be represented by one delegate who may be assisted by alternate delegates, advisors and experts.

(c) The expenses of each delegation shall be borne by the Contracting Party that has appointed the delegation. The Assembly may ask WIPO to grant financial assistance to facilitate the participation of delegations of Contracting Parties that are regarded as developing countries in conformity with the established practice of the General Assembly of the United Nations or that are countries in transition to a market economy.

(2) (a) The Assembly shall deal with matters concerning the maintenance and development of this Treaty and the application and operation of this Treaty.

(b) The Assembly shall perform the function allocated to it under Article 26(2) in respect of the admission of certain intergovernmental organizations to become party to this Treaty.

(c) The Assembly shall decide the convocation of any diplomatic conference for the revision of this Treaty and give the necessary instructions to the Director General of WIPO for the preparation of such diplomatic conference.

(3) (a) Each Contracting Party that is a State shall have one vote and shall vote only in its own name.

(b) Any Contracting Party that is an intergovernmental organization may participate in the vote, in place of its Member States, with a number of votes equal to the number of its Member States which are party to this Treaty. No such intergovernmental organization shall participate in the vote if any one of its Member States exercises its right to vote and vice versa.

(4) The Assembly shall meet in ordinary session once every two years upon convocation by the Director General of WIPO.

(5) The Assembly shall establish its own rules of procedure, including the convocation of extraordinary sessions, the requirements of a quorum and, subject to the provisions of this Treaty, the required majority for various kinds of decisions.

Article 25
International Bureau

The International Bureau of WIPO shall perform the administrative tasks concerning the Treaty.

Article 26
Eligibility for Becoming Party to the Treaty

(1) Any Member State of WIPO may become party to this Treaty.

(2) The Assembly may decide to admit any intergovernmental organization to become party to this Treaty which declares that it is competent in respect of, and has its own legislation binding on all its Member States on, matters covered by this Treaty and that it has been duly authorized, in accordance with its internal procedures, to become party to this Treaty.

(3) The European Community, having made the declaration referred to in the preceding paragraph in the Diplomatic Conference that has adopted this Treaty, may become party to this Treaty.

Article 27
Rights and Obligations under the Treaty

Subject to any specific provisions to the contrary in this Treaty, each Contracting Party shall enjoy all of the rights and assume all of the obligations under this Treaty.

Article 28
Signature of the Treaty

This Treaty shall be open for signature until December 31, 1997, by any Member State of WIPO and by the European Community.

Article 29
Entry into Force of the Treaty

This Treaty shall enter into force three months after 30 instruments of ratification or accession by States have been deposited with the Director General of WIPO.

Article 30
Effective Date of Becoming Party to the Treaty

This Treaty shall bind

(i) the 30 States referred to in Article 29, from the date on which this Treaty has entered into force;

(ii) each other State from the expiration of three months from the date on which the State has deposited its instrument with the Director General of WIPO;

(iii) the European Community, from the expiration of three months after the deposit of its instrument of ratification or accession if such instrument has been deposited after the entry into force of this Treaty according to Article 29, or, three months after the entry into force of this Treaty if such instrument has been deposited before the entry into force of this Treaty;

(iv) any other intergovernmental organization that is admitted to become party to this Treaty, from the expiration of three months after the deposit of its instrument of accession.

Article 31
Denunciation of the Treaty

This Treaty may be denounced by any Contracting Party by notification addressed to the Director General of WIPO. Any denunciation shall take effect one year from the date on which the Director General of WIPO received the notification.

Article 32
Languages of the Treaty

(1) This Treaty is signed in a single original in English, Arabic, Chinese, French, Russian and Spanish languages, the versions in all these languages being equally authentic.

(2) An official text in any language other than those referred to in paragraph (1) shall be established by the Director General of WIPO on the request of an interested party, after consultation with all the interested parties. For

the purposes of this paragraph, "interested party" means any Member State of WIPO whose official language, or one of whose official languages, is involved and the European Community, and any other intergovernmental organization that may become party to this Treaty, if one of its official languages is involved.

Article 33
Depositary

The Director General of WIPO is the depositary of this Treaty.

EUROPEAN UNION INTERNET COPYRIGHT DIRECTIVE

Directive 2001/29/EC of the European Parliament and of the Council of 22 May 2001 on the Harmonisation of Certain Aspects of Copyright and Related Rights in the Information Society

THE EUROPEAN PARLIAMENT AND THE COUNCIL OF THE EUROPEAN UNION,

Having regard to the Treaty establishing the European Community, and in particular Articles 47(2), 55 and 95 thereof,

Having regard to the proposal from the Commission,[1]

Having regard to the Opinion of the Economic and Social Committee,[2]

Acting in accordance with the procedure laid down in Article 251 of the Treaty,[3]

Whereas:

(1) The Treaty provides for the establishment of an internal market and the institution of a system ensuring that competition in the internal market is not distorted. Harmonisation of the laws of the Member States on copyright and related rights contributes to the achievement of these objectives.

(2) The European Council, meeting at Corfu on 24 and 25 June 1994, stressed the need to create a general and flexible legal framework at Community level in order to foster the development of the information society in Europe. This requires, *inter alia*, the existence of an internal market for new products and services. Important Community legislation to ensure such a regulatory framework is already in place or its adoption is well under way. Copyright and related rights play an important role in this context as they protect and stimulate the development and marketing of new products and services and the creation and exploitation of their creative content.

(3) The proposed harmonisation will help to implement the four freedoms of the internal market and relates to compliance with the fundamental principles of law and especially of property, including intellectual property, and freedom of expression and the public interest.

(4) A harmonised legal framework on copyright and related rights, through increased legal certainty and while providing for a high level of protection of intellectual property, will foster substantial investment in creativity

---

[1] OJ C 108, 7.4.1998, p. 6 and OJ C 180, 25.6.1999, p. 6.

[2] OJ C 407, 28.12.1998, p. 30.

[3] Opinion of the European Parliament of 10 February 1999 (OJ C 150, 28.5.1999, p. 171), Council Common Position of 28 September 2000 (OJ C 344, 1.12.2000, p. 1) and Decision of the European Parliament of 14 February 2001 (not yet published in the Official Journal). Council Decision of 9 April 2001.

and innovation, including network infrastructure, and lead in turn to growth and increased competitiveness of European industry, both in the area of content provision and information technology and more generally across a wide range of industrial and cultural sectors. This will safeguard employment and encourage new job creation.

(5) Technological development has multiplied and diversified the vectors for creation, production and exploitation. While no new concepts for the protection of intellectual property are needed, the current law on copyright and related rights should be adapted and supplemented to respond adequately to economic realities such as new forms of exploitation.

(6) Without harmonisation at Community level, legislative activities at national level which have already been initiated in a number of Member States in order to respond to the technological challenges might result in significant differences in protection and thereby in restrictions on the free movement of services and products incorporating, or based on, intellectual property, leading to a refragmentation of the internal market and legislative inconsistency. The impact of such legislative differences and uncertainties will become more significant with the further development of the information society, which has already greatly increased transborder exploitation of intellectual property. This development will and should further increase. Significant legal differences and uncertainties in protection may hinder economies of scale for new products and services containing copyright and related rights.

(7) The Community legal framework for the protection of copyright and related rights must, therefore, also be adapted and supplemented as far as is necessary for the smooth functioning of the internal market. To that end, those national provisions on copyright and related rights which vary considerably from one Member State to another or which cause legal uncertainties hindering the smooth functioning of the internal market and the proper development of the information society in Europe should be adjusted, and inconsistent national responses to the technological developments should be avoided, whilst differences not adversely affecting the functioning of the internal market need not be removed or prevented.

(8) The various social, societal and cultural implications of the information society require that account be taken of the specific features of the content of products and services.

(9) Any harmonisation of copyright and related rights must take as a basis a high level of protection, since such rights are crucial to intellectual creation. Their protection helps to ensure the maintenance and development of creativity in the interests of authors, performers, producers, consumers, culture, industry and the public at large. Intellectual property has therefore been recognised as an integral part of property.

(10) If authors or performers are to continue their creative and artistic work, they have to receive an appropriate reward for the use of their work, as must producers in order to be able to finance this work. The investment required to produce products such as phonograms, films or multimedia products, and

services such as 'on-demand' services, is considerable. Adequate legal protection of intellectual property rights is necessary in order to guarantee the availability of such a reward and provide the opportunity for satisfactory returns on this investment.

(11) A rigorous, effective system for the protection of copyright and related rights is one of the main ways of ensuring that European cultural creativity and production receive the necessary resources and of safeguarding the independence and dignity of artistic creators and performers.

(12) Adequate protection of copyright works and subject-matter of related rights is also of great importance from a cultural standpoint. Article 151 of the Treaty requires the Community to take cultural aspects into account in its action.

(13) A common search for, and consistent application at European level of, technical measures to protect works and other subject-matter and to provide the necessary information on rights are essential insofar as the ultimate aim of these measures is to give effect to the principles and guarantees laid down in law.

(14) This Directive should seek to promote learning and culture by protecting works and other subject-matter while permitting exceptions or limitations in the public interest for the purpose of education and teaching.

(15) The Diplomatic Conference held under the auspices of the World Intellectual Property Organisation (WIPO) in December 1996 led to the adoption of two new Treaties, the "WIPO Copyright Treaty" and the "WIPO Performances and Phonograms Treaty," dealing respectively with the protection of authors and the protection of performers and phonogram producers. Those Treaties update the international protection for copyright and related rights significantly, not least with regard to the so-called "digital agenda," and improve the means to fight piracy world-wide. The Community and a majority of Member States have already signed the Treaties and the process of making arrangements for the ratification of the Treaties by the Community and the Member States is under way. This Directive also serves to implement a number of the new international obligations.

(16) Liability for activities in the network environment concerns not only copyright and related rights but also other areas, such as defamation, misleading advertising, or infringement of trademarks, and is addressed horizontally in Directive 2000/31/EC of the European Parliament and of the Council of 8 June 2000 on certain legal aspects of information society services, in particular electronic commerce, in the internal market ("Directive on electronic commerce"),[1] which clarifies and harmonises various legal issues relating to information society services including electronic commerce. This Directive should be implemented within a timescale similar to that for the implementation of the Directive on electronic commerce, since that Directive provides

[1] OJ L 178, 17.7.2000, p. 1.

a harmonised framework of principles and provisions relevant *inter alia* to important parts of this Directive. This Directive is without prejudice to provisions relating to liability in that Directive.

(17) It is necessary, especially in the light of the requirements arising out of the digital environment, to ensure that collecting societies achieve a higher level of rationalisation and transparency with regard to compliance with competition rules.

(18) This Directive is without prejudice to the arrangements in the Member States concerning the management of rights such as extended collective licences.

(19) The moral rights of rightholders should be exercised according to the legislation of the Member States and the provisions of the Berne Convention for the Protection of Literary and Artistic Works, of the WIPO Copyright Treaty and of the WIPO Performances and Phonograms Treaty. Such moral rights remain outside the scope of this Directive.

(20) This Directive is based on principles and rules already laid down in the Directives currently in force in this area, in particular Directives 91/250/EEC,[(2)] 92/100/EEC,[(3)] 93/83/EEC,[(4)] 93/98/EEC[(5)] and 96/9/EC,[(6)] and it develops those principles and rules and places them in the context of the information society. The provisions of this Directive should be without prejudice to the provisions of those Directives, unless otherwise provided in this Directive.

(21) This Directive should define the scope of the acts covered by the reproduction right with regard to the different beneficiaries. This should be done in conformity with the acquis communautaire. A broad definition of these acts is needed to ensure legal certainty within the internal market.

(22) The objective of proper support for the dissemination of culture must not be achieved by sacrificing strict protection of rights or by tolerating illegal forms of distribution of counterfeited or pirated works.

(23) This Directive should harmonise further the author's right of communication to the public. This right should be understood in a broad sense covering all communication to the public not present at the place where the communication originates. This right should cover any such transmission or

---

[(2)] Council Directive 91/250/EEC of 14 May 1991 on the legal protection of computer programs (OJ L 122, 17.5.1991, p. 42). Directive as amended by Directive 93/98/EEC.

[(3)] Council Directive 92/100/EEC of 19 November 1992 on rental right and lending right and on certain rights related to copyright in the field of intellectual property (OJ L 346, 27.11.1992, p. 61). Directive as amended by Directive 93/98/EEC.

[(4)] Council Directive 93/83/EEC of 27 September 1993 on the coordination of certain rules concerning copyright and rights related to copyright applicable to satellite broadcasting and cable retransmission (OJ L 248, 6.10.1993, p. 15).

[(5)] Council Directive 93/98/EEC of 29 October 1993 harmonising the term of protection of copyright and certain related rights (OJ L 290, 24.11.1993, p. 9).

[(6)] Directive 96/9/EC of the European Parliament and of the Council of 11 March 1996 on the legal protection of databases (OJ L 77, 27.3.1996, p. 20).

retransmission of a work to the public by wire or wireless means, including broadcasting. This right should not cover any other acts.

(24) The right to make available to the public subject-matter referred to in Article 3(2) should be understood as covering all acts of making available such subject-matter to members of the public not present at the place where the act of making available originates, and as not covering any other acts.

(25) The legal uncertainty regarding the nature and the level of protection of acts of on-demand transmission of copyright works and subject-matter protected by related rights over networks should be overcome by providing for harmonised protection at Community level. It should be made clear that all rightholders recognised by this Directive should have an exclusive right to make available to the public copyright works or any other subject-matter by way of interactive on-demand transmissions. Such interactive on-demand transmissions are characterised by the fact that members of the public may access them from a place and at a time individually chosen by them.

(26) With regard to the making available in on-demand services by broadcasters of their radio or television productions incorporating music from commercial phonograms as an integral part thereof, collective licensing arrangements are to be encouraged in order to facilitate the clearance of the rights concerned.

(27) The mere provision of physical facilities for enabling or making a communication does not in itself amount to communication within the meaning of this Directive.

(28) Copyright protection under this Directive includes the exclusive right to control distribution of the work incorporated in a tangible article. The first sale in the Community of the original of a work or copies thereof by the rightholder or with his consent exhausts the right to control resale of that object in the Community. This right should not be exhausted in respect of the original or of copies thereof sold by the rightholder or with his consent outside the Community. Rental and lending rights for authors have been established in Directive 92/100/EEC. The distribution right provided for in this Directive is without prejudice to the provisions relating to the rental and lending rights contained in Chapter I of that Directive.

(29) The question of exhaustion does not arise in the case of services and on-line services in particular. This also applies with regard to a material copy of a work or other subject-matter made by a user of such a service with the consent of the rightholder. Therefore, the same applies to rental and lending of the original and copies of works or other subject-matter which are services by nature. Unlike CD-ROM or CD-I, where the intellectual property is incorporated in a material medium, namely an item of goods, every on-line service is in fact an act which should be subject to authorisation where the copyright or related right so provides.

(30) The rights referred to in this Directive may be transferred, assigned or subject to the granting of contractual licences, without prejudice to the relevant national legislation on copyright and related rights.

(31) A fair balance of rights and interests between the different categories of rightholders, as well as between the different categories of rightholders and users of protected subject-matter must be safeguarded. The existing exceptions and limitations to the rights as set out by the Member States have to be reassessed in the light of the new electronic environment. Existing differences in the exceptions and limitations to certain restricted acts have direct negative effects on the functioning of the internal market of copyright and related rights. Such differences could well become more pronounced in view of the further development of transborder exploitation of works and cross-border activities. In order to ensure the proper functioning of the internal market, such exceptions and limitations should be defined more harmoniously. The degree of their harmonisation should be based on their impact on the smooth functioning of the internal market.

(32) This Directive provides for an exhaustive enumeration of exceptions and limitations to the reproduction right and the right of communication to the public. Some exceptions or limitations only apply to the reproduction right, where appropriate. This list takes due account of the different legal traditions in Member States, while, at the same time, aiming to ensure a functioning internal market. Member States should arrive at a coherent application of these exceptions and limitations, which will be assessed when reviewing implementing legislation in the future.

(33) The exclusive right of reproduction should be subject to an exception to allow certain acts of temporary reproduction, which are transient or incidental reproductions, forming an integral and essential part of a technological process and carried out for the sole purpose of enabling either efficient transmission in a network between third parties by an intermediary, or a lawful use of a work or other subject-matter to be made. The acts of reproduction concerned should have no separate economic value on their own. To the extent that they meet these conditions, this exception should include acts which enable browsing as well as acts of caching to take place, including those which enable transmission systems to function efficiently, provided that the intermediary does not modify the information and does not interfere with the lawful use of technology, widely recognised and used by industry, to obtain data on the use of the information. A use should be considered lawful where it is authorised by the rightholder or not restricted by law.

(34) Member States should be given the option of providing for certain exceptions or limitations for cases such as educational and scientific purposes, for the benefit of public institutions such as libraries and archives, for purposes of news reporting, for quotations, for use by people with disabilities, for public security uses and for uses in administrative and judicial proceedings.

(35) In certain cases of exceptions or limitations, rightholders should receive fair compensation to compensate them adequately for the use made of their protected works or other subject-matter. When determining the form, detailed arrangements and possible level of such fair compensation, account should be taken of the particular circumstances of each case. When evaluating these circumstances, a valuable criterion would be the possible harm to the

rightholders resulting from the act in question. In cases where rightholders have already received payment in some other form, for instance as part of a licence fee, no specific or separate payment may be due. The level of fair compensation should take full account of the degree of use of technological protection measures referred to in this Directive. In certain situations where the prejudice to the rightholder would be minimal, no obligation for payment may arise.

(36) The Member States may provide for fair compensation for rightholders also when applying the optional provisions on exceptions or limitations which do not require such compensation.

(37) Existing national schemes on reprography, where they exist, do not create major barriers to the internal market. Member States should be allowed to provide for an exception or limitation in respect of reprography.

(38) Member States should be allowed to provide for an exception or limitation to the reproduction right for certain types of reproduction of audio, visual and audio-visual material for private use, accompanied by fair compensation. This may include the introduction or continuation of remuneration schemes to compensate for the prejudice to rightholders. Although differences between those remuneration schemes affect the functioning of the internal market, those differences, with respect to analogue private reproduction, should not have a significant impact on the development of the information society. Digital private copying is likely to be more widespread and have a greater economic impact. Due account should therefore be taken of the differences between digital and analogue private copying and a distinction should be made in certain respects between them.

(39) When applying the exception or limitation on private copying, Member States should take due account of technological and economic developments, in particular with respect to digital private copying and remuneration schemes, when effective technological protection measures are available. Such exceptions or limitations should not inhibit the use of technological measures or their enforcement against circumvention.

(40) Member States may provide for an exception or limitation for the benefit of certain non-profit making establishments, such as publicly accessible libraries and equivalent institutions, as well as archives. However, this should be limited to certain special cases covered by the reproduction right. Such an exception or limitation should not cover uses made in the context of on-line delivery of protected works or other subject-matter. This Directive should be without prejudice to the Member States' option to derogate from the exclusive public lending right in accordance with Article 5 of Directive 92/100/EEC. Therefore, specific contracts or licences should be promoted which, without creating imbalances, favour such establishments and the disseminative purposes they serve.

(41) When applying the exception or limitation in respect of ephemeral recordings made by broadcasting organisations it is understood that a broadcaster's own facilities include those of a person acting on behalf of and under the responsibility of the broadcasting organisation.

(42) When applying the exception or limitation for non-commercial educational and scientific research purposes, including distance learning, the non-commercial nature of the activity in question should be determined by that activity as such. The organisational structure and the means of funding of the establishment concerned are not the decisive factors in this respect.

(43) It is in any case important for the Member States to adopt all necessary measures to facilitate access to works by persons suffering from a disability which constitutes an obstacle to the use of the works themselves, and to pay particular attention to accessible formats.

(44) When applying the exceptions and limitations provided for in this Directive, they should be exercised in accordance with international obligations. Such exceptions and limitations may not be applied in a way which prejudices the legitimate interests of the rightholder or which conflicts with the normal exploitation of his work or other subject-matter. The provision of such exceptions or limitations by Member States should, in particular, duly reflect the increased economic impact that such exceptions or limitations may have in the context of the new electronic environment. Therefore, the scope of certain exceptions or limitations may have to be even more limited when it comes to certain new uses of copyright works and other subject-matter.

(45) The exceptions and limitations referred to in Article 5(2), (3) and (4) should not, however, prevent the definition of contractual relations designed to ensure fair compensation for the rightholders insofar as permitted by national law.

(46) Recourse to mediation could help users and rightholders to settle disputes. The Commission, in cooperation with the Member States within the Contact Committee, should undertake a study to consider new legal ways of settling disputes concerning copyright and related rights.

(47) Technological development will allow rightholders to make use of technological measures designed to prevent or restrict acts not authorised by the rightholders of any copyright, rights related to copyright or the *sui generis* right in databases. The danger, however, exists that illegal activities might be carried out in order to enable or facilitate the circumvention of the technical protection provided by these measures. In order to avoid fragmented legal approaches that could potentially hinder the functioning of the internal market, there is a need to provide for harmonised legal protection against circumvention of effective technological measures and against provision of devices and products or services to this effect.

(48) Such legal protection should be provided in respect of technological measures that effectively restrict acts not authorised by the rightholders of any copyright, rights related to copyright or the *sui generis* right in databases without, however, preventing the normal operation of electronic equipment and its technological development. Such legal protection implies no obligation to design devices, products, components or services to correspond to technological measures, so long as such device, product, component or service does not otherwise fall under the prohibition of Article 6. Such legal protection should respect proportionality and should not prohibit those devices or activities which have

a commercially significant purpose or use other than to circumvent the technical protection. In particular, this protection should not hinder research into cryptography.

(49) The legal protection of technological measures is without prejudice to the application of any national provisions which may prohibit the private possession of devices, products or components for the circumvention of technological measures.

(50) Such a harmonised legal protection does not affect the specific provisions on protection provided for by Directive 91/250/EEC. In particular, it should not apply to the protection of technological measures used in connection with computer programs, which is exclusively addressed in that Directive. It should neither inhibit nor prevent the development or use of any means of circumventing a technological measure that is necessary to enable acts to be undertaken in accordance with the terms of Article 5(3) or Article 6 of Directive 91/250/EEC. Articles 5 and 6 of that Directive exclusively determine exceptions to the exclusive rights applicable to computer programs.

(51) The legal protection of technological measures applies without prejudice to public policy, as reflected in Article 5, or public security. Member States should promote voluntary measures taken by rightholders, including the conclusion and implementation of agreements between rightholders and other parties concerned, to accommodate achieving the objectives of certain exceptions or limitations provided for in national law in accordance with this Directive. In the absence of such voluntary measures or agreements within a reasonable period of time, Member States should take appropriate measures to ensure that rightholders provide beneficiaries of such exceptions or limitations with appropriate means of benefiting from them, by modifying an implemented technological measure or by other means. However, in order to prevent abuse of such measures taken by rightholders, including within the framework of agreements, or taken by a Member State, any technological measures applied in implementation of such measures should enjoy legal protection.

(52) When implementing an exception or limitation for private copying in accordance with Article 5(2)(b), Member States should likewise promote the use of voluntary measures to accommodate achieving the objectives of such exception or limitation. If, within a reasonable period of time, no such voluntary measures to make reproduction for private use possible have been taken, Member States may take measures to enable beneficiaries of the exception or limitation concerned to benefit from it. Voluntary measures taken by rightholders, including agreements between rightholders and other parties concerned, as well as measures taken by Member States, do not prevent rightholders from using technological measures which are consistent with the exceptions or limitations on private copying in national law in accordance with Article 5(2)(b), taking account of the condition of fair compensation under that provision and the possible differentiation between various conditions of use in accordance with Article 5(5), such as controlling the number of reproductions. In order to prevent abuse of such measures, any technological measures applied in their implementation should enjoy legal protection.

(53) The protection of technological measures should ensure a secure environment for the provision of interactive on-demand services, in such a way that members of the public may access works or other subject-matter from a place and at a time individually chosen by them. Where such services are governed by contractual arrangements, the first and second subparagraphs of Article 6(4) should not apply. Non-interactive forms of online use should remain subject to those provisions.

(54) Important progress has been made in the international standardisation of technical systems of identification of works and protected subject-matter in digital format. In an increasingly networked environment, differences between technological measures could lead to an incompatibility of systems within the Community. Compatibility and interoperability of the different systems should be encouraged. It would be highly desirable to encourage the development of global systems.

(55) Technological development will facilitate the distribution of works, notably on networks, and this will entail the need for rightholders to identify better the work or other subject-matter, the author or any other rightholder, and to provide information about the terms and conditions of use of the work or other subject-matter in order to render easier the management of rights attached to them. Rightholders should be encouraged to use markings indicating, in addition to the information referred to above, *inter alia* their authorisation when putting works or other subject-matter on networks.

(56) There is, however, the danger that illegal activities might be carried out in order to remove or alter the electronic copyright-management information attached to it, or otherwise to distribute, import for distribution, broadcast, communicate to the public or make available to the public works or other protected subject-matter from which such information has been removed without authority. In order to avoid fragmented legal approaches that could potentially hinder the functioning of the internal market, there is a need to provide for harmonised legal protection against any of these activities.

(57) Any such rights-management information systems referred to above may, depending on their design, at the same time process personal data about the consumption patterns of protected subject-matter by individuals and allow for tracing of on-line behaviour. These technical means, in their technical functions, should incorporate privacy safeguards in accordance with Directive 95/46/EC of the European Parliament and of the Council of 24 October 1995 on the protection of individuals with regard to the processing of personal data and the free movement of such data.[1]

(58) Member States should provide for effective sanctions and remedies for infringements of rights and obligations as set out in this Directive. They should take all the measures necessary to ensure that those sanctions and remedies are applied. The sanctions thus provided for should be effective,

[1] OJ L 281, 23.11.1995, p. 31.

proportionate and dissuasive and should include the possibility of seeking damages and/or injunctive relief and, where appropriate, of applying for seizure of infringing material.

(59) In the digital environment, in particular, the services of intermediaries may increasingly be used by third parties for infringing activities. In many cases such intermediaries are best placed to bring such infringing activities to an end. Therefore, without prejudice to any other sanctions and remedies available, rightholders should have the possibility of applying for an injunction against an intermediary who carries a third party's infringement of a protected work or other subject-matter in a network. This possibility should be available even where the acts carried out by the intermediary are exempted under Article 5. The conditions and modalities relating to such injunctions should be left to the national law of the Member States.

(60) The protection provided under this Directive should be without prejudice to national or Community legal provisions in other areas, such as industrial property, data protection, conditional access, access to public documents, and the rule of media exploitation chronology, which may affect the protection of copyright or related rights.

(61) In order to comply with the WIPO Performances and Phonograms Treaty, Directives 92/100/EEC and 93/98/EEC should be amended,

HAVE ADOPTED THIS DIRECTIVE:

CHAPTER I

OBJECTIVE AND SCOPE

Article 1

Scope

1. This Directive concerns the legal protection of copyright and related rights in the framework of the internal market, with particular emphasis on the information society.

2. Except in the cases referred to in Article 11, this Directive shall leave intact and shall in no way affect existing Community provisions relating to:

(a) the legal protection of computer programs;

(b) rental right, lending right and certain rights related to copyright in the field of intellectual property;

(c) copyright and related rights applicable to broadcasting of programmes by satellite and cable retransmission;

(d) the term of protection of copyright and certain related rights;

(e) the legal protection of databases.

CHAPTER II

RIGHTS AND EXCEPTIONS

Article 2

Reproduction right

Member States shall provide for the exclusive right to authorise or prohibit direct or indirect, temporary or permanent reproduction by any means and in any form, in whole or in part:

(a) for authors, of their works;

(b) for performers, of fixations of their performances;

(c) for phonogram producers, of their phonograms;

(d) for the producers of the first fixations of films, in respect of the original and copies of their films;

(e) for broadcasting organisations, of fixations of their broadcasts, whether those broadcasts are transmitted by wire or over the air, including by cable or satellite.

Article 3

Right of communication to the public of works and right of making available to the public other subject-matter

1. Member States shall provide authors with the exclusive right to authorise or prohibit any communication to the public of their works, by wire or wireless means, including the making available to the public of their works in such a way that members of the public may access them from a place and at a time individually chosen by them.

2. Member States shall provide for the exclusive right to authorise or prohibit the making available to the public, by wire or wireless means, in such a way that members of the public may access them from a place and at a time individually chosen by them:

(a) for performers, of fixations of their performances;

(b) for phonogram producers, of their phonograms;

(c) for the producers of the first fixations of films, of the original and copies of their films;

(d) for broadcasting organisations, of fixations of their broadcasts, whether these broadcasts are transmitted by wire or over the air, including by cable or satellite.

3. The rights referred to in paragraphs 1 and 2 shall not be exhausted by any act of communication to the public or making available to the public as set out in this Article.

Article 4

Distribution right

1. Member States shall provide for authors, in respect of the original of their works or of copies thereof, the exclusive right to authorise or prohibit any form of distribution to the public by sale or otherwise.

2. The distribution right shall not be exhausted within the Community in respect of the original or copies of the work, except where the first sale or other transfer of ownership in the Community of that object is made by the rightholder or with his consent.

Article 5

Exceptions and limitations

1. Temporary acts of reproduction referred to in Article 2, which are transient or incidental [and] an integral and essential part of a technological process and whose sole purpose is to enable:

(a) transmission in a network between third parties by an intermediary, or

(b) a lawful use

of a work or other subject-matter to be made, and which have no independent economic significance, shall be exempted from the reproduction right provided for in Article 2.

2. Member States may provide for exceptions or limitations to the reproduction right provided for in Article 2 in the following cases:

(a) in respect of reproductions on paper or any similar medium, effected by the use of any kind of photographic technique or by some other process having similar effects, with the exception of sheet music, provided that the rightholders receive fair compensation;

(b) in respect of reproductions on any medium made by a natural person for private use and for ends that are neither directly nor indirectly commercial, on condition that the rightholders receive fair compensation which takes account of the application or non-application of technological measures referred to in Article 6 to the work or subject-matter concerned;

(c) in respect of specific acts of reproduction made by publicly accessible libraries, educational establishments or museums, or by archives, which are not for direct or indirect economic or commercial advantage;

(d) in respect of ephemeral recordings of works made by broadcasting organisations by means of their own facilities and for their own broadcasts; the preservation of these recordings in official archives may, on the ground of their exceptional documentary character, be permitted;

(e) in respect of reproductions of broadcasts made by social institutions pursuing non-commercial purposes, such as hospitals or prisons, on condition that the rightholders receive fair compensation.

(3) Member States may provide for exceptions or limitations to the rights provided for in Articles 2 and 3 in the following cases:

(a) use for the sole purpose of illustration for teaching or scientific research, as long as the source, including the author's name, is indicated, unless this turns out to be impossible and to the extent justified by the non-commercial purpose to be achieved;

(b) uses, for the benefit of people with a disability, which are directly related to the disability and of a non-commercial nature, to the extent required by the specific disability;

(c) reproduction by the press, communication to the public or making available of published articles on current economic, political or religious topics or of broadcast works or other subject-matter of the same character, in cases where such use is not expressly reserved, and as long as the source, including the author's name, is indicated, or use of works or other subject-matter in connection with the reporting of current events, to the extent justified by the informatory purpose and as long as the source, including the author's name, is indicated, unless this turns out to be impossible;

(d) quotations for purposes such as criticism or review, provided that they relate to a work or other subject-matter which has already been lawfully made available to the public, that, unless this turns out to be impossible, the source, including the author's name, is indicated, and that their use is in accordance with fair practice, and to the extent required by the specific purpose;

(e) use for the purposes of public security or to ensure the proper performance or reporting of administrative, parliamentary or judicial proceedings;

(f) use of political speeches as well as extracts of public lectures or similar works or subject-matter to the extent justified by the informatory purpose and provided that the source, including the author's name, is indicated, except where this turns out to be impossible;

(g) use during religious celebrations or official celebrations organised by a public authority;

(h) use of works, such as works of architecture or sculpture, made to be located permanently in public places;

(i) incidental inclusion of a work or other subject-matter in other material;

(j) use for the purpose of advertising the public exhibition or sale of artistic works, to the extent necessary to promote the event, excluding any other commercial use;

(k) use for the purpose of caricature, parody or pastiche;

(l) use in connection with the demonstration or repair of equipment;

(m) use of an artistic work in the form of a building or a drawing or plan of a building for the purposes of reconstructing the building;

(n) use by communication or making available, for the purpose of research or private study, to individual members of the public by dedicated terminals on the premises of establishments referred to in paragraph 2(c) of works and other subject-matter not subject to purchase or licensing terms which are contained in their collections;

(o) use in certain other cases of minor importance where exceptions or limitations already exist under national law, provided that they only concern analogue uses and do not affect the free circulation of goods and services within the Community, without prejudice to the other exceptions and limitations contained in this Article.

4. Where the Member States may provide for an exception or limitation to the right of reproduction pursuant to paragraphs 2 and 3, they may provide similarly for an exception or limitation to the right of distribution as referred to in Article 4 to the extent justified by the purpose of the authorised act of reproduction.

5. The exceptions and limitations provided for in paragraphs 1, 2, 3 and 4 shall only be applied in certain special cases which do not conflict with a normal exploitation of the work or other subject-matter and do not unreasonably prejudice the legitimate interests of the rightholder.

CHAPTER III

PROTECTION OF TECHNOLOGICAL MEASURES AND RIGHTS-MANAGEMENT INFORMATION

Article 6

Obligations as to technological measures

1. Member States shall provide adequate legal protection against the circumvention of any effective technological measures, which the person concerned carries out in the knowledge, or with reasonable grounds to know, that he or she is pursuing that objective.

2. Member States shall provide adequate legal protection against the manufacture, import, distribution, sale, rental, advertisement for sale or rental, or possession for commercial purposes of devices, products or components or the provision of services which:

(a) are promoted, advertised or marketed for the purpose of circumvention of, or

(b) have only a limited commercially significant purpose or use other than to circumvent, or

(c) are primarily designed, produced, adapted or performed for the purpose of enabling or facilitating the circumvention of,

any effective technological measures.

3. For the purposes of this Directive, the expression "technological measures" means any technology, device or component that, in the normal course of its operation, is designed to prevent or restrict acts, in respect of works or other subject-matter, which are not authorised by the rightholder of any copyright or any right related to copyright as provided for by law or the *sui generis* right provided for in Chapter III of Directive 96/9/EC. Technological measures shall be deemed "effective" where the use of a protected work or other subject-matter is controlled by the rightholders through application of an access control or protection process, such as encryption, scrambling or other transformation of the work or other subject-matter or a copy control mechanism, which achieves the protection objective.

4. Notwithstanding the legal protection provided for in paragraph 1, in the absence of voluntary measures taken by rightholders, including agreements between rightholders and other parties concerned, Member States shall take appropriate measures to ensure that rightholders make available to the beneficiary of an exception or limitation provided for in national law in accordance with Article 5(2)(a), (2)(c), (2)(d), (2)(e), (3)(a), (3)(b) or (3)(e) the means of benefiting from that exception or limitation, to the extent necessary to benefit from that exception or limitation and where that beneficiary has legal access to the protected work or subject-matter concerned.

A Member State may also take such measures in respect of a beneficiary of an exception or limitation provided for in accordance with Article 5(2)(b), unless reproduction for private use has already been made possible by rightholders to the extent necessary to benefit from the exception or limitation concerned and in accordance with the provisions of Article 5(2)(b) and (5), without preventing rightholders from adopting adequate measures regarding the number of reproductions in accordance with these provisions.

The technological measures applied voluntarily by rightholders, including those applied in implementation of voluntary agreements, and technological measures applied in implementation of the measures taken by Member States, shall enjoy the legal protection provided for in paragraph 1.

The provisions of the first and second subparagraphs shall not apply to works or other subject-matter made available to the public on agreed contractual terms in such a way that members of the public may access them from a place and at a time individually chosen by them.

When this Article is applied in the context of Directives 92/100/EEC and 96/9/EC, this paragraph shall apply: *mutatis; mutandis*.

Article 7

Obligations concerning rights-management information

1. Member States shall provide for adequate legal protection against any person knowingly performing without authority any of the following acts:

(a) the removal or alteration of any electronic rights-management information;

(b) the distribution, importation for distribution, broadcasting, communication or making available to the public of works or other subject-matter protected under this Directive or under Chapter III of Directive 96/9/EC from which electronic rights-management information has been removed or altered without authority,

if such person knows, or has reasonable grounds to know, that by so doing he is inducing, enabling, facilitating or concealing an infringement of any copyright or any rights related to copyright as provided by law, or of the *sui generis* right provided for in Chapter III of Directive 96/9/EC.

2. For the purposes of this Directive, the expression "rights-management information" means any information provided by rightholders which identifies the work or other subject-matter referred to in this Directive or covered by the *sui generis* right provided for in Chapter III of Directive 96/9/EC, the author or any other rightholder, or information about the terms and conditions of use of the work or other subject-matter, and any numbers or codes that represent such information.The first subparagraph shall apply when any of these items of information is associated with a copy of, or appears in connection with the communication to the public of, a work or other subject-matter referred to in this Directive or covered by the *sui generis* right provided for in Chapter III of Directive 96/9/EC.

CHAPTER IV

COMMON PROVISIONS

Article 8

Sanctions and remedies

1. Member States shall provide appropriate sanctions and remedies in respect of infringements of the rights and obligations set out in this Directive and shall take all the measures necessary to ensure that those sanctions and remedies are applied. The sanctions thus provided for shall be effective, proportionate and dissuasive.

2. Each Member State shall take the measures necessary to ensure that rightholders whose interests are affected by an infringing activity carried out

on its territory can bring an action for damages and/or apply for an injunction and, where appropriate, for the seizure of infringing material as well as of devices, products or components referred to in Article 6(2).

3. Member States shall ensure that rightholders are in a position to apply for an injunction against intermediaries whose services are used by a third party to infringe a copyright or related right.

Article 9

Continued application of other legal provisions

This Directive shall be without prejudice to provisions concerning in particular patent rights, trade marks, design rights, utility models, topographies of semi-conductor products, type faces, conditional access, access to cable of broadcasting services, protection of national treasures, legal deposit requirements, laws on restrictive practices and unfair competition, trade secrets, security, confidentiality, data protection and privacy, access to public documents, the law of contract.

Article 10

Application over time

1. The provisions of this Directive shall apply in respect of all works and other subject-matter referred to in this Directive which are, on 22 December 2002, protected by the Member States' legislation in the field of copyright and related rights, or which meet the criteria for protection under the provisions of this Directive or the provisions referred to in Article 1(2).

2. This Directive shall apply without prejudice to any acts concluded and rights acquired before 22 December 2002.

Article 11

Technical adaptations

1. Directive 92/100/EEC is hereby amended as follows:

   (a) Article 7 shall be deleted;

   (b) Article 10(3) shall be replaced by the following:

   "3. The limitations shall only be applied in certain special cases which do not conflict with a normal exploitation of the subject-matter and do not unreasonably prejudice the legitimate interests of the rightholder."

2. Article 3(2) of Directive 93/98/EEC shall be replaced by the following:

   "2. The rights of producers of phonograms shall expire 50 years after the fixation is made. However, if the phonogram has been lawfully published within this period, the said rights shall expire

50 years from the date of the first lawful publication. If no lawful publication has taken place within the period mentioned in the first sentence, and if the phonogram has been lawfully communicated to the public within this period, the said rights shall expire 50 years from the date of the first lawful communication to the public.

"However, where through the expiry of the term of protection granted pursuant to this paragraph in its version before amendment by Directive 2001/29/EC of the European Parliament and of the Council of 22 May 2001 on the harmonisation of certain aspects of copyright and related rights in the information society[*] the rights of producers of phonograms are no longer protected on 22 December 2002, this paragraph shall not have the effect of protecting those rights anew."

Article 12

Final provisions

1. Not later than 22 December 2004 and every three years thereafter, the Commission shall submit to the European Parliament, the Council and the Economic and Social Committee a report on the application of this Directive, in which, *inter alia*, on the basis of specific information supplied by the Member States, it shall examine in particular the application of Articles 5, 6 and 8 in the light of the development of the digital market. In the case of Article 6, it shall examine in particular whether that Article confers a sufficient level of protection and whether acts which are permitted by law are being adversely affected by the use of effective technological measures. Where necessary, in particular to ensure the functioning of the internal market pursuant to Article 14 of the Treaty, it shall submit proposals for amendments to this Directive.

2. Protection of rights related to copyright under this Directive shall leave intact and shall in no way affect the protection of copyright.

3. A contact committee is hereby established. It shall be composed of representatives of the competent authorities of the Member States. It shall be chaired by a representative of the Commission and shall meet either on the initiative of the chairman or at the request of the delegation of a Member State.

4. The tasks of the committee shall be as follows:

(a) to examine the impact of this Directive on the functioning of the internal market, and to highlight any difficulties;

(b) to organise consultations on all questions deriving from the application of this Directive;

(c) to facilitate the exchange of information on relevant developments in legislation and case-law, as well as relevant economic, social, cultural and technological developments;

---

[*] OJ L 167, 22.6.2001, p. 10.

(d) to act as a forum for the assessment of the digital market in works and other items, including private copying and the use of technological measures.

Article 13

Implementation

1. Member States shall bring into force the laws, regulations and administrative provisions necessary to comply with this Directive before 22 December 2002. They shall forthwith inform the Commission thereof.

When Member States adopt these measures, they shall contain a reference to this Directive or shall be accompanied by such reference on the occasion of their official publication. The methods of making such reference shall be laid down by Member States.

2. Member States shall communicate to the Commission the text of the provisions of domestic law which they adopt in the field governed by this Directive.

Article 14

Entry into force

This Directive shall enter into force on the day of its publication in the *Official Journal of the European Communities.*

Article 15

Addresses

This Directive is addressed to the Member States.

Done at Brussels, 22 May 2001.

For the European Parliament
The President
N. FONTAINE

For the Council
The President
M. WINBERG

THE WHITE PAPER: INTELLECTUAL PROPERTY AND THE NATIONAL INFORMATION INFRASTRUCTURE[*] (including H.R. 2441/S. 1284, 104th Cong., 2d Sess.)

THE REPORT OF THE WORKING GROUP ON INTELLECTUAL PROPERTY RIGHTS

Bruce A. Lehman

Assistant Secretary of Commerce and
Commissioner of Patents and Trademarks

CHAIR

INFORMATION INFRASTRUCTURE TASK FORCE

Ronald H. Brown

Secretary of Commerce

CHAIR

SEPTEMBER 1995

INTRODUCTION

In February 1993, President Clinton formed the Information Infrastructure Task Force (IITF) to articulate and implement the Administration's vision for the National Information Infrastructure (NII). The IITF is chaired by Secretary of Commerce Ronald H. Brown and consists of high-level representatives of the Federal agencies that play a role in advancing the development and application of information technologies. Guided by the principles for government action described in *NII Agenda for Action*[1] and *GII Agenda for Cooperation*,[2] the participating agencies are working with the private sector, public interest groups, Congress, and State and local governments to develop comprehensive telecommunications and information policies and programs that will promote the development of the NII and best meet the country's needs.

To drive these efforts, the IITF is organized into three committees: the Telecommunications Policy Committee, which formulates Administration positions on relevant telecommunications issues; the Committee on Applications and Technology, which coordinates Administration efforts to develop, demonstrate and promote applications of information technologies in key areas; and the Information Policy Committee, which addresses critical information policy

---

[*] Including selected footnotes only.—*Eds.*

[1] Information Infrastructure Task Force, *National Telecommunications and Information Administration, National Information Infrastructure: Agenda for Action* (Sept. 1993).

[2] Information Infrastructure Task Force, *Global Information Infrastructure: Agenda for Cooperation* (Feb. 1995).

issues that must be dealt with if the NII is to be fully deployed and utilized. In addition, the IITF established a Security Issues Forum to assess the security needs and concerns of users, service providers, information providers, State and local governments and others. Finally, the U.S. Advisory Council on the National Information Infrastructure (NII Advisory Council) was established within the Department of Commerce to advise the Secretary of Commerce on a national strategy for promoting the development of the NII.

The Working Group on Intellectual Property Rights, which is chaired by Assistant Secretary of Commerce and Commissioner of Patents and Trademarks Bruce A. Lehman, was established within the Information Policy Committee to examine the intellectual property implications of the NII and make recommendations on any appropriate changes to U.S. intellectual property law and policy.

This Report represents the Working Group's examination and analysis of each of the major areas of intellectual property law, focusing primarily on copyright law and its application and effectiveness in the context of the NII.[5] The approach of this Report is to discuss the application of the existing copyright law and to recommend only those changes that are essential to adapt the law to the needs of the global information society. By providing a generalized legal framework, based on the extensive analysis and discussion of the way in which the law has been and should be interpreted, we can lay the groundwork for the rapid and efficient development of the NII.

To prepare this Report, the Working Group drew upon expertise within the participating departments and agencies of the Federal government. In addition, the Working Group received and considered views of the public, including those of the NII Advisory Council.

The Working Group held a public hearing in November 1993, at which 30 witnesses testified. The Working Group also solicited written comments and received some 70 statements during a public comment period which closed on December 10, 1993. Following its review of the public comments and analysis of the issues, the Working Group released a preliminary draft of its report ("Green Paper") on July 7, 1994.[10] The Working Group issued the report in preliminary draft form to ensure broad dissemination and ample opportunity for public comment prior to making final recommendations and issuing this

---

[5] The "National Information Infrastructure," as it is discussed in this Report, encompasses digital, interactive services now available, such as the Internet, as well as those contemplated for the future. To make the analyses more concrete, however, the Working Group has, in many instances, evaluated the intellectual property implications of activity on the Internet, the superstructure whose protocols and rules effectively create (or permit the creation of) a "network of networks." This reflects neither an endorsement of the Internet nor a derogation of any other existing or proposed network or service that may be available via the NII, but, rather, an acknowledgment that a currently functioning structure lends itself more readily to legal analysis than a hypothetical construct based on future developments.

[10] *See* Information Infrastructure Task Force, Working Group on Intellectual Property Rights, Intellectual Property and the National Information Infrastructure: A Preliminary Draft of the Report of the Working Group on Intellectual Property Rights (July 1994).

Report. Thousands of copies of the Green Paper were distributed in paper form as well as electronically via the IITF Bulletin Board.[11]

Following the release of the Green Paper, the Working Group heard testimony from the public in four days of hearings in Chicago, Los Angeles and Washington, D.C., in September 1994. In addition, more than 1,500 pages of written comments on the Green Paper and reply comments were filed, in paper form and through the Internet, by more than 150 individuals and organizations-representing more than 425,000 members of the public-during the comment period, which extended over four months.

The Working Group convened a Conference on Fair Use (CONFU) to bring together copyright owner and user interests to discuss fair use issues and, if possible, to develop guidelines for uses of copyrighted works by librarians and educators. Some 60 interest groups are participants in the Conference and have been meeting regularly since September 1994 in sessions that are open to the public. The Working Group also kicked off a Copyright Awareness Campaign (CAC) in March 1995. Approximately 40 participating individuals and organizations are coordinating their educational efforts and joining with the Working Group and the Department of Education to raise public awareness of copyright. Meetings of the Campaign are also open to the public.

Interested parties had numerous opportunities to submit their views on the intellectual property implications of the development and use of the NII and on the Working Group's Green Paper, including its preliminary findings and recommendations. The open process instituted by the Working Group resulted in a well-developed, voluminous record indicating the views of a wide variety of interested parties, including various electronic industries, service providers, the academic, research, library and legal communities, and individual creators, copyright owners and users, as well as the computer software, motion picture, music, broadcasting, publishing and other information and entertainment industries.

The special intellectual property concerns and issues raised by the development and use of the NII are the subject of this Report.[14] It does not, however, provide all of the answers. It may not even present all of the questions. There is much that we do not-and cannot-now know about how the NII will develop. Technology is advancing at such an incredible pace that issues will certainly continue to arise in the future, perhaps demanding more comprehensive legislation. However, because there is much that we do know, the fact that future

[11] The IITF Bulletin Board can be accessed through the Internet by pointing the Gopher Client to iitf.doc.gov or by telnet to iitf.doc.gov (log in as gopher). The Bulletin Board is also accessible at 202-501-1920 using a personal computer and a telephone modem.

[14] This Report does not attempt to address all existing intellectual property issues. For instance, current debates over protection of the design of useful articles and whether or to what extent certain aspects of computer programs are or should be protected under copyright law are not covered by this Report. Likewise, certain patent issues, such as pre-grant publication and reexamination, are not addressed.

developments will raise additional issues not currently ripe should not deter us from addressing those that are.[15]

BACKGROUND

Intellectual property is a subtle and esoteric area of the law that evolves in response to technological change. Advances in technology particularly affect the operation and effectiveness of copyright law. Changes in technology generate new industries and new methods for reproduction and dissemination of works of authorship, which may present new opportunities for authors, but also create additional challenges. Copyright law has had to respond to those challenges, from Gutenberg's moveable type printing press to digital audio recorders and everything in between-photocopiers, radio, television, videocassette recorders, cable television and satellites.

Uses of computer technology-such as digitization-and communications Technology-such as fiber optic cable—have had an enormous impact on the creation, reproduction and dissemination of copyrighted works. The merger of computer and communications technology into an integrated information technology has made possible the development of the National Information Infrastructure which will generate both unprecedented challenges and important opportunities for the copyright marketplace.

An information infrastructure already exists, but it is not integrated into a whole. Telephones, televisions, radios, computers and fax machines are used every day to receive, store, process, perform, display and transmit data, text, voice, sound and images in homes and businesses throughout the country. Fiber optics, wires, cables, switches, routers, microwave networks, satellites and other communications technologies currently connect telephones, computers and fax machines. The NII of tomorrow, however, will be much more than these separate communications networks; it will integrate them into an advanced high-speed, interactive, broadband, digital communications system. Computers, telephones, televisions, radios, fax machines and more will be linked by the NII, and users will be able to communicate and interact with other computers, telephones, televisions, radios, fax machines and more—all in digital form.[18]

The NII has tremendous potential to improve and enhance our lives. It can increase access to a greater amount and variety of information and entertainment resources that can be delivered quickly and economically from and to virtually anywhere in the world in the blink of an eye. For instance, hundreds of channels of "television" programming, thousands of musical recordings,

---

[15] In the process of preparing this Report, the Working Group constantly received and evaluated information concerning a large variety of technological and other developments that bear on the NII and intellectual property rights in works distributed thereon. In April 1995, the Working Group was compelled to place the Report in concrete form, and, thus, to stop adjusting the text with respect to just received news. As a result, the Working Group has elected to: (a) pose in some detail — but not try to definitively answer — certain questions, and (b) not discuss every possible technological development of which it recently became aware. We are confident that the legislative and political processes will offer the opportunity for additional comments from both the U.S. Government and interested parties.

[18] These devices will be linked not only to each other (computer to computer, for example) but will also be cross-linked (computer to television set).

and literally millions of "magazines" and "books" can be made available to homes and businesses across the United States and around the world.[19]

The NII can provide access to rich cultural resources around the world, transforming and expanding the scope and reach of the arts and humanities. It will provide opportunities for the development of new markets for cultural products. It can broaden our cultural experiences through diversity of content, and increase our understanding of other societies.

The NII can support our education systems by, for example, linking students and educators in remote locations around the world. It can also improve the nation's health care systems by increasing public awareness of health issues, providing continuing education of health care professionals, and allowing patients to take a more active role in their own health care.

The NII can dramatically increase the opportunity for democratic participation in government. The Task Force has shown some of the potential in its work. For instance, the IITF Bulletin Board makes available copies of Task Force reports, testimony, speeches, meeting schedules and minutes, hearing notices, transcripts, and other documents related to the work of the Administration and opportunities for public participation. The Task Force has also accepted comments from the public through the Internet and has conducted an on-line public conference.

Individuals and entities that heretofore have been predominately consumers of works can now become authors and providers through the NII. It can put easier, more sophisticated communication and publishing tools in the hands of the public, increasing the ability to communicate with, and disseminate works of authorship to, others.

The NII can boost the ability of U.S. firms to compete and succeed in the global economy, thereby generating more jobs for Americans. It can spur economic growth. More than half of the U.S. work force is in information-based jobs, and the telecommunications and information sector is growing faster than any other sector of the U.S. economy. New job opportunities can be created in the processing, organizing, packaging and dissemination of the information and entertainment products flowing through the NII.

The NII can provide benefits to authors and consumers by reducing the time between creation and dissemination. It will open additional markets for authors. If authors choose to enter those new markets, it will provide a wider variety and greater number of choices for consumers, which should increase competition and reduce prices. The availability of these benefits is by no means assured, however. Authors are wary of entering this market because doing so exposes their works to a higher risk of piracy and other unauthorized uses than any of the traditional, current modes of dissemination.

[19] The United States and other countries are working toward the development of an advanced Global Information Infrastructure (GII) that "will allow us to share information, to connect, and to communicate as a global community." And as that information moves through international channels, "[p]rotecting intellectual property is absolutely essential." *See* Remarks Prepared for Delivery by Vice President Al Gore at the International Telecommunications Union in Buenos Aires, Argentina (March 21, 1994).

Therefore, authors may withhold their works from this environment. Further, even if authors choose not to expose their works to this more risky environment, the risk is not eliminated. Just one unauthorized uploading of a work onto a bulletin board, for instance—unlike, perhaps, most single reproductions and distributions in the analog or print environment—could have devastating effects on the market for the work.

Thus, the full potential of the NII will not be realized if the education, information and entertainment products protected by intellectual property laws are not protected effectively when disseminated via the NII. Creators and other owners of intellectual property rights will not be willing to put their interests at risk if appropriate systems-both in the U.S. and internationally—are not in place to permit them to set and enforce the terms and conditions under which their works are made available in the NII environment. Likewise, the public will not use the services available on the NII and generate the market necessary for its success unless a wide variety of works are available under equitable and reasonable terms and conditions, and the integrity of those works is assured. All the computers, telephones, fax machines, scanners, cameras, keyboards, televisions, monitors, printers, switches, routers, wires, cables, networks and satellites in the world will not create a successful NII, if there is no content. What will drive the NII is the content moving through it.

Ensuring consumer access to and enjoyment of both copyrighted works and new technologies is an attainable goal, and recent experience has confirmed this.[22] For example, the introduction of digital audio tape recorders recently posed significant problems for copyright owners. Congress responded to the increased threat of rampant unauthorized use with legislation that incorporated both technological and legal measures to protect the interests of both consumers and copyright owners.[23]

---

[22] *See, e.g.*, Sony Corp. v. Universal City Studios, Inc., 464 U.S. 417, 430–31 nn.11–12 (1984) (hereinafter Sony) (discussing significance of changes in technology and their effect on copyright law); *Final Report of the National Commission on New Technological Uses of Copyrighted Works* (hereinafter CONTU Final Report) at 3 (reporting about the issues raised by photocopiers and computers back in 1978, in language that is equally applicable today) (citations omitted):

> The ownership and control of information and the means of disseminating it are emerging as national and international policy issues. Concerns about the impact on individual freedom posed by the control of the flow of information are at the forefront of public debate. The adequacy of the legal structure to cope with the pace and rate of technological change frequently has been called into question.

[23] Congress enacted the Audio Home Recording Act of 1992, which combined legal and technological protection for sound recordings. *See* 17 U.S.C. 1001 et seq. (Supp. V 1993). The Audio Home Recording Act requires a serial copy management system in all digital audio recording devices and digital audio interface devices imported, manufactured or distributed in the United States. Such a system allows unlimited first generation digital copying of sound recordings, but prevents the making of digital copies from copies. The Act prohibits the importation, manufacture or distribution of any device, or the offering or performance of service, the primary purpose of which is to circumvent any program or circuit which implements a serial copy management system. The Act also establishes a royalty system through which importers and manufacturers of digital audio recording devices and digital audio recording media make royalty payments on each device or medium they distribute. Such payments are collected by the Copyright Office and distributed annually to record companies, performers, music publishers and songwriters.

Advances in digital technology and the rapid development of electronic networks and other communications technologies raise the stakes considerably. Any two-dimensional work can readily be "digitized"—i.e., translated into a digital code (usually a series of zeros and ones). The work can then be stored and used in that digital form. This dramatically increases: the ease and speed with which a work can be reproduced; the quality of the copies (both the first and the hundredth "generation" are virtually identical); the ability to manipulate and change the work; and the speed with which copies (authorized and unauthorized) can be "delivered" to the public. Works also can be combined easily with other works into a single medium, such as a CD-ROM, which contributes to a blurring of the lines that typically divide types of works and the rights and limitations applicable thereto.

The establishment of high-speed, high-capacity electronic information systems makes it possible for one individual, with a few key strokes, to deliver perfect copies of digitized works to scores of other individuals—or to upload a copy to a bulletin board or other service where thousands of individuals can download it or print unlimited "hard" copies. The emergence of integrated information technology is dramatically changing, and will continue to change, how people and businesses deal in and with information and entertainment products and services, and how works are created, reproduced, distributed, adapted, displayed, performed, owned, licensed, managed, presented, organized, sold, accessed, used and stored. This leads, understandably, to a call for adaptation of—or change in—the law.

Thomas Jefferson stated:

> I am not an advocate for frequent changes in laws and constitutions. But laws and institutions must go hand and hand with the progress of the human mind. As that becomes more developed, more enlightened, as new discoveries are made, new truths discovered and manners and opinions change, with the change of circumstances, institutions must advance also to keep pace with the times. We might as well require a man to wear still the coat which fitted him when a boy....[24]

Our task is to determine whether the coat still fits in this new information age. An effective intellectual property regime must (1) ensure that users have access to the broadest feasible variety of works by (2) recognizing the legitimate rights and commercial expectations of persons and entities whose works are used in the NII environment.

For more than two centuries, copyright law, with periodic amendment, has provided protection for an increasing variety of works of authorship. The most recent complete revision of the law—The Copyright Act of 1976—was enacted in response to "significant changes in technology [that had] affected

---

[24] *See* Inscription at the Jefferson Memorial, Washington, D.C. As Secretary of State, Thomas Jefferson was the first head of the U.S. Patent Office.

the operation of the copyright law."[26] The legislative history of the 1976 Act notes that those changes had "generated new industries and new methods for the reproduction and dissemination of copyrighted works, and the business relations between authors and users [had] evolved new patterns."[27]

We are once again faced with significant changes in technology that upset the balance that currently exists under the Copyright Act. Our goal is to maintain the existing balance.

Some assert that copyright protection should be reduced in the NII environment. The public wants information to be free and unencumbered on the NII, it is argued, and the law should reflect the public interest. Without doubt, this is a valid concern. Information per se should not be protected by copyright law—nor is it. Facts and ideas from any work of authorship may be freely copied and distributed; the Copyright Act expressly excludes such information from the scope of the protection it accords. The copyright law should also serve the public interest—and it does. While, at first blush, it may appear to be in the public interest to reduce the protection granted works and to allow unfettered use by the public, such an analysis is incomplete. Protection of works of authorship provides the stimulus for creativity, thus leading to the availability of works of literature, culture, art and entertainment that the public desires and that form the backbone of our economy and political discourse. If these works are not protected, then the marketplace will not support their creation and dissemination, and the public will not receive the benefit of their existence or be able to have unrestricted use of the ideas and information they convey.

Others assert that technological advances justify reduced protection. Since computer networks now make unauthorized reproduction, adaptation, distribution and other uses of protected works so incredibly easy, it is argued, the law should legitimize those uses or face widespread flouting. This argument is not valid. Technology makes many things possible. Computer networks can be and have been used to embezzle large sums of money and to commit other crimes. Yet, these acts are prohibited by law. Simply because a thing is possible does not mean that it should be condoned.

Finally, there are those who argue that intellectual property laws of any country are inapplicable to works on the NII or GII because all activity using these infrastructures takes place in "Cyberspace," a sovereignty unto itself that should be self-governed by its inhabitants, individuals who, it is suggested, will rely on their own ethics—or "netiquette"—to determine what uses of works, if any, are improper. First, this argument relies on the fantasy that users of the Internet, for instance, are somehow transported to "chat rooms" and other locations, such as virtual libraries. While such conceptualization helps to put

---

[26] *See* H.R. Rep. No. 1476, 94th Cong., 2d Sess. 47 (1976) (hereinafter *House Report*) ("During the past half century a wide range of new techniques for capturing and communicating printed matter, visual images, and recorded sounds have come into use, and the increasing use of information storage and retrieval devices, communications satellites, and laser technology promises even greater changes in the near future.").

[27] *See* House Report at 47.

in material terms what is considered rather abstract, activity on the Internet takes place neither in outer space nor in parallel, virtual locations. Satellite, broadcast, fax and telephone transmissions have not been thought to be outside the jurisdiction of the nations from which or to which they are sent. Computer network transmissions have no distinguishing characteristics warranting such other-world treatment. Further, such a legal free-for-all would transform the GII into a veritable copyright Dodge City. As enticing as this concept may seem to some users, it would hardly encourage creators to enter its confines.

Nonetheless, content providers are currently experimenting with a number of business models in the networked environment, and it is already clear that a wide variety of such models may coexist. Some content providers will choose not to enforce all-or any-of their rights; others may change their business practices. For instance, some newspaper publishers are selling individual articles using electronic payment mechanisms, in addition to selling subscriptions and individual issues. Some software companies are making their "client" software freely available for individual use in an effort to increase the market share of their "server" software. Some hypermedia magazine publishers on the World Wide Web are choosing to give away their product but charge sponsors for advertising space. A number of information service providers are charging for the use of the search engines that add value to freely available public domain content.

Some content providers will not be motivated by any commercial considerations. For instance, certain scientific communities are working together to create archives of freely available electronic pre-prints on the Internet. The copyright law allows copyright owners to exercise the rights granted to them, to license their rights to others, or to give them away. Those creators who wish to dedicate their works to the public domain may, of course, do so notwithstanding the availability of protection under the Copyright Act. Nothing in the law prevents those who do not wish to claim copyright from waiving their rights and allowing unrestricted reproduction, distribution and other use of their works. Indeed, notices to that effect are not uncommon on the Internet.

The absence on the NII of copyrighted works for which authors do wish to exercise their rights— fully or to some limited extent—under the copyright law, of course, would not necessarily result in its demise. The Internet, for instance, could continue to serve as a communications tool and resource for Government, public domain and works of willing authors. However, unless the framework for legitimate commerce is preserved and adequate protection for copyrighted works is ensured, the vast communications network will not reach its full potential as a true, global marketplace. Copyright protection is not an obstacle in the way of the success of the NII; it is an essential component. Effective copyright protection is a fundamental way to promote the availability of works to the public.

Preserving the framework does not require, however, a dramatic increase in authors' rights, such as more limited or no further applicability of the fair use doctrine in the NII environment. Some have argued that because it may now be technically feasible to "meter" each use of a copyrighted work, and to charge a user a fee for the use, the concept of fair use has no place in the NII environment. They argue equally that other limitations on rights should be abolished or narrowed for similar reasons. The Working Group believes that weakening copyright owners' rights in the NII is not in the public interest; nor would a dramatic increase in their rights be justified.

With no more than minor clarification and limited amendment, the Copyright Act will provide the necessary balance of protection of rights—and limitations on those rights—to promote the progress of science and the useful arts.[29] Existing copyright law needs only the fine tuning that technological advances necessitate, in order to maintain the balance of the law in the face of onrushing technology. There must be, however, effort in three disciplines—law, technology and education—to successfully address the intellectual property issues raised by the development and use of the NII.

* * * * * *

IV. RECOMMENDATIONS

A. Copyright

It is difficult for intellectual property laws to keep pace with technology. When technological advances cause ambiguity in the law, courts look to the law's underlying purposes to resolve that ambiguity. However, when technology gets too far ahead of the law, and it becomes difficult and awkward to adapt the specific statutory provisions to comport with the law's principles, it is time for reevaluation and change. "Even though the 1976 Copyright Act was carefully drafted to be flexible enough to be applied to future innovations, technology has a habit of outstripping even the most flexible statutes."[529]

> From its beginning, the law of Copyright has developed in response to significant changes in technology. Indeed, it was the invention of a new form of copying equipment—the printing press—that gave rise to the original need for copyright protection. Repeatedly, as new developments have occurred in this country, it has been the Congress that has fashioned the new rules that new technology made necessary.[530]

The Working Group has examined the adequacy of the Copyright Act to cope with the pace of technological changes. In applying the law to new uses, media and technology, the issues presented vary. Certain issues merely require an explanation of the application of the current law, and clearly are appropriately covered. Others present rights or limitations that clearly fit within the spirit of the law but the letter of the law is in need of clarification to avoid uncertainty and unnecessary litigation. Still others need new solutions. Technology

---

[29] The Working Group believes that no revision of the patent, trademark or trade secret law is warranted at this time.

[529] H.R. Rep. No. 101-735, 101st Cong., 2d Sess. 7 (1990) (report accompanying legislation granting copyright owners of computer software an exclusive rental right).

[530] *Sony*, [464 U.S. 417,] at 430–31 [(1984)].

has altered the balance of the Copyright Act—in some instances, in favor of copyright owners and in others, in favor of users. The goal of these recommendations is to accommodate and adapt the law to technological change so that the intended balance is maintained and the Constitutional purpose is served.

While it is not advisable to propose amendment of the law with every technological step forward, neither is it appropriate to blindly cling to the status quo when the market has been altered.

> Sound policy, as well as history, supports our consistent deference to Congress when major technological innovations alter the market for copyrighted materials. Congress has the constitutional authority and the institutional ability to accommodate fully the varied permutations of competing interests that are inevitably implicated by such new technology.[532]

Throughout more than 200 years of history, with periodic amendment, United States law has provided the necessary copyright protection for the betterment of our society. The Copyright Act is fundamentally adequate and effective. In a few areas, however, it needs to be amended to take proper account of the current technology. The coat is getting a little tight. There is no need for a new one, but the old one needs a few alterations.

1. The Transmission of Copies and Phonorecords

a. The Distribution Right

The Copyright Act gives a copyright owner the exclusive right "to distribute copies or phonorecords of the copyrighted work" to the public. It is not clear under the current law that a transmission can constitute a distribution of copies or phonorecords of a work. Yet, in the world of highspeed, communications systems, it is possible to transmit a copy of a work from one location to another. This may be the case, for instance, when a computer program is transmitted from one computer to ten other computers. When the transmission is complete, the original copy typically remains in the transmitting computer and a copy resides in the memory of, or in storage devices associated with, each of the other computers.[535] The transmission results essentially in the distribution of ten copies of the work. However, the extent of the distribution right under the present law may be somewhat uncertain and subject to challenge. Therefore, the Working Group recommends that the Copyright Act be amended to expressly recognize that copies or phonorecords of works can be distributed to the public by transmission, and that such transmissions fall within the exclusive distribution right of the copyright owner.

The proposed amendment does not create a new right. It is an express recognition that, as a result of technological developments, the distribution

[532] *Sony*, at 431.

[535] In contrast, a "standard" distribution of a copy necessarily divests the distributor of his copy. In the case of a distribution by transmission, the distributor generally retains his copy of the work and a reproduction is distributed.

right can be exercised by means of transmission—just as the reproduction, public performance and public display rights may be.[536]

It is argued by some that the existing right of distribution encompasses transmissions of copies and that no amendment is necessary. Indeed, the distribution right, as set forth in Section 106(3) of the Copyright Act, can be—and, in at least one case, has been—interpreted to include transmissions which distribute copies of works to, for example, the memories of computers. Transmission, it is argued, is logically and legally a means of distribution. The Working Group has no argument with such an interpretation; it properly conforms to the intent of the distribution right and, we believe, is correct from both a practical and legal standpoint.

Others suggest that amendment of the law may not be necessary because even if the distribution right does not cover the distribution of reproductions by transmission, the reproduction right is clearly implicated and that will protect the copyright owner. However, the fact that more than one right may be involved in infringing activity does not, and should not, mean that only one right should apply. Each of the exclusive rights is distinct and separately alienable and different parties may be responsible for infringements or licensing of different rights—and different rights may be owned by different people. Because transmissions of copies may constitute both a reproduction and a distribution of a work, transmissions of copies should not constitute the exercise of just one of those rights. Indeed, those licensed only to reproduce a work should not be entitled to also distribute the work through transmission—thereby displacing the market for the copyright owner or his distribution licensee.

Infringement takes place when any one of the rights is violated: where, for example, a printer reproduces copies without selling them or a retailer sells copies without having anything to do with their reproduction.[539]

Clearly, not all transmissions of copies of copyrighted works will fall within the copyright owner's exclusive distribution right. Moreover, even if a transmission of a copy falls within the scope of the right, it is not necessarily unlawful. First, the distribution must be a distribution *to the public*. The case law interpreting "publication" provides guidance as to what constitutes distribution to the public.[540] If a distribution would not constitute a publication of

---

[536] It has been suggested that recognition of distribution by transmission may diminish the public performance right. However, if a work is publicly performed by transmission, then there has been a public performance—whether or not the distribution right is or is not also involved. The fact that some transmissions may constitute a reproduction and distribution of copies to the public does not mean that transmissions that constitute public performances are not public performances. The scope of the public performance right is not diminished by the recognition that a transmission may fall within the scope of the distribution right. If a copy of a motion picture is transmitted to a computer's memory, for instance, and in the process, the sounds are capable of being heard and the images viewed as they are received in memory, then the public performance right may well be implicated as well. *See* 17 U.S.C. § 101 (1988) (definition of "perform").

[539] House Report at 61.

[540] ... The term "public" as used in connection with the distribution right is not coincident with the meaning assigned to that term in connection with the public performance or public display right.

the work, then it would likely be found to be outside the scope of the copyright owner's distribution right. Therefore, the transmission of a copyrighted work from one person to another in a private e-mail message would not constitute a distribution to the public.[541] Second, all of the limitations, exemptions and defenses that currently apply to the distribution right and allow users to distribute certain copies to the public or to distribute copies under certain circumstances will continue to apply. For example, any exercise of one of the exclusive rights may be fair use—including the reproduction and distribution of copies by transmission.

Some are of the view that the current language of the Act does not encompass distribution by transmission. They argue that the proposed amendment expands the copyright owner's rights without a concomitant expansion of the limitations on those rights. However, since transmissions of copies already clearly implicate the reproduction right, it is misleading to suggest that the proposed amendment of the distribution right would expand the copyright owner's rights into an arena previously unprotected.

Further, even if the premise is correct (that the amendment expands the distribution right), the conclusion that the limitations of that right are not similarly expanded is invalid. The limitations on the right—which place certain distributions to the public outside the scope of the copyright owner's right—would necessarily expand to also place similar distributions by means of transmission outside the scope of the right.

Nevertheless, there is no reason to treat works that are distributed in copies to the public by means of transmission differently than works distributed in copies to the public by other, more conventional means.[542] Copies distributed via transmission are as tangible as any distributed over the counter or through the mail. Through each method of distribution, the consumer receives a tangible copy of the work.

When the public performance right was initially granted, it was thought to encompass only "live," in-person performances. When it became clear that copyrighted works could be publicly performed by other means—i.e., broadcast and, later, cable transmissions—the law was clarified. The same is true today with respect to the distribution right. Transmission is a means of distribution of copies, just as it can be a means of performance. However, the differences of opinion summarized above underscore the need for clarification and legal certainty. The costs and risks of litigation to define more clearly the right—and the time achieving such clarity would take—would discourage and delay use of the NII.

(b) Related Definitional Amendments

The Working Group also recommends other related amendments to two definitions.

---

[541] If copies of works are offered to the public—even though they may be distributed one copy at a time—it would likely constitute distribution to the public. *See* 17 U.S.C. § 101 (1988) (definition of "publication") ...

[542] In the future, transmission may become the conventional means of distribution.

To "Transmit"

As explained above, under current technology, a copy of a work may be transmitted. However, the Copyright Act defines only what it is to transmit a performance or display of a work. Therefore, the Working Group recommends that the definition of "transmit" in Section 101 of the Copyright Act be amended to include a definition of a transmission of a reproduction.[543] How to delineate between these types of transmissions is a difficult issue to resolve. The transmissions themselves hold no clues; one type often looks the same as the other during the transmission. If the transmitter intends to transmit a performance of the work, as well as to distribute a reproduction of it—or if the receiver is able to hear or see a performance of the work in the course of receiving a copy of it—what rights are exercised by the transmission? A transmission could be a transmission of a reproduction or a performance or both. The resolution of these issues should rest upon the specific facts of the case. Such issues will typically be clarified between rights-holders and users in appropriate license arrangements. If confusion or disagreement exists in a specific context, the courts—rather than Congress— are in the better position to determine which, if any, exclusive rights are involved in a particular transmission. Courts regularly make such determinations in other cases where rights overlap.[544]

"Publication"

The legislative history of the Copyright Act makes clear that "any form of dissemination in which a material object does not *change hands* ... is not a publication no matter how many people are exposed to the work."[545] Thus, a work that is only displayed or performed via the NII would not be considered published, no matter how many people have access to the display or performance, because a material object—a copy of the work—does not change hands. However, in the case of transmissions of reproductions, the recipients of the transmissions receive copies of the work (i.e., copies of the work have been distributed) — although they may not have "changed hands" in the literal sense.

Whether the transmission of copies of works is clearly within the scope of the distribution right is also a problem with respect to the act of publication by the transmission of copies. Indeed, the definition of "publication" incorporates the language used to describe the distribution right, which the Working Group's proposal amends.[547] Publication largely turns on whether the work has

[543] Under the proposed definition, to transmit a reproduction is to distribute it by any device or process whereby a copy or phonorecord of the work is fixed beyond the place from which it was sent.

[544] To delineate between those transmissions that are communications of performances or displays and those that are distributions of reproductions, one may look at both ends of the transmission. Did the transmitter intend to communicate a performance or display of the work or, rather, to distribute a reproduction of the work? Did the receiver simply hear or see the work or rather/also receive a copy of it? Did the receiver simply receive a copy or was it possible for her to hear or see it as well? License rates and terms will assist in determining the intent of the parties.

[545] *See* House Report at 138 (emphasis added).

[547] Under the current law, the distribution right is identified as the right "to distribute copies or phonorecords of the copyrighted work to the public by sale or other transfer of ownership, or by rental, lease, or lending." *See* 17 U.S.C. § 106(3) (1988).

been distributed to the public. Thus, if copies of a work may be distributed to the public by transmission, then a work may be published by the transmission of copies to the public. Therefore, consistent with the proposed amendment of the distribution right, the Working Group recommends that the definition of "publication" in Section 101 of the Copyright Act be amended to recognize that a work may be published through the distribution of copies of the work to the public by transmission.[548]

The effects under the law of a work being considered published (rather than unpublished) generally are negative from the viewpoint of the copyright owner. Published works, for example: (1) must be deposited in the Library of Congress; (2) are subject to more limitations on the exclusive rights, including a broader application of fair use; (3) must meet certain author nationality or domicile requirements to be eligible for protection; and (4) must bear a copyright notice if published before March 1, 1989. However, the designation of works distributed to the public by transmission as published will be important in the case of works distributed first—or solely-on-line. The deposit requirement will aid in the preservation of those works, which otherwise might be updated or revised on-line, destroying—or at least obscuring—the original published versions. This may be particularly critical in preserving the scholarly and scientific record.ilable for reference, partially because of the deposit requirement, but primarily because subsequent versions do not override the originals—which is possible in the on-line environment.

Just as not all distributions of copies by transmission will constitute distributions to the public (and fall within the distribution right), not all transmissions of copies will constitute publication. Private e-mail messages would not be regarded as published. Neither would other restricted transmissions of copies, such as those in a typical corporate setting, where transmissions of copies within the company computer network are restricted as to further distribution. However, as in the print environment, the distribution of copies to a small group under circumstances where further distribution is authorized would publish the work.[553]

(c) The Importation Provisions

The Working Group also recommends that the prohibitions on importation be amended to reflect the fact that, just as copies of copyrighted works can be distributed by transmission in the United States, they can also be imported into the U.S. by transmission. If an infringing literary work, for instance, were physically shipped into the U.S. in the form of a paper copy, a CD-ROM disk or

[548] Under the law of the United Kingdom, making a work available to the public by means of an electronic retrieval system constitutes publication. *See* Copyright, Designs and Patents Act of 1988, § 175(1)(b).

[553] *See* White v. Kimmell, 193 F.2d 744 (9th Cir. 1952) (unrestricted circulation of 200 copies of a manuscript to friends and acquaintances published the work); Continental Casualty Co. v. Beardsley, 253 F.2d 702 (2d Cir. 1958) (distribution of approximately 100 sets of forms to corporate officers and surety companies for possible purchase of more constituted publication).

even stored on a memory chip, then it would be an infringing importation if the statutory conditions existed.

Cross-border transmission of copies of copyrighted works should be subject to the same restrictions as shipping them by airmail. Just as the distribution of copies of a copyrighted work is no less a distribution than the distribution of copies by mail, the international transmission of copies of copyrighted works is no less an importation than the importation by airmail.

Although we recognize that the U.S. Customs Service cannot, for all practical purposes, enforce a prohibition on importation by transmission, given the global dimensions of the information infrastructure of the future, it is important that copyright owners have the other remedies for infringements of this type available to them. Therefore, the Working Group recommends that Section 602 of the Copyright Act be amended to include importation by carriage or shipping of copies as well as by transmission of them.

2. Public Performance Right for Sound Recordings

Transmissions of sound recordings will certainly supplement and may eventually replace the current forms of distribution of phonorecords. In the very near future, consumers will be able to receive digital transmissions of sound recordings on demand—for performance in the home or for downloading—from the so-called "celestial jukebox." The legal nature of such transmissions—whether they are performances or distributions—has been widely debated. As discussed above, the Working Group recommends that Section 106 of the Copyright Act be amended to make clear that copies or phonorecords can be distributed by transmission. However, many of these transmissions will clearly constitute exercise of the public performance right—a right which the Copyright Act fails to grant to copyright owners of sound recordings.[555]

The lack of a public performance right in sound recordings under U.S. law is an historical anomaly that does not have a strong policy justification—and certainly not a legal one. Sound recordings are the only copyrighted works that are capable of being performed that are not granted that right. Therefore, for example, to transmit a performance of a sound recording without infringement liability, an audio-on-demand service acting as a "celestial jukebox" must obtain a license from, and pay a royalty to, the copyright owner of the underlying musical work (i.e., the person or entity who owns the rights in the notes and the lyrics), but it does not have to obtain permission from, or pay a license fee to, the copyright owner of the sound recording or the performer. The Working Group believes that this inequity should be rectified.

Public performance rights are granted in many foreign markets. Due to the lack of a performance right in the United States, U.S. performers and

[555] Some transmissions that clearly constitute public performances may, in effect, substitute for distributions in the future. If consumers are offered a service through which they can receive a performance of any sound recording at any time, they may stop buying phonorecords. The market for distributed phonorecords may shrink to include only the providers of that service to consumers.

record companies are denied their fair share of foreign royalty pools for the public performance of U.S. sound recordings in some countries and are in danger of losing access to their share in others.

By granting performance rights in sound recordings, the United States will treat the creators of these culturally and economically important copyrighted works the same as all other works capable of being publicly performed. This legislation will provide increased incentive for the creators of sound recordings to produce and disseminate more works, thereby expanding consumer choice. In addition, the enactment of these rights will strengthen the hand of Government negotiators and private advocates seeking a fair share of foreign royalty pools.

Some argue that copyright owners of sound recordings should not be granted a public performance right because they derive some indirect benefit from the public performance of their works. This argument is based on the theory that the public performance of a work increases the sales of reproductions of that work. Therefore, the copyright owner gets an indirect benefit (i.e., increased sales of reproductions) from the so-called "free advertising" that public performances provide. This, in fact, may be true in some cases. However, it is not a valid policy argument against providing sound recording copyright owners with the full panoply of exclusive rights other copyright owners enjoy.

The exercise of one right often increases the value of the exercise of another right, but we do not restrict any other copyright owners from exercising all of his or her rights. For instance:

— The copyright owner of the musical composition embodied in a sound recording is paid both when recordings of the composition are sold and when the composition is publicly performed—even though the public performance might increase the number of records sold and thus benefit the copyright owner.

— Serial excerpts from a novel that are published in a magazine might increase sales of the book, but the magazine nonetheless must obtain permission from the author of the book.

— The copyright owner of that novel may also increase his book sales when a motion picture based on the novel is released. However, no one suggests that the motion picture company should not have to pay the copyright owner of the novel for the right to turn it into a movie, just because the movie might indirectly benefit the copyright owner.

The copyright owners of sound recordings should be able to decide for themselves, as do all other copyright owners, if "free advertising" is sufficient compensation for the use of their works. If the users' arguments regarding the benefit copyright owners derive from the public performance of their sound recordings are correct, the users should be able to negotiate a very low rate for a license to do so.

It also has been argued that the copyright owners of sound recordings should not be granted the "exclusive" right that all other copyright owners enjoy, but instead be subject to a compulsory license, so that they cannot act as a "gatekeeper" to the licensing of performances of the musical works embodied in sound recordings. It is asserted that while a copyright owner of a sound recording with an exclusive public performance right could block the performance of the musical work by denying a license to publicly perform the sound recording, the copyright owner of the musical work could not. This argument is based on the incorrect assumption that copyright owners of musical works are not granted exclusive public performance rights. Section 106(4) of the Copyright Act clearly grants exclusive rights to the copyright owners of musical works, and, while virtually all music performance licensing is handled for those copyright owners by performing rights societies on a nonexclusive basis, the copyright owners could license their performance rights on an exclusive basis if they chose to do so.[556]

Two bills introduced in the 104th Congress would grant a very limited performance right in sound recordings.[557] A *full* public performance right—*particularly* with respect to all *digital* transmissions—is warranted. There is no just reason to afford a lower level of protection to one class of creative artists. Further, *any* special limitations on this right weakens our position internationally. The digital communications revolution—the creation of advanced information infrastructures—is erasing the distinctions among different categories of protected works and the uses made of them.

3. Library Exemptions

The copyright law carefully balances the rights of copyright owners with the legitimate needs of users. Nowhere is this balancing more apparent than in the exemptions that are intended to permit libraries reasonable use of copyrighted works to serve the legitimate demands of their patrons. Many have expressed concern that the special exemptions for libraries in Section 108 of the Copyright Act are no longer relevant in the digital era. Libraries, of course, may make fair use of any copyrighted works pursuant to the provisions of Section 107. Section 108, however, provides additional exemptions specifically for libraries and archives. On the one hand, there are those who believe that since licensing of transactions of works in digital form will be a feature of the digital distribution systems of the future, there is no need for library exceptions. Each copying transaction will be cheap and libraries can simply pay for all of the copying in which they engage. On the other hand, there are those who believe that unrestricted copying in libraries should be the rule, without the special conditions and limitations set forth in Section 108.

The Working Group agrees with neither those who would delete the exemptions for library copying nor those who would permit wholesale copying in libraries. It believes that there is an important public interest in exempting certain library uses of copyrighted works and that the public interest is no less important—and, indeed, may be more important—when such use involves

[556] If the copyright owners of sound recordings abused the exclusivity that the law should provide, the solution would lie in the enforcement of the antitrust laws— where the music licensing problems have been addressed—not in the reduction of rights under the Copyright Act.

[557] *See* S. 227, 104th Cong., 1st Sess. (1995); H.R. 1506, 104th Cong., 1st Sess. (1995).

digital technology. It also believes that there is an equally important interest in recognizing the legitimate interests of copyright owners in licensing uses of their works through voluntary systems.

Therefore, notwithstanding the legislative history of the 1976 Act which clearly intended that Section 108 did not permit digital reproduction,[559] the Working Group believes that it is important to expand the exemption so that digital copying by libraries and archives is permitted under certain circumstances. In supporting this departure from the generally accepted view of the scope and intention of Section 108, the Working Group believes that the law must preserve the role of libraries and archives in the digital era.

Libraries and archives are the trustees of our collective knowledge and must be able to make use of digital technology to preserve the Nation's heritage and scholarship. Therefore, the Working Group recommends that the library exemptions be amended: (1) to accommodate the reality of the computerized library by allowing the preparation of three copies of works in digital form, with no more than one copy in use at any time (while the others are archived); (2) to recognize that the use of a copyright notice on a published copy of a work is no longer mandatory; and (3) to authorize the making of digital copies for purposes of preservation.[560]

4. Reproduction for the Visually Impaired

The NII offers real opportunities to many visually impaired people to participate in learning, communication and discourse to a greater extent than when only conventional modes of communication are available. With the aid of software and computer equipment that is widely available, people now have the capacity to view text on CD-ROM on screen in a "large-type" format even if the publisher did not include such a feature, but the publication and distribution of large-type editions remains very important. To ensure fair access to all manner of printed materials, it is necessary to amend the copyright law.

The laws of many Berne Convention countries contain express exemptions from liability for the unauthorized manufacture and distribution of Braille or other editions designed to assist the visually impaired.[561] The Working Group believes that similar provisions should be included in the Copyright Act, and has modeled its proposal on the Australian law, so as to maintain private rights while recognizing certain readers' special needs. The proposed amendment

---

[559] The legislative history makes it clear that digital uses are generally not encompassed by Section 108: "Under this exemption, for example, a repository could make photocopies of manuscripts by microfilm or electrostatic process, but *could not reproduce the work in 'machine-readable' language* for storage in an information system." House Report at 75; Senate Report at 67 (emphasis added). The Senate Report also speaks precisely of "the *photocopying* needs of ... multi-county regional systems." *Id.* at 70 (emphasis added).

[560] The Working Group believes that replacement copies may be digital in nature, and may be made under this provision only when an unused replacement is not available in either digital or analog form.

[561] *See, e.g.*, Section 53D of the Australian law (privilege conditioned on copyright owner's abstention from market for Braille edition); Section 18 of the Finnish law (Braille editions and talking books may be manufactured "for use by lending libraries for blind persons"); Section 80 of the Portuguese law (Braille editions may be manufactured if not for profit).

would provide an exemption for non-profit organizations to reproduce and distribute to the visually impaired—at cost-Braille, large type, audio or other editions of previously published literary works in forms intended to be perceived by the visually impaired, provided that the owner of the exclusive right to distribute the work in the United States has not entered the market for such editions during the first year following first publication of the work.[562]

5. Criminal Offenses

Although the Copyright Act provides criminal penalties when the infringement is willful and is for purposes of commercial advantage or private financial gain, the dismissal of the criminal charges in *United States v. LaMacchia* demonstrates a serious lacuna in the criminal copyright provisions: it does not now reach even the most wanton and malicious large-scale endeavors to copy and provide on the NII limitless numbers of unauthorized copies of valuable copyrighted works unless the copier seeks profits. Since there is virtually no cost to the infringer, certain individuals are willing to make such copies (or assist others in making them) for reasons other than monetary reward. For example, someone who believes that all works should be free in Cyberspace can easily make and distribute thousands of copies of a protected work and may have no desire for commercial advantage or private financial gain.

The Working Group agrees with the *LaMacchia* court: Criminal as well as civil penalties should probably attach to willful, multiple infringements of copyrighted software even absent a commercial motive on the part of the infringer. One could envision ways that the copyright law could be modified to permit such prosecution. But, "[i]t is the legislature, not the Court which is to define a crime, and ordain its punishment."

Therefore, the Working Group generally supports the amendments to the copyright law and the criminal law (which sets out sanctions for criminal copyright violations) set forth in S. 1122, introduced in the 104th Congress by Senators Leahy and Feingold following consultations with the Justice Department. The bill would make it a criminal offense to willfully infringe a copyright by reproducing or distributing copies with a retail value of $5,000 or more. By setting a monetary threshold and requiring willfulness, the bill ensures that merely casual or careless conduct resulting in distribution of only a few copies will not be subject to criminal prosecution and that criminal charges will not be brought unless there is a significant level of harm to the copyright owner's rights.[565]

---

[562] The visually impaired were the only users with a disability who provided comments or testimony concerning a need for a narrow exemption to ensure the availability of literary works in a usable form. By its recommendation of such an exemption for the visually impaired, the Working Group does not intend to dismiss the possibility that other disabled users may have needs of which it has not been made aware and, therefore, has not considered.

[565] ... [T]he idea/expression dichotomy and the limitations on the exclusive rights, including fair use, address First Amendment concerns ... . *See also* Harper & Row, Publishers, Inc. v. Nation Enterprises, 471 U.S. 539, 560 (1985) ("First Amendment protections [are] embodied in the [Copyright] Act's distinction between copyrightable expression and uncopyrightable facts and ideas, and the latitude for scholarship and comment traditionally afforded by fair use").

6. Technological Protection

The ease of infringement and the difficulty of detection and enforcement will cause copyright owners to look to technology, as well as the law, for protection of their works. However, it is clear that technology can be used to defeat any protection that technology may provide. The Working Group finds that legal protection alone will not be adequate to provide incentive to authors to create and to disseminate works to the public. Similarly, technological protection likely will not be effective unless the law also provides some protection for the technological processes and systems used to prevent or restrict unauthorized uses of copyrighted works.

The Working Group finds that prohibition of devices, products, components and services that defeat technological methods of preventing unauthorized use is in the public interest and furthers the Constitutional purpose of copyright laws. Consumers of copyrighted works pay for the acts of infringers; copyright owners have suggested that the price of legitimate copies of copyrighted works may be higher due to infringement losses suffered by copyright owners. The public will also have access to more copyrighted works via the NII if they are not vulnerable to the defeat of protection systems.

Therefore, the Working Group recommends that the Copyright Act be amended to include a new Chapter 12, which would include a provision to prohibit the importation, manufacture or distribution of any device, product or component incorporated into a device or product, or the provision of any service, the primary purpose or effect of which is to avoid, bypass, remove, deactivate, or otherwise circumvent, without authority of the copyright owner or the law, any process, treatment, mechanism or system which prevents or inhibits the violation of any of the exclusive rights under Section 106. The provision will not eliminate the risk that protection systems will be defeated, but it will reduce it.

The proposed prohibition is intended to assist copyright owners in the protection of their works.[566] The Working Group recognizes, however, that copyright owners may wish to use such systems to prevent the unauthorized reproduction, for instance, of their works, but may also wish to allow some users to deactivate the systems. Furthermore, certain uses of copyrighted works are not unlawful under the Copyright Act. Therefore, the proposed legislation prohibits only those devices or products, the primary purpose or effect of which is to circumvent such systems *without authority*. That authority may be granted by the copyright owner or by limitations on the copyright owner's rights under the Copyright Act.

It has been suggested that the prohibition is incompatible with fair use. First, the fair use doctrine does not require a copyright owner to allow or to facilitate unauthorized access or use of a work. Otherwise, copyright owners

---

[566] Legislation of a similar type has been introduced with respect to technological protection of audiovisual works. *See, e.g.*, S. 1096, 102d Cong., 1st Sess., 137 Cong. Rec. S. 6034 (1991); H.R. 3568, 101st Cong., 1st Sess., 135 Cong. Rec. H. 7924 (1989).

could not withhold works from publication; movie theatres could not charge admission or prevent audio or video recording; museums could not require entry fees or prohibit the taking of photographs. Indeed, if the provision of access and the ability to make fair use of copyrighted works were required of copyright owners—or an affirmative right of the public—even passwords for access to computer databases would be considered illegal. Second, if the circumvention device is primarily intended and used for legal purposes, such as fair use, the device would not violate the provision, because a device with such purposes and effects would fall under the "authorized by law" exemption.

Concern has also been expressed with regard to the ability to defeat technological protection for copies of works not protected by copyright law, such as those whose term of protection has expired or those in the public domain for other reasons (such as ineligibility for protection). However, devices whose primary purpose and effect is to defeat the protection for such works would not violate the provision. The proposed provision exempts all devices, products and services primarily intended and used for legal purposes, which would include the reproduction and distribution of copies of works in the public domain. Further, a protection system on copies of works in the public domain would not qualify with respect to such copies as a system which "prevents or inhibits the violation of any of the exclusive rights of the copyright owner under Section 106." Works in the public domain are not protected by copyright, and thus have no copyright owner or exclusive rights applicable to them. Finally, while technological protection may be applied to copies of works in the public domain, such protection attaches only to those particular copies-not to the underlying work itself.[567]

It has also been suggested that the provision places an unwarranted burden on manufacturers. The proposed amendment would impose no requirement on manufacturers to accommodate any protection systems, such as those required in Chapter 10 of manufacturers of digital audio recording devices.[568]

The provision would only prohibit the manufacture of circumvention devices.[569]

[567] Copies of the work in the marketplace free from copyright protection could be freely reproduced (and, in fact, the lower distribution costs of the NII may encourage increased availability of public domain works). Further, technological protection that restricts the ability to reproduce the work by technical means does not prevent reproduction by other means (such as quoting, manually copying, etc.).

[568] However, the Working Group does encourage the equipment manufacturing and copyright industries to work together on bilateral solutions for other types of recording devices and categories of works. In response to a request from Congressional leaders, representatives of the motion picture industry and the consumer electronics industry are presently drafting a joint legislative proposal addressing legal and technical measures pertaining to consumer recording of motion pictures. This proposal would set forth a technical means to be applied that would respect the legitimate commercial expectations of copyright owners and the reasonable and customary copying practices of consumers.

[569] Some have suggested that while manufacturers will surely know the primary purpose of the devices they produce, they may inadvertently find themselves liable for devices which they intended for legal purposes, but which have the incidental effect of circumventing copyright protection systems. For a manufacturer to find himself in this situation, the device would have to fail to be used primarily for the purpose for which it was sold, and be primarily used, to the surprise of its

Neither does the proposed amendment require copyright owners to use technological protection, or, if they do, to employ any particular type. Copyright owners should be free to determine what level or type of protection (if any) is appropriate for their works, taking into consideration cost and security needs, and different consumer and market preferences. Moreover, there is no evidence that one technological protection system could—or should—take care of all types of works. Legislation of this type is not unprecedented. The Copyright Act already protects sound recordings and musical works by prohibiting the circumvention of any program or circuit that implements a serial copy management system or similar system included in digital audio recording devices and digital audio interface devices. Section 1002 provides:

> No person shall import, manufacture, or distribute any device, or offer or perform any service, the primary purpose or effect of which is to avoid, bypass, remove, deactivate, or otherwise circumvent any program or circuit which implements, in whole or in part, a [serial copy management system or similar system].[570]

The Communications Act includes a similar provision:

> Any person who manufactures, assembles, modifies, imports, exports, sells, or distributes any electronic, mechanical, or other device or equipment, knowing or having reason to know that the device or equipment is primarily of assistance in the unauthorized decryption of satellite cable programming, or is intended for any other activity prohibited by [Section 605(a)] shall be fined not more than $500,000 for each violation, or imprisoned for not more than 5 years for each violation, or both. For purposes of all penalties and remedies established for violations of this paragraph, the prohibited activity established herein as it applies to each such device shall be deemed a separate violation.[571]

Precedent for this type of legislation is also found in the international arena. The NAFTA requires each party to make it a criminal offense to "manufacture, import, sell, lease or otherwise make available a device or system that is primarily of assistance in decoding an encrypted program-carrying satellite signal without the authorization of the lawful distributor of such signal...."[572] In 1988, the United Kingdom enacted legislation prohibiting the manufacture,

---

manufacturer, for defeating protection systems. It is likely that such a situation would occur rarely, if ever. (It would be self-defeating for copyright owners to begin using a protection system that an existing device could defeat.) However, the chapter contains an "innocent violation" provision for just such a case. A court would have the ability to reduce or eliminate altogether any damages for which the manufacturer would otherwise be liable, to avoid an unfair result but still protect the copyright owner.

570 17 U.S.C. § 1002(c) (Supp. V 1993).

571 47 U.S.C. § 605(e)(4) (1988).

572 *See* NAFTA, at art. 1707(a). The NAFTA also requires parties to make it a civil offense to "receive, in connection with commercial activities, or further distribute, an encrypted program-carrying satellite signal that has been decoded without the authorization of the lawful distributor of the signal or to engage in any activity prohibited under [the criminal provisions]." *See* NAFTA, at art. 1707(b).

distribution or sale of a device designed or adapted to circumvent copy-protection systems.[573]

7. Copyright Management Information

In the future, the copyright management information associated with a Work—such as the name of the copyright owner and the terms and conditions for uses of the workf—may be critical to the efficient operation and success of the NII. Copyright management information will serve as a kind of license plate for a work on the information superhighway, from which a user may obtain important information about the work. The accuracy of such information will be crucial to the ability of consumers to find and make authorized uses of copyrighted works on the NII. Reliable information will also facilitate efficient licensing and reduce transaction costs for licensable uses of copyrighted works (both fee-based and royalty-free).

The public should be protected from false information about who created the work, who owns rights in it, and what uses may be authorized by the copyright owner. Therefore, the Working Group recommends that the Copyright Act be amended to prohibit the provision, distribution or importation for distribution of copyright management information known to be false and the unauthorized removal or alteration of copyright management information. Under the proposed amendment, copyright management information is defined as the name and other identifying information of the author of a work, the name and other identifying information of the copyright owner, terms and conditions for uses of the work, and such other information as the Register of Copyrights may prescribe by regulation—to provide adequate flexibility in the future.[574]

While the proposed amendment does not require copyright owners to provide copyright management information, it does require that when such information is included, it be accurate. However, the Working Group encourages copyright owners to include the information to enable consumers to more easily find and make authorized uses of copyrighted works. Nor does it specify standardized formats or content, although private sector initiatives in this area are underway and are also encouraged by the Working Group. Finally, it does not require transmitting entities to include the copyright information as part of their transmission of a work where such information has been included in the work.[575] However, such a proposal deserves further consideration.

The proposal prohibits the falsification, alteration or removal of any copyright management information—not just that which is included in or digitally linked to the copyrighted work. Many users will obtain such information from public registers, where the integrity of such information will be no less

---

[573] *See* Copyright, Designs and Patents Act of 1988, Part VII, § 296.

[574] Other information that may become important to the efficient operation of the NII includes the country of origin of the work, the year of creation or first publication, a description of the work, the name and other identifying information of licensees and standardized codes.

[575] While a transmitting entity may not remove the copyright management information, if such information is not included in the normal course of the transmission (such as when a work in digital form is broadcast through analog transmission), no violation would occur.

important. The proposal also contains a knowledge requirement; therefore, inadvertent falsification, alteration or removal would not be a violation.[576]

B. PATENT

The present law governing the eligibility of inventions for patent protection and the enforcement of patent rights appears adequate to address the needs of inventors and the public with regard to technology used on the NII. The NII will increase the accessibility and content of the body of prior art, which in turn will affect patentability determinations. The law governing information that properly is considered part of the prior art appears to be adequate to address new forms of "printed" publications; however, some issues related to the authenticity, including the date of origination, the contents as originally disclosed, and the extent of dissemination of electronically disseminated publications, deserve further study.

The Working Group recommends that the Patent and Trademark Office obtain public input related to measures that can be adopted to ensure the authenticity of electronically—disseminated publications, particularly with respect to verifying the contents and date of first public dissemination of the publication, and evaluating the substantive value of the information contained in the publication as to its role in patentability determinations.

The Working Group also recommends that the PTO explore the feasibility of establishing requirements or standards that would govern authentication of the date and contents of electronically—disseminated information for purposes of establishing their use as prior art. Such standards would assist in patentability determinations, whether they occur before the PTO or before a court. To develop such standards, the PTO should invite public comment and work with other interested Federal agencies working on authentication standards outside the direct sphere of the patent system.

C. TRADEMARK

The Nice Agreement Concerning the International Classification of Goods and Services for the Purposes of the Registration of Marks must be sufficiently flexible to accommodate the changing goods and services available in connection with the NII and the GII. Such flexibility is essential to the owners of marks identifying goods and services connected with the NII and the GII, as well as to the continued viability of the International Classification system in the electronic information age. Therefore, the Working Group recommends that the Patent and Trademark Office, in the context of WIPO experts meetings on the International Classification system, propose changes to the International Classification system to ensure that the system reflects the goods and services of modern information technology. Additionally, the Working Group recommends that the Patent and Trademark Office regularly update its Manual for the Identification of Goods and Services to reflect new goods and services used on or in connection with the NII and GII.

---

576 For criminal liability, both knowledge and the intent to defraud are required.

Appendix 1
Proposed Legislation
NII Copyright Protection Act of 1995
104th Congress, 1st Session
[S. 1284/H.R. 2441]

A BILL

To amend title 17 to adapt the copyright law to the digital, networked environment of the National Information Infrastructure, and for other purposes.

Be it enacted by the Senate and House of Representatives of the United States of America in Congress assembled,

SEC. 1 SHORT TITLE.

This Act may be cited as the "NII Copyright Protection Act of 1995."

SEC. 2 TRANSMISSION OF COPIES.

(a) DISTRIBUTION.—Section 106(3) of title 17, United States Code, is amended by striking "or by rental, lease, or lending" and inserting "by rental, lease, or lending, or by transmission."

(b) DEFINITIONS.— Section 101 of title 17, United States Code, is amended—

(1) in the definition of "publication" by striking "or by rental, lease, or lending" in the first sentence and insert "by rental, lease, or lending, or by transmission"; and

(2) in the definition of "transmit" by inserting at the end thereof the following: "To `transmit' a reproduction is to distribute it by any device or process whereby a copy or phonorecord of the work is fixed beyond the place from which it was sent."

(c) IMPORTATION.—Section 602 of title 17, United States Code, is amended by inserting "whether by carriage of tangible goods or by transmission," after "Importation into the United States."

SEC. 3 EXEMPTIONS FOR LIBRARIES AND THE VISUALLY IMPAIRED.

(a) LIBRARIES.—Section 108 of title 17, United States Code, is amended—

(1) in subsection (a) by deleting "one copy or phonorecord" and inserting in lieu thereof "three copies or phonorecords";

(2) in subsection (a) by deleting "such copy or phonorecord" and inserting in lieu thereof "no more than one of such copies or phonorecords";

(3) by inserting at the end of subsection (a)(3) "if such notice appears on the copy or phonorecord that is reproduced under the provisions of this section";

(4) in subsection (b) by inserting "or digital" after "facsimile" and by inserting "in facsimile form" before "for deposit for research use"; and

(5) in subsection (c) by inserting "or digital" after "facsimile."

(b) VISUALLY IMPAIRED.—Title 17, United States Code, is amended by adding the following new section:

§ 108A. Limitations on exclusive rights: Reproduction for the Visually Impaired

> Notwithstanding the provision of section 106, it is not an infringement of copyright for a non-profit organization to reproduce and distribute to the visually impaired, at cost, a Braille, large type, audio or other edition of a previously published literary work in a form intended to be perceived by the visually impaired, provided that, during a period of at least one year after the first publication of a standard edition of such work in the United States, the owner of the exclusive right to distribute such work in the United States has not entered the market for editions intended to be perceived by the visually impaired.

SEC. 4 COPYRIGHT PROTECTION SYSTEMS AND COPYRIGHT MANAGEMENT INFORMATION.

Title 17, United States Code, is amended by adding the following new chapter:

Chapter 12.—COPYRIGHT PROTECTION AND MANAGEMENT SYSTEMS
Sec.

1201. Circumvention of Copyright Protection Systems

1202. Integrity of Copyright Management Information

1203. Civil Remedies

1204. Criminal Offenses and Penalties

1201. Circumvention of Copyright Protection Systems

No person shall import, manufacture or distribute any device, product, or component incorporated into a device or product, or offer or perform any service, the primary purpose or effect of which is to avoid, bypass, remove, deactivate, or otherwise circumvent, without the authority of the copyright owner or the law, any process, treatment, mechanism or system which prevents or inhibits the violation of any of the exclusive rights of the copyright owner under section 106.

1202. Integrity of Copyright Management Information

(a) FALSE COPYRIGHT MANAGEMENT INFORMATION.—No person shall knowingly provide copyright management information that is false, or knowingly publicly distribute or import for public distribution copyright management information that is false.

(b) REMOVAL OR ALTERATION OF COPYRIGHT MANAGEMENT INFORMATION.—No person shall, without authority of the copyright owner or the law, (i) knowingly remove or alter any copyright management information, (ii) knowingly distribute or import for distribution copyright management information that has been altered without authority of the copyright owner or the law, or (iii) knowingly distribute or import for distribution copies or phonorecords from which copyright management information has been removed without authority of the copyright owner or the law.

(c) DEFINITION.—As used in this chapter, "copyright management information" means the name and other identifying information of the author of a work, the name and other identifying information of the copyright owner, terms and conditions for uses of the work, and such other information as the Register of Copyrights may prescribe by regulation.

1203. Civil Remedies

(a) CIVIL ACTIONS.—Any person injured by a violation of Sec. 1201 or 1202 may bring a civil action in an appropriate United States district court for such violation.

(b) POWERS OF THE COURT.—In an action brought under subsection (a), the court—

(1) may grant temporary and permanent injunctions on such terms as it deems reasonable to prevent or restrain a violation;

(2) at any time while an action is pending, may order the impounding, on such terms as it deems reasonable, of any device or product that is in the custody or control of the alleged violator and that the court has reasonable cause to believe was involved in a violation;

(3) may award damages under subsection (c);

(4) in its discretion may allow the recovery of costs by or against any party other than the United States or an officer thereof;

(5) in its discretion may award reasonable attorney's fees to the prevailing party; and

(6) may, as part of a final judgment or decree finding a violation, order the remedial modification or the destruction of any device or product involved in the violation that is in the custody or control of the violator or has been impounded under subsection (2).

(c) AWARD OF DAMAGES.—

(1) IN GENERAL.—Except as otherwise provided in this chapter, a violator is liable for either (i) the actual damages and any additional profits of the violator, as provided by subsection (2) or (ii) statutory damages, as provided by subsection (3).

(2) ACTUAL DAMAGES.—The court shall award to the complaining party the actual damages suffered by him or her as a result of the

violation, and any profits of the violator that are attributable to the violation and are not taken into account in computing the actual damages, if the complaining party elects such damages at any time before final judgment is entered.

(3) STATUTORY DAMAGES.—

(A) At any time before final judgment is entered, a complaining party may elect to recover an award of statutory damages for each violation of section 1201 in the sum of not less than $200 or more than $2,500 per device, product, offer or performance of service, as the court considers just.

(B) At any time before final judgment is entered, a complaining party may elect to recover an award of statutory damages for each violation of section 1202 in the sum of not less than $2,500 or more than $25,000.

(4) REPEATED VIOLATIONS.—In any case in which the injured party sustains the burden of proving, and the court finds, that a person has violated section 1201 or 1202 within three years after a final judgment was entered against that person for another such violation, the court may increase the award of damages up to triple the amount that would otherwise be awarded, as the court considers just.

(5) INNOCENT VIOLATIONS.—The court in its discretion may reduce or remit altogether the total award of damages in any case in which the violator sustains the burden of proving, and the court finds, that the violator was not aware and had no reason to believe that its acts constituted a violation.

1204. Criminal Offenses and Penalties

Any person who violates section 1202 with intent to defraud shall be fined not more than $500,000 or imprisoned for not more than 5 years, or both.

SEC. 5 CONFORMING AMENDMENTS.

(a) Table of Sections.— The table of sections for chapter 1 of title 17, United States Code, is amended by inserting after the item relating to section 108 the following: 108A. Limitations on exclusive rights: Reproduction for the Visually Impaired.

(b) Table of Chapters.— The table of chapters for title 17, United States Code, is amended by adding at the end the following:

12. COPYRIGHT PROTECTION AND MANAGEMENT SYSTEMS. ... 1201.

SEC. 6 EFFECTIVE DATE.

This Act, and the amendments made by this Act, shall take effect on the date of the enactment of this Act.

PART THREE

LEGISLATIVE HISTORIES

SYNOPSIS

HOUSE REPORT ON THE COPYRIGHT ACT OF 1976
H.R. Rep. No. 94-1476, 94th Cong., 2d Sess. (1976), *reprinted in* 1976 U.S.C.C.A.N. 5659

SECTIONAL ANALYSIS AND DISCUSSION

SECTION 101. DEFINITIONS

The significant definitions in this section will be mentioned or summarized in connection with the provisions to which they are most relevant.

SECTION 102. GENERAL SUBJECT MATTER OF COPYRIGHT

"Original Works of authorship"

The two fundamental criteria of copyright protection — originality and fixation in tangible form — are restated in the first sentence of this cornerstone provision. The phrase "original works of authorship," which is purposely left undefined, is intended to incorporate without change the standard of originality established by the courts under the [Copyright Act of 1909]. This standard does not include requirements of novelty, ingenuity, or [a]esthetic merit, and there is no intention to enlarge the standard of copyright protection to require them.

In using the phrase "original works of authorship," rather than "all the writings of an author" now in section 4 of the [1909 Act], the committee's purpose is to avoid exhausting the constitutional power of Congress to legislate in this field, and to eliminate the uncertainties arising from the latter phrase. Since the [1909 Act] language is substantially the same as the empowering language of the Constitution, a recurring question has been whether the statutory and the constitutional provisions are coextensive. If so, the courts would be faced with the alternative of holding copyrightable something that Congress clearly did not intend to protect, or of holding constitutionally incapable of copyright something that Congress might one day want to protect. To avoid these equally undesirable results, the courts have indicated that "all the writings of an author" under the [1909 Act] is narrower in scope than the "writings" of "authors" referred to in the Constitution. The bill avoids this dilemma by using a different phrase — "original works of authorship" — in characterizing the general subject matter of statutory copyright protection.

The history of copyright law has been one of gradual expansion in the types of works accorded protection, and the subject matter affected by this expansion has fallen into two general categories. In the first, scientific discoveries and technological developments have made possible new forms of creative expression that never existed before. In some of these cases the new expressive forms — electronic music, filmstrips, and computer programs, for example — could be regarded as an extension of copyrightable subject matter Congress had already intended to protect, and were thus considered copyrightable from the outset without the need of new legislation. In other cases, such as photographs, sound recordings, and motion pictures, statutory enactment was deemed necessary to give them full recognition as copyrightable works.

Authors are continually finding new ways of expressing themselves, but it is impossible to foresee the forms that these new expressive methods will take. The bill does not intend either to freeze the scope of copyrightable technology or to allow unlimited expansion into areas completely outside the present congressional intent. Section 102 implies neither that that subject matter is unlimited nor that new forms of expression within that general area of subject matter would necessarily be unprotected.

The historic expansion of copyright has also applied to forms of expression which, although in existence for generations or centuries, have only gradually come to be recognized as creative and worthy of protection. The first copyright statute in this country, enacted in 1790, designated only "maps, charts, and books": major forms of expression such as music, drama, and works of art achieved specific statutory recognition only in later enactments. Although the coverage of the [1909 Act] is very broad, and would be broadened further by the explicit recognition of all forms of choreography, there are unquestionably other areas of existing subject matter that this bill does not propose to protect but that future Congresses may want to.

Fixation in tangible form

As a basic condition of copyright protection, the bill [and, as enacted, the Copyright Act of 1976] perpetuates the existing requirement that a work be fixed in a "tangible medium of expression," and adds that this medium may be one "now known or later developed," and that the fixation is sufficient if the work "can be perceived, reproduced, or otherwise communicated, either directly or with the aid of a machine or device." This broad language is intended to avoid the artificial and largely unjustifiable distinctions, derived from cases such as *White-Smith [Music] Publishing Co. v. Apollo Co., 209 U.S. 1 (1908)*, under which statutory copyrightability in certain cases has been made to depend upon the form or medium in which the work is fixed. Under the bill it makes no difference what the form, manner, or medium of fixation may be — whether it is in words, numbers, notes, sounds, pictures, or any other graphic or symbolic indicia, whether embodied in a physical object in written, printed, photographic, sculptural, punched, magnetic, or any other stable form, and whether it is capable of perception directly or by means of any machine or device "now known or later developed."

Under the bill, the concept of fixation is important since it not only determines whether the provisions of the statute apply to a work, but it also represents the dividing line between common law and statutory protection. As will be noted in more detail in connection with section 301, an unfixed work of authorship, such as an improvisation or an unrecorded choreographic work, performance, or broadcast, would continue to be subject to protection under State common law or statute, but would not be eligible for Federal statutory protection under section 102.

The bill seeks to resolve, through the definition of "fixation" in section 101, the status of live broadcasts — sports, news coverage, live performances of music, etc. — that are reaching the public in unfixed form but that are simultaneously being recorded. When a football game is being covered by four television cameras, with a director guiding the activities of the four cameramen and choosing which of their electronic images are sent out to the public and in what order, there is little doubt that what the cameramen and the director are doing constitutes "authorship." The further question to be considered is whether there has been a fixation. If the images and sounds to be broadcast are first recorded (on a video tape, film, etc.) and then transmitted, the recorded work would be considered a "motion picture" subject to statutory protection against unauthorized reproduction or retransmission of the broadcast. If the program content is transmitted live to the public while being recorded at the same time, the case would be treated the same; the copyright owner would not be forced to rely on common law rather than statutory rights in proceeding against an infringing user of the live broadcast.

Thus, assuming it is copyrightable — as a "motion picture" or "sound recording," for example — the content of a live transmission should be accorded statutory protection if it is being recorded simultaneously with its transmission. On the other hand, the definition of "fixation" would exclude from the concept purely evanescent or transient reproductions such as those projected briefly on a screen, shown electronically on a television or other cathode ray tube, or captured momentarily in the "memory" of a computer.

Under the first sentence of the definition of "fixed" in section 101, a work would be considered "fixed in a tangible medium of expression" if there has been an authorized embodiment in a copy or phonorecord and if that embodiment "is sufficiently permanent or stable" to permit the work "to be perceived, reproduced, or otherwise communicated for a period of more than transitory duration." The second sentence makes clear that, in the case of "a work consisting of sounds, images, or both, that are being transmitted," the work is regarded as "fixed" if a fixation is being made at the same time as the transmission.

Under this definition "copies" and "phonorecords" together will comprise all of the material objects in which copyrightable works are capable of being fixed. The definitions of these terms in section 101, together with their usage in section 102 and throughout the bill, reflect a fundamental distinction between the "original work" which is the product of "authorship" and the multitude of material objects in which it can be embodied. Thus, in the sense of the bill, a "book" is not a work of authorship, but is a particular kind of "copy." Instead, the author may write a "literary work," which in turn can be embodied in a wide range of "copies" and "phonorecords," including books, periodicals, computer punch cards, microfilm, tape recordings, and so forth. It is possible to have an "original work of authorship" without having a "copy" or "phonorecord" embodying it, and it is also possible to have a "copy" or "phonorecord" embodying something that does not qualify as an "original work of authorship." The two essential elements — original work and tangible object — must merge through fixation in order to produce subject matter copyrightable under the statute.

Categories of copyrightable works

[The following excerpt from the House Report refers to "seven" categories of works of authorship. As a result of Public Law 101-650, 101st Cong., 2d Sess., 104 Stat. 5089, signed into law by Pres. George H.W. Bush on December 1, 1990, an eighth category — "architectural works" — was added to § 102 of the Act.]

The second sentence of section 102 lists seven [now eight] broad categories which the concept of "works of authorship" is said to "include." The use of the word "include," as defined in section 101, makes clear that the listing is "illustrative and not limitative," and that the seven categories do not necessarily exhaust the scope of "original works of authorship" that the bill is intended to protect. Rather, the list sets out the general area of copyrightable subject matter, but with sufficient flexibility to free the courts from rigid or outmoded concepts of the scope of particular categories. The items are also overlapping in the sense that a work falling within one class may encompass works coming within some or all of the other categories. In the aggregate, the list covers all classes of works now specified in section 5 of title 17 [of the 1909 Act]; in addition, it specifically enumerates "pantomimes and choreographic works."

Of the seven items listed, four [now five, including "architectural works"] are defined in section 101. The three undefined categories — "musical works," "dramatic works," and "pantomimes and choreographic works" — have fairly settled meanings. There is no need, for example, to specify the copyrightability of electronic or concrete music in the statute since the form of a work would no longer be of any importance, nor is it necessary to specify that "choreographic works" do not include social dance steps and simple routines.

The four items defined in section 101 are "literary works," "pictorial, graphic, and sculptural works," "motion pictures and audiovisual works," and "sound recordings." In each of these cases, definitions are needed not only because the meaning of the term itself is unsettled but also because the distinction between "work" and "material object" requires clarification. The term "literary works" does not connote any criterion of literary merit or qualitative value: it includes catalogs, directories, and similar factual, reference, or instructional works and compilations of data. It also includes computer data bases, and computer programs to the extent that they incorporate authorship in the programmer's expression of original ideas, as distinguished from the ideas themselves.

Correspondingly, the definition of "pictorial, graphic, and sculptural works" carries with it no implied criterion of artistic taste, [a]esthetic value, or intrinsic quality. The term is intended to comprise not only "works of art" in the traditional sense but also works of graphic art and illustration, art reproductions, plans and drawings, photographs and reproductions of them, maps, charts, globes, and other cartographic works, works of these kinds intended for use in advertising and commerce, and work[s] of "applied art." There is no intention whatever to narrow the scope of the subject matter now characterized in [the 1909 Act] section 5(k) as "prints or labels used for articles of merchandise." However, since this terminology suggests the material object in which a work is embodied rather than the work itself, the bill does not mention this category separately.

In accordance with the Supreme Court's decision in *Mazer v. Stein*, 347 U.S. 201 (1954), works of "applied art" encompass all original pictorial, graphic, and sculptural works that are intended to be or have been embodied in useful articles, regardless of factors such as mass production, commercial exploitation, and the potential availability of design patent protection. The scope of exclusive rights in these works is given special treatment in section 113, to be discussed below.

The committee has added language to the definition of "pictorial, graphic, and sculptural works" in an effort to make clearer the distinction between works of applied art protectible under the bill and industrial designs not subject to copyright protection. The declaration that "pictorial, graphic, and sculptural works" include "works of artistic craftsmanship insofar as their form but not their mechanical or utilitarian aspects are concerned" is classic language; it is drawn from Copyright Office regulations promulgated in the 1940s and expressly endorsed by the Supreme Court in the *Mazer* case.

The second part of the amendment states that "the design of a useful article ... shall be considered a pictorial, graphic, or sculptural work only if, and only to the extent that, such design incorporates pictorial, graphic, or sculptural features that can be identified separately from, and are capable of existing independently of, the utilitarian aspects of the article." A "useful article" is defined as "an article having an intrinsic utilitarian function that is not merely to portray the appearance of the article or to convey information." This part of the amendment is an adaptation of language added to the Copyright Office Regulations in the mid-1950s in an effort to implement the Supreme Court's decision in the *Mazer* case.

In adopting this amendatory language, the committee is seeking to draw as clear a line as possible between copyrightable works of applied art and uncopyrighted works of industrial design. A two-dimensional painting, drawing, or graphic work is still capable of being identified as such when it is printed on or applied to utilitarian articles such as textile fabrics, wallpaper, containers, and the like. The same is true when a statue or carving is used to embellish an industrial product or, as in the *Mazer* case, is incorporated into a product without losing its ability to exist independently as a work of art. On the other hand, although the shape of an industrial product may be aesthetically satisfying and valuable, the committee's intention is not to offer it copyright protection under the bill. Unless the shape of an automobile, airplane, ladies' dress, food processor, television set, or any other industrial product contains some element that, physically or conceptually, can be identified as separable from the utilitarian aspects of that article, the design would not be copyrighted under the bill. The test of separability and independence from "the utilitarian aspects of the article" does not depend upon the nature of the design — that is, even if the appearance of an article is determined by [a]esthetic (as opposed to functional) considerations, only elements, if any, which can be identified separately from the useful article as such are copyrightable. And, even if the three-dimensional design contains some such element (for example, a carving on the back of a chair or a floral relief design on silver flatware), copyright protection would extend only to that element, and would not cover the over-all configuration of the utilitarian article as such.

[The portion of the House Report concerning architectural works has been omitted, in light of the 1990 amendments adding such works to the catalog of protectible works in § 102(a).]

The committee has considered, but chosen to defer, the possibility of protecting the design of typefaces. A "typeface" can be defined as a set of letters, numbers, or other symbolic characters, whose forms are related by repeating design elements consistently applied in a notational system and are intended to be embodied in articles whose intrinsic utilitarian function is for use in composing text or other cognizable combinations of characters. The committee does not regard the design of typeface, as thus defined, to be a copyrightable "pictorial, graphic, or sculptural work" within the meaning of this bill and the application of the dividing line in section 101.

Enactment of Public Law 92-140 in 1971 marked the first recognition in American copyright law of sound recordings as copyrightable works. As defined in section 101, copyrightable "sound recordings" are original works of authorship comprising an aggregate of musical, spoken, or other sounds that have been fixed in tangible form. The copyrightable work comprises the aggregation of sounds and not the tangible medium of fixation. Thus, "sound recordings" as copyrightable subject matter are distinguished from "phonorecords," the latter being physical objects in which sounds are fixed. They are also distinguished from any copyrighted literary, dramatic, or musical works that may be reproduced on a "phonorecord."

As a class of subject matter, sound recordings are clearly within the scope of the "writings of an author" capable of protection under the Constitution, and the extension of limited statutory protection to them was too long delayed. Aside from cases in which sounds are fixed by some purely mechanical means without originality of any kind, the copyright protection that would prevent the reproduction and distribution of unauthorized phonorecords of sound recordings is clearly justified.

The copyrightable elements in a sound recording will usually, though not always, involve "authorship" both on the part of the performers whose performance is captured and on the part of the record producer responsible for setting up the recording session, capturing and electronically processing the sounds, and compiling and editing them to make the final sound recording. There may, however, be cases where the record producer's contribution is so minimal that the performance is the only copyrightable element in the work, and there may be cases (for example, recordings of birdcalls, sounds of racing cars, *et cetera*) where only the record producer's contribution is copyrightable.

Sound tracks of motion pictures, long a nebulous area in American copyright law, are specifically included in the definition of "motion pictures," and excluded in the definition of "sound recordings." To be a "motion picture," as defined, requires three elements: (1) a series of images, (2) the capability of showing the images in certain successive order, and (3) an impression of motion when the images are thus shown. Coupled with the basic requirements of original authorship and fixation in tangible form, this definition encompasses a wide range of cinematographic works embodied in films, tapes, video disks, and other media. However, it would not include: (1) unauthorized fixation of live performances or telecasts, (2) live telecasts that are not fixed simultaneously with their transmission, or (3) filmstrips and slide sets which, although consisting of a series of images intended to be shown in succession, are not capable of conveying an impression of motion.

On the other hand, the bill equates audiovisual materials such as filmstrips, slide sets, and sets of transparencies with "motion pictures" rather than with "pictorial, graphic, and sculptural works." Their sequential showing is closer to a "performance" than to a "display," and the definition of "audiovisual works," which applies also to "motion pictures," embraces works consisting of a series of related images that are by their nature, intended for showing by means of projectors or other devices.

Nature of copyright

Copyright does not preclude others from using the ideas or information revealed by the author's work. It pertains to the literary, musical, graphic, or artistic form in which the author expressed intellectual concepts. Section 102(b) makes clear that copyright protection does not extend to any idea, procedure, process, system, method of operation, concept, principle, or discovery, regardless of the form in which it is described, explained, illustrated, or embodied in such work.

Some concern has been expressed lest copyright in computer programs should extend protection to the methodology or processes adopted by the programmer, rather than merely to the "writing" expressing his ideas. Section 102(b) is intended, among other things, to make clear that the expression adopted by the programmer is the copyrightable element in a computer program, and that the actual processes or methods embodied in the program are not within the scope of the copyright law.

Section 102(b) in no way enlarges or contracts the scope of copyright protection under the present law. Its purpose is to restate, in the context of the new single Federal system of copyright, that the basic dichotomy between expression and idea remains unchanged.

SECTION 103. COMPILATIONS AND DERIVATIVE WORKS

Section 103 complements section 102: a compilation or derivative work is copyrightable if it represents an "original work of authorship" and falls within one or more of the categories listed in section 102. Read together, the two sections make plain that the criteria of copyrightable subject matter stated in section 102 apply with full force to works that are entirely original and to those containing preexisting material. Section 103(b) is also intended to define, more sharply and clearly than does section 7 of the [1909 Act], the important interrelationship and correlation between protection of preexisting and of "new" material in a particular work. The most important point here is one that is commonly misunderstood today: copyright in a "new version" covers only the material added by the later author, and has no effect one way or the other on the copyright or public domain status of the preexisting material.

Between them the terms "compilations" and "derivative works," which are defined in section 101, comprehend every copyrightable work that employs preexisting material or data of any kind. There is necessarily some overlapping between the two, but they basically represent different concepts. A "compilation" results from a process of selecting, bringing together, organizing, and arranging previously existing material of all kinds, regardless of whether the individual items in the material have been or ever could have been subject to copyright. A "derivative work," on the other hand, requires a process of recasting, transforming, or adapting "one or more preexisting works"; the "preexisting work" must come within the general subject matter of copyright set forth in section 102, regardless of whether it is or was ever copyrighted.

The second part of the sentence that makes up section 103(a) deals with the status of a compilation or derivative work unlawfully employing preexisting copyrighted material. In providing that protection does not extend to "any part of the work in which such material has been used unlawfully," the bill prevents an infringer from benefiting, through copyright protection, from committing an unlawful act, but preserves protection for those parts of the work that do not employ the preexisting work. Thus, an unauthorized translation of a novel could not be copyrighted at all, but the owner of copyright in an anthology of poetry could sue someone who infringed the whole anthology, even though the infringer proves that publication of one of the poems was unauthorized. Under this provision, copyright could be obtained as long as the use of the preexisting work was not "unlawful," even though the consent of the copyright owner had not been obtained. For instance, the unauthorized reproduction of a work might be "lawful" under the doctrine of fair use or an applicable foreign law, and if so the work incorporating it could be copyrighted.

SECTION 104. NATIONAL ORIGIN

Section 104 … sets forth the basic criteria under which works of foreign origin can be protected under the U.S. copyright law …

SECTION 105. U.S. GOVERNMENT WORKS

Scope of the prohibition

The basic premise of section 105 … is … that works produced for the U.S. Government by its officers and employees should not be subject to copyright. The provision applies the principle equally to unpublished and published works.

The general prohibition against copyright in section 105 applies to 'any work of the United States Government,' which is defined in section 101 as 'a work prepared by an officer or employee of the United States Government as part of that person's official duties.' Under this definition a Government official or employee would not be prevented from securing copyright in a work written at that person's own volition and outside his or her duties, even though the subject matter involves the Government work or professional field of the official or employee. Although the wording of the definition of 'work of the United States Government' differs somewhat from that of the definition of 'work made for hire,' the concepts are intended to be construed in the same way. ...

The prohibition on copyright protection for United States Government works is not intended to have any effect on protection of these works abroad. Works of the governments of most other countries are copyrighted. There are no valid policy reasons for denying such protection to United States Government works in foreign countries, or for precluding the Government from making licenses for the use of its works abroad.

The effect of section 105 is intended to place all works of the United States Government, published or unpublished, in the public domain. ...

SECTION 106. EXCLUSIVE RIGHTS IN COPYRIGHTED WORKS

[This report refers below to the "five fundamental rights" under § 106, and to the several sections following § 106 in Chapter 1 of the 1976 Act as "sections 107 through 118." Subsequent amendments to the Act have added a new right under § 106 (the § 106(6) right to perform sound recordings by means of digital audio transmissions), and four new limitations on the § 106 rights (in §§ 119 through 122).]

General scope of copyright

The five [now six] fundamental rights that the bill gives to copyright owners — the exclusive rights of reproduction, adaptation, publication, performance, and display [plus the DART right in § 106(6)] — are stated generally in section 106. These exclusive rights, which comprise the so-called "bundle of rights" that is a copyright, are cumulative and may overlap in some cases. Each of the [six] enumerated rights may be subdivided indefinitely and, as discussed below in connection with section 201, each subdivision of an exclusive right may be owned and enforced separately.

The approach of the bill is to set forth the copyright owner's exclusive rights in broad terms in section 106, and then to provide various limitations, qualifications, or exemptions in the [16] sections that follow. Thus, everything in section 106 is "made subject to sections 107 through [122]," and must be read in conjunction with those provisions.

The exclusive rights accorded to a copyright owner under section 106 are "to do and to authorize" any of the activities specified in the [six] numbered clauses. Use of the phrase "to authorize" is intended to avoid any questions as to the liability of contributory infringers. For example, a person who lawfully acquires an authorized copy of a motion picture would be an infringer if he or she engages in the business of renting it to others for purposes of unauthorized public performance.

Rights of reproduction, adaptation, and publication

The first three clauses of section 106, which cover all rights under a copyright except those of performance and display, extend to every kind of copyrighted work. The exclusive rights encompassed by these clauses, though closely related, are independent; they can generally be characterized as rights of copying, recording, adaptation, and publishing. A single act of infringement may violate all of these rights at once, as where a publisher reproduces, adapts, and sells copies of a person's copyrighted work as part of a publishing venture. Infringement takes place when any one of the rights is violated: where, for example, a printer reproduces copies without selling them or a retailer sells copies without having anything to do with their reproduction. The references to "copies or phonorecords," although in the plural, are intended here and throughout the bill to include the singular (1 U.S.C. § 1).

Reproduction. — Read together with the relevant definitions in section 101, the right "to reproduce the copyrighted work in copies or phonorecords" means the right to produce a material object in which the work is duplicated, transcribed, imitated, or simulated in a fixed form from which it can be "perceived, reproduced, or otherwise communicated, either directly or with the aid of a machine or device." As under the [1909 Act], a copyrighted work would be infringed by reproducing it in whole or in any substantial part, and by duplicating it exactly or by imitation or simulation. Wide departures or variations from the copyrighted work would still be an infringement as long as the author's "expression" rather than merely the author's "ideas" [is] taken. An exception to this general principle, applicable to the reproduction of copyrighted sound recordings, is specified in section 114.

"Reproduction" under clause (1) of section 106 is to be distinguished from "display" under clause (5). For a work to be "reproduced," its fixation in tangible form must be "sufficiently permanent or stable to permit it to be perceived, reproduced, or otherwise communicated for a period of more than transitory duration." Thus, the showing of images on a screen or tube would not be a violation of clause (1), although it might come within the scope of clause (5).

Preparation of derivative works. — The exclusive right to prepare derivative works, specified separately in clause (2) of section 106, overlaps the exclusive right of reproduction to some extent. It is broader than that right, however, in the sense that reproduction requires fixation in copies or phonorecords, whereas the preparation of a derivative work, such as a ballet, pantomime, or improvised performance, may be an infringement even though nothing is ever fixed in tangible form.

To be an infringement the "derivative work" must be "based upon the copyrighted work," and the definition in section 101 refers to "a translation, musical arrangement, dramatization, fictionalization, motion picture version, sound recording, art reproduction, abridgment, condensation, or any other form in which a work may be recast, transformed, or adapted." Thus, to constitute a violation of section 106(2), the infringing work must incorporate a portion of the copyrighted work in some form; for example, a detailed commentary on a work or a programmatic musical composition inspired by a novel would not normally constitute infringements under this clause.

Use in information storage and retrieval systems. — [*See* § 117.]

Public distribution. — Clause (3) of section 106 establishes the exclusive right of publication: the right "to distribute copies or phonorecords of the copyrighted work to the public by sale or other transfer of ownership, or by rental, lease, or lending." Under this provision, the copyright owner would have the right to control the first public distribution of an authorized copy or phonorecord of his work, whether by sale, gift, loan, or some rental or lease arrangement. Likewise, any unauthorized public distribution of copies or phonorecords that were unlawfully made would be an infringement. As section 109 makes clear, however, the copyright owner's rights under section 106(3) cease with respect to a particular copy or phonorecord once he has parted with ownership of it.

Performing rights and the "for profit" limitation. — The right of public performance under section 106(4) extends to "literary, musical, dramatic, and choreographic works, pantomimes, and motion pictures and other audiovisual works and sound recordings" and, unlike the equivalent provisions now in effect, is not limited by any "for profit" requirement. The approach of the bill, as in many foreign laws, is first to state the public performance right in broad terms, and then to provide specific exemptions for educational and other nonprofit uses.

This approach is more reasonable than the outright exemption of the 1909 statute. The line between commercial and "nonprofit" organizations is increasingly difficult to draw. Many "nonprofit" organizations are highly subsidized and capable of paying royalties, and the widespread public exploitation of copyrighted works by public broadcasters and other noncommercial organizations is likely to grow. In addition to these trends, it is worth noting that performances and displays are continuing to supplant markets for printed copies and that in the future a broad "not for profit" exemption could not only hurt authors but could dry up their incentive to write.

The exclusive right of public performance is expanded to include not only motion pictures, including works recorded on film, videotape, and video disks, but also audiovisual works such as filmstrips and sets of slides. This provision of section 106(4), which is consistent with the assimilation of motion pictures to audiovisual works throughout the bill, is also related to amendments of the definitions of "display" and "perform" discussed below. The important issue of performing rights in sound recordings is discussed in connection with section 114.

Right of public display. — Clause (5) of section 106 represents the first explicit statutory recognition in American copyright law of an exclusive right to show a copyrighted work, or an image of it, to the public. The existence or extent of this right under the [1909 Act] is uncertain and subject to challenge. The bill would give the owners of copyright in "literary, musical, dramatic, and choreographic works, pantomimes, and pictorial, graphic, or sculptural works," including the individual images of a motion picture or other audiovisual work, the exclusive right "to display the copyrighted work publicly."

Definitions

Under the definitions of "perform," "display," "publicly," and "transmit" in section 101, the concepts of public performance and public display cover not only the initial rendition or showing, but also any further act by which that rendition or showing is transmitted or communicated to the public. Thus, for example: a singer is performing when he or she sings a song; a broadcasting network is performing when it transmits his or her performance (whether simultaneously or from records); a local broadcaster is performing when it transmits the network broadcast; a cable television system is performing when it retransmits the broadcast to its subscribers; and any individual is performing whenever he or she plays a phonorecord embodying the performance or communicates the performance by turning on a receiving set. Although any act by which the initial performance or display is transmitted, repeated, or made to recur would itself be a "performance" or "display" under the bill, it would not be actionable as an infringement unless it were done "publicly," as defined in section 101. Certain other performances and displays, in addition to those that are "private," are exempted or given qualified copyright control under sections 107 through [122].

To "perform" a work, under the definition in section 101, includes reading a literary work aloud, singing or playing music, dancing a ballet or other choreographic work, and acting out a dramatic work or pantomime. A performance may be accomplished "either directly or by means of any device or process," including all kinds of equipment for reproducing or amplifying sounds or visual images, any sort of transmitting apparatus, any type of electronic retrieval system, and any other techniques and systems not yet in use or even invented.

The definition of "perform" in relation to "a motion picture or other audiovisual work" is "to show its images in any sequence or to make the sounds accompanying it audible." The showing of portions of a motion picture, filmstrip, or slide set must therefore be sequential to constitute a "performance" rather than a "display," but no particular order need be maintained. The purely aural performance of a motion picture sound track, or of the sound portions of an audiovisual work, would constitute a performance of the "motion picture or other audiovisual work"; but, where some of the sounds have been reproduced separately on phonorecords, a performance from the phonorecord would not constitute performance of the motion picture or audiovisual work.

The corresponding definition of "display" [in § 101] covers any showing of a "copy" of the work, "either directly or by means of a film, slide, television image, or any other device or process." Since "copies" are defined as including the material object "in which the work is first fixed," the right of public display applies to original works of art as well as to reproductions of them. With respect to motion pictures and other audiovisual works, it is a "display" (rather than a "performance") to show their "individual images nonsequentially." In addition to the direct showings of a copy of a work, "display" would include the projection of an image on a screen or other surface by any method, the transmission of an image by electronic or other means, and the showing of an image on a cathode ray tube, or similar viewing apparatus connected with any sort of information storage and retrieval system.

Under clause (1) of the definition of "publicly" in section 101, a performance or display is "public" if it takes place "at a place open to the public or at any place where a substantial number of persons outside of a normal circle of a family and its social acquaintances is gathered." One of the principal purposes of the definition was to make clear that, contrary to the decision in *Metro-Goldwyn-Mayer Distributing Corp. v. Wyatt*, 21 C.O. Bull. 203 (D. Md. 1932), performances in "semipublic" places such as clubs, lodges, factories, summer camps, and schools are "public performances" subject to copyright control. The term "a family" in this context would include an individual living alone, so that a gathering confined to the individual's social acquaintances would normally be regarded as private. Routine meetings of businesses and governmental personnel would be excluded because they do not represent the gathering of a "substantial number of persons."

Clause (2) of the definition of "publicly" in section 101 makes clear that the concepts of public performance and public display include not only performances and displays that occur initially in a public place, but also acts that transmit or otherwise communicate a performance or display of the work to the public by means of any device or process. The definition of "transmit" — to communicate a performance or display "by any device or process whereby images or sound are received beyond the place from which they are sent" — is broad enough to include all conceivable forms and combinations of wired or wireless communications media, including but by no means limited to radio and television broadcasting as we know them. Each and every method by which the images or sounds comprising a performance or display are picked up and conveyed is a "transmission," and if the transmission reaches the public in [any] form, the case comes within the scope of clauses (4) or (5) of section 106.

Under the bill, as under the [1909 Act], a performance made available by transmission to the public at large is "public" even though the recipients are not gathered in a single place, and even if there is no proof that any of the potential recipients was operating his receiving apparatus at the time of the transmission. The same principles apply whenever the potential recipients of the transmission represent a limited segment of the public, such as the occupants of hotel rooms or the subscribers of a cable television service. Clause (2) of the definition of "publicly" is applicable "whether the members of the public capable of receiving the performance or display receive it in the same place or in separate places and at the same time or at different times."

SECTION 107. FAIR USE

General background of the problem

The judicial doctrine of fair use, one of the most important and well-established limitations on the exclusive right of copyright owners, would be given express statutory recognition for the first time in section 107. The claim that a defendant's acts constituted a fair use rather than an infringement has been raised as a defense in innumerable copyright actions over the years, and there is ample case law recognizing the existence of the doctrine and applying it. The examples enumerated [in] the Register's 1961 Report, while by no means exhaustive, give some idea of the sort of activities the courts might regard as fair use under the circumstances: "quotation of excerpts in a review or criticism for purposes of illustration or comment; quotation of short passages in a scholarly or technical work, for illustration or clarification of the author's observations; use in a parody of some of the content of the work parodied; summary of an address or article, with brief quotations, in a news report; reproduction by a library of a portion of a work to replace part of a damaged copy; reproduction by a teacher or student of a small part of a work to illustrate a lesson; reproduction of a work in legislative or judicial proceedings or reports; incidental and fortuitous reproduction, in a newsreel or broadcast, of a work located in the scene of an event being reported."

Although the courts have considered and ruled upon the fair use doctrine over and over again, no real definition of the concept has ever emerged. Indeed, since the doctrine is an equitable rule of reason, no generally applicable definition is possible, and each case raising the question must be decided on its own facts. On the other hand, the courts have evolved a set of criteria which, though in no case definitive or determinative, provide some gauge for balancing the equities. These criteria have been stated in various ways, but essentially they can all be reduced to the four standards which have been adopted in section 107:

> (1) the purpose and character of the use, including whether such use is of a commercial nature or is for non-profit educational purposes; (2) the nature of the copyrighted work; (3) the amount and substantiality of the portion used in relation to the copyrighted work as a whole; and (4) the effect of the use upon the potential market for or value of the copyrighted work.

These criteria are relevant in determining whether the basic doctrine of fair use, as stated in the first sentence of section 107, applies in a particular case:

> Notwithstanding the provisions of section 106, the fair use of a copyrighted work, including such use by reproduction in copies or phonorecords or by any other means specified by that section, for purposes such as criticism, comment, news reporting, teaching (including multiple copies for classroom use), scholarship, or research, is not an infringement of copyright.

The specific wording of section 107 as it now stands is the result of a process of accretion, resulting from the long controversy over the related problems of fair use and the reproduction (mostly by photocopying) of copyrighted material for educational and scholarly purposes. For example, the reference to fair use "by reproduction in copies or phonorecords or by any other means" is mainly intended to make clear that the doctrine has as much application to photocopying and taping as to older forms of use; it is not intended to give these kinds of reproduction any special status under the fair use provision or to sanction any reproduction beyond the normal and reasonable limits of fair use. Similarly, the newly-added reference to "multiple copies for classroom use" is a recognition that, under the proper circumstances of fairness, the doctrine can be applied to reproductions of multiple copies for the members of a class.

The committee has amended the first of the criteria to be considered—"the purpose and character of the use"—to state explicitly that this factor includes a consideration of "whether such use is of a commercial nature or is for non-profit educational purposes." This amendment is not intended to be interpreted as any sort of not-for-profit limitation on educational uses of copyrighted works. It is an express recognition that, as under the [1909 Act], the commercial or non-profit character of an activity, while not conclusive with respect to fair use, can and should be weighed along with other factors in fair use decisions.

General intention behind the provision

The statement of the fair use doctrine in section 107 offers some guidance to users in determining when the principles of the doctrine apply. However, the endless variety of situations and combinations of circumstances that can [a] rise in particular cases precludes the formulation of exact rules in the statute. The bill endorses the purpose and general scope of the judicial doctrine of fair use, but there is no disposition to freeze the doctrine in the statute, especially during a period of rapid technological change. Beyond a very broad statutory explanation of what fair use is and some of the criteria applicable to it, the courts must be free to adapt the doctrine to particular situations on a case-by-case basis. Section 107 is intended to restate the present judicial doctrine of fair use, not to change, narrow, or enlarge it in any way.

Intention as to classroom reproduction

Although the works and uses to which the doctrine of fair use is applicable are as broad as the copyright law itself, most of the discussion of section 107 has centered around questions of classroom reproduction, particularly photocopying. ...

The Committee ... adheres to its ... conclusion [in a 1967 report] that 'a specific exemption freeing certain reproductions of copyrighted works for educational and scholarly purposes from copyright control is not justified.' At the same time the Committee recognizes, as it did in 1967, that there is a 'need for greater certainty and protection for teachers.' In an effort to meet this need the Committee has not only adopted further amendments to section 107, but has also amended section 504(c) to provide innocent teachers and other non-profit users of copyrighted material with broad insulation against unwarranted liability for infringement. ...

At the Judiciary Subcommittee hearings in June 1975, Chairman Kastenmeier and other members urged the parties to meet together independently in an effort to achieve a meeting of the minds as to permissible educational uses of copyrighted material. The response to these suggestions was positive, and a number of meetings of three groups, dealing respectively with classroom reproduction of printed material, music, and audio-visual material, were held beginning in September 1975.

In a joint letter to Chairman Kastenmeier, dated March 19, 1976, the representatives of the Ad Hoc Committee of Educational Institutions and Organizations on Copyright Law Revision, and of the Authors League of American, Inc., and the Association of American Publishers, Inc., stated:

You may remember that in our letter of March 8, 1976 we told you that the negotiating teams representing authors and publishers and the Ad Hoc Group had reached tentative agreement on guidelines to insert in the Committee Report covering educational copying from books and periodicals ...We are now happy to tell you that the agreement has been approved by the principals and we enclose a copy herewith. We had originally intended to translate the agreement into language suitable for inclusion in the legislative report dealing with Section 107, but we have since been advised by committee staff that this will not be necessary.... [T]he agreement refers only to copying from books and periodicals, and it is not intended to apply to musical or audiovisual works.The full text of the agreement is as follows:

AGREEMENT ON GUIDELINES FOR CLASSROOM COPYING IN NOT-FOR-PROFIT EDUCATIONAL INSTITUTIONS WITH RESPECT TO BOOKS AND PERIODICALS

The purpose of the following guidelines is to state the minimum and not the maximum standards of educational fair use under Section 107 ... The parties agree that the conditions determining the extent of permissible copying for educational purposes may change in the future; that certain types of copying permitted under these guidelines may not be permissible in the future; and conversely that in the future other types of copying not permitted under these guidelines may be permissible under revised guidelines.

Moreover, the following statement of guidelines is not intended to limit the types of copying permitted under the standards of fair use under judicial decision and which are stated in Section 107 of the Copyright Revision Bill. There may be instances in which copying which does not fall within the guidelines stated below may nonetheless be permitted under the criteria of fair use.

GUIDELINES

I. *Single Copying for Teachers*

A single copy may be made of any of the following by or for a teacher at his or her individual request for his or her scholarly research or use in teaching or preparation to teach a class:

A. A chapter from a book;

B. An article from a periodical or newspaper;

C. A short story, short essay or short poem, whether or not from a collective work;

D. A chart, graph, diagram, drawing, cartoon or picture from a book, periodical, or newspaper;

II. *Multiple Copies for Classroom Use*

Multiple copies (not to exceed in any event more than one copy per pupil in a course) may be made by or for the teacher giving the course for classroom use or discussion; provided that:

A. The copying meets the tests of brevity and spontaneity as defined below; and,

B. Meets the cumulative effect test as defined below; and,

C. Each copy includes a notice of copyright

Definitions

Brevity

(i) Poetry: (a) A complete poem if less than 250 words and if printed on not more than two pages or, (b) from a longer poem, an excerpt of not more than 250 words.

(ii) Prose: (a) Either a complete article, story or essay of less than 2,500 words, or (b) an excerpt from any prose work of not more than 1,000 words or 10% of the work, whichever is less, but in any event a minimum of 500 words. (Each of the numerical limits stated in 'i' and 'ii' above may be expanded to permit the completion of an unfinished line of a poem or of an unfinished prose paragraph.)

(iii) Illustration: One chart, graph, diagram, drawing, cartoon or picture per book or per periodical issue.

(iv) 'Special' works: Certain work in poetry, prose or in 'poetic prose' which often combine language with illustrations and which are intended sometimes for children and at other times for a more general audience fall short of 2,500 words in their entirety.

Paragraph 'ii' above notwithstanding such 'special works' may not be reproduced in their entirety; however, an excerpt comprising not more than two of the published pages of such special work and containing not more than 10% of the words found in the text thereof, may be reproduced.

Spontaneity

(i) The copying is at the instance and inspiration of the individual teacher, and

(ii) The inspiration and decision to use the work and the moment of its use for maximum teaching effectiveness are so close in time that it would be unreasonable to expect a timely reply to a request for permission.

Cumulative Effect

(i) The copying of the material is for only one course in the school in which the copies are made.

(ii) Not more than one short poem, article, story, essay or two excerpts may be copied from the same author, nor more than three from the same collective work or periodical volume during one class term.

(iii) There shall not be more than nine instances of such multiple copying for one course during one class term. (The limitations stated in 'ii' and 'iii' above shall not apply to current news periodicals and newspapers and current news sections of other periodicals.)

III. *Prohibitions as to I and II Above*

Notwithstanding any of the above, the following shall be prohibited:

(A) Copying shall not be used to create or to replace or substitute for anthologies, compilations or collective works. Such replacement or substitution may occur whether copies of various works or excerpts therefrom are accumulated or reproduced and used separately.

(B) There shall be no copying of or from works intended to be 'consumable' in the course of study or of teaching. These include workbooks, exercises, standardized tests and test booklets and answer sheets and like consumable material.

(C) Copying shall not:

(a) substitute for the purchase of books, publishers' reprints or periodicals;

(b) be directed by higher authority;

(c) be repeated with respect to the same item by the same teacher from term to term.

(D) No charge shall be made to the student beyond the actual cost of the photocopying.

Agreed MARCH 19, 1976.

Ad Hoc Committee of Copyright Law Revision:

By SHELDON ELLIOTT STEINBACH.

Author-Publisher Group:

Authors League of America:

By IRWIN KARP, Counsel.

Association of American Publishers, Inc.

By ALEXANDER C. HOFFMAN,

Chairman, Copyright Committee.

In a joint letter dated April 30, 1976, representatives of the Music Publishers' Association of the United States, Inc., the National Music Publishers' Association, Inc., the Music Teachers National Association, the Music Educators National Conference, the National Association of Schools of Music, and the Ad Hoc Committee on Copyright Law Revision, wrote to Chairman Kastenmeier as follows:

> "During the hearings on H.R. 2223 in June 1975, you and several of your subcommittee members suggested that concerned groups should work together in developing guidelines which would be helpful to clarify Section 107 of the bill. Representatives of music educators and music publishers delayed their meetings until guidelines had been developed relative to books and periodicals. Shortly after that work was completed and those guidelines were forwarded to your subcommittee, representatives of the undersigned music organizations met together with representatives of the Ad Hoc Committee on Copyright Law Revision to draft guidelines relative to music.
>
> "We are very pleased to inform you that the discussions thus have been fruitful on the guidelines which have been developed. Since private music teachers are an important factor in music education, due consideration has been given to the concerns of that group.
>
> "We trust that this will be helpful in the report on the bill to clarify Fair Use as it applies to music."

The text of the guidelines accompanying this letter is as follows:

GUIDELINES FOR EDUCATIONAL USES OF MUSIC

The purpose of the following guidelines is to state the minimum and not the maximum standards of educational fair use under Section 107 of HR 2223. The parties agree that the conditions determining the extent of permissible copying for educational purposes may change in the future; that certain types of copying permitted under these guidelines may not be permissible in the future, and conversely that in the future other types of copying not permitted under these guidelines may be permissible under revised guidelines.

Moreover, the following statement of guidelines is not intended to limit the types of copying permitted under the standards of fair use under judicial decision and which are stated in Section 107 of the Copyright Revision Bill. There may be instances in which copying which does not fall within the guidelines stated below may nonetheless be permitted under the criteria of fair use.

A. Permissible Uses

1. Emergency copying to replace purchased copies which for any reason are not available for an imminent performance provided purchased replacement copies shall be substituted in due course.

2. (a) For academic purposes other than performance, multiple copies of excerpts of works may be made, provided that the excerpts do not comprise

a part of the whole which would constitute a performable unit such as a section, movement or aria, but in no case more than (10% of the whole work. The number of copies shall not exceed one copy per pupil.

(b) For academic purposes other than performance, a single copy of an entire performable unit (section, movement, aria, etc.) that is, (1) confirmed by the copyright proprietor to be out of print or (2) unavailable except in a larger work, may be made by or for a teacher solely for the purpose of his or her scholarly research or in preparation to teach a class.

3. Printed copies which have been purchased may be edited or simplified provided that the fundamental character of the work is not distorted or the lyrics, if any, altered or lyrics added if none exist.

4. A single copy of recordings of performances by students may be made for evaluation or rehearsal purposes and may be retained by the educational institution or individual teacher.

5. A single copy of a sound recording (such as a tape, disc or cassette) of copyrighted music may be made from sound recordings owned by an educational institution or an individual teacher for the purpose of constructing aural exercises or examinations and may be retained by the educational institution or individual teacher. (This pertains only to the copyright of the music itself and not to any copyright which may exist in the sound recording.)

B. Prohibitions

1. Copying to create or replace or substitute for anthologies, compilations or collective works.

2. Copying of or from works intended to be 'consumable' in the course of study or of teaching such as workbooks, exercises, standardized tests and answer sheets and like material.

3. Copying for the purpose of performances, except as in A(1) above.

4. Copying for the purpose of substituting for the purchase of music, except as in A(1) and A(2) above.

5. Copying without inclusion of the copyright notice which appears on the printed copy.

The problem of off-the-air taping for nonprofit classroom use of copyrighted audiovisual works incorporated in radio and television broadcasts has proved to be difficult to resolve. The Committee believes that the fair use doctrine has some limited application in this area, but it appears that the development of detailed guidelines will require a more thorough exploration than has so far been possible of the needs and problems of a number of different interests affected, and of the various legal problems presented. Nothing in section 107 or elsewhere in the bill is intended to change or prejudge the law on the point. On the other hand, the Committee is sensitive to the importance of the problem, and urges the representative of the various interests, if possible under the leadership of the Register of Copyrights, to continue their discussions actively and in a constructive spirit. If it would be helpful to a solution, the Committee is receptive to undertaking further consideration of the problem in a future Congress.

The Committee appreciates and commends the efforts and the co-operative and reasonable spirit of the parties who achieved the agreed guidelines on books and periodicals and on music. Representatives of the American Association of University Professors and of the Association of American Law Schools have written to the Committee strongly criticizing the guidelines, particularly with respect to multiple copying, as being too restrictive with respect to classroom situations at the university and graduate level. However, the Committee notes that the Ad Hoc group did include representatives of higher education, that the stated 'purpose of the ... guidelines is to state the minimum and not the maximum standards of educational fair use' and that the agreement acknowledges 'there may be instances in which copying which does not fall within the guidelines ... may nonetheless be permitted under the criteria of fair use.'

The Committee believes the guidelines are a reasonable interpretation of the minimum standards of fair use. Teachers will know that copying within the guidelines is fair use. Thus, the guidelines serve the purpose of fulfilling the need for greater certainty and protection for teachers. The Committee expresses the hope that if there are areas where standards other than these guidelines may be appropriate, the parties will continue their efforts to provide additional specific guidelines in the same spirit of good will and give and take that has marked the discussion of this subject in recent months.

Reproduction and uses for other purposes

The concentrated attention given the fair use provision in the context of classroom teaching activities should not obscure its application in other areas. It must be emphasized again that the same general standards of fair use are applicable to all kinds of uses of copyrighted material, although the relative weight to be given them will differ from case to case. ...

SECTION 108. REPRODUCTION BY LIBRARIES AND ARCHIVES

Notwithstanding the exclusive rights of the owners of copyright, section 108 provides that under certain conditions it is not an infringement of copyright for a library or archives, or any of its employees acting within the scope of their employment, to reproduce or distribute not more than one copy or phonorecord of a work, provided (1) the reproduction or distribution is made without any purpose of direct or indirect commercial advantage and (2) the collections of the library or archives are open to the public or available not only to researchers affiliated with the library or archives, but also to other persons doing research in a specialized field, and (3) the reproduction or distribution of the work includes a notice of copyright.

Under this provision, a purely commercial enterprise could not establish a collection of copyrighted works, call itself a library or archive, and engage in for-profit reproduction and distribution of photocopies. Similarly, it would not be possible for a non-profit institution, by means of contractual arrangements with a commercial copying enterprise, to authorize the enterprise to carry out copying and distribution functions that would be exempt if conducted by the non-profit institution itself.

The reference to "indirect commercial advantage" has raised questions as to the status of photocopying done by or for libraries or archival collections within industrial, profit-making, or proprietary institutions (such as the research and development departments of chemical, pharmaceutical, automobile, and oil corporations, the library of a proprietary hospital, the collections owned by a law or medical partnership, etc.).

There is a direct interrelationship between this problem and the prohibitions against "multiple" and "systematic" photocopying in section 108(g)(1) and (2). Under section 108, a library in a profit-making organization would not be authorized to:

> (a) use a single subscription or copy to supply its employees with multiple copies of material relevant to their work; or
>
> (b) use a single subscription or copy to supply its employees, on request, with single copies of material relevant to their work, where the arrangement is "systematic" in the sense of deliberately substituting photocopying for subscription or purchase; or
>
> (c) use "interlibrary loan" arrangements for obtaining photocopies in such aggregate quantities as to substitute for subscriptions or purchase of material needed by employees in their work.

Moreover, a library in a profit-making organization could not evade these obligations by installing reproducing equipment on its premises for unsupervised use by the organization's staff.

Isolated, spontaneous making of single photocopies by a library in a for-profit organization, without any systematic effort to substitute photocopying for subscriptions or purchases, would be covered by section 108, even though the copies are furnished to the employees of the organization for use in their work. Similarly, for-profit libraries could participate in interlibrary arrangements for exchange of photocopies, as long as the production or distribution was not "systematic." These activities, by themselves, would ordinarily not be considered "for direct or indirect commercial advantages," since the "advantage" referred to in this clause must attach to the immediate commercial motivation behind the reproduction or distribution itself, rather than to the ultimate profit-making motivation behind the enterprise in which the library is located. On the other hand, section 108 would not excuse reproduction or distribution if there were a commercial motive behind the actual making or distributing of the copies, if multiple copies were made or distributed, or if the photocopying activities were "systematic" in the sense that their aim was to substitute for subscriptions or purchases. ...

SECTION 109. EFFECT OF TRANSFER OF PARTICULAR COPY OR PHONORECORD

Effect on further disposition of copy or phonorecord

Section 109(a) restates and confirms the principle that, where the copyright owner has transferred ownership of a particular copy or phonorecord of a work, the person to whom the copy or phonorecord is transferred is entitled to dispose of it by sale, rental, or any other means. Under this principle, which has been established by the court decisions and section 27 of the [1909 Act], the copyright owner's exclusive right of public distribution would have no effect upon anyone who owns "a particular copy or phonorecord lawfully made under this title" and who wishes to transfer it to someone else or to destroy it.

Thus, for example, the outright sale of an authorized copy of a book frees it from any copyright control over its resale price or other conditions of its future disposition. A library that has acquired ownership of a copy is entitled to lend it under any conditions it chooses to impose. This does not mean that conditions on future disposition of copies or phonorecords, imposed by a contract between their buyer and seller, would be unenforceable between the parties as a breach of contract, but it does mean that they could not be enforced by an action for infringement of copyright. Under section 202, however, the owner of the physical copy or phonorecord cannot reproduce or perform the copyrighted work publicly without the copyright owner's consent.

To come within the scope of section 109(a), a copy or phonorecord must have been 'lawfully made under this title,' though not necessarily with the copyright owner's authorization. For example, any resale of an illegally 'pirated' phonorecord would be an infringement, but the disposition of a phonorecord legally made under the compulsory licensing provisions of section 115 would not.

Effect o[f] display of copy

Subsection (b) [now (c)] of section 109 deals with the scope of the copyright owner's exclusive right to control the public display of a particular "copy" of a work (including the original or prototype copy in which the work was first fixed). Assuming, for example, that a painter has sold the only copy of an original work of art without restrictions, would it be possible for him to restrain the new owner from displaying it publicly in galleries, shop windows, on a projector, or on television?

Section 109[(c)] adopts the general principle that the lawful owner of a copy of a work should be able to put his copy on public display without the consent of the copyright owner. As in cases arising under section 109(a), this does not mean that contractual restrictions on display between a buyer and seller would be unenforceable as a matter of contract law.

The exclusive right of public display granted by section 106(5) would not apply where the owner of a copy wishes to show it directly to the public, as in a gallery or display case, or indirectly, as through an opaque projector. Where the copy itself is intended for projection, as in the case of a photographic slide, negative, or transparency, the public projection of a single image would be permitted as long as the viewers are "present at the place where the copy is located."

On the other hand, section 109[(c)] takes account of the potentialities of the new communications media, notably television, cable and optical transmission devices, and information storage and retrieval devices, for replacing printed copies with visual images. First of all, the public display of an image of a copyrighted work would not be exempted from copyright control if the copy from which the image was derived were outside the presence of the viewers. In other words, the display of a visual image of a copyrighted work would be an infringement if the image were transmitted by any method (by closed or open circuit television, for example, or by a computer system) from one place to members of the public located elsewhere.

Moreover, the exemption would extend only to public displays that are made "either directly or by the projection of no more than one image at a time." Thus, even where the copy and the viewers are located at the same place, the simultaneous projection of multiple images of the work would not be exempted. For example, where each person in a lecture hall is supplied with a separate viewing apparatus, the copyright owner's permission would generally be required in order to project an image of a work on each individual screen at the same time.

The committee's intention is to preserve the traditional privilege of the owner of a copy to display it directly, but to place reasonable restrictions on the ability to display it indirectly in such a way that the copyright owner's market for reproduction and distribution of copies would be affected. Unless it constitutes a fair use under section 107, or unless one of the special provisions of section 110 or 111 is applicable, projection of more than one image at a time, or transmission of an image to the public over television or other communication channels, would be an infringement for the same reasons that reproduction in copies would be. The concept of "the place where the copy is located" is generally intended to refer to a situation in which the viewers are present in the same physical surroundings as the copy, even though they cannot see the copy directly.

Effect of mere possession of copy or phonorecord

Subsection (c) [now (d)] of section 109 qualifies the privileges specified in subsections (a) and [(c)] by making clear that they do not apply to someone who merely possesses a copy or phonorecord without having acquired ownership of it. Acquisition of an object embodying a copyrighted work by rental, lease, loan, or bailment carries with it no privilege to dispose of the copy under section 109(a) or to display it publicly under section 109[(c)]. To cite a familiar example, a person who has rented a print of a motion picture from the copyright owner would have no right to rent it to someone else without the owner's permission.

Burden of proof in infringement actions

During the course of its deliberations on this section, the committee's attention was directed to a recent court decision holding that the plaintiff in an infringement action had the burden of establishing that the allegedly infringing copies in the defendant's possession were not lawfully made or acquired ... *American International Pictures, Inc. v. Foreman*, 400 F. Supp. 928 (S.D. Alabama 1975) [*rev'd*, 576 F.2d 661 (5th Cir. 1978)]. The committee believes that the court's decision, if followed, would place a virtually impossible burden on copyright owners. The decision is also inconsistent with the established legal principle that the burden of proof should not be placed upon a litigant to establish facts particularly within the knowledge of his adversary. The defendant in such actions clearly has the particular knowledge of how possession of the particular copy was acquired, and should have the burden of providing this evidence to the court. It is the intent of the committee, therefore, that in an action to determine whether a defendant is entitled to the privilege established by section 109(a) and [(c)], the burden of proving whether a particular copy was lawfully made or acquired should rest on the defendant.

SECTION 110. EXEMPTIONS OF CERTAIN PERFORMANCES AND DISPLAYS

Clauses (1) through (4) of section 110 deal with performances and exhibitions that are now generally exempt under the 'for profit' limitation or other provisions of the copyright law, and that are specifically exempted from copyright liability under this legislation. Clauses (1) and (2) between them are intended to cover all of the various methods by which performance or displays in the course of systematic instruction take place.

Face-to-face teaching activities

Clause (1) of section 110 is generally intended to set out the conditions under which performances or displays, in the course of instructional activities other than educational broadcasting, are to be exempted from copyright control. The clause covers all types of copyrighted works, and exempts their performance or display 'by instructors or pupils in the course of face-to-face teaching activities of a nonprofit educational institution,' where the activities take place 'in a classroom or similar place devoted to instruction.'

There appears to be no need for a statutory definition of 'face-to-face' teaching activities to clarify the scope of the provision. 'Face-to-face teaching activities' under clause (1) embrace instructional performances and displays that are not 'transmitted.' The concept does not require that the teacher and students be able to see each other, although it does require their simultaneous presence in the same general place. Use of the phrase 'in the course of face-to-face teaching activities' is intended to exclude broadcasting or other transmissions from an outside location into classrooms, whether radio or television and whether open or closed circuit. However, as long as the instructor and pupils are in the same building or general area, the exemption would extend to the use of devices for amplifying or reproducing sound and for projecting visual images. The 'teaching activities' exempted by the clause encompass systematic instruction of a very wide variety of subjects, but they do not include performances or displays, whatever their cultural value or intellectual appeal, that are given for the recreation or entertainment of any part of their audience.

Works affected.— Since there is no limitation on the types of works covered by the exemption, teachers or students would be free to perform or display anything in class as long as the other conditions of the clause are met. They could read aloud from copyrighted text material, act out a drama, play or sing a musical work, perform a motion picture or filmstrip, or display text or pictorial material to the class by means of a projector. However, nothing in this provision is intended to sanction the unauthorized reproduction of copies or phonorecords for the purpose of classroom performance or display, and the clause contains a special exception dealing with performances from unlawfully made copies of motion pictures and other audiovisual works, to be discussed below.

Instructors or pupils.— To come within clause (1), the performance or display must be 'by instructors or pupils,' thus ruling out performances by actors, singers, or instrumentalists brought in from outside the school to put on a program. However, the term 'instructors' would be broad enough to include guest lecturers if their instructional activities remain confined to classroom situations. In general, the term 'pupils' refers to the enrolled members of a class.

Nonprofit educational institution.— Clause (1) makes clear that it applies only to the teaching activities 'of a nonprofit educational institution,' thus excluding from the exemption performances or displays in profit-making institutions such as dance studios and language schools.

Classroom or similar place.— The teaching activities exempted by the clause must take place 'in a classroom or similar place devoted to instruction.' For example, performances in an auditorium or stadium during a school assembly, graduation ceremony, class play, or sporting event, where the audience is not confined to the members of a particular class, would fall outside the scope of clause (1), although in some cases they might be exempted by clause (4) of section 110. The 'similar place' referred to in clause (1) is a place which is 'devoted to instruction' in the same way a classroom is; common examples would include a studio, a workshop, a gymnasium, a training field, a library, the stage of an auditorium, or the auditorium itself, if it is actually used as a classroom for systematic instructional activities.

Motion pictures and other audiovisual works.— The final provision of clause (1) deals with the special problems of performances from unlawfully-made copies of motion pictures and other audiovisual works. The exemption is lost where the copy being used for a classroom performance was 'not lawfully made under this title' and the person responsible for the performance knew or had reason to suspect as much. This special exception to the exemption would not apply to performances from lawfully-made copies, even if the copies were acquired from someone who had stolen or converted them, or if the performances were in violation of an agreement. However, though the performance would be exempt under section 110(1) in such cases, the copyright owner might have a cause of action against the unauthorized distributor under section 106(3), or against the person responsible for the performance for breach of contract.

Projection devices.— As long as there is no transmission beyond the place where the copy is located, both section 109(b) and section 110(1) would permit the classroom display of a work by means of any sort of projection device or process.

Instructional broadcasting

Works affected.— The exemption for instructional broadcasting provided by section 110(2) would apply only to 'performance of a nondramatic literary or musical work or display of a work.' Thus, the copyright o[w]ner's permission would be required for the performance on educational television or radio of a dramatic work, of a dramatico-musical work such as an opera or musical comedy, or of a motion picture. Since, as already explained, audiovisual works such as filmstrips are equated with motion pictures, their sequential showing would be regarded as a performance rather than a display and would not be exempt under section 110(2). The clause is not intended to limit in any way the copyright owner's exclusive right to make dramatizations, adaptations, or other derivative works under section 106(2). Thus, for example, a performer could read a nondramatic literary work aloud under section 110(2), but the copyright owner's permission would be required for him to act it out in dramatic form.

Systematic instructional activities.— Under section 110(2) a transmission must meet three specified conditions in order to be exempted from copyright liability. The first of these, as provided by subclause (A), is that the performance or display must be 'a regular part of the systematic instructional activities of a governmental body or a nonprofit educational institution.' The concept of 'systematic instructional activities' is intended as the general equivalent of 'curriculums,' but it could be broader in a case such as that of an institution using systematic teaching methods not related to specific course work. A transmission would be a regular part of these activities if it is in accordance with the pattern of teaching established by the governmental body or institution. The use of commercial facilities, such as those of a cable service, to transmit the performance or display, would not affect the exemption as long as the actual performance or display was for nonprofit purposes.

Content of transmission.— Subclause (B) requires that the performance or display be directly related and of material assistance to the teaching content of the transmission.

Intended recipients.— Subclause (C) requires that the transmission is made primarily for:

(i) Reception in classrooms or similar places normally devoted to instruction, or

(ii) Reception by persons to whom the transmission is directed because their disabilities or other special circumstances prevent their attendance in classrooms or similar places normally devoted to instruction, or

(iii) Reception by officers or employees of governmental bodies as a part of their official duties or employment.

In all three cases, the instructional transmission need only be made 'primarily' rather than 'solely' to the specified recipients to be exempt. Thus, the transmission could still be exempt even though it is capable of reception by the public at large. Conversely, it would not be regarded as made 'primarily' for one of the required groups of recipients if the principal purpose behind the transmission is reception by the public at large, even if it is cast in the form of instruction and is also received in classrooms. Factors to consider in determining the 'primary' purpose of a program would include its subject matter, content, and the time of its transmission.

Paragraph (i) of subclause (C) generally covers what are known as 'in-school' broadcasts, whether open- or closed-circuit. The reference to 'classrooms or similar places' here is intended to have the same meaning as that of the phrase as used in section 110(1). The exemption in paragraph (ii) is intended to exempt transmissions providing systematic instruction to individuals who cannot be reached in classrooms because of 'their disabilities or other special circumstances.' Accordingly, the exemption is confined to instructional broadcasting that is an adjunct to the actual classwork of nonprofit schools or is primarily for people who cannot be brought together in classrooms such as preschool children, displaced workers, illiterates, and shut-ins.

There has been some question as to whether or not the language in this section of the bill is intended to include instructional television college credit courses. These telecourses are aimed at undergraduate and graduate students in earnest pursuit of higher educational degrees who are unable to attend daytime classes because of daytime employment, distance from campus, or some other intervening reason. So long as these broadcasts are aimed at regularly enrolled students and conducted by recognized higher educational institutions, the committee believes that they are clearly within the language of section 110(c)(C)(ii). Like night school and correspondence courses before them, these telecourses are fast becoming a valuable adjunct of the normal college curriculum.

The third exemption in subclause (C) is intended to permit the use of copyrighted material, in accordance with the other conditions of section 110(2), in the course of instructional transmissions for Government personnel who are receiving training 'as a part of their official duties or employment.'

Religious services

The exemption in clause (3) of section 110 covers performances of a nondramatic literary or musical work, and also performances 'of dramatico-musical works of a religious nature'; in addition, it extends to displays of works of all kinds. The exemption applies where the performance or display is 'in the course of services at a place of worship or other religious assembly.' The scope of the clause does not cover the sequential showing of motion pictures and other audiovisual works. ...

To be exempted under section 110(3) a performance or display must be 'in the course of services,' thus excluding activities at a place of worship that are for social, educational, fund raising, or entertainment purposes. Some performances of these kinds could be covered by the exemption in section 110(4), discussed next. Since the performance or display must also occur 'at a place of worship or other religious assembly,' the exemption would not extend to religious broadcasts or other transmissions to the public at large, even where the transmissions were sent from the place of worship. On the other hand, as long as services are being conducted before a religious gathering, the exemption would apply if they were conducted in places such as auditoriums; outdoor theaters, and the like.

Certain other nonprofit performances

In addition to the educational and religious exemptions provided by clauses (1) through (3) of section 110, clause (4) contains a general exception to the exclusive right of public performance that would cover some, though not all, of the same ground as the present 'for profit' limitation.

Scope of exemption.— The exemption in clause (4) applies to the same general activities and subject matter as those covered by the 'for profit' limitation today: public performances of nondramatic literary and musical works. However, the exemption would be limited to public performances given directly in the presence of an audience whether by means of living performers, the playing of phonorecords, or the operation of a receiving apparatus, and would not include a 'transmission to the public.' Unlike the clauses (1) through (3) and (5) of section 110, but like clauses (6) through (8), clause (4) applies only to performing rights in certain works, and does not affect the exclusive right to display a work in public.

No profit motive.— In addition to the other conditions specified by the clause, the performance must be 'without any purpose of direct or indirect commerical advantage.' This provision expressly adopts the principle established by the court decisions construing the 'for profit' limitation: that public performances given or sponsored in connection with any commercial or profit-making enterprises are subject to the exclusive rights of the copyright owner even though the public is not charged for seeing or hearing the performance.

No payment for performance.— An important condition for this exemption is that the performance be given 'without payment of any fee or other compensation for the performance to any of its performers, promoters, or organizers.' The basic purpose of this requirement is to prevent the free use of copyrighted material under the guise of charity where fees or percentages are paid to performers, promoters, producers, and the like. However, the exemption would not be lost if the performers, directors, or producers of the performance, instead of being paid directly 'for the performance,' are paid a salary for duties encompassing the performance. Examples are performances by a school orchestra conducted by a music teacher who receives an annual salary, or by a service band whose members and conductors perform as part of their assigned duties and who receive military pay. The committee believes that performances of this type should be exempt, assuming the other conditions in clause (4) are met, and has not adopted the suggestion that the word 'salary' be added to the phrase referring to the 'payment of any fee or other compensation.'

Admission charge.— Assuming that the performance involves no profit motive and no one responsible for it gets paid a fee, it must still meet one of two alternative conditions to be exempt. As specified in subclauses (A) and (B) of section 110(4), these conditions are: (1) that no direct or indirect admission charge is made, or (2) that the net proceeds are 'used exclusively for educational, religious, or charitable purposes and not for private financial gain.' Under the second of these conditions, a performance meeting the other conditions of clause (4) would be exempt even if an admission fee is charged, provided any amounts left 'after deducting the reasonable costs of producing the performance' are used solely for bona fide educational, religious, or charitable purposes. In cases arising under this second condition, and as provided in subclause (B), where there is an admission charge, the copyright owner is given an opportunity to decide whether and under what conditions the copyrighted work should be performed; otherwise, owners could be compelled to make involuntary donations to the fund-raising activities of causes to which they are opposed. The subclause would thus permit copyright owners to prevent public performances of their works under section 110(4)(B) by serving notice of objection, with the reasons therefor, at least seven days in advance.

Mere reception in public

Unlike the first four clauses of section 110, clause (5) [of section 110] applies to performances and displays of all types of works, and its purpose is to exempt from copyright liability anyone who merely turns on, in a public place, an ordinary radio or television receiving apparatus of a kind commonly sold to members of the public for private use.

The basic rationale of this clause is that the secondary use of the transmission by turning on an ordinary receiver in public is so remote and minimal that no further liability should be imposed. In the vast majority of these cases no royalties are collected today, and the exemption should be made explicit in the statute. This clause has nothing to do with cable television systems and the exemptions would be denied in any case where the audience is charged directly to see or hear the transmission.

[Section 110(5) should be read in light of *Twentieth Century Music Corp. v. Aiken*, 422 U.S. 151 (1975).] The defendant [in *Aiken*], owner and operator of a fast-service food shop in downtown Pittsburgh, had "a radio with outlets to four speakers in the ceiling," which he apparently turned on and left on throughout the business day. Lacking any performing license, he was sued for copyright infringement by two ASCAP members. He lost in the District Court, won a reversal in the Third Circuit Court of Appeals, and finally prevailed, by a margin of 7-2, in the Supreme Court.

The *Aiken* decision is based squarely on the two Supreme Court decisions dealing with cable television. In *Fortnightly Corp. v. United Artists*, 393 U.S. 390, and again in *Teleprompter Corp. v. CBS*, 415 U.S. 394, the Supreme Court held that a CATV operator was not "performing," within the meaning of the 1909 statute, when it picked up broadcast signals off the air and retransmitted them to subscribers by cable. The *Aiken* decision extends this interpretation of the scope of the 1909 statute's right of "public performance for profit" to a situation outside the CATV context and, without expressly overruling the decision in *Buck v. Jewell-La Salle Realty Co.*, 283 U.S. 191 (1931), effectively deprives it of much meaning under the [1909 Act] … .

The majority of the Supreme Court in the *Aiken* case based its decision on a narrow construction of the word "perform" in the 1909 statute. This basis for the decision is completely overturned by the present bill and its broad definition of "perform" in section 101. The Committee has adopted the language of section 110(5), with an amendment expressly denying the exemption in situations where "the performance or display is further transmitted beyond the place where the receiving apparatus is located"; in doing so, it accepts the traditional, pre-*Aiken*, interpretation of the *Jewell-La Salle* decision, under which public communication by means other than a home receiving set, or further transmission of a broadcast to the public, is considered an infringing act.

[The remaining clauses of § 110, as enacted in 1976, concerned agricultural fairs, retail sales of phonorecords, and transmissions to handicapped audiences.]

SECTION 111. SECONDARY TRANSMISSIONS

Introduction and general summary

The complex and economically important problem of "secondary transmissions" is considered in section 111. For the most part, the section is directed at the operation of cable television systems and the terms and conditions of their liability for the retransmission of copyrighted works. However, other forms of secondary transmissions are also considered, including apartment house and hotel systems, wired instructional systems, common carriers, nonprofit "boosters" and translators, and secondary transmissions of primary transmissions to controlled groups.

Cable television systems are commercial subscription services that pick up broadcasts of programs originated by others and retransmit them to paying subscribers. A typical system consists of a central antenna which receives and amplifies television signals and a network of cables through which the signals are transmitted to the receiving sets of individual subscribers. In addition to an installation charge, the subscribers pay a monthly charge for the basic service averaging about six dollars. A large number of these systems provide automated programming. A growing number of CATV systems also originate programs, such as movies and sports, and charge additional fees for this service (pay-cable).

The number of cable systems has grown very rapidly since their introduction in 1950, and now [in 1976] totals about 3,450 operating systems, servicing 7,700 communities… .

Pursuant to two decisions of the Supreme Court (*Fortnightly Corp. v. United Artists Television, Inc.*, 392 U.S. 390 (1968), and *Teleprompter Corp. v. CBS, Inc.*, 415 U.S. 394 (1974)), under the 1909 copyright law, the cable television industry has not been paying copyright royalties for its retransmission of over-the-air broadcast signals. Both decisions urged the Congress, however, to consider and determine the scope and extent of such liability in the pending [Copyright Act of 1976]. ...

In general [and subject to various requirements, limitations and exemptions omitted in the present excerpt], the committee believes that cable systems are commercial enterprises whose basic retransmission operations are based on the carriage of copyrighted program material and that copyright royalties should be paid by cable operators to the creators of such programs. The committee recognizes, however, that it would be impractical and unduly burdensome to require every cable system to negotiate with every copyright owner whose work was retransmitted by a cable system. Accordingly, [the bill establishes] a compulsory copyright license [subject to royalties to be decided by Copyright Royalty Judges, as the statute has been amended since to provide] for the retransmission of those over-the-air broadcast signals that a cable system is authorized to carry pursuant to the rules and regulations of the FCC.

SECTION 112. EPHEMERAL RECORDINGS

Section 112 of the bill concerns itself with a special problem that is not dealt with in the [1909 Act] but is the subject of provisions in a number of foreign statutes and in the revisions of the Berne Convention since 1948. This is the problem of what are commonly called "ephemeral recordings": copies or phonorecords of a work made for purposes of later transmission by a broadcasting organization legally entitled to transmit the work. In other words, where a broadcaster has the privilege of performing or displaying a work either because he is licensed or because the performance or display is exempted under the statute, the question is whether he should be given the additional privilege of recording the performance or display to facilitate its transmission. The need for a limited exemption in these cases because of the practical exigencies of broadcasting has been generally recognized, but the scope of the exemption has been a controversial issue.

[The remainder of this section describes limited exceptions to the § 106(1) reproduction right allowed by the Act when the copy or phonorecord is made for purposes of later performance or display, including certain privileges with respect to instructional broadcasts, transmissions by public broadcasters, religious broadcasts, and transmissions to the handicapped.]

SECTION 113. REPRODUCTION OF PICTORIAL, GRAPHIC, AND SCULPTURAL WORKS IN USEFUL ARTICLES

Section 113 deals with the extent of copyright protection in "works of applied art." The section takes as its starting point the Supreme Court's decision in *Mazer v. Stein*, 347 U.S. 201 (1954), and the first sentence of subsection (a) restates the basic principle established by that decision. The rule of *Mazer*, as affirmed by the bill, is that copyright in a pictorial, graphic, or sculptural work will not be affected if the work is employed as the design of a useful article, and will afford protection to the copyright owner against the unauthorized reproduction of his work in useful as well as nonuseful articles. The terms "pictorial, graphic, and sculptural works" and "useful article" are defined in section 101, and these definitions are discussed above in connection with section 102.

The broad language of section 106(1) and of subsection (a) of section 113 raises questions as to the extent of copyright protection for a pictorial, graphic, or sculptural work that portrays, depicts, or represents an image of a useful article in such a way that the utilitarian nature of the article can be seen. To take the example usually cited, would copyright in a drawing or model of an automobile give the artist the exclusive right to make automobiles of the same design?

The 1961 Report of the Register of Copyrights stated, on the basis of judicial precedent, that "copyright in a pictorial, graphic, or sculptural work, portraying a useful article as such, does not extend to the manufacture of the useful article itself," and recommended specifically that "the distinctions drawn in this area by existing court decisions" not be altered by the statute. The Register's Supplementary Report, at page 48, cited a number of these decisions, and explained the insuperable difficulty of finding "any statutory formulation that would express the distinction satisfactorily." Section 113(b) reflects the Register's conclusion that "the real need is to make clear that there is no intention to change the present law with respect to the scope of protection in a work portraying a useful article as such."

Section 113(c) provides that it would not be an infringement of copyright, where a copyright work has been lawfully published as the design of useful articles, to make, distribute or display pictures of the articles in advertising, in feature stories about the articles, or in the news reports. ...

SECTION 114. SCOPE OF EXCLUSIVE RIGHTS IN SOUND RECORDINGS

Subsection (a) of Section 114 specifies that the exclusive rights of the owner of copyright in a sound recording are limited to the rights to reproduce the sound recording in copies or phonorecords, to prepare derivative works based on the copyrighted sound recording, and to distribute copies or phonorecords of the sound recording to the public. Subsection (a) states explicitly that the owner's rights 'do not include any right of performance under section 106(4).' ...

Subsection (b) of section 114 makes clear that statutory protection for sound recordings extends only to the particular sounds of which the recording consists, and would not prevent a separate recording of another performance in which those sounds are imitated. Thus, infringement takes place whenever all or any substantial portion of the actual sounds that go to make up a copyrighted sound recording are reproduced in phonorecords by repressing, transcribing, recapturing off the air, or any other method, or by reproducing them in the soundtrack or audio portion of a motion picture or other audiovisual work. Mere imitation of a recorded performance would not constitute a copyright infringement even where one performer deliberately sets out to simulate another's performance as exactly as possible.

Under section 114, the exclusive right of owner of copyright in a sound recording to prepare derivative works based on the copyrighted sound recording is recognized. However, in view of the expressed intention not to give exclusive rights against initiative or simulated performances and recordings, … [s] ection 114(b) provides that the 'exclusive right of the owner of copyright in a sound recording under clause (2) of section 106 is limited to the right to prepare a derivative work in which the actual sounds fixed in the sound recording are rearranged, remixed, or otherwise altered in sequence or quality.' …

SECTION 115. COMPULSORY LICENSE FOR PHONORECORDS

The … present law, establishing a system of compulsory licensing for the making and distribution of phonorecords of copyrighted music, [is] retained with a number of modifications and clarifications in section 115 of the bill. Under these provisions, which represented a compromise of the most controversial issue of the 1909 act, a musical composition that has been reproduced in phonorecords with the permission of the copyright owner may generally be reproduced in phonorecords by another person, if that person notifies the copyright owner and pays a specified royalty.

The fundamental question of whether to retain the compulsory license or to do away with it altogether was a major issue during earlier stages of the program for general revision of the copyright law. At the hearings it was apparent that the argument on this point had shifted, and the real issue was not whether to retain the compulsory license but how much the royalty rate under it should be. … The Committee's conclusion … remains the same as in [its 1967 report on the same subject]: 'that a compulsory licensing system is still warranted as a condition for the rights of reproducing and distributing phonorecords of copyrighted music,' but 'that the present system is unfair and unnecessarily burdensome on copyright owners, and that the present statutory rate is too lo[w].' …

SECTION 116. PERFORMANCE ON COIN-OPERATED PLAYERS

General background of the problem

No provision of the present law has attracted more heated denunciations and controversy than the so-called jukebox exemption of section 1(e). This paragraph, which has remained unchanged since its enactment in 1909, provides that— "The reproduction or rendition of a musical composition by or upon coin-operated machines shall not be deemed a public performance for profit unless a fee is charged for admission to the place where such reproduction or rendition occurs."

This blanket exemption has been widely and vigorously condemned as an anachronistic 'historical accident' and in terms such as 'unconscionable,' 'indefensible,' 'totally unjustified,' and 'grossly discriminatory.' …

The committee's basic conclusions can be summarized as follows:

1. The present blanket jukebox exemption should not be continued. Whatever justification existed for it in 1909 exists no longer, and one class of commercial users of music should not be completely absolved from liability when none of the others enjoys any exemption.

2. Performances on coin-operated phonorecord players should be subject to a compulsory license (that is, automatic clearance) with statutory fees. Unlike other commercial music users, who have been subject to full copyright liability from the beginning and have made the necessary economic and business adjustments over a period of time, the whole structure of the jukebox industry has been based on the existence of the copyright exemption.

3. The most appropriate basis for the compulsory license is a statutory per box fee, with a mechanism for periodic review and adjustment of the per box fee. Such a mechanism is afforded by the Copyright Royalty Commission. ...

SECTION 117. COMPUTER USES

As the program for general revision of the copyright law has evolved, it has become increasingly apparent that in one major area the problems are not sufficiently developed for a definitive legislative solution. This is the area of computer uses of copyrighted works: the use of a work "in conjunction with automatic systems capable of storing, processing, retrieving, or transferring information." The Commission on New Technological Uses [of Copyrighted Works] is, among other things, now engaged in making a thorough study of the emerging patterns in this field and it will, on the basis of its findings, recommend definitive copyright provisions to deal with the situation. ...

[For the results of the CONTU study, its disposition by Congress and subsequent amendments, see § 117 of the current statute.]

SECTION 118. NONCOMMERCIAL BROADCASTING

... The Committee is cognizant of the intent of Congress ... that encouragement and support of noncommercial broadcasting is in the public interest. It is also aware that public broadcasting may encounter problems not confronted by commercial broadcasting enterprises, due to such factors as the special nature of programming, repeated use of programs, and, of course, limited financial resources. Thus, the Committee determined that the nature of public broadcasting does warrant special treatment in certain areas ...

In general, ... copyright owners and public broadcasters [should] be encouraged to reach voluntary private agreements. ...

Copyright owners and public broadcasting entities that do not reach voluntary agreement are bound by the terms and rates established voluntary agreement are bound by the terms and rates established by the Commission ...

SECTION 201. OWNERSHIP OF COPYRIGHT

Initial ownership

Two basic and well-established principles of copyright law are restated in section 201(a): that the source of copyright ownership is the author of the work, and that, in the case of a "joint work," the coauthors of the work are likewise coowners of the copyright. Under the definition of section 101, a work is "joint" if the authors collaborated with each other, or if each of the authors prepared his or her contribution with the knowledge and intention that it would be merged with the contributions of other authors as "inseparable or interdependent parts of a unitary whole." The touchstone here is the intention, at the time the writing is done, that the parts be absorbed or combined into an integrated unit, although the parts themselves may be either "inseparable" (as in the case of a novel or painting) or "interdependent" (as in the case of a motion picture, opera, or the words and music of a song). The definition of "joint work" is to be contrasted with the definition of "collective work," also in section 101, in which the elements of merger and unity are lacking; there the key elements are assemblage or gathering of "separate and independent works ... into a collective whole."

The definition of "joint works" has prompted some concern lest it be construed as converting the authors of previously written works, such as plays, novels, and music, into coauthors of a motion picture in which their work is incorporated. It is true that a motion picture would normally be a joint rather than a collective work with respect to those authors who actually work on the film, although their usual status as employees for hire would keep the question of coownership from coming up. On the other hand, although a novelist, playwright, or songwriter may write a work with the hope or expectation that it will be used in a motion picture, this is clearly a case of separate or independent authorship rather than one where the basic intention behind the writing of the work was for motion picture use. In this case, the motion picture is a derivative work within the definition of that term, and section 103 makes plain that copyright in a derivative work is independent of, and does not enlarge the scope of rights in, any pre-existing material incorporated in it. There is thus no need to spell this conclusion out in the definition of "joint work."

There is also no need for a specific statutory provision concerning the rights and duties of the coowners of a work; court-made law on this point is left undisturbed. Under the bill, as under the [1909 Act], coowners of a copyright would be treated generally as tenants in common, with each coowner having an independent right to use or license the use of a work, subject to a duty of accounting to the other coowners for any profits.

Works made for hire

Section 201(b) of the bill adopts one of the basic principles of the ... law [under the 1909 Act]: that in the case of works made for hire the employer is considered the author of the work, and is regarded as the initial owner of copyright unless there has been an agreement otherwise. The subsection also requires that any agreement under which the employee is to own rights be in writing and signed by the parties.

The work-made-for-hire provisions of this bill represent a carefully balanced compromise, and as such they do not incorporate the amendments proposed by screenwriters and composers for motion pictures. Their proposal was for the recognition of something similar to the "shop right" doctrine of patent law: with some exceptions, the employer would acquire the right to use the employee's work to the extent needed for purposes of his regular business, but the employee would retain all other rights as long as he or she refrained from the authorizing of competing uses. However, while this change might theoretically improve the bargaining position of screenwriters and others as a group, the practical benefits that individual authors would receive are highly conjectural. The presumption that initial ownership rights vest in the employer for hire is well established in American copyright law, and to exchange that for the uncertainties of the shop right doctrine would not only be of dubious value to employers and employees alike, but might also reopen a number of other issues.

The status of works prepared on special order or commission was a major issue in the development of the definition of "works made for hire" in section 101, which has undergone extensive revision during the legislative process. The basic problem is how to draw a statutory line between those works written on special order or commission that should be considered as "works made for hire," and those that should not. The definition now provided by the bill represents a compromise which, in effect, spells out those specific categories of commissioned works that can be considered "works made for hire" under certain circumstances. ...

Contributions to collective works

Subsection (c) of section 201 deals with the troublesome problem of ownership of copyright in contributions to collective works, and the relationship between copyright ownership in a contribution and in the collective work in which it appears. The first sentence establishes the basic principle that copyright in the individual contribution and copyright in the collective work as a whole are separate and distinct, and that the author of the contribution is, as in every other case, the first owner of copyright in it. Under the definitions in section 101, a "collective work" is a species of "compilation" and, by its nature, must involve the selection, assembly, and arrangement of "a number of contributions." Examples of "collective works" would ordinarily include periodical issues, anthologies, symposia, and collections of the discrete writings of the same authors, but not cases, such as a composition consisting of words and music, a work published with illustrations or front matter, or three one-act plays, where relatively few separate elements have been brought together. Unlike the contents of other types of "compilations," each of the contributions incorporated in a "collective work" must itself constitute a "separate and independent" work, therefore ruling out compilations of information or other uncopyrightable material and works published with editorial revisions or annotations. Moreover, as noted above, there is a basic distinction between a "joint work," where the separate elements merge into a unified whole, and a "collective work," where they remain unintegrated and disparate. ...

The second sentence of section 201(c), in conjunction with the provisions of section 404 dealing with copyright notice, will preserve the author's copyright in a contribution even if the contribution does not bear a separate notice in the author's name, and without requiring any unqualified transfer of rights to the owner of the collective work. This is coupled with a presumption that, unless there has been an express transfer of more, the owner of the collective work acquires "only the privilege of reproducing and distributing the contribution as part of that particular collective work, any revision of that collective work, and any later collective work in the same series."

The basic presumption of section 201(c) is fully consistent with ... law and practice [under the 1909 Act], and represents a fair balancing of equities. At the same time, the last clause of the subsection, under which the privilege of republishing the contribution under certain limited circumstances would be presumed, is an essential counterpart of the basic presumption. Under the language of this clause a publishing company could reprint a contribution from one issue in a later issue of its magazine, and could reprint an article from a 1980 edition of an encyclopedia in a 1990 revision of it; the publisher could not revise the contribution itself or include it in a new anthology or an entirely different magazine or other collective work.

Transfer of ownership

The principle of unlimited alienability of copyright is stated in clause (1) of section 201(d). Under that provision the ownership of a copyright, or of any part of it, may be transferred by any means of conveyance or by operation of law, and is to be treated as personal property upon the death of the owner. The term "transfer of copyright ownership" is defined in section 101 to cover any "conveyance, alienation, or hypothecation," including assignments, mortgages, and exclusive licenses, but not including nonexclusive licenses. ...

Clause (2) of subsection (d) contains the first explicit statutory recognition of the principle of divisibility of copyright in our law. This provision, which has long been sought by authors and their representatives, and which has attracted wide support from other groups, means that any of the exclusive rights that go to make up a copyright, including those enumerated in section 106 and any subdivision of them, can be transferred and owned separately. The definition of "transfer of copyright ownership" in section 101 makes clear that the principle of divisibility applies whether or not the transfer is "limited in time or place of effect," and another definition in the same section provides that the term "copyright owner," with respect to any one exclusive right, refers to the owner of that particular right. The last sentence of section 201(d)(2) adds that the owner, with respect to the particular exclusive right he or she owns, is entitled "to all of the protection and remedies accorded to the copyright owner by this title." ...

SECTION 202. DISTINCTION BETWEEN OWNERSHIP OF COPYRIGHT AND MATERIAL OBJECT

The principle restated in section 202 is a fundamental and important one: that copyright ownership and ownership of a material object in which the copyrighted work is embodied are entirely separate things. Thus, transfer of a material object does not of itself carry any rights under the copyright, and this includes transfer of the copy or phonorecord—the original manuscript, the photographic negative, the unique painting or statue, the master tape recording, etc.—in which the work was first fixed. Conversely, transfer of a copyright does not necessarily require the conveyance of any material object.

As a result of the interaction of this section and the provisions of sections 204(a) and 301, the bill would change a common law doctrine exemplified by the decision in *Pushman v. New York Graphic Society, Inc.*, 287 N.Y. 302, 39 N.E.2d 249 (1942). Under that doctrine, authors or artists are generally presumed to transfer common law literary property rights when they sell their manuscript or work of art, unless those rights are specifically reserved. This presumption would be reversed under the bill, since a specific written conveyance of rights would be required in order for a sale of any material object to carry with it a transfer of copyright.

SECTION 203. TERMINATION OF TRANSFERS AND LICENSES

The problem in general

The provisions of section 203 are based on the premise that the reversionary provisions of the [1909 Act] section on copyright renewal (17 U.S.C. sec. 24) should be eliminated, and that the proposed law should substitute for them a provision safeguarding authors against unremunerative transfers. A provision of this sort is needed because of the unequal bargaining position of authors, resulting in part from the impossibility of determining a work's value until it has been exploited. Section 203 reflects a practical compromise that will further the objectives of the copyright law while recognizing the problems and legitimate needs of all interests involved.

Scope of the provision

Instead of being automatic, as is theoretically the case [when a renewal has been claimed under the 1909 Act], the termination of a transfer or license under section 203 [of the 1976 Act] would require the serving of an advance notice within specified time limits and under specified conditions. However, although affirmative action is needed to effect a termination, the right to take this action cannot be waived in advance or contracted away. Under section 203(a) the right of termination would apply only to transfers and licenses executed after the effective date of the new statute [*i.e.*, January 1, 1978], and would have no retroactive effect.

The right of termination would be confined to *inter vivos* transfers or licenses executed by the author, and would not apply to transfers by the author's successors in interest or to the author's own bequests. The scope of the right would extend not only to any "transfer of copyright ownership," as defined in section 101, but also to non-exclusive licenses. The right of termination would not apply to "works made for hire," which is one of the principal reasons the definition of that term assumed importance in the development of the bill.

Who can terminate a grant

Two issues emerged from the disputes over section 203 as to the persons empowered to terminate a grant: (1) the specific classes of beneficiaries in the case of joint works; and (2) whether anything less than unanimous consent of all those entitled to terminate should be required to make a termination effective. The bill to some extent reflects a compromise on these points, including a recognition of the dangers of one or more beneficiaries being induced to "hold out" and of unknown children or grandchildren being discovered later. The provision can be summarized as follows:

1. In the case of a work of joint authorship, where the grant was signed by two or more of the authors, majority action by those who signed the grant, or by their interests, would be required to terminate it.

2. There are three different situations in which the shares of joint authors, or of a dead author's widow or widower, children, and grandchildren, must be divided under the statute: (1) The right to effect a termination; (2) the ownership of the terminated rights; and (3) the right to make further grants of reverted rights. The respective shares of the authors, and of a dead author's widow or widower, children, and grandchildren, would be divided in exactly the same way in each of these situations. The terms "widow," "widower," and "children" are defined in section 101 in an effort to avoid problems and uncertainties that have arisen under the present renewal section.

3. The principle of *per stirpes* representation would also be applied in exactly the same way in all three situations. Take, for example, a case where a dead author left a widow, two living children, and three grandchildren by a third child who is dead. The widow will own half of the reverted interests, the two children will each own 16 2/3 percent, and the three grandchildren will each own a share of roughly 5 1/2 percent. But who can exercise the right of termination? Obviously, since she owns 50 percent, the widow is an essential party, but suppose neither of the two surviving children is willing to join her in the termination; is it enough that she gets one of the children of the dead child to join, or can the dead child's interest be exercised only by the action of a majority of his children? Consistent with the *per stirpes* principle, the interest of a dead child can be exercised only as a unit by majority action of his surviving children. Thus, even though the widow and one grandchild would own 55 1/2 percent of the reverted copyright, they would have to be joined by another child or grandchild in order to effect a termination or a further transfer of reverted rights. This principle also applies where, for example, two joint authors executed a grant and

one of them is dead; in order to effect a termination, the living author must be joined by a *per stirpes* majority of the dead author's beneficiaries. The notice of termination may be signed by the specified owners of termination interests or by "their duly authorized agents," which would include the legally appointed guardians or committees of persons incompetent to sign because of age or mental disability.

When a grant can be terminated

Section 203 draws a distinction between the date when a termination becomes effective and the earlier date when the advance notice of termination is served. With respect to the ultimate effective date, section 203(a)(3) provides, as a general rule, that a grant may be terminated during the 5 years following the expiration of a period of 35 years from the execution of the grant. As an exception to this basic 35-year rule, the bill also provides that "if the grant covers the right of publication of the work, the period begins at the end of 35 years from the date of publication of the work under the grant or at the end of 40 years from the date of execution of the grant, whichever term ends earlier." This alternative method of computation is intended to cover cases where years elapse between the signing of a publication contract and the eventual publication of the work.

The effective date of termination, which must be stated in the advance notice, is required to fall within the 5 years following the end of the applicable 35- or 40-year period, but the advance notice itself must be served earlier. Under section 203(a)(4)(A), the notice must be served "not less than two or more than ten years" before the effective date stated in it.

As an example of how these time-limit requirements would operate in practice, we suggest two typical contract situations:

Case 1: Contract for theatrical production signed on September 2, 1987. Termination of grant can be made to take effect between September 2, 2022 (35 years from execution) and September 1, 2027 (end of 5-year termination period). Assuming that the author decides to terminate on September 1, 2022 (the earliest possible date), the advance notice must be filed between September 1, 2012 and September 1, 2020.

Case 2: Contract for book publication executed on April 10, 1980; book finally published on August 23, 1987. Since contract covers the right of publication, the 5-year termination period would begin on April 10, 2020 (40 years from execution) rather than April 10, 2015 (35 years from execution) or August 23, 2022 (35 years from publication). Assuming that the author decides to make the termination effective on January 1, 2024, the advance notice would have to be served between January 1, 2014, and January 1, 2022.

Effect of termination

Section 203(b) makes clear that, unless effectively terminated within the applicable 5-year period, all rights covered by an existing grant will continue unchanged, and that rights under other Federal, State, or foreign laws are unaffected. However, assuming that a copyright transfer or license is terminated under section 203, who are bound by the termination and how are they affected?

Under the bill, termination means that ownership of the rights covered by the terminated grant reverts to everyone who owns termination interests on the date the notice of termination was served, whether they joined in signing the notice or not. In other words, if a person could have signed the notice, that person is bound by the action of the majority who did; the termination of the grant will be effective as to that person, and a proportionate share of the reverted rights automatically vests in that person. Ownership is divided proportionately on the same *per stirpes* basis as that provided for the right to effect termination under section 203(a) and, since the reverted rights vest on the date notice is served, the heirs of a dead beneficiary would inherit his or her share.

Under clause (3) of subsection (b), majority action is required to make a further grant of reverted rights. A problem here, of course, is that years may have passed between the time the reverted rights vested and the time the new owners want to make a further transfer; people may have died and children may have been born in the interim. To deal with this problem, the bill looks back to the date of vesting; out of the group in whom rights vested on that date, it requires the further transfer or license to be signed by "the same number and proportion of the owners" (though not necessarily the same individuals) as were then required to terminate the grant under subsection (a). If some of those in whom the rights originally vested have died, their "legal representatives, legatees, or heirs at law" may represent them for this purpose and, as in the case of the termination itself, any one of the minority who does not join in the further grant is nevertheless bound by it.

An important limitation on the rights of a copyright owner under a terminated grant is specified in section 203(b)(1). This clause provides that, notwithstanding a termination, a derivative work prepared earlier may "continue to be utilized" under the conditions of the terminated grant; the clause adds, however, that this privilege is not broad enough to permit the preparation of other derivative works. In other words, a film made from a play could continue to be licensed for performance after the motion picture contract had been terminated but any remake rights covered by the contract would be cut off. For this purpose, a motion picture would be considered as a "derivative work" with respect to every "preexisting work" incorporated in it, whether the preexisting work was created independently or was prepared expressly for the motion picture.

Section 203 would not prevent the parties to a transfer or license from voluntarily agreeing at any time to terminate an existing grant and negotiating a new one, thereby causing another 35-year period to start running. However, the bill seeks to avoid the situation that has arisen under the present renewal provision, in which third parties have bought up contingent future interests as a form of speculation. Section 203(b)(4) would make a further grant of rights that revert under a terminated grant valid "only if it is made after the effective date of the termination." An exception, in the nature of a right of "first refusal," would permit the original grantee or a successor of such grantee to negotiate a new agreement with the persons effecting the termination at any time after the notice of termination has been served.

Nothing contained in this section or elsewhere in this legislation is intended to extend the duration of any license, transfer or assignment made for a period of less than thirty-five years. If, for example, an agreement provides an earlier termination date or lesser duration, or if it allows the author the right of cancelling or terminating the agreement under certain circumstances, the duration is governed by the agreement. Likewise, nothing in this section or legislation is intended to change the existing state of the law of contracts concerning the circumstances in which an author may cancel or terminate a license, transfer, or assignment.

Section 203(b)(6) provides that, unless and until termination is effected under this section, the grant, "if it does not provide otherwise," continues for the term of copyright. This section means that, if the agreement does not contain provisions specifying its term or duration, and the author has not terminated the agreement under this section, the agreement continues for the term of the copyright, subject to any right of termination under circumstances which may be specified therein. If, however, an agreement does contain provisions governing its duration—for example, a term of fifty years—and the author has not exercised his or her right of termination under the statute, the agreement will continue according to its terms—in this example, for only fifty years. The quoted language is not to be construed as requiring agreements to reserve the right of termination.

SECTIONS 204, 205. EXECUTION AND RECORDATION OF TRANSFERS

Section 204 is a somewhat broadened and liberalized counterpart of sections 28 and 29 of the [1909 Act]. Under subsection (a), a transfer of copyright ownership (other than one brought about by operation of law) is valid only if there exists an instrument of conveyance, or alternatively a "note or memorandum of the transfer," which is in writing and signed by the copyright owner "or such owner's duly authorized agent." Subsection (b) makes clear that a notarial or consular acknowledgment is not essential to the validity of any transfer, whether executed in the United States or abroad. However, the subsection would liberalize the conditions under which certificates of acknowledgment of documents executed abroad are to be accorded *prima facie* weight, and would give the same weight to domestic acknowledgments under appropriate circumstances.

The recording and priority provisions of section 205 are intended to clear up a number of uncertainties arising from sections 30 and 31 of the [1909 Act] and to make them more effective and practical in operation. Any "document pertaining to a copyright" may be recorded under subsection (a) if it "bears that actual signature of the person who executed it," or if it is appropriately certified as a true copy. However, subsection (c) makes clear that the recorded document will give constructive notice of its contents only if two conditions are met: (1) the document or attached material specifically identifies the work to which it pertains so that a reasonable search under the title or registration number would reveal it, and (2) registration has been made for the work. Moreover, even though the Register of Copyrights may be compelled to accept for recordation documents that on their face appear self-serving or colorable, the Register should take care that their nature is not concealed from the public in the Copyright Office's indexing and search reports.

... The one- and three-month grace periods provided in subsection [(d)] are a reasonable compromise between those who want a longer hiatus and those who argue that any grace period makes it impossible for a *bona fide* transferee to rely on the record at any particular time.

Under subsection [(e)] of section 205, a nonexclusive license in writing and signed, whether recorded or not, would be valid against a later transfer, and would also prevail as against a prior unrecorded transfer if taken in good faith and without notice. Objections were raised by motion picture producers, particularly to the provision allowing unrecorded nonexclusive licenses to prevail over subsequent transfers, on the ground that a nonexclusive license can have drastic effects on the value of a copyright. On the other hand, the impracticalities and burdens that would accompany any requirement of recordation of nonexclusive licenses outweigh the limited advantages of a statutory recordation system for them.

SECTION 301. FEDERAL PREEMPTION OF RIGHTS EQUIVALENT TO COPYRIGHT

Single Federal system

Section 301, one of the bedrock provisions of the bill, would accomplish a fundamental and significant change in the present law [*i.e.*, the 1909 Act]. Instead of a dual system of "common law copyright" for unpublished works and statutory copyright for published works, which has been the system in effect in the United States since the first copyright statute in 1790, the bill adopts a single system of Federal statutory copyright from creation. Under section 301 a work would obtain statutory protection as soon as it is "created" or, as that term is defined in section 101, when it is "fixed in a copy or phonorecord for the first time." Common law copyright protection for works coming within the scope of the statute would be abrogated, and the concept of publication would lose its all—embracing importance as a dividing line between common law and statutory protection and between both of these forms of legal protection and the public domain.

By substituting a single Federal system for the present anachronistic, uncertain, impractical, and highly complicated dual system, the bill would greatly improve the operation of the copyright law and would be much more effective in carrying out the basic constitutional aims of uniformity and the promotion of writing and scholarship. The main arguments in favor of a single Federal system can be summarized as follows:

> 1. One of the fundamental purposes behind the copyright clause of the Constitution, as shown in Madison's comments in THE FEDERALIST, was to promote national uniformity and to avoid the practical difficulties of determining and enforcing an author's rights under the differing

laws and in the separate courts of the various States. Today, when the methods for dissemination of an author's work are incomparably broader and faster than they were in 1789, national uniformity in copyright protection is even more essential than it was then to carry out the constitutional intent.

2. "Publication," perhaps the most important single concept under the [1909 Act], also represents its most serious defect. Although at one time, when works were disseminated almost exclusively through printed copies, "publication" could serve as a practical dividing line between common law and statutory protection, this is no longer true. With the development of the 20th-century communications revolution, the concept of publication has become increasingly artificial and obscure. To cope with the legal consequences of an established concept that has lost much of its meaning and justification, the courts have given "publication" a number of diverse interpretations, some of them radically different. Not unexpectedly, the results in individual cases have become unpredictable and often unfair. A single Federal system would help to clear up this chaotic situation.

3. Enactment of section 301 would also implement the "limited times" provision of the Constitution, which has become distorted under the traditional concept of "publication." Common law protection in "unpublished" works is now perpetual, no matter how widely they may be disseminated by means other than "publication"; the bill would place a time limit on the duration of exclusive rights in them. The provision would also aid scholarship and the dissemination of historical materials by making unpublished, undisseminated manuscripts available for publication after a reasonable period.

4. Adoption of a uniform national copyright system would greatly improve international dealings in copyrighted material. No other country has anything like our present dual system. In an era when copyrighted works can be disseminated instantaneously to every country on the globe, the need for effective international copyright relations, and the concomitant need for national uniformity, assume ever greater importance.

Under section 301, the statute would apply to all works created after its effective date [*i.e.*, January 1, 1978], whether or not they are ever published or disseminated. With respect to works created before [that date] and still under common law protection, section 303 of the statute would provide protection from that date on, and would guarantee a minimum period of statutory copyright.

Preemption of State Law

The intention of section 301 is to preempt and abolish any rights under the common law or statutes of a State that are equivalent to copyright and that extend to works coming within the scope of the Federal copyright law. The declaration of this principle in section 301 is intended to be stated in the clearest and most unequivocal language possible, so as to foreclose any conceivable misinterpretation of its unqualified intention that Congress shall act preemptively, and to avoid the development of any vague borderline areas between State and Federal protection.

Under section 301(a), all "legal or equitable rights that are equivalent to any of the exclusive rights within the general scope of copyright as specified by section 106" are governed exclusively by the Federal copyright statute if the works involved are "works of authorship that are fixed in a tangible medium of expression and come within the subject matter of copyright as specified by sections 102 and 103." All corresponding State laws, whether common law or statutory, are preempted and abrogated. Regardless of when the work was created and whether it is published or unpublished, disseminated or undisseminated, in the public domain or copyrighted under the Federal statute, the States cannot offer it protection equivalent to copyright. Section 1338 of title 28, United States Code, also makes clear that any action involving rights under the Federal copyright law would come within the exclusive jurisdiction of the Federal courts. The preemptive effect of section 301 is limited to State laws; as stated expressly in subsection (d) of section 301, there is no intention to deal with the question of whether Congress can or should offer the equivalent of copyright protection under some constitutional provision other than the patent-copyright clause of article 1, section 8.

As long as a work fits within one of the general subject matter categories of sections 102 and 103, the bill prevents the States from protecting it even if it fails to achieve Federal statutory copyright because it is too minimal or lacking in originality to qualify, or because it has fallen into the public domain. On the other hand, section 301(b) explicitly preserves common law copyright protection for one important class of works: works that have not been "fixed in any tangible medium of expression." Examples would include choreography that has never been filmed or notated, an extemporaneous speech, "original works of authorship" communicated solely through conversations or live broadcasts, and a dramatic sketch or musical composition improvised or developed from memory and without being recorded or written down. As mentioned above in connection with section 102, unfixed works are not included in the specified "subject matter of copyright." They are therefore not affected by the preemption of section 301, and would continue to be subject to protection under State statute or common law until fixed in tangible form.

The preemption of rights under State law is complete with respect to any work coming within the scope of the bill, even though the scope of exclusive rights given the work under the bill is narrower than the scope of common law rights in the work might have been. ...

In a general way subsection (b) of section 301 represents the obverse of subsection (a). It sets out, in broad terms and without necessarily being exhaustive, some of the principal areas of protection that preemption would not prevent the States from protecting. Its purpose is to make clear, consistent with the 1964 Supreme Court decisions in *Sears, Roebuck & Co. v. Stiffel Co.*, 376 U.S. 225, and *Compco Corp. v. Day-Brite Lighting, Inc.*, 376 U.S. 234, that preemption does not extend to causes of action, or subject matter outside the scope of the revised Federal copyright statute.

The numbered clauses of subsection (b) list three general areas left unaffected by the preemption: (1) subject matter that does not come within the subject matter of copyright; (2) causes of action arising under State law before the effective date of the statute; and (3) violations of rights that are not equivalent to any of the exclusive rights under copyright.

[For reasons that will appear shortly, the Report's discussion of § 301(b) is omitted.]

A unique and difficult problem is presented with respect to the status of sound recordings fixed before February 12, 1972, the effective date of the amendment bringing recordings fixed after that date under Federal copyright protection. In its testimony during the 1975 hearings, the Department of Justice pointed out that, under section 301 as then written:

> This language could be read as abrogating the anti-piracy laws now existing in 29 states relating to pre-February 15, 1972 sound recordings on the grounds that these statutes proscribe activities violating rights "equivalent to ... the exclusive rights within the general scope of copyright. ... " Certainly such a result cannot have been intended for it would likely effect the immediate resurgence of piracy of pre-February 15, 1972 sound recordings.The Department recommended that section 301(b) be amended to exclude sound recordings fixed prior to February 15, 1972 from the effect of the preemption.

The Senate adopted this suggestion when it passed S. 22. The result of the Senate amendment would be to leave pre-1972 sound recordings as entitled to perpetual protection under State law, while post-1972 recordings would eventually fall into the public domain as provided in the bill.

The committee recognizes that, under recent court decisions, pre-1972 recordings are protected by State statute or common law, and that [they] should not all be thrown into the public domain instantly upon the coming into effect of the new law. However, it cannot agree that they should in effect be accorded perpetual protection, as under the Senate amendment, and it has therefore revised clause (4) [now codified as § 301(c) of the Copyright Act of 1976] to establish a future date for the pre-emption to take effect. The date chosen is February 15, 2047, which is 75 years from the effective date of the statute extending Federal protection to recordings.

Subsection (c) [now (d)] makes clear that nothing contained in Title 17 annuls or limits any rights or remedies under any other Federal statute.

SECTION 302. DURATION OF COPYRIGHT IN WORKS CREATED AFTER EFFECTIVE DATE

In general

[The following excerpt from the House Report discusses the policy justifications for the since-extended basic term of copyright originally adopted in the 1976 Act: life-plus-50 years (together with a term of 75 years from publication or 100 years from creation, whichever is shorter, for certain works). In 1998, Congress enacted the Sonny Bono Copyright Term Extension Act ("CTEA"), extending the basic term of protection to life-plus-70 years (and bumping up the alternative term to 95 years from publication or 120 from creation, whichever is shorter).]

The debate over how long a copyright should last is as old as the oldest copyright statute and will doubtless continue as long as there is a copyright law. With certain exceptions, there appears to be strong support for the principle, as embodied in the bill, of a copyright term consisting of the life of the author and 50 years after his death. In particular, the authors and their representatives stressed that the adoption of a life-plus-50 term was by far their most important legislative goal in copyright law revision. The Register of Copyrights now regards a life-plus-50 term as the foundation of the entire bill.

Under the [1909 Act,] statutory copyright protection begins on the date of publication (or on the date of registration in unpublished form) and continues for 28 years from that date; it may be renewed for a second 28 years, making a total potential term of 56 years in all cases. The principal elements of this system—a definite number of years, computed from either publication or registration, with a renewal feature—have been a part of the U.S. copyright law since the first statute in 1790. The arguments for changing this system to one based on the life of the author can be summarized as follows:

> 1. The present 56-year term is not long enough to insure an author and his dependents the fair economic benefits from his works. Life expectancy has increased substantially, and more and more authors are seeing their works fall into the public domain during their lifetimes, forcing later works to compete with their own early works in which copyright has expired.
>
> 2. The tremendous growth in communications media has substantially lengthened the commercial life of a great many works. A short term is particularly discriminatory against serious works of music, literature, and art, whose value may not be recognized until after many years.
>
> 3. Although limitations on the term of copyright are obviously necessary, too short a term harms the author without giving any substantial benefit to the public. The public frequently pays the same for works in the public domain as it does for copyrighted works, and the only result is a commercial windfall to certain users at the author's expense. In some cases the lack of copyright protection actually restrains dissemination of the work, since publishers and other users cannot risk investing in the work unless assured of exclusive rights.
>
> 4. A system based on the life of the author would go a long way toward clearing up the confusion and uncertainty involved in the vague concept of "publication," and would provide a much simpler, clearer method for computing the term. The death of the author is a definite, determinable event, and it would be the only date that a potential user would have to worry about. All of a particular author's works, including

successive revisions of them, would fall into the public domain at the same time, thus avoiding the present problems of determining a multitude of publication dates and of distinguishing "old" and "new" matter in later editions. The bill answers the problems of determining when relatively obscure authors died, by establishing a registry of death dates and a system of presumptions.

5. One of the worst features of the [1909 Act] is the provision for renewal of copyright. A substantial burden and expense, this unclear and highly technical requirement results in incalculable amounts of unproductive work. In a number of cases it is the cause of inadvertent and unjust loss of copyright. Under a life-plus-50 system the renewal device would be inappropriate and unnecessary.

6. Under the preemption provisions of section 301 and the single Federal system they would establish, authors will be giving up perpetual, unlimited exclusive common law rights in their unpublished works, including works that have been widely disseminated by means other than publication. A statutory term of life-plus-50 years is no more than a fair recompense for the loss of these perpetual rights.

7. A very large majority of the world's countries have adopted a copyright term of the life of the author and 50 years after the author's death. Since American authors are frequently protected longer in foreign countries than in the United States, the disparity in the duration of copyright has provoked considerable resentment and some proposals for retaliatory legislation. Copyrighted works move across national borders faster and more easily than virtually any other economic commodity, and with the techniques now in common use this movement has in many cases become instantaneous and effortless. The need to conform the duration of U.S. copyright to that prevalent throughout the rest of the world is increasingly pressing in order to provide certainty and simplicity in international business dealings. Even more important, a change in the basis of our copyright term would place the United States in the forefront of the international copyright community. Without this change, the possibility of future United States adherence to the Berne Copyright Union would evaporate, but with it would come a great and immediate improvement in our copyright relations. All of these benefits would accrue directly to American and foreign authors alike.

The need for a longer total term of copyright has been conclusively demonstrated. It is true that a major reason for the striking statistical increase in life expectancy since 1909 is the reduction in infant mortality, but this does not mean that the increase can be discounted. Although not nearly as great as the total increase in life expectancy, there has been a marked increase in longevity, and with medical discoveries and health programs for the elderly this trend shows every indication of continuing. If life expectancy in 1909, which was in the neighborhood of 56 years, offered a rough guide to the length of copyright protection, then life expectancy in the 1970s, which is well over 70 years, should offer a similar guide; the Register's 1961 Report included statistics indicating that something between 70 and 76 years was then the average equivalent of life-plus-50 years. A copyright should extend beyond the author's lifetime, and judged by this standard the present term of 56 years is too short.

The arguments as to the benefits of uniformity with foreign laws, and the advantages of international comity that would result from adoption of a life-plus-50 term, are also highly significant. ...

A point that has concerned some educational groups arose from the possibility that, since a large majority (now about 85 percent) of all copyrighted works are not renewed, a life-plus-50 year term would tie up a substantial body of material that is probably of no commercial interest but that would be more readily available for scholarly use if free of copyright restrictions. ...

It is true that today's ephemera represent tomorrow's social history, and that works of scholarly value, which are now falling into the public domain after 29 years, would be protected much longer under the bill. Balanced against this are the burdens and expenses of renewals, the near impossibility of distinguishing between types of works in fixing a statutory term, and the extremely strong case in favor of a life-plus-50 system. Moreover, it is important to realize that the bill would not restrain scholars from using any work as source material or from making "fair use" of it; the restrictions would extend only to the unauthorized reproduction or distribution of copies of the work, its public performance, or some other use that would actually infringe the copyright owner's exclusive rights. The advantages of a basic term of copyright enduring for the life of the author and for 50 years after the author's death outweigh any possible disadvantages.

Basic copyright term

Under subsection (a) of section 302, a work "created" on or after the effective date of the revised statute would be protected by statutory copyright "from its creation" and, with exceptions to be noted below, "endures for a term consisting of the life of the author and 50 years after the author's death."

Under this provision, as a general rule, the life-plus-50 term would apply equally to unpublished works, to works published during the author's lifetime, and to works published posthumously. ...

Joint Works

Since by definition a "joint work" has two or more authors, a statute basing the term of copyright on the life of the author must provide a special method of computing the term of "joint works." Under the system in effect in many foreign countries, the term of copyright is measured from the death of the last survivor of a group of joint authors, no matter how many there are. The bill adopts this system as the simplest and fairest of the alternatives for dealing with the problem.

Anonymous works, pseudonymous works, and works made for hire

Computing the term from the author's death also requires special provisions to deal with cases where the authorship is not revealed or where the "author" is not an individual. Section 302(c) therefore provides a special term for anonymous works, pseudonymous works, and works made for hire: 75 years from publication or 100 years from creation, whichever is shorter. The definitions in section 101 make the status of anonymous and pseudonymous works depend on what is revealed on the copies or phonorecords of a work; a work is "anonymous" if "no natural person is identified as author," and is "pseudonymous" if "the author is identified under a fictitious name."

Section 302(c) provides that the 75- and 100-year terms for an anonymous or pseudonymous work can be converted to the ordinary life-plus-50 term if "the identity of one or more authors ... is revealed" in special records maintained for this purpose in the Copyright Office. The term in such cases would be "based on the life of the author or authors whose identity has been revealed." Instead of forcing a user to search through countless Copyright Office records to determine if an author's identity has been revealed, the bill sets up a special registry for the purpose, with requirements concerning the filing of identifying statements that parallel those of the following subsection (d) with respect to statements of the date of an author's death.

The alternative terms established in section 302(c)-75 years from publication or 100 years from creation, whichever expires first—are necessary to set a time limit on protection of unpublished material. For example, copyright in a work created in 1978 and published in 1988 would expire in 2063 (75 years from publication). A question arises as to when the copyright should expire if the work is never published. Both the Constitution and the underlying purposes of the bill require the establishment of an alternative term for unpublished work and the only practicable basis for this alternative is "creation." Under the bill a work created in 1980 but not published until after 2005 (or never published) would fall into the public domain in 2080 (100 years after creation). ...

Records and presumption as to author's death

Subsections (d) and (e) of section 302 together furnish an answer to the practical problems of how to discover the death dates of obscure or unknown authors. Subsection (d) provides a procedure for recording statements that an author died, or that he was still living, on a particular date, and also requires the Register of Copyrights to maintain obituary records on a current basis. Under subsection (e) anyone who, after a specified period, obtains certification from the Copyright Office that its records show nothing to indicate that the author is living or died less than 50 years before, is entitled to rely upon a presumption that the author has been dead for more than 50 years. The period specified in subsection (e)—75 years from publication or 100 years from creation—is purposely uniform with the special term provided in subsection (c).

SECTION 303. PREEXISTING WORKS UNDER COMMON LAW PROTECTION

Theoretically, at least, the legal impact of section 303 would be far reaching. Under it, every "original work of authorship" fixed in tangible form that is in existence would be given statutory copyright protection as long as the work is not in the public domain in this country. The vast majority of these works consist of private material that no one is interested in protecting or infringing, but section 303 would still have practical effects for a prodigious body of material already in existence.

Looked at another way, however, section 303 would have a genuinely restrictive effect. Its basic purpose is to substitute statutory for common law copyright for everything now protected at common law, and to substitute reasonable time limits for the perpetual protection now available. In general, the substituted time limits are those applicable to works created after the effective date of the law; for example, an unpublished work written in 1945 whose author dies in 1980 would be protected under the statute from the effective date through 2030 (50 years after the author's death).

A special problem under this provision is what to do with works whose ordinary statutory terms will have expired or will be nearing expiration on the effective date. The committee believes that a provision taking away subsisting common law rights and substituting statutory rights for a reasonable period is fully in harmony with the constitutional requirements of due process, but it is necessary to fix a "reasonable period" for this purpose. Section 303 provides that under no circumstances would copyright protection expire before December 31, 2002, and also attempts to encourage publication by providing 25 years more protection (through 2027) if the work were published before the end of 2002.

[The CTEA extended the term of protection for works published before 2003 by 20 years, i.e., through 2047.]

SECTION 304. DURATION OF SUBSISTING COPYRIGHTS

The arguments in favor of lengthening the duration of copyright apply to subsisting as well as future copyrights. The bill's basic approach is to increase the present 56-year term to 75 years in the case of copyrights subsisting in both their first and their renewal terms.

Copyrights in their first term

Subsection (a) of section 304 reenacts and preserves the renewal provision, now in section 24 of the [1909 Act], for all of the works presently in their first 28-year term. A great many of the present expectancies in these cases are the subject of existing contracts, and it would be unfair and immensely confusing to cut off or alter these interests. Renewal registration will be required during the 28th year of the copyright but the length of the renewal term will be increased from 28 to 47 years.

Although the bill preserves the language of the [1909 Act] renewal provision without any change in substance, the committee intends that the reference to a "posthumous work" in this section has the meaning given to it in *Bartok v. Boosey & Hawkes, Inc.*, 523 F.2d 941 (2d Cir. 1975)—one as to which no copyright assignment or other contract for exploitation of the work has occurred during an author's lifetime, rather than one which is simply first published after the author's death.

Copyrights in their renewal term

Renewed copyrights that are subsisting in their second term at any time during the period between December 31, 1976, and December 31, 1977, inclusive, would be extended under section 304(b) to run for a total of 75 years. This provision would add another 19 years to the duration of any renewed copyright whose second term started during the 28 years immediately preceding the effective date of the act (January 1, 1978). In addition, it would extend by varying lesser amounts the duration of renewal copyrights already extended under Public Laws 87-668, 89-142, 90-416, 91-147, 91-555, 92-170, 92-566, and 93-573, all of which would otherwise expire on December 31, 1976. The subsection would also extend the duration of renewal copyrights whose second 28-year term is scheduled to expire during 1977. In none of these cases, however, would the total terms of copyright for the work be longer than 75 years.

Subsection (b) also covers the special situation of a subsisting first-term copyright that becomes eligible for renewal registration during the year before the [1976 Act] comes into effect. If a renewal registration is not made before the effective date [*i.e.*, January 1, 1978], the case is governed by the provisions of section 304(a). If a renewal registration is made during the year before the new law takes effect [*i.e.*, 1977], however, the copyright would be treated as if it were already subsisting in its second term and would be extended to the full period of 75 years without the need for further renewal.

[Under the CTEA, any copyright secured in 1923 still in its renewal term on the effective date of the Act (October 27, 1998) was extended to run for a total of 95 years from the date copyright originally was secured.]

Termination of grants covering extended term

An issue underlying the 19-year extension of renewal terms under both subsections (a) and (b) of section 304 is whether, in a case where their rights have already been transferred, the author or the dependents of the author should be given a chance to benefit from the extended term. ... [This] term represents a completely new property right, and there are strong reasons for giving the author, who is the fundamental beneficiary of copyright under the Constitution, an opportunity to share in it.

... In the case of either a first-term or renewal copyright already subsisting when the new statute becomes effective, any grant of rights covering the renewal copyright in the work, executed before the effective date, may be terminated under conditions and limitations [provided in this subsection]. Except for transfers and licenses covering renewal copyrights already extended under Public Laws 87-668, 89-142, 90-141, 90-416, 91-147, 91-555, 92-170, 92-566, and 93-573, which would become subject to termination immediately upon the coming into effect of the revised law, the 5-year period during which termination could be made effective would start 56 years after copyright was originally secured.

... [T]he right of termination under section 304(c) extends [both] to grants executed [by the author and to grants executed] by those beneficiaries of the author who can claim renewal under the [1909 Act]: his or her widow or widower, children, executors, or next of kin.

[The provision to permit termination of grants made by beneficiaries is necessary because,] under the present renewal provisions, any statutory beneficiary of the author can make a valid transfer or license of future renewal rights, which is completely binding if the author is dead and the person who executed the grant turns out to be the proper renewal claimant. Because of this, a great many contingent transfers of future renewal rights have been obtained from widows, widowers, children, and next of kin, and a substantial number of these will be binding. After the present 28-year renewal period has ended, a statutory beneficiary who has signed a disadvantageous grant of this sort should have the opportunity to reclaim the extended term. ...

[Under the CTEA, even if, prior to 1998, the author or successor did not timely exercise the right to recapture the initial 19 years of the extended term, such a person is afforded a "second bite" at the termination apple by virtue of new § 304(d).]

SECTION 305. YEAR END EXPIRATION OF TERMS

Under section 305, which has its counterpart in the laws of most foreign countries, the term of copyright protection for a work extends through December 31 of the year in which the term would otherwise have expired. This will make the duration of copyright much easier to compute, since it will be enough to determine the year, rather than the exact date, of the event from which the term is based.

Section 305 applies only to "terms of copyright provided by sections 302 through 304," which are the sections dealing with duration of copyright. It therefore has no effect on the other time periods specified in the bill; and, since they do not involve "terms of copyright," the periods provided in section 304(c) with respect to termination of grants are not affected by section 305.

The terminal date section would change the duration of subsisting copyrights under section 304 by extending the total terms of protection under subsections (a) and (b) to the end of the 75th year from the date copyright was secured. A copyright subsisting in its first term on [January 1, 1978] would run through December 31 of the 28th year and would then expire unless renewed. Since all copyright terms under the bill expire on December 31, and since section 304(a) requires that renewal be made "within one year prior to the expiration of the original term of copyright," the period for renewal registration in all cases will run from December 31 through December 31. ...

SECTION 401. NOTICE ON VISUALLY-PERCEPTIBLE COPIES

A requirement that the public be given formal notice of every work in which copyright is claimed was a part of the first U.S. copyright statute enacted in 1790, and since 1802 our copyright laws have always provided that the published copies of copyrighted works must bear a specified notice as a condition of protection. Under the [1909 Act,] the copyright notice serves four principal functions:

(1) It has the effect of placing in the public domain a substantial body of published material that no one is interested in copyrighting;

(2) It informs the public as to whether a particular work is copyrighted;

(3) It identifies the copyright owner; and

(4) It shows the date of publication.

Ranged against these values of a notice requirement are its burdens and unfairness to copyright owners. One of the strongest arguments for revision of the [1909 Act] has been the need to avoid the arbitrary and unjust forfeitures now resulting from unintentional or relatively unimportant omissions or errors in the copyright notice. It has been contended that the disadvantages of the notice requirement outweigh its values and that it should therefore be eliminated or substantially liberalized.

The fundamental principle underlying the notice provisions of the bill is that the copyright notice has real values which should be preserved, and that this should be done by inducing use of notice without causing outright forfeiture for errors or omissions. Subject to certain safeguards for innocent infringers, protection would not be lost by the complete omission of copyright notice from large numbers of copies or from a whole edition, if registration for the work is made before or within 5 years after publication. Errors in the name or date in the notice could be corrected without forfeiture of copyright.

Sections 401 and 402 set out the basic notice requirements of the bill, the former dealing with "copies from which the work can be visually perceived," and the latter covering "phonorecords" of a "sound recording." The notice requirements established by these parallel provisions apply only when copies or phonorecords of the work are "publicly distributed." No copyright notice would be required in connection with the public display of a copy by any means, including projectors, television, or cathode ray tubes connected with information storage and retrieval systems, or in connection with the public performance of a work by means of copies or phonorecords, whether in the presence of an audience or through television, radio, computer transmission, or any other process. ...

Subsections (a) of both section 401 and section 402 require that a notice be used whenever the work "is published in the United States or elsewhere by authority of the copyright owner." The phrase "or elsewhere," which does not appear in the [1909 Act], makes the notice requirements applicable to copies or phonorecords distributed to the public anywhere in the world, regardless of where and when the work was first published. ...

Subsection (b) of section 401, which sets out the form of notice to appear on visually-perceptible copies, retains the basic elements of the notice under the [1909 Act]: the word "Copyright," the abbreviation "Copr.," or the symbol "'©"; the year of first publication; and the name of the copyright owner. The year of publication, which is still significant in computing the term and determining the status of a work, is required for all categories of copyrightable works. Clause (2) of subsection (b) makes clear that, in the case of a derivative work or compilation, it is not necessary to list the dates of publication of all preexisting material incorporated in the work ... Clause (3) establishes that a recognizable abbreviation or a generally known alternative designation may be used instead of the full name of the copyright owner.

By providing simply that the notice "shall be affixed to the copies in such manner and location as to give reasonable notice of the claim of copyright," subsection (c) follows the flexible approach of the Universal Copyright Convention. The further provision empowering the Register of Copyrights to set forth in regulations a list of examples of "specific methods of affixation and positions of the notice on various types of works that will satisfy this requirement" will offer substantial guidance and avoid a good deal of uncertainty. ...

SECTION 402. NOTICE ON PHONORECORDS OF SOUND RECORDINGS

A special notice requirement, applicable only to the subject matter of sound recordings, is established by section 402. Since the bill protects sound recordings as separate works, independent of protection for any literary or musical works embodied in them, there would be a likelihood of confusion if the same notice requirements applied to sound recordings and to the works they incorporate. Like the present law, therefore, section 402 thus sets forth requirements for a notice to appear on the "phonorecords" of "sound recordings" that are different from the notice requirements established by section 401 for the "copies" of all other types of copyrightable works. Since "phonorecords" are not "copies," there is no need to place a section 401 notice on "phonorecords" to protect the literary or musical works embodied in the records.

In general, the form of the notice specified by section 402(b) consists of the symbol "℗" the year of first publication of the sound recording; and the name of the copyright owner or an admissible variant. ... [T]he notice for a copyrighted sound recording may be affixed to the surface, label, or container of the phonorecord "in such manner and location as to give reasonable notice of the claim of copyright." ...

SECTION 403. NOTICE FOR PUBLICATIONS INCORPORATING UNITED STATES WORKS

... In cases where a Government work is published or republished commercially, it has frequently been the practice to add some "new matter" in the form of an introduction, editing, illustrations, etc., and to include a general copyright notice in the name of the commercial publisher. This in no way suggests to the public that the bulk of the work is uncopyrightable and therefore free for use.

To make the notice meaningful rather than misleading, section 403 requires that, when the copies or phonorecords consist "preponderantly of one or more works of the United States Government," the copyright notice (if any) identify those parts of the work in which copyright is claimed. A failure to meet this requirement would be treated as an omission of the notice, subject to the provisions of section 405.

SECTION 404. NOTICE FOR CONTRIBUTIONS TO COLLECTIVE WORKS

In conjunction with the provisions of section 201(c), section 404 deals with ... the notice requirements applicable to contributions published in periodicals and other collective works. The basic approach of the section is threefold:

(1) To permit but not require a separate contribution to bear its own notice;

(2) To make a single notice, covering the collective work as a whole, sufficient to satisfy the notice requirement for the separate contributions it contains, even if they have been previously published or their ownership is different; and

(3) To protect the interests of an innocent infringer of copyright in a contribution that does not bear its own notice, who has dealt in good faith with the person named in the notice covering the collective work as a whole.As a general rule, under this section, the rights in an individual contribution to a collective work would not be affected by the lack of a separate copyright notice, as long as the collective work as a whole bears a notice. ...

Under section 404(b), a separate contribution that does not bear its own notice, and that is published in a collective work with a general notice containing the name of someone other than the copyright owner of the contribution, is treated as if it has been published with the wrong name in the notice. The case is governed by section 406(a), which means that an innocent infringer who in good faith took a license from the person named in the general notice would be shielded from liability to some extent.

SECTION 405. OMISSION OF COPYRIGHT NOTICE

Effect of omission on copyright protection

The provisions of section 405(a) make clear that the notice requirements of sections 401, 402, and 403 are not absolute and that, [contrary to the provisions of the 1909 Act,] the outright omission of a copyright notice[, albeit a notice still required under the 1976 Act from its effective date, January 1, 1978, until the effective date of the Berne Convention Implementation Act, March 1, 1989, would not] automatically forfeit protection and throw the work into the public domain. This not only represents a major change in the theoretical framework of American copyright law, but it also seems certain to have immediate practical consequences in a great many individual cases. Under the [1976 Act as originally enacted], a work published without any copyright notice will still be subject to statutory protection for at least 5 years, whether the omission was partial or total, unintentional or deliberate.

Under the general scheme of the [1976 Act], statutory copyright protection is secured automatically when a work is created, and is not lost when the work is published, even if the copyright notice is omitted entirely. Subsection

(a) of section 405 provides that omission of notice, whether intentional or unintentional, does not invalidate the copyright if either of two conditions is met:

(1) if "no more than a relatively small number" of copies or phonorecords have been publicly distributed without notice; or

(2) if registration for the work has already been made, or is made within 5 years after the publication without notice, and a reasonable effort is made to add notice to copies or phonorecords publicly distributed in the United States after the omission is discovered.

Thus, if notice is omitted from more than a "relatively small number" of copies or phonorecords, copyright is not lost immediately, but the work will go into the public domain if no effort is made to correct the error or if the work is not registered within 5 years. ...

The basic notice requirements set forth in sections 401(a) and 402(a) are limited to cases where a work is published "by authority of the copyright owner" and, in prescribing the effect of omission of notice, section 405(a) refers only to omission "from copies or phonorecords publicly distributed by authority of the copyright owner." The intention behind this language is that, where the copyright owner authorized publication of the work, the notice requirements would not be met if copies or phonorecords are publicly distributed without a notice, even if he expected a notice to be used. However, if the copyright owner authorized publication only on the express condition that all copies or phonorecords bear a prescribed notice, the provisions of section 401 or 402 and of section 405 would not apply since the publication itself would not be authorized. This principle is stated directly in section 405(a)(3).

SECTION 406. ERROR WITH RESPECT TO NAME OR DATE IN NOTICE

In addition to cases where notice has been omitted entirely, it is common under the present law for a copyright notice to be fatally defective because the name or date has been omitted or wrongly stated. Section 406 is intended to avoid technical forfeitures in these cases, while at the same time inducing use of the correct name and date and protecting users who rely on erroneous information. ...

SECTION 407. DEPOSIT FOR THE LIBRARY OF CONGRESS

The provisions of section[s] 407 through 411 of the bill mark another departure from the [1909 Act]. Under [that law], deposit of copies for the collections of the Library of Congress and deposit of copies for purposes of copyright registration have been treated as the same thing. The bill's basic approach is to regard deposit and registration as separate though closely related: deposit of copies or phonorecords for the Library of Congress is mandatory, but exceptions can be made for material the Library neither needs nor wants; copyright registration is not generally mandatory, but is a condition of certain remedies for copyright infringement. Deposit for the Library of Congress can be, and in the bulk of cases undoubtedly will be, combined with copyright registration.

The basic requirement of the deposit provision, section 407, is that within 3 months after a work has been published with notice of copyright in the United States, the "owner of copyright or of the exclusive right of publication" must deposit two copies or phonorecords of the work in the Copyright Office. The Register of Copyrights is authorized to exempt any category of material from the deposit requirements. Where the category is not exempted and deposit is not made, the Register may demand it; failure to comply would be penalized by a fine.

Under the [1909 Act,] deposits for the Library of Congress must be combined with copyright registration, and failure to comply with a formal demand for deposit and registration results in complete loss of copyright. Under section 407 of the bill, the deposit requirements can be satisfied without ever making registration, and subsection (a) makes clear that deposit "is not a condition of copyright protection." A realistic fine, coupled with the increased inducements for voluntary registration and deposit under other sections of the bill, seems likely to produce a more effective deposit system than the present one. The bill's approach will also avoid the danger that, under a divisible copyright, one copyright owner's rights could be destroyed by another owner's failure to deposit. ...

Deposits under section 407, although made in the Copyright Office, are "for the use or disposition of the Library of Congress." Thus, the fundamental criteria governing regulations issued under section 407(c), which allows exemptions from the deposit requirements for certain categories of works, would be the needs and wants of the Library.

[The remaining provisions of section 407 deal with specialized deposit requirements, and provide that persons failing to make a deposit within three months after the Register's demand shall be liable for: (1) a fine of not more than $250 for each work; (2) the reasonable cost of the Library of Congress acquiring the desired copies or phonorecords; and (3) a fine of $2,500 in the event of willful or repeated failure to comply with a deposit demand.]

SECTION 408. COPYRIGHT REGISTRATION IN GENERAL

Permissive registration

Under section 408(a), registration of a claim to copyright in any work, whether published or unpublished, can be made voluntarily by "the owner of copyright or of any exclusive right in the work" at any time during the copyright term. The claim may be registered in the Copyright Office by depositing the copies, phonorecords, or other material specified by subsection (b) and (c), together with an application and fee. Except where, under section 405(a), registration is made to preserve a copyright that would otherwise be invalidated because of omission of the notice, registration is not a condition of copyright protection.

Deposit for purpose of copyright registration

In general, and subject to various exceptions, the material to be deposited for copyright registration consists of one complete copy or phonorecord of an unpublished work, and two complete copies or phonorecords of the best edition in the case of a published work. ...

With respect to works published in the United States, a single deposit could be used to satisfy the deposit requirements of section 407 and the registration requirements of section 408, if the application and fee for registration are submitted at the same time and are accompanied by "any additional identifying material" required by regulations. To serve this dual purpose the deposit and registration would have to be made simultaneously. ...

Corrections and amplifications

Another unsatisfactory aspect of the present law is the lack of any provision for correcting or amplifying the information given in a completed registration. Subsection (d) of section 408 would remedy this by authorizing the Register to establish "formal procedures for the filing of an application for supplementary registration," in order to correct an error or amplify the information in a copyright registration. ...

SECTION 409. APPLICATION FOR REGISTRATION

The various clauses of section 409, which specify the information to be included in an application for copyright registration, are intended to give the Register of Copyrights authority to elicit all of the information needed to examine the application and to make a meaningful record of registration. ...

SECTION 410. REGISTRATION OF CLAIM AND ISSUANCE OF CERTIFICATE

The first two subsections of section 410 set forth the two basic duties of the Register of Copyrights with respect to copyright registration: (1) to register the claim and issue a certificate if the Register determines that "the material deposited constitutes copyrightable subject matter and that the other legal and formal requirements of this title have been met," and (2) to refuse registration and notify the applicant if the Register determines that "the material deposited does not constitute copyrightable subject matter or that the claim is invalid for any other reason."

Subsection (c) deals with the probative effect of a certificate of registration issued by the Register under subsection (a). Under its provisions, a certificate is required to be given *prima facie* weight in any judicial proceedings if the registration it covers was made "before or within five years after first publication of the work"; thereafter the court is given discretion to decide what evidentiary weight the certificate should be accorded. ...

Under section 410(c), a certificate is to "constitute *prima facie* evidence of the validity of the copyright and of the facts stated in the certificate."... It is true that, unlike a patent claim, a claim to copyright is not examined for basic validity before a certificate is issued. On the other hand, endowing a copyright claimant who has obtained a certificate with a rebuttable presumption of the validity of the copyright does not deprive the defendant in an infringement suit of any rights; it merely orders the burdens of proof. The plaintiff should not ordinarily be forced in the first instance to prove all of the multitude of facts that underlie the validity of the copyright unless the defendant, by effectively challenging them, shifts the burden of doing so to the plaintiff.

Section 410(d) … makes the effective date of registration the day when an application, deposit, and fee "which are later determined by the Register of Copyrights or by a court of competent jurisdiction to be acceptable for registration" have all been received. Where the three necessary elements are received at different times the date of receipt of the last of them is controlling, regardless of when the Copyright Office acts on the claim. …

SECTION 411. REGISTRATION AS PREREQUISITE TO INFRINGEMENT SUIT

… [A] copyright owner who has not registered his claim can have a valid cause of action against someone who has infringed his copyright, but he cannot enforce his right in the courts until he has made registration. …

… [A] rejected claimant who has properly applied for registration [and been refused] may maintain an infringement suit if notice of it is served on the Register of Copyrights. The Register is authorized, though not required, to enter the suit within 60 days; the Register would be a party on the issue of registrability only, and a failure by the Register to join the action would "not deprive the court of jurisdiction to determine that issue."

SECTION 412. REGISTRATION AS PREREQUISITE TO CERTAIN REMEDIES

The need for section 412 arises from two basic changes the bill will make in [registration law under the 1909 Act]:

> (1) Copyright registration for published works, which is useful and important to users and the public at large, would no longer be compulsory, and should therefore be induced in some practical way.
>
> (2) The great body of unpublished works now protected at common law would automatically be brought under copyright and given statutory protection. The remedies for infringement presently available at common law should continue to apply to these works under the statute, but they should not be given special statutory remedies unless the owner has, by registration, made a public record of his copyright claim.

Under the general scheme of the bill, a copyright owner whose work has been infringed before registration would be entitled to the remedies ordinarily available in infringement cases: an injunction on terms the court considers fair, and his actual damages plus any applicable profits not used as a measure of damages. However, section 412 would deny any award of the special or "extraordinary" remedies of statutory damages or attorney's fees where infringement of copyright in an unpublished work began before registration or where, in the case of a published work, infringement commenced after publication and before registration (unless registration has been made within a grace period of three months after publication). These provisions would be applicable to works of foreign and domestic origin alike.

SECTION 501. INFRINGEMENT OF COPYRIGHT

The bill, unlike the [1909 Act], contains a general statement of what constitutes infringement of copyright. Section 501(a) identifies a copyright infringer as someone who "violates any of the exclusive rights of the copyright owner as provided by sections 106 through [122]" of the bill, or who imports copies or phonorecords in violation of section 602. Under the latter section an unauthorized importation of copies or phonorecords acquired abroad is an infringement of the exclusive right of distribution under certain circumstances.

The principle of the divisibility of copyright ownership, established by section 201(d), carries with it the need in infringement actions to safeguard the rights of all copyright owners and to avoid a multiplicity of suits. Subsection (b) of section 501 enables the owner of a particular right to bring an infringement action in that owner's name alone, while at the same time insuring to the extent possible that the other owners whose rights may be affected are notified and given a chance to join the action.

The first sentence of subsection (b) empowers the "legal or beneficial owner of an exclusive right" to bring suit for "any infringement of that particular right committed while he or she is the owner of it." A "beneficial owner" for this purpose would include, for example, an author who had parted with legal title to the copyright in exchange for percentage royalties based on sales or license fees.

The second and third sentences of section 501(b), which supplement the provisions of the Federal Rules of Civil Procedure, give the courts discretion to require the plaintiff to serve notice of the plaintiff's suit on "any person shown, by the records of the Copyright Office or otherwise, to have or claim an interest in the copyright"; where a person's interest "is likely to be affected by a decision in the case," a court order requiring service of notice is mandatory. As under the Federal rules, the court has discretion to require joinder of "any person having or claiming an interest in the copyright"; but, if any such person wishes to become a party, the court must permit that person's intervention.

In addition to cases involving divisibility of ownership in the same version of a work, section 501(b) is intended to allow a court to permit or compel joinder of the owners of rights in works upon which a derivative work is based.

[The remaining subsections of § 501 are specialized provisions concerning standing with respect to secondary transmissions by cable systems and satellite carriers.]

Vicarious liability for infringing performances

The committee has considered and rejected an amendment to this section intended to exempt the proprietors of an establishment, such as a ballroom or night club, from liability for copyright infringement committed by an independent contractor, such as an orchestra leader. A well-established principle of copyright law is that a person who violates any of the exclusive rights of the copyright owner is an infringer, including persons who can be considered related or vicarious infringers. To be held a related or vicarious infringer in the case of performing rights, a defendant must either actively operate or supervise the operation of the place wherein the performances occur, or control the content of the infringing program, and expect commercial gain from the operation and either direct or indirect benefit from the infringing performance. The committee has decided that no justification exists for changing existing law, and causing a significant erosion of the public performance right.

SECTION 502. INJUNCTIONS

Section 502(a) reasserts the discretionary power of courts to grant injunctions and restraining orders, whether "preliminary," "temporary," "interlocutory," "permanent," or "final," to prevent or stop infringements of copyright … .

SECTION 503. IMPOUNDING AND DISPOSITION OF INFRINGING ARTICLES

The two subsections of section 503 deal respectively with the courts' power to impound allegedly infringing articles during the time an action is pending, and to order the destruction or other disposition of articles found to be infringing. In both cases the articles affected include "all copies or phonorecords" which are claimed or found "to have been made or used in violation of the copyright owner's exclusive rights," and also "all plates, molds, matrices, masters, tapes, film negatives, or other articles by means of which such copies of phonorecords may be reproduced." The alternative phrase "made or used" in both subsections enables a court to deal as it sees fit with articles which, though reproduced and acquired lawfully, have been used for infringing purposes such as rentals, performances, and displays.

Articles may be impounded under subsection (a) "at any time while an action under this title is pending," thus permitting seizures of articles alleged to be infringing as soon as suit has been filed and without waiting for an injunction. The same subsection empowers the court to order impounding "on such terms as it may deem reasonable." …

… Section 503(b) … giv[es] the court discretion to order "destruction or other reasonable disposition" of the articles found to be infringing. Thus, as part of its final judgment or decree, the court could order the infringing articles sold, delivered to the plaintiff, or disposed of in some other way that would avoid needless waste and best serve the ends of justice.

SECTION 504. DAMAGES AND PROFITS

In general

A cornerstone of the remedies sections and of the [1976 Act] as a whole is section 504, the provision dealing with recovery of actual damages, profits, and statutory damages … .

Subsection (a) ... establish[es] the liability of a copyright infringer for either "the copyright owner's actual damages and any additional profits of the infringer," or statutory damages. Recovery of actual damages and profits under section 504(b) or of statutory damages under section 504(c) is alternative and for the copyright owner to elect; ... the plaintiff in an infringement suit is not obliged to submit proof of damages and profits and may choose to rely on the provision for minimum statutory damages. However, there is nothing in section 504 to prevent a court from taking account of evidence concerning actual damages and profits in making an award of statutory damages within the range set out in subsection (c).

Actual damages and profits

In allowing the plaintiff to recover "the actual damages suffered by him or her as a result of the infringement," plus any of the infringer's profits "that are attributable to the infringement and are not taken into account in computing the actual damages," section 504(b) recognizes the different purposes served by awards of damages and profits. Damages are awarded to compensate the copyright owner for losses from the infringement, and profits are awarded to prevent the infringer from unfairly benefiting from a wrongful act. Where the defendant's profits are nothing more than a measure of the damages suffered by the copyright owner, it would be inappropriate to award damages and profits cumulatively, since in effect they amount to the same thing. However, in cases where the copyright owner has suffered damages not reflected in the infringer's profits, or where there have been profits attributable to the copyrighted work but not used as a measure of damages, subsection (b) authorizes the award of both.

The language of the subsection makes clear that only those profits "attributable to the infringement" are recoverable; where some of the defendant's profits result from the infringement and other profits are caused by different factors, it will be necessary for the court to make an apportionment. However, the burden of proof is on the defendant in these cases; in establishing profits the plaintiff need prove only "the infringer's gross revenue," and the defendant must prove not only "his or her deductible expenses" but also "the element of profit attributable to factors other than the copyrighted work."

Statutory damages

Subsection (c) of section 504 makes clear that the plaintiff's election to recover statutory damages may take place at any time during the trial before the court has rendered its final judgment. The remainder of clause (1) of the subsection represents a statement of the general rates applicable to awards of statutory damages. Its principal provisions may be summarized as follows:

> 1. As a general rule, where the plaintiff elects to recover statutory damages, the court is obliged to award between $250 and $10,000 [now $750 and $30,000, respectively, as a result of statutory amendments adopted by Congress in 1999]. It can exercise discretion in awarding an amount within that range but, unless one of the exceptions provided by

clause (2) is applicable, it cannot make an award of less than $[750] or of more than $[30,000] if the copyright owner has chosen recovery under section 504(c).

2. Although, as explained below, an award of minimum statutory damages may be multiplied if separate works and separately liable infringers are involved in the suit, a single award in the $[750] to $[30,000] range is to be made "for all infringements involved in the action." A single infringer of a single work is liable for a single amount between $[750] and $[30,000], no matter how many acts of infringement are involved in the action and regardless of whether the acts were separate, isolated, or occurred in a related series.

3. Where the suit involves infringement of more than one separate and independent work, minimum statutory damages for each work must be awarded. For example, if one defendant has infringed three copyrighted works, the copyright owner is entitled to statutory damages of at least $[2,250] and may be awarded up to $[90,000]. Subsection (c)(1) makes clear, however, that, although they are regarded as independent works for other purposes, "all the parts of a compilation or derivative work constitute one work" for this purpose. Moreover, although the minimum and maximum amounts are to be multiplied where multiple "works" are involved in the suit, the same is not true with respect to multiple copyrights, multiple owners, multiple exclusive rights, or multiple registrations. This point is especially important since, under a scheme of divisible copyright, it is possible to have the rights of a number of owners of separate "copyrights" in a single "work" infringed by one act of a defendant.

4. Where the infringements of one work were committed by a single infringer acting individually, a single award of statutory damages would be made. Similarly, where the work was infringed by two or more joint tortfeasors, the bill would make them jointly and severally liable for an amount in the $[750] to $[30,000] range. However, where separate infringements for which two or more defendants are not jointly liable are joined in the same action, separate awards of statutory damages would be appropriate.Clause (2) of section 504(c) provides for exceptional cases in which the maximum award of statutory damages could be raised from $[30,000] to $[150,000], and in which the minimum recovery could be reduced from $[750] to $[200]. The basic principle underlying this provision is that the courts should be given discretion to increase statutory damages in cases of willful infringement and to lower the minimum where the infringer is innocent. The language of the clause makes clear that in these situations the burden of proving willfulness rests on the copyright owner and that of proving innocence rests on the infringer, and that the court must make a finding of either willfulness or innocence in order to award the exceptional amounts. ... In addition to the general "innocent infringer" provision, clause (2) deals with the special situation of teachers, librarians, archivists, and public

broadcasters, and the nonprofit institutions of which they are a part. Section 504(c)(2) provides that, where such a person or institution infringed copyrighted material in the honest belief that what they were doing constituted fair use, the court is precluded from awarding any statutory damages. It is intended that, in cases involving this provision, the burden of proof with respect to the defendant's good faith should rest on the plaintiff.

SECTIONS 505 THROUGH 5[10]. MISCELLANEOUS PROVISIONS ON INFRINGEMENT AND REMEDIES

... Under section 505 the awarding of costs and attorney's fees is left to the court's discretion, and the section also makes clear that neither costs nor attorney's fees can be awarded to or against "the United States or an officer thereof."

[The Report next discusses § 506 of the House Bill, which was eventually modified in conference to conform more nearly to the Senate Bill. As adopted, subsection (a) makes it a criminal offense to infringe a copyright "willfully and for purposes of commercial advantage or private financial gain." Under 18 U.S.C. § 2319, the penalty for criminal infringement may in some circumstances be quite severe: a fine of up to $250,000, imprisonment for up to five years, or both. In addition, subsection (b) of § 506 provides for mandatory forfeiture and destruction of all infringing copies or phonorecords and the devices used to produce them. Subsections (c), (d) and (e) also outlaw fraudulent use of a copyright notice, fraudulent removal of a notice, and false representations in connection with a copyright application. The penalty, in each case, is a fine of up to $2,500.]

Section 507 ... establishes a three-year statute of limitations for [civil actions and a five-year period for criminal proceedings].

Section 508 ... establish[es] a method for notifying the Copyright Office and the public of the filing and disposition of copyright cases ... .

[What is now § 509 of the Act provides for seizure and forfeiture to the United States in certain instances of criminal infringement.]

Section 5[10] [deals exclusively with remedies] for alteration of programming by cable systems ...

SECTION 601. MANUFACTURING REQUIREMENT

The requirement in general

A chronic problem in efforts to revise the copyright statute for the past 85 years has been the need to reconcile the interests of the American printing industry with those of authors and other copyright owners. The scope and impact of the 'manufacturing clause,' which came into the copyright law as a compromise in 1891, have been gradually narrowed by successive amendments.

[Congress passed a liberalized version of § 601 in 1976 but allowed it to lapse in 1986.]

SECTION 602. INFRINGING IMPORTATION

Scope of the section

Section 602 ... deals with two separate situations: importation of "piratical" articles (that is, copies or phonorecords made without any authorization of the copyright owner), and unauthorized importation of copies or phonorecords that were lawfully made. The general approach of section 602 is to make unauthorized importation an act of infringement in both cases, but to permit the United States Customs Service to prohibit importation only of "piratical" articles.

Section 602(a) first states the general rule that unauthorized importation is an infringement merely if the copies of phonorecords "have been acquired outside the United States," but then enumerates three specific exceptions: (1) importation under the authority or for the use of a governmental body, but not including material for use in schools or copies of an audiovisual work imported for any purpose other than archival use; (2) importation for the private use of the importer of no more than one copy or phonorecord of a work at a time, or of articles in the personal baggage of travelers from abroad; or (3) importation by nonprofit organizations "operated for scholarly, educational, or religious purposes" of "no more than one copy of an audiovisual work solely for archival purposes, and no more than five copies or phonorecords of any other work for its library lending or archival purposes." The bill specifies that the third exception does not apply if the importation "is part of an activity consisting of systematic reproduction or distribution, engaged in by such organization in violation of the provisions of section 108(g)(2)."

If none of the three exemptions applies, any unauthorized importer of copies or phonorecords acquired abroad could be sued for damages and enjoined from making any use of them, even before any public distribution in this country has taken place.

Importation of "piratical" copies

Section 602(b) retains the [1909 Act's] prohibition against importation of "piratical" copies of phonorecords — those whose making "would have constituted an infringement of copyright if this title had been applicable." Thus, the Customs Service could exclude copies or phonorecords that were unlawful in the country where they were made; it could also exclude copies or phonorecords which, although made lawfully under the domestic law of that country, would have been unlawful if the U.S. copyright law could have been applied. A typical example would be a work by an American author which is in the public domain in a foreign country because that country does not have copyright relations with the United States; the making and publication of an authorized edition would be lawful in that country, but the Customs Service could prevent the importation of any copies of that edition.

Importation for infringing distribution

The second situation covered by section 602 is that in which the copies or phonorecords were lawfully made but their distribution in the United States would infringe the U.S. copyright owner's exclusive rights. As already said, the mere act of importation in this situation would constitute an act of infringement and could be enjoined. However, in cases of this sort, it would be impracticable for the United States Customs Service to attempt to enforce the importation prohibition, and section 602(b) provides that, unless a violation of the manufacturing requirements is also involved, the Service has no authority to prevent importation, "where the copies or phonorecords were lawfully made." The subsection would authorize the establishment of a procedure under which copyright owners could arrange for the Customs Service to notify them whenever articles appearing to infringe their works are imported.

SECTION 603. ENFORCEMENT OF IMPORTATION PROHIBITIONS

The importation prohibitions of both sections 601 and 602 would be enforced under section 603 ... Subsection (a) would authorize the Secretary of the Treasury and the United States Postal Service to make regulations for this purpose, and subsection (c) provides for the disposition of excluded articles.

Subsection (b) of section 603 deals only with the prohibition against importation of 'piratical' copies or phonorecords, and is aimed at solving problems that has arisen under the present statute. Since the United States Customs Service is often in no position to make determinations as to whether particular articles are 'piratical,' section 603(b) would permit the Customs regulations to require the person seeking exclusion either to obtain a court order enjoining importation, or to furnish proof of his claim and to post bond.

SECTIONS 701 THROUGH 710. ADMINISTRATIVE PROVISIONS

Chapter 7, entitled "Copyright Office," sets forth the administrative and housekeeping provisions of the bill ... .

Retention and disposition of deposited articles

A recurring problem in the administration of the copyright law has been the need to reconcile the storage limitations of the Copyright Office with the continued value of deposits in identifying copyrighted works. Aside from its indisputable utility to future historians and scholars, a substantially complete collection of both published and unpublished deposits, other than those selected by the Library of Congress, would avoid the many difficulties encountered when copies needed for identification in connection with litigation or other purposes have been destroyed. The basic policy behind section 704 is that copyright deposits should be retained as long as possible, but that the Register of Copyrights and the Librarian of Congress should be empowered to dispose of them under appropriate safeguards when they decide that it has become necessary to do so.

Under subsection (a) of section 704, any copy, phonorecord, or identifying material deposited for registration, whether registered or not, becomes "the property of the United States Government." This means that the copyright owner or person who made the deposit cannot demand its return as a matter of right, even in rejection cases, although the provisions of sections 407 and

408 are flexible enough to allow for special arrangements in exceptional cases. On the other hand, Government ownership of deposited articles under section 704(a) carries with it no privileges under the copyright itself; use of a deposited article in violation of the copyright owner's exclusive rights would be infringement.

With respect to published works, section 704(b) makes all deposits available to the Library of Congress "for its collections, or for exchanges or transfer to any other library"; where the work is unpublished, the Library is authorized to select any deposit for its own collections or for transfer to the National Archives of the United States or to a Federal records center. ...

The Committee added a new subsection (c) to section 704, under which the Register is authorized to make microfilm or other recorded copies of copyright deposits before transferring or otherwise disposing of them.

For deposits not selected by the Library, subsection (d) provides that they, or "identifying portions or reproductions of them," are to be retained under Copyright Office control "for the longest period considered practicable and desirable" by the Register and the Librarian. When and if they ultimately decide that retention of certain deposited articles is no longer "practicable and desirable," the Register and Librarian have joint discretion to order their "destruction or other disposition." Because of the unique value and irreplaceable nature of unpublished deposits, the subsection prohibits their intentional destruction during their copyright term, unless a facsimile reproduction has been made.

Subsection (e) of section 704 establishes a new procedure under which a copyright owner can request retention of deposited material for the full term of copyright. The Register of Copyrights is authorized to issue regulations prescribing the fees for this service and the "conditions under which such requests are to be made and granted."

Catalog of copyright entries

Section 707(a) of the bill retains the [1909 Act's] basic requirement that the Register compile and publish catalogs of all copyright registrations at periodic intervals, but provides for "discretion to determine, on the basis of practicability and usefulness the form and frequency of publication of each particular part." This provision will in no way diminish the utility or value of the present catalogs, and the flexibility of approach, coupled with use of the new mechanical and electronic devices now becoming available, will avoid waste and result in a better product.

Copyright Office fees

The schedule of fees set out in section 708 reflects a general increase in the fees of the Copyright Office from those established by the Congress in 1965. ... The section also contains new fee provisions needed because of new requirements or services established under the bill, and subsection (a)(11) authorizes the Register to fix additional fees, on the "basis of the cost of providing the service," "for any other special services requiring a substantial amount of time or expense. ... "

Reproduction for the blind and handicapped

Section 710 directs the Register of Copyrights to establish by regulation forms and procedures by which the copyright owners of certain categories of works may voluntarily grant to the Library of Congress a license to reproduce and distribute copies or phonorecords of the work solely for the use of the blind and physically handicapped.

CHAPTER 8. COPYRIGHT ROYALTY COMMISSION

Chapter 8 establishes a Copyright Royalty Commission for the purpose of periodically reviewing and adjusting statutory royalty rates for use of copyrighted materials pursuant to compulsory licenses provided in sections 111 (secondary transmissions by cable systems), 115 (mechanical royalties) and 116 (jukebox) of the bill. In addition, the Commission will make determinations as to reasonable terms and rates of royalty payments as provided in section 118 (public broadcasting), and to resolve disputes over the distribution of royalties paid pursuant to the statutory licenses in sections 111 and 116.

[Chapter 8 of Title 17 as enacted in 1976 has been superseded by amendment, and the Commission has been replaced by Copyright Royalty Judges. For details, see the current statute.]

SENATE REPORT ON BERNE CONVENTION IMPLEMENTATION ACT OF 1988
S. Rep. No. 100-352, 100th Cong., 2d Sess. (1988), *reprinted in* 1988 U.S.C.C.A.N. 3706

...

I. PURPOSE

The Berne Convention Implementation Act of 1988 amends title 17, United States Code, to make the changes to the U.S. copyright law that are necessary for the United States to adhere to the Berne Convention for the Protection of Literary and Artistic Works signed at Berne, Switzerland, on September 9, 1886, and all acts, protocols, and revisions thereto.

II. LEGISLATIVE HISTORY

A. REASONS FOR JOINING THE BERNE CONVENTION

The Berne Convention for the Protection of Literary and Artistic Works, better known as the Berne Convention, is the highest internationally recognized standard for the protection of works of authorship of all kinds. U.S. membership in the Berne Convention will secure the highest available level of multilateral copyright protection for U.S. artists, authors and other creators. Adherence will also ensure effective U.S. participation in the formulation and management of international copyright policy.

Adherence to the Convention is in the national interest because it will ensure a strong, credible U.S. presence in the global marketplace. The United States is the world's largest exporter of copyright material. At a time when the United States is suffering a large overall trade deficit, works protected by copyright—such as books, sound recordings, motion pictures, and computer software—routinely generate a trade surplus. ... Adherence by the United States to the Berne Convention is a significant opportunity to reduce the impact of copyright piracy on our world trade position.

For more than 100 years, the Berne Convention has been the major multilateral agreement governing international copyright relations. The Berne Union has 77 members, including most of the free market countries, a number of developing nations, and several nations of the Eastern Bloc. The United States and the Soviet Union are conspicuously absent from this list. The United States and the Soviet Union, along with another 78 States, belong to the Universal Copyright Convention (UCC), which has lower standards of copyright protection. Both Berne and the UCC are administered by United Nations Agencies; Berne by the World Intellectual Property Organization (WIPO) and the UCC by the United Nations Educational Scientific and Cultural Organization (UNESCO). Fifty-three states adhere to both, and the United States has copyright relations, either through the UCC, certain other multilateral agreements, or bilaterally, with almost 100 countries.

The Berne Convention assures higher levels of protection than the UCC. Protection under both treaties is based on the general concept of 'national treatment,' which requires each member State to accord to nationals of other member States the same level of copyright protection provided to its own citizens. The national treatment obligation under the UCC is general, and its minimum levels of protection are not sufficient to deter piracy of U.S. works. While the Berne Convention is also grounded in the concept of national treatment, it is superior to the UCC because it also requires that generally well—specified minimum rights be guaranteed under the laws of member states for works originating in other member states. Among these are: duration of copyright for life of the author plus 50 years, and rights of translation, reproduction, public performance, broadcasting, adaptation and arrangement. Thus, Berne assures the highest level of protection in the countries that are the largest users of American copyrighted works.

While bilateral copyright agreements are important, there are clear advantages to a multilateral approach. First, adherence to Berne will immediately give the United States copyright relations with 24 countries with which no current relations exist. A twenty-fifth country, the Peoples Republic of China, with more than a billion potential users of American works, has given strong signals that it is considering adherence to Berne. Second, bilateral arrangements often suffer from lack of certainty or varying standards, and are more likely to be dishonored. Protection of U.S. works under bilateral agreements, moreover, is often problematic. The standards in these agreements vary widely, they lack the credibility and authority of an international convention like Berne, and sometimes they are simply ignored.

Berne adherence will also secure high-level protection for U.S. copyright holders by eliminating the need to rely on the so-called 'back-door' to Berne protection. Article 3(1) of the Berne Convention extends protection to the works of authors of non-Berne countries, like the United States, if the works are published simultaneously in the country of origin and in a Berne country. Many U.S. copyright owners have attempted to obtain Berne protection through simultaneous publication of their works in the United States and in the nearest Berne country market, Canada.

In fact, simultaneous publication is expensive and uncertain. Only large U.S. companies can afford the substantial expense of attempting simultaneous publication in a Berne country. Article 3(3) of the Berne Convention defines publication as making a sufficient number of copies of the work available to the public in the Berne member country where it is published. This is difficult or impossible for many U.S. publishers and for most individual authors, artists and composers, for whom Berne protection through the 'back door' is not economically feasible. Also, while the 1948 Brussels version of the Convention defined simultaneous publication as publication in two or more countries within 30 days, some Berne States, like Canada, have not adhered to the Brussels text and consequently may require publication within a shorter period of time. Proving simultaneous publication in a foreign court can be expensive, burdensome, and fraught with uncertainty. ...

Another reason that U.S. copyright owners may not safely rely on 'back door' protection is that the Berne Convention allows its members to retaliate against the works of non-member States obtaining protection through this means. The capacity of Berne members to retaliate is not remote. Under the Canadian copyright law, for example, it is illegal to import books within 14 days of their first publication in another country. This provision, which is not generally enforced, was enacted to prohibit American publishers from using Canada as a source of 'back door' Berne protection. The risk of such retaliation may increase if the United States remains outside the Berne Union while U.S. publishers seek to obtain 'back door' protection.

Adherence to the Berne Convention is also necessary to ensure effective U.S. participation in the formulation and management of international copyright policy. New technologies like satellites, photocopiers, computers, and video and audio recorders have 'internationalized' intellectual property to an unprecedented extent. When the United States withdrew from UNESCO in 1984, it gave up its vote in the UNESCO General Conference, the body that makes decisions on the programs of the UNESCO Copyright Division. Participation by the United States in an effective international copyright organization like the Berne Union is essential.

The U.S. Copyright Office, Administration representatives, and members of Congressional committees have recognized the importance to U.S. copyright holders of decisions taken under the auspices of the WIPO and, at the national level, states of the Berne Union. U.S. representatives have attended Berne revision and other Berne conferences, but as passive observers with no direct voice and only indirect influence on the deliberations. The limitations were described poignantly by Barbara Ringer, former Register of Copyrights, in her analysis of the 1967 Stockholm Conference to revise Berne:

> From the outset of the conference it was obvious that the developing countries were well organized and prepared to fight, and that the developed countries were in disarray. Such open negotiations as there were took place in a febrile atmosphere of crisis and bitter debate, but most of the real decisions were made in camera, between the principal negotiations from India and the United Kingdom. The large American observer delegation was generally aware of what was going on, and was concerned with both the form the Protocol was taking and the danger that the whole Conference might blow up. Although Abraham L. Kaminstein, the U.S. Register of Copyrights, made an 'intervention' at the Conference, commenting on the course of events, the American delegates were Berne outsiders with no real influence upon the outcome.

Ringer, *The Role of the United States in International Copyright—Past, Present and Future,* 56 Geo. L. J. 1050, 1070 (1968). U.S. adherence to Berne will give our officials the right to participate fully in the administration and management of the Convention. Since revision of the Convention requires a unanimous vote, the United States could, if it joins Berne, prevent any decision detrimental to U.S. interests.

Membership in Berne also will serve to strengthen the credibility of the U.S. position in trade negotiations with countries where piracy is not uncommon. Thailand, a Berne member, is a good example. Thai officials repeatedly highlight the inconsistency of U.S. efforts to persuade the Thai government to combat piracy of U.S. work when we do not belong to Berne. They add that while the United States has so far failed to join Berne, it nonetheless claims Berne benefits through the 'back door' and urges other nations to conform to Berne standards. Adherence can only heighten U.S. credibility and raise the likehood that other nations will enter the Convention or increase existing levels of copyright protection.

Berne adherence will also complement a major trade policy goal of the United States—to formulate an intellectual property code within the General Agreement on Tariffs and Trade (the GATT). An intellectual property code, including a section on copyrights, within the GATT must be drawn from the fundamental economic rights established in the Berne Convention and adequate and effective copyright laws.

The United States has an unparalleled stake in preserving Berne's high levels of copyright protection. The development of a GATT intellectual property code, while a commendable goal, is no substitute for U.S. adherence to the Berne Convention. The U.S. position for inclusion of Berne—level copyright standards within a GATT intellectual property code may be seriously undermined if the United States is advocating this position from outside the Berne Union.

B. ACTION PRECEDING COMMITTEE PASSAGE OF S. 1301

For almost one hundred years, differences between U.S. law and Berne Convention standards kept our nation from joining the Convention. However, in the last two decades, changes in American law and in the Berne standards have narrowed that gap. S. 1301 makes the last remaining changes to the copyright law to reconcile the difference between Berne standards and U.S. law so that the United States can join Berne. ...

[The report goes on to discuss, and to provide section-by-section analyses, of such matters as architectural works and moral rights, both of which would be addressed in subsequent legislation, and formalities, which were dealt with by the BCIA itself. See also the overviews of the BCIA and GATT/TRIPS provided in Part Two of this Supplement.]

HOUSE REPORT ON THE VISUAL ARTISTS RIGHTS ACT OF 1990
H.R. Rep. 101-514, 101st Cong., 2nd Sess. (1990), *reprinted in* 1990 U.S.C.C.A.N. 6915

...

I. PURPOSE OF THE LEGISLATION

H.R. 2690, the Visual Artists Rights Act of 1990, protects both the reputations of certain visual artists and the works of art they create. It provides these artists with the rights of "attribution" and "integrity." The former ensures that artists are correctly identified with the works of art they create, and that they are not identified with works created by others. The latter allows artists to protect their works against modifications and destructions that are prejudicial to their honor or reputations.

These rights are analogous to those protected by Article 6bis of the Berne Convention, which are commonly known as "moral rights." "The theory of moral rights is that they result in a climate of artistic worth and honor that encourages the author in the arduous act of creation."[1] Artists' rights are consistent with the purpose behind the copyright laws[2] and the Constitutional provision they implement: "To promote the Progress of Science and useful Arts.***"[3]

...

III. BACKGROUND

After almost 100 years of debate, the United States joined the Berne Convention, effective in March 1989. While the Convention is the premier international copyright convention, consensus over United States adherence was slow to develop in large part because of debate over the requirements of Article 6bis. The principal question was whether that article required the United States to enact new laws protecting moral rights. Certain proprietary groups were also concerned that even if new laws were not required, the very fact of adherence could work a gradual but substantial change in the American copyright system and the protections accorded authors. While some (chiefly motion picture directors and screenwriters) argued that adherence to Berne required the enactment of new laws, the vast majority of those using adherence contended that existing laws, both Federal and State, statutory and common, were sufficient to comply with the requirements of the Convention.[4]

---

[1] The Visual Artists Rights Act of 1989; Hearings on H.R. 2690 Before the Subcommittee on Courts, Intellectual Property, and the Administration of Justice of the House Committee on the Judiciary, 101st Cong., 1st Sess. (1989) (hereinafter cited as Subcommittee Hearings) (statement of the Honorable Ralph Oman, Register of Copyrights [hereinafter cited as "Oman Statement"] at 3.)

[2] 17 U.S.C. 101 et seq.

[3] U.S. Const. art. I, §8, cl. 8.

[4] *See generally* H. Rept. No. 609, 100th Cong., 2d Sess. 32–40 (1988); Oman Statement, *supra* note 1, at 13–17.

The Congress agreed with the latter viewpoint and therefore enacted legislation to implement the Convention's requirements[5] without also enacting additional moral rights laws.

The Congress concluded, however, that adherence to the Berne Convention did not end the debate about whether the United States should adopt artists' rights laws, and the Subcommittee on Courts, Intellectual Property, and the Administration of Justice continued its review of the issue in hearing sheld in June.[6]

While the Berne Convention implementation debate crystallized attempts by artists to obtain protection for their creations, efforts to enact artists' rights laws had begun well before that time. Bills seeking to protect visual artists dated from 1979,[7] and H.R. 2400, introduced in the 100th Congress,[8] was designed to grant film directors and screenwriters certain moral rights. Adherence to the Convention did not end the efforts in support of these and similar bills.

The complaints underlying these efforts are similar in both the visual arts and film arenas, but the factual contexts in which these complaints arise are distinct. Under the American copyright system, an artist who transfers a copy of his or her work to another may not, absent a contractual agreement, prevent that person from destroying the copy or collect damages after the fact. Further, with respect to modifications of a work, only an artist who retains the copyright in his or her work is able to invoke title 17 rights in defense of the integrity of that work, and then only where a modification amounts to the creation of a derivative work.

Visual artists, such as painters and sculptors, have complained that their works are being mutilated and destroyed, that authorship of their works is

---

[5] Berne Convention Implementation Act of 1988, Pub. L. No. 100-568, 102 Stat. 2853 (1988).

[6] H. Rept. No. 609, 100th Cong., 2d Sess. 32–40 (1988); Oman Statement, supra note 1, at 13–17. The Visual Artists Rights Act of 1987: Hearings on H.R. 3221 Before the Subcommittee on Courts, Civil Liberties, and the Administration of Justice of the House Committee on the Judiciary, 100th Cong., 2d Sess. (1988); The Film Integrity Act of 1987: Hearings on H.R. 2400 Before the Subcommittee on Courts, Civil Liberties, and the Administration of Justice of the House Committee on the Judiciary, 100th Cong., 2d Sess. (1988). In addition to the hearings, Chairman Kastenmeier and Representative Carlos Moorhead, the ranking Republican on the Subcommittee, requested that the United States Copyright Office conduct a study of the state of moral rights in the film industry. Letter from the Honorable Robert W. Kastenmeier, Chairman, Subcommittee on Courts, Intellectual Property, and the Administration of Justice, and the Honorable Carlos Moorhead to the Honorable Ralph Oman, Register of Copyrights, Feb. 25, 1988. That study concluded that "[t]he Subcommittee should seriously consider a unified federal system of moral rights protection ... [and that] strong arguments can be made for creating ... [such a] system." Report of the Register of Copyrights, Technological Alterations to Motion Pictures 176–77 (March 1989) (hereinafter cited as "Copyright Office Report").

[7] *See, e.g.*, H.R. 288, 96th Cong., 1st Sess. 125 Cong. Rec. 164 (1979); H.R. 2908, 97th Cong., 1st Sess., 127 Cong. Rec. 691 (1981); H.R. 1521, 98th Cong., 1st Sess., 129 Cong. Rec. 2414 (1983); H.R. 5772, 99th Cong., 2d Sess., 132 Cong. Rec. 32,704 (1986); S. 2796, 99th Cong., 2d Sess., 132 Cong. Rec. S12,185 (daily ed. Sept. 9, 1986); S. 1619, 100th Cong., 1st Sess., 133 Cong. Rec. S11,470 (daily ed. Aug. 6, 1987); H.R. 3221, 100th Cong., 1st Sess., 133 Cong. Rec. E3425 (daily ed. Aug. 7, 1987).

[8] H.R. 2400, 100th Cong., 1st Sess., 133 Cong. Rec. 12,412 (1987).

being misattributed, and that the American copyright system does not enable them to share in any profits upon resale of their works. Directors, screenwriters, and other creative contributors to motion pictures, have complained that without their consent, films originally shot with the special characteristics of the wide screen in mind are being electronically recomposed for viewing on smaller television screens (panned and scanned), and films are being speeded up or slowed down (time compressed or expanded) to fit into television broadcast slots.

Where an individual creating a work typically retains the economic rights in it, such as a visual artist does, an additional grant of rights such as those accorded by H.R. 2690 will not impede distribution of the work. By contrast, those who participate in a collaborative effort, such as an audiovisual work, do not typically own the economic rights. Instead, audiovisual works are generally works-made-for-hire.[9] Granting these artists the rights of attribution and integrity might conflict with the distribution and marketing of these works.

Motion pictures and other audiovisual works are generally produced and exploited in multiple copies. They are leased for theatrical and non-theatrical exhibition, licensed for broadcasting, shown on airplanes, and sold as videocassettes. Each market has its own commercial and technological configuration that affects how the work will appear when presented. In contrast, the works of visual art covered by H.R. 2690 are limited to originals: works created in single copies or in limited editions. They are generally not physically transformed to suit the purposes of different markets. Further, when an original of a work of visual art is modified or destroyed, it cannot be replaced. This is not the case when one copy of a work produced in potentially unlimited copies is altered.

These critical factual and legal differences in the way visual arts and audiovisual works are created and disseminated have important practical consequences. They have led the Congress to consider the claims of these artists separately, and have facilitated the progress of legislation to protect the rights of visual artists.

H.R. 2690 therefore acknowledges and is premised on these distinctions. It responds to comments on the issue of visual artists' rights elicited at the Subcommittee's earlier hearings.[10] Those hearings revealed a consensus that the bill's scope should be limited to certain carefully defined types of works and artists, and that if claims arising in other contexts are to be considered, they must be considered separately.

H.R. 2690 creates a uniform Federal system of rights for certain visual artists. This system is akin to the uniform copyright system codified in the 1976

[9] 17 U.S.C. 101.

[10] The Berne Convention Implementation Act: Hearings on H.R. 1623 Before the Subcommittee on Courts, Civil Liberties and the Administration of Justice of the House Committee on the Judiciary, 100th Cong., 1st & 2d Sess. (1987–88); The Visual Artists Rights Act of 1987: Hearings on H.R. 3221 Before the Subcommittee on Courts, Civil Liberties, and the Administration of Justice of the House Committee on the Judiciary, 100th Cong., 2d Sess. (188).

Copyright Act.[11] While 11 States have enacted artists' rights laws,[12] John Koegel, a practitioner who has represented various artistic interests, noted at the Subcommittee's hearings that those laws are a "'patchwork' of rules which by itself vitiates somewhat the single, unified system of copyright. Artists, lawyers, courts, and even the owners of works deserve a single set of rules on this subject."[13]

The Committee agrees, and notes that the 11 State statutes have operated successfully and that they "have not engendered a blizzard of litigation, nor an outcry of opposition from groups who might be adversely affected by them."[14] Because of its limited nature, H.R. 2690 protects the legitimate interests of visual artists without inhibiting the rights of copyright owners and users, and without undue interference with the successful operation of the American copyright system.

As Professor Jane Ginsburg testified at the Subcommittee hearings:

> This bill represents an important initiative in the domain of moral rights, an area that [the] Berne Implementation Act left open to future development. The prompt attention to artists' interests in securing attribution for and the integrity of their works that Congress has shown by this, and similar, bills should prove gratifying not only to the artistic community, but also to the American public that enjoys the benefits of access to artistic creations, and to our partners in the Berne Union.[15]

The Register of Copyrights further elucidated the importance of H.R. 2690:

> H.R. 2690 brings U.S. law into greater harmony with laws of other Berne countries. Numerous developed and developing countries provided by positive law for moral rights. Enactment of moral rights legislation serves another important Berne objective—that of harmonizing national copyright laws.[16]

The Committee notes that H.R. 2690 has bipartisan support and was approved by the Committee without opposition.

---

[11] 17 U.S.C. 101 *et seq.*

[12] Cal. Civ. Code §§ 980–990; Conn. Gen. Stat. Ann. §§ 42-116s to 42-116t; Ill. Ann. Stat. ch. 1211/2 paras. 1401–1408; La. Rev. Staat. Ann. §§ 51:2151–51:2156; Me. Rev. Stat. Ann. tit. 27 § 303; Mass. Gen. Laws Ann. ch. 231 §§ 85S; N.J. Stat. Ann. §§ 2A:24A-1 to 2A:24-8; N.M. Stat. Ann. §§ 56-11-1 to 56-11-3; N.Y. Arts & Cult. Aff. Law §§ 11.01–16.01; Pa. Stat. Ann. tit. 73 §§ 2101–2110; R.I. Gen. Laws §§ 5-62-2 to 5-62-6.

[13] Subcommittee Hearings, supra note 1 (statement of John B. Koegel, Esq. [hereinafter cited as "Koegel Statement"] at 6).

[14] Subcommittee Hearings, *supra* note 1 (statement of the Honorable John E. Frohnmayer, Chairman, National Endowment for the Arts [hereinafter cited as "Frohnmayer Statement"] at 2).

[15] Subcommittee Hearings, *supra* note 1 (statement of Prof. Jane C. Ginsburg [hereinafter cited as "Ginsburg Statement"] at 3).

[16] Oman Statement, *supra* note 1, at 37; see also, Ginsburg Statement, supra note 21, at 3; 2 M. Nimmer on Copyright, 8.21[A][2][b] (1989): "[B]y its minimalist approach, the United States leaves itself open to the charge that it is failing to comply with some of Berne's provisions. Prudential behavior dictates that, in order to reap the benefits that flow from appearing to be moral, the U.S. must undertake activities that will be perceived to be moral." *Id.* at 8-254 to 55 (emphasis in original); Frohnmayer Statement, *supra* note 20, at 3–4.

IV. SECTION-BY-SECTION ANALYSIS

Short Title. — Section 1 of the bill sets forth its short title, the "Visual Artists Rights Act of 1990."

Definition of Covered Works. — Section 2 of the bill amends 17 U.S.C. 101 to define a "work of visual art." The authors[17] of these works are accorded the rights of attribution and integrity set forth in new 17 U.S.C. 106A. The definition of a work of visual art is a critical underpinning of the limited scope of the bill. As Representative Markey testified, "I would like to stress that we have gone to extreme lengths to very narrowly define the works of art that will be covered *** [T]his legislation covers only a very select group of artists.***"[18]

The definition is not synonymous with any other definition in the Copyright Act and, in particular, it is narrower than the definition of "pictorial, graphic, and scuptural works" set forth in 17 U.S.C. 101. It encompasses certain paintings, drawings, prints, sculpture, and finally, still photographic images produced for exhibition purposes only. In all cases, these works are covered only in single copies or in limited editions of 200 or fewer copies. See discussion below.

The courts should use common sense and generally accepted standards of the artistic community in determining whether a particular work falls within the scope of the definition. Artists may work in a variety of media, and use any number of materials in creating their works. Therefore, whether a particular work falls within the definition should not depend on the medium or materials used. For example, the term "painting" includes murals, works created on canvas, and the like.[19]

The term "sculpture" includes, but is not limited to, castings, carvings, modelings, and constructions.[20] Similarly, the term "print" includes works such as lithographs, serigraphs, and etchings.[21] The latter term does not, however, cover photographic prints, which are covered separately.

The photographs encompassed by the definition are those still photographic images produced for exhibition purposes. The bill covers both positives (for example, prints, contact sheets, and transparencies such as slides) and negatives (negative photographic images or transparent material used for

---

[17] The term "author" as used in this report incorporates those persons, if the author is deceased, "to whom copyright in such work passes by bequest of the author or by the applicable laws of interstate succession." *See, e.g.*, proposed 17 U.S.C. 106A(d)(2).

[18] Subcommittee Hearings, *supra* note 1 (statement of the Honorable Edward Markey) [hereinafter cited as "Markey Statement"] at 2).

[19] In a recent case interpreting the California Art Preservation Act, a court held that murals are not protected, but urged an appeal to clarify the issue. Los Angeles Times, March 8, 1990, at part B, p. 10, col. 1. H.R. 2690 clearly encompasses works such as murals within the definition of "painting." However, protection for such works may well be qualified by the rules set forth in proposed section 113(d), relating to works incorporated in buildings.

[20] The Complete Guide to Sculpture, Modeling and Ceramic Techniques and Materials 8 (Midgley ed. 1986).

[21] T. Newman, Innovative Printmaking 1–2 (1977).

printing positives) of a photograph. The limitation to "still" photographic images is intended to ensure that "moving" images, such as those appearing in motion pictures and other audiovisual works, are not protected under the bill. In fact, those categories of works are expressly excluded pursuant to subparagraph (1)(A)(i) of the definition of a work of visual art. See discussion infra.

The limited approach of the bill precludes coverage of all photographs. Thus the bill both narrowly defines the kinds of photographs covered and, through the exclusions set forth in subparagraphs (A) and (B) of the definition of a work of visual art, specifically denies protection to others. For example, many photographs are produced for use by newspapers and magazines and for other non-exhibition purposes and are specifically excluded by the definition of covered photographs. In addition, these photographs are often works-made-for-hire, which subsection (B) of the definition specifically excludes. See discussion infra.

The nature or location of the exhibition is not relevant to the determination of whether the photograph is produced only for exhibition purposes. In addition, it is the initial purpose for which the image is produced that controls whether a photograph is covered. Thus a qualifying photograph will not fall outside the ambit of the bill's protection simply because it is later used for non-exhibition purposes. Proposed section 106A(c)(3) excludes any reproduction of a qualifying photograph in a different context, such as a newspaper or magazine. However, the making and distribution of the reproduction would not deprive the photographer of protection for the original single copy of the photograph or for any limited edition of it.

Single Copies and Limited Editions. — The bill covers only single copies and limited editions of 200 or fewer. The latter is a familiar concept in the artistic community. Limited editions, as opposed to reproductions, are comprised of multiple originals of the same work[22] and are thus deserving of special protection. As Professor Ginsburg testified:

> The bill recognizes the special value inherent in the original or limited edition copy of a work of art. The original or few copies with which the artist was most in contact embody the artist's "personality" far more closely than subsequent mass produced images. Accordingly, the physical existence of the original itself possesses an importance independent from any communication of its contents by means of copies. ... Were the original defaced or destroyed, we would still have the copies, we would all know what the work looked like, but, I believe, we would all agree that the original's loss deprives us of something uniquely valuable.[23]

Numbering and Marking Requirement — The act of numbering and marking serves to define the subject matter of the legislation. There are significant differences between marked and numbered editions, and other works of the

[22] Id. at 20.

[23] Ginsburg Statement, supra note 21, at 4.

visual arts distributed in finite numbers of copies but without the pledge inherent in marking and numbering that replication of the work is to be limited. This pledge is important to the artist and to the buyer, and it is with respect to these works that the dangers of mutilation and destruction are most acute.

While the bill covers only numbered and marked limited editions, the Committee does not intend to create a rigid requirement akin to the copyright notice required by earlier copyright laws.[24] Numbering and marking serves the primary purpose of the bill, which is to limit the works to which its protection extends. It is an additional advantage that numbering and marking also provides purchasers with notice of the work's protected status.

Numbering and marking is also consistent with current practice in the artistic community. Artists creating limited editions in there types of works usually break their molds, strike their plates, or otherwise destroy the materials from which additional original copies of the work may be made.[25] State fraud laws reinforce this practice by generally prohibiting additions to a limited edition.[26]

Different rules apply depending on the kind of work. Limited editions of paintings, drawings, prints, and photographs must be signed and consecutively numbered by the author. Limited editions of sculptural works must also be consecutively numbered, but because of the nature of these works, the bill permits the author to either sign the pieces or place equivalent identifying marks on them.

To distinguish between the photographs covered by the bill and those produced for use by newspapers, magazines, and for other non-exhibition purposes, or that are otherwise excluded, photographers must sign single copies of their covered works. As noted, this will also provide adequate notice to those to whom photographs are transferred about whether the photographs are protected.

In comparison, single copies of paintings, drawings, prints, and sculptures need not be signed. Even without a signature, these works may easily be distinguished from other works excluded from coverage, and subsequent transferees of paintings, drawings, prints, and sculpture should always have adequate notice that these types of works fall within the ambit of the bill's protections.

Courts should be flexible in determining whether the placement of the numbering and marking is adequate to serve the purposes described above. Artists need not deface the work itself in numbering and marking. For example, placement on the back of the work or on the matting surrounding it is sufficient.

Burden of Proof. — Consistent with the general rule that the plaintiff has the burden of establishing the basic elements of a cause of action, the author ordinarily has the burden of showing that the particular work falls within the

---

[24] 17 U.S.C. 401–406 (1976 ed.); 17 U.S.C. 19 (1909).

[25] Ted Crawford, Legal Guide for the Visual Artist 95-8 (Allworth Press 1990).

[26] *See, e.g.*, Cal. Civ. Code S S 1740–1745.5; Ill. Ann. Stat. ch. 1211/2 S S 361–368.

definition set forth in the bill. In general, for example, a photographer will have the burden of showing that a photographic image is produced for exhibition purposes and a printmaker who creates a limited edition must show that the edition consists of 200 or fewer copies.

Exclusions from Covered Works — The definition of a work of visual art specifically excludes certain works and thus helps ensure the limited application of the legislation. These exclusions, set forth in subparagraphs (A), (B), and (C) of the definition, work in trandem with the exclusions set forth in proposed section 106A. They are self-explanatory and reinforce the premise of the bill: to cover only those works described in the definition of a work of visual art and therefore to protect only originals of those works of art. Proposed subsections (A) and (B) distinguish covered works of visual art from other works that are denied protection, such as newspapers, audiovisual works, applied art, and maps. While subparagraph (A)(iii) also excludes any portions or parts of these types of works, a new and independent work created from snippets of these materials, such as a collage, is of course not excluded.

The exclusion set forth in subparagaph (C) makes the bill's scope consistent with current copyright law, but granting protection to only those works subject to copyright protection under title 17. This avoids any tension between the public's ability to exploit the work under the copyright law and the rights granted under this Act.

The Rights of Attribution and Integrity. — Section 3 of the bill creates a new section 106A of title 17, which accords the rights of attribution and integrity to authors of covered works. These rights:

> promote *** the interests of artists and public alike. [They] benefit artists by assuring their rights to recognition for the works they have created and by protecting the works themselves against destruction or mutilation. These safeguards may enhance the creative environment in which artists labor. Equally important, these safeguards enhance our cultural heritage. The attribution right not only affords basic fairness to artists, it promotes the public interest by increasing available information concerning artworks and their provenance, and by helping ensure that that information is accurate. The integrity right helps preserve artworks intact for all of us to enjoy.[27]

The rights of attribution and integrity are independent of the exclusive rights provided to owners of copyrights by 17 U.S.C. 106, and they in no way interfere with ordinary commerce in works of art by art dealers, auction houses, and others similarly situated. Moreover, these rights are granted subject to 17 U.S.C. 107, which limits section 106's exclusive rights pursuant to the fair use doctrine. See discussion *infra*.

Proposed section 106A(a)(1) creates a right of attribution that extends not only to the right to be identified as the author of a work, or to prevent use

[27] Ginsburg Statement, *supra* note 21, at 4.

of the author's name when he or she is improperly identified as the author of a work of visual art, but also to the right to publish anonymously or under a pseudonym.[28] Section 106A(a)(2) provides that an author shall have the right to prevent the use of his or her name in connection with a work of visual art that has been modified in a way that would violate the right of integrity set forth in proposed section 106A(a)(3).

New section 106A(a)(3) sets forth a right of integrity, which is subject to the limitations set forth in proposed section 113(d), relating to works attached to buildings. See discussion infra. Section 106A(a)(3) provides that an author shall have the right to prevent certain modifications of the work, including distortions, mutilations, and destruction. Modifications are prohibited only if they would be prejudicial to the author's honor or reputation, and if they are the result of an intentional or negligent act or omission with respect to the covered work.

The first criterion is analogous to the standard required by the Berne Convention: harm to the author's honor or reputation. As John Koegel testified:

> An artist's professional and personal identity is embodied in each work created by that artist. Each work is a part of his/her reputation. Each work is a form of personal expression (oftentimes painstakingly and earnestly recorded). It is a rebuke to the dignity of the visual artist that our copyright law allows distortion, modification and even outright permanent destruction of such efforts.[29]

H.R. 2690 as introduced established a virtual per se standard with regard to protecting works of recognized stature. The Committee believes that a per se standard is inappropriate. It therefore endorses the Subcommittee's decision at markup to delete this language and to use the "honor and reputation" standard of the Berne Convention with regard to all covered works. First, the Committee recognizes that the original standard would have increased litigation by creating a battle of expert witnesses over whether a particular work had a recognized stature. Second, by deleting the language, the bill makes clear that to be protected, an author need not prove a pre-existing standing in the artistic community. The Committee appreciates that less well-known or appreciated artists also have honor and reputations worthy of protection. The deletion of this language is consistent with the fact that, throughout history, many works now universally acknowledged as masterpieces have been rejected and often misunderstood by the general public at the time they were created.[30]

The Berne Convention's standard of harm to "'honour or reputation' does impose certain limitations, leaving a considerable scope for interpretation by

---

[28] Final Report of the Ad Hoc Working Group on U.S. Adherence to the Berne Convention, reprinted in 10 Colum.—Vla J. Law & Arts 1 (1986) (hereinafter referred to as "Ad Hoc Working Group Final Report") at 550.

[29] Koegel Statement, *supra* note 19, at 8.

[30] H. Potterton, National Gallery London 32, 124–125, 157, 160, 168, Thames and Hudson Co. (1977).

national legislation."[31] The Committee believes that the best approach to construing the term "honor or reputation" in H.R. 2690 is to focus on the artistic or professional honor or reputation of the individual as embodied in the work that is protected. The standard used is not analogous to that of a defamation case, where the general character of the plaintiff is at issue. In a suit for a violation of the rights accorded under H.R. 2690, any evidence with regard to the latter is irrelevant.

The formulation for determining whether harm to honor or reputation exists must of necessity be flexible.[32] The trier of fact must examine the way in which a work has been modified and the professional reputation of the author of the work. Rules 701–706 of the Federal Rules of Evidence permit expert testimony on the issue of whether the modification affects the artist's honor or reputation. While no per se rule exists, modification of a work of recognized stature will generally establish harm to honor or reputation.

Some Berne members do not include destruction of a work within the right of integrity because, theoretically, once the work no longer exists, there can be no effect on an artist's honor or reputation. Other Berne members, however, do protect against destruction. Even assuming that the Berne Convention does not require protection against destruction of works, it is clear that the Convention simply sets a floor for protection and does not prohibit member countries from providing additional rights.[33] By providing for the right of attribution and by protecting against both mutilation and destruction, H.R. 2690 follows the preservation model enacted by some States. This model recognizes that destruction of works of art has a detrimental effect on the artist's reputation, and that it also represents a loss to society.[34] The bill furthers the preservation concept and provides in the most effective way for the protection of the work by giving the artist the right of integrity and the power to enforce it.

Kenneth Snelson provided the Subcommittee with a compelling example of the need for the kind of protection extended by H.R. 2690. Mr. Snelson, who is today a widely known and well-regarded artist, created the first two of a series of sculptural towers in 1962–64, and sold them to the New York World's Fair. At the conclusion of the World's Fair, the pieces, which were the then-unkown Mr. Snelson's first major commission, were sold for scrap metal without his knowledge. If H.R. 2690 had been the law at the time, Mr. Snelson's

---

[31] Ricketson, the Berne Convention for the protection of literary and artistic works: 1886–1986 (1987) (hereinafter cited as "Ricketson") at 471. While the precise scope and application of the rights provided by the Berne Convention and proposed section 106A may differ, it may still be useful to refer to various authoritative sources on Berne for a description of the nature and importance of these rights. *See, e.g.*, W.I.P.O. Guide to the Berne Convention for the Protection of Literary Works (Paris Act 1971) [hereinafter cited as W.I.P.O. guide], Article 6bis at 41–44; W.I.P.O., Glossary of Terms of the Law of Copyright and Neighboring Rights (1982); 2 M. Nimmer on Copyright 8.21 [A][2] (1989); Ad Hoc Working Group Final Report, *supra* note 34, at 547–52; Copyright Office Report, *supra* note 11, at 77–8, 84.

[32] See W.I.P.O. Guide, *supra* note 37, at 42.

[33] *See generally* Ricketson, supra note 37, at 470.

[34] Oman Statement, supra note 1, at 4–7.

works would have been protected, because the bill protects lesser-known authors, and because it covers destruction as well as modification.

State of Mind. — H.R. 2690 as introduced did not require a particular state of mind, nor did it expressly require a nexus between a destruction, distortion, mutilation, or other modification of a work and any subsequent harm to the author's reputation or honor. The Committee endorses the amendment in the nature of a substitute, which clarifies that the right of integrity extends only to intentional and negligent acts or omissions, and that those acts or omissions must have been committed with respect to the work at issue. Thus, for example, while an author may assert the integrity right where his or her work is destroyed in a fire caused for the purpose of collecting insurance on the work, the author may not assert the right where the fire is caused by someone accidentally forgetting to turn off a coffee pot.

Holder of the Rights. — Because artists' rights are separate from economic rights, proposed section 106A(b) grants the rights of attribution and integrity to the author, rather than to the copyright holder (unless the artist is also the copyright holder).

Joint Works. — Consistent with current copyright law,[35] subsection (b) makes authors of a joint work of visual art coowners of the rights it confers. The consequences of coownership are the same in this context as they are with respect to section 106 rights. Authors of a joint work are therefore tenants in common.[36]

Exclusions from Rights Granted. — Proposed section 106A(c) takes into account current practices of the artistic community and supplements the exclusions set forth in the definition of a work of visual art. For example, according to proposed subsection (c)(1), a modification due to the passage of time or to the inherent nature of the materials used by the author does not violate the right of integrity, unless the modification is the result of gross negligence in maintaining or protecting the work. In addition, subsection (c)(2) excludes a modification due to conservation efforts and to the presentation of the work, including lighting and placement, unless the modification was grossly negligent. Generally, the removal of a work from a specific location comes within the exclusion because the location is a matter of presentation, unless the work cannot be removed without causing the kinds of modifications described in proposed subsection 106A(a)(3).[37] Under subsection (c)(2), galleries and museums continue to have normal discretion to light, frame, and place works of art. However, conduct that goes beyond presentation of a work to physical modification of it is actionable. For example, Representative Markey described the actions of two Australian entrepreneurs who cut Picasso's "Trois Femmes" into hundreds of pieces and sold them as "original Picasso pieces."[38] This is clearly

[35] 17 U.S.C. 201(a).

[36] H. Rep. No. 1476, 94th Cong., 2d Sess. 121 (1976).

[37] See discussion of proposed section 113 infra.

[38] Markey Statement, supra note 24, at 2.

not a presentation question. On the other hand, the Committee believes that the presentation exclusion would operate to protect a Canadian shopping center that temporarily bedecked a sculpture of geese in flight with ribbons at Christmas time.[39]

Proposed subsection (c)(3) sets forth a final exemption, relating to certain works specifically excluded from the definition of a work of visual art. It makes clear that the bill protects original works in single copies and limited editions, and that it does not protect reproductions, depictions, portrayals, and similar uses of works of visual art that are embodied in works such as audiovisual works, books, and similar works that are excluded from protection by subparagraphs (A) and (B) of the definition of a work of visual art. Copyright owners and users are insulated from liability under H.R. 2690 under these circumstances. For example, a newspaper, book, or magazine may include a photograph of a painting or a piece of sculpture. A motion picture may include a scene in an art gallery. The exclusion from the definition of a work of visual art would be of little or no value if these industries could be held liable under section 106A for the manner in which they depict, portray, reproduce, or otherwise make use of such a work. Moreover, because such actions do not affect the single or limited edition copy, imposing liability in these situations would not further the paramount goal of the legislation: to preserve and protect certain categories of original works of art.

Term of Protection. — Proposed section 106A(d) relates to the duration of the rights of attribution and integrity. Subsection (d)(1) encompasses works created after the law's effective date. Subsection (d)(2) encompasses a narrow class of works created before the effective date, but in which the author still holds the copyright.[40] In either case, the term of protection is consistent with current copyright terms for economic rights. For the former kinds of works, the term of protection is the life of the author plus 50 years. For the latter, the term is coextensive with that provided for the economic rights relating to the work.[41]

Similarly, subsection (d)(3) provides that the term for joint works is concurrent with the copyright term for joint works, which is the life of the last surviving author plus 50 years.[42]

As in current copyright law, all terms run to the end of the calendar year of the year in which they expire.[43]

Waiver, Assignment, and Transfer. — Although the section 106A rights of attribution and integrity are separate from the economic rights granted in

[39] Snow v. The Eaton Centre, Ltd., 70 Can. Pat. Rptr. 2d 105 (Ont. High Ct. 1982.).

[40] The bill as introduced covered works created before, but not published until after, the effective date. In the context of visual arts, this standard was not easily applied. Letter Edged in Black Press, Inc. v. Public Building Comm'n of Chicago, 320 F. Supp. 1303 (N.D.Ill. 1970). The amendment in the nature of a substitute therefore changed the coverage. The bill does not, however, apply to acts committed before the date of enactment.

[41] 17 U.S.C. 302–304.

[42] 17 U.S.C. 302(b).

[43] 17 U.S.C. 305.

section 106, the issue of whether section 106A rights are waivable, assignable, or transferable has important economic consequences.

Proposed subsection (e)(1) permits an author to waive the rights of attribution and integrity. The Committee recognizes that these rights are personal to the author and that, because of a relatively weak economic position, the author may be required to bargain away those rights. It also recognizes that routine waivers of the rights will eviscerate the law. On the other hand, the Committee believes that to proscribe waiver would be to inhibit normal commercial practices. Professor Ginsburg testified that:

> Arguably, the best recognition of moral rights would countenance no waivers. This position, however, is probably too extreme for the U.S. system, nor does Berne require it. As a practical matter, moreover, despite their formal prohibition, de facto waivers are likely to occur. The artist is better protected under a regime requiring specificity of waivers than under one where an ideologically pure no-waiver law is rarely in fact observed.[44]

The Committee agrees. Waivers and the circumstances surrounding them must be narrowly circumscribed. Waivers will be valid only if the parties follow the rules set forth in subsection (e)(1).

In general, the bill's waiver provision permits the author to hold harmless specific activity that in the absence of a waiver would violate the law. However, a waiver applies only to the specific person to whom waiver is made. That person may not subsequently transfer the waiver to a third party. Any third parties must obtain waivers directly from the author.

The author must expressly agree to the waiver in a written instrument, and must sign that instrument. The writing must specifically identify the work and the uses of the work to which the waiver applies. The waiver will apply only to that work and those uses. The bill does not permit blanket waivers.

The amendment in the nature of a substitute clarifies that one joint author of a work may waive the rights of attribution and integrity and thereby bind all other joint authors. This rule, set forth in proposed subsection (e)(1), is consistent with current practice under title 17, in which one joint author may exploit the economic rights in a work, subject only to a duty to account to other joint authors for any profits earned from that exploitation.[45] Similarly, if a joint author waives the right of attribution or integrity in exchange for compensation, that joint author has a duty to account to the other joint authors.[46]

The specific controls over the exercise of waiver should adequately protect authors. These protections would not be available if assignment and transfer of the rights of attribution and integrity were permitted. Further, an assignment or transfer of these rights to third parties would be contrary to the

---

[44] Ginsburg Statement, supra note 21, at 13.

[45] Oddo v. Ries, 743 F. 2d 630 (9th Cir. 1984).

[46] *Id.*

personal nature of the rights, and to the Committee's objective of strictly controlling the circumstances under which the author chooses to exercise them. Subsection (e)(1) therefore proscribes assignment and transfer.

Ownership of Rights After Author's Death. — Pursuant to proposed subsection (e)(2), the rights of attribution and integrity, and the authority to waive them, vest after the author's death in those people named in the author's will. If the author's will does not dispose of the rights, they will vest through intestate succession. State laws on testacy and intestacy will govern these situations.

Effect of Transfer of Rights. — Proposed subsection (e)(3) provides that transfer of a copy of the work or of any economic rights in that work does not effect a transfer of any rights provided under section 106A; nor does such transfer effectuate a waiver of those rights. This principle is consistent with current practice under 17 U.S.C. 202.

Conversely, a waiver properly entered into does not transfer any ownership rights in the physical copy of the work, or any of the exclusive rights granted under section 106.

Works Incorporated Into Buildings. — Section 4 of the bill amends 17 U.S.C. 113 to create special rules for removal of works incorporated into buildings. Drawn from similar provisions in the California statute,[47] the amendment covers two separate situations. First, it covers works that cannot be removed without the removal causing the kinds of modifications described in proposed section 106A(a)(3). Second, it covers works that can be removed without the removal causing such harm to the work.

The former situation is addressed in proposed section 113(d)(1), which provides that the rights granted pursuant to paragraphs (2) and (3) of section 106A(a) shall not apply where the author and the building owner, notwithstanding their recognition that the work cannot be removed without harm, have signed a written instrument permitting installation of the work. The purpose of this provision is to ensure that the author is made fully aware of the circumstances surrounding the installation and potential removal of the work and has nevertheless knowingly subjected the work to possible modifications that would otherwise be actionable under section 106A.

The Committee recognizes, however, that some installations will have occurred prior to the effective date of the law, and that they will not have been accompanied by written agreements. Therefore, to protect valid understandings of the law as it existed at the time of those installations, proposed section 113(d)(1)(B) provides that a written agreement is not required with respect to these works. The Committee believes, however, that the better rule is to require written agreements, and therefore subsection (d)(1)(B) requires such agreements for all installations occurring after the Act's effective date.

The amendment in the nature of a substitute clarifies and simplifies the procedure applicable to works incorporated into buildings by deleting more

[47] Cal. Civ. Code §987.

cumbersome language contained in the bill as introduced. In particular, the bill as introduced attempted specifically to acknowledge the interests of subsequent owners of the buildings at issue. The amendment recognizes that such language is superfluous. Proposed section 113(d) sets forth a general rule that authors of works of visual art incorporated into buildings are protected under section 106A. When an author and building owner agree to the installation in a particular building, the agreement in effect extends to all subsequent owners of that building. Whether the rights set forth in paragraphs (2) and (3) of section 106A(a) apply is controlled not by who owns the building at any given time, but by the fact of installation of a work in a building and the circumstances surrounding that installation.

The second category addressed by proposed section 113(d) encompasses those works that are incorporated into buildings but that may be removed without causing the modifications described in section 106A(a)(3). Under these circumstances, the rights of attribution and integrity apply to any effort of the building owner to remove the work, unless the owner makes a diligent, good faith effort to notify the author in writing that the author but is unable to do so, or the owner notifies the author in writing but the author fails to respond within 90 days, by either removing the work or paying for its removal. In these cases, the rights of attribution and integrity will not be available to an author wishing to sue for their violation. The bill presumes that an attempt to notify the author by registered mail constitutes a diligent, good faith effort.

The legislation recognizes that building owners may find it difficult to locate authors whose works have been incorporated into buildings. Proposed section 113(d)(3) therefore directs the Register of Copyrights to establish a system permitting authors of works of visual art to record their identities and addresses with the Copyright Office. This system will inure to the benefit both of authors seeking to protect their rights and of building owners attempting diligently, and in good faith, to notify these authors of proposed removals.

Preemption. — Section 5 of the bill follows the principles set forth in and amends 17 U.S.C. 301, the preemption section of the Copyright Act. Witnesses at the Subcommittee hearings strongly supported the enactment of a uniform Federal law and the concomitant preemption of State law where appropriate. As the Register of Copyrights noted, "A single Federal system is preferable to State statutes or municipal ordinances on moral rights because creativity is stimulated more effectively on a uniform, national basis."[48]

For preemption to occur under current section 301, two criteria must be met. First, the rights sought to be vindicated under State law must be fixed in a tangible medium of expression and fall within the subject matter of copyright as specified in section 102 or 103 of title 17. Second, the rights must be equivalent to legal or equitable rights granted under section 106 of that title. Only if both criteria are met will State law be preempted.

---

[48] Oman Statement, supra note 1, at 36; Koegel Statement, supra note 19, at 6.

Similarly, pursuant to the amendments made by H.R. 2690, preemption will occur when, with respect to works of visual art falling within the subject matter described in 17 U.S.C. 102, as further defined by the amendment to section 101, a State seeks to grant legal or equitable rights equivalent to those embodied in proposed section 106A.

Consistent with current law on preemption for economic rights, the new Federal law will not preempt State causes of action relating to works that are not covered by the law, such as audiovisual works, photographs produced for non-exhibition purposes, and works in which the copyright has been transferred before the effective date. Similarly, State artists' rights laws that grant rights not equivalent to those accorded under the proposed law are not preempted, even when they relate to works covered by H.R. 2690. For example, the law will not preempt a cause of action for a misattribution of a reproduction of a work of visual art or for a violation of a right to a resale royalty. Further, State law causes of action such as those for misappropriation, unfair competition, breach of contract, and deceptive trade practices, are not currently preempted under section 301, and they will not be preempted under the proposed law.

On the other hand, if a State attempts to grant an author the rights of attribution or integrity for works of visual art as defined in this Act, those laws will be preempted. For example, the new law will preempt a State law granting the right of integrity in paintings or sculpture, even if the State law is broader than Federal law, such as by providing a right of attribution or integrity with respect to covered works without regard to injury to the author's honor or reputation.

Standing and Remedies. — Section 6(a) of the bill simply amends section 501(a) of title 17 to add those authors covered by new section 106A to those entitled under section 501 to bring actions for violations of the rights granted under title 17. It thereby makes all title 17 remedies (except the criminal sanctions provided by section 506) available to those authors, and ensures that any reference to copyright in title 17 (excluding that in section 506) also includes section 106A(a) rights. H.R. 2690 therefore provides for monetary damages, and for injunctive relief to prevent future harm. The same standards that the courts presently use to determine whether such relief is appropriate for violations of section 106 rights will apply to violations of section 106A rights as well.

Criminal Penalties. — Section 6(b) of the bill amends 17 U.S.C. 506 to exclude criminal penalties from the remedies available for a violation of section 106A. The Committee believes that the civil penalties provided in title 17 are adequate to redress any violations of the rights of attribution and integrity.

Registration. — Section 6(c) of the bill amends sections 411 and 412 of title 17 to provide that registration is not a prerequisite to suit for violations of section 106A or to obtaining the remedies available for such violations. As Professor Ginsburg noted in the Subcommittee's hearings, "moral rights are particularly inapt subject matter for imposition of formalities. Moral rights claims go to creators' reputations, not to rights of economic exploitation."[49]

---

[49] Ginsburg Statement, supra note 21, at 13.

Fair Use. — Section 7 of the bill amends 17 U.S.C. 107, and states that section 107's fair use provisions apply to violations of new section 106A as well as to violations of section 106. The Committee does not want to preclude fair use claims in this context. However, it recognizes that it is unlikely that such claims will be appropriate given the limited number of works covered by the Act, and given that the modification of a single copy or limited edition of a work of visual art has different implications for the fair use doctrine than does an act involving a work reproduced in potentially unlimited copies.

Copyright Office Studies. — Section 8 of the bill requires the Copyright Office to conduct two studies, on the issues of waiver and resale royalties.

Section 8(a) of the bill directs the Copyright Office to review the operation of the waiver provisions set forth in section 106A(c) of the Act, and to report its preliminary results two years after the date of enactment, and its final results five years after enactment. The Committee intends to ensure that the waiver provisions serve to facilitate current practices while not eviscerating the protections provided by the proposed law. It is important, therefore, for the Congress to know whether waivers are being automatically obtained in every case involving a covered work of visual art, whether any imbalance in the economic bargaining power of the parties serves to compel artists to waive their rights, and whether the parties are properly adhering to the strict rules governing waivers.

Section 8(b) of the bill directs the Copyright Office, in consultation with the National Endowment for the Arts, to study the feasibility of implementing a system that provides authors with a share of the profits from any resale of their works, or any similar system that would achieve the same objective of "allowing an author of a work of art to share monetarily in the enhanced value of that work." The Committee intends that the Copyright Office consult with all appropriate and interested governmental and private sector individuals and organizations. The Office is directed to make a report to the Congress 18 months after enactment.

H.R. 3221, introduced in the 100th Congress, granted authors the rights of attribution and integrity, but it also provided that artists could share in any profits from resale of their works. This was a controversial provision,[50] which was not included in H.R. 2690. Instead, the Committee believes that the Congress should await the results of the Copyright Office study before deciding whether any such provision is appropriate.

Effective Date. — Section 9 of the bill sets forth the Act's effective date. In general, the rights created under section 106A will apply to works created before, but in which the copyright has not been transferred by, the effective date. That date is six months after enactment, except that the Copyright Office studies shall commence immediately upon enactment. Second, proposed section

[50] The Visual Artists Rights Act of 1987: Hearings on H.R. 3221 Before the Subcommittee on Courts, Civil Liberties, and the Administration of Justice of the House Committee on the Judiciary, 100th Cong., 2d Ses. (1988).

106A's rights will apply to all works created on or after the effective date. However, acts that would otherwise violate the right of integrity but that occurred before the effective date will not give rise to a cause of action under the proposed law. The Committee recognizes that the law modifies important understandings and responsibilities of the parties, and that it would not be appropriate to apply new standards to conduct occurring before the effective date. Since the effective date is six months after the date of enactment, the new law provides adequate notice to those who possess covered works of the authors' rights of attribution and integrity. ...

HOUSE REPORT ON THE ARCHITECTURAL WORKS COPYRIGHT PROTECTION ACT OF 1990 H.R. Rep. No. 101-735, 101st Cong., 2d Sess. (1990), *reprinted in* 1990 U.S.C.C.A.N. 6935

...

DISCUSSION

The Architectural Works Protection Act of 1990 is a result of United States adherence to the Berne Convention for the Protection of Literary and Artistic Works ... on March 1, 1989. ...

Article 2(1) of the Berne Convention requires member countries to provide copyright for "works of architecture" — the constructed design of buildings. This category of subject matter is distinct from "illustrations, plans, sketches and three-dimensional works relative to architecture," which are also required to be protected under Article 2(1). The current U.S. Copyright Act expressly includes "diagrams, models, and technical drawings, including architectural plans" as a species of protected "pictorial, graphic, and sculptural work."[51] It does not, however, expressly protect "works of architecture," although this Committee's Report accompanying the 1976 Copyright Act contemplated that at least selected works of architecture — those containing elements physically or conceptually separable from their utilitarian function — would be protected to the extent of their separability.[52]

[In conjunction with consideration of the Berne Convention Implementation Act, the House Subcommittee on Courts, Civil Liberties, and the Administration of Justice requested that the Copyright Office undertake a full review of including in the Act express statutory protection for architectural works.]

On June 19, 1989, [Register of Copyrights Ralph] Oman delivered his report. ...[53] While the Register noted the strong professional disagreement within the Copyright Office over the existence of copyright for the design of works of architecture under the 1976 Act, he concluded, and the entire staff concurred, that the Berne Convention required such protection. ...

... [T]he Committee concluded that the design of a work of architecture is a "writing" under the Constitution and fully deserves protection under the Copyright Act. Protection for works of architecture should stimulate excellence in design, thereby enriching our public environment in keeping with the constitutional goal. ...

---

[51] The reference to "architectural plans" was added by the Berne Convention Implementation Act of 1988. ...

[52] H.R. Rep. No. 94-1476, 94th Cong., 2d Sess. 55 (1976).

[53] *Copyright in Works of Architecture: A Report of the Register of Copyrights* (June 1989).

SECTION-BY-SECTION ANALYSIS

Section 201. Short Title

This section provides that this title may be cited as the "Architectural Works Copyright Protection Act of 1990."

Section 202. Definitions

Section 202 adds a new definition ("architectural work") to the Copyright Act and amends an existing definition ("Berne Convention work").

Subsection (a) amends section 101 of title 17, United States Code, to provide a definition of the subject matter protected by the bill, "architectural works." An "architectural work" is defined as "the design of a building as embodied in any tangible medium of expression, including a building, architectural plans, or drawings." The work includes "the overall form as well as the arrangement and composition of spaces and elements in the design, but does not include individual standard features."

The definition has two components. First, it states what is protected. Second, it specifies the material objects in which the architectural work may be embodied: the protected work in the design of a building. The term "design" includes the overall form as well as the arrangement and composition of spaces and elements in the design. The phrase "arrangement and composition of spaces and elements" recognizes that: (1) creativity in architecture frequently takes the form of a selection, coordination, or arrangement of unprotectible elements into an original, protectible whole; (2) an architect may incorporate new, protectible design elements into otherwise standard, unprotectible building features; and (3) interior architecture may be protected.

Consistent with other provisions of the Copyright Act and Copyright Office regulations, the definition makes clear that protection does not extend to individual standard features, such as common windows, doors, and other staple building components. A grant of exclusive rights in such features would impede, rather than promote, the progress of architectural innovation. The provision is not, however, intended to exclude from the copyright in the architectural work any individual features that reflect the architect's[54] creativity. ...

The Committee [amended] the definition of architectural work [as contained in the architectural works protection bill as originally filed by deleting] the phrase "or three-dimensional structure." This phrase was included in [the bill] to cover cases where architectural works [are] embodied in innovative structures that defy easy classification. Unfortunately, the phrase also could be interpreted as covering interstate highway bridges, cloverleafs, canals, dams, and pedestrian walkways. The Subcommittee examined protection for these

[54] Protection is not limited to architects. Any individual creating an architectural work is entitled to exercise the exclusive rights granted under the bill, without regard to professional training or state licensing requirements. The general provisions of the Copyright Act governing ownership and transfer of copyrighted works shall apply equally to architectural works.

works, some of which form important elements of this nation's transportation system, and determined that copyright protection is not necessary to stimulate creativity or prohibit unauthorized reproduction.

The sole purpose of legislating at this time is to place the United States unequivocally in compliance with its Berne Convention obligations. Protection for bridges and related nonhabitable three-dimensional structures is not required by the Berne Convention. Accordingly, the question of copyright protection for these works can be deferred to another day. As a consequence, the phrase "or three-dimensional structures" was deleted from the definition of architectural work and from all other places in the bill.

This deletion, though, raises more sharply the question of what is meant by the term "building." Obviously, the term encompasses habitable structures such as houses and office buildings. It also covers structures that are used, but not inhabited, by human beings, such as churches, pergolas, gazebos, and garden pavilions. ...

Section 203. Subject Matter of Copyright

This provision amends section 102, title 17, United States Code, to create a new category of protected subject matter: "architectural works." By creating a new category of protectible subject matter in new section 102(a)(8), and, therefore, by deliberately not encompassing architectural works as pictorial, graphic, or sculptural works in existing section 102(a)(5), the copyrightability of architectural works shall not be evaluated under the separability test applicable to pictorial, graphic, or sculptural works embodied in useful articles. There is considerable scholarly and judicial disagreement over how to apply the separability test,[55] and the principal reason for not treating architectural works as pictorial, graphic, or sculptural works is to avoid entangling architectural works in this disagreement.[56]

The Committee does not suggest, though, that in evaluating the copyrightability or scope of protection for architectural works, the Copyright Office or the courts should ignore functionality. A two-step analysis is envisioned. First, an architectural work should be examined to determine whether there are original design elements present, including overall shape and interior architecture. If such design elements are present, a second step is reached to examine whether the design elements are functionally required. If the design elements are not functionally required, the work is protectible without regard to physical or conceptual separability. As a consequence, contrary to the Committee's report accompanying the 1976 Copyright Act with respect to industrial products, the aesthetically pleasing overall shape of an architectural work could be protected under this bill.

---

[55] See Perlmutter, *Conceptual Separability and Copyright in the Design of Useful Articles*, 37 J. COPYRIGHT SOC'Y 339 (1990), for a helpful review of this issue.

[56] Monumental, nonfunctional works of architecture are currently protected under section 102(a)(5) of title 17 as sculptural works. These works are, nevertheless, architectural works, and as such, will now be protected exclusively under section 102(a)(8).

The proper scope of protection for architectural works is distinct from registrability. Functional considerations may, for example, determine only particular design elements. Protection would be denied for the functionally determined elements, but would be available for the nonfunctional determined elements. Under such circumstances, the Copyright Office should issue a certificate of registration, letting the courts determine the scope of protection. In each case, the courts must be free to decide the issue upon the facts presented, free of the separability conundrum presented by the useful articles doctrine applicable for pictorial, graphic, and sculptural works. Evidence that there is more than one method of obtaining a given functional result may be considered in evaluating registrability or the scope of protection.

The proposed legislation incorporates the general standards of originality applicable for all other copyrightable subject matter. …

… [D]eterminations of infringement of architectural works are to be made according to the same standard applicable to all other forms of protected subject matter. The references in the definition of "architectural work" to "overall form," and to the nonprotectibility of "individual standard features" are not intended to indicate that a higher standard of similarity is required to prove infringement of an architectural work, or that the scope of protection of architectural works is limited to verbatim or near-verbatim copying. These definitional provisions are intended merely to give the courts some guidance regarding the nature of the protected matter. The extent of protection is to be made on an *ad hoc* basis.

Section 204. Scope of Exclusive Rights [i]n Architectural Works

Section 204 creates a new section 120 of title 17, United States Code, limiting the exclusive rights in architectural works.

Subsection (a) of new section 120 permits the unauthorized "making, distributing, or public display of pictures, painting, photographs, or other pictorial representation of the work, if the building in which the work is embodied is located in or ordinarily visible from a public place." Similar exceptions are found in many Berne member countries, and serve to balance the interests of authors and the public. …

Subsection (b) … permits the owner of a building embodying a protected architectural work to "make or authorize the making of alterations to such building, and to destroy or authorize the destruction of such building" without the copyright owner's consent. With respect to the right to destroy a building embodying a protected architectural work, the provision is consistent with existing section 109(a) of title 17 … [but] the Committee believed it advisable to spell out expressly the limitations contained in section 120(b).

The Committee considered the question of moral rights for architectural works. None of the witnesses at the Subcommittee's March 14, 1990 hearing testified in favor of an express statutory grant of such rights. Accordingly, the bill does not contain an express or implied statutory grant of moral rights. …

Section 205. Preemption

Section 205 amends section 301(b) of title 17 ... by adding a new paragraph (4). The new provision provides that state and local landmark, historic preservation, zoning, or building codes relating to architectural works protected under section 102(a)(8) are not preempted by the Copyright Act. ...

Section 206. Effective Date

The bill is prospective, protecting: (1) "architectural works created on or after the date of enactment"; and (2) "architectural works that on the date of enactment are unconstructed and embodied in unpublished plans or drawings." This latter form of protection is subject to possible termination on December 31, 2002 depending on whether the work has been constructed by that date, and is derived from the bill's definition of architectural work. Under the definition, an architectural work can be embodied in any tangible medium of expression, including architectural plans or drawings. An architectural work that has not been constructed before the date of enactment, but which has been embodied in plans or drawings which themselves are unpublished on the date of enactment, is protected under the bill against unauthorized construction that occurs on or after the date of enactment.[57] The result does not violate prohibitions against retroactivity. ...

This provision does, however, raise the question of term of protection. To aid copyright owners, the public, and the courts, the Committee believes it would be helpful to explain in some detail the various terms of protection that will vest under the bill.

Architectural Works created on or after the date of enactment

These works will be governed by section 302 of title 17, United States Code: that is, works created by individuals will have a copyright measured by the life of the author plus 50 years; works created under a work-made-for-hire arrangement, anonymously, or under a pseudonym will have a copyright measured from 100 years from creation or 75 years from publication, whichever occurs first. ...

Architectural Works unconstructed on the date of enactment

The term of protection for architectural works unconstructed on the date of enactment and embodied in unpublished plans or drawings will be governed by sections 302 and 303 of title 17, United States Code. In order to encourage authors of architectural works to construct their unpublished creations, a provisional cut-off date of December 31, 2002, has been provided: works that would

[57] The Subcommittee deliberately limited this provision to architectural works embodied in unpublished plans or drawings, rather than using the broader term "any tangible medium of expression" contained in the definition of "architectural work." The purpose of the exception is to encourage architects who have kept drawings and plans private to disclose them free of fear that disclosure will result in lack of protection against a substantially similar constructed architectural work.

ordinarily be eligible for a term of protection continuing past that date will lose protection on that date if the architectural work has not been constructed. The actual term will vary depending upon a number of factors, including whether the work was created by an individual, or under a work-made-for hire arrangement, or whether the work is published before December 31, 2002, but two basic categories may be identified. Within each category, two examples are given, illustrating the relevant principle governing the calculation of term.

1. *Works created by individuals.* — These works will be governed in the first instance by the life plus 50 years *post mortem auctoris* term in section 302 of title 17, United States Code:

> A. Author dies in 1990. Term will expire in 2040 under section 302; however, under the bill the term will expire on December 31, 2002 unless the architectural work is constructed by that date.
>
> B. Author died in 1940. Under section 303, the term will expire on December 31, 2002 unless the architectural work is constructed and published before that date, in which case protection will expire on December 31, 2027.

2. *Works created under work-made-for-hire.* — These works will be governed in the first instance by the term set forth in section 302 of title 17, United States Code: 100 years from the date of creation; the 75 year term for published works made-for-hire will not apply, since the provisions of section 6 of the proposed legislation are limited to architectural works that are unconstructed on the date of enactment.

> A. Work is created in 1902. Term will expire on December 31, 2002, unless the work is constructed and published before that date, in which case the term will expire on December 31, 2027.
>
> B. Work is created in 1950. Term will expire [in] 2050, unless the work is not constructed by December 31, 2002, in which case protection will expire on that date.

[The terms of protection referenced in the foregoing examples were extended by 20 years by the Sonny Bono Copyright Term Extension Act in 1998. Nonetheless, under § 303 of the Copyright Act, the "magic date" by which architectural works protected by unpublished plans or drawings must be constructed in order to obtain additional protection remains December 31, 2002, at which point their protection would be extended through December 31, 2047.]

HOUSE REPORT ON THE COPYRIGHT TERM EXTENSION ACT (1998)
H.R. Rep. 105-452, 105th Cong., 2nd Sess., reproduced at 1998 WL 120160

...

PURPOSE AND SUMMARY

H.R. 2589, the "Copyright Term Extension Act," will extend the term of copyright protection in all copyrighted works that have not fallen into the public domain by twenty years.

BACKGROUND AND NEED FOR LEGISLATION

Pursuant to Article I, Section 8 of the United States Constitution, Title 17 of the United States Code gives the owners and authors of creative works an exclusive right to keep others from their work for a limited period of time through copyright protection.

The term of copyright protection varies depending on the type of work. Under current law, most creative works receive copyright protection for the life of the author plus fifty years. In a work created by two or more authors, the copyright term endures for the life of the last surviving author plus fifty years. In the case of anonymous works, pseudonymous works, and works made for hire, the copyright term endures for a period of seventy-five years from the year of its publication, or a term of one hundred years from its creation, whichever expires first. A work made for hire is a work prepared by an employee in the scope of his employment or a work that is specifically commissioned for use in certain types of works, such as a collective work or motion picture.

Upon the expiration of the copyright term, the work falls into the public domain. This means that anyone may perform the work, display the work, make copies of the work, distribute copies of the work, and create derivative works based on the work without first having to get authorization from the copyright holder. Essentially, the copyright holder no longer has the exclusive ability to exploit the work to their financial gain and no longer "owns" the work.

The United States has international obligations to protect copyrights as well. The Berne Convention, originally drafted in 1886, is the international treaty which mandates basic copyright protection rules for its member countries. Currently there are over 100 countries that are members of the convention. The United States became a member in 1989. Under the Berne Convention, member countries must protect copyright for a term of life of the author plus fifty years. Under "the rule of the shorter term", member states need only protect the work of foreign authors to the same extent that they would be protected in their country of origin.

In 1995, the European Union extended the copyright term for all of its member states from life of the author plus fifty years to life of the author plus seventy years. As the world leader in the export of intellectual property, this has profound effects for the United States if it does not extend copyright term as well.

European Union countries, which are huge markets for U.S. intellectual property, would not have to provide twenty years of copyright protection to U.S. works and the U.S. would lose millions of dollars in export revenues. Extending copyright term to life of the author plus seventy years means that U.S. works will generally be protected for the same amount of time as works created by European Union authors. Therefore, the United States will ensure that profits generated from the sale of U.S. intellectual property abroad will come back to the United States.

Extending copyright protection will be an incentive for U.S. authors to continue using their creativity to produce works, and provide copyright owners generally with the incentive to restore older works and further disseminate them to the public. Authors will be able to pass along to their children and grandchildren the financial benefits of their works. ...

SECTION-BY-SECTION ANALYSIS AND DISCUSSION

SECTION 1. SHORT TITLE

This section states that this bill may be cited as the "Copyright Term Extension Act."

SECTION 2. DURATION OF COPYRIGHT PROVISIONS

Subsection (a), Preemption With Respect to Other Laws

Section 301(c) of the current copyright statute contains an exception to the general preemption of state common law and statutory copyright. The exception "grandfathers" state common law and statutory protection for sound recordings against record piracy for 75 years from February 15, 1972, the date the federal copyright statute was amended to first grant federal protection for sound recordings. Because this bill will extend the total term of protection for pre-1978 copyrighted works by 20 years, to a total of 95 years, a similar 20-year extension is be given to the "grandfathered" pre-February 15, 1972 sound recordings in H.R. 2589.

Subsection (b), Duration of Copyright: Works created on or After January 1, 1978

Section 302(a) of the current copyright statute grants a basic term of life-plus-50-years; in the case of joint works, Section 302(b) measures the "life" by that of the longest surviving co-author. The bill makes both terms life-plus-70-years. Section 302(c) of the current statute grants a term of 75 years from publication or 100 years from creation (whichever expires first) in the cases of works made for hire, anonymous and pseudonymous works (as there is no known "life" to be measured in those cases). The bill extends those terms by 20 years, to 95 years from publication or 120 years from creation, whichever expires first. Section 302(e) of the current statute establishes a presumption with respect to an author's death: if a search of Copyright Office records made after 75 years from publication or 100 years from creation of a work does not disclose that the author died within the past 50 years, the author is presumed dead for at least 50 years and no infringement action will lie. The bill extends all those time periods by 20 years.

Subsection (c), Duration of Copyright: Works Created but Not Published or Copyrighted Before January 1, 1978

Prior to January 1, 1978, state common law copyright for unpublished works was perpetual. The 1976 Copyright Act preempted such perpetual common law protection, and the perpetual term for unpublished works protected by common law on January 1, 1978 transformed to the life-plus-50-years (or other applicable) term. However, because some of those unpublished works were written by authors who had been dead for more than 50 years on January 1, 1978, it was thought unfair to thrust those works into the public domain immediately (which would have been the effect if the life-plus-50-year term were applied). Section 303 of the current law gave those unpublished works a minimum of 25 years of protection until December 31, 2002. In order to provide an incentive to make those works available to the public, an additional 25 years was provided if the work was published before December 31, 2002, making the potentially available term last through the year 2027. In the 104th Congress, the bill H.R. 989 extended both of these dates. H.R. 2589 leaves unaffected the ordinary term for section 303 works, so that protection expires at the latest in the year 2002. These older works by definition have not been subject to commercial exploitation, so that the benefit from extending the term of protection for this category of works do not outweigh the detriments from limiting public access to these often historically significant works. However, works in this category that are published before the year 2002 would have protection until the year 2047, an extra twenty years beyond the current possible term.

Subsection (d), Duration of Copyright: Subsisting Copyrights

Subsection (d)(1) In General

This section amends Section 304(a) which deals with copyrights in their first term on January 1, 1978. Under current law, works in their first term are eligible for a renewal term of 47 years. H.R. 2589 will extend the renewal term of copyright protection by twenty years making it a 67 year renewal term. This section also amends Section 304(b) which deals with copyrights in their renewal term before January 1, 1978. Under current law, works in their renewal term before January 1, 1978, received a term of seventy-five years from the date copyright was originally secured. This bill would extend that term to ninety-five years from the date copyright was originally secured. This bill also subjects to termination any exclusive or nonexclusive transfers or licenses of works in their renewal term in certain circumstances. This is to allow the original authors of works and their beneficiaries to benefit from the extended copyright protection.

Subsection (d)(2), Copyright Renewal Act of 1992 Amendment

In 1992, Public Law 102-307 (the Copyright Renewal Act of 1992) amended the then-current Section 304(a) to make renewals of pre-1978 works automatic rather than dependent on timely filing of a renewal application. Section 102(2) of Title I of Public Law 102-307 spoke of the effect of renewal "for a further term of 47 years" on grants of transfer or license made before the amendment went into effect. As the bill will make the renewal term 67 rather than 47 years, this provision of Public Law 102-307 is accordingly amended, to avoid any implication that a shorter term still applies to some older works.

SECTION 3. TERMINATION OF TRANSFERS AND LICENSES COVERING EXTENDED RENEWAL TERM

This section amends Sections 203(a)(2) and 304(c)(2) by allowing an author's executor to receive his entire termination interest in the event that the author's widow, widower, children, or grandchildren are not living, or in the absence of a will, the author's next of kin shall own the author's entire termination interest.

SECTION 4. REPRODUCTION BY LIBRARIES AND ARCHIVES

This section is designed to permit libraries and archives to make certain uses of copyrighted material, including in digital form, during the 20-year extension, in certain circumstances. This is an exemption for libraries and archives, or other nonprofit educational institution, allowing them to reproduce, distribute, display, or perform a copy of a work or phonorecord for purposes of preservation, scholarship, or research. However, the exemption applies only where the entity has determined after reasonable investigation, that none of the following conditions apply: (1) that the work is subject to normal commercial exploitation, (2) a copy of the work can be obtained at a reasonable price, and (3) the copyright owner or its agents have provided notice that either of the first two conditions apply. This exemption would allow library users the benefit of access to published works that are not commercially exploited or otherwise reasonably available during the extended term.

SECTION 5. VOLUNTARY NEGOTIATION REGARDING DIVISION OF ROYALTIES

This is a new provision containing a Sense of Congress that the parties involved in the making of motion pictures should negotiate voluntarily and in good faith to decide amongst themselves the amount of remuneration to be divided between them for the amounts received as a result of this bill. ...

[As enacted ultimately by Congress, the bill contained also Title II, the "Fairness in Music Licensing Act of 1998," amending, *inter alia*, 17 U.S.C. § 110(5).]

HOUSE REPORT ON THE DIGITAL MILLENNIUM COPYRIGHT ACT (1998)
H.R. Rep. 105-551(I), 105th Cong., 2nd Sess. 1998, reproduced at 1998 WL 261605

...

PURPOSE AND SUMMARY

H.R. 2281 contains two titles. The first, entitled the "WIPO Copyright Treaties Implementation Act," implements World Intellectual Property Organization sponsored copyright agreements signed by the United States. The second, entitled the "On-Line Copyright Infringement Liability Limitation Act," limits the liability on-line and Internet service providers may incur as a result of transmissions containing copyrighted works traveling through systems and networks under their control.

[As enacted ultimately after conference committee consideration of competing bills from the House and the Senate, the bill contained three more titles. Title III concerned an exemption from copyright infringement liability for computer maintenance or repair. Title IV included miscellaneous provisions with respect to such matters as ephemeral recordings, libraries and archives, and distance education. Title V provided protection for "certain original designs," namely, of vessel hulls.]

BACKGROUND AND NEED FOR THE LEGISLATION

The "WIPO Copyright Treaties Implementation Act"

The digital environment now allows users of electronic media to send and retrieve perfect reproductions of copyrighted material easily and nearly instantaneously, to or from locations around the world. With this evolution in technology, the law must adapt in order to make digital networks safe places to disseminate and exploit copyrighted works.

In Geneva, Switzerland, in December, 1996, a Diplomatic Conference was convened under the auspices of the World Intellectual Property Organization ("WIPO"), to negotiate new multilateral treaties to protect copyrighted material in the digital environment and to provide stronger international protection to performers and producers of phonograms. In addition to the digital issues, the latter is important to provide guarantees abroad of the same strong protection for American records, tapes, and compact discs abroad that is provided domestically.

The conference produced two treaties, the "WIPO Copyright Treaty" and the "WIPO Performances and Phonograms Treaty," which were adopted by consensus by over 150 countries. The treaties will ensure adequate protection for American works in countries around the world at a time when borderless digital means of dissemination are becoming increasingly popular. While such rapid dissemination of perfect copies will benefit both U.S. owners and consumers, it will unfortunately also facilitate pirates who aim to destroy the value of American intellectual property.

The successful negotiation of the treaties brings with it the need for domestic implementing legislation. Title I of this bill contains two substantive additions to U.S. domestic law, in addition to some technical changes, to bring the law into compliance with the treaties so that they may be ratified appropriately.

The treaties do not require any change in the substance of copyright rights or exceptions in U.S. law. They do, however, require two technological adjuncts to the copyright law, intended to ensure a thriving electronic marketplace for copyrighted works on the *10 Internet. The treaties address the problems posed by the possible circumvention of technologies, such as encryption, which will be used to protect copyrighted works in the digital environment and to secure on-line licensing systems. To comply with the treaties, the U.S. must make it unlawful to defeat technological protections used by copyright owners to protect their works. This would include preventing unauthorized access as well as the manufacture and sale of devices primarily designed to decode encrypted copyrighted material. Further, the U.S. must, under the treaties, make it unlawful to intentionally provide false information, or to deliberately alter or delete information provided by a copyright owner which identifies a work, its owner or performer, and the terms and conditions for its use.

When copyrighted material is adequately protected in the digital environment, a plethora of works will be distributed and performed over the Internet. In order to protect the owner, copyrighted works will most likely be encrypted and made available to consumers once payment is made for access to a copy of the work. There will be those who will try to profit from the works of others by decoding the encrypted codes protecting copyrighted works, or engaging in the business of providing devices or services to enable others to do so. A new "Section 1201" to the Copyright Act is required by both WIPO Treaties to make it unlawful to engage in such activity. The changes contained in the new Section 1201 are meant to parallel similar types of protection afforded by Federal telecommunications law and state laws. Just as Congress acted in the areas of cable television and satellite transmissions to prevent unauthorized interception and descrambling of signals, it is now necessary to address the on-line environment.

While there are no objections to preventing piracy on the Internet, it is not easy to draw the line between legitimate and non-legitimate uses of decoding devices, and to account for devices which serve legitimate purposes. The bill, as reported, presents a reasonable compromise by preventing only the manufacture or sale of devices that: (1) are "primarily designed" to grant free, unauthorized access to copyrighted works; (2) have only limited commercially significant purpose or use other than to grant such free access; or (3) are intentionally marketed for use in granting such free access. This would not include normal household devices such as Videocasette Recorders or personal computers, since such devices are not "primarily designed" to circumvent technological protections granting access to copyrighted works, have obvious and numerous commercially significant purposes and uses other than circumventing such protections, and are not intentionally marketed to circumvent such protections. It would however, prevent a manufacturer from making a device that is primarily designed for such a purpose and labeling it as a common household device.

A new "Section 1202" to the Copyright Act is required by both WIPO Treaties to ensure the integrity of the electronic marketplace by preventing fraud and misinformation. The section prohibits intentionally providing false copyright management information, such as the title of a work or the name of its author, with the intent to induce, enable, facilitate or conceal infringement. It also prohibits the deliberate deleting or altering copyright management *11 information. This section will operate to protect consumers from misinformation as well as authors and copyright owners from interference with the private licensing process.

The "On-Line Copyright Infringement Liability Limitation Act"

The "On-Line Copyright Infringement Liability Limitation Act" addresses concerns raised by a number of on-line service and Internet access providers regarding their potential liability when infringing material is transmitted online through their services. While several judicially created doctrines currently address the question of when liability is appropriate, providers have sought greater certainty through legislation as to how these doctrines will apply in the digital environment.

Title II of this bill codifies the core of current case law dealing with the liability of on-line service providers, while narrowing and clarifying the law in other respects. It offers the advantage of incorporating and building on those judicial applications of existing copyright law to the digital environment that have been widely accepted as fair and reasonable.

The bill distinguishes between direct infringement and secondary liability, treating each separately. This structure is consistent with evolving case law, and appropriate in light of the different legal bases for and policies behind the different forms of liability.

As to direct infringement, liability is ruled out for passive, automatic acts engaged in through a technological process initiated by another. Thus, the bill essentially codifies the result in the leading and most thoughtful judicial decision to date: *Religious Technology Center v. Netcom On-line Communications Services, Inc.*, 907 F. Supp. 1361 (N.D. Cal. 1995). In doing so, it overrules those aspects of *Playboy Enterprises, Inc. v. Frena*, 839 F. Supp. 1552 (M.D. Fla. 1993), insofar as that case suggests that such acts by service providers could constitute direct infringement, and provides certainty that Netcom and its progeny, so far only a few district court cases, will be the law of the land.

As to secondary liability, the bill changes existing law in two primary respects: (1) no monetary relief can be assessed for the passive, automatic acts identified in *Religious Technology Center v. Netcom On-line Communications Services, Inc.*; and (2) the current criteria for finding contributory infringement or vicarious liability are made clearer and somewhat more difficult to satisfy. Injunctive relief will, however, remain available, ensuring that it is possible for copyright owners to secure the cooperation of those with the capacity to prevent ongoing infringement. Failure to qualify for the exemption or limitation does not mean that the provider is necessarily an infringer or liable for monetary damages. If the exemption or limitation does not apply, the doctrines of existing law will come into play, and liability will only attach to the extent that the court finds that the requirements for direct infringement, contributory infringement or vicarious liability have been met, that the conduct is not excused by any other exception or limitation, and that monetary remedies are appropriate. Where monetary remedies remain available under the bill, the ordinary rules for courts to follow in setting the amounts of those remedies will still apply. This includes the remittal of statutory damages under paragraph 504*12 (c)(2) for non-profits and public broadcasting entities based on the reasonable belief that the infringing act was a fair use.

Safeguards in the bill include language intended to guard against interference with privacy; a provision ensuring that nonprofit institutions such as universities will not be prejudiced when they determine that an allegedly infringing use is fair use; a provision protecting service providers from lawsuits when they act to assist copyright owners in limiting or preventing infringement; and a provision requiring payment of costs incurred when someone knowingly makes false accusations of on-line infringement.

[Because the DMCA, as enacted, was amended extensively, the bill's section-by-section analysis is omitted here.]

PART FOUR

NEW TEXT AND CASE LAW

SYNOPSIS

Chapter 2

PREREQUISITES FOR COPYRIGHT PROTECTION

§ 2.02 ORIGINALITY

[F] The Idea-Expression Dichotomy

USAGE: On pages 122–123, SUBSTITUTE the following for the text of Note (4):

(4) *Possible meanings of* Baker v. Selden. Along the way to exculpating Baker, the principal case offers us not one but several holdings. The most straightforward is its concluding statement that "blank account books are not the subject of copyright." Most courts, as well as the U.S. Copyright Office in its Regulations, 37 C.F.R. § 202.1(c) (barring protection for "blank forms ... which are designed for recording information and do not in themselves convey information"), appear to have accepted this proposition. There are, of course, problems in applying it. *Compare Utopia Provider Systems, Inc. v. Pro-Med Clinical Systems, LLC*, 596 F.3d 1313 (11th Cir. 2010) (denying copyright in hospital emergency room charts) *and Bibbero Systems, Inc. v. Colwell Systems, Inc.*, 893 F.2d 1104 (9th Cir. 1990) (denying copyright in medical claim forms), *with Kregos v. Associated Press*, 937 F.2d 700 (2d Cir. 1991) (blank form for recording nine pitching statistics was subject to copyright). For a comprehensive overview of the blank forms doctrine, see *Advanz Behavioral Management Resources, Inc. v. Miraflor*, 21 F. Supp. 2d 1179 (C.D. Cal. 1998). Where it applies to bar protection, "[t]he Blank Form Doctrine is ... simply an expression of the basic principle 'that originality ... is the touchstone of copyright protection ...' ... Like the telephone directory white pages at issue in *Feist*, blank forms cannot be copyrighted because they are 'works in which the creative spark is utterly lacking or so trivial as to be virtually nonexistent. ...'" *Hollister Inc. v. Uarco Inc.*, 39 U.S.P.Q. 2d (BNA) 1542 (N.D. Ill. 1996) (quoting *Feist*). In other words, however new and useful Selden's accounting system (the idea) may be, the forms (their expression) don't measure up.

But does the Supreme Court's opinion, read in its entirety, bear out the conclusion that this is the actual holding of *Baker*?

Chapter 3

WORKS OF AUTHORSHIP

§ 3.01 ORIGINAL WORKS OF AUTHORSHIP UNDER § 102

[D] Pictorial, Graphic, and Sculptural Works

USAGE: On pages 174–175, SUBSTITUTE the following text for the paragraph beginning with the last two lines of page 174:

The same principles apply to more specialized maps, such as site plans for development. In *Sparaco v. Lawler, Matusky, Skelly, Engineers LLP*, 303 F.3d 460 (2d Cir. 2002), for example, the court held that, while a surveyor's use of standard cartographic symbols to represent existing physical features was not original, detailed plans for proposed physical improvements (such as creation of parking lots, drives, curbs, and walkways; placement of utilities; creation of fire lanes, fences, walls, and security gates; and landscaping) constituted protected expression. In so holding, the court distinguished an earlier case rejecting copyright in plans that conveyed only general ideas about how a site might be developed. *See Attia v. Society of the New York Hospital*, 201 F.3d 50 (2d Cir. 1999). *See also Peter F. Gaito Architecture LLC v. Simone Development Corp.*, 602 F.3d 57 (2d Cir. 2010) (allegedly copied matter consisted solely of "generalized notions of where to place functional elements," and concepts and ideas "common to countless other urban high-rise residential developments").

§ 3.03 DERIVATIVE WORKS AND COMPILATIONS UNDER § 103

[B] Derivative Works

USAGE: On page 235, SUBSTITUTE the following for the first paragraph of Note (13):

(13) Under § 103(a), copyright in a derivative work "does not extend to any part of the work in which [the preexisting] material has been used unlawfully." This provision sometimes denies copyright to a derivative work that otherwise would meet the standard of sufficient originality. *See, e.g., Palladium Music, Inc. v. EatSleepMusic, Inc.*, 398 F.3d 1193 (10th Cir. 2005) (holding karaoke sound recording copyrights invalid and unenforceable for failure to obtain compulsory or consensual licenses from the copyright owners of the underlying musical works). Note, however, that permission does not have to be granted in writing; an implied nonexclusive license (discussed in § 4.02 below) will suffice. *See Latimer v. Roaring Toyz, Inc.*, 601 F.3d 1224 (11th Cir. 2010) (assuming photos of custom-painted motorcycles were derivative works of the artwork, copyrights were nonetheless valid, because artist was aware that the motorcycles would be photographed for promotional purposes).

Chapter 4

OWNERSHIP AND TRANSFERS

§ 4.01 INITIAL OWNERSHIP

[B] Works Made for Hire

USAGE: On page 274, SUBSTITUTE the following for the second paragraph of Note (5):

Take another look at *CCNV*'s "nonexhaustive list of [*Restatement (Second) of Agency* § 220(2)] factors" which a court should take into account in determining whether someone is an employee or an independent contractor. Which factors (if any) should be weighted most heavily? *See, e.g.*, *Carter v. Helmsley-Spear, Inc.*, 71 F.3d 77 (2d Cir. 1995) (looking, in particular, to payroll formalities); *Aymes v. Bonelli*, 980 F.2d 857 (2d Cir. 1992) (ranking factors and noting that "every case since *Reid* ... has found the hired party to be an independent contractor where the hiring party failed to extend benefits or pay social security taxes"); *Kirk v. Harter*, 188 F.3d 1005 (8th Cir. 1999) (noting that no single factor is determinative, but treating financial relationship, including tax treatment, as highly probative). *But see JustMed, Inc. v. Byce*, 600 F.3d 1118 (9th Cir. 2010) (finding programmer was an employee, despite the fact that he worked at home, was not paid benefits, and did not have taxes withheld). Note that failing to identify the work as made "for hire" on the registration certificate is not dispositive. *See Pritchett v. Pound*, 473 F.3d 217 (5th Cir. 2006).

[C] Joint Works

USAGE: On pages 291–292, SUBSTITUTE the following for the text of Note (8):

(8) Besides requiring simultaneity between intention and creation, *Childress* says that the putative coauthors' collective intent to create a joint work must have included not just a common "state of mind regarding the unitary nature of the finished work," but also an "intent ... to regard themselves as co-authors." Is this the same as insisting, as the trial judge did (with the Second Circuit's retroactive blessing), that the parties have "entertain[ed] in their minds the concept of joint authorship, whether or not they understood precisely the legal consequences of that relationship"? What is the statutory basis for this elaboration of the intent standard, and how is it to be applied? *See, e.g.*, *Gaylord v. U.S.*, 595 F.3d 1364 (Fed. Cir. 2010) (holding Gaylord was sole author of the Korean War Veterans Memorial sculpture, and that contributions of others were more in the nature of "suggestions and criticism").

How helpful is Judge Newman's gloss that, "[i]n many instances, a useful test will be whether, in the absence of contractual agreements concerning listed authorship, each participant intended that all would be identified as coauthors"? Realistically, how reliable is a test based on understandings about "billing" or "credit"? Imagine the case of a ghost-written memoir, published under the celebrity subject's name, to which the "ghost" contributes the greatest share of protectible expression. Would the *Childress* approach to intent assign sole authorship to the celebrity? *See Childress*, n.7.

§ 4.02 TRANSFERS OF RIGHTS

[C] Decisional Law

USAGE: On page 308, ADD the following after Note (3):

(3A) Does the text of § 204(a) leave room for any implied exceptions to the writing requirement? In *Latin American Music Co. v. ASCAP*, 593 F.3d 95 (1st Cir. 2010), West Side Music Co. granted an exclusive license to LAMCO in 1982 in writing, but allegedly rescinded the transfer orally before ASCAP acquired West Side's copyrights in 1993. The court held that § 204(a) "applies to the transfer or grant of copyright ownership, *not* to the termination of such a transfer or grant" (emphasis in original). Because, under New York law, a contract with no stated duration may be terminated upon reasonable notice, the court held that the oral termination was sufficient. Does this decision give sufficient weight to the Congressional policy for requiring transfers of copyright ownership to be in writing?

USAGE: On page 310, ADD the following text to the end of Note (10):

Although one court has stated that "implied licenses are found only in narrow circumstances," *Estate of Hevia v. Portrio Corp.*, 602 F.3d 34 (1st Cir. 2010), a growing number of cases have found implied licenses to exist. *See, e.g.*, *Estate of Hevia* (evidence that deceased architect granted implied license to development company that he co-owned with his partner was "compelling"); *Latimer v. Roaring Toyz, Inc.*, 601 F.3d 1224 (11th Cir. 2010) (artist granted implied license to make and display photos of custom motorcycle artwork, and photographer in turn granted an implied license to display photos at media event).

[E] Recordation

USAGE: On page 315, SUBSTITUTE the following for the first paragraph of the section entitled "Priority Between Conflicting Transfers":

Section 205(d) (as redesignated by the Berne Convention Implementation Act of 1988) establishes priorities of copyright ownership between conflicting transfers of copyrights, including any combination of conflicting assignments and exclusive licenses, taken in good faith. Suppose, for example, that *A*, a songwriter, assigned to *B* the copyright to his song in 1981, and then, in 1995, conveyed the same rights to *C*, who took without actual knowledge of the prior transfer to *B*. Who owns the copyright? Under the terms of § 205(d), the first transferee, *B*, will prevail if he records within one month after execution of the agreement (two months, if the agreement was executed outside the country). When the one-month grace period expires, the two transferees become competitors in a race to record. If *B*, the first transferee, loses and *C* is the first to record, *C* rather than *B* becomes the owner of the copyright in the song. *See, e.g.*, *Banco Popular de Puerto Rico, Inc. v. Latin American Music Co.*, 685 F. Supp. 2d 259 (D.P.R. 2010).

Chapter 5

DURATION AND TERMINATIONS

§ 5.02 TERMINATIONS OF TRANSFERS

[D] The Mechanics of Termination

USAGE: On page 373, at the end of *"Step One – Which Statute Applies?"*, add the following paragraph:

A query, however. Suppose that, on December 31,1977, Author ("A") signed an agreement with Publisher ("P") to write and deliver to P a work of nonfiction, granting to P "all of [A's] right, title, and interest said work." In 1978, A wrote the work and duly delivered the manuscript to P, which promptly published it. If and when A wished to terminate the grant to P, which set of Title 17's termination provisions applies: § 304(c),(d) or § 203?

On March 29, 2010, the Copyright Office published in the Federal Register a notice of public inquiry and request for comments regarding what the Office described as a possible "gap in termination provisions." *See* 75 Fed. Reg. 15390. It will be interesting to see what comments the Office receives – and what action, ultimately, it takes (or urges Congress to take) in response to its inquiry.

Chapter 6

PUBLICATION AND FORMALITIES

§ 6.02 NOTICE

[A] Introduction

USAGE: On page 412, note that the caption to the chart on this page should read:

NOTICE PROVISIONS FOR PUBLISHED WORKS UNDER THE 1909, 1976, AND BERNE CONVENTION IMPLEMENTATION ACTS

The caption apparently was omitted inadvertently in the composition of this edition of the casebook.

§ 6.03 DEPOSIT AND REGISTRATION

[B] Concepts and Procedures

USAGE: On page 432–433, SUBSTITUTE the following for the text of Note (11):

(11) *Incentives to registration.* Although permissive, registration is rewarded handsomely under the 1976 Act. The most important incentive is that registration is a prerequisite to the filing of a civil action for infringement for United States works. As amended in 2008, the language of § 411(a) seems straightforward enough: "no civil action ... shall be instituted until ... registration of the copyright claim has been made. ..."

But what, exactly, is meant by "has been made"? An interesting split has developed on this question. Some courts treat the submission of an application, accompanied by payment of the required fee and deposit of the requisite copies, as sufficient compliance. *See, e.g.*, *Apple Barrel Productions, Inc. v. Beard*, 730 F.2d 384 (5th Cir. 1984); *Cosmetic Ideas, Inc. v. IAC/Interactive Corp.*, 606 F.3d 612 (9th Cir. 2010). Other courts hold that the prerequisite is not satisfied until the Copyright Office has acted on the application. *See, e.g.*, *LaResolana Architects v. Clay Realtors Angel Fire*, 416 F.3d 1195 (10th Cir. 2005) (collecting cases); *M.G.B. Homes, Inc. v. Ameron Homes, Inc.*, 903 F.2d 1486 (11th Cir. 1990). (The dispute turns, in part, on § 410(d), which provides that the effective date of a copyright registration is the date on which the application and supporting materials are received by the Copyright Office, rather than the later date on which the application is determined to be acceptable for registration.) Many of the courts adhering to the latter position, however, allow the plaintiff to file an amended complaint once the registration in fact issues, thus curing the jurisdictional problem. *See, e.g., M.G.B. Homes*, 903 F.2d at 1489. Some courts adhering to the former position have taken an even more generous approach. *See, e.g., Positive Black Talk, Inc. v. Cash Money Records, Inc.*, 394 F.3d 357 (5th Cir. 2004) (finding defect cured when Copyright Office received complete application four days after action was filed, despite the fact that plaintiff never filed an amended or supplemental pleading). The dispute could make a difference if, for example, the statute of limitations expires before the amended complaint is filed. *See Morgan v. Hanna Holdings, Inc.*, 635 F. Supp. 2d 404 (W.D. Pa. 2009).

Despite the near-unanimous opinion of the Courts of Appeals to the contrary, the U.S. Supreme Court recently held that § 411(a) is not "jurisdictional," so that failure to register does not deprive the trial court of subject-matter jurisdiction. *Reed Elsevier, Inc. v. Muchnick*, 130 S. Ct. 1237 (2010). The ruling revived a proposed settlement of a class action that included both registered and unregistered copyrights; and it gives a boost to those courts that have held that a lack of registration may be "cured." However, the Court did not expressly resolve the circuit split noted above; and it also specifically "decline[d] to address whether § 411(a)'s registration requirement is a mandatory precondition to suit that ... district courts may or should enforce sua sponte by dismissing copyright infringement claims involving unregistered works."

USAGE: On page 438, SUBSTITUTE the following for the first paragraph of Note (20):

(20) *Registration and the BCIA*. Under the "two-tier" approach to registration adopted in the Berne Convention Implementation Act of 1988, as amended by the Uruguay Round Agreements Act of 1994, only "United States works" must be registered before an infringement suit is commenced. § 411(a). Works from a Berne or WTO nation other than the United States are excused from compliance with the registration formality for § 411 jurisdictional purposes, but continue to be subject to it for purposes of gaining the benefits available under §§ 406, 410 and 412. Is this consistent with Article 5 of the Berne Convention, which bars conditioning the "exercise" or "enjoyment" of copyright, as to works for which protection is claimed under the treaty, on compliance with any national law formality? *Cf. Elsevier, B.V. v. UnitedHealth Group, Inc.*, 93 U.S.P.Q.2d (BNA) 1408 (S.D.N.Y. 2010) (§ 412 is not inconsistent with the Supremacy Clause, because the Berne Convention is not a self-executing treaty and is therefore valid only to the extent implemented in domestic law).

Chapter 7

EXCLUSIVE RIGHTS AND THEIR LIMITATIONS

§ 7.01 OVERVIEW

[C] Statutory (or "Compulsory") Licenses

USAGE: On page 450, ADD the following text to the end of the first full paragraph:

Note that the CRJs have already survived a challenge under the Appointments Clause of the U.S. Constitution. *See Live365, Inc. v. Copyright Royalty Board*, 94 U.S.P.Q.2d (BNA) 1418 (D.D.C. 2010).

§ 7.04 THE PUBLIC DISTRIBUTION RIGHT

[C] Import and Export Rights

USAGE: On pages 517–518, SUBSTITUTE the following for the three paragraphs beginning with the last paragraph at the bottom of page 517:

In response to the argument that this interpretation would render the importation right a nullity, the Court noted that § 109(a) is limited to copies and phonorecords "lawfully made under this title." "Lawfully made" means made either with the permission of the copyright owner or under some exemption, such as the § 115 compulsory license or fair use. "Under this title" must refer to Title 17, because that is the title in which §602(a) is codified; and, because the Copyright Act generally is not extraterritorial in its application (see § 8.04, below), the phrase "lawfully made under this title" must mean goods lawfully manufactured in the United States. On this logic, gray market copies manufactured outside the United States might be lawfully made, either by the copyright owner or a licensee, but they would not be lawfully made under Title 17. Rather, they would be lawfully made under the copyright laws of the other country; and the first-sale doctrine would therefore not limit the importation right for such copies. *See Omega S.A. v. Costco Wholesale Group*, 541 F.3d 982 (9th Cir. 2008), *cert. granted*, 130 S. Ct. 2089 (2010); *see also Pearson Education, Inc. v. Liu*, 656 F. Supp. 2d 407 (S.D.N.Y. 2009) (criticizing this result on policy grounds, but following *Quality King* as binding authority).

This resolution makes sense, particularly when one compares the phrase "lawfully made under this title" in § 109 with the phrase "if this title had been applicable" in § 602(b) (and in newly-enacted § 602(a)(2)). But does that mean that copies lawfully manufactured abroad can *never* be subject to the first-sale doctrine, even if lawfully imported and sold in the U.S. with the permission of the copyright owner? When faced with this dilemma, most courts have ignored the "plain language" of the statute, suggesting that "§ 109(a) can apply to copies not made in the United States so long as an authorized first sale occurred here." *Omega*, 541 F.3d at 986, *citing Denbicare U.S.A., Inc. v. Toys R Us, Inc.*, 84 F.3d 1143, 1150 (9th Cir. 1996).

What effect would you expect the rule in *Quality King* to have on international commerce in copyrighted works? In the short run, authorized distributors may be discouraged from vigorously promoting their products as competition from discounters begins to erode their profit margins. How will manufacturers respond? The alternatives are unappealing. Enforcement of contractual provisions against errant distributors abroad is, to put it mildly, impractical. Raising the price of goods sold overseas would render them uncompetitive in the foreign market. In the long run, U.S. copyright owners who consider it necessary to maintain wide price disparities between their domestic and international markets may decide to manufacture copies for the export market abroad, resulting in a loss of U.S. manufacturing jobs. Perhaps for this reason, the U.S. Supreme Court granted *certiorari* to review the decision in *Omega*, despite the negative recommendation of the Solicitor General. The case will be argued in the October 2010 Term.

§ 7.05 THE PUBLIC PERFORMANCE RIGHT

[A] Public Performances

[7] Performance Rights in Sound Recordings

USAGE: On page 536, ADD the following after the end of the second full paragraph:

The controversy over public performance rights for sound recordings resurfaced in 2009, with the introduction in the House and Senate of bills that, for the first time in U.S. history, would require terrestrial broadcasters to pay royalties for sound recordings similar to those paid by digital broadcasters. The bills received a boost in April 2010 when the Obama administration announced its support for the measure. You can read the text of the proposed legislation in Part One of this Supplement and follow the progress of the legislation at *www.copyright.gov/legislation*.

[B] Secondary Transmissions

USAGE: On pages 553–554, SUBSTITUTE the following for the last paragraph of the subsection:

In May 2009, after months of wrangling and three temporary extensions, Congress finally reached agreement on an extension of the existing § 119 license for another five years, with more limited amendments than those recommend by the Copyright Office. The Satellite Television Extension and Localism Act (STELA) of 2010 was signed by President Obama on May 27, 2010. Among other provisions, it expands the definition of "unserved households" for purposes of importing distant network signals; and it lifts an injunction previously entered against satellite provider DISH Network, on the condition that it provide local-to-local retransmission into all 210 Designated Market Areas in the United States. You can read the text of the legislation at *www.copyright.gov/legislation*.

Chapter 8

INFRINGEMENT ACTIONS

§ 8.02 FRAMING THE LAWSUIT

[A] Jurisdictional Matters

USAGE: On page 607, SUBSTITUTE the following for the first paragraph of Note (5):

(5) The second prong of the *Harms* test presents perhaps fewer difficulties. Judge Friendly would have the federal courts take jurisdiction under § 1338(a) in instances in which the complaint "*asserts a claim requiring construction of the Act.*" In *Harms* itself, this standard was not met because the question of ownership of the copyright depended entirely on interpretation of the contract at issue. But where the question of ownership requires an interpretation of the "work made for hire" or "joint work" provisions of the Copyright Act (*see generally* Chapter 4), federal subject matter jurisdiction is proper. *See, e.g.*, *Merchant v. Levy*, 92 F.3d 51 (2d Cir. 1996); *Goodman v. Lee*, 815 F.2d 1030 (5th Cir. 1987). Indeed, one court has held that there may be federal jurisdiction over such state-law claims as misappropriation of trade secrets and conversion, if the question of ownership overlaps with the "work made for hire" provisions of the federal Copyright Act. *See JustMed, Inc. v. Byce*, 600 F.3d 1118 (9th Cir. 2010).

USAGE: On page 610, SUBSTITUTE the following text for the first full paragraph:

What happens if the federal copyright claim is dismissed on motion prior to trial — the situation addressed in § 1367(c)(3)? The usual course is to dismiss the state claims as well, without prejudice to re-filing in state court. *See, e.g., Utopia Provider Systems, Inc. v. Pro-Med Clinical Systems, LLC*, 596 F.3d 1313 (11th Cir. 2010) (district court did not abuse its discretion in dismissing state-law claims); *but see Batiste v. Island Records, Inc.*, 179 F.3d 217, 227 (5th Cir. 1999) ("[a]lthough we have stated that our 'general rule' is to decline to exercise jurisdiction over pendent state law claims when all federal claims are dismissed or otherwise eliminated from a case prior to trial, this rule is neither mandatory nor absolute") (reversing District Court's dismissal of remaining state law claims).

USAGE: On pages 611–612, SUBSTITUTE the following text for the three paragraphs headed "Registration and class actions" and "Registration and declaratory judgments":

Registration and class actions. As we learned earlier, a copyright must be registered (or registration must be denied) before an infringement action may be brought, although courts disagree whether that failure may be "cured" by amendment. *See* § 6.03 above. Most courts agreed, however, that a failure to register the copyright deprives the court of subject-matter jurisdiction over the claim. As a result, in *In Re Literary Works in Electronic Databases Copyright*

Litigation, 509 F.3d 116 (2d Cir. 2007), a divided panel held that the district court did not have jurisdiction to certify a class action including thousands of works for which the copyright was not registered. The Supreme Court, however, reversed, holding that lack of registration does not deprive the district court of jurisdiction. *Reed Elsevier, Inc. v. Muchnick*, 130 S. Ct. 1237 (2010). The ruling revives the proposed class-action settlement, which now will be reviewed on its merits. The Court expressly declined to decide, however, whether "district courts may or should enforce [§ 411(a)'s registration requirement] *sua sponte* by dismissing copyright infringement claims involving unregistered works."

Registration and declaratory judgments. Sometimes a potential defendant will file an action seeking a declaratory judgment of non-infringement. As you may remember from first-year civil procedure, however, the statute authorizing district courts to grant declaratory judgments (28 U.S.C. § 2201) is *not* an independent basis for subject-matter jurisdiction in federal courts. Instead, courts must analyze whether they *would have* jurisdiction over a *hypothetical* action that would have been filed in the absence of § 2201.

Because federal courts have subject-matter jurisdiction over actions for infringement, most courts have found no barrier to actions seeking such a declaratory judgment. But in *Stuart Weitzman, LLC v. Microcomputer Resources, Inc.*, 542 F.3d 859 (11th Cir. 2008), the court held that because it would not have had jurisdiction over an infringement action unless the copyright was registered, it could not entertain an action for a declaratory judgment unless the copyright was registered (even though the alleged infringer has no control over registration). The Supreme Court's subsequent opinion in *Reed Elsevier* undercuts this rationale and, presumably, implicitly overrules the result. Otherwise, the ruling would create a disincentive for copyright owners to register, and it would leave alleged infringers in the Eleventh Circuit with no means of resolving a threatened infringement suit.

[B] Other Procedural Matters

USAGE: On page 621–622, SUBSTITUTE the following text for the paragraph labeled "Pleading":

Pleading. Like every other pleading that an attorney prepares, the complaint in a copyright infringement action requires thoughtful consideration — and, usually, a little practice — if it is to be done properly. Rule 8(a)(2) of the Federal Rules of Civil Procedure requires a short and plain statement that the pleader is entitled to relief, so as to give the opposing party fair notice of the claim. Courts typically have required the plaintiff to provide adequate allegations of the following elements: (1) a specification of the work at issue; (2) a statement that plaintiff owns the copyright in the work; (3) a statement that a registration has been obtained if required (i.e., for "United States works"); and, (4) a specification of the acts by which defendant violated the plaintiff's rights and during what time period. *See Elektra Entertainment Group, Inc. v. Barker*, 551 F. Supp. 2d 234, 238 (S.D.N.Y. 2008). Under the Supreme Court's opinions in *Bell Atlantic Corp. v. Twombly*, 550 U.S. 544 (2007) and *Ashcroft v. Iqbal*,

129 S. Ct. 1937 (2009), however, additional facts may be required when necessary to render the claim plausible. *See, e.g.*, *Weinstein Co. v. Smokewood Ent. Group, LLC*, 664 F. Supp. 2d 332 (S.D.N.Y. 2009) (allegation of non-exclusive license did not meet *Iqbal*'s plausibility standard); *Phillips v. Murdock*, 543 F. Supp. 2d 1219 (D. Haw. 2008) (dismissing claim based solely on statements in defendant's advertisements as impermissible speculation); *but see Arista Records, LLC v. Doe 3*, 604 F.3d 110 (2d Cir. 2010) (*Twombly* and *Iqbal* do not impose a heightened pleading standard); *CoStar Realty Info., Inc. v. Field*, 612 F. Supp. 2d 660 (D. Md. 2009) (plaintiff need only allege that it owns a valid copyright and that the defendant copied original expression). You should also note the existence of F.R.C.P. Form 19 ("Complaint for Copyright Infringement and Unfair Competition"),[1] as amended in 2007. The answer must, of course, plead any affirmative defenses on which the defendant intends to rely. F.R.C.P. 8(c)

§ 8.03 PROVING THE CLAIM

[C] Improper Appropriation

USAGE: On page 693, SUBSTITUTE the following for the text of Note (10):

(10) *Reactions to* Altai. *Altai* can be criticized as being overly restrictive in its vision of software copyright, as well as for doing a better job of articulating standards and procedures than of applying them. All the same, the criteria articulated in *Altai* apparently satisfied a previously unmet need. Since 1992, each circuit newly confronting the choice between the *Whelan* and *Altai* approaches has adopted the latter, in one form or another. *See, e.g.*, *Gates Rubber Co. v. Bando Chemical Industries, Ltd.*, 9 F.3d 823 (10th Cir. 1993); *Apple Computer, Inc. v. Microsoft Corp.*, 35 F.3d 1435 (9th Cir. 1994) (similar standard "differently articulated"); *Engineering Dynamics, Inc., v. Structural Software, Inc.*, 26 F.3d 1335 (5th Cir. 1994); *MiTek Holdings, Inc. v. Arce Engineering Co.*, 89 F.3d 1548 (11th Cir. 1996); *Mitel, Inc. v. Iqtel, Inc.*, 124 F.3d 1366 (10th Cir. 1997); *Computer Management Assistance Co. v. Robert F. DeCastro, Inc.*, 220 F.3d 396 (5th Cir. 2000); and *General Universal Systems, Inc. v. Lee*, 379 F.3d 131 (5th Cir. 2004); *cf. R.C. Olmstead, Inc. v. CU Interface, LLC*, 606 F.3d 262 (6th Cir. 2010) ("All of the evidence offered by Olmstead clearly lacks the abstraction and filtration elements."). Only the Third Circuit stubbornly clings to *Whelan*, rejecting an argument based on *Altai* that interoperability justifies a certain amount of copying. *See Dun*

---

[1] Were you not aware that the Supreme Court has promulgated a form complaint for copyright actions? You are in good company:

CHIEF JUSTICE ROBERTS: We have forms for copyright infringement actions?

[COUNSEL]: You do. ...

(Laughter.)

CHIEF JUSTICE ROBERTS: Live and learn.

Reed Elsevier, Inc. v. Muchnick, No. 08-103, Transcript of Argument at 16 (Oct. 7, 2009).

& Bradstreet Software Services, Inc. v. Grace Consulting, Inc., 307 F.3d 197 (3rd Cir. 2002).

USAGE: On page 705, ADD the following text at the end of Note (4):

Indeed, some courts have held that where the works in question are attached to the complaint, a court may properly determine lack of substantial similarity as a matter of law. *See Peter F. Gaito Architecture, LLC v. Simone Development Corp.*, 602 F.3d 67 (2d Cir. 2010).

Chapter 9

SECONDARY LIABILITY

§ 9.01 CONTRIBUTORY INFRINGEMENT AND VICARIOUS LIABILITY

[B] Case Law

USAGE: On pages 735–736, SUBSTITUTE the following for the text of Notes (4) and (5):

(4) How easy is it to distinguish the two forms of 'secondary' liability? Consider the different circumstances in which the two theories might be invoked. For example, what if you are going after an employee/officer/director of a small incorporated business that has been engaging in widespread infringements of your client's product line? What are the potential strengths and weaknesses of "vicarious" and "contributory" liability in these circumstances? *See Softel, Inc. v. Dragon Medical & Scientific Communications, Inc.*, 118 F.3d 955, 971 (2d Cir. 1997) (derivative claims against defendant company's president dismissed); *MDY Industries, LLC v. Blizzard Entertainment, Inc.*, 616 F. Supp. 2d 958 (D. Ariz. 2009) (principal of MDY supervised infringing activities and personally profited from their success); *Arista Records LLC v. Lime Group LLC*, 2010 U.S. Dist. LEXIS 46638 (S.D.N.Y. 2010) (defendant's CEO and sole Director directed and benefitted from infringing activity); *Burdick v. Koerner*, 988 F. Supp. 1206 (E.D. Wis. 1998) (contributory and vicarious liability claims against defendant company's board members dismissed on various grounds).

(5) From the copyright litigator's standpoint, it is sometimes highly desirable to be able to reach the parent corporation of an allegedly infringing subsidiary. Under which version of derivative liability are you most likely to be able to accomplish this result? *See Goes Lithography Co. v. Banta Corp.*, 26 F. Supp. 2d 1042 (N.D. Ill. 1998) (distinguishing and criticizing *Broadcast Music, Inc. v. Hartmarx Corp.*, 1988 U.S. Dist. LEXIS 13298 (N.D. Ill. 1988), which presumes the parent corporation's right to control the subsidiary's infringing activities as part of a contributory infringement analysis). *See also UMG Recordings, Inc. v. Veoh Networks, Inc.*, 2009 WL 334022 (C.D. Cal. 2009) (claims against investors in defendant dismissed; exercising ownership interest to select directors without actual control or culpable conduct is not a material contribution); *Arista Records v. Lime Group* (although formally separate, parent and subsidiary were operated as a single company).

§ 9.03 SECONDARY LIABILITY ON THE INTERNET

[C] Peer-to-Peer File Sharing

USAGE: On pages 770–771, SUBSTITUTE the following for the text of Note (9):

(9) As we saw in § 9.02, the *Sony* standard can be understood as applied to both contributory *and* vicarious liability — or to contributory liability only. In *Grokster*, the Ninth Circuit had relied on *Sony* to absolve the defendants of both. Given the tack that it took on "inducement," however, the Supreme Court did not reach the issue of vicarious infringement. After *Grokster*, how should a court deal with a case in which the issue of a technology provider's vicarious liability is inescapably presented? In *Arista Records LLC v. Lime Group LLC*, 2010 U.S. Dist. LEXIS 46638 (S.D.N.Y. 2010), the District Court refused to extend *Sony* to vicarious liability. Should it have?

In *Arista Records*, the District Court held that defendant LimeWire was liable for inducement under *Grokster* for creating and distributing file-sharing software. The court systematically reviewed evidence that LimeWire was aware of substantial infringement by users, purposefully marketed LimeWire to former Napster users, optimized its features to facilitate searches for copyrighted music recordings, depended on infringement for its economic success, and considered but failed to implement filtering to mitigate infringement. Despite this evidence, however, the court held that there was a genuine issue of material fact with regard to contributory infringement, because it was unclear whether LimeWire was "capable of substantial non-infringing use" under *Sony*. Did *Grokster* establish inducement as a separate category of secondary liability, or is it more properly viewed as a type of contributory infringement? If the former, does *Sony* still apply without change to the category of contributory infringement?

Chapter 10

FAIR USE AND AFFIRMATIVE DEFENSES

§ 10.02 THE FUNDAMENTALS OF FAIR USE

[B] Analyzing Fair Use Today

USAGE: On page 823, SUBSTITUTE the following text for the first full paragraph, i.e., the third paragraph of Note (13):

For a contrary view, see *Salinger v. Colting*, 641 F. Supp. 2d 250 (S.D.N.Y. 2009) (preliminarily enjoining U.S. publication of defendant's novel, *60 Years Later: Coming Through the Rye*, in which a senior citizen known simply as "Mr. C" escapes from an retirement home and reencounters a world of "phonies," including a reclusive, self-protective character named "Salinger"), *vacated on other grounds*, 2010 U.S. App. LEXIS 8956 (2d Cir. 2010) (agreeing that "Defendants are not likely to prevail in their fair use defense"). In concluding that the defendant was unlikely to show that the new work transformed *The Catcher in the Rye*, the District Court placed considerable weight on the fact that the defendant's marketing materials described the book as a "sequel" instead of a "parody" or "critique."

§ 10.03 CONCEPTUAL ISSUES IN FAIR USE

[C] Effect on the Market Under § 107(4)

USAGE: On pages 854–855, SUBSTITUTE the following for the text of Note (4):

(4) What should be the result when there is only a "market of one"? In *Gaylord v. United States*, 85 Fed. Cl. 59 (2008), *rev'd*, 595 F.3d 1364 (Fed. Cir. 2010), the sculptor of the Korean War Veterans Memorial sued the U.S. Postal Service for using a photograph of his sculpture on a postage stamp. The trial court found that the use would have little effect on the market for the work, because Gaylord "has made only limited attempts to commercialize his copyright." In so holding, did the court ignore a poten tial market for licensing an image of the sculpture for the stamp itself? Ultimately, the Federal Circuit held that the use was not fair, *despite* affirming the finding that there was no adverse effect on the potential market.

[D] Photocopying, Guidelines, and "Personal Reproduction"

[3] Modern Technology and "Personal Reproduction"

USAGE: On page 863, SUBSTITUTE the following text for the first paragraph:

The debate concerning personal copies was reignited in 1998, when Napster introduced software that enabled peer-to-peer file sharing of music files in the MP3 digital format. Ultimately, as we know from *Metro-Goldwyn-Mayer Studios, Inc. v. Grokster, Ltd.*, 545 U.S. 913 (2005) (discussed in § 9.03), the U.S. Supreme Court assumed (and the defendants conceded) that downloading a copyrighted sound recording for personal use was an infringement and was not a fair use. Despite some academic criticism, courts that have analyzed the issue have unanimously agreed. *See Arista Records, LLC v. Doe 3*, 604 F.3d 110 (2d Cir. 2010); *BMG Music v. Gonzalez*, 430 F.3d 888 (7th Cir. 2005); *Sony BMG Music Ent. v. Tenenbaum*, 672 F. Supp. 2d 217 (D. Mass. 2009); *but see* Lunney, *Brief of Amici Curiae Law Professors in Support of Respondents in Metro-Goldwyn-Mayer Studios, Inc. v. Grokster, Ltd.*, 545 U.S. 913 (2005), available on LEXIS at 2004 U.S. Briefs 480 (contending that "[t]he predominant use of P2P file-sharing software ... appears to be fair"); Schaumann, *Copyright Infringement and Peer-to-Peer Technology*, 28 Wm. Mitchell L. Rev. 1001, 1028–39 (2002) (concluding that making music files available to others is an unlawful distribution, but that downloading music files for personal use is either a fair use or immunized by § 1008).

Chapter 11

REMEDIES, PREEMPTION, AND RELATED BODIES OF LAW

§ 11.01 REMEDIES UNDER FEDERAL LAW

[B] Non-Monetary Relief

[1] Preliminary and Permanent Injunctions

USAGE: On pages 904–913, SUBSTITUTE the following case and amended Notes and Questions for the *Paramount Pictures* case and the Notes and Questions following:

SALINGER v. COLTING

United States Court of Appeals, Second Circuit
2010 U.S. App. LEXIS 8956 (2010)

CALABRESI, Circuit Judge:

Defendants-Appellants ... appeal from an order ... granting Plaintiff-Appellee J.D. Salinger's[1] motion for a preliminary injunction. The District Court's judgment is VACATED and REMANDED.

BACKGROUND

I.

Salinger published *The Catcher in the Rye* in 1951. *Catcher* is a coming-of-age story about a disaffected sixteen-year-old boy, Holden Caulfield, who after being expelled from prep school wanders around New York City for several days before returning home. ...

Catcher was an instant success. It was on the *New York Times* best-seller list for over seven months and sold more than one million copies in its first ten years. To date it has sold over 35 million copies, influenced dozens of literary works, and been the subject of "literally reams of criticism and comment." ...

Inseparable from the *Catcher* mystique is the lifestyle of its author, Salinger. ... Salinger has not published since 1965 and has never authorized any new narrative involving Holden or any work derivative of *Catcher*. ... Salinger has never permitted, and has explicitly instructed his lawyers not to allow, adaptations of his works. He has, however, remained in the public

[1] We note that Plaintiff-Appellee J.D. Salinger died during the pendency of this appeal. ... Colleen M. Salinger and Matthew R. Salinger, trustees of the J.D. Salinger Literary Trust, [have been] substituted for Salinger as Appellees. For reasons of convenience, however, we will continue to refer to Salinger as "Plaintiff" or "Appellee" in this opinion.

spotlight through a series of legal actions to protect his intellectual property. Salinger has registered and duly renewed his copyright in *Catcher* with the U.S. Copyright Office.

II.

Defendant-Appellant Fredrik Colting wrote *60 Years Later: Coming Through the Rye* under the pen name "John David California." Colting published *60 Years Later* ... in England on May 9, 2009. Copies were originally scheduled to be available in the United States on September 15, 2009. Colting did not seek Salinger's permission to publish *60 Years Later*.

60 Years Later tells the story of a 76-year-old Holden Caulfield, referred to as "Mr. C," in a world that includes Mr. C's 90-year-old author, a "fictionalized Salinger." ... [Despite Colting's claim that *60 Years Later* was a post-modern commentary on or criticism of *Catcher* and/or Salinger, the District Court noted that the cover of the U.K. edition describes the novel as "a marvelous sequel to one of our most beloved classics."]

III.

On July 1, 2009, the District Court granted Salinger's motion for a preliminary injunction, barring Defendants from "manufacturing, publishing, distributing, shipping, advertising, promoting, selling, or otherwise disseminating any copy of [*60 Years Later*], or any portion thereof, in or to the United States." *Salinger v. Colting*, 641 F. Supp. 2d 250, 269 (S.D.N.Y. 2009). In doing so, it found that (1) Salinger has a valid copyright in *Catcher* and the Holden Caulfield character, (2) absent a successful fair use defense, Defendants have infringed Salinger's copyright in both *Catcher* and the Holden Caulfield character, (3) Defendants' fair use defense is likely to fail, and (4) a preliminary injunction should issue. ...

... Because Salinger had established a *prima facie* case of copyright infringement, and in light of how the District Court, understandably, viewed this Court's precedents, the District Court presumed irreparable harm without discussion. *Id.* at 268 (citing *ABKCO Music, Inc. v. Stellar Records, Inc.*, 96 F.3d 60, 66 (2d Cir. 1996)).

DISCUSSION

We hold that, although the District Court applied our Circuit's long-standing standard for preliminary injunctions in copyright cases, our Circuit's standard is inconsistent with the "test historically employed by courts of equity" and has, therefore, been abrogated by *eBay, Inc. v. MercExchange, LLC*, 547 U.S. 388, 390 (2006). ...

I.

The Copyright Act of 1976 authorizes courts to "grant temporary and final injunctions on such terms as [they] may deem reasonable to prevent or restrain infringement of a copyright." 17 U.S.C. § 502(a). And, as the District

Court stated, this Court has long issued preliminary injunctions in copyright cases upon a finding of (a) irreparable harm and (b) either (1) likelihood of success on the merits or (2) sufficiently serious questions going to the merits to make them a fair ground for litigation and a balance of hardships tipping decidedly toward the party requesting the preliminary relief. *See, e.g., NXVIM Corp. v. Ross Inst.*, 364 F.3d 471, 476 (2d Cir. 2004). ...

Thus, once a plaintiff establishes a likelihood of success on the merits, the only additional requirement is a showing that the plaintiff will be irreparably harmed if the preliminary injunction does not issue. And traditionally, this Court has presumed that a plaintiff likely to prevail on the merits of a copyright claim is also likely to suffer irreparable harm if an injunction does not issue. *See, e.g., Richard Feiner & Co. v. Turner Entm't Co.*, 98 F.3d 33, 34 (2d Cir. 1996). ...

This Court has applied this presumption in several ways. Some decisions have interpreted the presumption to mean that a plaintiff likely to prevail on the merits does not need to make a detailed showing of irreparable harm. Other cases have discussed the presumption as though it applies automatically and is irrebutable. A few decisions, by contrast, have found the presumption rebuttable where the plaintiff delayed in bringing the action seeking an injunction. ...

Under any of these articulations, however, this Court has nearly always issued injunctions in copyright cases as a matter of course upon a finding of likelihood of success on the merits. *Cf.* Mark A. Lemley & Eugene Volokh, *Freedom of Speech and Injunctions in Intellectual Property Cases*, 48 Duke L.J. 147, 19 (1998) ("The ostensibly four-factor test collapses ... to a simple inquiry into likelihood of success on the merits. If that can be demonstrated, a preliminary injunction is the expected remedy.") ...

II.

Defendants do not claim that the District Court failed to apply this Circuit's longstanding preliminary injunction standard. Rather, they argue both that this standard is an unconstitutional prior restraint on speech and that it is in conflict with the Supreme Court's decision in by *eBay, Inc. v. MercExchange, LLC*, 547 U.S. 388 (2006). We agree that *eBay* abrogated parts of this Court's preliminary injunction standard in copyright cases, and accordingly, this case must be remanded to the District Court to reevaluate Salinger's preliminary injunction motion. In light of that holding, we need not decide whether the preliminary injunction issued by the District Court constituted an unconstitutional prior restraint on speech.

eBay involved the propriety of a permanent injunction after a finding of patent infringement. ... [The District Court held] that "the evidence of the plaintiff's willingness to license its patents, its lack of commercial activity in practicing the patents, and its comments to the media as to its intent with respect to enforcement of its patent rights, are sufficient to rebut the presumption that it will suffer irreparable harm if an injunction does not issue." 275 F. Supp. 2d at 712. The Federal Circuit reversed on appeal, applying a "general rule ... that a permanent injunction will issue once infringement and validity have been adjudged." *MercExchange, LLC v. eBay, Inc.*, 401 F.3d 1323, 1338 (Fed. Cir. 2005). The court cited for this rule *Richardson v. Suzuki Motor Co.*, which equates the "general rule" with a rule that "[i]n matters involving patent rights, irreparable harm has been presumed when a clear showing has been made of patent validity and infringement." 868 F.2d 1226, 1246–47 (Fed. Cir. 1989). ...

Writing for a unanimous Court, Justice Thomas held that neither the District Court nor the Federal Circuit correctly applied the equitable factors:

> According to well-established principles of equity, a plaintiff seeking a permanent injunction must satisfy a four-factor test before a court may grant such relief. A plaintiff must demonstrate: (1) that it has suffered an irreparable injury; (2) that remedies available at law, such as monetary damages, are inadequate to compensate for that injury; (3) that, considering the balance of hardships between the plaintiff and defendant, a remedy in equity is warranted; and (4) that the public interest would not be disserved by a permanent injunction.

eBay, 547 U.S. at 391. Although the courts below had articulated the correct standard, they had both, albeit in different ways, applied "broad classifications" that were inconsistent with traditional equitable principles. *Id.* at 393. ...

We hold today that *eBay* applies with equal force (a) to preliminary injunctions (b) that are issued for alleged copyright infringement. First, nothing in the text or the logic of *eBay* suggests that its rule is limited to patent cases. On the contrary, *eBay* strongly indicates that the traditional principles of equity it employed are the presumptive standard for injunctions in any context. ...

Moreover, the Court expressly relied upon copyright cases in reaching its conclusion. In response to the Federal Circuit's reasoning that the Patent Act's right to exclude justifies the preference for injunctive relief, ... the Court emphasized that it "has consistently rejected invitations to replace traditional equitable considerations with a rule that an injunction automatically follows a determination that a copyright has been infringed." *Id.* at 392–93 (citing *New York Times Co. v. Tasini*, 533 U.S. 483, 505 (2001); *Campbell*, 510 U.S. at 578 n.10; *Dun v. Lumberman's Mutual Credit Ass'n*, 209 U.S. 20, 23–24 (1908)). Whatever the underlying issues and particular circumstances of the cases cited by the Court in *eBay*, it seems clear that the Supreme Court did not view patent and copyright injunctions as different in kind, or as requiring different standards.

Nor does *eBay* ... permit an easier grant of a preliminary than of a permanent injunction. First, as mentioned above, one of the two cases *eBay* relied upon in stating the traditional equitable test involved a preliminary injunction. *See Amoco Prod.*, 480 U.S. at 542; *see also id.* at 546 n.12 ("The standard for a preliminary injunction is essentially the same as for a permanent injunction with the exception that the plaintiff must show a likelihood of success on the merits rather than actual success."). Second, in *Winter* [*v. Natural Resources Defense Counsel*, 129 S. Ct. 365 (2008)], the Supreme Court in fact applied *eBay* in a case involving a preliminary injunction. Reversing the Ninth Circuit, ... the Court stated: "Issuing a preliminary injunction based only on a possibility of irreparable harm is inconsistent with our characterization of injunctive relief as an extraordinary remedy that may only be awarded upon a clear showing that the plaintiff is entitled to such relief." *Winter*, 129 S. Ct. at 375–76. And, using broad, unqualified language, the Court discussed the preliminary injunction standard as follows:

> A preliminary injunction is an extraordinary remedy never awarded as of right. In each case, courts must balance the competing claims of injury and must consider the effect on each party of the granting or withholding of the requested relief. In exercising their sound discretion, courts of equity should pay particular regard for the public consequences in employing the extraordinary remedy of injunction.

Id. at 376–77. ...

III.

This Court's pre-*eBay* standard for when preliminary injunctions may issue in copyright cases is inconsistent with the principles of equity set forth in *eBay*. ... Therefore, in light of *Winter* and *eBay*, we hold that a District Court must undertake the following inquiry in determining whether to grant a plaintiff's motion for a preliminary injunction in a copyright case. First, as in most other kinds of cases in our Circuit, a court may issue a preliminary injunction in a copyright case only if the plaintiff has demonstrated "either (a) a likelihood of success on the merits or (b) sufficiently serious questions going to the merits to make them a fair ground for litigation and a balance of hardships tipping decidedly in the [plaintiff]'s favor." *NXIVM Corp.*, 364 F.3d at 476. ... Second, the court may issue the injunction only if the plaintiff has demonstrated "that he is likely to suffer irreparable injury in the absence of an injunction." *Winter*, 129 S. Ct. at 374. The court must not adopt a "categorical" or "general" rule or presume that the plaintiff will suffer irreparable harm (unless such a "departure from the long tradition of equity practice" was intended by Congress). *eBay*, 547 U.S. at 391, 393–94. Instead, the court must actually consider the injury the plaintiff will suffer if he or she loses on the preliminary injunction but ultimately prevails on the merits, paying particular attention to whether the "remedies available at law, such as monetary damages, are inadequate to compensate for that injury." *eBay*, 547 U.S. at 391. ... Third, a court must consider the balance of hardships between the plaintiff and defendant and issue the injunction only if the balance of hardships tips in the plaintiff's favor. *Winter*, 129 S. Ct. at 374; *eBay*, 547 U.S. at 391. Finally, the court must ensure that the "public interest would not be disserved" by the issuance of a preliminary injunction. *eBay*, 547 U.S. at 391; *accord Winter*, 129 S. Ct. at 374.

A.

The first consideration in the preliminary injunction analysis is the probability of success on the merits. In gauging this, we emphasize that courts should be particularly cognizant of the difficulty of predicting the merits of a copyright claim at a preliminary injunction hearing. *See* Lemley & Volokh, *supra,* at 201–02 ("When deciding whether to grant a TRO or a preliminary injunction, the judge has limited time for contemplation. The parties have limited time for briefing. Preparation for a typical copyright trial, even a bench trial, generally takes many months; the arguments about why one work isn't substantially similar in its expression to another, or about why it's a fair use of another, are often sophisticated and fact-intensive, and must be crafted with a good deal of thought and effort."). This difficulty is compounded significantly when a defendant raises a colorable fair use defense. ...

B.

Next, the court must consider whether the plaintiff will suffer irreparable harm in the absence of a preliminary injunction, and the court must assess the balance of hardships between the plaintiff and defendant. Those two items, both of which consider the harm to the parties, are related. The relevant harm is the harm that (a) occurs to the parties' legal interests and (b) cannot be remedied after a final adjudication, whether by damages or a permanent injunction. The plaintiff's interest is, principally, a property interest in the copyrighted material. But as the Supreme Court has suggested, a copyright holder might also have a First Amendment interest in *not* speaking. *See Harper & Row Publishers, Inc. v. Nation Enterprises*, 471 U.S. 539, 559 (1985). The defendant to a copyright suit likewise has a property interest in his or her work to the extent that work does not infringe the plaintiff's copyright. And a defendant also has a core First Amendment interest in the freedom to express him or herself, so long as that expression does not infringe the plaintiff's copyright.

But the above-identified interests are relevant only to the extent that they are not remediable after a final adjudication. Harm might be irremediable, or irreparable, for many reasons, including that a loss is difficult to replace or difficult to measure, or that it is a loss that one should not be expected to suffer. In the context of copyright infringement cases, the harm to the plaintiff's property interest has often been characterized as irreparable in light of possible market confusion. And courts have tended to issue injunctions in this context because "to prove the loss of sales due to infringement is ... notoriously difficult." *Omega Importing Corp. v. Petri-King Camera Co.*, 451 F.2d 1190, 1195 (2d Cir. 1971) (Friendly, C.J.). Additionally, "[t]he loss of First Amendment freedoms," and hence infringement of the right *not* to speak, "for even minimal periods of time, unquestionably constitutes irreparable injury." *Elrod v. Burns*, 427 U.S. 347, 373 (1976).

After *eBay*, however, courts must not simply presume irreparable harm. Rather, plaintiffs must show that, on the facts of their case, the failure to issue an injunction would actually cause irreparable harm. This is not to say that most copyright plaintiffs who have shown a likelihood of success on the merits would not be irreparably harmed absent preliminary injunctive relief. As an empirical matter, that may well be the case, and the historical tendency to issue preliminary injunctions readily in copyright cases may reflect just that. *See* H. Tomás Gómez-Arostegui, *What History Teaches Us About Copyright Injunctions and the Inadequate-Remedy-at-Law Requirement*, 81 S. Cal. L. Rev. 1197, 1201 (2008) (concluding, after a thorough historical analysis, that "the historical record suggests that in copyright cases, legal remedies were deemed categorically inadequate"). As Chief Justice Roberts noted, concurring in *eBay*:

> From at least the early 19th century, courts have granted injunctive relief upon a finding of infringement in the vast majority of patent cases. This "long tradition of equity practice" is not surprising, given the difficulty of protecting a right to *exclude* through monetary remedies. ... This historical practice, as the Court holds, does not *entitle* a patentee to [an] ... injunction or justify a *general rule* that such injunctions should issue. ... At the same time, there is a difference between exercising equitable discretion pursuant to the established four-factor test and writing on an entirely clean slate. ... When it comes to discerning and applying those standards, in this area as others, a page of history is worth a volume of logic.

547 U.S. at 395 (quotation marks omitted).

But by anchoring the injunction standard to equitable principles, albeit with one eye on historical tendencies, courts are able to keep pace with innovation in this rapidly changing technological area. Justice Kennedy, responding to Justice Roberts, made this very point as to patent injunctions in his *eBay* concurrence. ... Justice Kennedy concluded that changes in the way parties use patents may now mean that "legal damages [are] sufficient to compensate for the infringement." *Id.*

C.

Finally, courts must consider the public's interest. The object of copyright law is to promote the store of knowledge available to the public. But to the extent it accomplishes this end by providing individuals a financial incentive to contribute to the store of knowledge, the public's interest may well be already accounted for by the plaintiff's interest.

The public's interest in free expression, however, is significant and is distinct from the parties' speech interests. *See Pacific Gas & Elec. Co. v. Public Utilities Commission of Cal.*, 475 U.S. 1, 8 (1986). "By protecting those who wish to enter the marketplace of ideas from government attack, the First Amendment protects the public's interest in receiving information." *Id.* Every injunction issued before a final adjudication on the merits risks enjoining speech protected by the First Amendment. Some uses, however, will so patently infringe another's copyright, without giving rise to an even colorable fair use defense, that the likely First Amendment value in the use is virtually nonexistent.

IV.

Because the District Court considered only the first of the four factors that, under *eBay* and our holding today, must be considered before issuing a preliminary injunction, we vacate and remand the case. But in the interest of judicial economy, we note that there is no reason to disturb the District Court's conclusion as to the factor it did consider — namely, that Salinger is likely to succeed on the merits of his copyright infringement claim.

Most of the matters relevant to Salinger's likelihood of success on the merits are either undisputed or readily established in his favor. Thus, Defendants do not contest either that Salinger owns a valid copyright in *Catcher* or that they had actual access to *Catcher*. And while they argue only that *60 Years Later* and *Catcher* are not substantially similar, that contention is manifestly meritless. ...

More serious is Defendants' assertion of a fair use defense. And at this preliminary stage, we agree with the District Court that Defendants will not likely be able to make out such a defense. The District Court ... found that "[i] t is simply not credible for Defendant Colting to assert now that his primary purpose was to critique Salinger and his persona, while he and his agents' previous statements regarding the book discuss no such critique, and in fact reference various other purposes behind the book." *Salinger*, 641 F. Supp. 2d at 262. Such a finding is not clear error. ... [W]hen we consider the District Court's credibility finding together with all the other facts in this case, we conclude, with the District Court, that Defendants are not likely to prevail in their fair use defense.

CONCLUSION

In this preliminary injunction case, the District Court erred by not applying the equitable standard outlined by the Supreme Court in *eBay, Inc. v. MercExchange, LLC* and *Winter v. Natural Resources Defense Counsel*. Accordingly, we vacate and remand for further proceedings consistent with this opinion. ...

NOTES AND QUESTIONS

(1) *Permanent injunctions*. Section 502(a) provides that a court *may* "grant temporary and final injunctions on such terms as it may deem reasonable to prevent or restrain infringement of a copyright." Despite the permissive language of the statute, however, virtually all courts were willing to presume the existence of irreparable harm. "[T]he traditional formulation [was] to characterize as an abuse of discretion the denial of a permanent injunction when liability has been established and there is a threat of continuing infringement." 4 NIMMER ON COPYRIGHT § 14.06[B] (2010). Only occasionally did one see suggestions that "where great public injury would be worked by an injunction ... the courts could follow cases in other areas of property law, and award damages or a continuing royalty [*i.e.*, what would amount to a judicially created compulsory license] instead of an injunction in such special circumstances." *Id.*

(2) As the Second Circuit indicates in *Salinger*, the Supreme Court's opinion in *eBay v. MercExchange*, 547 U.S. 388 (2006), a patent case, has changed the game entirely. As stated in *Salinger*, *eBay* held that it was improper to presume irreparable harm in patent cases. At least three other Circuits have held, along with *Salinger*, that the *eBay* standard applies with equal force in copyright cases. *See CoxCom, Inc. v. Chaffee*, 536 F.3d 101, 112 (1st Cir. 2008); *Peter Letterese & Assocs. v. World Institute of Scientology Enters. Int'l*, 533 F.3d 1287, 1323 (11th Cir. 2008); *Christopher Phelps & Assocs. v. Galloway*, 492 F.3d 532, 543 (4th Cir. 2007). All three of those cases, however, involved *permanent* injunctions. *Salinger* is the first appellate opinion to address how the *eBay* standard should be applied in considering a *preliminary* injunction.

(3) *Preliminary injunctions*. Even before the Supreme Court's opinion in *eBay*, a majority of the Circuits were using the standard four-part preliminary injunction test familiar to you from other areas of the law. They considered:

(a) the significance of the threat of irreparable harm to the plaintiff if the injunction is not granted;

(b) the balance between this harm and the injury that granting the injunction would inflict on the defendant;

(c) the probability that the plaintiff will succeed on the merits; and

(d) promotion of the public interest.

For an example of the four-part test applied in a copyright case, see *Lakedreams v. Taylor*, 932 F.2d 1103 (5th Cir. 1991) (dispute over the design of a T-shirt illustrating the genealogy of the mythical Schitt family, "whose members had names that evoked one or another inelegant image").

(4) How is the traditional four-factor test affected by *eBay*? At the least, *eBay* seems to require an affirmative showing of irreparable harm (or at least the probability of irreparable harm). It seems that a mere "possibility" of irreparable harm is no longer sufficient, even if the other factors weigh in the movant's favor. Second, because *eBay* involved a permanent injunction, success on the merits was already established and was not expressly discussed. Instead, the *eBay* court lists an inadequate remedy at law as the second factor (moving the balance of hardships to the third factor). Does that mean an inadequate remedy at law is now a factor *in addition to* probable success on the merits? How is an inadequate remedy at law different from irreparable harm? Isn't it the lack of an adequate remedy at law that makes any likely harm "irreparable"?

(5) By contrast, prior to *eBay* the Second and Ninth Circuits, the nation's two premier copyright courts, both employed a "streamlined" preliminary injunction standard that specified more precisely how the various factors would be weighed against one another. *Salinger* notes the standard formerly employed by the Second Circuit: The movant must show (a) a possibility of irreparable

harm *and* (b) *either* (1) a likelihood of success on the merits or sufficiently serious questions going to the merits to make them a fair ground of litigation *and* a balance of hardships tipping decidedly in the movant's favor.

The Ninth Circuit used a slightly different standard, requiring that "a plaintiff seeking preliminary injunctive relief must demonstrate 'either a likelihood of success on the merits and the possibility of irreparable injury ... or that serious questions going to the merits were raised and that the balance of hardships tips sharply in its favor.'" *Cadence Design Sys., Inc. v. Avant! Corp.*, 125 F.3d 824, 826 (9th Cir. 1997), *quoting Sega Enters. Ltd. v. Accolade, Inc.*, 977 F.2d 1510, 1517 (9th Cir. 1992.) Was there really any significant difference between the Second and Ninth Circuit standards? What was the role of the public interest in the Second and Ninth Circuits?

(6) Despite the holding in *eBay*, the Second Circuit seems reluctant to abandon its previous standard entirely. Thus, in adapting the *eBay* standard to preliminary injunctions, the *Salinger* court expressly retains the second half of its pre-*eBay* formula, requiring "either (a) a likelihood of success on the merits or (b) sufficiently serious questions going to the merits to make them a fair ground for litigation and a balance of hardships tipping decidedly in the [plaintiff]'s favor." But then, under its third factor, the *Salinger* court states that a court may "issue the injunction only if the balance of hardships tips in the plaintiff's favor." What is the point of retaining the "balance of hardships" formulation in two different places in the test?

(7) *Irreparable injury*. Following *eBay* and *Salinger*, irreparable harm may no longer be presumed, but must be proven. In what circumstances will irreparable injury be found to be lacking? Some guidance may be found in those few pre-*eBay* cases in which the presumption of irreparable harm was found to be rebutted. Suppose, for example, that the plaintiff had known of the defendant's infringing uses for an extended period but had taken no legal steps until the present filing to bring them to an end. *See Bourne Co. v. Tower Records, Inc.*, 976 F.2d 99 (2d Cir. 1992) (no injunction re Disney's use of songs from movie "Pinocchio" in videocassette trailer advertisements); *Richard Feiner & Co. v. Turner Entertainment Co.*, 98 F.3d 33 (2d Cir. 1996) (delay in suing is "suggestive of a lack of irreparable harm"). The Ninth Circuit has stated (in *Cadence Design*) that there may be other situations, as well: *e.g.*, "[w]here the plaintiff has not been harmed, where any harm is *de minimis*, or where the defendant acted with innocent intent, relying on lack of copyright notice; *cf. Belushi v. Woodward*, 598 F. Supp. 36, 37 (D.D.C 1984) (denying injunction where one photograph in the defendant's book infringed the plaintiff's copyright)." 125 F.3d at 829.

(8) *Balance of hardships*. Under the third factor in *Salinger*, the court must consider the balance of hardships, and find that the probable harm to the plaintiff if the injunction is not issued outweighs the probable harm to the defendant if the injunction is issued wrongfully. Under what circumstances will a court find that this factor weighs in the defendant's favor? Note that prior to *eBay*, many courts were reluctant to rely on this factor. *See, e.g.*, *Apple*

Computer, Inc. v. Franklin Computer Corp., 714 F.2d 1240, 1255 (3d Cir. 1983) (if the balance of harm were given too much weight, "a knowing infringer would be permitted to construct its business around its infringement").

(9) *The public interest*. Generally, the "public interest" factor has not figured prominently in decisions about preliminary injunctive relief in copyright cases, even in those Circuits which retained it as an element of the four-part test. As one Circuit stated, "Since Congress has elected to grant certain exclusive rights to the owner of a copyright in a protected work, it is virtually axiomatic that the public interest can only be served by upholding copyright protections and, correspondingly, preventing the misappropriation of the skills, creative energies, and resources which are invested in the protected work." *Apple v. Franklin* at 1254.

Sometimes, however, the "public interest" factor (closely linked to considerations of copyright policy) may come into play. *See, e.g., Silverstein v. Penguin Putnam, Inc.*, 368 F.3d 77 (2d Cir. 2004) (even if plaintiff's selection of poems by Dorothy Parker was original, it would be an abuse of discretion to grant an injunction against publication of a book of Parker's complete poems that infringed that selection); *Abend v. MCA, Inc.*, 863 F.2d 1465, 1479 (9th Cir. 1988) (despite a finding of infringement, withdrawal of film *Rear Window* would cause public injury as well as injustice to the film's owners, and an award of damages would vindicate the plaintiff's interests), *aff'd on other grounds sub nom., Stewart v. Abend*, 495 U.S. 207 (1990) (discussed in § 5.01 above) (carefully describing Court of Appeals' discussion of remedies as "not relevant to the issue on which we granted *certiorari*"); *and Greenberg v. National Geographic Society*, 244 F.3d 1267, 1275 (11th Cir. 2001) (discussed in § 4.01 above) (urging the District Court "to consider alternatives, such as mandatory license fees, in lieu of foreclosing the public's computer-aided access to" *The Complete National Geographic* on CD-ROM).

(10) For the most practical of reasons, many copyright infringement cases are never litigated beyond the preliminary injunction stage. Perhaps for this reason, opinions on motions for preliminary injunctions sometimes seem difficult to distinguish from opinions on the merits. If *Salinger* goes to trial, what will be left to decide?

Does the frequency with which litigation is wound up, one way or another, after a grant of preliminary injunctive relief pose any risks to the integrity of copyright law? Can you identify any aspects of the infringement or fair use analysis in the *Salinger* opinion which seem controversial to you? Is a District Court more likely to "stretch" its legal analysis in a preliminary injunction opinion than in a final decision on the merits?

(11) *Burden of proof*. In *Perfect 10, Inc. v. Amazon.com, Inc.*, 487 F.3d 701, 714 (9th Cir. 2007), the court initially held that although defendant Google had the burden of introducing evidence on its affirmative defenses of fair use and § 512, Perfect 10 retained the ultimate burden of demonstrating a likelihood of overcoming those defenses in order to obtain a preliminary injunction. Several months later, however, the court amended its opinion to hold that once

Perfect 10 had satisfied its burden of demonstrating a likelihood of success on the merits, the burden shifted to Google to demonstrate a likelihood of success on its affirmative defense. 508 F.3d 1146, 1158 (9th Cir. 2007). Which party *should* bear the burden when an affirmative defense is raised in defense to a motion for a preliminary injunction?

(12) *Scope of the injunction*. The *Perfect 10* court also held that even though § 411(a) requires registration before an infringement suit may be commenced, a preliminary injunction could issue as to both registered and unregistered works. *Id.* at 1154 n.1, citing *Olan Mills, Inc. v. Linn Photo Co.*, 23 F.3d 1345, 1349 (8th Cir. 1994). This holding is consistent with the Supreme Court's subsequent ruling in *Reed Elsevier, Inc. v. Muchnick*, 130 S. Ct. 1237 (2010), that failure to register a work does not deprive the court of subject-matter jurisdiction. See § 6.03 of the casebook. May a court also enjoin copying of works that have not yet been created? In answering, consider the language of the statute itself, which empowers a court to issue injunctions "on such terms as it may deem reasonable to prevent or restrain infringement of *a copyright*." § 502(a) (emphasis added). *See Pacific & Southern Co. v. Duncan*, 572 F. Supp. 1186 (N.D. Ga. 1983) (videotaping of future news broadcasts by clipping service enjoined); *Walt Disney Co. v. Powell*, 897 F.2d 565 (D.C. Cir. 1990) (in view of "history of continuing infringement and a significant threat of future infringement," trial court properly enjoined future infringement of works owned by plaintiff but not in suit). What steps should be taken by counsel for the successful plaintiff in an infringement action, prior to the entry of judgment, to maximize the client's protection under any proposed injunctive relief?

(11) *Injunctions and technology*. Should grants of preliminary injunctive relief be granted more sparingly in cases involving dissemination of expression through new technologies? For example, the trial court in the *Betamax* case, *Universal City Studios, Inc. v. Sony Corp. of America*, 480 F. Supp. 429, 464 (C.D. Cal. 1979), *rev'd*, 659 F.2d 963 (9th Cir. 1981), *rev'd*, 464 U.S. 417 (1984), denied the plaintiffs' request for a preliminary injunction stating that "[t]his is a doubtful case [and a]n injunction would deprive the public of a new technology capable of noninfringing uses." That result was that VCRs were widely adopted by the public before the Supreme Court rendered its decision. But in *A&M Records, Inc. v. Napster, Inc.*, 239 F.3d 1004 (9th Cir. 2001), the Ninth Circuit dismissed the defendants' suggestion that it should impose a compulsory royalty payment schedule rather than restricting the scope of its services.

(12) *Prior restraint*. Are preliminary injunctions in copyright cases constitutionally permissible, in any case? See the provocative article by Mark Lemley & Eugene Volokh, *Freedom of Speech and Injunctions in Intellectual Property Cases*, 48 Duke L.J. 147 (1998), cited in *Salinger*, questioning preliminary injunctions in copyright cases under the "prior restraint" doctrine. How — if at all — should courts take account of the professors' argument? Should it matter if the injunction in question is being sought in an effort to silence speech with which the plaintiff disagrees for political or ideological

reasons? *See, e.g.*, *Religious Tech. Ctr. v. F.A.C.T.NET, Inc.*, 901 F. Supp. 1519 (D. Col. 1995) (action brought by the Church of Scientology against critics distributing its proprietary scriptures on the Internet).

Consider the initial ruling in *SunTrust Bank v. Houghton Mifflin Co.*, 252 F.3d 1165 (11th Cir. 2001). After hearing the appeal from the grant of preliminary injunctive relief, an Eleventh Circuit panel ruled, from the bench, that "the entry of a preliminary injunction in this copyright case was an abuse of discretion in that it represents an unlawful prior restraint in violation of the First Amendment." (In its subsequent written opinion at 268 F.3d 1257, however, the court did not mention the prior restraint doctrine.)

(13) *Miscellaneous*. By virtue of § 502(a)'s express reference to 28 U.S.C. § 1498, neither a preliminary nor a permanent injunction may issue against the United States. Once issued, an injunction may be served and enforced anywhere in the United States. § 502(b).

[C] Damages

[2] Statutory or "In Lieu" Damages

USAGE: On page 934, ADD the following paragraph to the end of Note (3):

Note that under §§ 401(d) and 402(d), a defendant cannot claim to be an "innocent" infringer for purposes of calculating statutory damages if proper notice appears on the copies or phonorecords of the work to which the defendant had access. *See, e.g.*, *Maverick Recording Co. v. Harper*, 598 F.3d 193 (5th Cir. 2010) (rule satisfied if published CDs bore proper notice, even though infringing audio files which defendant downloaded did not; subjective intent is irrelevant).

USAGE: On page 935, ADD the following note after the end of Note (5):

(5A) How should statutory damages for peer-to-peer file sharing be calculated? In *Capitol Records, Inc. v. Thomas-Rasset*, 680 F. Supp. 2d 1045 (D. Minn. 2010), defendant was found to have willfully infringed 24 songs. The first jury awarded statutory damages of $9,250 per song, for a total award of $222,000. After the court ordered a new trial (for incorrect jury instructions on liability), the second jury awarded statutory damages of $80,000 per song, for a total award of $1,920,000. The trial judge held that the award was grossly excessive, and it granted a remittitur to $2,250 per song (three times the minimum amount of statutory damages), for a total award of $54,000. *See also Sony BMG Music Ent'mt v. Tenenbaum*, 93 U.S.P.Q.2d (BNA) 1867 (2009) (30 songs infringed; jury award of $22,500 per song, for a total award of $675,000).

USAGE: On page 935, SUBSTITUTE the following for the first paragraph of Note (6):

(6) *The number of infringements.* In addition to assessing damages for a willful infringement, the court in *Krypton* was confronted with the problem of deciding the number of infringements that would serve as the basis for statutory damages. In this regard, consider those portions of § 504(c)(1) and its legislative history that concern multiple infringements. Are they intended to govern situations in which the copyright holder joins, in a single action, a series of claims for infringements of his/her rights in multiple works? If not, what situations are governed by § 504(c)(1)? *See Bryant v. Media Right Prods.*, 603 F.3d 135 (2d Cir. 2010) (one award of statutory damages per album, as a "compilation," rather than per song). *But see WB Music Corp. v. RTV Communication Group, Inc.*, 445 F.3d 538 (2d Cir. 2006) (§ 504(c)(1) applies only to a compilation made by the copyright owner, and does not apply to a new compilation of 13 songs made by the defendant, so separate awards of statutory damages per song was appropriate). What if eight registrations are obtained for eight episodes of a popular television program, where the basic plot continues throughout all eight episodes? Would your answer change if a book written as a unitary work was later adapted for television as a series of eight episodes? *See Twin Peaks Prods., Inc. v. Publ'ns Int'l, Ltd.*, 996 F.2d 1366, 1381 (2d Cir. 1993). You also may wish to consider a later episode in the *Feltner* saga itself: *MCA Television Ltd. v. Feltner*, 89 F.3d 766 (11th Cir. 1996) (TV series episodes considered as separate works for statutory damages purposes, leading to a total award of $9 million and a vigorous dissent).

USAGE: On page 936, SUBSTITUTE the following for the second paragraph of Note (7):

Do you agree that economic viability should be the standard? What does it mean to say that a work is economically viable? And who is to make this determination? *See also Bryant* (refusing to recognize an exception to the "one award per compilation" rule for parts of a compilation having independent economic value).

PART FIVE

CUMULATIVE BIBLIOGRAPHY

SYNOPSIS

Chapters 1 and 12
COPYRIGHT'S LANDSCAPE AND HORIZON

Reference Works

H. Abrams, The Law of Copyright §§ 1.1 to 1.35, 19.1 to 19.24 (2008)

P. Goldstein, Goldstein on Copyright §§ 1.0 to 1.16, 18.0, 18.3, 18.6 to 18.9 (3d ed. 2005)

M. Leaffer, Understanding Copyright Law §§ 1.01 to 1.14, 12.01 to 12.14 (5th ed. 2010)

M. Nimmer & D. Nimmer, Nimmer on Copyright, 1-OV, §§ 1.12, 17.01 to 17.13, 18.01 to 18.09 (2010)

W. Patry, Patry on Copyright §§ 1:1 to 1:115, 2:1 to 2:63, 23:1 to 23:76, 24:1 to 24:50 (2010)

Copyright and Related Bodies of Law

M. Adelman & D. Dunner, Patent Law Perspectives (2nd ed. 1982 & Supp. 2009)

L. Altman & M. Pollack, Callmann on Unfair Competition, Trademarks, and Monopolies (4th ed. 2007 & Supp. 2009)

F. Cate, Privacy in the Information Age (1997)

D. Chisum, Patents (1997 & Supp. 2010)

A. Gilson Lalonde, Gilson on Trademarks (rev. ed. 2007 & Supp. 2010)

R. Harmon, Patents and the Federal Circuit (9th ed. 2009)

M. Jager, Trade Secrets Law (1985 & Supp. 2010)

R. Lind, P. Acton, T. Selz, & M. Simensky, Entertainment Law: Legal Concepts and Business Practices (3d ed. 2006 & Supp. 2009)

A. Lindey, Lindey on Entertainment, Publishing and the Arts: Agreements and the Law (3d ed. 2004 & Supp. 2010)

J.T. McCarthy, McCarthy on Trademarks and Unfair Competition (4th ed. 1996 & Supp. 2010)

C.R. McManis, Intellectual Property and Unfair Competition in a Nutshell (6th ed. 2009)

R. Milgrim, Milgrim on Licensing (1990 & Supp. 2010)

R. Milgrim, Milgrim on Trade Secrets (1997 & Supp. 2010)

J. Mills, R. Highley & D. Reiley, Patent Law Fundamentals (2d ed. 2002 & Supp. 2010)

C. Moy, Moy's Walker on Patents (4th ed. 2003 & Supp. 2009)

M. Petry, Taxation of Intellectual Property and Technology (2006 & Supp. 2010)

F. Schechter, The Historical Foundations of the Law Relating to Trademarks (1925)

D. Welkowitz, Trademark Dilution: Federal, State and International Law (2002 & Supp. 2009)

Karjala, *Distinguishing Patent and Copyright Subject Matter*, 35 Comm. L. Rev. 439 (2003)

Kwall, *The Attribution Right in the United States: Caught in the Crossfire Between Copyright and Section 43(A)*, 77 Wash. L. Rev. 985 (2002)

Litman, *Copyright Law as Communications Policy: Convergence of Paradigms and Cultures War Stories*, 20 Cardozo Arts & Ent. L.J. 337 (2002)

Long, *Information Costs in Patent and Copyright*, 90 Va. L. Rev. 465 (2004)

Welkowitz & Ochoa, *Teaching Rights of Publicity: Blending Copyright and Trademark, Common Law and Statutes, and Domestic and Foreign Law*, 52 St. Louis U. L.J. 905 (2008)

Copyright Law History

A. Birrell, Seven Lectures on the Law and History of Copyright in Books (1971)

B. Bugbee, Genesis of American Patent and Copyright Law (1967)

A. Clark, The Movement for International Copyright in Nineteenth Century America (1960)

G. Curtis, A Treatise on the Law of Copyright (1847)

R. Deazley, On the Origin of the Right to Copy: Charting the Movement of Copyright Law in Eighteenth-Century Britain (1695–1775) (2004)

R. Deazley, Rethinking Copyright: History, Theory, and Language (2006)

E. Drone, A Treatise on the Law of Property in Intellectual Productions (1879)

D. Eisenstein, The Printing Revolution in Early Modern Europe (1993)

J. Feather, Publishing, Piracy and Politics: An Historical Study of Copyright in Britain (1994)

J. Gaines, Contested Culture: The Image, the Voice, and the Law (1991)

P. Goldstein, Copyright's Highway: From Gutenberg to the Celestial Jukebox (2d ed. 2003)

N. Netanel, Copyright's Paradox (2008)

D.P. Nord, J.S. Rubin & M. Schudson, The Enduring Book: Print Culture in Postwar America (2009)

L. R. Patterson, Copyright in Historical Perspective (1968)

F. Pierce, A UNIFIED FIELD THEORY OF COPYRIGHT (1870)

M. Rose, AUTHORS AND OWNERS: THE INVENTION OF COPYRIGHT (1993)

E. Samuels, THE ILLUSTRATED STORY OF COPYRIGHT (2000)

D. Saunders, AUTHORSHIP AND COPYRIGHT (1992)

C. Seville, LITERARY COPYRIGHT REFORM IN EARLY VICTORIAN ENGLAND: THE FRAMING OF THE 1842 COPYRIGHT ACT (1999)

B. Sherman & A. Strowel, OF AUTHORS AND ORIGINS: ESSAYS ON COPYRIGHT LAW (1994)

T. Solberg, COPYRIGHT IN CONGRESS, 1789–1904: A BIBLIOGRAPHY, AND CHRONOLOGICAL RECORD OF ALL PROCEEDINGS (1905)

E. Walterscheid, THE NATURE OF THE INTELLECTUAL PROPERTY CLAUSE: A STUDY IN HISTORICAL PERSPECTIVE (2002)

L. Zemer, THE IDEA OF AUTHORSHIP IN COPYRIGHT (2007)

Abrams, *The Historic Foundation of American Copyright Law: Exploding the Myth of Common Law Copyright,* 29 Wayne L. Rev. 1119 (1983)

Aoki, *Authors, Inventors and Trademark Owners: Private Intellectual Property and the Public Domain (Parts I & II),* 18 Colum.-VLA J.L. & Arts, 1 & 191 (1994–1995)

Aoki, *Neocolonialism, Anticommons Property, and Biopiracy in the (Not-So-Brave) New World Order of International Intellectual Property*, 6 Ind. J. Global L. Stud. 11 (1998)

Austin, *Does the Copyright Clause Mandate Isolationism?*, 26 Colum.-VLA J.L. & Arts 17 (2002)

Band & Weinstein, *The Blackmun Papers: A Peek Behind the Scenes of a Quarter Century of Supreme Court Jurisprudence*, 28 Colum. J.L. & Arts 315 (2005)

Baker, *First Amendment Limits on Copyright*, 55 Vand. L. Rev. 13 (2003)

Bedingfield, *Copyrighting Medieval Literature: Editing and Publishing the Pre-modern Public Domain*, 28 Col. J. Law & Arts 213 (2005)

Benkler, *Through the Looking Glass: Alice and the Constitutional Foundations of the Public Domain*, 66 Law & Contemp. Probs. 173 (2003)

Bentley, *R. v The Author: From Death Penalty to Community Service,* 32 Colum. J.L. & Arts 1 (2008)

Bently, *Copyright, Translations, and Relations Between Britain and India in the Nineteenth and Early Twentieth Centuries*, 82 Chi.-Kent L. Rev. 1181 (2007)

Birnhack, *The Idea of Progress in Copyright Law,* 1 Buff. Intell. Prop. L.J. 3 (2001)

Bracha, *The Ideology of Authorship Revisited: Authors, Markets, and Liberal Values in Early American Copyright,* 118 Yale L.J. 186 (2008)

Cotter, *Gutenberg's Legacy: Copyright, Censorship, and Religious Pluralism*, 91 Cal. L. Rev. 323 (2003)

Crawford, *Pre-Constitutional Copyright Statutes,* 23 Bull. Copyright Soc'y 11 (1975)

Deazley, Capitol Records v. Naxos of America *(2005): Just Another Footnote in the History of Copyright?*, 53 J. Copyright Soc'y 23 (2005)

Dutfield & Suthersanen, *The Innovation Dilemma: Intellectual Property and the Historical Legacy of Cumulative Creativity*, Intell. Prop. Q. 379 (Fall 2004)

Eilenberg, *Mortal Pages: Wordsworth and the Reform of Copyright,* 56 Eng. Lit. Hist. 351 (1989)

Epstein, Liberty v. Property? *Cracks in the Foundation of Copyright Law*, 42 San Diego L. Rev. 1 (2005)

Farley, *The Lingering Effects of Copyright's Response to the Invention of Photography*, 65 U. Pitt. L Rev. 385 (2004)

Foster, *Prelude to Compatibility between Human Rights and Intellectual Property*, 9 Chi. J. Int'l L. 171 (2008)

Geller, *Copyright History and the Future: What's Culture Got to Do With It?*, 40 J. Copyright Soc'y 209 (2000)

Ginsburg, *A Tale of Two Copyrights: Literary Property in Revolutionary France and America,* 64 Tul. L. Rev. 991 (1990)

Ginsburg, *How Copyright Got a Bad Name for Itself*, 26 Colum.-VLA J.L. & Arts 61 (2002)

Ginsburg, *The Author's Place in the Future of Copyright,* 45 Willamette L. Rev. 381 (2008)

Ginsburg, *"Une Chose Publique"?: The Author's Domain and the Public Domain in Early British, French and U.S. Copyright Law*, 65 Cambridge L.J. 636 (2006)

Goldman, *The History of U.S.A. Copyright Law Revision from 1901 to 1954*, Copyright Law Revision Study No. 1 (1960)

Goldstein, *Copyright's Commons*, 29 Col. J. L & Arts 1 (2005)

Hamilton, *Copyright at the Supreme Court: A Jurisprudence of Deference*, 40 J. Copyright Soc'y 317 (2000)

Hughes, *Copyright and Incomplete Historiographies of Piracy, Propertization, and Thomas Jefferson*, 79 S. Cal. L. Rev. 993 (2006)

Hughes, *Locke's 1694 Memorandum (and More Incomplete Copyright Historiographies)*, 27 Cardozo Arts & Ent. L.J. 555 (2010)

Hulsebosch, *An Empire of Law: Chancellor Kent and the Revolution in Books in the Early Republic,* 60 Ala. L. Rev. 377 (2009)

Jaszi, *Towards a Theory of Copyright: The Metamorphoses of Authorship,* 1991 Duke L.J. 455

Joyce, *"A Curious Chapter in the History of Judicature":* Wheaton v. Peters *and the Rest of the Story (of Copyright in the New Republic)*, 42 Hous. L. Rev. 325 (2005)

Joyce, *Copyright (and Its Master) in Historical Perspective*, 10 J. Intell. Prop. L. 239 (2003)

Joyce, *The Rise of the Supreme Court Reporter: An Institutional Perspective on Marshall Court Ascendancy,* 83 Mich. L. Rev. 1291 (1985)

Kastenmeier, *Copyright in an Era of Technological Change: A Political Perspective,* 14 Colum.-VLA J.L. & Arts 1 (1989)

Kidwell, *Congressman Robert Kastenmeier and Professor John Stedman: A Thirty-Five Year Relationship,* 55 Law & Contemp. Probs. 129 (1992)

Kitch, *Property Rights in Inventions, Writings, and Marks,* 13 Harv. J. L. & Pub. Pol'y 119 (1990)

Lauriat, *Charles Reade's Roles in the Drama of Victorian Dramatic Copyright,* 33 Colum. J.L. & Arts 35 (2009)

Lessig, *Copyright's First Amendment,* 48 UCLA L. Rev. 1057 (2001)Leval, *An Assembly of Idiots?*, 34 Conn. L. Rev. 1049 (2002)

Litman, *Copyright as Myth,* 53 U. of Pitts. L. Rev. 235 (1991)

Litman, *Copyright, Compromise and Legislative History,* 72 Cornell L. Rev. 857 (1987)

Litman, *Creative Reading*, 70 Law & Contemp. Probs. 175 (2007)

Litman, *The Public Domain*, 39 Emory L.J. 965 (1990)

Litman, *War and Peace (in Copyright),* 53 J. Copyright Soc'y 1 (2005)

McGinty, *First Amendment Rights to Protected Expression: What Are The Traditional Contours of Copyright Law?,* 23 Berkeley Tech. L.J. 1099 (2008)

Merges, *Symposium on Law in the Twentieth Century: One Hundred Years of Solicitude: Intellectual Property Law, 1900–2000,* 88 Calif. L. Rev. 2187 (2000)

Mosoff, *Is Copyright Property?,* 42 San Diego L. Rev. 29 (2005)

Nachbar, *Constructing Copyright's Mythology*, 6 Green Bag 2d 37 (2002)

Netanel, Maharam of Padua v. Guistiniani: *The Sixteenth Century Origins of the Jewish Law of Copyright*, 44 Hous. L. Rev. 821 (2007)

Ochoa, *1984 and Beyond: Two Decades of Copyright Law*, 20 Santa Clara Computer & High Tech. L.J. 167 (2003)

Ochoa & Rose, *The Anti-Monopoly Origins of the Patent and Copyright Clause*, 49 J. Copyright Soc'y 675 (2002)

Okediji, *Through the Years: The Supreme Court and the Copyright Clause*, 30 Wm. Mitchell L. Rev. 1633 (2004)

Olson, *The Iron Law of Consensus: Congressional Responses to Proposed Copyright Reforms Since the 1909 Act,* 36 J. Copyright Soc'y 109 (1989)

Oman, *Bob Kastenmeier and the Legislative Process:* Sui Generis *and Proud of It,* 55 Law & Contemp. Probs. 241 (1992)

Oman, *The Copyright Clause: "A Charter For A Living People,"* 17 U. Balt. L. Rev. 99 (1987)

O'Rourke, *A Brief History of Author-Publisher Relations and the Outlook for the 21st Century*, 50 J. Copyright Soc. 425 (2003)

Patterson, *Copyright and "the Exclusive Right" of Authors,* 1 J. Intell. Prop. L. 1 (1993)

Patterson & Birch, *A Unified Theory of Copyright*, 46 Hous. L. Rev. 215 (Joyce ed. 2009)

Patterson & Joyce, *Copyright in 1791: An Essay Concerning the Founders' View of the Copyright Power Granted to Congress in Article I, Section 8, Clause 8 of the U.S. Constitution*, 52 Emory L.J. 101 (2003)

Patterson & Joyce, *Monopolizing the Law: The Scope of Copyright Protection for Law Reports and Statutory Compilations,* 36 UCLA L. Rev. 719 (1989)

Patterson, *The Statute of Anne: Copyright Misconstrued,* 3 Harv. J. on Legis. 223 (1966)

Patterson, *Understanding the Copyright Clause*, 40 J. Copyright Soc'y 365 (2000)

Picker, *From Edison to the Broadcast Flag: Mechanisms of Consent and Refusal and the Propertization of Copyright*, 70 U. Chi. L. Rev. 281 (2003)

Prager, *The Early Growth and Influence of Intellectual Property*, 34 J. Pat. Off. Soc'y 106 (1952)

Raskind, *Grading the Performance of a Legislator,* 55 Law & Contemp. Probs. 267 (1992)

Reese, *Is the Public Domain Permanent? Congress' Power to Grant Exclusive Rights in Unpublished Public Domain Works*, 30 Colum. J.L. & Arts 531 (2007)

Remington, *Robert W. Kastenmeier: Copyright Legislator Par Excellence,* 55 Law & Contemp. Probs. 297 (1992)

Rose, *The Public Domain: Nine-Tenths of the Law: The English Copyright Debates and the Rhetoric of the Public Domain,* 66 Law & Contemp. Probs. 225 (2003)

Samuelson, *Economic and Constitutional Influences on Copyright Law in the United States*, 23 Eur. Intell. Prop. Rev. 409 (2001)

Seville, *Authors as Copyright Campaigners: Mark Twain's Legacy*, 55 J. Copyright Soc'y 283 (2008)

Suchman, *Invention and Ritual: Notes on the Interrelation of Magic and Intellectual Property in Preliterate Societies,* 89 Colum. L. Rev. 1264 (1989)

Temple, Johnson & Macpherson, *Cultural Authority and the Construction of Literary Property,* 5 Yale J. of L. & Human. 355 (1993)

VerSteeg, *The Roman Law Roots of Copyright*, 59 Md. L. Rev. 522 (2000)

Walterscheid, *The Preambular Argument: The Dubious Premise of* Eldred v. Ashcroft, 44 Idea 331 (2004)

Walterscheid, *Understanding the Copyright Act of 1790 — The Issue of Common Law Copyright in America and the Modern Interpretation of the Copyright Power,* 53 J. Copyright Soc'y 313 (2005)

Wicher, *The Ghost of* Donaldson v. Beckett: *An Inquiry into the Constitutional Distribution of Powers over the Law of Literary Property in the United States (Parts I and II),* 9 Bull. Copyright Soc'y 102 & 194 (1961–62)

Zemer, *The Copyright Moment*, 43 San Diego L. Rev. 247 (2006)

Zimmerman, *Authorship without Ownership: Reconsidering Incentives in a Digital Age*, 52 DePaul L. Rev. 1121 (2003)

Copyright in a Changing World

J. Band & M. Katoh, INTERFACES ON TRIAL: INTELLECTUAL PROPERTY AND INTEROPERABILITY IN THE GLOBAL SOFTWARE INDUSTRY (1995)

R. Barker, COPYRIGHT: THE NEW INTERNATIONAL CONVENTIONS (1971)

A. Bogsch, THE LAW OF COPYRIGHT UNDER THE UNIVERSAL COPYRIGHT CONVENTION (3d rev. ed. 1968)

P. Drahos with J. Braithwaite, INFORMATION FEUDALISM: WHO OWNS THE KNOWLEDGE ECONOMY (2003)

M. Ficsor, THE LAW OF COPYRIGHT AND THE INTERNET: THE 1996 WIPO TREATIES, THEIR INTERPRETATION AND IMPLEMENTATION (2002)

P.E. Geller, INTERNATIONAL COPYRIGHT LAW AND PRACTICE (2003 & Supp. 2008)

D. Gervais, THE TRIPS AGREEMENT: DRAFTING HISTORY AND ANALYSIS (3d ed. 2008)

C. Hesse, PUBLISHING AND CULTURAL POLITICS IN REVOLUTIONARY PARIS, 1789–1810 (1991)

T. Kupferman & M. Foner, eds., UNIVERSAL COPYRIGHT CONVENTION ANALYZED (1955)

S. Ladas, THE INTERNATIONAL PROTECTION OF LITERARY AND ARTISTIC PROPERTY (1938)

C. Masouye, GUIDE TO THE BERNE CONVENTION (WIPO 1978)

C. Masouye, GUIDE TO THE ROME CONVENTION AND TO THE PHONOGRAMS CONVENTION (WIPO 1981)

J. Reinbothe, THE WIPO TREATIES, 1996: THE WIPO COPYRIGHT TREATY AND THE WIPO PERFORMANCE AND PHONOGRAMS TREATY: COMMENTARY AND LEGAL ANALYSIS (2002)

S. Ricketson & J. Ginsburg, INTERNATIONAL COPYRIGHT AND NEIGHBOURING RIGHTS: THE BERNE CONVENTION AND BEYOND (2d ed. 2006)

M. Ryan, KNOWLEDGE DIPLOMACY: GLOBAL COMPETITION AND THE POLITICS OF INTELLECTUAL PROPERTY (1998)

T. Solberg, THE PRESENT INTERNATIONAL COPYRIGHT SITUATION: THREATS OF REPRISAL (1934)

T. Solberg, THE UNITED STATES AND INTERNATIONAL COPYRIGHT (1929)

S. Stewart & H. Sandison, INTERNATIONAL COPYRIGHT AND NEIGHBOURING RIGHTS (2d ed. 1989)

Antezana, *The European Union Internet Copyright Directive as Even More Than It Envisions: Toward a Supra-EU Harmonization of Copyright Policy and Theory*, 26 B.C. Int'l & Comp. L. Rev. 415 (2003)

Austin, *The Berne Convention as a Canon of Construction: Moral Rights after Dastar,* 61 N.Y.U. Ann. Surv. Am. L. 111 (2005)

Barbosa, *International Copyright Law and Litigation: A Mechanism for Improvement*, 11 Marq. Intell. Prop. L. Rev. 82 (2007)

Barbosa, *Revisiting International Copyright Law*, 8 Barry L. Rev. 43 (2007)

Bitton, *Exploring European Union Copyright Policy Through the Lens of the Database Directive,* 23 Berkeley Tech. L.J. 1411 (2008)

Boytha, *Some Private International Law Aspects of the Protection of Authors' Rights,* 24 Copyright 399 (Oct. 1988)

Braegelmann, *Copyright Law in and under the Constitution: A Comparison between American and German Constitutional Copyright Law,* 27 Cardozo Arts & Ent. L.J. 99 (2009)

Brenner-Beck, *Do As I Say, Not As I Did (Economic Development of Less Developed Countries and the Protection of Intellectual Property),* 11 UCLA Pac. Basin L.J. 84 (1992)

Burrell & Weatherall, *Export Controversy? Reactions to the Copyright Provisions of the U.S.-Australia Free Trade Agreement: Lessons for U.S. Trade Policy,* 2008 U. Ill. J.L. Tech. & Pol'y 259

Carson, *Making the "Making Available" Right Available,* 33 Colum. J.L. & Arts 135 (2010)

Cate, *Global Information Policymaking and Domestic Law*, 1 Ind. J. Global Leg. Stud. 467 (1994)

Chinni, *Droit D'Auteur Versus the Economics of Copyright: Implications for American Law of Accession to the Berne Convention,* 14 W. New Eng. L. Rev. 145 (1992)

Choi, *Development of Copyright Protection in Korea: Its History, Inherent Limits, and Suggested Solutions*, 28 Brooklyn J. Int'l L. 643 (2003)

Cornish, *The International Relations of Intellectual Property,* 52 Cambridge L.J. 16 (1993)

Crawford, *First Do No Harm: The Problem of Spyware,* 20 Berkeley Tech. L. J. 1433 (2005)

Crawford, *Internet Think*, 5 J. Telecomm. & High Tech. L.467 (2007)

Crawford, *Network Rules*, 70 Law & Contemp. Probs. 512 (2007)

Crawford, *Shortness of Vision: Regulatory Ambition in the Digital Age,* 74 Fordham L. Rev. 695 (2005)

Crawford, *The Internet and the Project of Communications Law*, 55 UCLA L. Rev. 359 (2007)

Cronin, *Genius in a Bottle: Perfume, Copyright and Human Perception*, 56 J. Copyright Soc'y 427 (2009)

Das, *Intellectual Property Dispute, GATT, WIPO: Of Playing by the Game Rules and Rules of the Game*, 35 Idea 149 (1994)

Davis, *Some Realism About Indigenism*, 11 Cardozo J. Int. & Comp. L. 815 (2003)

Dietz, *The Harmonization of Copyright in the European Community,* 16 IIC 379 (1985)

Dimmock & Punniyamoorthy, *Fair Dealing: A User Right or a Defence,* 22 Can. Intell. Prop. Rev. 11 (2005)

Dinwoodie, *A New Copyright Order: Why National Courts Should Create Global Norms,* 149 U. Pa. L. Rev. 469 (2000)

Dinwoodie, *The Development and Incorporation of International Norms in the Formation of Copyright Law,* 62 Ohio St. L.J. 733 (2001)

Dinwoodie, *International Intellectual Property Litigation: A Vehicle for Resurgent Comparativist Thought?,* 49 Am. J. Comp. L. 429 (2001)

Dittrich, *The Practical Application of the Rome Convention,* 26 Bull. Copyright Soc'y 287 (1979)

Doherty & Griffiths, *The Harmonization of European Union Copyright Law for the Digital Age*, 22 E.I.P.R. 17 (2000)

Dox, *Trade, Competition and Intellectual Property — TRIPS and its Antitrust Counterparts,* 29 Vand. J. Transnat'l L. 481 (1996)

Dreier, *The Role of the ECJ for the Development of Copyright in the European Community*, 54 J. Copyright Soc'y 183 (2007)

Dreier & von Lewinski, *The European Community's Activities in the Field of Copyright,* 39 J. Copyright Soc'y 96 (1991)

Dreyfuss & Lowenfeld, *Two Achievements of the Uruguay Round: Putting TRIPS and Dispute Settlement Together,* 27 Va. J. Int'l L. 275 (1997)

Dutfield, *TRIPS-Related Aspects of Traditional Knowledge*, 33 Case West. Res. J. Int'l L. 233 (2001)

Final Report of the Ad Hoc Working Group on U.S. Adherence to the Berne Convention, reprinted in 10 Colum.-VLA J.L. & Arts 513 (1986)

Fitzpatrick, *Copyright Imbalance: U.S. and Australian Responses to the WIPO Digital Copyright Treaty*, 22 E.I.P.R. 214 (2000)

Garilov, *The Legal Protection of Folklore,* 20 Copyright 76 (1984)

Garza Barbosa, *The Philosophical Approaches to Intellectual Property and Legal Transplants, The Mexican Supreme Court and NAFTA Article 1705,* 31 Hous. J. Int'l L. 515 (2009)

Geiger, *From Berne to National Law, Via the Copyright Directive: The Dangerous Mutations of the Three-Step Test,* 29 E.I.P.R. 486 (2007)

Geller, *Can the GATT Incorporate Berne Whole?*, 4 World Intell. Prop. Rep. 193 (1990)

Geller, *Conflicts of Law in Cyberspace: Rethinking International Copyright,* J. Copyright Soc'y 103 (1996)

Geller, *Copyright Protection in the Berne Union: Analyzing the Issues,* 5 Intell. Prop. J. 1 (1989)

Geller, *Harmonizing Copyright-Contract Conflicts Analyses,* 25 Copyright 49 (1989)

Geller, *Legal Transplants in International Copyright: Some Problems of Method,* 13 UCLA Pac. Basin L.J. 199 (1994)

Gervais, *Spiritual But Not Intellectual?: The Protection of Sacred Intangible Traditional Knowledge*, 11 Cardozo J. Int. & Comp. L. 467 (2003)

Gibbons & Wang, *Striking the "Rights" Balance Among Private Incentives and Public Fair Uses in the United States and China,* 7 J. Marshall Rev. Intell. Prop. L. 488 (2008)

Ginsburg, *Colors in Conflicts: Moral Rights and the Foreign Exploitation of Colorized U.S. Motion Pictures,* 36 J. Copyright Soc'y 81 (1988)

Ginsburg, *International Copyright: From a "Bundle" of National Copyright Laws to a Supranational Code?*, 40 J. Copyright Soc'y 265 (2000)

Ginsburg, *The Concept of Authorship in Comparative Copyright Law*, 52 DePaul L. Rev. 1063 (2003)

Ginsburg & Kernochan, *One Hundred and Two Years Later: The United States Adheres to the Berne Convention,* 13 Colum.-VLA J.L. & Arts 1 (1988)

Ginsburg & Sirinelli, *Author, Creation and Adaptation in Private International Law and French Domestic Law: Reflections Based on the* Huston *Case (i),* 150 Revue Internationale de Droit D'Auteur [R.I.D.A.] 2 (1991)

Goswami & Nandi, *Naming the Unnamed: Intellectual Property Rights of Women Artists from India,* 16 Am. U.J. Gender Soc. Pol'y & L. 257 (2008)

Graves, *Globalization, Treaty Powers, and the Limits of the Intellectual Property Clause*, 50 J. Copyright Soc'y 199 (2003)

Gutsche, *Equitable Remuneration for Authors in Germany — How the German Copyright Act Secures Their Rewards*, 50 J. Copyright Soc'y 257 (2003)

Halbert, *The World Intellectual Property Organization: Past, Present and Future*, 54 J. Copyright Soc'y 253 (2007)

Hamilton, *The TRIPS Agreement: Imperialistic, Outdated, and Overprotective,* 29 Vand. J. Transnat'l L. 613 (1996)

Handler & Rolph, *"A Real Pea Souper": The Panel Case and the Development of the Fair Dealing Defences to Copyright Infringement in Australia*, 27 Melbourne U.L. Rev. 381 (2003)

Hayhurst, *The Canadian Supreme Court on Copyright:* CCH Canadian Ltd. v. Law Society of Upper Canada, 41 Can. Bus. L.J. 134 (2004)

Heald, *Mowing the Playing Field: Addressing Information Distortion and Asymmetry in the TRIPS Game*, 88 Minn. L. Rev. 249 (2003)

Helfer, *Adjudicating Copyright Claims Under the TRIPs Agreement: The Case for a European Human Rights Analogy,* 39 Harv. Int'l L.J. 357 (1998)

Hennessey, *Protection of Intellectual Property in China (30 Years and More): A Personal Reflection*, 46 Hous. L. Rev. 1257 (2009)

Huet & Ginsburg, *Computer Programs in Europe: A Comparative Analysis of the 1991 EC Software Directive,* 30 Colum. J. Transnat'l L. 327 (1992)

Hugenholtz, *Why the Copyright Directive is Unimportant, and Possibly Invalid*, 22 Eur. Intell. Prop. Rev. 499 (2000)

Jacobs, *Work-for-Hire and the Moral Right Dilemma in the European Community: A U.S. Perspective,* 16 B.C. Int'l & Comp. L. Rev. 29 (1993)

Jaszi, *GATT or WIPO? New Ways in the International Protection of Intellectual Property (Symposium at Ringberg Castle, July 13–16, 1989)* (F.-K. Beier & G. Schricker, eds., IIC Studies 1989)

Jaszi & Woodmansee, *The Ethical Reaches of Authorship,* 95 S. Atlantic 947 (1996)

Jehoram, *The Nature of Neighboring Rights of Performing Artists, Phonogram Producers and Broadcasting Organizations*, 15 Colum.-VLA J. L. & Arts 75 (1990)

Jehoram, *Shall the Perfume Scent Decision of the Dutch Supreme Court Conquer the EU and Then the World or Will It Perish?*, 54 J. Copyright Soc'y 571 (2007)

Jolliffe, Sartorio & Chenoweth, *The Dawn of a New Era of Balance in Canadian Copyright Law,* 22 Can. Intell. Prop. Rev. 17 (2005)

Kerever, *Copyright: The Achievements and Future Development of European Legal Culture,* 26 Copyright 130 (Apr. 1990)

Klement, *Protecting Television Show Formats Under Copyright Law: New Developments in Common Law and Civil Law Countries*, 29 E.I.P.R. 52 (2007)

Lafuze & Stanford, *An Overview of Section 337 of the Tariff Act of 1983: A Primer for Practice Before the International Trade Commission,* 25 J. Marshall L. Rev. 159 (1992)

Leaffer, *International Copyright from an American Perspective,* 43 Ark. L. Rev. 373 (1990)

Leaffer, *Protecting American Intellectual Property Abroad: Toward a New Multilateralism,* 76 Iowa L. Rev. 273 (1991)

Liang, *Beyond the Copyright Act: The Fair Use Doctrine Under Chinese Judicial Opinions*, 56 J. Copyright Soc'y 695 (2009)

Lin, *The U.S.-Taiwan Copyright Agreement: Cooperation or Coercion?,* 11 UCLA Pac. Basin L.J. 155 (1992)

Lindner, *Revival of Rights v. Protection of Acquired Rights: The Interpretation of Article 10(3) of the Duration Directive by the European Court of Justice in the Butterfly Case*, 22 E.I.P.R. 133 (2000)

Lipton, *Copyright in the Digital Age: A Comparative Survey,* 27 Rutgers Computer & Tech. L.J. 333 (2001)

Long, *Copyright and the Uruguay Round Agreements: A New Era of Protection or an Illusory Promise?*, 22 AIPLA Q.J. 531 (1994)

Long, *"Globalization": A Future Trend or a Satisfying Mirage?,* 49 J. Copyright Soc'y 357 (2001)

Luder, *The Next Ten Years in E.U. Copyright: Making Markets Work,* 18 Fordham Intell. Prop. Media & Ent. L.J. 1 (2007)

Lupo, *International Trade Commission Section 337 Proceedings and Their Applicability to Copyright Ownership,* 32 J. Copyright Soc'y 193 (1985)

McManis, *Taking TRIPS on the Information Superhighway: International Intellectual Property Protection and Emerging Computer Technology,* 41 Vill. L. Rev. 207 (1996)

Mehra, *Copyright, Control, and Comics: Japanese Battles Over Downstream Limits on Content*, 56 Rutgers L. Rev. 181 (2003)

Mizaras, *Lithuanian Copyright: Historical and Modern Aspects and Trends of Development, 2007*, 54 J. Copyright Soc'y 829 (2007)

Mouchet, *Problems of the "Domaine Public Payant,"* 8 Colum.-VLA J. L. & Arts 137 (1983)

Munzer & Raustiala, *The Uneasy Case for Intellectual Property Rights in Traditional Knowledge,* 27 Cardozo Arts & Ent. L.J. 37 (2009)

Naser & Muhaisen, *Intellectual Property: An Islamic Perspective*, 56 J. Copyright Soc'y 571 (2009)

Netanel, *Asserting Copyright's Democratic Principles in the Global Arena,* 51 Vand. L. Rev. 217 (1998)

Netanel, *The Next Round: The Impact of the WIPO Copyright Treaty on TRIPS Dispute Settlement,* 37 Va. J. Int'l L. 441 (1997)

D. Nimmer, *GATT's Entertainment: Before and NAFTA*, 15 Loy. L.A. Ent. L.J. 133 (1995)

D. Nimmer, *A Tale of Two Treaties*, 22 Colum.-VLA J.L. & Arts 1 (1997)

D. Nimmer, *Nation, Duration, Violation, Harmonization: An International Copyright Proposal for the United States,* 55 Law & Contemp. Probs. 211 (1992)

Nordemann, *The U.S. "Works-for-Hire" Doctrine before German Courts — Rejection and Reception*, 53 J. Copyright Soc'y 603 (2006)

Okediji, *Copyright and Public Welfare in Global Perspective,* 7 Ind. J. Global Leg. Stud. 117 (1999)

Okediji, *Knowledge Creation Systems on the International Stage: The Regulation of Creativity under the WIPO Internet Treaties*, 77 Fordham L. Rev. 2379 (2009)

Okediji, *The Regulation of Creativity under the WIPO Internet Treaties*, 77 Fordham L. Rev. 2379 (2009)

Okediji, *TRIPS Dispute Settlement and the Sources of (International) Copyright Law*, 49 J. Copyright Soc'y 585 (2001)

Patry, *The United States and International Copyright Law: From Berne to* Eldred, 40 Hous. L. Rev. 749 (2003)

Pelz, 2009, *Global Warming Trend? The Creeping Indulgence of Fair Use in International Copyright Law*, 17 Tex. Intell. Prop. L.J. 267 (2009)

Perlmutter, *Future Directions in International Copyright*, 16 Cardozo Arts & Ent. L.J. 369 (1998)

Perlmutter, *Participation in the International Copyright System as a Means to Promote the Progress of Science and Useful Arts*, 36 Loy. L.A. L. Rev. 323 (2002)

Raskind, *Protecting Computer Software in the European Economic Community: The Innovative New Directive,* 18 Brooklyn J. Int'l L. 729 (1992)

Reichman, *Enforcing the Enforcement Procedures of the TRIPS Agreement,* 37 Va. J. Int'l L. 335 (1997)

Reichman, *Intellectual Property in International Trade: Opportunities and Risks of a GATT Connection,* 22 Vand. J. Transnat'l L. 747 (1989)

Reinbothe & Von Lewinski, *The WIPO Treaties 1996: Ready to Come into Force,* 24 E.I.P.R. 199 (2002)

Remington, *The Ever-Whirling Cycle of Change: Copyright and Cyberspace,* 3 N.C.J.L. & Tech. 213 (2002)

Rinaldo, *The Scope of Copyright Protection in the United States Under Existing Inter-American Relations: Abrogation of the Need for U.S. Protection Under the Buenos Aires Convention by Reliance Upon the U.C.C.,* 22 Bull. Copyright Soc'y 417 (1975)

Ringer, *The Role of the United States in International Copyright — Past, Present and Future,* 65 Geo. L.J. 1065 (1968)

Ruiz, Lapena & Clark, *The Protection of Traditional Knowledge in Peru: A Comparative Perspective*, 3 Wash. U. Global L. Studies L. Rev. 755 (2004)

Sackville, *Legal Protection of Indigenous Culture in Australia*, 11 Cardozo J. Int. & Comp. L. 711 (2003)

Samuelson, *The U.S. Digital Agenda at WIPO,* 37 Va. J. Int'l L. 369 (1997)

Schwartz, *Recent Developments in the Copyright Regimes of the Soviet Union and Eastern Europe,* 38 J. Copyright Soc'y 123 (1991)

Scott, *A Comparative View of Copyright as Cultural Property in Japan and the United States*, 20 Temp. Int'l & Comp. L.J. 283 (2006)

Simone, *Protection of American Copyrights in Books on Taiwan,* 35 J. Copyright Soc'y 115 (1988)

Sobel, *The Framework of International Copyright,* 8 Cardozo Arts & Ent. L.J. 1 (1989)

Solberg, *The International Copyright Union,* 36 Yale L.J. 68 (1926)

Spangler, *When Indigenous Communities Go Digital: Protecting Traditional Cultural Expressions Through Integration of IP and Customary Law,* 27 Cardozo Arts & Ent. L. J. 709 (2010)

Sterling, *Space Copyright Law: The New Dimension: A Preliminary Survey and Proposals*, 54 J. Copyright Soc'y 345 (2007)

Story, *Burn Berne: Why the Leading International Copyright Convention Must Be Repealed,* 40 Hous. L. Rev. 763 (2003)

Symposium, *Fundamentals of International Copyright: The Impact of Berne,* 8 Cardozo Arts & Ent. L.J. 1 (1989)

Symposium, *Trade-Related Aspects of Intellectual Property,* 22 Vand. J. Transnat'l L. 689 (1989)

Tabatabai, *A Tale of Two Countries: Canada's Response to the Peer-to-Peer Crisis and What it Means for the United States,* 73 Fordham L. Rev. 2321 (2005)

Travis, *Opting Out of the Interent in the United States and the European Union: Copyright, Safe Harbors, and International Law,* 84 Notre Dame L. Rev. 331 (2008)

Turkewitz, *Authors' Rights Are Dead,* 38 J. Copyright Soc'y 41 (1990)

U.S. Copyright Office, *Circular 38a: International Copyright Relations of the United States* (continually updated)

Vathitphund, *Access to Knowledge Difficulties in Developing Countries: A Balanced Access to Copyrighted Works in the Digital Environment,* 24 Int'l Rev. L., Computer & Tech. 7 (2010)

Von Lewinski, *Copyright in the European Communities: The Proposed Harmonization Measures,* 28 Brooklyn J. Int'l L. 703 (1992)

Von Lewinski, *International Copyright Over the Last 50 Years — A Foreign Perspective,* 50 J. Copyright Soc'y 581 (2003)

Von Lewinski, *The Protection of Folklore,* 11 Cardozo J. Int'l & Comp. L. 747 (2003)

Westkamp, *Transient Copyright and Public Communication: The Creeping Evolution of Use and Access Rights in European Copyright Law,* 36 Geo. Wash. Int'l L. Rev. 1057 (2004)

Wong, *"Transformative" User-Generated Content in Copyright Law: Infringing Derivative Works or Fair Use?,* 11 Vand. J. Ent. & Tech. L. 1075 (2009)

Yu, *Four Common Misconceptions about Copyright Piracy,* 26 L.A. Int. & Comp. L. Rev. 127 (2003)

Yu, *The Copyright Divide,* 25 Cardozo L. Rev. 705 (2003)

Yu, *The Harmonization Game: What Basketball Can Teach About Intellectual Property and International Trade,* 26 Fordham Int. L.J. 218 (2003)

Yufeng & Ng, *Understanding the Great Qing Copyright Law of 1910,* 56 J. Copyright Soc'y 767 (2009)

Zheng & Pendleton, *A Response to United States Government Criticisms of the Chinese Copyright Law,* 7 E.I.P.R. 257 (1991)

Copyright and the Digital Challenge

G.P. Albert, Intellectual Property Law in Cyberspace (1999 & Supp. 2007)

J. Dratler, Jr., Cyberlaw: Intellectual Property in the Digital Millennium (2000 & Supp. 2008)

W. Fisher, Promises to Keep: Technology, Law, and the Future of Entertainment (2004)

T. Gillespie, Wired Shut: Copyright and the Shape of Digital Culture (2007)

L. Hilderbran, Inherent Vice: Bootleg Histories of Videotape and Copyright (2009)

D. Katsh, Law in a Digital World (1995)

J. Litman, Digital Copyright: Protecting Intellectual Property on the Internet (2001)

H. Perritt, Law and the Information Superhighway (2d. ed. 2001 & Supp. 2008)

M. Remington, *Napster* and the Digital Age: The Future of Copyright Law (2001)

Bambauer, *Cybersieves (Internet Censorship)*. 59 Duke L.J. 377 (2009)

Bartow, *Electrifying Copyright Norms and Making Cyberspace More Like a Book*, 48 Vill. L. Rev. 13 (2003)

Bartow, *Libraries in a Digital and Aggressively Copyrighted World: Retaining Patron Access through Changing Technologies*, 62 Ohio St. L.J. 821 (2001)

Bartow, *Our Data, Ourselves: Privacy, Propertization, and Gender*, 34 U.S.F. L. Rev. 633 (2000)

Bartow, *Pornography, Coercion, and Copyright Law,* 10 Vand. J. Ent. & Tech. L. 799 (2008)

Beard, *Clones, Bones and Twilight Zones: Protecting the Digital Persona of the Quick, the Dead and the Imaginary,* 16 Berkeley Tech. L.J. 1165 (2001)

T. Bell, *The Specter of Copyism v. Blockheaded Authors: How User-Generated Content Affects Copyright Policy*, 10 Vand. J. Ent. & Tech. L. 841 (2008)

Boyle, *Intellectual Property Policy Online: A Young Person's Guide,* 10 Harv. J. L. & Tech. 47 (1996)

Burk, *Muddy Rules for Cyberspace,* 21 Cardozo L. Rev. 121 (1999)

Burk, *The Mereology of Digital Copyright*, 18 Fordham Intell. Prop. Media & Ent. L.J. 711 (2008)

Burk, *The Trouble With Trespass*, 4 J. Small & Emerging Bus. L. 27 (2000)

Cate, *The First Amendment and the National Information Infrastructure*, 30 Wake Forest L. Rev 1 (1995)

Cate, *The Technological Transformation of Copyright Law*, 81 Iowa L. Rev. 1395 (1996)

Cavasos & Miles, *Copyright on the WWW: Linking and Liability*, 4 Rich. J.L. & Tech. 3 (1997)

J. Cohen, *A Right to Read Anonymously: A Closer Look at "Copyright Management" in Cyberspace,* 28 Conn. L. Rev. 981 (1996)

Craig, *The Development of Internet Education and the Role of Copyright Law*, 40 J. Copyright Soc'y 75 (2000)

Dallon, *The Problem With Congress and Copyright Law: Forgetting the Past and Ignoring the Public Interest,* 44 Santa Clara L. Rev. 365 (2004)

Durham, *Copyright and Information Theory: Toward An Alternative Model of "Authorship,"* 2004 B.Y.U. L. Rev. 69

Elkin-Koren, *Cyberlaw and Social Change: A Democratic Approach to Copyright Law in Cyberspace,* 14 Cardozo Arts & Ent. L.J. 215 (1996)

Feigin, *Architecture of Consent: Internet Protocols and Their Legal Implications*, 56 Stan. L. Rev. 901 (2004)

Field, *Copyright, Technology and Time: Perspectives on "Interactive" as a Term of Art in Copyright Law*, 50 J. Copyright Soc'y 59 (2003)

Gailey, *Who Owns Digital Rights? Examining the Scope of Copyright Protection for Electronically Distributed Works,* 18 Comm. & The Law 3 (1996)

Garon, *Media and Monopoly in the Information Age: Slowing the Convergence at the Marketplace of Ideas*, 17 Cardozo Arts & Ent. L.J. 491 (1999)

Gerhardt, *Plagiarism in Cyberspace: Learning the Rules of Recycling Content with a View Towards Nurturing Academic Trust in an Electronic World*, 12 Rich. J.L. & Tech. 10 (2006)

Ginsburg, *Putting Cars on the "Information Superhighway": Authors, Exploiters & Copyright in Cyberspace,* 95 Colum. L. Rev. 1466 (1995)

Halpern, *Copyright Law in the Digital Age: Malum in Se and Malum Prohibitum*, 4 Marq. Intell. Prop. L. Rev. 1 (2000)

Halpern, *The Digital Threat to the Normative Role of Copyright Law*, 62 Ohio St. L.J. 569 (2001)

Hardy, *Not So Different: Tangible, Intangible, Digital, and Analog Works and Their Comparison for Copyright Purposes,* 26 U. Dayton L. Rev. 211 (2001)

Hardy, *Property (and Copyright) in Cyberspace*, 1996 U. Chi. Legal F. 217

Hardy, *The Internet and the Law: Copyright and "New-Use" Technologies,* 23 Nova L. Rev. 657 (1999)

Hardy, *The Proper Legal Regime for "Cyberspace",* 55 U. Pitt. L. Rev. 993 (1994)

Hilty, *Five Lessons About Copyright in the Information Society: Reaction of the Scientific Community to Over-Protection and What Policy Makers Should Learn*, 53 J. Copyright Soc'y 103 (2005)

Jensen, *The More Things Change, the More They Stay the Same: Copyright, Digital Technology, and Social Norms*, 56 Stan. L. Rev. 531 (2003)

Johnson & Post, *Law and Borders: The Rise of the Law in Cyberspace*, 48 Stan. L. Rev. 1367 (1996)

Kaplan, *Copyright in the Digital Age,* 49 J. Copyright Soc'y 1 (2001)

Karjala, *Federal Preemption of Shrinkwrap and On-Line Licenses,* 22 U. Dayton L. Rev. 511 (1997)

Katsh & Rifkin, *The New Media and a New Model of Conflict Resolution: Copying, Copyright, and Creating,* 6 Notre Dame J.L., Ethics & Pub. Pol'y 49 (1992)

Ku, *Creative Destruction of Copyright:* Napster *and the New Economics of Digital Technology,* 69 U. Chi. L. Rev. 263 (2002)

Kurtz, *Symposium: Copyright and the Internet — World Without Borders,* 43 Wayne L. Rev. 117 (1996)

Lastowka, *User-Generated Content and Virtual Worlds,* 10 Vand. J. Ent. & Tech. L. 893 (2008)

Leaffer, *Protecting Authors' Rights in a Digital Age*, 27 U. Tol. L. Rev. 1 (1996)

Lee, *Culturally-Based Copyright Systems?: The U.S. and Korea in Conflict,* 79 Wash. U.L.Q. 1103 (2001)

Lee, *Warming Up to User-Generated Content*, 2008 U. Ill. L. Rev. 1459

M. Lemley, *Dealing With Overlapping Copyrights on the Internet,* 22 U. Dayton L. Rev. 547 (1997)

M. Lemley, *Place and Cyberspace*, 91 Cal. L. Rev. 521 (2003)

Litman, *Reforming Information Law in Copyright's Image,* 22 Dayton L. Rev. 587 (1997)

Litman, *Revising Copyright Law for the Information Age,* 75 Or. L. Rev. 19 (1996)

Liu, *Owning Digital Copies: Copyright Law and the Incidents of Copy Ownership,* 42 Wm. & Mary L. Rev. 1245 (2001)

Long, *When World Collide: The Uneasy Convergence of Creativity and Innovation*, 25 J. Marshall J. Computer & Info. L. 653 (2009)

Loundy, *Revising the Copyright Law for Electronic Publishing,* 14 J. Marshall J. Computer & Info. L. 1 (1995)

McCoy, *Cybertheft: Will Copyright Law Prevent Digital Tyranny on the Superhighway?,* 30 Wake Forest L. Rev. 169 (1995)

Menell, *Envisioning Copyright Law's Digital Future*, 46 N.Y.L. Sch. L. Rev. 63 (2002)

Menell, *Knowledge Accessibility and Preservation Policy for the Digital Age,* 44 Hous. L. Rev. 1013 (2007)

Menell, *The Challenges of Reforming Intellectual Property Protection for Computer Software,* 94 Colum. L. Rev. 2644 (1994)

Meurer, *Price Discrimination, Personal Use and Piracy: Copyright Protection for Digital Works,* 45 Buff. L. Rev. 845 (1997)

Montagnani, *A New Interface Between Copyright Law and Technology: How User-Generated Content Will Shape the Future of Online Distribution,* 26 Cardozo Arts & Ent. L.J. 719 (2009)

Mtima, *Protecting and Licensing Software: Copyright and Common Law Contract Considerations*, 22 Computer & Internet Law. 13 (2005)

Myers, *Defamation and the Quiescent Anarchy of the Internet: A Case Study of Cyber Targeting* (Defamation Discussion Forum), 110 Penn St. L. Rev. 667 (2006)

R. Nimmer & Krauthaus, *Copyright on the Information Superhighway: Requiem for a Middleweight,* 6 Stan. L. & Pol'y Rev. 25 (1994)

Ohm, *The Myth of the Super-User: Fear, Risk, and Harm Online*, 41 U.C. Davis L. Rev. 1327 (2009)

Patel, *'Authors v. Internet Archives': The Copyright Infringement Battle Over Web Pages*, 89 J. Pat. & Trademark Off. Soc'y 410 (2007)

Patterson, *The DMCA: A Modern Version of the Licensing Act of 1662*, 10 J. Intell. Prop. L. 33 (2002)

Perlmutter, *Convergence and the Future of Copyright,* 24 Colum.-VLA J.L. & Arts 163 (2001)

Pessach, *[Networked] Memory Institutions: Social Remembering, Privatization and Its Discontents*, 26 Cardozo Arts & Ent. L.J. 71 (2008)

Phillips, *Australia's Heritage Protection Act: An Alternative to Copyright in the Struggle to Protect Communal Interests in Authored Works of Folklore,* 18 Pac. Rim L. & Pol'y J. 547 (2009)

Post, *Symposium:* Napster *& Beyond: Protecting Copyright in the Digital Millennium — His* Napster's *Voice,* 20 Temp. Envtl. L. & Tech. J. 35 (2001)

Radin, *Property Evolving in Cyberspace,* 15 J. L. & Com. 509 (1996)

Reichman, *Electronic Information Tools: The Outer Edge of World Intellectual Property Law,* 17 U. Dayton L. Rev. 853 (1992)

Reidenberg, *The Rule of Intellectual Property Law in the Internet Economy*, 44 Hous. L. Rev. 1073 (2007)

Rice, *Digital Information as Property and Product:* ***U.C.C. Article 2B*****, 22** U. Dayton L. Rev. 621 (1997)

Samuelson, *Digital Media and the Changing Face of Intellectual Property Law,* 16 Rutgers Computer & Tech. L.J. 323 (1990)

Samuelson, *Privacy As Intellectual Property?,* 52 Stan. L. Rev. 1125 (2000)

Samuelson, *Toward a "New Deal" for Copyright in the Information Age*, 100 Mich. L. Rev. 1488 (2002)

Shipley, *Liability Issues Facing Online Businesses,* 36-WTR Ark. Law 20 (2001)

Sieber, *Digital Media: The Constitutionality of the DMCA Explored:* Universal City Studios, Inc. v. Corley & United States v. Elcom Ltd., 18 Berkeley Tech. L.J. 7 (2003)

Waelde & MacQueen, *From Entertainment to Education: The Scope of Copyright*, Intell. Prop. Q. 259 (Summer 2004)

Wagner, *On Software Regulation*, 78 S. Cal. L. Rev. 457 (2005)

Winn & Jondet, *A New Deal for End Users? Lessons from a French Innovation in the Regulation of Interoperability,* 51 Wm. & Mary L. Rev. 547 (2009)

Yu, *The Escalating Copyright Wars*, 32 Hofstra L.Rev. 907 (2004)

Zimmerman, *Copyright in Cyberspace: Don't Throw Out the Public Interest With the Bathwater,* 1994 Annual Survey of American Law 403.

Thinking and Talking About Copyright Law

Y. Benkler, THE WEALTH OF NETWORKS: HOW SOCIAL PRODUCTION TRANSFORMS MARKETS AND FREEDOM (2006)

S. Biegel, BEYOND OUR CONTROL? CONFRONTING THE LIMITS OF OUR LEGAL SYSTEM IN THE AGE OF CYBERSPACE (2001)

M. Boldrin & D. Levine, AGAINST INTELLECTUAL PROPERTY (2008)

J. Boyle, SHAMANS, SOFTWARE & SPLEENS: LAW AND THE CONSTRUCTION OF THE INFORMATION SOCIETY (1996)

J. Boyle, THE PUBLIC DOMAIN: ENCLOSING THE COMMONS OF THE MIND (2008)

C. Doctorow, CONTENT: SELECTED ESSAYS ON TECHNOLOGY, CREATIVITY, COPYRIGHT AND THE FUTURE OF THE FUTURE (2008)

A. Friedman, THE LAW OF HIGH TECHNOLOGY INNOVATION (1991)

H. Hansen, U.S. INTELLECTUAL PROPERTY LAW AND POLICY (2006)

M. Helprin, DIGITAL BARBARIANS: A WRITER'S MANIFESTO (2009)

M. Jussawalla, THE ECONOMICS OF INTELLECTUAL PROPERTY IN A WORLD WITHOUT FRONTIERS: A STUDY OF COMPUTER SOFTWARE (1992)

B. Kaplan, AN UNHURRIED VIEW OF COPYRIGHT (1967)

D. Lange & H.J. Powell, NO LAW: INTELLECTUAL PROPERTY IN THE IMAGE OF AN ABSOLUTE FIRST AMENDMENT (2008)

L. Lessig, CODE AND OTHER LAWS OF CYBERSPACE (1999)

L. Lessig, FREE CULTURE: HOW BIG MEDIA USES TECHNOLOGY AND THE LAW TO LOCK DOWN CULTURE AND CONTROL CREATIVITY (2004)

L. Lessig, REMIX: MAKING ART AND COMMERCE THRIVE IN THE HYBRID ECONOMY (2008)

L. Lessig, THE FUTURE OF IDEAS: THE FATE OF THE COMMONS IN A CONNECTED WORLD (2001)

C.B. MacPherson, THE POLITICAL THEORY OF POSSESSIVE INDIVIDUALISM (1962)

M. Mason, THE PIRATE'S DILEMMA: HOW YOUTH CULTURE IS REINVENTING CAPITALISM (2008)

A. Moore, INTELLECTUAL PROPERTY: MORAL, LEGAL & INTERNATIONAL DILEMMAS (1997)

D. Nimmer, COPYRIGHT: SACRED TEXT, TECHNOLOGY, AND THE DMCA (2003)

W. Patry, MORAL PANICS AND THE COPYRIGHT WARS (2009)

L. R. Patterson & S.W. Lindberg, THE NATURE OF COPYRIGHT: A LAW OF USERS' RIGHTS (1991)

A. Plant, THE NEW COMMERCE IN IDEAS AND INTELLECTUAL PROPERTY (1953)

S. Stewart, CRIMES OF WRITING: PROBLEMS IN THE CONTAINMENT OF REPRESENTATION (1991)

R. Towse, CREATIVITY, INCENTIVE AND REWARD: AN ECONOMIC ANALYSIS OF COPYRIGHT AND CULTURE IN THE INFORMATION AGE (2001)

M. Woodmansee, THE AUTHOR, THE ARTS, AND THE MARKET: REREADING THE HISTORY OF AESTHETICS (1993)

M. Woodmansee & P. Jaszi (eds.), THE CONSTRUCTION OF AUTHORSHIP: TEXTUAL APPROPRIATION IN LAW AND LITERATURE (1994)

P. Yu, INTELLECTUAL PROPERTY AND INFORMATION WEALTH: ISSUES AND PRACTICES IN THE DIGITAL AGE (2007)

Afori, *Human Rights and Copyright: The Introduction of Natural Law Considerations Into American Copyright Law*, 14 Fordham Intell. Prop. Media & Ent. L.J. 497 (2004)

Aoki, *Balancing Act: Reflections on Justice O'Connor's Intellectual Property Jurisprudence*, 44 Hous. L. Rev. 965 (2007)

Balganesh, *Debunking Blackstonian Copyright,* 118 Yale L.J. 1126 (2009)

Balganesh, *Foreseeability and Copyright Incentives,* 122 Harv. L. Rev. 1569 (2009)

Baker, *First Amendment Limits on Copyright*, 55 Vand. L. Rev. 891 (2002)

Bar-Gill & Parchomovsky, *A Marketplace for Ideas?*, 84 Tex. L. R. 395 (2005)

Barlow, *The Economy of Ideas*, 2.03 Wired 84 (Mar. 1994)

Barnett, *Is Intellectual Property Trivial?,* 157 U. Penn. L. Rev. 1691 (2009)

Bartow, *Fair Use and the Fairer Sex: Gender, Feminism, and Copyright Law*, 14 Am U. J. Gender Soc. Pol'y & L. 551 (2006)

Bartow, *The Hegemony of the Copyright Treatise*, 73 U. Cin. L. Rev. 581 (2004)

Bauer, *Refusals to Deal with Competitors by Owners of Patents and Copyrights: Reflections on the Image Technical and Xerox Decisions*, 55 DePaul L. Rev. 1211 (2006)

Beebe, *Intellectual Property Law and the Sumptuary Code,* 123 Harv. L. Rev. 809 (2010)

A. Bell & Parchomovsky, *The Evolution of Private and Open Access Property*, 10 Theoretical Inq. L. 77 (2009)

T. Bell, *Author's Welfare: Copyright as a Statutory Mechanism for Redistributing Rights*, 69 Brooklyn L. Rev. 229 (2003)

T. Bell, Copyright as Intellectual Privilege, 58 Syracuse L. Rev. 523 (2008)

T. Bell, Escape from Copyright: Market Success vs. Statutory Failure in the Protection of Expressive Works, 69 U. Cin. L. Rev. 741 (2001)

T. Bell, Prediction Markets for Promoting the Progress of Science and the Useful Arts, 14 Geo. Mason L. Rev. 37 (2006)

Benkler, *Free as the Air to Common Use: First Amendment Constraints on Enclosure of the Public Domain*, 74 N.Y.U. L. Rev. 354 (1999)

Benkler, *Siren Songs and Amish Children: Autonomy, Information, and Law,* 76 N.Y.U.L. Rev. 23 (2001)

Benkler, *The Public Domain: Through the Looking Glass: Alice and the Constitutional Foundations of the Public Domain,* 66 Law & Contemp. Prob. 173 (2003)

Besen & Kirby, *Private Copying, Appropriability and Optimal Copying Royalties,* 32 J. Law & Econ. 255 (1989)

Besen & Raskind, *An Introduction to the Law and Economics of Intellectual Property,* 5 J. Econ. Persp. 3 (1991)

Birnhack, *Copyright Law and Free Speech after* Eldred v. Ashcroft, 76 So. Cal. L. Rev. 1275 (2003)

Birnhack, *The Copyright Law and Free Speech Affair: Making-Up and Breaking-Up,* 43 IDEA 233 (2003)

Bohannan, *Reclaiming Copyright*, 23 Cardozo Arts & Ent. L.J. 567 (2006)

Boyle, *Cruel, Mean, or Lavish? Economic Analysis, Price Discrimination and Digital Intellectual Property*, 53 Vand. L. Rev. 2007 (2000)

Boyle, *A Theory of Law and Information: Copyright, Spleens, Blackmail, and Insider Trading,* 80 Cal. L. Rev. 1413 (1992)

Boyle, *The Second Enclosure Movement and the Construction of the Public Domain*, 33. Law & Contemp. Probs. 33 (2003)

Boytha, *The Justification of the Protection of Authors' Rights as Reflected in Their Historical Development,* 151 Revue Internationale de Droit D'Auteur [R.I.D.A.] 53 (1992)

Boytha, *Whose Right is Copyright?,* 6/7 GRUR Int'l 379 (1983)

Breyer, *The Uneasy Case for Copyright: A Study in Copyright of Books, Photocopies and Computer Programs,* 84 Harv. L. Rev. 281 (1970)

Breakey, *Natural Intellectual Property Rights and the Public Domain,* 73 Mod. L. Rev. 208 (2010)

Breyer, *Copyright: A Rejoinder,* 20 UCLA L. Rev. 75 (1972)

Burk, *Copyright and Feminism in Digital Media*, 14 Am U. J. Gender Soc. Pol'y & L. 519 (2006)

Burk, *Expression, Selection, Abstraction: Copyright's Golden Braid*, 55 Syracuse L. Rev. 593 (2005)

Burk, *Intellectual Property and the Firm,* 71 U. Chi. L. Rev. 3 (2004)

Burk, *Method and Madness in Copyright Law*, 2007 Utah L. Rev. 587

Cameron & Tomkowicz, *Competition Policy and Canada's New Breed of 'Copyright' Law*, 52 McGill L.J. 291 (2007)

Carrier, *Cabining Intellectual Property Through a Property Paradigm*, 54 Duke L.J. 1 (2004)

Chafee, *Reflections on the Law of Copyright,* 45 Colum. L. Rev. 503, 719 (1945)

Clark, *Intangibles, Appropriations, and Intellectual Property Law: The Problem(s) with Copyright for Native American Oral Traditions*, 38 Stud. L. Pol. & Soc'y 173 (2005)

J. Cohen, *The Law and Economics of Intellectual Property Rights: Copyright and the Perfect Curve*, 53 Vand. L. Rev. 1799 (2000)

J. Cohen, *The Place of the User in Copyright Law*, 74 Fordham L. Rev. 347 (2005)

Conley & Yoo, *Nonrivalry and Price Discrimination in Copyright Economics,* 157 U. Penn. L. Rev. 1801 (2009)

Coombe, *The Properties and the Politics of Possessing Identity: Native Claims in the Cultural Appropriation Controversy*, 6 Can. J. L. & Juris. 249 (1993)

Craig, *Reconstructing The Author-Self: Some Feminist Lessons for Copyright Law*, 15 Am. U.J. Gender Soc. Pol'y & L. 207 (2007)

Crane, *Intellectual Liability,* 88 Tex. L. Rev. 253 (2009)

Crews, *Looking Ahead and Shaping the Future: Provoking Change in Copyright Law*, 49 J. Copyright Soc'y 549 (2001)

Dallon, *The Problem with Congress and Copyright Law: Forgetting the Past and Ignoring the Public Interest*, 44 Santa Clara L. Rev. 365 (2004)

Depoorter, *Technology and Uncertainty: The Shaping Effect on Copyright Law,* 157 U. Penn. L. Rev. 1831 (2009)

Dietz, *Copyright in the Modern Technological World: A Mere Industrial Property Right?,* 39 J. Copyright Soc'y 83 (1991)

Dinwoodie, *Copyright Lawmaking Authority: An (Inter)Nationalist Perspective on the Treaty Clause*, 30 Colum. J.L. & Arts 355 (2007)

Driedman, *Standards as Intellectual Property: An Economic Approach,* 19 U. Dayton L. Rev. 1109 (1994)

Fagundes, *Crystals in the Public Domain*, 50 B.C. L. Rev. 139 (2009)

Fagundes, *Property Rhetoric and the Public Domain,* 94 Minn. L. Rev. 652 (2010)

Foster, *Invitation to a Discourse Regarding the History, Philosophy and Social Psychology of a Property Right in Copyright,* 21 Fla J. Int'l L. 171 (2009)

Frischmann, *An Economic Theory of Infrastructure and Commons Management*, 89 Minn. L. Rev. 917 (2005)

Frischmann, *Spillovers Theory and its Conceptual Boundaries,* 51 Wm. & Mary L. Rev. 801 (2009)

Fromer, *Claiming Intellectual Property,* 76 U. Chi. L. Rev. 719 (2009)

Garfield, *The Case for First Amendment Limits on Copyright Law*, 35 Hofstra L. Rev. 1169 (2007)

Garon, *Normative Copyright: A Conceptual Framework for Copyright Philosophy and Ethics,* 88 Cornell L. Rev. 1278 (2003)

Gasaway, *A Defense of the Public Domain: A Scholarly Essay,* 101 L. Libr. J. 451 (2009)

Geller, *Beyond the Copyright Crisis: Principles for Change*, 55 J. Copyright Soc'y 165 (2008)

Geist, *All Rights Reserved?: Cultural Monopoly and the Troubles with Copyright*, 10 Marq. Intell. Prop. L. Rev. 411 (2006)

Ghosh, *Decoding and Recoding Natural Monopoly, Deregulation, and Intellectual Property,* 2008 U. Ill. L. Rev. 1125

Ghosh, *The Fable of the Commons: Exclusivity and the Construction of Intellectual Property Markets*, 40. U.C. Davis L. Rev. 855 (2007)

Ghosh, *The Merits of Ownership, or, How I Learned to Stop Worrying and Love Intellectual Property: Review Essay of Lawrence Lessig, the Future of Ideas, and Siva Vaidhyanathan, Copyrights and Copywrongs*, 15 Harv. J.L. & Tech. 453 (2002)

Ginsburg, *Authors and Users in Copyright*, 45 J. Copyright Soc'y 1 (1997)

Ginsburg, *Creation and Commercial Value: Copyright Protection for Works of Information,* 90 Colum. L. Rev. 1865 (1990)

Ginsburg, *How Copyright Got a Bad Name For Itself,* 26 Colum.-VLA J.L. & Arts 61 (2002)

Goldstein, *Copyright,* 38 J. Copyright Soc'y (1991)

Goldstein, *Copyright and Its Substitutes*, 1997 Wis. L. Rev. 865 (1997)

Goodman, *Media Policy and Free Speech: The First Amendment at War with Itself,* 35 Hofstra L. Rev. 1211 (2007)

Gordon, *A Property Right in Self-Expression: Equality and Individualism in the Natural Law of Intellectual Property,* 102 Yale L.J. 1533 (1993)

Gordon, *An Inquiry into the Merits of Copyright: The Challenges of Consistency, Consent, and Encouragement Theory,* 41 Stan. L. Rev. 1343 (1989)

Gordon, *Assertive Modesty: An Economics of Intangibles,* 94 Colum. L. Rev. 2579 (1994)

Gordon, *Asymetric Market Failure and Prisoner's Dilemna in Intellectual Property,* 17 U. Dayton L. Rev. 853 (1992)

Gordon, *Copyright as Tort Law's Mirror Image: "Harms," "Benefits," and the Uses and Limits of Analogy,* 34 McGeorge L. Rev. 533 (2003)

Gordon, *Harmless Use: Gleaning from Fields of Copyrighted Works*, 77 Fordham L. Rev. 2411 (2009)

Gordon, *On Owning Information: Intellectual Property Law and the Restitutionary Impulse,* 78 Va. L. Rev. 149 (1992)

Gordon, *Render Copyright Unto Caesar: On Taking Incentives Seriously*, 71 U. Chi. L. Rev. 75 (2004)

Graves, *Private Rights, Public Uses, and the Future of the Copyright Clause,* 80 Neb. L. Rev. 64 (2001)

Greene, *Copyright, Culture & Black Music: A Legacy of Unequal Protection,* 21 Hastings Comm. & Ent. L.J. 339 (1999)

Greene, *'Copynorms,' Black Cultural Production, and the Debate Over African-American Reparation*, 25 Cardozo Arts & Ent. L.J. 1179 (2008)

Grimmelmann, *The Ethical Visions of Copyright*, 77 Fordham L. Rev. 2005 (2009)

Halpern, *Copyright Law in the Digital Age:* Malum In Se *and* Malum Prohibitum, 4 Marq. Intell. Prop. L. Rev. 1 (2000)

Hamilton, *Appropriation Art & the Imminent Decline in Authorial Control Over Copyrighted Works,* 42 J. Copyright Soc'y 93 (1994)

Hamilton, *Art and the Marketplace of Expression*, 17 Cardozo Arts & Ent. L.J. 167 (1999)

Hamilton, *The Jurisprudence of Information Flow: How the Constitution Constructs the Pathways of Information,* 25 Cardozo L. Rev. 267 (2003)

Hardy, *The Ancient Doctrine of Trespass to Web Sites*, 1996 J. Online L., Art. 7

Harmon, *Law, Art, and the Killing Jar,* 79 Iowa L. Rev. 367 (1994)

Harrison, *A Positive Externalities Approach to Copyright Law: Theory and Application*, 13 J. Intell. Prop. L. 1 (2005)

Heald, *Property Rights and the Efficient Exploitation of Copyrighted Works: An Empirical Analysis of Public Domain and Copyrighted Fiction Bestsellers*, 92 Minn. L. Rev. 1031 (2008)

Heald, *Reviving the Rhetoric of the Public Interest: Choir Directors, Copy Machines, and New Arrangements of Public Domain Music*, 46 Duke L.J. 241 (1996)

Hetcher, *Hume's Penguin, or, Yochai Benkler and the Nature of Peer Production*, 11 Vand. J. Ent. & Tech. L. 963 (2009)

Hetcher, *Using Social Norms to Regulate Fan Fiction and Remix Culture,* 157 U. Penn. L. Rev. 1869 (2009)

Hettinger, *Justifying Intellectual Property,* 18 Phil. & Pub. Aff. 31 (1989)

Horowitz, *Designing the Public Domain,* 122 Harv. L. Rev. 1489 (2009)

Hughes, *The Philosophy of Intellectual Property,* 77 Geo. L.J. 287 (1988)

Hughes, *"Recoding" Intellectual Property and Overlooked Audience Interests*, 77 Tex. L. Rev. 923 (1999)

Hurt & Schuchmàn, *The Economic Rationale of Copyright,* 56 Am. Econ. Rev. 42 (1966)

Jaszi, *Goodbye to All That — A Reluctant (and Perhaps Premature) Adieu to a Constitutionally-Grounded Discourse of Public Interest in Copyright Law,* 29 Vand. J. Transnat'l L. 595 (1996)

Jaszi, *On the Author Effect: Contemporary Copyright and Collective Creativity,* 10 Cardozo Arts & Ent. L.J. 293 (1992)

Johnson, *The Economics of Copying,* 93 J. Pol. Econ. 158 (1985)

Kasunic, *Preserving the Traditional Contours of Copyright*, 30 Colum. J.L. & Arts 397 (2007)

Katyal, *Performance, Property and the Slashing of Gender in Fan Fiction*, 14 Am. U. J. Gender Soc. Pol'y & L. 461 (2006)

Kauffman, *Exposing the Suspicious Foundations of Society's Primacy in Copyright Law: Five Accidents,* 10 Colum.-VLA J.L. & Arts 381 (1986)

Kreiss, *Accessability and Commercialization in Copyright Theory,* 43 U.C.L.A. L. Rev. 1 (1995)

Ku, Sun & Fan, *Does Copyright Law Promote Creativity? An Empirical Analysis of Copyright's Bounty,* 62 Vand. L. Rev. 1669 (2009)

Kurtz, *Commentary: Copyright and the Human Condition*, 40 U.C. Davis L. Rev. 1233 (2007)

Ladd, *The Harm of the Concept of Harm in Copyright,* 30 J. Copyright Soc'y 421 (1983)

Landes & Posner, *An Economic Analysis of Copyright Law,* 18 J. Leg. Stud. 325 (1989)

Lange, *At Play in the Fields of the Word: Copyright and the Construction of Authorship in the Post-Literate Millenium,* 55 Law & Contemp. Probs. 139 (1992)

Lange, *Recognizing the Public Domain,* 44 Law & Contemp. Probs. 147 (1981)

Lange, *Reimagining the Public Domain*, 66 Law & Contemp. Probs. 463 (2003)

Leaffer, *Life After* Eldred: *The Supreme Court and the Future of Copyright*, 30 Wm. Mitchell L. Rev. 1597 (2004)

Lee, *Freedom of the Press 2.0*, 42 Ga. L. Rev. 309 (2008)

Lee, *Guns and Speech Technologies: How the Right to Bear Arms Affects Copyright Regulations of Speech Technologies*, 17 Wm. & Mary Bill Rts. J. 1037 (2009)

K. Lemley, *The Innovative Medium Defense; A Doctinre to Promote the Multiple Goals of Copyright in the Wake of Advancing Digital Technologies*, 110 Penn. St. L. Rev. 111 (2005)

M. Lemley, *The Economics of Improvement in Intellectual Property Law*, 75 Tex. L. Rev. 989 (1997)

Lessig, *Innovating Copyright*, 20 Cardozo Arts & Ent. L.J. 611 (2002)

Lichtman, *Copyright as a Rule of Evidence,* 52 Duke L.J. 683 (2003)

Lipton, *Information Property: Rights and Responsibility*, 56 Fla. L. Rev. 135 (2004)

Litman, *Convergence of Paradigms and Cultures: War Stories,* Cardozo Arts & Ent. L.J. 337 (2002)

Litman, *Copyright and Information Policy,* 55 Law & Contemp. Probs. 185 (1992)

Litman, *Copyright, Compromise and Legislative History,* 72 Cornell L. Rev. 857 (1987)

Litman, *Copyright Legislation and Technological Change,* 68 Or. L. Rev. 275 (1989)

Litman, *Reforming Information Law in Copyright's Image,* 22 U. Dayton L. Rev. 587 (1997)

Litman, *The Copyright Revision Act of* 2026, 13 Marq. Intell. Prop. L. Rev. 249 (2009)

Litman, *The Exclusive Right to Read,* 75 Oreg. L. Rev. 299 (1996)

Litman, *The Public Domain,* 39 Emory L.J. 965 (1990)

Litman, *War Stories*, 20 Cardozo Arts & Ent. L.J. 337 (2002)

Liu, *Copyright and Breathing Space*, 30 Colum. J.L. & Arts 429 (2007)

Liu, *Copyright Law's Theory of the Consumer,* 44 B.C. L. Rev 397 (2003)

Liu, *Enabling Copyright Consumers,* 22 Berkeley Tech. L.J. 1099 (2007)

Liu, *Regulatory Copyright*, 83 N.C. L. Rev. 87 (2004)

Long, *Information Costs in Patent and Copyright*, 90 Va. L. Rev. 465 (2004)

Long, *First, "Let's Kill All the Intellectual Property Lawyers!": Musings on the Decline and Fall,of the Intellectual Property Empire,* 34 J. Marshall L. Rev. 851 (2001)

Loren, *The Pope's Copyright? Aligning Incentives with Reality by Using Creative Motivation to Shape Copyright Protection,* 69 La. L. Rev. 1 (2008)

Lunceford & Lunceford, *The Irrelevance of Copyright in the Public Mind*, 7 Nw. J. Tech. & Intell. Prop. 33 (2008)

Lunney, *Reexamining Copyright's Incentives -Access Paradigm,* 49 Vand. L. Rev. 483 (1996)

Madison, *Complexity and Copyright in Contradiction*, 18 Cardozo Arts & Ent. L.J. 125 (2000)

Madison, *Intellectual Property and Americana, or Why IP Gets the Blues,*18 Fordham Intell. Prop. Media & Ent. L.J. 677 (2008)

Madison, *Notes on a Geography of Knowledge,* 77 Fordham L. Rev. 2039 (2009)

Madison, *Where Does Creativity Come From? And Other Stories of Copyright,* 53 Case W. Res. 747 (2003)

Mathias, *Some Unhurried Reflections on Copyright,* 6 Cardozo Arts & Ent. L.J. 101 (1987)

McDonald, *Government Regulation or Other "Abridgements" of Scientific Research: The Proper Scope of Judicial Review Under the First Amendment*, 54 Emory L.J. 979 (2005)

McDonald, *Speech and Distrust: Rethinking the Content Approach to Protecting the Freedom of Expression*, 81 Notre Dame L. Rev. 1347 (2006)

McGowan, *Copyright Nonconsequentialism*, 69 Mo. L. Rev. 1 (2004)

McGowan, *Why the First Amendment Cannot Dictate Copyright Policy*, 65 U. Pitt. L. Rev. 281 (2004)

Menell, *Knowledge Accessibility and Preservation Policy for the Digital Age,* 44 Hous. L. Rev. 1013 (2007)

Merges, *A New Dynamism in the Public Domain*, 71 U. Chi. L. Rev. 183 (2004)

Merges, *Of Property Rules, Coase, and Intellectual Property,* 94 Colum. L. Rev. 2655 (1994)

Merges & Reynolds, *The Proper Scope of the Copyright and Patent Power,* 37 Harv. J. on Legis. 45 (2000)

Mtima, *Copyright Social Utility and Social Justice Interdependence: A Paradigm for Intellectual Property Empowerment and Digital Entrepreneurship*, 112 W. Va. L. Rev. 97 (2009)

Nachbar, *Judicial Review and the Quest to Keep Copyright Pure,* 2 J. Telecomm. & High Tech. L. 33 (2003)

Nadel, *How Current Copyright Law Discourages Creative Output: The Overlooked Impact of Marketing*, 19 Berkeley Tech. L.J. 785 (2004)

Netanel, *Copyright Alienability Restrictions and the Enhancement of Author Autonomy: A Normative Evaluation,* 24 Rutgers L.J. 347 (1993)

Netanel, *Copyright and a Democratic Civil Society,* 108 Yale L.J. 283 (1996)

Netanel, *Cyberspace Self-Governance: A Skeptical View from Liberal Democratic Theory,* 88 Calif. L. Rev. 395 (2000)

Netanel, *Locating Copyright Within The First Amendment Skein,* 54 Stan. L. Rev. 1 (2001)

Netanel, *Market Hierarchy and Copyright in Our System of Free Expression*, 53 Vand. L. Rev. 1879 (2000)

Netanel, *New Media in Old Bottles? Barron's Contextual First Amendment and Copyright in the Digital Age*, 76 Geo. Wash. L. Rev. 952 (2008)

Ng, *Authors and Readers: Conceptualizing Authorship in Copyright Law*, 30 Hastings Comm. & Ent. L.J. 377 (2008)

D. Nimmer, *Codifying Copyright Comprehensibly*, 51 UCLA L Rev. 1233 (2004)

D. Nimmer, *Copyright Law and the Restoration of Beauty*, 47 Osgoode Hall L.J. 553 (2009)

D. Nimmer, *The End of Copyright,* 48 Vand. L. Rev. 1385 (1995)

Ochoa, *Origins and Meanings of the Public Domain,* 28 Dayton L. Rev. 215 (2002)

Oliar & Sprigman, *There's No Free Laugh (Anymore): The Emergence of Intellectual Property Norms and Transformation of Stand-Up Comedy,* 94 Va. L. Rev. 1787 (2008)

Olson, *First Amendment Interests and Copyright Accommodations*, 50 B.C. L. Rev. 1393 (2009).

O'Rourke, *Essay: Evaluating Mistakes in Intellectual Property Law: Configuring the System to Account for Imperfection*, 4 J. Small & Emerging Bus. L. 167 (2000)

Palmer, *Intellectual Property: A Non-Posnerian Law and Economics Approach,* 12 Hamline L. Rev. 261 (1989)

Parchomovsky, *Towards an Integrated Theory of Intellectual Property,* 88 Va. L. Rev. 1455 (2002)

Patry, *Copyright and the Legislative Process: A Personal Perspective,* 14 Cardozo Arts & Ent. L.J. 139 (1996)

Patry, *Metaphors and Moral Panics in Copyright*, Intell. Prop. Q. 2008 1

Patry, *The Enumerated Powers Doctrine and Intellectual Property: An Imminent Constitutional Collision,* 67 Geo. Wash. L. Rev. 359 (1999)

Patterson, *Copyright in the New Millennium: Resolving the Conflict between Property Rights and Political Rights,* 62 Ohio St. L.J. 703 (2001)

Patterson & Birch, *A Unified Theory of Copyright*, 46 Hous. L. Rev. 215 (Joyce ed. 2009)

Pessach, *Copyright Law as a Silencing Restriction on Noninfringing Materials: Unveiling the Scope of Copyright's Diversity Externalities*, 76 So. Cal. L. Rev. 1067 (2003)

Pessach, *Reciprocal Share-Alike Exemptions in Copyright Law,* 30 Cardozo L. Rev. 1245 (2008)

Plant, *The Economic Aspects of Copyright in Books,* 1 Economica 167 (1934)

Radin, *Property and Personhood*, 34 Stan. L. Rev. 957 (1982)

Raskind, *The Continuing Process of Refining and Adapting Copyright Principles,* 14 Colum.-VLA J.L. & Arts 125 (1990)

Reichman, *Legal Hybrids Between the Patent and Copyright Paradigms,* 94 Colum. L. Rev. 2432 (1994)

Samuelson, *Enriching Discourse on Public Domains*, 55 Duke L.J. 783 (2006)

Samuelson, *Mapping the Digital Public Domain: Threats and Opportunities*, 66 Law & Contemp. Probs. 147 (2003)

Samuelson, *Preliminary Thoughts on Copyright Reform,* 2007 Utah L. Rev. 551

Schnably, *Property and Pragmatism: A Critique of Radin's Theory of Property and Personhood*, 45 Stan. L. Rev. 347 (1993)

Shipley, *Congressional Authority Over Intellectual Property Policy After* Eldred v. Ashcroft*: Deference, Empty Limitations, and Risks to the Public Domain*, 70 Alb. L. Rev. 1255 (2007)

Shur-Ofry, *Popularity as a Factor in Copyright Law,* 59 U. Toronto L.J. 525 (2009)

Sprigman, *Copyright and the Rule of Reason*, 7 J. Telecomm. & High Tech. L. 317 (2009)

Sprigman, *Indirect Enforcement of the Intellectual Property Clause*, 30 Colum. J.L. & Arts 565 (2007)

Stadler, *Copyright as Trade Regulation*, 155 U. Pa. L. Rev. 899 (2007)

Stadler, *Forging a Truly Utilitarian Copyright*, 91 Iowa L. Rev. 609 (2006)

Stadler, *Incentive and Expectation in Copyright*, 58 Hastings L.J. 433 (2007)

Sterk, *Intellectualizing Property: The Tenuous Connections Between Land and Copyright*, 83 Wash. U. L.Q. 417 (2005)

Sterk, *Rhetoric and Reality in Copyright Law,* 94 Mich. L. Rev. 1197 (1996)

Suchman, *Invention and Ritual: Notes on the Interrelation of Magic and Intellectual Property in Preliterate Societies,* 89 Colum. L. Rev. 1264 (1989)

Sunder, *The Invention of Traditional Knowledge*, 70 Law & Contemp. Probs. 97 (2007)

Swanson, *The Role of Disclosure in Modern Copyright Law,* 70 J. Pat. & Trademark Off. Soc'y 217 (1988)

Tatum, Spoo & Pope, *Does Gender Influence Attitudes Toward Copyright in the Filk Community?,* 18 Am. U.J. Gender Soc. Pol'y & L. 219 (2010)

Tehranian, *An Unhurried View of Copyright Reform: Bridging the Law / Norm Gap*, 2007 Utah L. Rev. 537 (2007)

Torremans, *Is Copyright a Human Right?*, 2007 Mich. St. L. Rev 271

Treiger-Bar-Am, *Kant on Copyright: Rights of Transformative Authorship*, 25 Cardozo Arts & Ent. L.J. 1059 (2008)

Trosow, *The Illusive Search for Justificatory Theories: Copyright, Commodification and Capital*, 16 Can. J.L. & Jurisprudence 217 (2003)

Troutt, *I Own Therefore I Am: Copyright, Personality, and Soul Music in the Digital Commons,* 20 Fordham Intell. Prop. Media & Ent. L.J. 373 (2010)

Tushnet, *Legal Fictions: Copyright, Fan Fiction, and a New Common Law*, 17 Loy. L.A. Ent. L.J. 651 (1997).

Tushnet, *Copyright as a Model for Free Speech Law: What Copyright Has in Common With Anti-Pornography Laws, Campaign Finance Reform, and Telecommunications Regulation*, 42 B.C. L. Rev. 1 (2000)

Tyerman, *The Economic Rationale for Copyright Protection for Published Books: A Reply to Professor Breyer,* 18 UCLA L. Rev. 1100 (1971)

Valkonen & White, *An Economic Model for the Incentive / Access Paradigm of Copyright, Propertization: An Argument in Support of the Orphan Works Act,* 29 Hastings Comm. & Ent. L.J. 359 (2007)

Van Houweling, *Distributive Values in Copyright,* 83 Tex. L. Rev. 1535 (2005)

Van Houweling, *Cultural Environmentalism and the Constructed Common*, 70 Law & Contemp. Probs. 23 (2007)

Vaver, *Intellectual Property Today: Of Myths and Paradoxes,* 69 Can. Bar Rev. 98 (1990)

VerSteeg, *Rhetoric and Law in Ovid's Orpheus,* 15 L. & Literature 395 (2003)

Waldron, *From Authors to Copiers: Individual Rights and Social Values in Intellectual Property,* 68 Chi.-Kent L. Rev. 847 (1993)

Wilde, *Replacing the Idea / Expression Metaphor With a Market-Based Analysis in Copyright Infringement Actions*, 16 Whittier L. Rev. 793 (1995)

Winslow, *Rapping on a Revolving Door: An Economic Analysis of Parody & Campbell v. Acuff-Rose Music, Inc.*, 69 S. Cal. L. Rev. 767 (1996)

Wong, *Toward an Alternative Normative Framework for Copyright: From Private Property to Human Rights,* 26 Cardozo Arts & Ent. L.J. 775 (2009)

Woodmansee, *The Genius and the Copyright,* 17 Eighteenth Century Studies 425 (1984)

Wu, *Copyright's Communications Policy*, 103 Mich. L. Rev. 278 (2004)

Yen, *A Preliminary Economic Analysis of* Napster*: Internet Technology, Copyright Liability, and The Possibility of Coasean Bargaining,* 26 U. Dayton L. Rev. 247 (2001)

Yen, *Copyright Opinions and Aesthetic Theory,* 71 S. Cal. L. Rev. 247 (1998)

Yen, Eldred, *the First Amendment, and Aggressive Copyright Claims*, 40 Hous. L. Rev. 673 (2003)

Yen, *Restoring the Natural Law: Copyright as Labor and Possession,* 51 Ohio St. L.J. 517 (1990)

Yen, *The Interdisciplinary Future of Copyright Theory,* 10 Cardozo Arts & Ent. L.J. 423 (1992)

Yen, *Western Frontier or Feudal Society?: Metaphors and Perceptions of Cyberspace*, 17 Berkeley Tech. L.J. 1207 (2002)

Yoo, *Copyright and Product Differentiation*, 79 N.Y.U. L. Rev. 212 (2004)

Yoo, *Copyright and Public Good Economics: A Misunderstood Relation*, 155 U. Pa. L. Rev. 635 (2007)

Zimmerman, *Is There a Right to Have Something to Say? One View of the Public Domain*, 73 Fordham L. Rev. (2004)

Chapter 2
PREREQUISITES FOR COPYRIGHT PROTECTION

Reference Works

H. Abrams, The Law of Copyright §§ 2.1 to 2.67, 8.1 to 8.7 (2008)

P. Goldstein, Goldstein on Copyright §§ 2.0 to 2.5, 18.4 (3d ed. 2005)

M. Leaffer, Understanding Copyright Law §§ 2.01 to 2.06, 2.13 to 2.14 (5th ed. 2010)

M. Nimmer & D. Nimmer, Nimmer on Copyright §§ 1.01 to 1.12, 2.01 to 2.02, 5.05 to 5.15 (2010)

W. Patry, Patry on Copyright §§ 3:1 to 3:45, 4:1 to 4:88 (2010)

Fixation

Brandriss, *Writing in Frost on a Window Pane: E-mail and Chatting on RAM and Copyright Fixation,* 43 J. Copyright Soc'y 237 (1996)

Damman, *Copyright of Computer Display Screens: Summary and Suggestions,* 9 Computer L.J. 417 (1989)

Heymann, *How to Write a Life: Some Thoughts on Fixation and the Copyright / Privacy Divide,* 51 Wm. & Mary L. Rev. 825 (2009)

McQueen, *"My tongue is mine ain": Copyright, the Spoken Word and Privacy*, 68 Mod. L.Q. 349 (2005)

Note, *Fixing Fixation: A Copyright With Teeth for Improvisational Performers,* 97 Colum. L. Rev. 1363 (1997)

Staines, *Idee or Idee Fixe?,* 50 Mod. L. Rev. 368 (1987)

Originality and Authorship Generally

Abrams, *Originality and Creativity in Copyright Law,* 55 Law & Contemp. Probs. 3 (1992)

Aoki, *(Intellectual) Property and Sovereignity: Notes Toward a Cultural Geography of Authorship,* 48 Stan. L. Rev. 1293 (1996)

Baade, *Photographer's Rights: Case for Sufficient Originality Test in Copyright,* 30 J. Marshall L. Rev. 149 (1996)

Booth & Yera, *Judicial Review, Copyrightability and the Register's Discretion: A New Direction?,* 7 U. Miami Ent. & Sports L. Rev. 255 (1990)

Brauneis, *The Transformation of Originality in the Progressive-Era Debate Over Copyright in News,* 27 Cardozo Arts & Ent. L.J.321 (2009)

Brown, *Eligibility for Copyright Protection: A Search for Principled Standards,* 70 Minn. L. Rev. 579 (1985)

Cameron, *In Defiance of* Bridgeman: *Claiming Copyright in Photographic Reproductions of Public Domain Works*, 15 Tex. Intell. Prop. L.J. 31 (2006)

Clifford, *Intellectual Property in the Era of Creative Computer Programs: Will the True Creator Please Stand Up?*, 71 Tul. L. Rev. 1675 (1997)

Craig, *Resisting 'Sweat' and Refusing* Feist: *Rethinking Originality After* CCH, 40 U.B.C. L. Rev. 69 (2007)

Dreier & Karnell, *Originality of the Copyrighted Work: A European Perspective,* 39 J. Copyright Soc'y 289 (1992)

Durham, *The Random Muse: Authorship and Indeterminacy,* 44 Wm. & Mary L. Rev. 569 (2002)

Durham, *Speaking of the World: Fact, Opinion and the Originality Standard of Copyright,* 33 Ariz. St. L.J. 791 (2001)

Dusollier, *Open Source and Copyleft: Authorship Reconsidered*, 26 Colum.-VLA J.L. & Arts 281 (2003)

Elkin-Koren, *Of Scientific Claims and Proprietary Rights: Lessons from the* Dead Sea Scrolls *Case,* 38 Hous. L. Rev. 445 (2001)

Field, *Originality: Does the Copyright Office Hide the Ball?*, 37 AIPLA Q.J. 425 (2009)

Gasaway, *Libraries, Users, and the Problems of Authorship in the Digital Age,* 52 DePaul L. Rev. 1193 (2003)

Ginsburg, *The Author's Place in the Future of Copyright*, 45 Willamette L. Rev. 381 (2009)

Goodman, *Media Policy and Free Speech: The First Amendment at War with Itself,* 35 Hofstra L. Rev. 1211 (2007)

Gorman, *Copyright Courts and Aesthetic Judgments: Abuse or Necessity?*, 25 Colum.-VLA J.L. & Arts 1 (2001)

Hughes, *Size Matters (or Should) in Copyright Law*, 74 Fordham L. Rev. 575 (2005)

Hussey, *The* Sine Qua Non *of Copyright*, 51 J. Copyright Soc'y 763 (2004)

Jaszi, *Toward a Theory of Copyright: The Metamorphosis of "Authorship,"* 41 Duke L.J. 455 (1991)

Johnson, *Statute of Anne-imals: Should Copyright Protect Sentient Nonhuman Creators?,* 15 Animal L. 15, (2008)

Judge & Gervais, *Of Silos and Constellations: Comparing Notions of Originality in Copyright Law,* 27 Cardozo Arts & Ent. L.J. 375 (2009)

Karjala, *Copyright and Misappropriation,* 17 U. Dayton L. Rev. 885 (1992)

Kremers, *Speaking With a Forked Tongue in the Global Debate on Traditional Knowledge and Genetic Resources: Are U.S. Intellectual Property Law and*

Policy Really Aimed at Meaningful Protection for Native American Cultures, 15 Fordham Intell. Prop. Media & Ent. L.J. 1 (2004)

Kwall, *Originality in Context*, 44 Hous. L. Rev. 871 (2007)

Lange, *At Play in the Fields of the Word: Copyright and the Construction of Authorship in the Post-Literate Millennium,* 55 Law & Contemp. Probs. 139 (1992)

Lanham, *Barbie and the Teacher of Righteousness: Two Lessons in the Economics of Attention,* 38 Hous. L. Rev. 499 (2001)

Mitchell, *Take Me out of the Ball Game? U.S. District Court Rejects Proprietary Rights in Player Names and Statistics*, 96 Trademark Rep. 1258 (2006)

Ng, *The Social Contract and Authorship: Allocating Entitlements in the Copyright System,* 19 Fordham Intell. Prop. Media & Ent. L.J. 413 (2009)

D. Nimmer, *Copyright in the Dead Sea Scrolls: Authorship and Originality,* 38 Hous. L. Rev. 1 (2001)

Oakes, *The Dead Sea Scrolls: A Live Copyright Controversy*, 38 Hous. L. Rev. 219 (2001)

Olson, *Copyright Originality*, 48 Mo. L. Rev. 29 (1983)

Oppenheimer, *Originality in Art Reproductions: "Variations" in Search of a Theme,* 26 Bull. Copyright Soc'y 1 (1978)

Parchomovsky & Stein, *Originality,* 95 Va. L. Rev. 1505 (2009)

Patterson, *Nimmer's Copyright in the Dead Sea Scrolls: A Comment*, 38 Hous. L. Rev. 431 (2001)

Reese, *Photographs of Public Domain Paintings: How, If at All, Should We Protect Them?,* 34 J. Corp. L. 1033 (2009)

Ricketson, *The Concept of Originality in Anglo-Australian Copyright Law,* 39 J. Copyright Soc'y 265 (1992)

Samuelson, *The Originality Standard for Literary Works Under U.S. Copyright Law,* 42 Am. J. Comp. L. 393 (1994)

Sookman, *Computer-Assisted Creation of Works Protected by Copyright,* 5 Intell. Prop. J. 165 (1990)

Stadler, *Relevant Markets for Copyrighted Works*. 34 J. Corp. L. 1059 (2009)

Stoddard, *Mother Nature as Muse: Copyright Protection for Works of Art and Photographs Inspired By, Based On, Or Depicting Nature*, 86 N.C. L. Rev. 572 (2008)

VerSteeg, *Defining "Author" for Purposes of Copyright,* 45 Am. U. L. Rev. 1323 (1996)

VerSteeg, *Intent, Originality, Creativity and Joint Authorship*, 68 Brook. L. Rev. 123 (2002)

VerSteeg, *Originality and Creativity in Copyright Law*, 1 Intellectual Property and Information Wealth: Issues and Practices in the Digital Age (2006)

VerSteeg, *Rethinking Originality (in Copyright)*, 34 Wm. & Mary L. Rev. 801 (1993)

VerSteeg, *Sparks in the Tinderbox:* Feist, *Creativity and the Legislative History of the 1976 Copyright Act*, 57 U. Pitt. L. Rev. 549 (1995)

Weinstein, *Ancient Works, Modern Dilemmas: The Dead Sea Scrolls Copyright Case*, 43 Am. U. L. Rev. 1637 (1994)

Wilkof, *Copyright, Moral Rights and the Choice of Law: Where Did the* Dead Sea Scrolls *Court Go Wrong?*, 38 Hous. L. Rev. 463 (2001)

Wojcik, *The Antithesis of Originality:* Bridgeman, *Image Licensors, and the Public Domain*, 30 Hastings Comm. & Ent. L.J. 257 (2008)

Woodmansee, *Response to David Nimmer*, 38 Hous. L. Rev. 231 (2001)

Zimmerman, *It's An Original!(?): In Pursuit of Copyright's Elusive Essence*, 28 Colum.-VLA J.L. & Arts 187 (2005)

The Idea/Expression Dichotomy

A. Cohen, *Copyright Law and the Myth of Objectivity: The Idea-Expression Dichotomy and the Inevitability of Artistic Value Judgments*, 66 Ind. L.J. 175 (1990)

Detterman, *The Scope of Copyright Protection for Computer Programs: Exploring the Idea-Expression Dichotomy*, 20 Intell. Prop. L. Rev. 399 (1988)

Gambrell, Hamilton & Hood, Whelan & Altai: *Protecting Software by Abusing Idea and Expression*, 11 Computer Law. 9 (1994)

Katz, *Expanded Notions of Copyright Protection: Idea Protection Within the Copyright Act*, 77 B.U. L. Rev. 873 (1997)

Kurtz, *Speaking to the Ghost: Idea and Expression in Copyright*, 47 U. Miami L. Rev. 1221 (1993)

Libott, *Round the Prickly Pear: The Idea-Expression Fallacy in a Mass Communications World*, 14 UCLA L. Rev. 735 (1967)

Malkan, *Rule-Based Expression in Copyright Law*, 57 Buff. L. Rev. 433 (2009)

Olson, *The Uneasy Legacy of Baker v. Selden*, 43 S.D. L. Rev. 604 (1998)

Patry, *The Enumerated Powers Doctrine and Intellectual Property: An Imminent Constitutional Collision*, 67 Geo. Wash. L. Rev. 359 (1999)

Reichman, *Computer Programs as Applied Scientific Know-How: Implication of Copyright Protection for Commercialized University Research*, 42 Vand. L. Rev. 639 (1989)

Samuels, *The Idea-Expression Dichotomy in Copyright Law,* 56 Tenn. L. Rev. 321 (1989)

Samuelson, *Why Copyright Law Excludes Systems and Processes from the Scope of Its Protection*, 85 Tex. L. Rev. 1921 (2007)

Spivack, *Does Form Follow Function? The Idea-Expression Dichotomy in Copyright Protection of Computer Software,* 35 UCLA L. Rev. 723 (1988)

Wilde, *Replacing the Idea / Expression Metaphor With a Market-Based Analysis in Copyright Infringement Actions,* 16 Whittier L. Rev. 793 (1995).

Yen, *A First Amendment Perspective on the Idea / Expression Dichotomy and Copyright in a Work's "Total Concept and Feel,"* 38 Emory L.J. 393 (1989)

Government Works

Cunningham, *Private Standards in Public Law: Copyright, Lawmaking and the Case of Accounting*, 74 Fordham L. Rev. 291 (2005).

Ghosh, *Copyright as Privatization: The Case of Model Codes,* 78 Tul. L. Rev. 653 (2004)

Ghosh, *Legal Code and the Need for a Broader Functionality Doctrine in Copyright,* 50 J. Copyright Soc'y 71 (2003)

Nadiff, *Copyrightability of Works of the Federal and State Governments Under the 1976 Act,* 29 St. Louis U. L.J. 91 (1984)

Patterson & Joyce, *Monopolizing the Law: The Scope of Copyright Protection for Law Reports and Statutory Compilations*, 36 UCLA L. Rev. 719 (1989)

Samuelson, *Questioning Copyrights in Standards*, 48 B.C. L. Rev. 193 (2007)

Trosow, *Copyright Protection for Federally Funded Research: Necessary Incentive or Double Subsidy?*, 22 Cardozo Arts & Ent. L.J. 613 (2004)

Valoir, *Deposition Transcripts: Are They Subject to Copyright Protection?*, 17 Intell. Prop. & Tech. L.J. 1 (2005)

Wittig, Zelenka, Smith, & Manz, *Government Works in an International Marketplace: The Copyright Issue,* 2002 Syracuse L. & Tech. J. 1 (2002)

Chapter 3

WORKS OF AUTHORSHIP

Reference Works

H. Abrams, THE LAW OF COPYRIGHT §§ 3.1 to 3.33, 20.1 to 20.37 (2008)

P. Goldstein, GOLDSTEIN ON COPYRIGHT §§ 2.6 to 2.16, 17.26 to 17.34 (3d ed. 2005)

M. Leaffer, UNDERSTANDING COPYRIGHT LAW §§ 2.07 to 2.12, 3.01 to 3.22 (5th ed. 2010)

M. Nimmer & D. Nimmer, NIMMER ON COPYRIGHT §§ 2.02 to 2.20, 3.01 to 3.08, 8A.13 to 8A.21 (2010)

W. Patry, PATRY ON COPYRIGHT §§ 3:46 to 3:164 (2010)

Literary Works Generally

M. Biagioli & P. Galison (eds.), SCIENTIFIC AUTHORSHIP (2003)

E.G. Perle & J.T. Williams, PERLE AND WILLIAMS ON PUBLISHING LAW HANDBOOK (3d ed. 1999 & 2007 Supp.)

R. Wincor, THE ART OF CHARACTER LICENSING (1996)

Abromson, *The Copyrightability of Sports Celebration Moves: Dance Fever or Just Plain Sick?*, 14 Marquette Sports L. Rev. 571 (2004)

Aoki, *Contradiction and Context in American Copyright Law,* 9 Cardozo Arts & Ent. L.J. 303 (1991)

Ariens, *The Ethics of Copyrighting Ethics Rules*, 36 U. Toledo L. Rev. 235 (2005)

Bartholomew, *Protecting the Performers: Setting a New Standard for Character Copyrightability,* 41 Santa Clara L. Rev. 341 (2001)

Beall, *Can Anyone Own a Piece of the Clock? The Troublesome Application of Copyright Law to Works of Historical Fiction, Interpretation, and Theory,* 42 Emory L.J. 253 (1993)

Bilder, *The Shrinking Back: The Law of Biography,* 43 Stan. L. Rev. 299 (1991)

Burcart, *No Title to Titles: An Analysis of the Lack of Copyright Protection for Literary Titles,* 32 Copyright L. Symp. (ASCAP) 75 (1986)

Cotter & Mirabole, *Written on the Body: Intellectual Property Rights in Tattoos, Makeup, and Other Body Art*, 10 UCLA Ent. L. Rev. 97 (2003)

Easton, *Who Owns "The First Rough Draft of History"? Reconsidering Copyright in News*, 27 Colum.-VLA J.L & Arts 521 (2004)

Effross, *Owning Enlightenment: Proprietary Spirituality in the "New Age" Marketplace*, 51 Buff. L. Rev. 483 (2003)

Ginsburg, *Sabotaging and Reconstructing History: A Comment on the Scope of Copyright Protection in Works of History After* Hoehling v. Universal City Studios, 29 J. Copyright Soc'y 647 (1982)

Gorman, *Fact or Fancy? The Implications for Copyright,* 29 J. Copyright Soc'y 560 (1982)

Hill, *Copyright Protection for Historical Research: A Defense of the Minority View,* 31 Copyright L. Symp. (ASCAP) 45 (1984)

Kidwell, *Open Records Laws and Copyright,* 1989 Wis. L. Rev. 1021

Kurtz, *Copyright: The Scenes a Faire Doctrine*, 41 Fla. L. Rev. 79 (1989)

Kurtz, *Digital Actors and Copyright — from the Polar Express to Simone*, 21 Santa Clara Computer & High Tech. L.J. 783 (2005)

Kurtz, *Protection for Titles of Literary Works in the Public Domain,* 37 Rutgers L. Rev. 53 (1984)

Kurtz, *The Independent Legal Lives of Fictional Characters,* 1986 Wis. L. Rev. 429

Kurtz, *The Methuselah Factor: When Characters Outlive Their Copyrights*, 11 U. Miami Ent. & Sports L. Rev. 437 (1994)

Lalor, *Copyrightability of Cartoon Characters,* 35 Idea 497 (1995)

Murray, *Copyrightability, Originality, and the End of the Scenes a Faire and Merger Doctrines for Visual Works*, 58 Baylor L. Rev. 779 (2006)

Nevins, *Copyright + Character = Catastrophe,* 39 J. Copyright Soc'y 303 (1992)

Poliakoff, *License to Copyright: The Ongoing Dispute Over the Ownership of James Bond*, 18 Cardozo Arts & Ent. L.J. 387 (2000)

Pollack, *Intellectual Property Protection for the Creative Chef, or How to Copyright a Cake: A Modest Proposal,* 12 Cardozo L. Rev. 1477 (1991)

Schwabach, *The Harry Potter Lexicon and the World of Fandom: Fan Fiction, Outsider Works, and Copyright,* 70 U. Pitt. L. Rev. 387 (2009)

Shipley & Hay, *Protecting Research: Copyright, Common Law Alternatives, and Federal Preemption,* 63 N.C.L. Rev. 125 (1984)

Stim, *E.T. Phone Home: The Protection of Literary Phrases,* 7 U. Miami Ent. & Sports L. Rev. 65 (1989)

Syn, *Copyright God: Enforcement of Copyright in the Bible and Religious Works,* 14 Regent U.L. Rev. 277 (2001)

Tannenbaum, *Uses of Titles for Copyright and Public Domain Works,* 6 Bull. Copyright Soc'y 64 (1958)

Tushnet, *Legal Fictions: Copyright, Fan Fiction & a New Common Law,* 17 Loy. L.A. Ent. L.J. 651 (1997)

Wang, *The Copyrightability of Legal Complaints*, B.C. L. Rev. 705 (2004)

Welkowitz, *Intellectual Property and DNA: Copyright and Trademark Applications,* 24 Whittier L. Rev. 473 (2002)

Software-Related Issues

S. Fishman, LEGAL GUIDE TO WEB & SOFTWARE DEVELOPMENT (5th ed. 2007)

R. Nimmer, THE LAW OF COMPUTER TECHNOLOGY: RIGHTS, LICENSES, LIABILITIES (2009)

R. Nimmer & H. Towle, THE LAW OF ELECTRONIC COMMERCIAL TRANSACTIONS (2003 & Supp. 2009)

Office of Technology Assessment, COMPUTER SOFTWARE: COPYRIGHT, PATENTS AND THE CHALLENGE OF TECHNOLOGICAL CHANGE (1993)

B. Sookman, COMPUTER, INTERNET AND ELECTRONIC COMMERCE LAW (2002 & Supp. 2009)

Amin, *The Lack of Protection Afforded Software Under the Current Intellectual Property Laws,* 43 Clev. St. L. Rev. 19 (1995)

Bobko, *Open-Source Software and the Demise of Copyright,* 27 Rutgers Computer & Tech. L.J. 51 (2001)

Butler, *Pragmatism in Software Copyright:* Computer Associates v. Altai, 6 Harv. J.L. & Tech. 183 (1992)

Capes, *The Software Copyright "Super Patent,"* 12 Computer Law. 8 (1995)

Cass, *Copyright, Licensing, and the "First Screen,"* 5 Mich. Telecomm. Tech. L. Rev. 35 (1999)

Clapes, Lynch & Steinberg, *Silicon Epics and Binary Bards: Determining the Proper Scope of Copyright Protection for Computer Programs,* 34 UCLA L. Rev. 1493 (1987)

J. Cohen, *Reverse Engineering and the Rise of Electronic Vigilantism: Intellectual Property Implications of "Lock-out" Programs*, 68 S. Cal. L. Rev. 1091 (1995)

Cook, *Music Publishers Slay Musicianship (Web Sites Hosting Guitar Tablature)*, 8 Tex. Rev. Ent. & Sports L. 101 (2007)

Derwin, *It Is Time to Put "Look and Feel" Out to Pasture,* 15 Hastings Comm. & Ent. L.J. 605 (1993)

Englund, *Idea, Process, or Protected Expression? Determining the Scope of Copyright Protection of the Structure of Computer Programs,* 88 Mich. L. Rev. 866 (1990)

Ginsburg, *Four Reasons and a Paradox: The Manifest Superiority of Copyright Over* Sui Generis *Protection of Computer Software,* 94 Colum. L. Rev. 2559 (1994)

Goldberg & Carson, *Copyright Protection for Artificial Intelligence Systems,* 39 J. Copyright Soc'y 57 (1991)

Gorman, *Comments on a Manifesto Concerning the Legal Protection of Computer Programs*, 5 Alb. L.J. Sci. & Tech. 277 (1996)

Graham & Zerbe, *Economically Efficient Treatment of Computer Software: Reverse Engineering, Protection & Disclosure,* 22 Rutgers Computer & Tech. L.J. 61 (1996)

Hamilton & Sabety, *Computer Science Concepts in Copyright Cases: The Path to a Coherent Law,* 10 Harv. J.L. & Tech. 239 (1997)

Hardy, *Six Copyright Theories for the Protection of Computer Object Programs*, 26 Ariz. L. Rev. 845 (1984)

Hardy, *The Copyrightability of New Works of Authorship: "XML Schemas" as an Example,* 38 Hous. L. Rev. 855 (2001)

Hardy, *The Policy, Law, and Facts of Copyrighting Computer Screen Displays: An Essay,* 11 Computer L.J. 371 (1992)

Hazen, *Contract Principles as a Guide for Protecting Intellectual Property Rights in Computer Software: The Limits of Copyright Protection, the Evolving Concept of Derivative Works, and the Proper Limits of Licensing Arrangements,* 20 U.C. Davis L. Rev. 105 (1986)

Kaplan, Apple v. Franklin *20 Years Later: Copyright and the Internet,* 22 Temp. Envtl. L. & Tech. J. 1 (2003)

Karjala, *A Coherent Theory for the Copyright Protection of Computer Software and Recent Judicial Interpretations*, 66 U. Cin. L. Rev. 53 (1997)

Karjala, *Copyright Law: Copyright Protection of Computer Program Structure,* 64 Brooklyn L. Rev. 519 (1998)

Karjala, *Copyright Protection of Computer Documents, Reverse Engineering, and Professor Miller*, 19 Dayton L. Rev. 975 (1994)

Karjala, *Lessons from the Computer Software Protection Debate in Japan,* 1984 Ariz. St. L.J. 53

Karjala, *Policy Considerations: Theoretical Foundations for the Protection of Computer Programs in Developing Countries*, 13 UCLA Pac. Basin L.J. 179 (1994)

Karjala, *The Relative Roles of Patent and Copyright in the Protection of Computer Programs*, 17 J. Marshall J. Computer & Info. L. 41 (1998)

Karjala, *Theoretical Foundations for the Protection of Computer Programs in Developing Countries,* 13 UCLA Pac. Basin L.J. 179 (1994)

Kasch, *The Semiconductor Chip Protection Act: Past, Present, and Future,* 7 High Tech. L.J. 71 (1992)

Kreiss, *Copyright Protection and Reverse Engineering of Software,* 19 U. Dayton L. Rev. 837 (1994)

Kreiss, *Section 117 of the Copyright Act (Computer Programs),* 1991 B.Y.U. L. Rev. 1497 (1991)

Last Frontier Conference Report, *Computer Software and Copyright Protection,* 30 Jurimetrics J. 15 (1989)

M. Lemley & O'Brien, *Encouraging Software Reuse,* 49 Stan. L. Rev. 255 (1997)

Levine, *Comment on* Bonito Boats *Follow-Up: The Supreme Court's Likely Rejection of Non-Literal Software Copyright Protection,* 6 Computer Law. 29 (1989)

Loren, *The Changing Nature of Derivative Works in the Face of New Technologies*, 4 J. Small & Emerging Bus. L. 57 (2000)

Lunney, Lotus v. Borland: *Copyright and Computer Programs,* 70 Tul. L. Rev. 2397 (1996)

Menell, *Tailoring Legal Protection for Computer Software,* 39 Stan. L. Rev. 1329 (1987)

Menell, *The Challenges of Reforming Intellectual Property Protection for Computer Software,* 94 Colum. L. Rev. 2644 (1994)

Miller, *Copyright Protection for Computer Programs, Databases, and Computer-Generated Works: Is Anything New Since CONTU?,* 106 Harv. L. Rev. 977 (1993)

R. Nimmer & P. Krauthaus, *Classification of Computer Software for Legal Protection: International Perspectives,* 21 Int'l Law. 733 (1987)

R. Nimmer & P. Krauthaus, *Copyright and Software Technology Infringement: Defining Third Party Development Rights,* 62 Ind. L.J. 13 (1986)

R. Nimmer & P. Krauthaus, *Software Copyright: Sliding Scales and Abstracted Expression,* 32 Hous. L. Rev. 317 (1995)

Oddi, *An Uneasier Case for Copyright Than for Patent Protection of Computer Programs,* 72 Neb. L. Rev. 351 (1993)

Patry, *Copyright and Computer Programs: A Failed Experiment and a Solution to a Dilemma*, 46 N.Y.L. Sch. L. Rev. 201 (2002)

Pollack, *The Right to Know?: Delimiting Database Protection at the Juncture of the Commerce Clause, the Intellectual Property Clause, and the First Amendment*, 17 Cardozo Arts &. Ent. L.J. 47 (1999)

Raskind, *The Uncertain Case for Special Legislation Protecting Computer Software,* 47 U. Pitt. L. Rev. 1131 (1986)

Reuveni, *On Virtual Worlds: Copyright and Contract Law at the Dawn of the Virtual Age*, 82 Ind. L.J. 261 (2007)

Samuelson, *Allocating Ownership Rights in Computer-Generated Works,* 47 U. Pitt. L. Rev. 1185 (1986)

Samuelson, Benson *Revisited: The Case Against Patent Protection for Algorithms and Other Computer Program-Related Works,* 39 Emory L.J. 1025 (1990)

Samuelson, *Comparing U.S. and EC Copyright Protection for Computer Programs: Are They More Different Than They Seem?,* 13 J.L. & Com. 279 (1994)

Samuelson, *Computer Programs, User Interfaces, and Section 102(b) of the Copyright Act of 1976: A Critique of* Lotus v. Paperback, 55 Law & Contemp. Probs. 311 (1992)

Samuelson, *CONTU Revisited: The Case Against Copyright Protection for Computer Programs in Machine-Readable Form,* 1984 Duke L.J. 663

Samuelson, *Creating a New Kind of Intellectual Property: Applying the Lessons of the Chip Law to Computer Programs,* 70 Minn. L. Rev. 471 (1985)

Samuelson, *How to Interpret the* Lotus *Decision (And How Not To),* 33 Comm. of the ACM 27 (1990)

Samuelson, *Modifying Copyrighted Software: Adjusting Copyright Doctrine to Accommodate a Technology,* 28 Jurimetrics J. 179 (1988)

Samuelson, *Reflections on the State of American Software Copyright Law and the Perils of Teaching It,* 13 Colum.-VLA J.L. & Arts 61 (1988)

Samuelson, *Some New Kinds of Authorship Made Possible by Computer and Some Intellectual Property Problems They Raise,* 53 U. Pitt. L. Rev. 685 (1992)

Samuelson, Davis, Kapor & Reichman, *A Manifesto Concerning the Legal Protection of Computer Programs,* 94 Colum. L. Rev. 2308 (1994)

Stern, *Copyright in Computer Programming Languages,* 17 Rutgers Computer & Tech. L.J. 321 (1991)

Stern, *Legal Protection for Screen Displays and Other User Interfaces for Computers: A Problem in Balancing Incentives for Creation Against Need for Free Access to the Utilitarian,* 14 Colum.-VLA J.L. & Arts 283 (1990)

Stern, *Scope-of-Protection Problems With Patents and Copyrights on Methods of Doing Business*, 10 Fordham Intell. Prop. Media & Ent. L.J. 105 (1999)

Tache, *Copyrightability of Computer Languages: Natural Expansion of Copyright Law or Destruction of the Copyright/Patent Distinction?,* 72 J. Pat. & Trademark Off. Soc'y 564 (1990)

Teter, *Merger and the Machines: An Analysis of the Pro-Compatibility Trend in Computer Software Copyright Cases,* 45 Stan. L. Rev. 1061 (1993)

Walker, *Protectable "Nuggets": Drawing the Line Between Idea and Expression in Computer Program Copyright Protection,* 44 J. Copyright Soc'y 79 (1996)

Weinreb, *Copyright for Functional Expression,* 111 Harv. L. Rev. 1149 (1998)

Wilkins, *Protecting Computer Programs as Compilations Under* Computer Associates v. Altai, 104 Yale L.J. 435 (1994)

Zimmerman, *Can Our Culture Be Saved? The Future of Digital Archiving,* 91 Minn. L. Rev. 989 (2007)

Musical Works and Sound Recordings

Arewa, *Blues Lives: Promise and Perils of Musical Copyright*, 27 Cardozo Arts & Ent. L.J. 573 (2010)

Arewa, *From J.C. Bach to Hip Hop: Musical Borrowing, Copyright and Cultural Context*, 84 N.C. L. Rev. 547 (2006)

Brauneis, *Copyright and the World's Most Popular Song*, 56 J. Copyright Soc'y 335 (2009)

Brylawski, *Motion Picture Soundtrack Music: A Gap or Gaff in Copyright Protection?,* 40 J. Copyright Soc'y 333 (1993)

Calamita, *Coming to Terms With the Celestial Juke Box: Keeping the Sound Recording Copyright Viable in the Digital Age,* 74 B.U. L. Rev. 505 (1994)

Carroll, *A Primer on U.S. Intellectual Property Rights Applicable to Music Information Retrieval Systems*, 2003 U. Ill. J.L. Tech. & Pol'y 313 (2003)

Carroll, *The Struggle for Music Copyright*, 57 Fla. L. Rev. 907 (2005)

Carroll, *Whose Music Is It Anyway?: How We Came to View Musical Expression as a Form of Property*, 72 U. Cinn. L. Rev. 1405 (2004)

Erlinger, *An Analog Solution in a Digital World: Providing Federal Copyright Protection for Pre-1972 Sound Recordings,* 16 UCLA Ent. L. Rev. 45 (2008)

Flavin, *A Digital Cry for Help: Internet Radio's Struggle to Survive a Second Royalty Rate Determination under the Willing Buyer / Willing Seller Standard,* 27 St. Louis U. Pub. L. Rev. 427 (2008)

Hall, *Blues and the Public Domain — No More Dues to Pay,* 42 J. Copyright Soc'y 215 (1995)

Heald, *Reviving the Rhetoric of the Public Interest: Choir Directors, Copy Machines, and New Arrangements of Public Domain Music*, 46 Duke L.J. 241 (1996)

Henslee, *Marybeth Peters Is Almost Right: An Alternative to Her Proposals to Reform the Compulsory License Scheme for Music,* 48 Washburn L.J. 107 (2008)

Kravis, *Does a Song by any Other Name Still Sound As Sweet?: Digital Sampling and its Copyright Implications,* 43 Am. U. L. Rev. 231 (1993)

Note, *Jazz Has Got Copyright Law and That Ain't Good*, 118 Harv. L. Rev. 1940 (2005)

Osterberg, *Should Sound Recordings Really be Treated Differently than Other Copyright Works?: The Illogic of* Bridgeport v. Dimension Films, 53 J. Copyright Soc'y 619 (2006)

Perritt, *New Architectures for Music: Law Should Get Out of the Way*, 29 Hastings Comm. & Ent. L.J. 259 (2007)

Rogoyski, *The Melody Machine: How to Kill Copyright and Other Problems with Protecting Discrete Musical Elements*, 88 J. Pat. & Trademark Off. Soc'y 347 & 403 (2006)

Schultz, *Live Performance, Copyright, and the Future of the Music Business*, 43 U. Rich. L. Rev. 685 (2009)

Self, *Digital Sampling: A Cultural Perspective*, 9 UCLA Ent. L. Rev. 247 (2002)

Zooesch, *"Discontented Blues": Jazz Arrangements and the Case for Improvements in Copyright Law*, 55 Cath. U. L. Rev. 867 (2006)

Dramatic Works, and Pantomimes & Choreographic Works

Abitabile & Picerno, *Dance and the Choreographer's Dilemma: A Legal and Cultural Perspective on Copyright Protection for Choreographic Works*, 27 Campbell L. Rev. 39 (2004)

Cramer, *Copyright Protection for Choreography: Can it Ever be "En Pointe"?*, 1 Syracuse J. Legis. & Pol'y 145 (1995)

de Quintana, *The Balancing Act: How Copyright and Customary Practices Protect Large Dance Companies Over Pioneering Choreographers*, 11 Vill. Sports & Ent. L.J. 139 (2004)

Fisher, *The Copyright in Choreographic Works: A Technical Analysis of the Copyright Act of 1976*, 31 Copyright L. Symp. (ASCAP) 145 (1984)

Hilgard, *Can Choreography & Copyright Waltz Together in the Wake of* Horgan v. MacMillan?, 27 U.C. Davis L. Rev. 757 (1994)

Lakes, *A* pas de deux *for Choreography and Copyright*, 80 N.Y.U. L. Rev. 1829 (2005)

Livingston, *Inspiration or Imitation: Copyright Protection for Stage Directions*, 50 B.C. L. Rev. 427 (2009)

Salter, *Taming the Trojan Horse: An Australian Perspective of Dramatic Authorship*, 56 J. Copyright Soc'y 789 (2009)

Varmer, *Copyright in Choreographic Works*, Copyright Office Study No. 28 (1960)

Wise, *Copyright Battles over Yoga's 5000-year-old Tradition*, 22 Ent. & Sports Law 18 (2005)

Yellin, *New Directions for Copyright: The Property Rights of Stage Directors*, 24 Colum.-VLA J.L. & Arts 317 (2001)

Pictorial, Graphic & Sculptural Works

Barton, *Back to the Beginning: a Revival of a 1913 Argument for Intellectual Property Protection for Fashion Design*, 35 J. Corp. L. 425 (2010)

Brown, *Copyright-like Protection for Designs*, 19 U. Balt. L. Rev. 308 (1989)

Brown, *Design Protection: An Overview*, 34 UCLA L. Rev. 1341 (1987)

Burgunder, *Product Design Protection After* Bonito Boats: *Where It Belongs and How It Should Get There*, 28 Am. Bus. L.J. 1 (1990)

Byron, *As Long as There's Another Way:* Pivot Point v. Charlene Products *as an Accidental Template for a Creativity-Driven Useful Articles Analysis*, 49 IDEA 147 (2009)

Denicola, *Applied Art and Industrial Design: A Suggested Approach to Copyright in Useful Articles*, 67 Minn. L. Rev. 707 (1983)

Derclaye, *Are Fashion Designers Better Protected in Continental Europe Than in the United Kingdom? A Comparative Analysis of the Recent*

Case Law in France, Italy and the United Kingdom, 13 J. World Intell. Prop. 315 (2010)

Fryer, *Industrial Design Protection in the United States of America-Present Situation and Plans for Revision,* 70 J. Pat. & Trademark Off. Soc'y 820 (1988)

Goldenberg, *The Long and Winding Road: A History of the Fight Over Industrial Design Protection in the United States*, 45 J. Copyright Soc'y 21 (1997)

Hamilton, *Art Speech*, 49 Vand. L. Rev. 73 (1996)

Hamilton, *Four Questions About Art*, 13 Cardozo Arts & Ent. L.J. 119 (1994)

Hemphill & Suk, *Remix and Cultural Production,* 61 Stan. L. Rev. 1227 (2009)

Lipton, *To © or Not to ©? Copyright and Innovation in the Digital Typeface Industry,* 43 U.C. Davis L. Rev. 143 (2009)

Lynch, *Copyright in Utilitarian Objects: Beneath Metaphysics,* 16 U. Dayton L. Rev. 647 (1991)

Oberman & Lloyd, *Copyright Protection for Photographs in the Age of New Technologies,* 2 B.U. J. Sci. & Tech. 10 (1996)

Perlmutter, *Conceptual Separability and Copyright in the Design of Useful Articles,* 37 J. Copyright Soc'y 339 (1990)

Polakovic, *Should the Bauhaus Be in the Copyright Doghouse? Rethinking Conceptual Separability,* 64 U. Colo. L. Rev. 871 (1993)

Raustiala & Sprigman, *The Piracy Paradox Revisited,* 61 Stan. L. Rev. 1201 (2009)

Reichman, *Design Protection After the Copyright Act of 1976: A Comparative View of the Emerging Interim Models,* 31 J. Copyright Soc'y 267 (1984)

Reichman, *Design Protection and the Legislative Agenda,* 55 Law & Contemp. Probs. 281 (1992)

Reichman, *Design Protection and the New Technologies: The United States Experience in a Transnational Perspective,* 19 U. Balt. L. Rev. 6 (1990)

Reichman, *Design Protection in Domestic and Foreign Copyright Law: From the Berne Revision of 1948 to the Copyright Act of 1976,* 1983 Duke L.J. 1143

Saroff, *Putting Intellectual Property Law on the Fairway: Toward an Expansion of Copyrighit Law to Golf Course Architecture*, 28 Colum. J.L. & Arts 379 (2005)

Silver, *A Bad Dream: In Search of a Legal Framework for Copyright Infringement Claims Involving Digital Imagery in Motion Pictures,* 35 Idea 407 (1995)

Sybert & Hulley, *Copyright Protection for "Useful Articles,"* 54 J. Copyright Soc'y 419 (2007)

VerSteeg, *Jurimetric Copyright: Future Shock for the Visual Arts,* 13 Cardozo Arts & Ent. L.J. 125 (1994)

Ward, *Copyrighting Context: Law for Plumbing's Sake,* 17 Colum.-VLA J.L. & Arts 159 (1993)

Whicher, *Originality, Cartography and Copyright,* 38 N.Y.U. L. Rev. 280 (1963)

Wolf, *Is There Any Copyright Protection for Maps after* Feist?, 39 J. Copyright Soc'y 224 (1992)

Wolf, *New Landscape in the Copyright Protection for Maps:* Mason v. Montgomery Data, Inc., 40 J. Copyright Soc'y 401 (1993)

Architectural Works

Ginsburg, *Copyright in the 101st Congress: Commentary on the Visual Artists' Rights Act and the Architectural Works Copyright Protection Act of 1990,* 14 Colum.-VLA J.L. & the Arts 477 (1990)

Hancks, *Copyright Protection for Architectural Design: A Conceptual and Practical Criticism,* 71 Wash. L. Rev. 177 (1996)

Newsam, *Architecture & Copyright — Separating the Poetic from the Prosaic,* 71 Tul. L. Rev. 1073 (1997)

Pollock, *The Architectural Works Copyright Protection Act: Analysis of Probable Ramifications and Arising Issues,* 70 Neb. L. Rev. 873 (1991)

Roberts, *There Goes My Baby: Buildings as Intellectual Property Under the Architectural Works Copyright Protection Act,* 21 Construction Law. 22 (Spr. 2001)

Scaglione, *Building upon the Architectural Works Protection Copyright Act of 1990,* 61 Fordham L. Rev. 193 (1992)

Shipley, *Copyright Protection for Architectural Works,* 37 S.C. L. Rev. 393 (1986)

Thiel, *The Architectural Works Copyright Protection Gesture of 1990, or, "Hey, That Looks Like My Building,"* 7 DePaul-LCA J. Art & Ent. L. 1 (1996)

Derivative Works

Abramowicz, *A Theory of Copyright's Derivative Right and Related Doctrines*, 90 Minn. L. Rev. 317 (2005)

Blaise, *Game Over: Issues Arising When a Copyright Work Is Licensed to Video Game Manufacturers*, 15 Alb. J.L. Sci. & Tech. 517 (2005)

Boyd, *Deriving Originality in Derivative Works: Considering the Quantum of Originality Needed to Attain Copyright Protection in a Derivative Work,* 40 Santa Clara L. Rev. 325 (1999)

Brandstetter, *The Lone Ranger: Have the Courts Unfairly Singled Out Musical Arrangements by Denying Them Protection as Derivative Works?,* 15 SPG Ent. & Sports Law. 1 (1997)

Comment, *Copyright and the Musical Arrangement: An Analysis of the Law and Problems Pertaining to This Specialized Form of Derivative Work,* 7 Pepperdine L. Rev. 125 (1979)

Durham, *Consumer Modification of Copyrighted Works*, 81 Ind. L.J. 851 (2006)

Goldstein, *Derivative Rights and Derivative Works in Copyright,* 30 J. Copyright Soc'y 209 (1982)

Loren, *The Changing Nature of Derivative Works in the Face of New Technologies*, 4 J. Small & Emerging Bus. L. 57 (2000)

Mtima, *So Dark the Con(tu) of Man: The Quest for a Software Derivative Work Right in Section 117,* 70 U. Pitt. L. Rev. 1 (2008)

Ochoa, *Copyright, Derivative Worksand Fixation: Is* Galoob *a Mirage, or Does the* Form(Gen) *of the Alleged Derivative Work Matter?*, 20 Santa Clara Computer & High Tech. L.J. 991 (2004)

Olin, *"Recoding" and the Derivative Works Entitlement: Addressing the First Amendment Challenge*, 119 Harv. L. Rev. 1488 (2006)

Ostertag, *The Use of Derivative Works After Copyright Termination — Does* Woods v. Bourne *Expose a Quagmire?,* 43 J. Copyright Soc'y 28 (1995)

Page, *The Works: Distinguishing Derivative Creations Under Copyright*, 5 Cardozo Arts & Ent. L.J. 415 (1986)

Prater, *When Museums Act Like Gift Shops: The Discordant Derivative Works Exception to the Termination Clause,* 17 Loy. L.A. Ent. L.J. 97 (1996)

Y'Barbo, *Aesthetic Ambition Versus Commercial Appeal: Adapting Novels to Film and the Copyright Law*, 10 St. Thomas L. Rev. 299 (1998)

Compilations

J. Baumgarten, FACT AND DATA PROTECTION AFTER *Feist* (1991)

R. Nimmer, THE LAW OF COMPUTER TECHNOLOGY: RIGHTS, LICENSES, LIABILITIES (2009)

Register of Copyrights, REPORT ON LEGAL PROTECTION FOR DATABASES (1997)

Aplin, *The EU Database Right: Recent Developments*, Intell. Prop. Q. 52 (Winter 2005)

Arden, *The Conflicting Treatments of Compilations of Facts under the United States and British Copyright Laws,* 19 AIPLA Q.J. 267 (1991)

Band & Kono, *The Database Protection Debate in the 106th Congress*, 62 Ohio. St. L.J. 869 (2001)

Baran, *Back to the Future: Learning from the Past in the Database Debate,* 62 Ohio St. L.J. 879 (2001)

Benkler, *The Role of Judicial Review in the Creation and Definition of Private Rights in Information*, 15 Berkeley Tech. L.J. 535 (2000)

Bolitho, *When Fantasy Meets the Courtroom: An Examination of the Intellectual Property Issues Surrounding the Burgeoning Fantasy Sports Industry*, 67 Ohio St. J. 911 (2006)

Cate, *The EU Data Protection Directive, Information Privacy, and the Public Interest*, 80 Iowa L. Rev. 431 (1995)

Denicola, *Copyright in Collections of Facts: A Theory for the Protection of Nonfiction Literary Works,* 81 Colum. L. Rev. 516 (1981)

Dreyfuss, *A Wiseguy's Approach to Information Products: Muscling Copyright and Patent into a Unitary Theory of Intellectual Property,* 1992 Sup. Ct. Rev. 195

Edwards, *Has the Dreaded Data Doomsday Arrived? Past, Present, and Future Effects of the European Union's Database Directive on Database and Information Availability in the European Union*, 39 Ga. L. Rev. 215 (2004)

Fortney, *Ending Copyright Claims in State Primary Legal Materials: Toward an Open Source Legal System,* 102 L. Libr. J. 59 (2010)

Gervais, *The Protection of Databases*, 82 Chi.-Kent L. Rev. 1109 (2007)

Ginsburg, *A Marriage of Convenience? A Comment on 'The Protection of Databases'*, 82 Chi.-Kent L. Rev. 1171 (2007)

Ginsburg, *Copyright, Common Law, and Sui Generis Protection of Databases in the United States and Abroad,* 66 U. Cin. L. Rev. 151 (1997)

Ginsburg, *Creation and Commercial Value: Copyright Protection of Works of Information,* 90 Colum. L. Rev. 1865 (1990)

Ginsburg, *Domestic and International Copyright Issues Implicated in the Compilation of a Multimedia Product*, 25 Seton Hall L. Rev. 1397 (1995)

Ginsburg, *No "Sweat"? Copyright and Other Protection of Works of Information after* Feist v. Rural Telephone, 92 Colum. L. Rev. 338 (1992)

Gordon, *Reality as Artifact: From* Feist *to Fair Use,* 55 Law & Contemp. Probs. 93 (1992)

Gorman, *Copyright Protection for the Collection and Representation of Facts,* 76 Harv. L. Rev. 1569 (1963)

Gorman, *The* Feist *Case: Reflections on a Pathbreaking Copyright Decision,* 18 Rutgers Computer & Tech. L.J. 731 (1992)

Grosheide, *Database Protection — The European Way,* 8 Wash. U. J.L. & Pol'y 39 (2002)

Hamilton, *Justice O'Connor's Opinion in* Feist Pub., Inc. v. Rural Telephone Service Co.*: An Uncommon Though Characteristic Approach,* 38 J. Copyright Soc'y 83 (1990)

Heald, *The Extraction/Duplication Dichotomy: Constitutional Line-Drawing in the Database Debate*, 62 Ohio St. L.J. 933 (2001)

Heald, *The Vices of Originality,* 1991 Sup. Ct. Rev. 143

Hughes, *Created Facts and the Flawed Ontology of Copyright Law*, 83 Notre Dame L. Rev. 43 (2007)

Hughes, *How Extra-Copyright Protection of Databases Can Be Constitutional,* 28 Dayton L. Rev. 159 (2002)

Karjala, *Copyright in Electronic Maps,* 35 Jurimetrics J. 395 (1995)

Kon, BHB/William Hill: *Europe's* Feist: *Court of Appel Confirmation Establishes Bright Lines*, 28 E.I.P.R. 60 (2006)

Leith & Fellows, *Enabling Free On-line Access to UK Law Reports: The Copyright Problem,* 18 Int'l J.L. Info. Tech. 72 (2010)

Lipton, *Balancing Private Rights and Public Policies: Reconceptualizing Property in Databases,* 18 Berkeley Tech. L.J. 773 (2003)

Litman, *After* Feist, 17 U. Dayton L. Rev. 607 (1992)

McManis, *Comparative Perspectives: Database Protection in the Digital Information Age,* 7 Roger Williams U.L. Rev. 7 (2001)

Mitten, *The Fantasy of Player Statistics Ownership: A Triple Play for the Public Domain:* Delaware Lottery to Motorola to C.B.C, 11 Chap. L. Rev. 569 (2008)

Patterson & Joyce, *Monopolizing the Law : The Scope of Copyright Protection for Law Reports and Statutory Compilations*, 36 UCLA L. Rev. 719 (1989)

Patry, *Copyright in Collections of Facts: A Reply,* 6 Comm. & The Law 11 (1984)

Perlmutter, *The Scope of Copyright in Telephone Directories: Keeping Listing Information in the Public Domain,* 38 J. Copyright Soc'y 1 (1990)

Pollack, *The Right to Know?: Delimiting Database Protection at the Juncture of the Commerce Clause, the Intellectual Property Clause and the First Amendment,* 17 Cardozo Arts & Ent. L.J. 47 (1999)

Raskind, *Assessing the Impact of* Feist, 17 U. Dayton L. Rev. 331 (1992)

Reichman, *Electronic Information Tools — The Outer Edge of World Intellectual Property Law,* 17 U. Dayton L. Rev. 797 (1992)

Reichman & Samuelson, *Intellectual Property Rights in Data?,* 50 Vand. L. Rev. 49 (1997)

Reichman & Uhlir, *A Contractually Reconstructed Research Commons for Scientific Data in a Highly Protectionist Intellectual Property Environment*, 66 Law & Contemp. Probs. 315 (2003)

Reichman & Uhlir, *Database Protection at the Crossroads: Recent Developments and Their Impact on Science and Technology*, 14 Berkeley Tech. L.J. 793 (1999)

Shipley, *Thin But Not Anorexic: Copyright Protection for Compilations and Other Fact Works,* 15 J. Intell. Prop. L. 91 (2007)

Symposium: *Copyright Protection for Computer Databases, CD-Roms and Factual Compilations*, 17 U. Dayton L. Rev. 323-629, 731–1018 (1992)

Wei, *Telephone Directories and Databases: The Policy at the Helm of Copyright Law and a Tale of Two Cities*, Intell. Prop. Q. 316 (Summer 2004)

Wood, *Copyrighting the Yellow Pages: Finding Originality in Factual Compilations,* 78 Minn. L. Rev. 1319 (1994)

Yen, *The Danger of Bootstrap Formalism in Copyright,* 5 J. Intell. Prop. L. 453 (1998)

Yen, *The Legacy of* Feist: *Consequences of the Weak Connection Between Copyright and the Economics of Public Goods,* 52 Ohio St. L.J. 1343 (1991)

Chapter 4
OWNERSHIP AND TRANSFERS

Reference Works

H. Abrams, THE LAW OF COPYRIGHT §§ 4.1 to 4.48, 10.67 to 10.73 (2008)

P. Goldstein, GOLDSTEIN ON COPYRIGHT §§ 4.1 to 4.3, 5.0 to 5.3, 5.6 to 5.7, 18.5 (3d ed. 2005)

M. Leaffer, UNDERSTANDING COPYRIGHT LAW §§ 5.01 to 5.15 (5th ed. 2010)

M. Nimmer & D. Nimmer, NIMMER ON COPYRIGHT §§ 5.01 to 5.04, 6.01 to 6.12, 6A.01 to 6A.05, 7.25, 10.01 to 10.15 (2010)

W. Patry, PATRY ON COPYRIGHT §§ 5:1 to 5:157 (2010)

Initial Ownership

C. Fisk, WORKING KNOWLEDGE: EMPLOYEE INNOVATION AND THE RISE OF CORPORATE INTELLECTUAL PROPERTY, 1800–1930 (2009)

C. McSherry, WHO OWNS ACADEMIC WORK?: BATTLING FOR CONTROL OF INTELLECTUAL PROPERTY (2001)

Angel & Tannenbaum, *Works for Hire Under S. 22,* N.Y.L. Sch. L. Rev. 209 (1976)

Birnhack, *Who Owns Bratz? The Integration of Copyright and Employment Law,* 20 Fordham Intell. Prop. Media & Ent. L.J. 95 (2009)

Braveman, *Duet of Disconent: Martha Graham and Her Non-Profit Battle Over Work for Hire*, 15 Loy. L.A. Ent. L. Rev. 471 (2005)

Brophy, *Joint Authorship Under the Copyright Law,* 16 Hastings Comm. & Ent. L.J. 451 (1994)

Cary, *Joint Ownership of Copyright*, Copyright Law Revision Study No. 12 (1958)

Chon, *New Wine Bursting from Old Bottles: Collaborative Internet Art, Joint Works, and Entrepreneurship,* 75 Or. L. Rev. 257 (1996)

Christy, *Stone Dead: Joint Authorship Battle Takes Centre Stage (United Kingdom)*, 142 Copyright World 17 (July 2004)

Ciolino, *How Copyrights Became Community Property (Sort Of): Through the* Rodrigue v. Rodrigue *Looking Glass,* 47 Loy. L. Rev. 631 (2001)

Ciolino, *Why Copyrights Are Not Community Property*, 60 La. L. Rev. 127 (1999)

Cochran, *It Takes Two to Tango!: Problems with Community Property Ownership of Copyrights and Patents in Texas*, 58 Baylor L.J. 407 (2006)

Dougherty, *Not a Spike Lee Joint? Issues in the Authorship of Motion Pictures Under U.S. Copyright Law*, 49 UCLA L. Rev. 225 (2001)

Dreyfuss, *Collaborative Research: Conflicts on Authorship, Ownership, and Accountability,* 53 Vand. L. Rev. 1162 (2000)

Dreyfuss, *The Creative Employee and the Copyright Act of 1976,* 54 U. Chi. L. Rev. 590 (1987)

Field, *From Custom to Law in Copyright*, 49 IDEA 125 (2008)

Gasaway, *Copyright Ownership & the Impact on Academic Libraries,* 13 DePaul-LCA J. Art & Ent. L. 277 (2003)

Ginsburg, *Copyright Without Borders? Choice of Forum and Choice of Law for Copyright Infringement in Cyberspace*, 15 Cardozo Arts & Ent. L.J. 153 (1997)

Gleik, *Who Owns What in the Digital World?,* 53 Case W. Res. 659 (2003)

Gordon, *Essay: Fine-Tuning* Tasini*: Privileges of Electronic Distribution and Reproduction,* 66 Brooklyn L. Rev. 473 (2000)

Gorman, *Copyright Conflicts on the University Campus,* 40 J. Copyright Soc'y 291 (2000)

Hamilton, *Commissioned Works as Works Made for Hire Under the 1976 Copyright Act: Misinterpretation and Injustice,* 135 U. Pa. L. Rev. 1281 (1987)

Hardy, *Copyright Law's Concept of Employment & What Congress Really Intended*, 35 J. Copyright Soc'y 210 (1988)

Hubbard, *Family Feud in the Entertainment Industry: Section 304(A) of the Copyright Act and Its Impact on Estate Distribution,* 21 Cardozo Arts & Ent. L.J. 407 (2003)

Hudis, *Software "Made for Hire": Make Sure It's Really Yours*, 44 J. Copyright Soc'y 8 (1996)

Hutchinson, *Can the Federal Courts Save Rock Music?: Why a Default Joint Authorship Rule Should Be Adopted to Protect Co-Authors Under United States Copyright Law*, 5 Tul. J. Tech. & Intell. Prop. 77 (2003)

Hyde & Hager, *Promoting the Copyright Act's Creator-Favoring Presumption: "Works Made For Hire" Under* Aymes v. Bonelli & Avtec Systems, Inc. v. Pfeiffer, 71 Denv. U.L. Rev. 693 (1994)

Jacob, *Tort Made for Hire – Reconsidering the* CCNV *Case*, 11 Yale J. L. & Tech. 96 (2009)

Jaffe, *Defusing the Time Bomb Once Again — Determining Authorship in a Sound Recording*, 53 J. Copyright Soc'y 139 (2005)

Johnson, *Reconciling Copyright Ownership Policies for Faculty-Authors in Distance Education*, 33 J.L. & Educ. 431 (2004)

Karlan, *Joint Ownership of Moral Rights*, 38 J. Copyright Soc'y 242 (1991)

Karp, ed., *Work Made for Hire — Practical Perspectives: A Roundtable Discussion,* 14 Colum.-VLA J.L. & Arts 507 (1990)

Kernochan, *Ownership and Control of Intellectual Property Rights in Audiovisual Works: Contracts and Practice*, 20 Colum.-VLA J. L. & Arts 359 (1996)

Kim, *Martha Graham, Professor Miller and the "Work for Hire" Doctrine: Undoing the Judicial Bind Created by the Legislature*, 13 J. Intell. Prop. L. 337 (2006)

Kreiss, *Scope of Employment and Being an Employee Under the Work-Made-For Hire Provision of the Copyright Law: Applying the Common-Law Agency Tests,* 40 Kan. L. Rev. 119 (1991)

Kwall, *"Author-Stories": Narrative's Implications for Moral Rights and Copyright's Joint Authorship Doctrine,* 75 S. Cal. L. Rev. 1 (2001)

Kwall, *Copyright Issues in Online Courses: Ownership, Authorship and Conflict,* 18 Computer & High Tech. L.J. 1 (2001)

LaFrance, *Authorship, Dominance, and the Captive Collaborator: Preserving the Rights of Joint Authors*, 50 Emory L.J. 193 (2001)

Lape, *A Narrow View of Creative Cooperation: The Current State of the Joint Work Doctrine,* 61 Alb. L. Rev. 43 (1997)

Lape, *Ownership of Copyrightable Works of University Professors: The Interplay Between the Copyright Act and University Copyright Policies,* 37 Vill. L. Rev. 223 (1992)

Meurer, *Too Many Markets or Too Few? Copyright Policy Toward Shared Works*, 77 So. Cal. L. Rev. 903 (2004)

Miller, *Photography and the Work For Hire Doctrine*, 1 Tex. Wesleyan L. Rev. 81 (1994)

Nevin, *No Business Like Business: Copyright Law, the Theater Industry, and the Dilemma of Rewarding Collaboration*, 53 Emory L.J. 1533 (2004)

Nevins, *To Split or Not to Split: Judicial Divisibility of the Copyright Interests of Authors and Others*, 40 Fam. L.Q. 499 (2006)

D. Nimmer, Menell & McGimsey, *Preexisting Confusion in Copyright's Work-for-Hire Doctrine,* 50 J. Copyright Soc'y 399 (2003)

Okamoto, *Musical Sound Recordings as Works Made for Hire: Money for Nothing and Tracks for Free*, 37 U.S.F. L. Rev. 783 (2003)

Packard, *Copyright or Copy Wrong: An Analysis of University Claims to Faculty Work,* 7 Comm. L. & Pol'y 275 (2002)

Perwin, *Drafting "Work for Hire" Agreements after* Community for Creative Non-Violence v. Reid, 14 Nova L. Rev. 459 (1990)

Reichman, *Overlapping Proprietary Rights in University-Generated Research Products: The Case of Computer Programs,* 1992 Colum.-VLA J.L. & Arts 51 (1992)

Rothstein, *Unilateral Settlements and Retroactive Transfers: A Problem of Copyright Co-Ownership*, 157 U. Pa. L. Rev. 881 (2009)

Roussel, *The Copyright of Salaried and Employed Authors: A Comparative Study of National Laws,* 26 Copyright 221 (1990)

Samuelson, *Allocating Ownership Rights in Computer-Generated Works,* 47 U. Pitt. L. Rev. 1185 (1986)

Samuelson, *Some New Kinds of Authorship Made Possible by Computers and Some Intellectual Property Questions They Raise*, 53 U. Pitt. L. Rev. 685 (1993)

Saville, *Peter Pan's Rights — "To Die Will Be an Awfully Big Adventure,"* 51 J. Copyright Soc'y 1 (2004)

Scully, *The Virtual Professorship: Intellectual Property Ownership of Academic Work in a Digital Era*, 35 McGeorge L. Rev. 227 (2004)

Spyke, *The Joint Works Dilemma: The Copyrightable Contribution Requirement and Co-Ownership Principles,* 40 J. Copyright Soc'y 463 (1993)

Varmer, *Works Made for Hire and on Commission*, Copyright Law Revision Study No. 13 (1960)

VerSteeg, *Copyright and the Educational Process: The Right of Teacher Inception,* 75 Iowa L. Rev. 381 (1990)

VerSteeg, *Intent, Originality, Creativity and Joint Authorship*, 8 Brook. L. Rev. 123 (2002)

Transfer and Recordation

Afori, *Implied License: An Emerging New Standard in Copyright Law,* 25 Santa Clara Computer & High Tech. L.J. 275 (2008)

Andrews, *Contracting Out of the Orphan Works Problem: How the Google Book Search Settlement Serves as a Private Solution to the Orphan Works Problem and Why It Should Matter to Policy Makers,* 19 S. Cal. Interdisc. L.J. 97 (2009)

Bartow, *Intellectual Property and Domestic Relations: Issues to Consider When There Is An Artist, Author, Inventor, or Celebrity in the Family*, 35 Fam. L.Q. 383 (2001)

Bramson, *Intellectual Property as Collateral: Patent, Trade Secrets, Trademarks and Copyrights,* 36 Bus. Law. 1567 (1981)

Brylawski, *The Role of Copyright in Acquisitions and Security Transactions,* 22 Beverly Hills B.A.J. 88 (1988)

Byrnes, *Copyright Licenses, New Technology and Default Rules: Converging Media, Diverging Courts?*, 20 Loy. L.A. Ent. L. Rev. 243 (2000)

Curtis, *Protecting Authors in Copyright Transfers: Revision Bill and the Alternatives,* 72 Colum. L. Rev. 799 (1972)

Goldstein, *Preempted State Doctrines, Involuntary Transfers and Compulsory Licenses: Testing the Limits of Copyright,* 24 UCLA L. Rev. 1107 (1977)

Haemmerli, *Insecurity Interests: Where Intellectual Property and Commercial Law Collide,* 96 Colum. L. Rev. 1645 (1996)

Huff, In re World Auxiliary Power Company: *A Look at Federal Preemption of State Law in the Perfection of Security Interests in Registered and Unregistered Copyrights*, 56 Ala. L. Rev. 917 (2005)

Jaszi, Tasini *and Beyond,* 23 Eur. Intell. Prop. L. Rev. 595 (2001)

Kaminstein, *Divisibility of Copyrights*, Copyright Law Revision Study No. 11 (1960)

Kreiss, *The "In Writing" Requirement for Copyright and Patent Transfers: Are the Circuits in Conflict?*, 26 Dayton L. Rev. 43 (2000)

Lange, *A Comment on* New York Times v. Tasini, 53 Case W. Res. 653 (2003)

Latman, *Recordation of Copyright Assignments and Licenses*, Copyright Law Revision Study No. 19 (1958)

Loren, *Untangling the Web of Music Copyrights,* 53 Case W. Res. 673 (2003)

MacQueen, *Abandoned, Orphaned or Property for Ever?, Copyright, Prescription and Personal Bar*, 14 Edinburgh L. Rev. 97 (2010)

Mtima, Tasini *and Its Progeny: The New Exclusive Right of Fair Use on the Electronic Publishing Frontier*, 14 Fordham Intell. Prop. Media & Ent. L.J. 369 (2004)

Nevine, *When an Author's Marriage Dies: The Copyright-Divorce Connection,* 37 J. Copyright Soc'y 382 (1990)

D. Nimmer, *Adams and Bits: Of Jewish Kings and Copyrights*, 71 S. Cal. L. Rev. 219 (1998)

R. Nimmer, *An Update on Financing With Intellectual Property as Collateral: Parts I and II*, 10 J. Proprietary Rts. 2 (1997) & 11 J. Proprietary Rts. 10 (1997)

Norgaard & Garcia, *The Ninth Circuit's Decisions in* Foad v. Musil Govan Azzalino *and* Gardner v. Nike, Inc. *: The Creation, Interpretation and Assignment of Copyright Licenses Under State and Federal Law*, 33 S.W.U. L. Rev. 347 (2004)

O'Rourke, *Bargaining in the Shadow of Copyright Law after* Tasini, Case W. Res. 605 (2003)

Polacheck, *The "UN-Worthy" Decision: The Characterization of a Copyright as Community Property,* 17 Hastings Comm. & Ent. L.J. 601 (1995)

Slavitt, *Fixation of Derivative Works in a Tangible Medium: Technology Forces a Reexamination*, 46 IDEA 37 (2005)

Smith, *General Intangible or Commercial Tort: Moral Rights and State-Based Intellectual Property as Collateral Under U.C.C. Revised Article 9*, 22 Emory Banr. Dev. J. 95 (2005)

Trefethen, *Copyright as Community Property*, 11 J. Contemp. Legal Issues 256 (2000)

Valkonen & White, *An Economic Model for the Incentive/Access Paradigm of Copyright Propertization: An Argument in Support of the Orphan Works Act*, 29 Hastings Comm. & Ent. L.J. 359 (2007)

VerSteeg, *Copyright and the Educational Process: The Right of Teacher Inception*, 75 Iowa L. Rev. 381 (1990)

Victoroff, *The Other Curse of the Werewolf: Interpreting Copyright Transfers Under U.S. and English Law,* 17 Whittier L. Rev. 215 (1995)

Ward, *The Perfection and Priority Rules for Security Interests in Copyrights, Patents, and Trademarks: The Current Structural Dissonance and Proposed Legislative Cures,* 53 Me. L. Rev. 391 (2001)

Chapter 5

DURATION AND TERMINATIONS

Reference Works

H. Abrams, THE LAW OF COPYRIGHT §§ 7.1 to 7.57, 11.1 to 11.62, 12.1 to 12.60 (2008)

P. Goldstein, GOLDSTEIN ON COPYRIGHT §§ 5.4 to 5.5, 6.0 to 6.3 (3d ed. 2005)

M. Leaffer, UNDERSTANDING COPYRIGHT LAW §§ 6.01 to 6.19 (5th ed. 2010)

M. Nimmer & D. Nimmer, NIMMER ON COPYRIGHT §§ 9.01 to 9.12, 9A.01 to 9A.07, 11.01 to 11.09 (2010)

W. Patry, PATRY ON COPYRIGHT §§ 7:1 to 7:63 (2010)

Duration of Copyright

Allen & Swift, *Shattering Copyright Law: Will James Stewart's* Rear Window *Become a Pain in the Glass?*, 22 Pac. L.J. 1 (1990)

Bard & Kurlantzick, *Copyright Duration at the Millennium*, 40 J. Copyright Soc'y 13 (2000)

Birnhack, *Copyright Law and Free Speech after* Eldred v. Ashcroft, 76 S. Cal. L. Rev. 1275 (2003)

Bradford, *Parody and Perception: Using Cognitive Research to Expand Fair Use in Copyright*, 46 B.C. L. Rev. 705 (2005)

Brauneis, *Copyright and the World's Most Popular Song*, 56 J. Copyright Soc'y 335 (2009)

Bricker, *Renewal and Extension of Copyright,* 29 S. Cal. L. Rev. 23 (1955)

H. Brown & D. Miller, *Copyright Term Extension: Sapping American Creativity*, 44 J. Copyright Soc'y 94 (1996)

R. Brown, *The Widening Gyre: Are Derivative Works Getting Out of Hand?*, 3 Cardozo Arts & Ent. L. Rev. 1 (1984)

Brownlee, *Recent Changes in the Duration of Copyright in the United States and European Union: Procedures and Policy,* 6 Fordham Intell. Prop. Media & Ent. L.J. 579 (1996)

Chafee, *Reflections on the Law of Copyright,* 45 Colum. L. Rev. 503, 719 (1945)

Claiborne, Golan v. Gonzales *and the Changing Balance between the First Amendment, Copyright Protection, and the Rest of the World,* 86 Denv. U.L. Rev. 1113 (2009)

Coenen & Heald, *Means / Ends Analysis in Copyright Law: Eldred v. Ashcroft in One Act*, 36 Loy. L.A. L. Rev. 99 (2002)

Colby, *Helen Sousa Albert, Mary Baker Eddy, and Otto Harbach — The Road to a Copyright Term of Life Plus 50 Years,* 6 Comm. & The Law 3 (1984)

Crews, *Copyright Duration and the Progressive Degeneration of a Constitutional Doctrine*, 55 Syracuse L. Rev. 189 (2005)

Davis, *Extending Copyright and the Constitution: "Have I Stayed Too Long?"*, 52 Fla. L. Rev. 989 (2000)

Epstein, *The Dubious Constitutionality of the Copyright Term Extension Act,* 36 Loy. L.A. L. Rev. 123 (2002)

Gard, *Unpublished Works in the Public Domain: The Opening of a New Frontier*, 54 J. Copyright Soc'y 439 (2007)

Gordon, *Authors, Publishers, and Public Goods: Trading Gold for Dross*, 36 Loy. L.A. L. Rev. 159 (2002)

Hamilton, *Copyright Duration Extension and the Dark Heart of Copyright,* 14 Cardozo Arts & Ent. L.J. 655 (1996)

Hart & Kaufman, *An Overview of the Copyright Renewal Amendment and its Impact on Renewal Practices Under U.S. Law,* 17 Colum.-VLA J.L. & Arts 311 (1994)

Hartnick, *Stanley Rothenberg, Final Thoughts on the Dickens Provision*, 54 J. Copyright Soc'y 565 (2007)

Heald & Sherry, *Implied Limits on the Legislative Power: The Intellectual Property Clause as an Absolute Constraint on Congress*, 2000 U. Ill. L. Rev. 1119 (2000)

Hughes, *Jurisprudential Vertigo: The Supreme Court's View of "Rear Window" Is for the Birds,* 60 Miss. L.J. 239 (1990)

Jaszi, *When Works Collide: Derivative Motion Pictures, Underlying Rights, and the Public Interest,* 28 UCLA L. Rev. 715 (1981)

Karjala, *Comment of U.S. Law Professors on the Copyright Office Term of Protection Study,* 12 Eur. Intell. Prop. Rev. 531 (1994)

Karjala, *Judicial Review of Copyright Term Extension Legislation*, 36 Loy. L.A. L. Rev. 199 (2002)

Karjala, *Congestion Externalities and Extended Copyright Protection*, 94 Geo. L.J. 1065 (2006)

Kreiss, *Abandoning Copyrights to Try to Cut Off Termination Rights,* 58 Mo. L. Rev. 85 (1993)

Kupferman, *Renewal of Copyright: Section 23 of the Copyright Act of 1909,* 44 Colum. L. Rev. 712 (1944)

Landes & Posner, *Indefinitely Renewable Copyright*, 70 U. Chi. L. Rev. (2003)

Ledford, *The Dream that Never Dies: Eldred v. Ashcroft, the Author, and the Search for Perpetual Copyright*, 84 Or. L. Rev. 665 (2005)

Lee, Eldred v. Ashcroft *and the (Hypothetical) Copyright Term Extension Act of 2020,* 12 Tex. Intell. Prop. L.J. 1 (2003)

Leval & Liman, *Are Copyrights for Authors or Their Children?*, 39 J. Copyright Soc'y 1 (1991)

Liu, *Copyright and Time: A Proposal*, 101 Mich. L. Rev. 409 (2002)

Merges & Reynolds, *The Proper Scope of the Copyright and Patent Power*, 37 Harv. J. on Legis. 45 (2000)

Miller, *Copyright Term Extension: Boon for American Creators and the American Economy,* 45 J. Copyright Soc'y 319 (1998)

Mimms, *Reversion and Derivative Works Under the Copyright Acts of 1909 and 1976,* 25 N.Y.L. Sch. L. Rev. 595 (1980)

Mulligan & Schultz, *Accessing the Law: Neglecting the National Memory: How Copyright Term Extensions Compromise the Development of Digital Archives,* 4 J. App. Prac. & Process 451 (2002)

Nachbar, *Intellectual Property and Constitutional Norms,* 104 Colum. L. Rev. 272 (2004)

Nevins, *Little Copyright Dispute on the Prairie: Unbumping the Will of Laura Ingalls Wilder*, 44 St. Louis L.J. 919 (2000)

Nevins, *The Magic Kingdom of Will Bumping: Where Estates Law and Copyright Law Collide,* J. Copyright Soc'y 77 (1988)

D. Nimmer, Corcovado: *Renewal's Second Coming or False Messiah?*, 1 UCLA Ent. L. Rev. 127 (1994)

D. Nimmer, *Refracting the Window's Light:* Stewart v. Abend *in Myth and in Fact*, 39 J. Copyright Soc'y 18 (1991)

Ochoa, *Copyright Duration: Theories and Practice*, *in* INTELLECTUAL PROPERTY AND INFORMATION WEALTH (2007)

Ochoa, *Patent and Copyright Term Extension and the Constitution: A Historical Perspective,* 49 J. Copyright Soc'y 19 (2001)

Patry, *The Copyright Term Extension Act of 1995: Or How Publishers Managed to Steal the Bread from Authors,* 14 Cardozo Arts & Ent. L.J. 661 (1996)

Patry, *The Failure of the American Copyright System: Protecting the Idle Rich,* 72 Notre Dame L. Rev. 907 (1997)

Patry & Posner, *Fair Use and Statutory Reform in the Wake of* Eldred, 92 Cal. L. Rev. 1639 (2004)

Patterson, Eldred v. Reno: *An Example of the Law of Unintended Consequences*, 8 J. Intell. Prop. L. 223 (2001)

Patterson, *What's Wrong with* Eldred? *An Essay on Copyright Jurisprudence*, 10 J. Intell. Prop. L. 345 (2003)

Pollack, *Dealing With Old Father William, or Moving From Constitutional Text to Constitutional Doctrine: Progress Clause Review of the Copyright Term Extension Act,* 36 Loy L.A. L. Rev. 337 (2002)

Posner, *How Long Should a Copyright Last?,* 50 J. Copyright Soc'y 1 (2003)

Reese, *Public but Private: Copyright's New Unpublished Public Domain,* 85 Tex. L. Rev. 485 (2007)

Reichman, *An Evaluation of the Copyright Extension Act of 1995: The Duration of the Limits of Cultural Policy,* 14 Cardozo Arts & Ent. L.J. 625 (1996)

Ricketson, *The Copyright Term,* 23 IIC 753 (1992)

Ringer, *Renewal of Copyright,* Copyright Law Revision Study No. 31 (1960)

Rosenbloum, *Give Me Liberty & Give Me Death: The Conflict Between Copyright Law and Estates Law,* 4 J. Intell. Prop. L. 163 (1996)

Samuelson, *The Constitutional Law of Intellectual Property After* Eldred, 50 J. Copyright Soc'y 547 (2003)

Schwartz & Treanor, Eldred *and* Lochner*: Copyright Term Extension and Intellectual Property as Constitutional Property,* 112 Yale L.J. 2331 (2003)

Segal, *Zombie Copyrights: Copyright Restoration Under the New Section 104A of the Copyright Act,* 13 Santa Clara Computer & High Tech. L.J. 71 (1997)

Shipley, *Congressional Authority Over Intellectual Property Policy After* Eldred v. Ashcroft*: Deference, Empty Limitations, and Risks to the Public Domain,* 70 Alb. L. Rev. 1255 (2007)

Spoo, *Ezra Pound's Copyright Statute: Perpetual Rights and the Problem of Heirs,* 56 UCLA L. Rev. 1775 (2009)

Symposium, *The Constitutionality of Copyright Term Extension: How Long is Too Long?,* 18 Cardozo Arts & Ent. L.J. 651 (2000)

Tor & Oliar, *Incentives to Create Under a "Lifetime-Plus-Years" Copyright Duration: Lessons From a Behavioral Economic Analysis for* Eldred v. Ashcroft, 36 Loy. L.A. L. Rev. 437 (2002)

Walterscheid, *Musings on the Copyright Power: A Critique of* Eldred v. Ashcroft, 14 Albany L.J. Sci. & Tech. 309 (2004)

Walterscheid, *The Remarkable-and Irrational-Disparity Between the Patent Term and the Copyright Term,* 83 J. Pat & Trademark Off. Soc'y 233 (2001)

Terminations of Transfers

Abrams, *Who's Sorry Now? Termination Rights and the Derivative Works Exception,* 62 U. Det. L. Rev. 181 (1985)

Bales, *The Grapes of Wrathful Heirs: Terminations of Transfers of Copyright and "Agreements to the Contrary",* 27 Cardozo Arts & Ent. L.J. 663 (2010)

Curtis, *Caveat Emptor in Copyright: A Practical Guide to the Termination Provisions of the New Copyright Code,* 25 Bull. Copyright Soc'y 19 (1977)

Curtis, *Protecting Authors in Copyright Transfers: Revision Bill § 203 and the Alternatives,* 72 Colum. L. Rev. 799 (1972)

Davis, *The Screenwriter's Indestructible Right to Terminate Her Assignment of Copyright: Once a Story Is "Pitched," A Studio Can Never Obtain All Copyrights in the Story*, 18 Cardozo Arts & Ent. L.J. 93 (2000)

Drisch & Fortnow, *Termination of Copyrights in Sound Recordings: Is There a Leak in the Record Company Vaults?*, 17 Colum.-VLA J.L. & Arts 211 (1993)

Gould, *Time's Up: Copyright Termination, Work-For-Hire and the Recording Industry*, 31 Colum. J.L. & Arts 91 (2007)

Kreiss, *Abandoning Copyright to Try to Cut Off Termination Rights,* 58 Mo. L. Rev. 85 (1993)

McGilvray, *Judicial Kryptonite? Superman and the Consideration of Moral Rights in American Copyright,* 32 Hastings Comm. & Ent. L.J. 319 (2010)

Menell & D. Nimmer, *Judicial Resistance to Copyright Law's Inalienable Right to Terminate Transfers,* 33 Colum. J.L. & Arts 227 (2010)

M. Nimmer, *Termination of Transfers Under the Copyright Act of 1976,* 125 U. Pa. L. Rev. 947 (1977)

Scott, *Oh Bother*: Milne, Steinbeck, *and an Emerging Circuit Split Over the Alienability of Copyright Termination Rights*, 14 J. Intell. Prop. L. 357 (2007)

Chapter 6

PUBLICATION AND FORMALITIES

Reference Works

H. Abrams, THE LAW OF COPYRIGHT §§ 8.8 to 8.47, 9.1 to 9.93, 10.1 to 10.66 (2008)

P. Goldstein, GOLDSTEIN ON COPYRIGHT §§ 3.0 to 3.19 (3d ed. 2005)

M. Leaffer, UNDERSTANDING COPYRIGHT LAW §§ 4.01 to 4.17, 7.01 to 7.17 (5th ed. 2010)

M. Nimmer & D. Nimmer, NIMMER ON COPYRIGHT §§ 4.01 to 4.13, 7.01 to 7.24, 7.26 to 7.28 (2010)

W. Patry, PATRY ON COPYRIGHT §§ 6:1 to 6:81 (2010)

Publication

Baumgarten & Meyer, *Effects of U.S. Adherence to the Berne Convention*, 3 World Intell. Prop. Rep. 73 (1989)

Brown, *Publication and Preemption in Copyright Law: Elegiac Reflections on* Goldstein v. California, 22 UCLA L. Rev. 1022 (1975)

Brylawski, *Publication: Its Role in Copyright Matters, Both Past and Present*, 31 J. Copyright Soc'y 507 (1984)

Cotter, *Toward a Functional Definition of Publication in Copyright Law*, 92 Minn. L. Rev. 1724 (2008)

Landau, *Music: "Publication," Musical Compositions, and the Copyright Act of 1909: Still Crazy After All These Years*, 2 Vand. J. Ent. L. & Prac. 29 (2000)

Landes, *Copyright Protection of Letters, Diaries, and Other Unpublished Works: An Economic Approach,* 21 J. Legal Stud. 79 (1992)

M. Nimmer, *Preface-The Old Copyright Act as a Part of the New Act,* 22 N.Y.L. Sch. L. Rev. 471 (1977)

Formalities

R. Wedgeworth & B. Ringer, THE LIBRARY OF CONGRESS ADVISORY COMMITTEE ON COPYRIGHT REGISTRATION AND DEPOSIT: REPORT OF THE CO-CHAIRS (1993)

Abromats, *Nondisclosure of Preexisting Works in Software Copyright Registrations: Inequitable Conduct in Need of a Remedy,* 32 Jurimetrics J. 571 (1992)

Arden, *The Questionable Utility of Copyright Notice: Statutory and Non Legal Incentives in the Post-Berne Era,* 24 Loy. U. Chi. L.J. 259 (1993)

Cole, *Of Copyright, Men, and a National Library,* 28 Q.J. Libr. Cong. 114 (1971)

Crews, *Legal Deposit in Four Countries: Laws and Library Services,* 80 Law Libr. J. 551 (1988)

Doyle, Cary, McCannon & Ringer, *Notice of Copyright*, Copyright Law Revision Study No. 7 (1960)

Fisher, *Reserving All Rights Beyond Copyright: Non-statutory Restrictive Notices,* 37 J. Copyright Soc'y 249 (1987)

Gasaway, *America's Cultural Record: A Thing of the Past*, 40 Hous. L. Rev. 643 (2003)

Geller, *Copyright Protection in the Berne Union: Analyzing the Issues,* 5 Intell. Prop. J. 1 (1989)

Gibson, *Once and Future Copyright*, 81 Notre Dame L. Rev. 167 (2005)

Grubb, *Status of Works Published in Violation of the Manufacturing Requirements of the 1909 Copyright Act After the Effective Date of the 1976 Copyright Law,* 27 J. Copyright Soc'y (1980)

Haynie, *So the Copyright Office Has Refused to Register Your Claim to Copyright-What Does It Mean and What Can You Do About It?,* 21 AIPLA Q.J. 70 (1993)

Hurwitz, *Omission of Copyright Notice Under Section 405(a): What Kind of Oxymoron Makes a Deliberate Error?*, 60 N.Y.U. L. Rev. 956 (1985)

Jelaso, *APA Abuse of Discretion Review as Applied to the Copyright Office: Is the Standard Meaningless?*, 5 Am. U. Admin. L.J. 485 (1991)

Joyce, *"A Curious Chapter in the History of Judicature":* Wheaton v. Peters *and the Rest of the Story (of Copyright in the New Republic)*, 42 Hous. L. Rev. 325 (2005)

Joyce, *The Rise of the Supreme Court Reporter: An Institutional Perspective on Marshall Court Ascendancy,* 83 Mich. L. Rev. 1291 (1985)

Kaplan, *The Registration of Copyright*, Copyright Law Revision Study No. 17 (1960)

Karp, *A Future Without Formalities,* 13 Cardozo Arts & Ent. L.J. 521 (1995)

Levine, *The End of Formalities: No More Second-Class Copyright Owners,* 13 Cardozo Arts & Ent. L.J. 553 (1995)

Lyons, *The Manufacturing Clause: A Legislative History,* 29 J. Copyright Soc'y 8 (1981)

McLain, *The Copyright Notice Requirement in the United States: A Proposed Amendment Concerning Deliberate Omissions of Notice,* 18 Loy. L. A. L. Rev. 689 (1985)

Metalitz, *Copyright Registration after* Feist: *New Rules and New Roles?,* 17 U. Dayton L. Rev. 763 (1992)

Ochoa, *Protection for Works of Foreign Origin Under the 1909 Copyright Act*, 26 Santa Clara Comp. & High Tech. L.J. 285 (2010)

Perlmutter, *Freeing Copyright From Formalities*, 13 Cardozo Arts & Ent. L.J. 565 (1995)

Peters, *The Copyright Office and the Formal Requirements of Registration of Claims to Copyright,* 17 U. Dayton L. Rev. 737 (1992)

Rosloff, *"Some Rights Reserved": Finding the Space Between All Rights Reserved and the Public Domain*, 33 Colum. J.L. & Arts 37 (2009)

Selkowitz, *A Well-Kept Secret: Informal Adjudication in the Copyright Office-A Freedom of Information Act Violation?,* 35 Admin. L. Rev. 133 (1983)

Sorkin, *The Futility of a Future Without Formalities,* 13 Cardozo Arts & Ent. L.J. 589 (1995)

Stim, *The Reform of Notice Omission:* Crumb v. A.A. Sales, Inc., 11 Colum.-VLA J.L. & Arts 635 (1987)

Y'Barbo, *On Section 411 of the Copyright Code and Determining the Proper Scope of a Copyright Registration*, 34 San Diego L. Rev. 343 (1997)

The Copyright Office

Abrams, *The Role of the Copyright Office: An Introduction*, 13 Cardozo Arts & Ent. L.J. 27 (1994)

Field, *Judicial Review of Copyright Examination*, 44 Idea 479 (2004)

Samuelson, *Will the Copyright Office Be Obsolete in the Twenty-First Century?*, 13 Cardozo Arts & Ent. L.J. 55 (1994)

Schwartz, *The Role of the Copyright Office in the Age of Information*, 13 Cardozo Arts & Ent. L.J. 69 (1994)

Chapter 7

EXCLUSIVE RIGHTS AND THEIR LIMITATIONS

Reference Works

H. Abrams, The Law of Copyright §§ 5.1 to 5.424 (2008)

P. Goldstein, Goldstein on Copyright §§ 7.0 to 7.18, 17.23 to 17.25 (3d ed. 2005)

M. Leaffer, Understanding Copyright Law §§ 8.01 to 8.32 (5th ed. 2010)

M. Nimmer & D. Nimmer, Nimmer on Copyright §§ 8.01 to 8.24, 8A.01 to 8A.12, 8B.01 to 8B.08, 8C.01 to 8C.05, 8D.01 to 8D.10, 8E.01 to 8E.05 (2010)

W. Patry, Patry on Copyright §§ 8:1 to 8:29, 9:1 to 9:3, 11:1 to 11:49, 12:1 to 12:31, 13:1 to 13:54, 14:1 to 14:123, 15:1 to 15:18, 16:1 to 16:47 (2010)

Overview

Cassler, *Copyright Compulsory Licenses: Are They Coming or Going?,* 37 J. Copyright Soc'y 231 (1990)

Field, *Limits to Administrative Appointments*, 50 Idea 121 (2009)

Françon, *The Future of Copyright,* 132 R.I.D.A. 2 (1987)

Goldstein, *Preempted State Doctrines, Involuntary Transfers and Compulsory Licenses: Testing the Limits of Copyright,* 24 UCLA L. Rev. 1107 (1977)

Kabat, *Proposal for a Worldwide Internet Collecting Society: Mark Twain and Samuel Johnson Licenses,* J. Copyright Soc'y (1998)

Kernochan, *Practical Limitations on Authors' Rights,* 24 Colum.-VLA J.L. & Arts 263 (2001)

Lim, *Copyright Under Siege: An Economic Analysis of the Essential Facilities Doctrine and the Compulsory Licensing of Copyrighted Works,* 17 Alb. L.J. Sci. & Tech. 481 (2007)

Madison, *Social Software, Groups and Governance,* 2006 Mich. St. L. Rev. 153 (2006)

Norek, *"You Can't Sing Without the Bling": The Toll of Excessive Sample License Fees on Creativity in Hip-Hop Music and the Need for a Compulsory Sound Recording Sample License System,* 11 UCLA Ent. L. Rev. 83 (2004)

Patterson, *A Response to Mr. Y'Barbo's Reply,* 5 J. Intell. Prop. L. 235 (1997)

Patterson & Birch, *Copyright and Free Speech,* 4 J. Intell. Prop. L. 1 (1996)

Ringer, *Copyright and the Future of Authorship,* 101 Lib. L.J. 229 (1976)

Tushnet, *My Library: Copyright and the Role of Institutions in a Peer-to-Peer World,* 53 U.C.L.A. L. Rev. 977 (2006)

Y'Barbo, *On Legal Protection for Electronic Texts: A Reply to Professor Patterson and Judge Birch,* 5 J. Intell. Prop. L. 195 (1997)

Exclusive Rights and Limitations in the Digital Age

Cate, *The Technological Transformation of Copyright Law,* 81 Iowa L. Rev. 1395 (1996)

J. Cohen, *A Right to Read Anonymously: A Closer Look at "Copyright Management" in Cyberspace,* 28 Conn. L. Rev. 981 (1996)

Ginsburg, *Domestic and International Copyright Issues Implicated in the Compilation of a Multimedia Product,* 25 Seton Hall L. Rev. 1397 (1995)

Harrison, *Rules of the Road for the Information Superhighway: Electronic Communication and the Law,* 35 Hous. Law. 58 (1997)

Jaszi, *Caught in the Net of Copyright,* 75 Or. L. Rev. 299 (1996)

M. Lemley, *Dealing With Overlapping Copyrights on the Internet,* 22 U. Dayton L. Rev. 547 (1997)

Litman, *Reforming Information Law in Copyright's Image,* 22 Dayton L. Rev. 587 (1997)

D. Nimmer, *Time and Space*, 38 IDEA 501 (1998)

Okediji, *Trading Posts in Cyberspace: Information Markets and the Construction of Proprietary Rights,* 44 B.C. L. Rev. 545 (2003)

Reese, *The First Sale Doctrine in the Era of Digital Networks,* 44 B.C. L. Rev. 557 (2003)

Samuelson, *Copyright and Freedom of Expression in Historical Perspective,* 10 J. Intell. Prop. L. 345 (2003)

Yong, *China's Regulations on the Right of Communication through the Information Network,* 54 J. Copyright Soc'y 525 (2007)

The Reproduction Right

Abramson, *Where's the Remote? The Importance of the Location of the Remote Control (and the One Who Uses It) in Determining Liability for Copyright Infringement for Remote Storage Dvrs (Digital Video Recorders),* 27 Cardozo Arts & Ent. L.J. 145 (2009)

Alexander, *The Concept of Reproduction and the "Temporary and Transient" Exception*, 68 Cambridge L.J. 520 (2009)

Bernfeld, *Free to Photocopy?: A Legislative History of Section 108, the Library Photocopying Provision of the Copyright Act of 1976*, 25 Legal Reference Serv. Q. 1 (2006)

Bloom, *Protecting Copyright Owners of Digital Music — No More Free Access to Cyber Tunes*, 45 J. Copyright Soc'y 179 (1997)

Dutfield, *TRIPS-Related Aspects of Traditional Knowledge,* 33 Case West. Res. J. Int'l L. 233 (2001)

Gasaway, *Amending the Copyright Act for Libraries and Society: The Section 108 Study Group*, 70 Alb. L. Rev. 1331 (2007)

Geller, *Reprography and Other Processes of Mass Use,* 38 J. Copyright Soc'y 21 (1990)

Gervais, *The Tangled Web of UGC: Making Copyright Sense of User-Generated Content*, 11 Vand. J. Ent. & Tech. L. 841 (2009)

Ginsburg, *Reproduction of Protected Works for University Research or Teaching,* 39 J. Copyright Soc'y 181 (1992)

Hardy, *Computer "RAM" Copies: A Hit or a Myth? Historical Perspectives on Caching as a Microcosm of Current Copyright Concerns*, 22 Dayton L. Rev. 423 (1997)

Reese, *Copyright and Internet Music Transmissions: Existing Law, Major Controversies, Possible Solutions,* 55 U. Miami L. Rev 237 (2001)

Rosenlund, *Compulsory Licensing of Musical Compositions for Phonorecords Under the Copyright Act of 1976,* 30 Hastings L.J. 683 (1979)

Schultz, *Reconciling Social Norms and Copyright Law: Strategies for Persuading People to Pay for Recorded Music*, 17 J. Intell. Prop. L. 59 (2009)

Yen, *Entrepreneurship, Copyright, and Personal Home Pages,* 75 Or. L. Rev. 331 (1996)

The Adaptation Right

Abramowicz, *A Theory of Copyright's Derivative Right and Related Doctrines*, 38 Intell. Prop. L. Rev. 537 (2006)

Black & Page, *Add-On Infringements: When Computer Add-Ons and Peripherals Should (and Should Not) Be Considered Infringing Derivative Works Under* Lewis Galoob Toys Inc. v. Nintendo of America Inc. *and Other Recent Decisions,* 15 Hastings Comm. & Ent. L.J. 615 (1993)

A. Cohen, *When Does a Work Infringe the Derivative Works Right of a Copyright Owner?*, 17 Cardozo Arts & Ent L.J. 623 (1999)

Gervais, *The Tangled Web of UGC: Making Copyright Sense of User-Generated Content*, 11 Vand. J. Ent. & Tech. L. 841 (2009)

Goldstein, *Derivative Rights and Derivative Works in Copyright,* 30 J. Copyright Soc'y 209 (1983)

Huggins, *The Judge's Order and the Rising Phoenix: The Role Public Interests Should Play in Limiting Author Copyrights in Derivative-Work Markets,* 95 Iowa L. Rev. 695 (2010)

Karjala, *Harry Potter, Tanya Grotter, and the Copyright Derivative Work*, 38 Ariz. St. L.J. 17 (2006)

Kreiss, *Section 117 of the Copyright Act,* [1991] BYU L. Rev. 1496

Lisby, *Web Site Framing: Copyright Infringement Through the Creation of an Unauthorized Derivative Work,* 6 Comm. L. & Pol'y 541 (2001)

Loren, *The Changing Nature of Derivative Works in the Face of New Technologies,* 4 J. Small & Emerging Bus. L. 57 (2000)

R. Nimmer & P. Krauthaus, *Copyright and Software Technology Infringement: Defining Third Party Development Rights,* 62 Ind. L.J. 13 (1986)

Ochoa, *Copyright, Derivative Works and Fixation: Is* Galoob *a Mirage, or Does the* Form(Gen) *of the Alleged Derivative Work Matter?*, 20 Santa Clara Computer & High Tech. L.J. 991 (2004)

Samuelson, *Modifying Copyrighted Software: Adjusting Copyright Doctrine to Accommodate a Technology,* 28 Jurimetrics J. 179 (1988)

Sanjek, *"Don't Have to DJ No More": Sampling and the "Autonomous" Creator,* 10 Cardozo Arts & Ent. L.J. 607 (1992)

Wurzer, *Infringement of the Exclusive Right to Prepare Derivative Works: Reducing Uncertainty,* 73 Minn. L. Rev. 1521 (1989)

Voegtli, *Rethinking Derivative Rights*, 63 Brooklyn L. Rev. 1213 (1997)

The Public Distribution Right

L. Pierredon-Fawcett & J. Kernochan, THE DROIT DE SUITE IN LITERARY AND ARTISTIC PROPERTY: A COMPARATIVE LAW STUDY (1991)

Alderman, *Resale Royalties in the United States for Fine Visual Artists: An Alien Concept,* 40 J. Copyright Soc'y 265 (1992)

Aplin, *Contemplating Australia's Digital Future*, 23 Eur. Intell. Prop. L. Rev. 565 (2001)

Carson, *Making the "Making Available" Right Available,* 33 Colum. J.L. & Arts 135 (2010)

Colby, *The First Sale Doctrine: The Defense That Never Was?,* 32 J. Copyright Soc'y 77 (1984)

Craig, *"Lending" Institutions: The Impact of the E-Book on the American Library System*, 2003 U. Ill. L. Rev. 1087

Delchin, *Musical Copyright Law: Past, Present and Future of Online Music Distribution*, 22 Cardozo Arts & Ent. L.J. 343 (2004)

Gervais, *Transmissions of Music on the Internet: An Analysis of the Copyright Laws of Canada, France, Germany, Japan, the United Kingdom, and the United States,* 34 Vand. J. Transnat'l L. 1363 (2001)

Getzels, *Importation of Out-Of-Print Works Under the Copyright Act of 1976,* 10 Fordham Int'l L.J. 782 (1987)

Gordon, *Essay: Fine-Tuning* Tasini*: Privileges of Electronic Distribution and Reproduction,* 66 Brooklyn L. Rev. 473 (2000)

Hansen, *Gray Market Goods: A Lighter Shade of Black*, 13 Brooklyn J. Int'l L. 2459 (1987)

Horowitz, *The Record Rental Amendment of 1984: A Case Study in the Effort to Adapt Copyright Law to New Technology,* 12 Law & Arts 31 (1987)

Kasunic, *Making Circumstantial Proof of Distribution Available*, 18 Fordham Intell. Prop. Media & Ent. L.J. 1145 (2008)

Kernochan, *The Distribution Right in the United States of America: Review and Reflections,* 42 Vand. L. Rev. 107 (1989)

Kim, *In Pursuit of Profit Maximization by Restricting Parallel Imports: The U.S. Copyright Owner and Taiwan Copyright Law,* 5 Pac. Rim L. & Pol'y J. 205 (1995)

Leaffer, *Parallel Importation and the Gray Market in the United States,* in 1 INTERNATIONAL INTELLECTUAL PROPERTY LAW AND POLICY, Chap. 37 (Hansen, ed., 1996)

Lovern, *Evaluating Resale Royalties for Used CDs,* 4 Kan. J.L. & Pub. Pol'y 113 (1994)

Neumann, *The Berne Convention and* Droit de Suite *Legislation in the United States: Domestic and International Consequences of Federal Incorporation of State Law for Treaty Implementation*, 16 Colum.-VLA J.L. & Arts 157 (1992)

Perlmutter, *Resale Royalties for Artists: An Analysis of the Register of Copyrights' Report,* 40 J. Copyright Soc'y 284 (1992)

Price, *Government Policy and Economic Security for the Artist: The Case of the* Droit de Suite, 77 Yale L.J. 1333 (1968)

Rice, *Licensing the Use of Computer Program Copies and the Copyright Act First Sale Doctrine,* 30 Jurimetrics J. 157 (1990)

Rubin, *Destined to Remain Grey: The Eternal Recurrence of Parallel Imports,* 26 Int'l Law. 579 (1992)

Seemann, *A Look at the Public Lending Right,* 30 Copyright L. Symp. (ASCAP) 71 (1983)

Weil, *Resale Royalties: Nobody Benefits,* ARTNews at 58 (Mar. 1978)

The Public Performance Right

A. Kohn & B. Kohn, KOHN ON MUSIC LICENSING (2002)

W. Krasilovsky, S. Shemel & J. Gross, THIS BUSINESS OF MUSIC: THE DEFINITIVE GUIDE TO THE MUSIC INDUSTRY (10th ed. 2007)

D. Passman, ALL YOU NEED TO KNOW ABOUT THE MUSIC BUSINESS (2009)

Bard & Kurlantzick, *A Public Performance Right in Recordings: How to Alter the Copyright System Without Improving It,* 43 Geo. Wash. L. Rev. 152 (1974)

Bertrand, *Performing Rights Societies: The Price Is Right "French-Style," or the* SACEM *Cases,* 3 Ent. L. Rev. 146 (1992)

Cantor, *How Many Guests May Attend a Wedding Reception Before ASCAP Shows Up? Or, What are the Limits of the Definition of Perform "Publicly" Under **17 U.S.C. § 101**?*, 27 Colum.-VLA J.L. & Arts 79 (2003)

Cochran, *Why Can't I Watch This Video Here?: Copyright Confusion and Performances of Videocassettes and Videodiscs in Libraries,* 15 Hastings Comm. & Ent. L.J. 837 (1993)

Crews, *Distance Education and Copyright Law: The Limits and Meaning of Copyright Policy*, 27 J.C. & U.L. 15 (2000)

Davis, *Practice before the Copyright Arbitration Royalty Panel in 17 USC § 111,* 5 Vand. J. Ent. L. & Prac. 11 (2003)

Day, *The Super Brawl: The History and Future of the Sound Recording Performance Right,* 16 Mich. Telecomm. & Tech. L. Rev. 179 (2009)

Deutsch, *Politics and Poker — Music Faces the Odds: A Ten-Year Retrospective,* 34 J. Copyright Soc'y 38 (1986)

Disch, *Compulsory Licensing of Blacked Out Professional Team Sporting Event Telecasts (PTSETS): Using Copyright Law to Mitigate Monopolistic Behavior,* 32 Harv. J. on Legis. 403 (1995)

D'Onofrio, *In Support of Performance Rights in Sound Recordings,* 29 UCLA L. Rev. 168 (1981)

Finkelstein, *The Composer and the Public Interest-Regulation of Performing Right Societies,* 19 Law & Contemp. Probs. 275 (1954)

Garner, United States v. ASCAP: *The Licensing Provisions of the Amended Final Judgment of 1950,* 23 Bull. Copyright Soc'y 119 (1976)

Gasaway, *Distance Learning and Copyright,* 49 J. Copyright Soc'y 195 (2001)

Gorman, *The Recording Musician and Union Power: A Case Study of the American Federation of Musicians,* 37 Sw. L.J. 697 (1983)

Hartnick, *The Network Blanket License Triumphant — The Fourth Round of the ASCAP-BMI / CBS Litigation,* 2 Comm. & The Law 49 (1980)

Helfer, *World Music on a U.S. Stage: A Berne / TRIPs and Economic Analysis of the Fairness in Music Licensing Act*, 80 B.U. L. Rev. 93 (2000)

Jackson, *From Broadcast to Webcast: Copyright Law and Streaming Media,* 11 Tex. Intell. Prop. L.J. 447 (2003)

Jehoram, *The Future of Copyright Collecting Societies*, 23 E.I.P.R. 134 (2001)

Jensen, *Is the Library Without Walls on a Collision Course With the 1976 Copyright Act?*, 85 Law Libr. J. 619 (1993)

Kernochan, *Music Performing Rights Organizations in the United States of America: Special Characteristics, Restraints, and Public Attitudes,* 10 Colum.-VLA J.L. & Arts 333 (1986)

Kheit, *Public Performance Copyrights: A Guide to Public Place Analysis,* 26 Rutgers Computer & Tech. L.J. 1 (1999)

Kim, *The Performers' Plight in Sound Recordings-Unique to the U.S.: A Comparative Study of the Development of Performers' Rights in the United States, England and France,* 10 Colum.-VLA J.L. & Arts 453 (1986)

Koenigsberg, *Performing Rights in Music and Performing Rights Organizations, Revisited,* 50 J. Copyright Soc'y 355 (2003)

Korman, *Performance Rights in Music Under Sections 110 and 118 of the 1976 Copyright Act,* 22 N.Y.L. Sch. L. Rev. 521 (1977)

Korman & Koenigsberg, *Performing Rights in Music and Performing Rights Societies,* 33 J. Copyright Soc'y 332 (1987)

Lipinski, *Legal Reform in an Electronic Age: Analysis and Critique of the Construction and Operation of S. 487, The Technology, Education and Copyright Harmonization (TEACH) Act of 2001,* 2003 BYU Educ. & L.J. 95 (2003)

Loren, *Paying the Piper*, 3 J. Small & Emerging Bus. L. 231 (1999)

Martin, *Compulsory License for Jukeboxes: Why the Song Could Not Remain the Same,* 37 J. Copyright Soc'y 262 (1990)

Martin, *The WIPO Performances and Phonograms Treaty: Will the U.S. Whistle a New Tune?,* 45 J. Copyright Soc'y 157 (1997)

Nagarajan, *Public Performance Rights in Sound Recordings and the Threat of Digitalization,* 77 J. Pat. & Trademark Off. Soc'y 721 (1995)

Perrone, *Small and Grand Performing Rights (Who Cared Before "Jesus Christ Superstar"?),* 20 Bull. Copyright Soc'y 19 (1972)

Scorese, *Performing Broadway Music: The Demon Grand Rights Traps,* 14 Colum.-VLA J.L. & Arts 123 (1989)

Shipley, *Copyright Law and Your Neighborhood Bar and Grill: Recent Developments in Performances and the Section 110(5) Exemption,* 29 Ariz. L. Rev. 475 (1987)

Sobel, *The Legal and Business Aspects of Motion Picture and Television Soundtrack Music*, 8 Loy. Ent. L.J. 231 (1988)

Timberg, *The Antitrust Aspects of Merchandising Modern Music: The ASCAP Consent Judgment of 1950,* 19 Law & Contemp. Probs. 294 (1954)

Tomlinson & Nielander, *Unchained Melody: Music Licensing in the Digital Age*, 6 Tex. Intell. Prop. L.J. 277 (1998)

Xalabarder, *Copyright and Digital Distance Education: The Use of Pre-existing Works in Distance Education Through the Internet*, 26 Colum. J.L. & Arts 101 (2003)

The Public Display Right

Goetzl & Sutton, *Copyright and the Visual Artist's Display Right: A New Doctrinal Analysis,* 9 Art & L. 15 (1984)

Moohr, *Going Once, Going Twice, Sold! Are Sales of Copyright Items Exposing Internet Auction Sites to Liability?,* 21 Loy. L.A. Ent. L.J. 97 (2000)

R. Nimmer, Perfect 10 *and Beyond*, 26 Computer & Internet Law. 20 (2009)

Reese, *The Public Display Right: The Copyright Act's Neglected Solution to the Controversy over RAM "Copies",* 2001 U. Ill. L. Rev. 83 (2001)

Miscellaneous Rights: In and Beyond Copyright

D. Sinacore-Guinn, Collective Administration of Copyrights and Neighboring Rights: International Practices, Procedures, and Organizations (1993)

Aplin, *Contemplating Australia's Digital Future*, 23 Eur. Intell. Prop. L. Rev. 565 (2001)

Armstrong, *Fair Circumvention,* 74 Brooklyn L. Rev. 1 (2008)

Bartow, *Arresting Technology: An Essay,* 1 Buff. Intell. Prop. L.J. 95 (2001)

Besek, *Anti-Circumvention Laws and Copyright: A Report from the Kernochan Center for Law, Media and the Arts*, 27 Colum. J.L. & Arts 385 (2004)

Burk, *Anticircumvention Abuse,* 50 UCLA L. Rev. 1095 (2003)

Burk, *Legal and Technical Standards in Digital Rights Management Technology*, 74 Fordham L. Rev.; 537 (2005)

Burk & J. Cohen, *Fair Use Infrastructure for Rights Management Systems,* 15 Harv. J.L. & Tech. 41 (2001)

Calandrillo & Davison, *The Dangers of the Digital Millennium Copyright Act: Much Ado About Nothing?*, 50 Wm. & Mary L. Rev. 349 (2008)

Carlisle, *The Audio Home Recording Act of 1992,* 1 J. Intell. Prop. L. 335 (1994)

J. Cohen, *DRM and Privacy,* 18 Berkeley Tech. L.J. 575 (2003)

J. Cohen, Lochner *in Cyberspace: The New Economic Orthodoxy of "Rights Management"*, 97 Mich. L. Rev. 462 (1998)

Craddock & McCullagh, *Designing Copyright TPM: A Mutuant Digital Copyright*, 13 Int'l J. L. & Info. Tech. 155 (2005)

Denicola, *Access Controls, Rights Protection, and Circumvention: Interpreting the Digital Millennium Copyright Act to Preserve Noninfringing Use*, 31 Colum. J.L. & Arts 209 (2008)

Ezra, *The Failure of the Broadcast Flag: Copyright Protection to Make Hollywood Happy*, 27 Comm.-Ent. 383 (2005)

Felten, *Protection from Copying or Protection from Competition?: The Digital Millennium Copyright Act and Its Legacy: A View From the Trenches,* 2002 U. Ill. J.L. Tech & Pol'y 289 (2002)

Field, *Copyright Co-Ownership in Cyberspace: The Digital Merger of Content and Technology in Digital Rights Management and E-Commerce,* 19 Ent. & Sports Law. 3 (Fall 2001)

Garon, *What If DRM Fails?,* 2008 Mich. St. L. Rev. 10

Gasaway, *The New Access Right and Its Impact on Libraries and Library Users,* 10 J. Intell. Prop. L. 269 (2003)

Ginsburg, *Copyright and Control Over New Technologies of Dissemination,* 101 Colum L. Rev. 1613 (2001)

Ginsburg, *From Having Copies to Experiencing Works: The Development of an Access Right in U.S. Copyright Law,* 50 J. Copyright Soc'y 113 (2003)

Ginsburg, *Legal Protection of Technological Measures Protecting Works of Authorship: International Obligations and the U.S. Experience*, 29 Col. J.L. & Arts 11 (2005)

Gorski, *The Future of the Digital Millennium Copyright Act (DMCA) Subpoena Power on the Internet in Light of the* Verizon *Cases*, 24 Rev. Litig. 149 (2005)

Hart, *The Copyright in the Information Society Directive: An Overview*, 24 Eur. Intell. Prop. L. Rev. 58 (2001)

Heide, *Access Control and Innovation Under the Emerging EU Electronic Commerce Framework,* 15 Berkeley Tech. L.J. 993 (2000)

Hurwitz, *A Proposal in Hindsight: Restoring Copyright's Delicate Balance by Reworking* ***17 U.S.C. Sec. 1201***, 13 U.C.L.A. Ent. L.J. 263 (2006)

Imfeld, *Playing Fair With Fair Use? The Digital Millennium Copyright Act's Impact on Encryption Researchers and Academicians,* 8 Comm. L. & Pol'y 111 (2003)

Kawamua, *Digital Audio Tape Technology: A Formidable Challenge to the American Copyright System,* 4 Am. U. J. Int'l L. & Pol'y 409 (1989)

P. Kitch, *DMCA Is OEM's Ticket to "Super-patenting the Unpatentable,"* 17 Intell. Property & Tech. L.J. 5 (2005)

Kurtlantzick & Pennino, *The Audio Home Recording Act of 1992 and the Formation of Copyright Policy,* 45 J. Copyright Soc'y 497 (1998)

Landau, *Has the Digital Millennium Copyright Act Really Created a New Exclusive Right of Access?: Attempting to Reach a Balance Between Users' and Content Providers' Rights,* 49 J. Copyright Soc'y 277 (2001)

Landau, *What If Anti-Bootlegging Statutes Are Upheld Under the Commerce Clause,* 2008 Mich. St. L. Rev. 153

Lastowka, *Free Access and the Future of Copyright,* 27 Rutgers Computer & Tech. L.J. 293 (2001)

M. Lemley & Reese, *Reducing Digital Copyright Infringement Without Restricting Innovation*, 56 Stan. L. Rev. 1345 (2004)

Lipton, *The Law of Unintended Consequences: The Digital Millennium Copyright Act and Interoperability*, 62 Wash. & Lee L. Rev. 487 (2005)

Liu, *The DMCA and the Regulation of Scientific Research,* 18 Berkeley Tech. L.J. 501 (2003)

Lunney, *The Death of Copyright: Digital Technology, Private Copying, and the Digital Millennium Copyright Act,* 87 Va. L. Rev. 813 (2001)

Macdonald, *Speed Bump on the Information Superhighway: Slowing Transmission of Digital Works to Protect Copyright Owners,* 63 La. L. Rev. 411 (2003)

McCullough, *Understanding the Impact of the Digital Millennium Copyright Act on the Open Source Model of Software Development,* 6 Marq. Intell. Prop. L. Rev. 91 (2002)

McKuin, *Home Audio Taping of Copyrighted Works and the Audio Home Recording Act of 1992: A Critical Analysis*, 16 Hastings Comm. & Ent. L.J. 311 (1994)

Madison, *Rights of Access and the Shape of the Internet,* 44 B.C. L. Rev. 433 (2003)

Marks & Turnbull, *Technical Protection Measures: The Intersection of Technology, Law and Commercial Licenses*, 22 E.I.P.R. 198 (2000)

Matesky, *The Digital Millennium Copyright Act and Non-Infringing Use: Can Mandatory Labeling of Digital Media Products Keep the Sky From Falling?*, 80 Chi.-Kent L. Rev. 515 (2005)

Menard, *And The Shirt Off Your Back:* Universal City Studios, *DCSS, and the Digital Millennium Copyright Act,* 27 Rutgers Computer & Tech. L.J. 371 (2001)

Mitchell, *Copyright, Congress, and Constitutionality: How The Digital Millennium Copyright Act Goes Too Far*, 79 Notre Dame L. Rev. 2115 (2004)

Nard, *The DMCA's Anti-Device Provisions: Impeding the Progress of the Useful Arts?,* 8 Wash. U. J.L. & Pol'y 19 (2002)

D. Nimmer, *Appreciating Legislative History: The Sweet and Sour Spots of the DMCA's Commentary,* 23 Cardozo L. Rev. 909 (2002)

D. Nimmer, *Aus der Neuen Welt*, 93 Nw. U. L. Rev. 195 (1998)

D. Nimmer, *Back from the Future: A Proleptic Review of the Digital Millennium Copyright Act,* 16 Berkeley Tech. L.J. 855 (2001)

D. Nimmer, *Ignoring the Public, Part I: On the Absurd Complexity of the Digital Audio Transmission Right,* 7 UCLA Ent. L. Rev. 189 (2000)

Ohm, *The Analog Hole and the Price of Music: An Empirical Study*, 5 J. Telecomm. & High Tech. L. 573 (2007)

Oliar, *Resolving Conflicts Among Congress' Powers Regarding Statutes' Constitutionality: The Case of Anti-Bootlegging Statutes*, 30 Colum. J.L. & Arts 467 (2007)

Parchomovsky & Goldman, *Fair Use Harbors*, 93 Va. L. Rev. 1483 (2007)

Patterson, *Copyright in the New Millennium: Resolving the Conflict Between Property Rights and Political Rights,* 62 Ohio St. L.J. 703 (2001)

Quinn, *An Unconstitutional Patent in Disguise: Did Congress Overstep its Constitutional Authority in Adopting Circumvention Prevention Provisions of the Digital Millennium Copyright Act?,* 41 Brandeis L.J. 33 (2002)

Reese, *Will Merging Access Controls and Rights Controls Undermine the Structure of Anticircumvention Law?,* 18 Berkeley Tech. L.J. 619 (2003)

Reichman, Dinwoodie & Samuelson, *A Reverse Notice and Takedown Regime to Enable Public Interest Uses of Technically Protected Copyrighted Works*, 22 Berkeley Tech. L.J. 981 (2007)

Rothchild, *Economic Analysis of Technological Protection Measures*, 84 Or. L. Rev. 489 (2005)

Sawicki, *Repeat Infringement in the Digital Millennium Copyright Act*, 73 U. Chi. L. Rev. 1455 (2006)

Seltzer, *The Broadcast Flag: It's Not Just TV*, 57 Fed. Comm. Bar J. 209 (2005)

Shah, *UK's Implementation of the Anti-Circumvention Provisions of the EU Copyright Directive: An Analysis,* 2004 Duke L. & Tech. Rev. 3 (2004)

Sharp, *Coming Soon to Pay-Per-View: How the Digital Millennium Copyright Act Enables Digital Content Owners to Circumvent Educational Fair Use,* 40 Am. Bus. L.J. 1 (2002)

Weinberg, *Digital TV, Copy Control, and Public Policy,* 20 Cardozo Arts & Ent. LJ 227 (2002)

Williams, *Congress Should Amend the Copyright Act to Protect Transactional Watermarks,* 2008, 23 Berkeley Tech. L.J. 1367 (2008)

Wong, *Cyber-Trespass and "Unauthorized Access" as Legal Mechanisms for Access Control: Lessons from the US Experience*, 14 Int'l J.L. & Info. Tech. 90 (2007)

Woodford, *Trusted Computing or Big Brother? Putting the Rights Back in Digital Rights Management*, 75 U. Colo. L. Rev. 253 (2004)

Xie, *The Regulation of Anti-Circumvention in China,* 54 J. Copyright Soc'y 545 (2007)

Yen, *What Federal Gun Control Can Teach Us About the DMCA's Ani-Trafficking Provisions,* 2003 Wis. L. Rev. 649 (2003)

Yu, *Anticircumvention and Anti-anticircumvention*, 84 Denv. U. L. Rev. 13 (2006)

Zieminski, *Game Over for Reverse Engineering? How the DMCA and Contracts Have Affected Innovation,* 13 J. Tech. L. & Pol'y 289 (2008)

Zimmerman, *Adrift in the Digital Millennium Copyright Act: The Sequel,* 26 U. Dayton L. Rev. 279 (2001)

Zohar, *Towards a Doctrine of "Fair Access" in Copyright: the Federal Circuit's Accord*, 46 IDEA 99 (2005)

Moral Rights

R. Kwall, The Soul of Creativity: Forging a Moral Rights Law for the United States (2009)

C. Lury, Cultural Rights: Technology, Legality, and Personality (1993)

J.H. Merryman & A. Elsen, S. Urice, Law, Ethics and the Visual Arts (5th ed. 2007)

U.S. Copyright Office, Waiver of Moral Rights in Visual Artworks (1996)

Adler, *Against Moral Rights*, 97 Calif. L. Rev. 263 (2009)

Aide, *A More Comprehensive Soul: Romantic Conceptions of Authorship and the Copyright Doctrine of Moral Rights,* 48 U. Toronto L. Rev. 211 (1990)

Barnett, *From New Technology to Moral Rights: Passive Carriers, Teletext, and Deletion as Copyright Infringement — The WGN Case,* 31 J. Copyright Soc'y 427 (1984)

Beyer, *Intentionalism, Art, and the Suppression of Innovation: Film Colorization and the Philosophy of Moral Rights*, 82 Nw. U. L. Rev. 1011 (1988)

Burton, *Artists' Moral Rights: Controversy and the Visual Artists' Rights Act,* 48 SMU L. Rev. 639 (1995)

Chang, *Revisiting the Visual Artists Rights Act of 1990: A Follow-up Survey about Awareness and Waiver*, 13 Tex. Intell. Prop. L.J. 129 (2005)

Ciolino, *Moral Rights and Real Obligations: A Property-Law Framework For the Protection of Authors' Moral Rights,* 69 Tul. L. Rev. 935 (1995)

Cotter, *Pragmatism, Economics, and the Droit Moral*, 76 N.C. L. Rev. 1 (1997)

Damich, *A Critique of the Visual Artists Rights Act of 1989,* 14 Nova L. Rev. 407 (1990)

Damich, *State "Moral Rights" Statutes: An Analysis and Critique,* 13 Colum.-VLA J.L. & Arts 291 (1989)

Damich, *The New York Artists' Authorship Rights Act: A Comparative Critique,* 84 Colum. L. Rev. 1733 (1984)

Damich, *The Right of Personality: A Common-Law Basis for the Protection of the Moral Rights of Authors,* 23 Ga. L. Rev. 1 (1988)

Damich, *The Visual Artists Rights Act of 1990: Toward a Federal System of Moral Rights Protection for Visual Art,* 39 Cath. U. L. Rev. 945 (1990)

DaSilva, Droit Moral *and the Amoral Copyright: A Comparison of Artists' Rights in France and the U.S.,* 28 Bull. Copyright Soc'y 1 (1980)

Davis, *State Moral Rights Law and the Federal Copyright System,* 4 Cardozo Arts & Ent. L.J. 233 (1986)

Dietz, *The Moral Right of the Author: Moral Rights and the Civil Law Countries,* 19 Colum.-VLA J.L. & Arts 199 (1995)

Dusollier, *Some Reflections on Copyright Management Information and Moral Rights,* 25 Colum.-VLA J.L. & Arts 377 (2003)

Dworkin, *The Moral Right of the Author: Moral Rights and the Common Law Countries,* 19 Colum.-VLA J.L. & Arts 229 (1995)

Francon & Ginsburg, *Authors' Rights in France: The Moral Right of the Creator of a Commissioned Work to Compel the Commissioning Party to Complete the Work,* 9 Colum.-VLA J.L. & Arts 381 (1981)

Ginsburg, *Copyright in the 101st Congress: Commentary on the Visual Artists' Rights Act and the Architectural Works Copyright Protection Act of 1990,* 14 Colum.-VLA J.L. & the Arts 477 (1990)

Ginsburg, *Reforms and Innovations Regarding Authors' and Performers' Rights in France,* 10 Colum.-VLA J.L. & Arts 83 (1985)

Ginsburg, *Suppression and Liberty: Have Moral Rights Come of (Digital) Age in the United States?,* 19 Cardozo Arts & Ent. L.J. 9 (2001)

Ginsburg, *The Right to Claim Authorship in U.S. Copyright and Trademarks Law,* 41 Hous. L. Rev. 263 (2004)

Ginsburg & Sirinelli, *Authors and Exploitations in International Private Law: The French Supreme Court and the Huston Film Colorization Controversy,* 15 Colum.-VLA J.L. & Arts 135 (1991)

Gorman, *Federal Moral Rights Legislation: The Need for Caution,* 14 Nova L. Rev. 421 (1990)

Gorman, *Visual Artists Rights Act of 1990,* 38 J. Copyright Soc'y 233 (1991)

Hanson & Santilli, *Authors' and Artists' Moral Rights: A Comparative Legal and Economic Analysis,* 26 J. Legal Stud. 95 (1997)

Hiatt, *The "Dirt" on Digital "Sanitizing": Droit Moral, Artistic Integrity and* The Directors Guild of America v. Cleanflicks, 30 Rutgers Computer & Tech. L.J. 375 (2004)

Hughes, *American Moral Rights and Fixing the* Dastar *'Gap'*, 2007 Utah L. Rev. 659

Karlen, *Joint Ownership of Moral Rights,* 38 J. Copyright Soc'y 242 (1991)

Karlen, *Moral Rights and Real Life Artists,* 15 Hastings Comm. & Ent. L.J. 929 (1993)

Kwall, *Copyright and the Moral Right: Is an American Marriage Possible?,* 38 Vand. L. Rev. 1 (1985)

Kwall, *How Fine Art Fares Post VARA,* 1 Marq. Intell. Prop. L. Rev. 1 (1997)

Kwall, *Originality in Context*, 44 Hous. L. Rev. 871 (2007)

Kwall, *Preserving Personality and Reputational Interests of Constructed Personas Through Moral Rights: A Blueprint for the Twenty-First Century,* 2001 U. Ill. L. Rev. 151

Kwall, *The Attribution Right in the United States: Caught in the Crossfire Between Copyright and Section 43A*, 77 Wash. L. Rev. 985 (2003)

LaFrance, *When You Wish Upon* Dastar: *Creative Provenance and the Lanham Act*, 38 Intell. Prop. L. Rev. 371 (2006)

Landau, Dastar v. Twentieth *Century Fox: The Need for Stronger Protection of Attribution Rights in the United States*, 61 N.Y.U. Surv. Am. L. 273 (2005)

Leaffer, *Of Moral Rights and Resale Royalties: The Kennedy Bill,* 7 Cardozo Arts & Ent. L.J. 234 (1989)

Lee, *Toward an American Moral Rights in Copyright,* 58 Wash. & Lee L. Rev. 795 (2001)

M. Lemley, *Rights of Attribution and Integrity in Online Communications,* 1995 J. Online L., Art 2, p. 40.

Merryman, *The Refrigerator of Bernard Buffet,* 27 Hastings L.J. 1023 (1976)

Merryman, *The Wrath of Robert Rauschenberg,* 40 J. Copyright Soc'y 241 (1992)

Netanel, *Alienability Restrictions and the Enhancement of Author Autonomy in United States and Continental Copyright Law,* 12 Cardozo Arts & Ent. L.J. 1 (1994)

Ong, *Why Moral Rights Matter: Recognizing the Intrinsic Value of Integrity Rights*, 26 Colum. J.L. & Arts 297 (2003)

Roeder, *The Doctrine of Moral Right: A Study in the Law of Artists, Authors and Creators,* 53 Harv. L. Rev. 554 (1940)

Rudoff, *The Dancer and the Dance: An Essay on Composers, Performers, and Integrity Rights,* 29 Alberta L. Rev. 884 (1991)

Sergent, *Building Reputational Capital: The Right of Attribution Under Section 43 of the Lanham Act*, 19 Colum.-VLA J. L. & Arts 45 (1995)

Serra, *"Tilted Arc" Destroyed,* 14 Nova L. Rev. 385 (1990)

Spellman & Schauer, *Artists' Moral Rights and the Psychology of Ownership*, 83 Tul. L. Rev. 661 (2009)

Stern, *A Matter of Life or Death: The Visual Artists Rights Act and the Problem of Postmortem Moral Rights*, 51 UCLA L. Rev. 849 (2004)

Strauss, *The Moral Right of the Author*, Copyright Law Revision Study No. 4 (1960)

Treece, *American Law Analogues of the Author's "Moral Right,"* 16 Am. J. Comp. L. 487 (1968)

Tushnet, *Naming Rights: Attribution and Law*, 2007 Utah L. Rev. 789

Tushnet, *Payment in Credit: Copyright Law and Subcultural Creativity*, 70 Law & Contemp. Probs. 135 (2007)

VerSteeg, *Federal Moral Rights for Visual Artists: Contract Theory and Analysis,* 67 Wash. L. Rev. 827 (1992)

Wang, *(Re)productive Rights: Copyright and Postmodern Art,* 14 Colum.-VLA J.L. & Arts 261 (1990)

Yonover, *The "Dissing" of Da Vinci: The Imaginary Case of* Leonardo v. Duchamp: *Moral Rights, Parody, and Fair Use,* 29 Val. U. L. Rev. 935 (1995)

Yonover, *The Precarious Balance: Moral Rights, Parody, and Fair Use,* 14 Cardozo Art & Ent. L.J. 79 (1996)

Chapter 8

INFRINGEMENT ACTIONS

Reference Works

H. Abrams, The Law of Copyright §§ 13.1 to 13.42, 13.49, 14.1 to 14.46, 19.19 to 19.24 (2008)

P. Goldstein, Goldstein on Copyright §§ 9.1 to 9.4, 10.0 to 10.6, 15.1 to 15.6, 16.1 to 16.6, 18.1 to 18.2 (3d ed. 2005)

M. Leaffer, Understanding Copyright Law §§ 9.01 to 9.06, 9.10 to 9.19 (5th ed. 2010)

M. Nimmer & D. Nimmer, Nimmer on Copyright §§ 12.01 to 12.03, 12.07 to 12.12, 13.01 to 13.03 (2010)

W. Patry, Patry on Copyright §§ 9:1 to 9:278, 17:1 to 17:223, 19:1 to 19:13, 21:1 to 21:39, 25:1 to 25:105 (2010)

Procedural Aspects Generally

Berman, Reese & Young, *State Accountability for Violations of Intellectual Property Rights: How to "Fix"* Florida Prepaid *(And How Not To),* 79 Tex. L. Rev. 1037 (2001)

Blair & Cotter, *The Elusive Logic of Standing Doctrine in Intellectual Property Law,* 74 Tul. L. Rev. 1323 (2000)

Bohannon & Cotter, *When the State Steals Ideas: Is the Abrogation of State Sovereign Immunity from Federal Infringement Claims Constitutional in Light of Seminole Tribe?*, 4 Fordham L. Rev. (1999)

A. Cohen, *"Arising Under" Jurisdiction and the Copyright Laws*, 44 Hastings L. Rev. 337 (1993)

J. Cohen, *Pervasively Distributed Copyright Enforcement*, 95 Geo. L.J. 1 (2006)

Cross, *Suing the States for Copyright Infringement,* 39 Brandeis L.J. 337 (2000–01)

Feldman, *An Examination of the Right to Jury Trial Where Copyright Statutory Damages Are Elected,* 21 Hofstra L. Rev. 261 (1992)

Ghosh, *Toward a Theory of Regulatory Takings for Intellectual Property: The Path Left Open After* College Savings v. Florida Prepaid, 37 San Diego L. Rev. 637 (2000)

Glauberman, *Citizen Suits Against States: The Exclusive Jurisdiction Dilemma*, 45 J. Copyright Soc'y 63 (1997)

Heald & Wells, *Remedies for the Misappropriation of Intellectual Property by State and Municipal Governments Before and After* Seminole Tribe: *The Eleventh Amendment and Other Immunity Doctrines*, 55 Wash. & Lee L. Rev. 849 (1998)

Hughes, *On the Logic of Suing One's Customers and the Dilemma of Infringement-based Business Models*, 22 Cardozo Arts & Ent. L.J. 725 (2005)

Kwall, *Governmental Use of Copyrighted Property: The Sovereign's Prerogative*, 67 Tex. L. Rev. 685 (1989)

Landau & Biederman, *The Case for a Specialized Copyright Court: Eliminating the Jurisdictional Advantage*, 21 Hastings Comm. & Ent. L.J. 717 (1999)

Latman & Tager, *Liability of Innocent Infringers of Copyright*, Copyright Law Revision Study No. 25 (1960)

K. Lemley, *Eliminating Value of Infringement: An Economic Analysis of Internal Transactions and Indirect External Transactions in Software Infringement Cases*, 45 IDEA 425 (2005)

Meltzer, *Overcoming Immunity: The Case of Federal Regulation of Intellectual Property,* 53 Stan. L. Rev. 1331 (2001)

Menell, *Economic Implications of State Sovereign Immunity from Infringement of Federal Intellectual Property Rights*, 33 Loy. L.A. L. Rev. 1399 (2000)

D. Nimmer, *Repeat Infringers*, 52 J. Copyright Soc'y 167 (2005)

Paetsch, *How to Admit E-mail and Web Pages into Evidence*, 94 Ill. B. J. 674 (2006)

Patry, *The Right to a Jury in Copyright Cases*, 29 J. Copyright Soc'y 139 (1981)

Shoiket, Creative Technology Ltd. v. Aztech System PTE, Ltd.: *Using Forum Non Conveniens to Dismiss a Copyright Infringement Action Brought by a Foreign Owner of U.S. Copyrights,* 31 U.S.F. L. Rev. 505 (1997)

Volokh, *Sovereign Immunity and Intellectual Property*, 73 S. Cal. L. Rev. 1161 (2000)

Volokh & McDonnell, *Freedom of Speech and Independent Judgment Review in Copyright Cases,* 107 Yale L.J. 2431 (1998)

Wanat, *Copyright and Contracts: The Subject Matter Jurisdiction of Federal Courts Under 28 U.S.C. § 1338(a),* 11 DePaul-LCA J. Art & Ent. L. 361 (2001)

Substantive Aspects Generally

Aoki, *Adrift in the Intertext: Authorship and Audience "Recoding" Rights,* 68 Chicago-Kent L. Rev. 805 (1993)

Arewa, *From J.C. Bach to Hip Hop: Musical Borrowing, Copyright and Cultural Context*, 84 N.C.L. Rev. 547 (2006)

Bisceglia, *Summary Judgment on Substantial Similarity in Copyright Actions,* 16 Hastings Comm. & Ent. L.J. 51 (1993)

Broaddus, *Eliminating the Confusion: A Restatement of the Test for Copyright Infringement*, 5 J. Art & Ent. L. 43 (1994)

Brown, *The Corporate Receipt Conundrum: Establishing Access in Copyright Infringement Actions,* 77 Minn. L. Rev. 1409 (1993)

Cadwell, *Expert Testimony, Scenes a Faire, and Tonal Music: A (Not So) New Test for Infringement*, 46 Santa Clara L. Rev. 137 (2005)

A. Cohen, *Masking Copyright Decisionmaking: The Meaninglessness of Substantial Similarity*, 20 U.C. Davis L. Rev. 719 (1987)

Dockins, *Internet Links: The Good, the Bad, the Tortious, and a Two-Part Test*, 36 U. Tol. L. Rev. 367 (2005)

Dogan, *Code Versus the Common Law*, 2 J. Telecomm. & High Tech. L. 73 (2003)

Druehwald, *Copyright Infringement of Musical Compositions: A Systematic Approach,* 26 Akron L. Rev. 15 (1992)

Ford, *Judging Expertise in Copyright Law*, 14 J. Intell. Prop. L. 1 (2006)

Francione, *Facing the Nation: The Standards for Copyright Infringement and Fair Use of Factual Works*, 134 U. Pa. L. Rev. 519 (1986)

Gherman, *Harmony and its Functionality: A Gloss on the Substantial Similarity Test in Music Copyrights*, 19 Fordham Intell. Prop. Media & Ent. L.J. 483 (2009)

Hartnick, *Summary Judgment in Copyright: From Cole Porter to Superman*, 3 Cardozo Arts & Ent. L.J. 53 (1984)

Jones, *Music Copyright in Theory and Practice: An Improved Approach for Determining Substantial Similarity*, 31 Duq. L. Rev. 277 (1993)

Kim, *Expert Testimony and Substantial Similarity: Facing the Music in (Music) Copyright Infringement Cases,* 19 Colum.-VLA J.L. & Arts 109 (1995)

Kegan, *Survey Evidence in Copyright Litigation*, 32 J. Copyright Soc'y 283 (1985)

Knowles & Palmieri, *Dissecting* Krofft: *An Expression of New Ideas in Copyright?*, 8 San Fern. V. L. Rev. 109 (1980)

Lape, *The Metaphysics of the Law: Bringing Substantial Similarity Down to Earth,* 98 Dick. L. Rev. 181 (1993)

Latman, *"Probative Similarity" as Proof of Copying: Towards Dispelling Some Myths in Copyright Infringement*, 90 Colum. L. Rev. 1187 (1990)

Litman, *Sharing and Stealing*, 27 Comm.-Ent. 1 (2004)

Morrison, Bridgeport *Redux: Digital Sampling and Audience Recoding,* 19 Fordham Intell. Prop. Media & Ent. L.J. 75 (2008)

Pever, *The Transfer of Media to Digital Form: Redefining the Copyright Infringement Test to Include Commercial Use as a Solution to Digital Copyright Infringement,* 31 Cap. U.L. Rev. 109 (2003)

Radin, *The Significance of Intent to Copy in a Civil Action for Copyright Infringement*, 54 Temp. L.Q. 1 (1981)

Schietinger, *How the Sixth Circuit Missed a Beat on Digital Music Sampling*, 55 DePaul L. Rev. 209 (2005)

Sher, *The Search for a Suitable Standard of Substantial Similarity: The Ninth Circuit's Application of the* Krofft *Test*, 25 U.C. Davis L. Rev. 229 (1991)

Sorensen & Sorensen, *Re-Examining the Traditional Legal Test of Literary Similarity: A Proposal for Content Analysis*, 37 Cornell L.Q. 638 (1952)

Taylor, *Common Errors as Evidence of Copying*, 22 Bull. Copyright Soc'y 444 (1975)

Wanat, *Copyright Law: Infringement of Musical Works and the Appropriateness of Summary Judgment under the Federal Rules of Civil Procedure, Rule 56(C)*, 39 U. Mem. L. Rev. 1037 (2009)

Wong, *Rocking and Ripping on the World Wide Web*, 3 Sing. Acad. L.J. 323 (2001)

Wright, *Hand, Posner, and the Myth of the Hand Formula*, 4 Theoretical Inq. L. 145 (2003)

Y'Barbo, *The Heart of the Matter: The Property Right Conferred by Copyright*, 49 Mercer L. Rev. 643 (1998)

Software Infringement

G.P. Albert, Intellectual Property Law in Cyberspace (1999 & 2007 Supp.)

R. Nimmer, The Law of Computer Technology: Rights, Licenses, Liabilities (2009)

H. Scott, Computer and Intellectual Property Crime: Federal and State Law (2001 & Supp. 2004)

Brown, *"Analytical Dissection" of Copyrighted Computer Software — Complicating the Simple and Confounding the Complex*, 25 Ariz. St. L.J. 801 (1993)

Clapes, Lynch & Steinberg, *Silicon Epics and Binary Bards: Determining the Proper Scope of Copyright Protection for Computer Programs*, 34 UCLA L. Rev. 1493 (1987)

J. Cohen, *Reverse Engineering and the Rise of Electronic Vigilantism: Intellectual Property Implications of "Lock-Out" Programs*, 68 S. Cal. L. Rev. 1091 (1995)

Dam, *Some Economic Considerations in the Intellectual Property Protection of Software*, 24 J. Legal Stud. 321 (1995)

Dogan & Liu, *Copyright Law and Subject Matter Specificity: The Case of Computer Software*, 61 N.Y.U. Ann. Surv. Am. L. 203 (2005)

Fox, *Harsh Realities: Substantial Similarity in the Reality Television Context*, 13 U.C.L.A. Ent. L. Rev. 223 (2006)

Goldstein, *Infringement of Copyright in Computer Programs*, 47 U. Pitt. L. Rev. 1119 (1986)

Gordon, *Copying to Compete: The Tension Between Copyright Protection and Antitrust Policy in Recent Non-Literal Computer Program Copyright Infringement Cases,* 15 J. Marshall J. Computer & Info. L. 171 (1996)

Hamilton & Sabety, *Computer Science Concepts in Copyright Cases: The Path to a Coherent Law,* 10 Harv. J.L. & Tech. 239 (1997)

Karjala, *Copyright Protection of Computer Software, Reverse Engineering, and Professor Miller,* 19 U. Dayton L. Rev. 975 (1994)

Litman, *Revising Copyright Law for the Information Age,* 75 Ore. L. Rev. 19 (1996)

Lowe, *A Square Peg in a Round Hole: The Proper Substantial Similarity Test for Nonliteral Aspects of Computer Programs,* 68 Wash. L. Rev. 351 (1993)

Lunney, Lotus v. Borland: *Copyright and Computer Programs,* 70 Tul. L. Rev. 2397 (1996)

Menell, *An Analysis of the Scope of Copyright Protection for Application Programs*, 41 Stan. L. Rev. 1045 (1989)

Menell, *Tailoring Legal Protection for Computer Software*, 41 Stan. L. Rev. 1329 (1987)

Miller, *Copyright Protection for Computer Programs, Databases, and Computer-Generated Works: Is Anything New Since CONTU?*, 106 Harv. L. Rev. 977 (1993)

D. Nimmer, *Brains and Other Paraphernalia of the Digital Age,* 10 Harv. J.L. & Tech. 1 (1996)

D. Nimmer, Bernacchi & Frischling, *A Structured Approach to Analyzing the Substantial Similarity of Computer Software in Copyright Infringement Cases*, 20 Ariz. St. L.J. 625 (1988)

Ogilvie, *Defining Computer Program Parts Under Learned Hand's Abstractions Test in Software Copyright Infringement Cases,* 91 Mich. L. Rev. 526 (1992)

Palmer & Vinje, *The E.C. Directive on the Legal Protection of Computer Software: New Law Governing Software Development,* 2 Duke J. Comp. & Int'l L. 65 (1992)

Patry, *Copyright and Computer Programs: It's All in the Definition*, 14 Cardozo Arts & Ent. L.J. 1 (1996)

Risch, *How Can* Whelan v. Jaslow *and* Lotus v. Borland *Both Be Right? Reexamining the Economics of Computer Software Reuse*, 17 J. Marshall J. Computer & Info. L. 511 (1999)

Rosen, *Virtual Reality: Copyrightable Subject Matter and the Scope of Judicial Protection,* 33 Jurimetrics J. 35 (1992)

Samuelson, *Computer Programs, User Interfaces, and Section 102(b) of the Copyright Act of 1976: A Critique of* Lotus v. Paperback, 6 High Tech. L.J. 209 (1991)

Samuelson, *The Nature of Copyright Analysis for Computer Programs: Copyright Law Professors' Brief Amicus Curiae in "Lotus v. Borland"*, 16 Hastings Comm. & Ent. L.J. 657 (1994)

Samuelson & Glushko, *Comparing the Views of Lawyers and User Interface Designers on the Software "Look and Feel" Law Suits*, 30 Jurimetrics J. 121 (1988)

Stevens, *Copyright Infringement of Computer Programs Stored on ROM Computer Chips,* 78 J. Patent & Trademark Off. Soc'y 640 (1996)

Teter, *Merger and the Machines: An Analysis of the Pro-Compatibility Trend in Computer Software Copyright Cases,* 45 Stan. L. Rev. 1061 (1993)

Wright, *Litigation as a Mechanism for Inefficiency in Software Copyright Law,* 39 UCLA L. Rev. 397 (1991)

Extraterritoriality and Conflicts of Laws

Austin, *Social Policy Choices and Choice of Law for Copyright Infringement in Cyberspace,* 79 Or. L. Rev. 575 (2000)

Bradley, *Territorial Intellectual Property Law in an Age of Globalism,* 37 Va. J. Int'l L. 505 (1997)

Chien-Hale, *Asserting U.S. Intellectual Property Rights in China: Expansion of Extraterritorial Jurisdiction*, 45 J. Copyright Soc'y 198 (1997)

Dinwoodie, *The Architecture of the International Intellectual Property System*, 77 Chi.-Kent L. Rev. 993 (2002)

Dreyfuss & Ginsburg, *Draft Convention on Jurisdiction and Recognition of Judgments in Intellectual Property Matters*, 77 Chi.-Kent L. Rev. 1065 (2002)

Geller, *Conflicts of Laws in Copyright Cases: Infringement and Onwership Issues*, 51 J. Copyright Soc'y 315 (2004)

Geller, *Conflicts of Laws in Cyberspace: Rethinking International Copyright*, 44 J. Copyright Soc'y 103 (1996)

Geller, *Harmonizing Copyright-Contract Conflicts Analyses,* 25 Copyright 49 (1989)

Ginsburg, *Copyright Without Borders? Choice of Forum and Choice of Law for Copyright Infringement in Cyberspace,* 15 Cardozo Arts & Ent. L.J. 153 (1997)

Ginsburg, *Extraterritoriality and Multiterritoriality in Copyright Infringement,* 37 Va. J. Int'l L. 587 (1997)

Ginsburg, *The Cyberian Captivity of Copyright: Territoriality and Authors' Rights in a Networked World,* 20 Santa Clara & High Tech. L.J. 185 (2003)

Goldsmith, *Against Cyberanarchy*, 65 U. Chi. L. Rev. 1199 (1998); *Post, Against "Against Cyberanarchy"*, 17 Berkeley Tech. L.J. 1365 (2002)

Goldstein (moderator), *Ideas Without Boundaries: Creating and Protecting Intellectual Property in the International Arena: Copyright's Long Arm: Enforcing U.S. Copyrights Abroad,* 24 Loy. L.A. Ent. L. Rev. 45 (2004)

Harkins, *Overcoming the Extraterritorial Bar to Bringing Copyright Actions: On Pleading Copyright Infringement to Protect Copyrighted Works from the Defendant that Ships Overseas for Distribution Abroad*, 17 Intell. Prop. & Tech. L.J. 1 (2005)

Kirios, *Territoriality and International Copyright Actions,* 22 Copyright L. Symp. (ASCAP) 53 (1977)

Koneru, *The Right to Authorize in U.S. Copyright Law: Questions of Contributory Infringement and Extraterritoriality,* 37 Idea 87 (1996)

Lee, *The New Canon: Using or Misusing Foreign Law to Decide Domestic Intellectual Property Claims*, 46 Harv. Int'l L.J. 1 (2005)

Morris, *Pirates of the Internet, at Intellectual Property's End with Torrents and Challenges for Choice of Law,* 17 Int'l J.L. & Info. Tech. 282 (2009)

M. Nimmer, *Who Is the Copyright Owner When the Laws Conflict?,* 5 IIC 62 (1974)

Patchel, *Software as a Commodity: International Licensing of Intellectual Property: Choice of Law and Software Licenses: A Framework for Discussion*, 26 Brooklyn J. Int'l L. 117 (2000)

Patry, *Choice of Law and International Copyright,* 48 Am. J. Comp. L. 383 (2000)

Wollman, *Maneuvering Through the Landmines of Multiterritorial Copyright Litigation: How to Avoid the Presumption Against Extraterritoriality When Attempting to Recover for the Foreign Exploitation of U.S. Copyrighted Works,* 104 W. Va. L. Rev. 343 (2002)

Xalabarder, *Choice of Law and Jurisdiction in the Digital Age,* 8 Ann. Surv. Int'l & Comp. L. 79 (2002)

Chapter 9

SECONDARY LIABILITY

Reference Works

H. Abrams, The Law of Copyright §§ 14.47 to 14.81 (2008)

P. Goldstein, Goldstein on Copyright §§ 8.0 to 8.3 (3d ed. 2005)

M. Leaffer, Understanding Copyright Law §§ 8.33 to 8.40, 9.07 to 9.08 (5th ed. 2010)

M. Nimmer & D. Nimmer, Nimmer on Copyright §§ 12.04, 12A.01 to 12A.19, 12B.01 to 12B.12 (2010)

W. Patry, Patry on Copyright §§ 21:40 to 21:90 (2010)

Contributory and Vicarious Infringement

Armstrong, Sony, Napster, *and* Aimster: *An Analysis of Dissimilar Application of the Copyright Law to Similar Technologies,* 13 DePaul-LCA J. Art & Ent. L. 1 (2003)

Band, *So What Does Inducement Mean?*, 22 Computer & Internet L. 1 (2005)

Band & Schruers, *Safe Harbors Against the Liability Hurricane: The Communications Decency Act and the Digital Millennium Copyright Act,* 20 Cardozo Arts & Ent. L.J. 295 (2002)

Bartholomew, *Cops, Robbers, and Search Engines: The Questionable Role of Criminal Law in Contributory Infringement Doctrine,* 2009 B.Y.U. L. Rev. 783

Bartholomew, *Copyright, Trademark and Secondary Liability After* Grokster, 32 Colum. J.L. & Arts 445 (2009)

Bartholomew & Tehranian, *The Secret Life of Legal Doctrine: The Divergent Evolution of Secondary Liability in Trademark and Copyright Law*, 21 Berkeley Tech. L.J. 1363 (2006)

Bartow, *Women in the Web of Secondary Liability and Internet Filtering*, 32 N. Ky. L. Rev. 2020 (2005)

Botein & Samuels, *Compulsory Licenses in Peer-to-Peer File Sharing: A Workable Solution?*, 30 S. Ill. L.J. 69 (2005)

Carmichael, *In Support of the White Paper: Why Online Service Providers Should Not Receive Immunity from Traditional Notions of Vicarious and Contributory Liability for Copyright Infringement*, 16 Loy. L.A. Ent. J.L. 759 (1996)

Carroll, *Disruptive Technology and Common Law Lawmaking: A Brief Analysis of* A & M Records, Inc. v. Napster, Inc., 9 Vill. Sports & Ent. L.J. 5 (2002)

J. Cohen, *Comment: Copyright's Public-Private Distinction* (response to article by Jessica Litman in Law Technology and the Arts Symposium: "Copyright and Personal Copying: *Sony v. Universal Studios* Twenty-One Years Later"), 55 Case W. Res. L. Rev. 963 (2005)

J. Cohen, *The Place of the User in Copyright Law* (Symposium: Law and the Information Society), 74 Fordham L. Rev. 347 (2005)

Dean, *Expanding the Doctrines of Vicarious and Contributory Copyright Infringement:* Fonovisa, Inc. v. Cherry Auction, Inc. *Targets the Primary Distribution Channels for Counterfeit Merchandise*, 4 Vill. Sports & Ent. L.J. 119 (1997)

Denster, *Fault-Based Libel and Copyright Infringement Liability for On-Line Content Providers and Bulletin Board Operators as "Information Distributors,"* 11 St. John's J. Legal Comment. 653 (1996)

Desai, *Big Entertainment Needs a Sequel to the Highly Anticipated Flop:* MGM v. Grokster, 41 Ga. L. Rev. 579 (2007)

Dogan, *Infringement Once Removed: The Perils of Hyperlinking to Infringing Content,* 87 Iowa L. Rev. 829 (2002)

Feder, *Is Betamax Obsolete?* Sony Corp. of America v. Universal City Studios, Inc. *in the Age of* Napster, 37 Creighton L. Rev. 859 (2004)

Ghosh, *Turning Gray into Green: Some Comments on* Napster, 23 Hastings Comm. & Ent. L.J. 563 (2001)

Gilbert & Katz, *When Good Value Chains Go Bad: The Economics of Indirect Liability for Copyright Infringement,* 52 Hastings L.J. 961 (2001)

Ginsburg, *Copyright Use and Excuse on the Internet*, 24 Colum.-VLA J.L. & Arts 1 (2000)

Ginsburg *Separating the* Sony *Sheep From the* Grokster *Goats: Reckoning the Future Business Plans of Copyright-Dependent Technology Entrepreneurs*, 50 Ariz. L. Rev. 577 (2008)

Glatstein, *Tertiary Copyright Liability*, 71 U. Chi. L. Rev. 1605 (2004)

Hamdani, *Who's Liable for Cyberwrongs?,* 87 Cornell L. Rev. 901 (2002)

Hamilton, *The Distant Drumbeat: Why the Law Still Matters in the Information Era*, 20 Cardozo Arts & Ent. L.J. 259 (2002)

Helman, *When Your Recording Agency Turns into an Agency Problem: The True Nature of the Peer-to-Peer Debate,* 50 Idea 49 (2009)

Hogberg, *The Search for Intent-based Doctrine of Secondary Liability in Copyright Law*, 106 Colum. L. Rev. 909 (2006)

Hollaar, *Liability for Inducement of Copyright Infringement: The Genie Is Out of the Bottle*, 8 J. Int. L. 18 (2004)

Honigsberg, *The Evolution and Revolution of* Napster, 36 U.S.F. L. Rev. 473 (2002)

Jackson, *One Step Forward, Two Steps Back: An Historical Analysis of Copyright Liability*, 20 Cardozo Arts & Ent. L.J. 367 (2002)

Karjala, *Access to Computer Programs Under the DMCA*, 25 J. Marshall J. Computer & Info. L. 641 (2009)

Katyal, *Filtering, Piracy Surveillance and Disobedience,* 32 Colum. J.L. & Arts. 401 (2009)

Ku, *Grokking* Grokster, 2005 Wis. L. Rev. 1217 (2005)

Ku, *The Creative Destruction of Copyright:* Napster *and the New Economics of Digital Technology*, 69 U. Chi. L. Rev. 263 (2002)

Lange, *Students, Music and the Net: A Comment on Peer-to-Peer File Sharing,* 2003 Duke L. & Tech. Rev. 21

Lee, *Decoding the DMCA Safe Harbors*, 32 Colum. J.L. & Arts 233 (2009)

M. Lemley & Reese, *A Quick and Inexpensive System for Resolving Peer-to-Peer Copyright Disputes*, 23 Cardozo Arts. & Ent. L.J. 1 (2005)

Lewis, *The Yellow Submarine Steers Clear of U.S. Copyright Law: The Ninth Circuit Reexamines the Doctrine of Contributory Infringement*, 18 Loy. L.A. Int'l & Comp. L.J. 371 (1996)

Lichtman & Landes, *Indirect Liability for Copyright Infringement: An Economic Perspective,* 16 Harv. J.L. & Tech. 395 (2003)

Litman, *The Sony Paradox*, 55 Case. W. Res. L. Rev. 917 (2005)

Malone, *Contributory Liability for Access Providers: Solving the Conundrum Digitization Has Placed on Copyright Laws*, 49 Fed. Comm. L.J. 491 (1997)

Mehra, *Software as Crime: Japan, the United States, and Contributory Copyright Infringement*, 79 Tulane L. Rev.(2004)

Menell, *Indirect Copyright Liability and Technological Innovation,* 32 Colum. J.L. & Arts 375 (2009)

Menell & Nimmer, *Legal Realism in Action: Indirect Copyright Liability's Continuing Tort Framework and* Sony's De Facto *Demise,* 55 UCLA L. Rev. 143 (2007)

Mota, *Napster: Facilitation of Sharing, Or Contributory and Vicarious Copyright Infringement?,* 2 Minn. Intell. Prop. Rev. 61 (2001)

Moye, *How Sony Survived: Peer-to-Peer Software,* Grokster, *and Contributory Copyright Liability in the Twenty-First Century*, 84 N.C. L. Rev. 646 (2006)

Mtima, *Whom the Gods Would Destroy: Why Congress Prioritized Copyright Protection over Internet Privacy in Passing the Digital Millennium Copyright Act,* 61 Rutgers L. Rev. 627 (2009)

Myers, *Speaking Frankly About Copyright Infringement on Computer Bulletin Boards: Lessons to be Learned from* Frank Music, Netcom, *and the White Paper,* 49 Vand. L. Rev. 439 (1996)

Netanel, *Impose a Noncommercial Use Levy to Allow Free Peer-to-Peer File Sharing,* 17 Harv. J.L. & Tech. 1 (2003)

D. Nimmer, *An Odyssey Through Copyright's Vicarious Defenses*, 73 N.Y.U. L. Rev. 162 (1998)

D. Nimmer & Menell, *Copyright's "Staple Article of Commerce" Doctrine: Patently Misguided*, 53 J. Copyright Soc'y 365 (2006)

Oddi, *Contributory Copyright Infringement: The Tort and Technology Tensions*, 64 Notre Dame L. Rev. 47 (1989)

Orbach, *Indirect Free Riding on the Wheels of Commerce: Dual-Use Technologies and Copyright Liability,* 57 Emory L.J. 409 (2008)

Perzanowski, *Rethinking Anticircumvention's Interoperability Policy,* 42 U.C. Davis L. Rev. 1549 (2009)

Picker, *Rewinding Sony: The Evolving Product, Phoning Home and the Duy of Ongoing Design*, 55 Case W. Res. L. Rev. 749 (2005)

Pomeroy, *Promoting the Progress of Science and the Useful Art in the Digital Domain: Copyright, Computer Bulletin Boards, and Liability for Infringement by Others*, 45 Emory L.J. 1035 (1996)

Reese, *The Relationship Between the ISP Safe Harbors and the Ordinary Rules of Copyright Liability,* 32 Colum. J.L. & Arts. 427 (2009)

Rushton & Jones, *The Tortoise and the Hare: Canadian Legislative Copyright Reforms Race Against Copyright Infringement Over Kazaa and Other New Generation Peer-to-Peer Networks*, 32 AIPLA Q. J. 197 (2004)

Schulman, *Internet Copyright Infringement Liability: Is an Online Access Provider More Like a Landlord or a Dancehall Operator?*, 27 Golden Gate U. L. Rev. 555 (1997)

Schultz, *The False Origin of the Induce Act*, 32 N. Ky. L. Rev. 527 (2005)

Scully, *Beyond* Napster — *Is It Just Music? Or Are Judicial Resolutions Ineffective in Digital Commerce?*, 15 Transnat'l Law. 313 (2002)

Self, *The Vicarious Liability of Trade Show Organizers for the Copyright Infringement of Exhibitors*, 5 Tex. Intell. Prop. L.J. 81 (1996)

Shah, *Modding the Web: Secondary Liability under Copyright and Web Modification Software in a Post-*Grokster *World*, 85 Tex. L. Rev. 703 (2007)

Stephens & Summer, *Catch 22: Internet Service Providers' Liability for Copyright Infringement Over the Internet*, 14 Computer Law. 1 (1997)

Yen, *Internet Service Provider Liability for Subscriber Copyright Infringement, Enterprise Liability, and the First Amendment*, 88 Geo. L.J. 1833 (2000)

Yen, *A Personal Injury Law Perspective on Copyright in an Internet Age,* 52 Hastings L.J. 929 (2001)

Yen, *A Preliminary Economic Analysis of* Napster*: Internet Technology, Copyright Liability, and The Possibility of Coasean Bargaining,* 26 U. Dayton L. Rev. 247 (2001)

Yen, Sony, *Tort Doctrines, and the Puzzle of Peer-to-Peer*, 55 Case W. Res. L. Rev. 815 (2005)

Yen, *Torts and the Construction of Inducement and Contributory Liability in* Amazon *and* Visa, 32 Colum. J.L. & Arts. 513 (2009)

Yen, *Third-party Copyright Liability after* Grokster, 91 Minn. L. Rev. 184 (2006)

Zittrain, *A History of Online Gatekeeping*, 19 Harv. J.L. & Techn. 255 (2006)

Chapter 10

FAIR USE AND AFFIRMATIVE DEFENSES

Reference Works

H. Abrams, THE LAW OF COPYRIGHT §§ 13.43 to 13.48, 15.1 to 15.136, 16.1 to 16.23 (2008)

P. Goldstein, GOLDSTEIN ON COPYRIGHT §§ 11.1 to 11.6, 12.1 to 12.3 (3d ed. 2005)

M. Leaffer, UNDERSTANDING COPYRIGHT LAW §§ 10.01 to 10.21 (5th ed. 2010)

M. Nimmer & D. Nimmer, NIMMER ON COPYRIGHT §§ 12.05 to 12.06, 13.04 to 13.09 (2010)

W. Patry, PATRY ON FAIR USE (2010)

W. Patry, PATRY ON COPYRIGHT §§ 10:1 to 10:160 (2010)

Development of the Fair Use Privilege

G. Davies, COPYRIGHT AND THE PUBLIC INTEREST (2d ed. 2002)

L.R. Patterson & S.W. Lindberg, THE NATURE OF COPYRIGHT: A LAW OF USERS' RIGHTS (1991)

S. Vaidhyanathan, COPYRIGHTS AND COPYWRONGS: THE RISE OF INTELLECTUAL PROPERTY AND HOW IT THREATENS CREATIVITY (2001)

Afori, *An Open Standard 'Fair Use' Doctrine: A Welcome Israeli Initiative*, 30 E.I.P.R. 85 (2008)

Anderson & Brown, *The Economics Behind Copyright Fair Use: A Principled and Predictable Body of Law,* 24 Loy. U. Chi. L.J. 143 (1993)

Beebe, *An Empirical Study of U.S. Copyright Fair Use Opinions, 1978–2005*, 156 U. Pa. L. Rev. 549 (2008)

Beebe, *Does Judicial Ideology Affect Copyright Fair Use Outcomes?: Evidence From the Fair Use Case Law*, Colum. J.L. & Arts 517 (2008)

Birch, *Copyright Fair Use: A Constitutional Imperative*, 54 J. Copyright Soc'y 139 (2007)

Bunker, *Advertising and Appropriation: Copyright and Fair Use in Advertising*, 54 J. Copyright Soc'y 167 (2008)

Ciolino, *Rethinking the Compatibility of Moral Rights and Fair Use*, 54 Wash. & Lee L. Rev. 33 (1997)

Cohen, *Fair Use in Copyright Law,* 6 Copyright L. Symp. (ASCAP) 42 (1955)

Conley, *Author, User, Scholar, Thief: Fair Use and Unpublished Works,* 9 Cardozo Arts & Ent. L.J. 15 (1990)

Cotter, *Fair Use and Copyright Overenforcement,* 93 Iowa L. Rev. 1271 (2008)

Dratler, *Distilling the Witches' Brew of Fair Use in Copyright Law*, 43 Miami L. Rev. 233 (1988)

Dursht, *Judicial Plagiariams: It May be Fair Use But Is It Ethical?*, 18 Cardozo L. Rev. 1253 (1996)

Fisher, *Reconstructing the Fair Use Doctrine,* 101 Harv. L. Rev. 1659 (1988)

Francione, *Facing* The Nation: *The Infringement and Fair Use of Factual Works,* 134 U. Pa. L. Rev. 519 (1986)

Gordon, *Fair Use as Market Failure: A Structural and Economic Analysis of the* Betamax *Case and Its Predecessors,* 82 Colum. L. Rev. (1982)

Gordon, *Fair Use: Threat or Threatened?*, 55 Case. W. Res. L. Rev. 903 (2005)

Gordon, *Market Failure and Intellectual Property: A Response to Professor Lunney*, 82 B.U. L. Rev. 1031 (2002)

Heymann, *Everything Is Transformative: Fair Use and Reader Response*, 31 Colum. J.L. & Arts 445 (2008)

Kasunic, *That All There Is? Reflections on the Nature of the Second Fair Use Factor,* 31 Colum. J.L. & Arts 529 (2008)

Lape, *Transforming Fair Use: The Productive Use Factor in Fair Use Doctrine*, 58 Alb. L. Rev. 677 (1995)

Latman, *Fair Use of Copyrighted Works*, Copyright Law Revision Study No. 14 (1960)

Leval, Campbell v. Acuff-Rose: *Justice Souter's Rescue of Fair Use,* 13 Cardozo Arts & Ent. L.J. 19 (1994)

Leval, *Fair Use or Foul?,* 36 J. Copyright Soc'y 167 (1989)

Leval, *Fair Use Rescued*, 44 UCLA L. Rev. 1449 (1997)

Leval, *Toward a Fair Use Standard,* 103 Harv. L. Rev. 1105 (1990)

Liu, *Two-Factor Fair Use?*, 31 Colum. J.L. & Arts 571 (2009)

Loren, *Redefining the Market Failure Approach to Fair Use in an Era of Copyright Permissions Systems,* 5 J. Intell. Prop. L. 1 (1997)

Lunney, *Fair Use and Market Failure:* Sony *Revisited*, 82 B.U. L. Rev. 975 (2002)

McJohn, *Fair Use and Privatization in Copyright,* 35 San Diego L. Rev. 61 (1998)

Miller, *Fair Use, Biographers, and Unpublished Works: Life After H.R. 4412,* 40 J. Copyright Soc'y 349 (1993)

Miner, *Exploiting Stolen Text: Fair Use or Foul Play?,* 37 J. Copyright Soc'y 1 (1989)

Morris, *Use of Copyrighted Images in Academic Scholarship and Creative Work: The Problems of New Technologies and Proposed Scholarly License,* 33 Idea 123 (1993)

Nelson, *The Fine Art of Reproduction: The Doctrine of Fair Use and Auction House Catalogues*, 18 Colum.-VLA J.L. & Arts 291 (1994)

Newman, *Not the End of History: The Second Circuit Struggles With Fair Use,* 37 J. Copyright Soc'y 12 (1989)

D. Nimmer, *"Fairest of Them All" and Other Fairy Tales of Fair Use*, 66 Law & Contemp. Probs. 263 (2003)

Patterson, Folsom v. Marsh *and Its Legacy,* 5 J. Intell. Prop. L. 431 (1998)

Patterson, *Understanding Fair Use,* 55 Law & Contemp. Probs. 249 (1992)

Patry, *Fair Use After* Sony *and* Harper & Row, 8 Comm. & The Law 21 (1986)

Raskind, *A Functional Interpretation of Fair Use*, 31 J. Copyright Soc'y 601 (1984)

Reese, *Transformativeness and the Derivative Work Right,* 31 Colum. J.L. & Arts 467 (2008)

Reid, *Fair Game: The Application of Fair Use Doctrine to Machinima*, 19 Fordham Intell. Prop. Media & Ent. L.J. 831 (2009)

Samuelson, *Unbundling Fair Uses*, 77 Fordham L. Rev. 2537 (2009)

Seltzer, *Exemptions and Fair Use in Copyright: The "Exclusive Rights" Tensions in the New Copyright Act,* 24 Bull. Copyright Soc'y 215 (1977)

Sobel, *Copyright and the First Amendment: A Gathering Storm?,* 19 Copyright L. Symp. (ASCAP) 43 (1971)

Tatum, Spoo & Pope, *Does Gender Influence Attitudes Toward Copyright in the Filk Community?,* 18 Am. U.J. Gender Soc. Pol'y & L. 219 (2010)

Tuchman, *Judge Leval's Transformation Standard: Can It Really Distinguish Foul from Fair?*, 51 J. Copyright Soc'y 101 (2004)

Tushnet, *User-Generated Discontent: Transformation in Practice,* 31 Colum. J.L. & Arts 497 (2008)

Weinreb, *Fair's Fair: A Comment on the Fair Use Doctrine,* 103 Harv. L. Rev. 1137 (1990)

Weinreb, *Fair Use and How It Got That Way,* 45 J. Copyright Soc. 634 (1998)

Williams, *Recent Second Circuit Opinions Indicate That Google's Library Project Is Not Transformative*, 25 Cardozo Arts & Ent. L.J. 303 (2007)

Wong, *"Transformative" User-Generated Content in Copyright Law: Infringing Derivative Works or Fair Use?*, 11 Vand. J. Ent. & Tech. L. 1075 (2009)

Wu, *Tolerated Use*, 31 Colum. J.L. & Arts 617 (2008)

Zissu, *Fair Use: From* Harper & Row *to* Acuff Rose, 42 J. Copyright Soc'y 7 (1994)

Fair Use, Free Speech, and Parody

Beck, *Copyright and the First Amendment: After the Wind Done Gone,* 5 Vand. J. Ent. L. & Prac. 5 (2003)

Berg, *Copying for Religious Reasons: A Comment on Principles of Copyright and Religious Freedom,* 21 Cardozo Arts & Ent. L.J. 287 (2003) J. Cohen, *Copyright's Public-Private Distinction*, 55 Case. W. Res. L. Rev. 963 (2005)

Farrell, *Fair Use of Copyrighted Material in Advertisement Parodies,* 92 Colum. L. Rev. 1550 (1992)

Gallo, *Barbie's Life in Plastic: It's Fantastic for First Amendment Protection — Or Is It?*, 29 U. Dayton L. Rev. 405 (2004)

Goldstein, *Copyright and the First Amendment,* 70 Colum. L. Rev. 983 (1970)

Kaplan, *Parody and the Fair Use Defense to Copyright Infringement: Appropriate Purpose and Object of Humor,* 26 Ariz. St. L.J. 857 (1994)

Ku, *Consumers and Creative Destruction: Fair Use Beyond Market Failure,* 18 Berkeley Tech. L.J. 589 (2003)

Lampke, *Why the Fair Use Defense of Free Speech or Parody Under the Anticybersquatting Consumer Protection Act Needs Judicial Review by the United States Supreme Court,* 11 Minn J.L. Sci. & Tech. 267 (2010)

Leval, Campbell v. Acuff-Rose: *Justice Souter's Rescue of Fair Use*, 13 Cardozo Arts & Ent. L.J. 19 (1994)

Light, *Parody, Burlesque and the Economic Rationale for Copyright,* 11 Conn. L. Rev. 615 (1979)

Litman, *The* Sony *Paradox*, 55 Case W. Res. L. Rev. 903 (2005)

McCausland, *Protecting 'A Fine Tradition of Satire': The New Fair Dealing Exception for Parady or Satire in the Australian Copyright Act*, 29 E.I.P.R. 287 (2007)

McLean, *All's Not Fair in Art and War: A Look at the Fair Use Defense After* Rogers v. Koons, 59 Brooklyn L. Rev. 373 (1993)

Mezei, *Fair Use and Culture: Comments on the Gowers Review*, 39 U. Tol. L. Rev. 653 (2008)

Merges, *Are You Making Fun of Me? Notes on Market Failure and the Parody Defense in Copyright,* 21 AIPLA Q.J. 305 (1993)

M. Nimmer, *Does Copyright Abridge the First Amendment Guarantees of Free Speech and Press?,* 17 UCLA L. Rev. 1180 (1970)

Ochoa, *Dr. Seuss, the Juice and Fair Use: How the Grinch Silenced a Parody,* 45 J. Copyright Soc'y 546 (1998)

Patterson, *Free Speech, Copyright, and Fair Use,* 40 Vand. L. Rev. 1 (1987)

Patterson & Birch, *Copyright and Free Speech Rights*, 4 J. Intell. Prop. L. 1 (1997)

Patry & Perlmutter, *Fair Use Misconstrued: Profit, Presumptions, and Parody,* 11 Cardozo Arts & Ent. L.J. 667 (1993)

Pessach, *Copyright Law as a Silencing Restriction on Noninfringing Materials: Unveiling the Scope of Copyright's Diversity Externalities,* 76 S. Cal. L. Rev. 1275 (2003)

Posner, *When Is Parody Fair Use?*, 21 J. Legal Stud. 67 (1992)

Rothman, *Liberating Copyright: Thinking Beyond Free Speech,* 95 Cornell L. Rev. 463 (2010)

Rushton & Jones, *The Tortoise and the Hare: Canadian Legislative Copyright Reforms Race Against Copyright Infringement Over Kazaa and Other New Generation Peer-to-Peer Networks*, 32 AIPLA Q. J. 197 (2004)

Samuelson, *Reviving* Zacchini: *Analyzing First Amendment Defenses in Right of Publicity and Copyright Cases,* 57 Tul. L. Rev. 836 (1983)

Tushnet, *Copy This Essay: How Fair Use Doctrine Harms Free Speech and How Copying Serves It*, 114 Yale L.J. 535 (2004)

Yen, *When Authors Won't Sell: Parody, Fair Use, and Efficiency in Copyright Law,* 62 U. Colo. L. Rev. 79 (1991)

Yonover, *The Precarious Balance: Moral Rights, Parody & Fair Use,* 14 Cardozo Arts & Ent. L.J. 79 (1996)

Zissu, *Funny Is Fair: The Case for According Increased Value to Humor in Copyright Fair Use Analysis*, 55 J. Copyright Soc'y 393 (2008)

Fair Use and Technology

Band, *Copyright Owners v. the Google Print Library Project*, 17 Ent. L. Rev. 21 (2006)

Bridy, *Why Pirates (Still) Won't Behave: Regulating P2P in the Decade after Napster,* 40 Rutgers L.J. 565 (2009)

J. Cohen, *Reverse Engineering and the Rise of Electronic Vigilantism: Intellectual Property Implications of "Lock-Out" Programs,* 68 S. Cal. L. Rev. 1091 (1995)

Douma, *Fair Use and Misuse: Two Guards at the Intersection of Copyrights and Trade Secret Rights Held in Software and Firmware,* 42 IDEA 37 (2002)

Durdik, *Reverse Engineering as a Fair Use Defense to Software Copyright Infringement,* 34 Jurimetrics J. 451 (1994)

Fraser, *The Conflict Between the First Amendment and Copyright Law and Its Impact on the Internet*, 16 Cardozo Arts & Ent. L.J. 1 (1998)

Gervais, *The Tangled Web of UGC: Making Copyright Sense of User-Generated* Content, 11 Vand. J. Ent. & Tech. L. 841 (2009)

Goldberg, *Now that the Future Has Arrived, Maybe the Law Should Take a Look: Multimedia Technology and its Interaction With the Fair Use Doctrine,* 44 Am. U.L. Rev. 919 (1995)

Ignatin, *Let the Hackers Hack: Allowing the Reverse Engineering of Copyrighted Computer Programs to Achieve Compatibility,* 140 U. Pa. L. Rev. 1999 (1992)

McJohn, *Fair Use of Copyrighted Software,* 28 Rutgers L.J. 593 (1997)

McManis, *Intellectual Property Protection and Reverse Engineering of Computer Programs in the United States and the European Community,* 8 High Tech. L.J. 25 (1993)

Menell, *Knowledge Accessibility and Preservation Policy for the Digital Age*, 44 Hous. L. Rev. 1013 (2007)

Morrow, *Practicing Reverse Engineering in an Era of Growing Constraints Under the Digital Millennium Copyright Act and Other Provisions,* 14 Alb. L.J. Sci. & Tech. 1 (2003)

Owen, *Interfaces and Interoperablity in* Lotus v. Borland: *A Market Oriented Approach to the Fair Use Doctrine,* 64 Fordham L. Rev. 2381 (1996)

Parchomovsky & Goldman, *Fair Use Harbors*, 93 Va. L. Rev. 1483 (2007)

Perkins, *Encryption Use: Law and Anarchy on the Digital Frontier*, 41 Hous. L. Rev. 1625 (2005)

Sag, *Copyright and Copy-Reliant Technology,* 103 Nw. U.L. Rev.1607 (2009)

Samuelson, *Fair Use for Computer Programs and Other Copyrightable Works in Digital Form: The Implications of* Sony, Galoob *and* Sega, 1 J. Intell. Prop. L. 49 (1993)

Samuelson, *The Generativity of* Sony v. Universal: *The Intellectual Property Legacy of Justice Blackmun*, 74 Fordham L. Rev. 1831 (2006)

Samuelson & Scotchmer, *The Law and Economics of Reverse Engineering,* 111 Yale L.J. 1575 (2002)

Szymanski, *Audio Pastiche: Digital Sampling, Intermeditate Copying, Fair Use,* 3 UCLA Ent. L. Rev. 271 (1996)

Toedt, *Oh, Pretty Woman: Muddying Software Copyright Even Further with "Transformative Fair Use",* 11 Computer L. 15 (1994)

Varmer, *Photoduplication of Copyrighted Materials by Libraries*, Copyright Law Revision Study No. 15 (1960)

Williams, *Can Reverse Engineering of Software Ever Be Fair Use? Application of* Campbell's *"Transformative Use" Concept,* 71 Wash. L. Rev. 255 (1996)

Fair Use in Corporations and Classrooms

K. Crews, Copyright, Fair Use, and the Challenge for Universities: Promoting the Progress of Higher Education (1993)

Bartow, *Educational Fair Use in Copyright: Reclaiming the Right to Copy Freely*, 60 U. Pitt. L. Rev. 149 (1998)

Bunker, *Advertising and Appropriation: Copyright and Fair Use in Advertising*, 54 J. Copyright Soc'y 167 (2007)

Crews, *Copyright at a Turning Point: Corporate Responses to the Changing Environment*, 3 J. Intell. Prop. L. 2177 (1996)

Dratler, *To Copy or Not to Copy: The Educator's Dilemma,* 19 J.L. & Educ. 1 (1990)

Gasaway, *Values Conflict in the Digital Environment: Librarians Versus Copyright Holders*, 24 Colum.-VLA J.L. & Arts 115 (2000)

Ginsburg, *Reproduction of Protected Works for University Research or Teaching,* 39 J. Copyright Soc'y 181 (1992)

Gorman, *Copyright Conflicts on the University Campus,* 40 J. Copyright Soc'y 291 (2000)

Hirtle, *Research, Libraries, and Fair Use: the Gentlemen's Agreement of 1935*, 53 J. Copyright Soc'y 545 (2006)

Issacs, *The Highest Form of Flattery?: Application of the Fair Use Defense against Copyright Claims for Unauthorized Appropriation of Litigation Documents*, 71 Mo. L. Rev. 391 (2006)

Kasunic, *Fair Use and the Educator's Right To Photocopy Copyrighted Material For Classroom Use,* 19 J.C. & U.L. 271 (1993)

Kreiss, *Copyright Fair Use of Standardized Tests,* 48 Rutgers L. Rev. 1043 (1996)

Miller, *Coursepacks & Copyright: Fair Use in* Princeton University Press v. Michigan Document Services, 23 J. C. & U. L. 525 (1997)

Miller, *Corporate Copyright Infringers Beware: Systematic Unauthorized Photocopying By For-Profit Corporations Does Not Constitute Fair Use:* American Geophysical Union v. Texaco, Inc., 30 Creighton L. Rev. 1521 (1997)

Patry, American Geophysical Union v. Texaco, Inc.: *Copyright and Corporate Photocopying,* 61 Brooklyn L. Rev. 429 (1995)

Patterson, *Regents Guide to Understanding Copyright and Educational Fair Use,* 5 J. Intell. Prop. L. 243 (1997)

Simon, *Teaching without Infringement: A New Model for Educational Fair Use,* 20 Fordham Intell. Prop. Media & Ent. L.J. 453 (2010)

Ster, *Photocopying & Fair Use: Exploring the Market for Scientific Journal Articles,* 30 Ind. L. Rev. 33 (1997)

Thau, *Copyright, Privacy, and Fair Use,* 24 Hofstra L. Rev. 179 (1995)

Thornburg, *The Impact of Copyright Law on Distance Education Programs: How Fair Use and the CONFU Guidelines May Shape the Future of Academia,* 27 S. Ill. U. L.J. 321 (2003)

Weinberg, *The Photocopying Revolution and the Copyright Crisis,* 38 Pub. Interest 99 (1975)

Fair Use and Copyright Policy

Bambauer, *Faulty Math: The Economics of Legalizing the Grey Album,* 59 Ala. L. Rev. 345 (2008)

Bartow, *Libraries in a Digital and Aggressively Copyrighted World: Retaining Patron Access through Changing Technologies,* 62 Ohio St. L.J. 821 (2001)

T. Bell, *Fair Use vs.* Fared *Use: The Impact of Automated Rights Management on Copyright's Fair Use Doctrine,* 76 N.C. L. Rev. 557 (1998)

Carroll, *Fixing Fair Use*, 85 N.C. L. Rev. 1037 (2007)

Casalini, *Harry Potter, Scientology, and the Mysterious Realm of Copyright Infringement: an Analyzing When Close is Too Close and When the Use is Fair,* 26 Touro L. Rev. 313 (2010)

Chander & Sunder, *Everyone's A Superhero: A Cultural Theory of 'Mary Sue' Fan Fiction as Fair Use*, 95 Cal. L. Rev. 597 (2007)

Coblenz, *Not for Entertainment Only: Fair Use and Fiction as Social Commentary*, 16 UCLA Ent. L. Rev. 265 (2009)

J. Cohen, *Comment: Copyright's Public-Private Distinction* (response to article by Jessica Litman in Law Technology and the Arts Symposium: "Copyright and Personal Copying: *Sony v. Universal Studios* Twenty-One Years Later"), 55 Case W. Res. L. Rev. 963 (2005)

J. Cohen, *Intellectual Privacy and Censorship of the Internet,* 8 Seton Hall Const. L.J. 693 (1998)

J. Cohen, *The Place of the User in Copyright Law*, 74 Fordham L. Rev. 347 (2005)

Craig, *The Development of Internet Education and the Role of Copyright Law,* 40 J. Copyright Soc'y 75 (2000)

Crews, *The Law of Fair Use and the Illusion of Fair-Use Guidelines*, 62 Ohio St. L.J. 599 (2001)

Dam, *Self-Help in the Digital Jungle*, 28 J. Legal Stud. 393 (1999)

Denicola, *Mostly Dead? Copyright Law in the New Millennium*, 40 J. Copyright Soc'y 193 (2000)

Dougherty, *All the World's Not a Stooge: The "Transformativeness" Test for Analyzing a First Amendment Defense to a Right of Publicity Claim Against Distribution of a Work of Art,* 27 Colum.-VLA J.L. & Arts 1 (2003)

Elliot, *Copyright Fair Use and Private Ordering: Are Copyright Holders and the Copyright Law Fanatical for Fansites?,* 11 DePaul-LCA J. Art & Ent. L. 329 (2001)

Gibson, *Risk Aversion and Rights Accretion in Intellectual Property Law*, 116 Yale L.J. 882 (2007)

Gold, *Fair Use and the First Amendment: Corporate Control of Copyright is Stifling Documentary-Making and Thwarting the Aims of the First Amendment*, 15 U. Balt. L.J. 1 (2006)

Goldstein, *Fair Use in a Changing World,* 50 J. Copyright Soc'y 133 (2003)

Gordon, *Excuse and Justification in the Law of Fair Use: Transactions Costs Have Always Been Part of the Story,* 50 J. Copyright Soc'y 149 (2003)

Gorman, *Copyright Conflicts on the University Campus*, 40 J. Copyright Soc'y 291 (2000)

Heide, *Copyright in the EU and U.S.: What "Access-Right"?,* 48 J. Copyright Soc'y 363 (2001)

Henslee, *You Can't Always Get What You Want, But If You Try Sometimes You Can Steal It and Call It Fair Use: A Proposal to Abolish the Fair Use Defense for Music,* 58 Cath. U.L. Rev. 663 (2009)

Hetcher, *Using Social Norms to Regulate Fan Fiction and Remix Culture,* 157 U. Penn. L. Rev. 1869 (2009)

Hughes, *Fair Use Across Time,* 50 UCLA L. Rev. 775 (2003)

Jaszi, *Copyright, Fair Use and Motion Pictures*, 2007 Utah L. Rev. 715

Johnston, *The Singer Did Not Approve this Message: Analyzing the Unauthorized Use of Copyrighted Music in Political Advertisements in* Jackson Browne v. John McCain, 27 Cardozo Arts & Ent. L.J. 687 (2010)

Landau, *Copyright, the First Amendment, and the Right of Publicity: The Expansion of "Transformative Uses"*, 21 No. 3 Computer & Internet Law. 13 (2004)

Lee, *Freedom of the Press 2.0*, 42 Ga. L. Rev. 309 (2008)

Leaffer, *The Uncertain Future of Fair Use in a Global Information Marketplace*, 62 Ohio St. L.J. 849 (2001)

Leland, *All's Fair in Love and News: How the Current Application of the Fair Use Doctrine Favors the Traditional Media Over Amateur Providers of News Content,* 8 Wake Forest Intell. Prop. L.J. 226 (2008)

Litman, *The* Sony *Paradox*, 55 Case. W. Res. L. Rev. 917 (2005)

Long, *Mashed Up Videos and Broken Down Copyright: Changing Copyright to Promote the First Amendment Values of Transformative Video*, 60 Okla. L. Rev. 317 (2007)

Madison, *A Pattern-Oriented Approach to Fair Use*, 45 Wm. & Mary L. Rev. 1525 (2004)

Mazzone, *Administering Fair Us*, 51 Wm. & Mary L. Rev. 395 (2009)

D. Nimmer, *A Modest Proposal to Streamline Fair Use Determinations*, 24 Cardozo Arts & Ent. L.J. 11 (2006)

D. Nimmer, *A Riff on Fair Use in the Digital Millennium Copyright Act*, 148 U. Pa. L. Rev. 673 (2000)

Noda, *Copyrights Retold: How Interpretive Rights Foster Creativity and Justify Fan-Based Activities*, 20 Seton Hall J. Sports & Ent. L. 131 (2010)

Okediji, *Givers, Takers, and Other Kinds of Users: A Fair Use Doctrine for Cyberspace,* 53 Fla. L. Rev. 107 (2001)

Okediji, *Toward an International Fair Use Doctrine*, 39 Colum. J. Transnat'l L. 75 (2000)

Parchomovsky & Goldman, *Fair Use Harbors*, 93 Va. L. Rev. 1483 (2007)

Patterson & Thomas, *Personal Use in Copyright Law: An Unrecognized Constitutional Right,* 50 J. Copyright Soc'y 475 (2003)

Pote, *Mashed-Up in Between: the Delicate Balance of Artists' Interests Lost Amidst the War on Copyright*, 88 N.C. L. Rev. 639 (2010)

Samuelson, *Unbundling Fair Uses,* 77 Fordham L. Rev. 2537 (2009)

Schwabach, *The Harry Potter Lexicon and the World of Fandom: Fan Fiction, Outsider Works, and Copyright,* 70 U. Pitt. L. Rev. 387 (2009)

Sharon, *Do Students Turn Over Their Rights When They Turn in Their Papers? A Case Study of Turnitin.Com (Plagiarism),* 26 Touro L. Rev. 207 (2010)

Siskind, *Crossing the Fair Use Line: The Demise and Revival of the Harry Potter Lexicon and its Implications for the Fair Use Doctrine in the Real World and on the Internet,* 27 Cardozo Arts & Ent. L.J. 291 (2009)

Stadler, *Relevant Markets for Copyrighted Works*, 34 J. Corp. L. 1059 (2009)

Stroude, *Complimentary Creation: Protecting Fan Fiction as Fair Use,* 14 Marq. Intell. Prop. L. Rev. 191 (2010)

Tehranian, *Et Tu, Fair Use? The Triumph of Natural-Law Copyright*, 38 U.C. Davis L. Rev. 465 (2005)

Tushnet, *Economies of Desire: Fair Use and Marketplace Assumptions*, 51 Wm. & Mary L. Rev. 513 (2009)

Tushnet, *My Fair Ladies: Sex, Gender, and Fair Use in Copyright*, 15 Am. U.J. Gender Soc. Pol'y & L. 273 (2007)

Von Lohmann, *Fair Use as Innovation Policy*, 23 Berkeley Tech. L.J. 829 (2008)

Wong, *"Transformative" User-Generated Content in Copyright Law: Infringing Derivative Works or Fair Use?*, 11 Vand. J. Ent. & Tech. L. 1075 (2009)

Affirmative Copyright Defenses

Aylward, *Copyright Law: The Fourth Circuit's Extension of the Misuse Doctrine to the Area of Copyright: A Misuse of the Misuse Doctrine? —* Lasercomb America, Inc. v. Reynolds, 17 U. Dayton L. Rev. 661 (1992)

Band & Levine, *You Say Misuse, I Say Fair Use ...,* 13 Computer L. 10 (1996)

T. Bell, *Codifying Copyright's Misuse Defense*, 2007 Utah L. Rev. 573

Childers, *State Sovereign Immunity and the Protection of Intellectual Property: Do Recent Congressional Attempts to "Level the Playing Field" Run Afoul of Current Eleventh Amendment Jurisprudence and Other Constitutional Doctrines?*, 82 N.C. L. Rev. 1067 (2004)

Clifford, *Simultaneous Copyright and Trade Secret Claims: Can the Copyright Misuse Defense Prevent Constitutional Doublethink?*, 104 Dick. L. Rev. 247 (2000)

Cotter, *Misuse*, 44 Hous. L. Rev. 901 (2007)

Davidson & Engisch, *Copyright Misuse and Fraud on the Copyright Office: An Escape for Infringers?*, 13 Computer Law. 14 (1996)

Didwania, *The Defense of Laches in Copyright Infringement Claims*, 75 U. Chi. L. Rev. 1227 (2008)

Fine, *Misuse and Antitrust Defenses to Copyright Infringement Actions,* 17 Hastings L.J. 315 (1965)

Frischmann & Moylan, *The Evolving Common Law Doctrine of Copyright Misuse: A Unified Theory and Its Application to Software*, 15 Berkeley Tech. L.J. 865 (2000)

Geraldi, *Misuse: An Equitable Defense to Intellectual Property Infringement Actions,* 14 Hastings Comm. & Ent. L.J. 235 (1992)

Hanna, *Misusing Antitrust: The Search for Functional Copyright Misuse Standards,* 46 Stan. L. Rev. 401 (1994)

Heald, *Payment Demands for Spurious Copyrights: Four Causes of Action,* 1 J. Intell. Prop. L. 259 (1994)

Hovenkamp, *Innovation and the Domain of Competition Policy*, 60 Ala. L. Rev. 103 (2009)

Judge, *Rethinking Copyright Misuse*, 37 Intell. Prop. L. Rev. 607 (2005)

Leaffer, *Engineering Competitive Policy and Copyright Misuse*, 19 Dayton L. Rev. 1087 (1994)

M. Lemley, *Antitrust Counterclaims in Patent and Copyright Infringement Cases,* 3 Tex. Intell. Prop. L.J. 1 (1994)

Mazzone, *Copyfraud*, 81 N.Y.U. L. Rev. 1026 (2006)

Paredes, *Copyright Misuse and Tying, Will Courts Stop Misusing Misuse?,* 9 High Tech. L.J. 271 (1994).

Susman, *Typing, Refusals to License, and Copyright Misuse: The Patent Misuse Model,* 36 J. Copyright Soc'y 300 (1989)

Webb & Locke, *Intellectual Property Misuses: Developments in the Misuse Doctrine*, 4 Harv. J.L. & Tech. 257 (1991)

Chapter 11

REMEDIES, PREEMPTION, AND RELATED BODIES OF LAW

Reference Works

H. Abrams, The Law of Copyright §§ 6.1 to 6.64, 17.1 to 17.67, 18.1 to 18.41 (2008)

P. Goldstein, Goldstein on Copyright §§ 13.0 to 13.4, 14.0 to 14.4, 17.0 to 17.22, 17.25 (3d ed. 2005)

M. Leaffer, Understanding Copyright Law 9.099to 9.15, 11.01 to 11.11 (5th ed. 2010)

M. Nimmer & D. Nimmer, Nimmer on Copyright §§ 8C.01 to 8C.05, 14.01 to 14.10, 15.01 to 15.07, 19D.01 to 19D.10 (2010)

W. Patry, Patry on Copyright §§ 18:1 to 18:60, 20:1 to 20:58, 22:1 to 22:223 (2010)

Remedies Under Federal Law

Alexander, *Discretionary Power to Impound and Destroy Infringing Articles: An Historical Perspective,* 29 J. Copyright Soc'y 479 (1982)

Amend, *The Geographical Scope of Injunctions in Intellectual Property Cases,* 77 Trademark Rep. 49 (1987)

Barker, *Grossly Excessive Penalties in the Battle Against Illegal File-Sharing: The Troubling Effects of Aggregating Minimum Statutory Damages of Copyright Infringement*, 83 Tex. L. Rev. (2004)

Berg, *Remedying the Statutory Damages Remedy for Secondary Copyright Infringement Liability: Balancing Copyright and Innovation in the Digital Age*, 56 J. Copyright Soc'y 265 (2009)

Blair & Cotter, *An Economic Analysis of Damages Rules in Intellectual Property Law*, 39 Wm. & Mary L. Rev. 1585 (1998)

Brown, *Civil Remedies for Intellectual Property Invasions,* 55 Law & Contemp. Probs. 45 (1992)

Brown, *The Operation of the Damages Provisions of the Copyright Law: An Exploratory Study*, Copyright Law Revision Study No. 23 (1958)

Ciolino, *Reconsidering Restitution in Copyright*, 48 Emory L.J. 1 (1999)

Coblenz, *Intellectual Property Crimes*, 9 Alb. L.J. Sci. & Tech. 235 (1999)

Erekosima & Koosed, *Intellectual Property Crimes*, 41 Am. Crim. L. Rev. 809 (2004)

Fonstad, *Protecting Fair Use with* Fogerty: *Toward a New Dual Standard,* 40 U. Mich. J.L. Reform 623 (2007)

…oad to No Warez: The No Electronic Theft Act and Criminal … Infringement,* 82 Or. L. Rev. 369 (2003)

…mez-Arostegui, *What History Teaches Us about Copyright Injunctions and the Inadequate-Remedy-at-Law Requirement,* 81 S. Cal. L. Rev. 1197 (2008)

Gomez-Arostegui, *Prospective Compensation in Lieu of a Final Injunction in Patent and Copyright Cases,* 78 Fordham L. Rev. 1661 (2010)

Greene, *Motion Picture Copyright Infringement and the Presumption of Irreparable Harm: Toward a Reevaluation of the Standard for Preliminary Injunctive Relief,* 31 Rutgers L.J. 173 (1999)

Hardy, *Criminal Copyright Infringement,* 11 Wm. & Mary Bill Rts. J. (2002)

Hyde, *A Reckless Disregard of the Ordinary Infringer?: Moving Toward A Balanced and Uniform Standard for Willful Copyright Infringement,* 35 U. Tol. L. Rev. 377 (2003)

Jaszi, *505 and All That — The Defendant's Dilemma,* 55 Law & Contemp. Probs. 107 (1993)

Latman, *Preliminary Injunctions in Patent, Trademark and Copyright Cases,* 60 Trademark Rep. 506 (1970)

M. Lemley & Volokh, *Freedom of Speech and Injunctions in Intellectual Property Cases,* 48 Duke L.J. 147 (1998)

Lindenberg-Woods, *Smoking Revolver: Criminal Copyright Infringement,* 27 Bull. Copyright Soc'y 63 (1979)

Loren, *Digitization, Commodification, Criminalization: The Evolution of Criminal Copyright Infringement and the Importance of the Willfulness Requirement*, 77 Wash. U. L. Q. 835 (1999)

Marcus & D. Nimmer, *Forum on Attorney's Fees in Copyright Cases: Are We Running Through the Jungle Now or Is the Old Man Still Stuck Down the Road?,* 39 Wm. & Mary L. Rev. 65 (1997)

Moohr, *The Crime of Copyright Infringement: An Inquiry Based on Morality, Harm, and Criminal Theory,* 83 B.U. L. Rev. 731 (2003)

D. Nimmer, *Repeat Infringers* (Copyright Infringement), 52 J. Copyright Soc'y 167 (2005)

Noonan & Raskin, *Intellectual Property Crimes,* 38 Am. Crim. L. Rev. 971 (2001)

Oakes, *Copyrights and Copyremedies: Unfair Use and Injunctions,* 38 J. Copyright Soc'y 63 (1990)

Oksanen & Valimaki, *Theory of Deterrence and Individual Behavior: Can Lawsuits Control File Sharing on the Internet?*, 3 Rev. L. & Econ. 1156 (2007)

Ossola, *Registration and Remedies: Recovery of Attorney's Fees and Statutory Damages Under the Copyright Reform Act,* 13 Cardozo Arts & Ent. L.J. 559 (1995)

Owens, *Impoundment Proceedings Under the Copyright Act: The Constitutional Infirmities,* 14 Hofstra L. Rev. 211 (1985)

Peterson, *The Knowledge to Act: Border Enforcement of Section 337 Exclusion Orders and the Need for Exclusion Order Disclosure Regulations,* 17 Fed. Cir. B.J. 607 (2008)

Rabinowitz, *Criminal Prosecution for Copyright Infringement of Unregistered Works: A Bite at an Unripe Apple?,* 49 Santa Clara L. Rev. 793 (2009)

Rusch, *Sentencing Guidelines for Copyright Pirates in the United States and the Hong Kong Special Administrative Region: A Comparative Perspective,* 26 Fordham Int'l L.J. 315 (2003)

Samuelson & Wheatland, *Statutory Damages in Copyright Law: A Remedy in Need of Reform*, 51 Wm. & Mary L. Rev. 439 (2009)

Saunders, *Criminal Copyright Infringement and the Copyright Felony Act,* 71 Denv. U. L. Rev. 671 (1994)

Thomas, *Willful Copyright Infringement: In Search of a Standard,* 65 Wash. L. Rev. 903 (1990)

Trunko, *Remedies for Copyright Infringement: Respecting the First Amendment,* 89 Colum. L. Rev. 1940 (1989)

Welkowitz & Ochoa, *The Terminator as Eraser: How Arnold Schwarzenegger Used the Right of Publicity to Terminate Non-Defamatory Political Speech,* 45 Santa Clara L. Rev. 651 (2005)

Woodin, *Copyrights and State Liability,* 76 Iowa L. Rev. 701 (1991)

Y'Barbo, *On Fee-Shifting and the Protection of Copyright,* 44 J. Copyright Soc'y 23 (1996)

Preemption

Abrams, *Copyright, Misappropriation, and Preemption: Constitutional and Statutory Limits of State Protection,* 1983 Sup. Ct. Rev. 509

Baird, *Common Law Intellectual Property and the Legacy of* International News Service v. Associated Press, 50 U. Chi. L. Rev. 411 (1983)

Bartow, *Open Access, Law, Knowledge, Copyrights, Dominance and Subordination*, 10 Lewis & Clark L. Rev. 869 (2006)

Bauer, *Addressing the Incoherency of the Preemption Provision of the Copyright Act of 1976*, 10 Vand. J. Ent. & Tech. L. 1 (2007)

T. Bell, *Misunderstanding* Dastar: *How the Supreme Court Unwittingly Revolutionized Copyright Preemption*, 65 Md. L. Rev. 206 (2006)

Bohannan, *Copyright Preemption of Contracts,* 67 Md. L. Rev. 616 (2008)

Bonser, *Preemption of "Shrink-Wrap" Legislation by the Copyright Act,* 37 Copyright L. Symp. (ASCAP) 127 (1990)

Brown, *Publication and Preemption in Copyright Law: Elegiac Reflections on* Goldstein v. California, 22 UCLA L. Rev. 1022 (1975)

Brown, *Unification: A Cheerful Requiem for Common Law Copyright,* 24 UCLA L. Rev. 1070 (1977)

Carroll, *Creative Commons and the New Intermediaries*, 2006 Mich. St. L. Rev. 45 (2006)

J. Cohen, *Copyright and the Jurisprudence of Self-Help*, 13 Berkeley Tech. L.J. 1089 (1998)

Comment, *Federal Copyright and State Trade Secret Protection: The Case for Partial Preemption,* 33 Am. U. L. Rev. 667 (1984)

Cotter & Dmitrieva, *Integrating the Right of Publicity with First Amendment and Copyright Preemption Analysis,* 33 Colum. J.L. & Arts 165 (2010)

Dabney, *State Law Protection of Intellectual Creations: Privacy and Preemption,* 38 Syracuse L. Rev. 653 (1987)

Diamond, *Preemption of State Law,* 25 Bull. Copyright Soc'y 204 (1978)

Douma, *The Uniform Computer Information Transactions Act and the Issue of Preemption of Contractual Provisions Prohibiting Reverse Engineering, Disassembly, or Decompilation,* 11 Alb. L.J. Sci. & Tech. 249 (2001)

Dreyfuss, *Do You Want to Know a Trade Secret? How Article 2B Will Make Licensing Trade Secrets Easier (But Innovation More Difficult)*, 87 Calif. L. Rev. 191 (1999)

Dusollier, *The Master's Tools v. the Master's House: Creative Commons v. Copyright*, 29 Colum. J.L & Arts 271 (2006)

Easterbrook, *Contract and Copyright*, 42 Hous. L. Rev. 953 (2005)

Elkin-Koren, *Copyrights in Cyberspace — Rights Without Laws?*, 73 Chi.-Kent. L. Rev. 1155 (1998)

Elkin-Koren, *What Contracts Cannot Do: The Limits of Private Ordering in Facilitating a Creative Commons*, 74 Fordham L. Rev. 375 (2005)

Fellmeth, *Control Without Interest: State Law Of Assignment, Federal Preemption, and the Intellectual Property License,* 6 Va. J.L. & Tech. 8 (2001)

Fetter, *Copyright Revision and the Preemption of State "Misappropriation" Law: A Study in Judicial and Congressional Interaction,* 27 Copyright L. Symp. (ASCAP) 1 (1982)

Fisher, *Property and Contract on the Internet*, 73 Chi.-Kent. L. Rev. 1203 (1998)

Francione, *The California Art Preservation Act and Federal Preemption by the 1976 Act — Equivalence and Actual Conflict,* 31 Copyright L. Symp. (ASCAP) 105 (1984)

Froomkin, *Article 2B as Legal Software for Electronic Contracting Operating System or Trojan Horse?*, 13 Berkeley Tech. L.J. 1023 (1998)

Gardiner, Bowers v. Baystate Technologies: *Using the Shrinkwrap Licence to Circumvent the Copyright Act and Escape Federal Preemption,* 11 U. Miami Bus. L. Rev. 105 (2003)

Garon, *Playing in the Virtual Arena: Avatars, Publicity, and Identity Reconceptualized Through Virtual Worlds and Computer Games,* 11 Chap. L. Rev. 465 (2008)

Gibbons, *Stop Mucking Up Copyright Law: A Proposal for a Federal Common Law of Contract*, 35 Rutgers L.J. (2004)

Ginsburg, *Authors as "Licensors" of "Informational Rights" Under U.C.C. Article 2B*, 13 Berkeley Tech. L.J. 945 (1998)

Goldstein, *Copyright and Its Substitutes*, 1997 Wis. L. Rev. 865

Goldstein, *Federal System Ordering of the Copyright Interest,* 69 Colum. L. Rev. 49 (1969)

Goldstein, *Preempted State Doctrines, Involuntary Transfers and Compulsory Licenses: Testing the Limits of Copyright,* 24 UCLA L. Rev. 1107 (1977)

Greene, *Intellectual Property Expansion: The Good, the Bad, and the Right of Publicity*, 11 Chap. L. Rev. 521 (2008)

Hansen, *The Right of Publicity Expands into Hallowed Ground:* Downing v. Abercrombe & Fitch *and the Preemption Power of the Copyright Act,* 71 UMKC L. Rev. 171 (2002)

Hardy, *Contracts, Copyright and Preemption in a Digital World*, 1 Rich. J.L. & Tech. 2 (1995)

Heald, *Federal Intellectual Property Law and the Economics of Preemption,* 76 Iowa L. Rev. 959 (1991)

Hyde & Sharrock, *A Decade Down the Road But Still Running Through the Jungle: A Critical Review of Post —* Fogerty *Fee Awards*, 52 U. Kan. L. Rev. 467 (2004)

Jorgensen & McIntyre-Cecil, *The Evolution of the Preemption Doctrine and Its Effect on Common Law Remedies,* 19 Idaho L. Rev. 85 (1983)

Karjala, *Federal Preemption of Shrinkwrap and On-Line Licenses,* 22 U. Dayton L. Rev. 511 (1997)

Kobayashi & Ribstein, *Uniformity, Choice of Law and Software Sales*, 8 Geo. Mason L. Rev. 261 (1999)

M. Lemley, *Beyond Preemption: The Law and Policy of Intellectual Property Licensing,* 87 Calif. L. Rev. 111 (1999)

M. Lemley, *Intellectual Property and Shrinkwrap Licenses,* 68 S. Cal. L. Rev. 1239 (1995)

Litman, *The Tales that Article 2B Tells,* 13 Berkeley Tech. L.J. 931 (1998)

Loren, *Building a Reliable Semicommons of Creative Works: Enforcement of Creative Commons Licenses and Limited Abandonment of Copyright*, 14 Geo. Mason L. Rev. 271 (2007)

Madison, *Legal-Ware: Contract and Copyright in the Digital Age,* 67 Fordham L. Rev. 1025 (1998)

Maher, *The Shrink-Wrap License: Old Problems in a New Wrapper,* 34 J. Copyright Soc'y 292 (1987)

McGowan, *Free Contracting, Fair Competition, and Article 2B: Some Reflections on Federal Competition Policy, Information Transactions, and "Aggressive Neutrality",* 13 Berkeley Tech. L.J. 1173 (1998)

McNamara, *Copyright Preemption: Effecting the Analysis Prescribed by Section 301,* 24 B.C. L. Rev. 963 (1983)

Merges, *Contracting into Liability Rules: Institutions Supporting Transactions in Intellectual Property Rights*, 84 Cal. L. Rev. 1293 (1997)

Moffat, *Super-Copyright: Contracts, Preemption, and the Structure of Copyright Policymaking,* 41 U.C. Davis L. Rev. 45 (2007)

Myers, *The Restatement's Rejection of the Misappropriation Tort: A Victory for the Public Domain*, 47 S.C. L. Rev. 673 (1996)

D. Nimmer, E. Brown & G. Frischling, *The Metamorphosis of Contract into Expand*, 87 Calif. L. Rev. 17 (1999)

R. Nimmer, *Article 2B: An Introduction*, 16 J. Marshall J. Computer & Info. L. 211 (1997)

R. Nimmer, *Breaking Barriers: The Relation Between Contract and Intellectual Property Law*, 13 Berkeley Tech. L.J. 827 (1998)

R. Nimmer, *Electronic Commerce: New Paradigms in Information Law*, 31 Idaho L. Rev. 937 (1995)

R. Nimmer, *Electronic Contracting: Legal Issues*, 14 J. Marshall J. Computer & Info. L. 211 (1996)

R. Nimmer, *Images and Contract Law — What Law Applies to Transactions in Information?*, 36 Hous. L. Rev. 1 (1999)

R. Nimmer, *Intangible Contracts: Thought of Hubs, Spokes, and Reinvigorating Article 2*, 35 Wm. & Mary L. Rev. 1337 (1994)

R. Nimmer, *International Information Transactions: An Essay on Law in an Information Society*, 26 Brooklyn J. Int'l L. 5 (2000)

R. Nimmer, *Licensing on the Global Information Infrastructure: Disharmony in Cyberspace*, 16 Nw. J. Int'l L. & Bus. 224 (1995)

R. Nimmer, *Through the Looking Glass: What Courts and UCITA Say About the Scope of Contract Law in the Information Age*, 38 Duq. L. Rev. 255 (2000)

R. Nimmer, *UCITA and the Continuing Evolution of Digital Licensing Law,* 21 No. 2 Computer & Internet Law. 10 (2004)

R. Nimmer, D. Cohn & E. Kirsch, *Licensing Contracts Under Article 2 of the Uniform Commercial Code: A Proposal*, 19 Rutgers Computer & Tech. L.J. 281 (1993)

Note, *The Single Publication Rule and Online Copyright: Tensions Between Broadcast, Licensing, and Defamation Law,* 123 Harv. L. Rev. 1315 (2010)

Ochoa, ETW Corp. v. Jireh Publishing, Inc.*: Introduction: Tiger Woods and the First Amendment,* 22 Whittier L. Rev. 381 (2000)

O'Connor, *"T's a Little Known Fact" that Copyright Law is in Conflict with the Right of Publicity,* 26 Touro L. Rev. 351 (2010)

Olson, *Common Law Misappropriation in the Digital Era*, 64 Mo. L. Rev. 837 (1999)

O'Rourke, *Copyright Preemption After the* ProCD *Case: A Market-Based Approach,* 12 Berkeley Tech. L.J. 53 (1997)

O'Rourke, *Drawing the Boundary Between Copyright and Contract: Copyright Preemption of Software License Terms,* 45 Duke L.J. 479 (1995)

O'Rourke, *Rethinking Remedies at the Intersection of Intellectual Property and Contract: Toward a Unified Body of Law*, 82 Iowa L. Rev. 1137 (1997)

Perzanowski, *The Penumbral Public Domain: Constitutional Limits on Quasi-Copyright Legislation*, 10 U. Pa. J. Const. L. 1081 (2008)

Reichman & Franklin, *Privately Legislated Intellectual Property Rights: Reconciling Freedom of Contract With Public Good Uses of Information*, 147 U. Pa. L. Rev. 875 (1999)

Rice, *Copyright and Contract: Preemption After* Bowers v. Baystate, 9 Roger Williams U.L. Rev. 595 (2004)

Rice, *Public Goods, Private Contract and Public Policy: Federal Preemption of Software License Prohibitions Against Reverse Engineering,* 53 U. Pitt. L. Rev. 543 (1992)

Romm, *The Fine Art of Preemption: Section 301 and the Copyright Act of 1976,* 60 Or. L. Rev. 287 (1981)

Rothman, *Copyright Preemption and the Right of Publicity,* 36 U.C. Davis L. Rev. 199 (2002)

Sandeen, Kewanee *Revisited: Returning to First Principles of Intellectual Property Law to Determine the Issue of Federal Preemption,* 12 Marq. Intell. Prop. L. Rev. 299 (2008)

Schechter, *The Unfairness of Click-On Software Licenses*, 46 Wayne L. Rev. 173 (2000)

Shipley, *Refusing to Rock the Boat, The* Sears/Compco *Preemption Doctrine Applied to* Bonito Boats v. Thundercraft, 25 Wake Forest L. Rev. 385 (1990)

Shipley, *Three Strikes and They're Out at the Old Ball Game: Preemption of Performers' Rights of Publicity Under the Copyright Act of 1976,* 20 Ariz. St. L.J. 369 (1988)

Shipley & Hay, *Protecting Research: Copyright, Common-Law Alternatives and Federal Pre-emption,* 63 N.C. L. Rev. 125 (1984)

Symposium, *Intellectual Property and Contract Law for the Information Age: The Impact of Article 2B of the Uniform Commercial Code on the Future of Information and Commerce*, 87 Calif. L. Rev. 1 (1999)

Tussey, *UCITA, Copyright, and Capture,* 21 Cardozo Arts & Ent. L.J. 319 (2003)

Wiley, Bonito Boats: *Uninformed But Mandatory Innovation Policy,* 1989 Sup. Ct. Rev. 283

Related Bodies of State and Federal Law (see also Chapter 1)

Andrews, *Reversing Copyright Misuse: Enforcing Contractual Prohibitions on Software Reverse Engineering*, 41 Hous. L. Rev. 975 (2004)

Band & Schruers, Datstar, *Attribution, and Plagiarism*, 33 AIPLA Q.J. 1 (2005)

Barnett, *First Amendment Limits on the Right of Publicity,* 30 Tort & Ins. L.J. 635 (1995)

Barrett, *The "Law of Ideas" Reconsidered,* 71 J. Pat. & Trademark Off. Soc'y 691 (1989)

Bartholomew, *Protecting the Performers: Setting a New Standard for Character Copyrightability*, 41 Santa Clara L. Rev. 341 (2001)

Basin & Rad, *"I Could Have Been a Fragrance Millionaire": Toward a Federal Idea Protection Act,* 56 J. Copyright Soc'y 731 (2009)

Beard, *Digital Replicas of Celebrities: Copyright, Trademark, and Right of Publicity Issues*, 23 U. Ark. Little Rock L. Rev. 197 (2000)

Bhatnagar, *Fantasy Liability: Publicity Law, the First Amendment, and Fantasy Sports,* 119 Yale L. J. 131 (2009)

Bloom, *Preventing the Misappropriation of Identity: Beyond the Right of Publicity,* 13 Hastings Comm. & Ent. L.J. 489 (1991)

Bohrer, *Strengthening the Distinction Between Copyright and Trademark: The Supreme Court Takes a Stand,* 2003 Duke L. & Tech. Rev. 23 (2003)

Brown, *Copyright and Its Upstart Cousins: Privacy, Publicity, Unfair Competition,* 33 J. Copyright Soc'y 301 (1986)

Chafee, *Unfair Competition,* 53 Harv. L. Rev. 1289 (1940)

Dougherty, *Foreword: The Right of Publicity Towards a Comparative and International Perspective*, 18 Loy. L.A. Ent. L.J. 421 (1998)

Felcher & Rubin, *Privacy, Publicity, and the Portrayal of Real People by the Media,* 88 Yale L.J. 1577 (1979)

Ginsburg, *The Right to Claim Authorship in U.S. Copyright and Trademarks Law,* 41 Hous. L. Rev. 263 (2004)

Gordon, *Harmless Use: Gleaning from Fields of Copyrighted* Works, 77 Fordham L. Rev. 2411 (2009)

Grady, *A Positive Economic Theory of the Right of Publicity,* 1 UCLA Ent. L. Rev. 97 (1994)

Haemmerli, *Whose Who? The Case for a Kantian Right of Publicity*, 49 Duke L.J. 383 (1999)

Hricik, *Remedies of the Infringer: The Use By the Infringer of Implied and Common Law Federal Rights, State Law Claims, and Contract to Shift Liability for Infringement of Patents, Copyrights, and Trademarks,* 28 Tex. Tech. L. Rev. 1027 (1997)

Hylton, *Baseball Cards and the Birth of the Right of Publicity: The Curious Case of* Haelen Laboratories v. Topps Chewing Gum, 12 Marq. Sports L.Q. 273 (2001)

Kaplan, *Performer's Right and Copyright: The* Capitol Records *Case*, 69 Harv. L. Rev. 409 (1956)

Karjala, *Copyright and Misappropriation,* 17 U. Dayton L. Rev. 885 (1992)

Karjala, *Misappropriation as a Third Intellectual Property Paradigm,* 94 Colum. L. Rev. 2594 (1994)

Kwall, *Fame*, 73 Ind. L.J. 1 (1997)

Kwall, *The Right of Publicity v. the First Amendment: A Property and Liability Rule Analysis,* 70 Ind. L.J. 47 (1994)

LaFrance, *Something Borrowed, Something New: The Changing Role of Novelty in Idea Proteciton Law*, 37 Intell. Prop. L. Rev. 679 (2005)

Leaffer, *The Right of Publicity: A Comparative Perspective*, 70 Alb. L. Rev. 1357 (2007)

Loren, *Slaying the Leather-Winged Demons in the Night: Reforming Copyright Owner Contracting With Clickwrap Misuse*, 30 Ohio N.U. L. Rev. 495 (2004)

Madison, *The Legitimacy of Open Source and Other Software Licenses*, 8 J. Internet L. 1 (2005)

Madison, *Reconstructing the Software License*, 35 Loy. U. Chi. L.J. 275 (2003)

Malkan, *Stolen Photographs: Personality, Publicity, and Privacy,* 75 Tex. L. Rev. 779 (1997)

Marks, *An Assessment of the Copyright Model in the Right of Publicity Cases*, 32 Copyright L. Symp. (ASCAP) 1 (1986)

Mazzone & Moore, *The Secret Life of Patents*, 48 Washburn L.J. 33 (2008)

McCarthy, *The Human Persona as Commercial Property: The Right of Publicity*, 19 Colum.-VLA J.L. & Arts 129 (1995)

Moffat, *Mutant Copyrights and Backdoor Patents: The Problem of Overlapping Intellectual Property Protection*, 19 Berkeley Tech. L.J. 1473 (2004)

M. Nimmer, *The Right of Publicity*, 19 L. & Contemp. Probs. 203 (1954)

O'Rourke, *Bargaining in the Shadow of Copyright Law*, 53 Case West. Res. L. Rev. 605 (2003)

Pagano, *"Origin of Goods": Delving Into* Dastar Corp. v. Twentieth Century Fox Films Corp., 19 St. John's J. Legal Comment. 2421 (2005)

Patterson, *Copyright Overextended: A Preliminary Inquiry into the Need for a Federal Statute of Unfair Competition*, 17 U. Dayton L. Rev. 385 (1992)

Raskind, *The Misappropriation Doctrine as a Competitive Norm of Intellectual Property Law*, 75 Minn. L. Rev. 875 (1991)

Saunders, *A Crusade in the Public Domain: The* Dastar *Decision*, 30 Rutgers Computer & Tech. L.J. 161 (2004)

Sease, *Misappropriation is Seventy-Five Years Old: Should We Bury It or Revive It?*, 70 N.D. L. Rev. 781 (1994)

Singer, *The Right of Publicity: Star Vehicle or Shooting Star?*, 10 Cardozo Arts & Ent. L.J. 1 (1991)

Towse, *The Singer or the Song? Developments in Performers' Rights from the Perspective of a Cultural Economist*, 3 Rev. L. & Econ. 1158 (2008)

Volokh, *Freedom of Speech and the Right of Publicity*, 40 Hous. L. Rev. 903 (2003)

Welkowitz & Ochoa, *The Terminator as Eraser: How Arnold Schwarzenegger Used the Right of Publicity to Terminate Non-Defamatory Political Speech*, 45 Santa Clara L. Rev. 651 (2005)

Zimmerman, *Fitting Publicity Rights into Intellectual Property and Free Speech Theory: Sam, You Made the Pants Too Long!*, 10 DePaul-LCA J. Art & Ent. L. & Pol'y 283 (2000)

Zimmerman, *Money as a Thumb on the Constitutional Scale: Weighing Speech Against Publicity Rights*, 50 B.C. L. Rev. 1503 (2009)